# THE FALL AND RISE OF THE *Stately Home*

*Reproduction of the Frontispiece to our Christmas Number.*

ALNWICK.   EATON.

In Liquidation.                    NOVEMBER 25th, 1905.

# THE
# BRITISH ARISTOCRACY

## CATALOGUE OF
# CASTLES, ESTATES
### AND OTHER EFFECTS.

## To be Sold by Private Treaty
### WITH IMMEDIATE POSSESSION OR FOR FUTURE DELIVERY.

# GLOGOUL & FAULMANN,
## ESTATE AGENTS,
## PALL MALL, S.W.

CHATSWORTH.   WARWICK.

WHAT WE ARE COMING TO: A SALE CATALOGUE OF A.D. 1905.

Stately Home: W.T. Stead's gloomy forecast of aristocratic liquidation ten years hence, 'The Splendid Paupers', published in the Christmas 1894 number of the *Review of*

# THE FALL AND RISE OF THE

## *Stately Home*

### PETER MANDLER

YALE UNIVERSITY PRESS

*New Haven & London*

Designed by Gillian Malpass
Printed and bound in Great Britain by Biddles Ltd, Guildford and Kings Lynn

**Library of Congress Cataloging-in-Publication Data**

Mandler, Peter.
    The fall and rise of the stately home / Peter Mandler.
    Includes bibliographical references and index.
    ISBN 0-300-06703-8
    1. Historic buildings – England – Conservation and restoration – History.   2. Architecture, Domestic – England – Conservation and restoration – History.   3. Country homes – England – Conservation and restoration – History.   4. Dwellings – England – Conservation and restoration – History.   5. Manors – England – Conservation and restoration – History.   6. Cultural property, Protection of – England – History.   7. Aristocracy (Social class) – England – History.   8. Architecture and society – England – History.   9. Art and society – England – History.   10. Tourist trade – England – History.   I. Title.
DA655.M26   1997
363.6'9'0942 – dc20
96-24203

CIP

A catalogue record for this book is available from the British Library

*For Ruth*

CONTENTS

# The Stately Homes and England

The stately homes of England, it is now often claimed, are that country's greatest contribution to Western civilization. They are the quintessence of Englishness: they epitomize the English love of domesticity, of the countryside, of hierarchy, continuity and tradition. Their aristocratic owners have built them up lovingly over centuries and kept them intact in times of adversity in order to bequeath to future generations this unique embodiment of the English character. They have always been open to visitors, their enjoyment shared by their owners with a wider public. So perhaps it is entirely natural that they should lie today at the heart of the 'national heritage', the people's inheritance of art and history.

These are the clichés of the present day: but how true are they? Have country houses always been accepted as quintessential symbols of Englishness? Have their owners, in turn, played a role as custodians of the national heritage? How true is it even to say that country houses have always been open to the public? Given the outpouring of writing about life *within* the walls the country house – about its art and architecture, its collections and gardens, the attitudes and habits of its owners, their families and servants – it is surprising how little we know about the view of the country house from *outside*. How has a nation growing ever more urban, commercial and democratic over the past two hundred years viewed these islands of aristocratic heritage in its midst? Today the stately homes are widely accepted as a crucial part of the national heritage, but it has not always been so, and how the aristocratic heritage came to be part of the national heritage is a longer, more erratic and more exciting story than the clichés of serene continuity would suggest.

If the clichés have gone largely unexamined, it is because the critics as well as the promoters of the country-house heritage have tended to adopt them. The critics do not, of course, agree that the English country house is such a pre-eminent treasure; they feel that admiration of it detracts from appreciation of other parts of the heritage (including urban and industrial artefacts) and saps the vitality of modern art and industry. But critics will still often argue that an élite of country-house owners and admirers has succeeded in imposing its taste, its heritage on the nation. Over the past two hundred years, aristocratic culture has been preserved, and with it some remnants of aristocratic wealth and authority, at the expense of democracy and modernity.

What the apparently opposed assessments of enthusiasts and critics share is the view that 'culture' and 'heritage' are matters shaped very largely by the rich and powerful. These élites, whose rule was relatively unchallenged in the eighteenth century, have in the nineteenth and twentieth centuries been threatened by urbanization, industrialization, democracy and mass culture. But – so the argument goes – whereas economic and political power have had gradually to be ceded to the masses, in the sphere of culture élite control has been refined and extended, and this has often taken the form of mechanisms to preserve the élite's idea of 'heritage'. From the late nineteenth century onwards particularly, new cultural institutions have been established to protect a narrow sliver of culture in the guise of 'national heritage': from the National Gallery to the National Trust, from the fake village that is the suburb to the idealized country house, the dominant classes of English society have been able to define a national heritage that stands as a rampart against modern life.

This book tells a very different story about the emergence of a 'national heritage' and the aristocracy's contribution to it. It does so by putting both heritage and the aristocracy back into the wider frame of English history. Elite culture is not something apart from or floating above the social, economic, political and cultural history of the nation: it is shaped by the marketplace, by government, by popular attitudes and prejudices as well as by the internal culture of the élite itself. This is particularly true of those elements of high culture that are proposed to the nation as *its* heritage, and more true still of the country house. For the country house on its estate has never been solely a matter of taste: it is also an economic unit subject to the vicissitudes of agriculture and the land and art markets, an asset subject to taxation, a target for political attacks on the rich and privileged and an object of planning law and government intervention.

Putting the country house into this wider context turns a story of stasis and preservation into a story of change. Modern English history is marked by continuity – undisrupted by the wars, revolutions and nation-building of the Continent – but it is a continuity achieved only by slow, continuous and sometimes remorseless change. Far from making the English peculiarly conscious of their history, this process of continuous change has often resulted in neglect and even contempt for the past. Newer nations have had to invent a past for themselves and have put a high political priority on protecting the remnants of their history from the ravages of economic development. They see historical consciousness as the handmaiden of national consciousness, and thus an integral part of modern life. Aristocratic mansions on the Continent, the villas, châteaux and Schlosses, have been officially protected since the nineteenth century as *national* rather than specifically aristocratic property.

The English have not been immune from these sentiments, particularly in periods of rapid economic change. For a time in the nineteenth century, it looked as if they might take the same approach to the older country houses, preserving them as symbols of the whole nation's history; but the underlying continuities of English history meant that such preservation was not necessary or even desirable. In England the national history has been more taken for granted, political interventions in the 'heritage' have been resisted and commercial development has been put above other considerations. 'Heritage' and 'progress' have been counterposed to each other, and although this has caused a minority of aesthetes to rally around 'heritage', for the rest of society progress has, until recently, been given the clear priority.

The English aristocracy have on the whole shared these attitudes. Their continuity – their remarkable success in preserving wealth and authority into the twentieth century – has been achieved by respecting and steering change, not resisting it. When, in the nineteenth century, the nation showed an interest in some of their houses as symbols of national history and identity, they accommodated that interest for a time, but like the rest of society ultimately they put economic progress above national heritage. At their insistence, country houses remained private homes, even if that entailed their destruction. It is only recently that a change of heart has been wrought on both sides. So the story of the country house and of the national heritage is, like the story of the nation itself, a story of change: changing economic and political arrangements, which bring with them changing attitudes to the national history, and a changing relationship between the nation and its historic ruling class.

Until the early nineteenth century, country houses were private homes of the aristocracy, admired as art objects principally by their owners and their immediate circle. Their role in the national heritage properly begins in the early nineteenth century, when the market for cultural products formerly confined to a much smaller élite starts to expand rapidly. Suddenly the country house was caught up in the drive to recover a truly popular and national history, an impulse that England shared with the Continent (and with Wales, Scotland and Ireland). In this period, the older stately homes were popularized as symbols of the common national history shared by all classes, in contrast to newer, showier houses that represented recent aristocratic exclusivity. The older houses were viewed, much like the châteaux and Schlosses, not as private homes but as common property: they were the 'mansions of England', not merely of their aristocratic owners. The owners, as befitted a progressive, adaptive élite, accommodated themselves to this view. They indulged a rapidly growing audience for national history in its desire to write about, read about and indeed to visit the mansions of England: the mid-nineteenth century was the first great age of country-house visiting.

This consensus fractured towards the end of the nineteenth century. The mass audience was now too large and too diverse for the rather cosy view of English history propagated earlier in the century. The period up to the First World War was characterized by an increasingly commercial culture and by mounting social and political conflict. Public opinion was less interested in history of any kind and less willing to accept aristocratic leadership. In this second phase, the position of the country house changed dramatically. Its historic value was at a discount and its material and political value as a symbol of aristocratic wealth and privilege drew heavy fire. Even lovers of art and architecture attacked the aristocracy as 'barbarians', and their homes as 'fortresses of barbarism'. Owners, still seeking to accommodate rather than to struggle against modernity, tended to withdraw themselves and their homes from the public sphere.

After the First World War, the public valuation of the country house continued to deteriorate. Country-house visiting virtually ended as owners closed, abandoned or demolished their homes. In this third phase grand mansions were derided as 'white elephants', both by their owners and the wider public. To a commercially minded public, their uselessness made it more difficult, not easier to respect their past. Those who *were* interested in the national heritage located it in features that seemed more durable and more central to the modern English character: the ordinary countryside, the cottage and the village.

Finally, between the Second World War and the 1970s, the current began gradually to shift yet again. Having been stripped of most of its political power and a great deal of its economic might, the aristocracy was no longer a target of great public enmity or suspicion. A more balanced attitude to its place in the national history was possible. In another of its long series of adaptations, the aristocracy for the first time began systematically to exploit its historical and artistic possessions both as public-relations gimmicks and as economic assets. Growing numbers of owners declared 'open house' and sought to profit from a gentle resurgence of popular interest in history of all kinds. In the last twenty years, this popular interest in history has exploded and has fixed particularly on the 'treasure houses' of the aristocracy as the centrepiece of the English heritage. While this may tell us a good deal about the present state of the culture, we should not be overawed. The country house has not always hung over us, nor has its current popularity been imposed on a passive and manipulated people. How we got here from there – a crooked path – is the story this book sets out to tell.[1]

# STOWE:

## A
# DESCRIPTION

Of the Magnificent

# HOUSE and GARDENS

Of the RIGHT HONOURABLE

# RICHARD,
# EARL TEMPLE,

## Viscount and Baron COBHAM,

One of his Majesty's most honourable Privy Council, and Knight of the most Noble Order of the Garter.

Embellished with a General PLAN of the GARDENS, and also a separate PLAN of each BUILDING, with PERSPECTIVE VIEWS of the same.

---

## A NEW EDITION,

With all the Alterations and Improvements that have been made therein, to the present Time.

With the DESCRIPTION of the Inside of the House.

---

*Here Order in Variety we see,*
*Where all Things differ, yet where all agree.*   POPE.

---

## LONDON:

Printed for JOHN RIVINGTON in *St. Paul's Church-yard*; B. SEELEY in *Buckingham*; and T. HODGKINSON at the *New Inn* at *Stowe*. 1763.

*The Description of the House and Gardens, without the Plans and Views of the Temples, may be had alone, Price Six-pence.*

---

1   Stowe was one of the few eighteenth-century country houses to have a proper tourist trade, with rival guidebooks, frequently reprinted.

# Houses of Taste (to 1815)

Before the early nineteenth century, country houses could be valued as symbols of power, as places of comfort and convenience for their owners, as repositories of fashionable taste in art or architecture or furnishing, but not as part of a national heritage. An understanding of heritage – a physical legacy of the past belonging, however abstractly, to the citizenry of the present by virtue of its contribution to national history – requires both a feeling for the past and the existence of a cultural nation. Georgian England had the first only imperfectly, the second hardly at all.

On the contrary, the story of the Georgian country house and the country house-owning class is, at least until the middle of the eighteenth century, a story of a progressive distancing both from history and from the rest of the community. The widening gap in wealth and power between the landowning élite and the rest of the nation since the civil wars manifested itself physically in new houses cut off from both the past and the people. Large landowners deserted their ancestral castles – many of which had been ruined or damaged in the domestic strife of the seventeenth century – and their old manor houses – too small and too cosily ensconced in a village group, next to church and rectory and labourers' cottages. The business of the estate was increasingly professionalized and carried on by stewards and agents, from separate estate offices, forming a buffer between landlords and tenants and, *a fortiori*, labourers. Thus absolved of many of its old social and economic functions, the country house was freed for higher aesthetic functions commensurate with its owner's growing sophistication. Central to those new aesthetic functions would be that of carrying the very message of the owner's status, not as part of a historically rooted organic community, but as a somewhat lonely possessor and modernizer.[1]

Physically, the country house was removed from the village and emparked in hundreds or perhaps thousands of acres of depopulated private space. Sometimes, as in the notorious case of Milton Abbas in Dorset, the village was removed from the country house and resited outside the park gates; more often, an entirely new situation was found for the house, more elevated and topographically varied than the protected sites appropriate to the older manor houses. Around the park were built miles of protective wall punctuated by gates and lodges and, in some cases, fortifications that were at least visual if not physical deterrents.[2] The surrounding countryside was excluded; when Georgian country-house owners had themselves portrayed outdoors, it was nearly always in the park, rather than in the fields.[3]

Inside the park, house and pleasure grounds could be constructed and reconstructed to suit changing fashions. In the first half of the eighteenth century, these fashions were largely determined by the accepted canons of classical art and literature, the currency of an élite education and foreign travel. Whether or not country-house classicism was quite as alienating to the humbler classes as the Victorians thought – '[their] cold and proud Palladianism seems to forbid approach', felt the Gothic architect Gilbert Scott – these brilliantly geometric classical boxes were unmistakable symbols of taste and refinement to the *cognoscenti*.

The quality of tasteful display was still more evident on the inside. The scale and disposition of rooms was often calculated first, before domestic requirements, to suit the housing of the great collections of classical marbles, 'Grand Manner' continental paintings, books, manuscripts and whatever else had been caught by the beady eye of the Grand Tour magpie. Vanbrugh's vast temples of art at Blenheim and Castle Howard were so jammed with paintings and statuary that visitors sometimes wondered where the owners were accommodated, and the hollow cube of Wilton House had to be filled in with a cloister to create more room for the famous marbles. The effect spilled over outdoors; early eighteenth-century parks, before the taste for landscape caught on, were dotted with temples and follies and columns and pavilions, not only as eyecatchers or picnic spots but also to display more works of art, especially the more durable bits of marble.

The urge to show off the booty of erudition and travel posed an interesting problem for the culturally ambitious country-house owner of the mid-eighteenth century. His collections had to be seen and admired for his skill and taste as a connoisseur to be fully appreciated; he had therefore to ensure that his impregnable fortifications were just sufficiently permeable to admit any visitors able to assess, appreciate and, preferably, report on his achievements. He too had to travel to

2  'Cold and proud Palladianism': the north front of Kedleston Hall, designed by Robert Adam, a symbol of refinement to the Georgians but too exclusive for Victorian tastes (painting attrib. to George Cuitt).

keep an eye on his rivals, to spot emerging fashions, to broaden his knowledge and hone his discrimination. So a remarkable apparatus of country-house visiting grew up, held in check only by the still-considerable physical barriers to travel and the desire for a degree of domestic privacy on the part of the owners. Visitors were carefully vetted at the lodge gates, their dress, servants, conveyances and calling-cards checked for suitability, before they were shown around house and grounds by the housekeeper, a maid or gardener. From the 1760s, guidebooks to individual properties began to appear, including multiple guides produced by rival local firms in the case of Stowe.[4] Because so many owners were absent in the summer months – at Bath or a local spa, or on the country-house tour themselves – visiting could be carried on with considerable freedom at that time of the year. Again, the two or three most popular houses had to organize visiting by confining it to stated days and hours, to minimize inconvenience to family members in residence, or simply to allow the servants to get on with their work.[5]

   To some extent, this practice must have begun to break down the boundary that nominally separated the cultivated few and the rude many. The culture of connoisseurship must have been flexible enough to admit some outsiders of acquired cultivation, and the willingness to admit those who aspired only to spectatorship, not participation, is some indication of the openness and confidence of the eighteenth-century landed élite. By the middle of the century, aesthetic ideals were already adapting to take account of this openness; but it is hard to say how extensive country-house connoisseurship was in this period. Esther Moir, the first scholar to survey the full range of published and unpublished accounts of country-house tours, concluded that domestic touring remained 'the prerogative of the governing classes . . . the nobility and gentry', and that this was particularly true of visitors to the great houses.[6]

More recently, a greater appreciation of the size and diversity of the propertied classes, which encompassed many of the middling ranks of professionals and tradesmen, has led writers on country-house visiting to paint a picture of a more motley, almost democratic tourist trade – a picture that inevitably looks very modern and encourages us to assimilate Georgian tourists to the late twentieth-century heritage industry. But this picture owes more to optimistic speculation – and, in the case of our contemporary stately-home promoters, a desire to invent a tradition – than to any new evidence unearthed since Moir's day. Apart from a second-hand report from one genteel traveller, Mrs Lybbe Powys (herself a country-house owner), that over 2,000 people had signed their names in the Wilton lodge book in the year she made her visit (1776), the only piece of hard evidence yet uncovered is the annual average of under three hundred visitors whom Horace Walpole recorded as visiting Strawberry Hill in the 1780s and 1790s.[7] For a house that was the *dernier cri* of newly fashionable Gothicism, and situated within an easy ride of London, Strawberry Hill's three hundred sounds like something of an upper limit for all but a small number of houses. Only the promoters of Stowe, Blenheim and Wilton found it necessary to reprint their guidebooks at all in the fifty-year period between 1760 and 1810, and only about two dozen houses in the whole country had printed guidebooks of any kind. Most of the really popular houses lay on a few well-travelled routes – safe and comparatively smooth – in a belt between London and Bath. It will not do to minimize the barriers of distance, expense, cultivation and deference that kept all but a relatively small number outside the boundary, and confined the country-house world in all senses to a minority within a minority.[8]

Coming on the heels of country-housing touring, and in some ways connected to it, is a shift in the élite world's aesthetics that might also be interpreted ambiguously as both an opening out to the nation and a revaluation of the national past. From the 1750s onwards, but especially from the 1790s, it is impossible to mistake the weakening of the classical canon as an integument binding and defining a cultural élite. All sorts of informalities, engaging the heart and the eye rather than the intellect and potentially linking up a much wider cultural nation, are in evidence: at first in the rather mannered form of the Picturesque, then in the less-disciplined outbursts that are known as Romanticism. The Picturesque first appears as a newly emotional response to the visual qualities of landscape in the second third of the eighteenth century. Though initially inspired by the 'Grand Manner' landscapes of seventeenth-century French and Italian painters – Claude Lorrain, Gaspard and Nicolas Poussin, Salvator Rosa – and therefore likely to be at first another affectation of Grand Tourists, a taste for the texture and rhythm of landscape inevitably moved high culture away from classical norms. Wildness, irregularity, the play of light and shadow – all gained in value at the expense of formality, symmetry and flatness. The Picturesque also dovetailed neatly with the more unsettling mid-century fashion for an honest and exploratory emotional response in daily life – what contemporaries called 'sensibility' – prompting newly opened eyes to drift from the continental landscapes on the walls indoors to the English landscape outside.

The way in which the Picturesque helped polite taste become more English and less cosmopolitan can be clearly detected in the shifting gaze of country-house tourism. Under the influence of the Picturesque, a wider range of English sites became acceptable to polite tourists. The wilds of the Peak District around Chatsworth, for instance, which had been held to be a rude distraction from the classical house around 1700, by the mid-eighteenth century were found to provide curious contrasts to the well-manicured house and garden, and by the late eighteenth century to hold aesthetic value of their own. This shift of priorities gave an immense impetus to the art of landscape architecture, as owners scrambled to alter their parks to complement their houses and later to alter their houses to complement their parks. It also stimulated native art, the highly finished landscapes of Gainsborough, the new school of watercolour painters and more widely circulated engravings of English scenes. When war halted the Grand Tour in the 1790s, the process was completed; the Picturesque was, willy-nilly, domesticated. The Reverend William Gilpin made his name in the closing years of the century by writing a series of tours designed to help travellers and artists find the Picturesque at home – the Wye Valley, the Lake District and rugged parts of Wales and Scotland being favoured places – and a serious theoretical struggle broke out between Uvedale Price and Richard Payne Knight over the

Picturesque qualities of the English landscape: were they intrinsically appealing to human perception, or could they be appreciated only by the eye properly trained in art and literature?

The effect of these aesthetic changes in opening up the cultural nation was clear but limited. Undoubtedly landscape tourism was an easier proposition for a wider section of the propertied classes than country-house tourism had been; furthermore, the extended land-scaped parks of the Picturesque period were designed to accommodate more visitors.[9] The earlier editions of Gilpin's tours left his Latin tags untranslated, but by the turn of the century this piece of elegance was thought too abstruse.[10] Victorian observers credited the Picturesque as a sign that their late-Georgian predecessors were awakening to sensibility and intuition – those universal, God-given qualities – but on the other hand they suspected it of disingenuousness, of being just another virtuoso's pose. Gilpin was widely held to be as cold and heartless as his classical predecessors; and it is indeed possible to view the Picturesque as principally a private amusement of owner-aesthetes. Walpole, Price and Knight were all country-house owners whose greatest happiness lay in manipulating their own properties to suit their theories. Walpole's Gothicked-up Strawberry Hill, Knight's estate at Downton in Shropshire, and Price's artificially natural landscaping at Foxley in Herefordshire were crafted in much the same spirit as moved their strictly classical predecessors: they were show-pieces of their owners' taste and sensibility. The preciousness of this competition made it an easy target for such early nineteenth-century satirists as Thomas Love Peacock, who caricatured Knight and Price in *Headlong Hall* (1816), and William Combe, whose *Tours of Dr. Syntax in Search of the Picturesque* (1809–21) were aimed straight at Gilpin, a clergyman and younger son unable to afford his own Picturesque landscape and so forced to seek it elsewhere.[11]

In other words, the Picturesque's cult of 'nature' could be just as artificial and exclusive as the most formidable classicism. The Picturesque did not demolish the wall separating the country-house park from the outside world; in some ways, it heightened it. Knight recommended the careful placing of trees to shield the Picturesque eye from the hideously regular hedges that disfigured the real agricultural landscape, and Gilpin advised the Picturesque planner to hide scenes of human labour: 'the lazy cowherd resting on his pole or the peasant lolling on a rock may be allowed . . . but the characters most suited to these scenes of grandeur are . . . figures in long, folding draperies; gypsies; banditti.'[12] Others, such as Price, were readier to include the agricultural landscape (if properly tended and improved) within the ambit of the Picturesque.[13]

Another potentially nationalistic effect of the Picturesque upon élite aesthetics was a renewed consciousness of English traditions in art and architecture, which had been obscured by the classical revival. In part this was only a random consequence of the fracturing of the Palladian consensus: old English styles proliferated, but so did Egyptian, Greek, Romanesque, Italian and continental Gothic styles. The formal aspects of the Picturesque encouraged architects and their patrons to roam the world in search of architectural features that produced the correct effects of mass, light and shadow, whatever their provenance or history, yielding the 'copyism' that dominated the architectural world before the High Victorian Gothic Revival temporarily reasserted discipline.[14] Still, Picturesque copyism did stimulate curiosity about the architectural forms that were closest to home. Horace Walpole's *Anecdotes of Painting* (1762) made a genuine contribution to English Gothic scholarship, and antiquarianism, hitherto considered a peculiarly antisocial pastime, was increasingly conceded to have some real use. 'The Study of Antiquities is generally considered either as confined within the compass of mere curiosity', wrote Thomas Burgess in 1780, 'or as dry and uninteresting . . . [but] the prejudice attending this study seems to be disappearing, from the liberal manner in which it is by many now conducted'.[15]

Again, however, later generations often doubted whether Georgian antiquarians had any deep-seated *feeling* for the past. A few exceptions, such as the modest and intimate Thomas Gray – he of the wildly popular 'Elegy on a Country Churchyard' – would be hailed by the Victorians as their emotional precursors. But exceptions prove rules, and the Victorians thought the proud and boastful Horace Walpole – who appropriated and publicized many of Gray's Gothic discoveries – to be far more typical of his generation. True, the cult of sensibility invited the traveller to view relics of the past in order to elicit certain feelings, but these were not feelings of identification or sympathy. On the contrary, relics were meant to transmit moral messages about the transgressions of our ancestors: they were images of superstition, of shattered ambition, of hubris punished. At its most intimate, a relic might be a *memento mori* – a reminder that the present and past share at least one quality, transitoriness – or it might induce an 'impolite' *frisson* of evil or danger, but these feelings could not with propriety be sustained for long or appreciated too grossly.

Because they induced the desired sensations, ruins were almost always to be preferred to intact buildings. Tintern Abbey, a highlight of the picturesque Wye Valley tour, afforded the viewer moderate doses of 'pleasurable sadness', piety and *memento mori*, as well as the aesthetic pleasures of irregularity and apparent naturalness. So, too, did Fountains Abbey in Yorkshire, until, that is, its owner William Aislabie trimmed and tailored the ruins the better to fit alongside his Neo-classical pleasure gardens at Studley Royal. Aislabie's landscaping attracted a good deal of criticism from the more up-to-date advocates of the Picturesque, and Gilpin's pious defence of a ruin as 'a sacred thing . . . a work of nature' is often cited as an earlier glimmering of modern heritage thinking. But Gilpin's concerns were still determinedly formal and aesthetic. What he wanted was a good-looking ruin. He was hardly interested in the abbey that had been Fountains, the monks who built and worshipped in it. Men can make buildings any day – he and his copyist friends could make an abbey – but ruins were more difficult: 'A Goth may deform [a ruin]; but it exceeds the

3   The ruins of Fountains Abbey were carefully trimmed and landscaped to suit the tastes of tourists in search of the Picturesque, portrayed here by Samuel Hieronymus Grimm towards the end of the eighteenth century.

power of art to amend.' Yet if nature had not produced the desired effect, men could still help it along: Gilpin found the regularities of Tintern disappointing and urged its owner, the Duke of Beaufort, to untidy it with a few judicious hammer-blows.[16]

Gilpin's aesthetic approach to ruins suggests an explanation for the Picturesque Norman and Gothic exteriors in which many late eighteenth- and early nineteenth-century country-house owners clothed their homes. Were they symbolic of a sudden surge of fellow-feeling passing from landed élite to the rest of the nation, a landed élite 'drunk with Romanticism', as Kenneth Clark once put it, yearning to identify itself with its more hospitable and paternalistic ancestors and thereby with its social inferiors? Edmund Burke, whose paeans to the 'noble and venerable' castle of the State and its physical analogue the 'magnificent ancient country seats of the nobility' were widely influential in the 1790s, certainly thought otherwise. His ideal of the country house and of the owning class was that they should stand as a 'natural rampart', not separate from society but nevertheless towering over it, if the British were to escape the miserable fate of their French counterparts.[17] George III, the most consistent patron of the new style, agreed heartily; for him the Gothic was a new discipline that might fill the void left by the crumbling of the classical consensus. 'I never thought I should have adopted Gothic instead of Grecian architecture', he wrote in 1803, 'but the bad taste of the last fifty years has so entirely corrupted the professors of the latter, I have taken to the former.' The effect of James Wyatt's Gothic castles at Kew and Windsor may have been 'national', but it was surely not intended to invite the nation inside but rather to keep it out.[18] Some patrons of the early Gothic Revival may have had more positive or sentimental motives, but for most the message was fairly brutal and straightforward. Great hulking castles such as Robert Smirke built for the violent Tory lords Lowther and Somers (Lowther Castle, 1806; Eastnor Castle, 1810) were only paternalist in the awe-inspiring, strap-wielding sense.[19]

This disciplinary twist given to the Gothic by aristocrats, their architects and spokesmen, points to the limits on aristocratic participation in the unfolding of English culture in the Napoleonic era. As Linda Colley has shown, aristocrats were eager to be seen as the natural military and political leaders of a united, constitutional and Protestant nation, at war with a French Catholic despotism. But while military and political leadership came easily to them – at least during the war – cultural leadership was more difficult. Their longstanding commitment to the classical, cosmopolitan taste that they shared with

4  'Great hulking castles': Lowther Castle, designed by Robert Smirke.

French aristocrats was not easily shaken off.[20] Wyatt and Smirke's castles were exceptions; most new country houses continued to be built in a classical style, however 'corrupted', until the 1840s.[21] Most aristocratic art collections remained continental in their flavour, if anything more so after 1815, when British buyers benefited from a flood of sales in the war-ravaged lands across the Channel.[22]

Furthermore, as already noted, for half a century or more, there was a persistent tension in élite culture between the continuing prestige of classical formality and the impulse – sometimes optimistic and progressive, sometimes neurotic and defensive – to join a broader community of the soul, to assist in forming a cultural nation. That tension was only aggravated by the political storms of revolution, war and postwar dissent. Many who embraced the informal and emotional nationalism of the Picturesque in the relatively relaxed atmosphere of the *status quo ante* 1789 either recoiled from it thereafter or tried to reproduce within it the strict hierarchies and exclusivity of the classical. Something of this sort happened to the Romantic poets of the Wordsworth, Southey and Coleridge generation, artists who launched themselves as naturalizers, simplifiers, radicalizers of poetry, but then tried to re-locate themselves politically once the glow of the French Revolution wore off. To put this in a country-house context, Wordsworth moved from singleminded rhapsodizing on the socially undifferentiated land-scape to a new appreciation, after the war, of the Gothic rampart of Lowther Castle.[23]

There *was* a new sense of responsibility spreading through the landed élite from the 1790s, but it took moral and economic rather than aesthetic and cultural forms; in fact, to later observers, the early nineteenth-century aristocracy appeared to have abdicated its cultural role in favour of philistine (though morally praiseworthy) projects of religious uplift and agricultural improvement.[24] Moral and economic improvement seemed the most compelling tasks if the aristocracy's traditional political and economic leadership was to be preserved. What cultural activity persisted was drably conservative, loyalty to older eighteenth-century tastes lingering in muted and debased forms, increasingly detached from the cultural life of the nation as a whole.[25]

However, nation-forming is very rarely a one-way street, and to tell the story of that formation from the top down would be to tell only half a story, or less. If aristocratic impulses to create a national culture and foster an idea of national heritage were frozen by deep-seated fears and ambivalences – and thus overtaken by more disciplinary enter-prises – they were also swamped by a wave of sensibility sweeping up rather than down the social scale. For moving into the nineteenth century, we find ourselves in the midst of a great revolution, not so much in élite as in popular culture. It is here that the two elements necessary to the making of a national heritage should be sought: the growth of a cultural nation and that nation's identification with the past. Very soon after they were built, the Picturesque houses and castles were to be buried under a deluge of criticism as inauthentic, barbarous, unfeeling. The impetus for this critique came not, as is sometimes supposed, from the pedantry and sectarianism of an élite current, the Oxford Movement and its ancillaries, but from a much wider and deeper source, the very large body of opinion that was now mobilized in search of history rather than taste. What exercised so many of the early Victorians, before and beyond Pugin, was the arrogance of a narrow caste in thinking, with Gilpin, that anyone could build an abbey. As for destroying an abbey, that crime – which Gilpin had thought to indict only at 'the court of Taste' – would soon be prosecuted at the court of public opinion.

THE

MANSIONS

OF

ENGLAND

IN THE

OLDEN TIME

BY

Joseph Nash

A.D. 1839.

5   Joseph Nash's *Mansions of England in the Olden Time* (first series, 1839): even the title page was illustrated with a genuine Tudor detail, from the doorway at East Barsham Hall, Norfolk.

PART I

# Mansions of England, 1815–1880

The stately homes of England,
  How beautiful they stand!
Amidst their tall ancestral trees,
  O'er all the pleasant land.
The deer across their greensward bound,
  Through shade and sunny gleam,
And the swan glides past them with the sound
  Of some rejoicing stream . . .

The free, fair Homes of England!
  Long, long, in hut and hall,
May hearts of native proof be rear'd
  To guard each hallow'd wall!
And green for ever be the groves,
  And bright the flowery sod,
Where first the child's glad spirit loves
  Its country and its God!

—Felicia Hemans, 'The Homes of
England' (1828)

6  Communal ritual in the Olden Time: Joseph Nash's painting *The May-Pole* in a cheap engraving.

## CHAPTER 1

# The Victorian Idea of Heritage

Where did the Victorian idea of heritage come from? A conventional view ascribes it to that growing élite uneasiness triggered by the French Revolution and the accelerating pace of social and economic change, which first unleashed the Picturesque and then Romanticism and culminated in a successful confidence trick by which aristocratic culture was preserved but identified with 'the nation'. As Linda Colley has put it, 'the primacy of the polite vision' was maintained, but in the early nineteenth century 'exercised and rationalised' in a different way, such that aristocratic possessions 'were presented as a public benefit, as an asset to the nation'. Everywhere across Europe aristocracies were being ousted and dispossessed, but 'only in Great Britain did it prove possible to float the idea that aristocratic property was in some magical and strictly intangible way *the people's property* also'.[1]

But aristocratic culture was not preserved. The Victorian idea of heritage rejected the 'cold and proud Palladianism' and even the instrumental neo-medievalism of the early Gothic Revival. Instead, the heritage consciousness of the nineteenth century was predicated on the construction of a national culture that drew on a much longer and more varied national history, in *opposition* to the exclusive élite fashions of the preceding century and a half. Historical consciousness, far from being an élite plot to imprison a dynamic society in older patterns of deference and tradition, was one of the crucial ways in which popular culture enfranchised itself and became part of a cultural nation. A national history was rediscovered and used to correct the social imbalance of the 'polite vision' of the eighteenth century.

Neither, however, was the Victorian idea of heritage anti-aristocratic. Victorian culture, like Victorian politics, was in general liberal, inclusive and proudly non-revolutionary. Its idea of heritage sought to echo the honest and equitable relations between aristocracy and people that were thought to have been established in the gradual dismantling of a corrupt and authoritarian State between the 1820s and the 1840s. The aristocratic past was part of the national past – a leading part in many eras – and was celebrated alongside the socially humbler histories of craftsmanship, the arts, science and technology. But the aristocratic past had to be retrieved selectively so as to provide a historical basis, not for the imagined fopperies, corruptions and pro-fanities of the eighteenth century, but for the fair, civilized, prosperous and above all *English* nineteenth century.

Aristocratic property did become the people's property, in some impressively substantive ways. This identity of interests was undoubt-edly subtle and is hard for posterity to read, resting like so much else in Victorian society on unwritten and unspoken compromises or meetings-of-mind between an ancient landed élite and an increasingly prosperous commercial society. But it was not mystified; it entailed a much more thorough and popular investigation of the aristocratic past than was possible on the Continent, where, in fact, much aristocratic property *was* public property (dispossessed in France, protected by the State elsewhere) and yet public interest in it was restricted by, among other factors, the limits to the cultural nation.

## The Origins of National Heritage

In the first few decades of peace after 1815 something like a cultural revolution took place, as much from below as from above, which overwhelmed the vagrant impulses of élite culture and permanently changed the form and content of cultural production. It is here – in the new institutions and creations of the mass-culture industry – that an understanding of the peculiar sensibility for the past that had gripped the nation by the 1840s should be sought.

Walter Scott was the pioneer. His first great verse epic, *The Lay of the Last Minstrel*, appeared in 1805, a tribute set in the mid-sixteenth century to the fading manners and morals of the Middle Ages; there followed *Marmion* (1808), *The Lady of the Lake* (1810), *Rokeby* (1813) and others in much the same mould, and then the breakthrough to a new audience with the adoption of the novel form in *Waverley* (1814). By the time of *Ivanhoe* (1819) and *Kenilworth* (1821), each new Scott novel was ensured such widespread popularity that its messages and motifs were instantly adopted at all levels of the culture market: in theatre, opera, at the light as well as the heavy end of the novel market, in static, gaslit panoramas or in dramatic representations staged at popular pleasure-gardens and other open-air sites, in the Royal

WAVERLEY NOVELS.

VOL. XXII.

KENILWORTH.

"Is it not of an absolute fancy Janet?
"Nay my lady", replied Janet, if you consult my poor judg-
ment, it is, methinks, over gawdy for a graceful habit."

C.R.Leslie,R.A.                                        W.H.Watt

PRINTED FOR ROBERT CADELL, EDINBURGH.
AND WHITTAKER & Cº LONDON.
1831.

7  The national heritage enters popular culture: Walter Scott's *Kenilworth*,
illustrated by C.R. Leslie for the bestselling Cadell edition of 1831.

Academy and Water-Colour Painters' showrooms, in the engravers' studios and private art galleries.

Scott had deliberately set out to court a wider audience. Taking some inspiration from Southey and Coleridge, though also from his researches into popular ballads and pre-modern poetry, he had adopted simpler, more informal verse forms, suited to narrative and description as much as to high-flying word-play and elevated diction. His poems and novels adopted strong narrative lines that borrowed themes both from early English literature – chivalry, martial heroism, courtly love – and from recent popular culture – the romances, horrors and crime stories of chapbooks and broadsheets. Above all, Scott's works were suffused with intimacy and locality. His heroes – even if knights and princes – spoke a common person's language and were prey to a common person's doubts, strengths and passions. Their deeds – even if acts of military leadership or kingly governance – were played out on a meticulously described local landscape, with features and character instantly recognizable to natives and visitors alike. Scott himself attributed the appeal of his poetry to this quality of 'locality':

> A very commonplace and obvious epithet, when applied to a scene which we have been accustomed to view with pleasure, recalls to us not merely the local scenery, but a thousand little nameless associations, which we are unable to separate or define . . . Tell a peasant an ordinary tale of robbery and murder, and perhaps you may fail to interest him; but to excite his terrors, you assure him that it happened on the very heath he usually crosses, or to a man whose family he has known . . .[2]

The speed and success with which Scott's devices were taken up across such a wide array of media suggests that the cultural nation was already in waiting, marking time until a pioneer made a venture. But there were also specific technological innovations that must share the credit. Steam printing was first introduced at *The Times* in 1814, though it took a while to supersede the hand presses. In visual representation, as Stephen Bann and Patricia Anderson have recently demonstrated, the changes were particularly sudden and dramatic. Woodcuts had long provided a means for the mass dissemination of simple and dramatic printed images, a medium splendidly exploited by Thomas Bewick, but the technical limitations of which seemed generally to condemn it to serve only crude popular taste. Engraving on copper, which made possible fine-art reproduction, was comparatively expensive and could only yield some thousand impressions of each plate. The introduction of engraving on steel in 1822 abolished this distinction almost at a stroke, and made possible tens of thousands of impressions of the quality formerly confined to copper-engraving. With the innovation of stereotyping in 1827, woodcuts could be incorporated into the body of a printed text and the popular illustrated book and magazine were born. There followed lithography and lithotinting, which further improved the quality of mass-produced reproductions, and electrotyping, which allowed steel engravings as well as woodcuts to be mass-produced with text.[3]

Just as important as these technological innovations, however, were the commercial initiatives that established a modern culture industry. Scott's sales in the thousands at the high prices then common for copyright works – raised higher still by his success, to 31s. for a new novel – opened the eyes of entrepreneurs to the possibilities of cheap publishing. John Limbird developed two new fields, the general-circulation non-fiction magazine (*The Mirror of Literature, Amusement and Instruction*, 1823) and the cheap novel, as cheap as sixpence a volume, from the mid-1820s. *The Mirror* for some years held a circulation of about 80,000, suggesting a readership of hundreds of thousands, which must, for the first time, have linked cultural consumers from at least the skilled working class up to those at the top of the hierarchy. From around 1823, illustrated annuals began to proliferate. These volumes, much favoured as Christmas presents between lovers and family members, combined engravings of popular contemporary oil paintings with a hotchpotch of Romantic poetry, historical and silver-fork fiction and moral and sentimental tales. Single titles sold 10–15,000 copies at a price about two-thirds below that of new novels. The annuals in turn provided a pool of inexpensive sub-Romantic literature for reprinting in the cheap weeklies and monthlies churned out by an ever-widening circle of religious, political and purely commercial groups.[4] By the late 1820s, Charles Knight had extended Limbird's innovations further in enterprises aimed explicitly at a working-class audience by the Society for the Diffusion of Useful Knowledge. His *Penny Magazine*, first issued in December 1832, peaked early with a circulation of 200,000 – a readership probably over a million – and instantly spawned a fleet of imitators, some directed at specific sectors of the market, but many still reaching across the classes with the commercial goal of a permanent mass market for pictures, stories and factual matter.[5]

The miscellaneous readership of these publications, combined with the diversity of sources on which they drew, militated against great uniformity of style or content in the new mass-publishing world of the

1820s. However, precisely because it did spring up so rapidly, and was very largely dependent on the models provided by Scott and a few of the more successful Romantic poets, there was more cohesiveness in this little world and more homogeneity of voice than might be expected. Writers, artists and publishers were very often provincial grammar-school boys drawn to London by the outbreak of peace and by the new opportunities in cultural production. Inspired by Scott and the Romantics, they were wedded further to these sources by their acknowledged market appeal. Alaric Watts, for instance, originally from Leicester and educated at grammar school in Kent, drifted between various Grub Street literary, teaching and clerical jobs until he had a triumph for the publishers Hurst and Robinson with the *Literary Souvenir*, one of the earliest annuals, which first appeared in November 1824.

Watts was unusual in that he had some high-society connections which got him his early jobs and may have contributed to his lifelong Toryism. Most of his peers were humbler, and at least started out professing a loose, bohemian liberalism, anti-oligarchical, populist and improving. At the radical end of the spectrum stood William and Mary Howitt, Nottingham Quakers who ran a chemist's business until their friendship with Watts yielded enough literary income to make a go of that life in London.[6] Midway between Watts and the Howitts, politically, stood their mutual friend Samuel Carter Hall, son of a bankrupt army officer, who also made his literary reputation as editor of an early annual, *The Amulet*, from 1826. He was best known for the *Art Journal*, the first and for a long time the only magazine devoted to contemporary British art, which he ran virtually single-handed from its launching (as the *Art-Union*) in 1839 until his retirement in 1880. Although personally aloof and, in later life, conservative – his friends guyed him as 'Shirt Collar' Hall, and Dickens is said to have modelled the pompous social-climber Mr Pecksniff in *Martin Chuzzlewit* on him – in the thirties and forties at least he was a leading proselytizer for culture for the masses, active not only in commercial ventures but in the Early Closing movement to free shopworkers for improving leisure activities, and an advocate of municipal galleries and museums.[7] His close collaborator Llewellynn Jewitt, son of a Derbyshire schoolmaster, came to London to engrave for Charles Knight and was drawn into the same array of causes as Hall, ultimately returning to Derby to found a popular newspaper, the *Derby Telegraph*.[8] It was Jewitt who introduced Hall to another engraver, F. W. Fairholt, the son of penniless German immigrants, whom he had met while working for

Knight on the *Penny Magazine* and who became the chief engraver and assistant editor of Hall's *Art Journal*.[9]

Few of these names have survived in the literary or artistic canon, precisely because they were devoted more to copying and disseminating than to producing original work of their own. Dickens, very much a part of this world, is perhaps the single exception. His friend and successor as editor of the popular monthly *Bentley's Miscellany*, William Harrison Ainsworth, might be regarded as a second, though his reputation has survived more on the strength of the volume and vigour of his output than on its literary ambitions. Ainsworth, grammar-school boy from Manchester and a solicitor's son, also gravitated to London in search of a literary career, wrote his first novel (*Sir John Chiverton*, 1826) explicitly in imitation of Scott, made a living by editing the inevitable annual (*The Keepsake*, from 1828), and then *Bentley's*, until his own novels became roaring successes in the late 1830s. Like Dickens, he serialized these novels in his own magazine, which mixed fiction with the kind of non-fictional historical, social and topographical material that had been the staple of the popular illustrated magazine since the 1820s.[10]

If Ainsworth and his fellows did not aspire to great art, they did consciously set about the construction of a visual and literary world in which, potentially, the whole nation could be accommodated. At its most ambitious – particularly in its early stages – the culture industry aimed to draw in the whole of the working class. This was certainly Charles Knight's ambition with the *Penny Magazine*, and to judge from his peak circulation figures he was remarkably successful. Like most Victorian agents of 'elevation' and 'improvement', of course, the culture industry found it easier to reach the most skilled manual workers and especially non-manual workers on the borderlands between the working and middle classes. Knight judged his customers to embrace 'the schoolboy, the apprentice, the milliner, the factory girl, the clerk, and the small shopkeeper'.[11] As the market broadened, so the opportunities for specialization grew, and the likelihood that the market would become segmented; there was not one market, not one cultural identity, but many. But until the mid-nineteenth century there persisted a central segment of the culture industry that generated products for general consumption – that could be picked up and enjoyed by shopgirl and clubman alike – for whom a uniform 'serious' cultural style had to be devised.[12]

The Gothic and the Picturesque provided materials better suited to the task than anything élite culture had previously offered, but they

still had to be redrawn to suit the new cultural world. Above all, they
had to be made less exclusive, not so much anti-aristocratic as non-
aristocratic, that is, popular and national, 'warmer and more genial', in
Ainsworth's phrase.[13] Scott had given a lead. People of all social ranks
had to be heard speaking a common language and sharing common
customs and experiences. What is now thought of as Victorian sentimentalism was often simply a determination to bring elevated figures
down to a universal level. The melodrama, a favourite Victorian mode
in fiction and poetry as well as in the theatre, nearly always featured
aristocrats courting working-class maids or labouring men discovered
in the end to be aristocrats switched at birth. Similarly, Scott's zeal for
local verisimilitude was widely adopted to assert the distinctive character of the different parts of England against the metropolitan tendency to aestheticize and anthropologize them. London-based artists
and writers of this period, who often had genuine provincial pedi-
grees, were always careful to emphasize how many miles they had
travelled to check local details, how they had sketched on site to
guarantee accuracy, how they had consulted local experts and antiquaries on matters of lore and custom.[14]

Historical settings and trappings were integral to this new style.
Why should this have been? It was certainly not a phenomenon
confined to Britain; popular spectacle and reading in France and
Germany also embraced a highly detailed and melodramatic historical
style from the 1820s. The recourse to history does seem to be a
common feature of rapidly growing cultural markets, struggling to free
themselves from forms and values hitherto the province of an élite. In
these circumstances the past can be appealed to both for its golden
ages (when, it could be claimed, widespread participation was once
common) or simply as a common resource of all classes (a demotic
story unrestricted by arcane knowledge or linguistic barriers). One
writer on nationalism has gone so far as to claim that 'history
alone . . . can furnish the bases of ethnic identity and the psychic
reassurance of communal security that goes with it'.[15]

Whatever the truth of this, it is clearly not necessary to explain the
Victorian turn to history – as British historians, less comfortable with
cultural nationalism than their French or German counterparts, tend to
do – by reference to ruling-class anxieties about the pace of social
change and the fear of political upheaval. The use of history is not
necessarily prescriptive or conservative, and is often very far from
being a device of social control. On the contrary, élite culture's
longstanding disregard of national history in favour of classicism and
cosmopolitanism gave the past an intrinsically democratic appear-

ance.[16] Long before the early Victorian period of cultural democrati-zation, political radicals had made arguments for constitutional change based on the idea of a lost 'ancient constitution', more popular and national, which had been subverted in the recent past but which could still be reconstructed. It was a natural instinct for advocates (*not* opponents) of change in a highly stable and hierarchical society to seek a pedigree, a tradition for their programme. In much the same way, the Victorian culture industry called into existence an old world to redress the balance of the new.

This motive can clearly be seen in the ways in which Victorian popular culture's identification with the past diverged from the parallel but different identifications developing in élite culture. Both eight-eenth-century antiquarianism and Scott's fictional extensions had dwelt heavily upon the Middle Ages. Aesthetes had enjoyed the thrill of tasting such forbidden fruits as Catholic piety, morbidity and decay; Scott had tried to rehabilitate the medieval from some of these asso-ciations by playing up the purity, simplicity and high ideals of chivalry, and his themes persisted in élite culture throughout the nineteenth century. As Mark Girouard has shown, chivalric models of leadership were adopted, with varying degrees of seriousness, by an aristocracy anxious to recast itself in a more serious and pious mode, so that the anxieties that had produced the Gothic Picturesque did indeed pro-duce a more historically accurate Gothicism in the mid-Victorian period. So useful was chivalry for this purpose that it quickly became detached from its medieval roots and spread widely throughout élite Victorian culture in modern dress, on the playing fields of the public schools, in the decoration and design of public buildings and country houses, and, ultimately, on the battlefields of Flanders.[17]

Intellectuals had their own uses for medievalism. Clerics wishing to revive the Church of England could look to a medieval priesthood for inspiration and refurbish the rotting medieval churches that dotted the countryside. Closely linked to the medieval movement in the Church was the rise of professional historical scholarship and antiquarianism, often pioneered by clergymen. A network of antiquarian societies grew out of the Oxford Movement within the Church, from the late 1830s. Scholarship soon acquired a momentum of its own, developing archival and archaeological techniques that could be applied to all ages, but of course the challenge was greater the more obscure the subject, and scholars had a tendency to move ever further backwards rather than forwards in time, to Roman and Celtic studies as well as the medieval.[18] Scholarly antiquarianism and Gothicism became indis-solubly linked and both found a considerable audience in polite

8 Chivalric medievalism aimed at an upper-class Tory audience: detail from Daniel Maclise's *The Chivalric Vow of the Ladies and the Peacock* (1835).

society. By the 1820s, the prestige series of engravings on classical or Picturesque lines – often depicting country houses set in landscape – that had dominated the top end of the market for the preceding century were giving way to series featuring medieval ruins, churches and cathedrals of the kind pioneered by John Carter and John Britton.[19]

The mass-culture industry, however, was motivated by quite different interests and thus dealt in different products. The purity and self-abnegation of the cult of chivalric leadership and the technicalities and obscurities of medieval scholarship were of limited use to their mass audience. They needed a past with which ordinary people could identify, which offered parallels and prefigurations of modern society, not medieval retreats from the problems of modernity, a past that fed the burgeoning appetites of the new consumer. Scott had, as always, given a lead. His early epics, though looking backwards to the glory days of chivalry, had been predominantly set in what the early Victorians came to think of as 'the Olden Time', broadly the period between medieval rudeness and aristocratic over-refinement, the time of the Tudors and early Stuarts. By the time of *The Abbot* (1820) and *Kenilworth* (1821), he had seen the potential and embraced the Olden Time wholeheartedly, though never exclusively. Scott's medievalism continued to reappear in mock tournaments and other élite cultural displays, but the images and tropes that resonated most durably in popular culture were his Olden Time set-pieces: the sixteenth-century settings for the swashbuckling of the early epic poems; key events in the life of Mary Queen of Scots taken from *The Abbot*; the great festivities for Queen Elizabeth at the close of *Kenilworth*; Cromwell's coming face-to-face with the portrait of Charles I in *Woodstock*. Thereafter, much of what has loosely been called early Victorian 'medievalism' is really set in the Olden Time.

By the 1840s there was a clear distinction between scholarly and popular antiquarianism, with the latter much more closely tied to a mass market and consequently to the Olden Time. There was, in fact, an institutional split within the antiquarian community, between the Archaeological Institute – dominated by the fanatical Gothicist J.H. Parker – and the British Archaeological Association – in whose ranks could be found such men as Thomas Wright, Samuel Carter Hall, F.W. Fairholt, Harrison Ainsworth and others producing a more eclectic range of material for the popular market.[20] Whereas Scott had distributed himself equitably between medieval and Olden Time settings, Ainsworth hitched his novels firmly to the sixteenth and seventeenth centuries, setting only two before Henry VII's time and eighteen in the Tudor and early Stuart periods.[21] At the Royal Academy, where the painters were shifting from reliance on aristocratic patronage to the 'new money' that also meant the new taste, there was a dramatic move away from the classics, portraiture and Grand Manner style towards history painting, but also from the 1830s a marked shift in the subject-matter of history painting from the Middle Ages to the Tudors and Stuarts.[22] The anniversary of the Battle of Hastings in 1866 was hardly noticed except by a few scholars, but the Shakespeare tercentenary in 1864 and the Hampden and Milton bicentenaries in 1843 and 1874 were national events.[23] Increasingly, the Gothic became the mode by which popular Victorian writers induced terror, suspense and alienation – following established trends in popular as well as élite culture – but the Olden Time became the Victorians' common heritage, the past in which the whole nation saw itself.[24]

The appeal of the Olden Time was various and complex. It benefited from being neither medieval nor modern, neither barbaric nor over-refined, neither too distant nor too recent. Victorian popular writers were very clear about the Olden Time's positive qualities. Prominent among them was the vision of social connection, of nascent nationhood, that it conveyed. Earlier, radicals who had deployed the 'ancient constitution' to argue for constitutional change had looked askance at what they called Tudor authoritarianism in suppressing old English liberties and appropriating the people's land and money. But as constitutional change became a reality – non-Anglicans gained civil rights in 1827–9, and the franchise was remodelled, if not on a democratic at least on a non-traditional basis, in 1832 – political medievalism lost its usefulness.[25] Tudor authoritarianism could now be viewed in a new light as nation-building, establishing equality under the law and a genuinely national religion in the form of English Protestantism, and, by enforcing the peace, putting an end to baronial rule, allowing talent and merit to flourish. Force of arms, the prerogative of the chivalric few, gave way to culture and commerce, the occupations of the many. Simplicity and self-denial yielded to diversity and a degree of self-indulgence.

The stress laid on culture and commerce was popular but not anti-aristocratic. Until the late nineteenth century, when anti-aristocratic themes rose to prominence in both working and middle-class politics, the nation had room for all sorts. Indeed, popular antiquarians were keen to include an aristocracy that had demonstrated its national bona fides.[26] Culture and commerce in the Olden Time were popular occupations that relied on aristocratic patronage, and the point of connection was emphasized. Not surprisingly, writers for the Victorian culture industry put the promotion of art and literature high on the list of Olden Time virtues, but perhaps less predictable is the praise showered on the ruling classes – even by radicals such as Howitt – for their encouragement of domestic talent in the fine arts. Elizabeth and Drake, Pembroke and Shakespeare, Sir Philip Sidney and Edmund Spenser formed statesman-artist couplets that were crucial to popular antiquarian writing. The image of the minstrel, first exploited by Scott, carried the same message at a slightly different level: the minstrel was kept by the prince to record and repeat the body of common lore.

The cross-class nature of commerce was conveyed in a slightly different way. It was not until later in the century that the Olden Time's contribution to modern capitalism and industrialism as the first age of discovery and entrepreneurship would be emphasized, and then principally by antiquarians in industrial sections of the country, especially Yorkshire.[27] Popular antiquarians earlier in the century were instead at pains to show that the Olden Time was a period of extending consumption, luxury and display. Loving descriptions of fancy dress – the ruffs and farthingales beloved of Victorian history painters – and feasting and overblown interior decoration not only made for brighter pictures and more vivid stories, but also drew explicit parallels with the Victorians' own love of richness and intricacy in dress and design. The Olden Time had put firmly behind it the crudity and barbarity of the Middle Ages, but it had not yet embraced the exclusiveness of fashion and taste. Aristocratic display in the Olden Time served communal purposes: public rituals, like the great royal peregrinations, seasonal rituals like Maying and the Yuletide, and especially the daily responsibility of hospitality. Great men kept open house for dependants and strangers alike, thus continuing to discharge the charitable functions of the Catholic Church dissolved by the Reformation. There is no more frequently depicted Olden Time scene than the feast in the great hall, all classes assembled together in the consumption of beer and the Roast Beef of Old England and in collective appreciation of the noise of the band, the harping of the minstrel, the florid carving in wood and stone, the capering of the fool, the fluttering of banners, and the peacock displays of satin, brocade and fine linen.[28]

Undoubtedly the most important aspect of the Olden Time to the public, and the craftsmen who re-created it for them, was its familiarity. Nearly every popular writer and artist laboured, after Scott's example, to present both the mighty and the meek of Olden Time as intimate and domestic creatures, just like their Victorian audience.

9    Joseph Nash's impression of Christmas festivities in the Olden Time at Haddon Hall: nobility, household and retainers join together, drinking from the wassail-bowl and enjoying the mummers, morris-dancers, hobby-horse, dragon, giant and 'salvage man' (the club-bearing figure at centre).

What is more, popular antiquarians insisted – against much scholarly carping – that this humanizing of the past was their own finest and most necessary achievement. It was not only that they were legitimating their own culture by demonstrating its affinities with the past; they were also engaged in a kind of scholarship themselves by rediscovering the human qualities of past ages buried under what William Howitt called 'the dust of ages and heaviness of antiquarian rubbish'.[29] They did not consider that they were inventing a past to fit their own preoccupations, but rather were reanimating a past that had been flattened and edited for exclusive purposes by virtuosi and aesthetes. A surprising array of opinion shared this view. The *Penny Magazine*, the trailblazer in providing culture for the million, naturally defended historical re-creation on the rather utilitarian ground that it extended the audience:

we hold it to be so great an advantage that multitudes should realize impressions (which are seldom contrary to truth) concerning historical places, persons, and circumstances, of which they would otherwise have had no impression at all, that none of the minor evils to the few who have subsequent occasion to discover that the writer dressed the facts, which he found naked, before he offered them to notice, are sufficient to neutralize it.[30]

Thomas Carlyle, who had no interest in defending mass acculturation simply for its own sake, thought that historical recreations actually represented a higher truth, 'unknown to writers of history and others, till so taught: that the bygone ages of the world were actually filled with living men, not by protocols, state papers, controversies and abstractions of men.'[31] This was, of course, the view of the popular antiquarians themselves.

Insisting as they did on the affiliations between past and present, popular antiquarians rarely considered themselves vulnerable to a charge of nostalgia or conservatism. Their recovery of the past was so closely connected in their minds to the building of a mass audience for culture that they could only see the enterprise as this-worldly and highly useful.[32] On the contrary, the promotion of lost traditions in English arts and letters was a salutary recognition of the dramatic changes in economy and society that had produced the popular culture market. Comparatively uninterested in extending popular access to high aristocratic culture, they turned instead to what high aristocratic culture had until recently rejected, the national past. 'It can scarcely be a question whether we – that is, the public – desire to see what is usually called "the good old times" revivified in reality', insisted the *Art Journal* in July 1857, and yet

> it is quite certain there is no class of pictures which more powerfully arrest the attention than works that recall them. Who would care to hang on his wall a representation of a dinner at the Freemasons' Tavern or the Trafalgar, or of an aristocratic gathering at Almack's, or of the interior of a church in Belgravia during service? The eye and the mind alike shrink from such pictorial inanities; with all our love of the advantages among which we live, and with all our appreciation of the comforts, social and political, that surround us on every side, we revert with no little pride and pleasure to what our ancestors were, and to what they did . . .[33]

The historical school *was* contemporary culture. Scott and the Romantics, Leslie and Frith and the history painters were great artists who had picked up the thread that led back to Shakespeare and Spenser, Holbein and Van Dyck, but which had been dropped in the interval by virtuosi and exquisites.

The Olden Time held its spell over popular taste for a very long time by modern standards of evanescent fashion. The persistence of this style must owe something to its association with the new forms of cultural consumption and thus to the loyalty of a newly enfranchised audience. Art historians argue that Victorian artists were held captive by this audience, whose purchases of framed engravings and illustrated magazines kept up the prestige and incomes of living artists practising the popular styles. Few artists were brave enough to break free of this cosy relationship, and the cross-class nature of the cultural nation meant that few aristocratic or *haut bourgeois* patrons were interested in supporting artistic experiments. The dominant mood in the Royal Academy as late as the 1870s, when its popularity was at its height, was still caught by history painters in the Leslie and Frith mould – one of the most popular was Leslie's son – whose subjects were so often Shakespearean and Elizabethan and whose style was accessible, realistic and 'literary', rather than painterly.[34]

The rise of the cultural nation and the growth of a sense of history were therefore all of a piece. An idea of heritage, of a past belonging to the present, grew naturally out of this junction, if only at first on a fairly abstract level. But popular antiquarians did not shy away from expressing this idea more concretely as well. They were nearly all advocates of extending public access to those relics of the past that might legitimately fall within the public realm. Sir Samuel Rush Meyrick, for instance, a scholarly antiquary with strong popular inclinations, was instrumental in the organization and display of the armour collections in the Tower of London, which were first opened to the public in 1828 – an Olden Time show, not a medieval one, as the collections were exclusively Tudor and Stuart.[35] Ten years later, Ainsworth used his sensational novel, *The Tower of London*, also set in the Olden Time, to promote the refurbishment and cheap public opening of the most historic sections of the Tower, and in 1839 Howitt was a motive force behind the free opening of Hampton Court Palace with its valued Tudor associations.[36] Contemporaries attributed the incredible popularity of the Tower and Hampton Court to Ainsworth's writings, the work of the history painters and, especially, the wide circulation of the new illustrated magazines.[37] By the 1850s, Hampton Court and the Tower had become the most visited historic buildings in the country, drawing respectively over 200,000 and 100,000 visitors a year.[38]

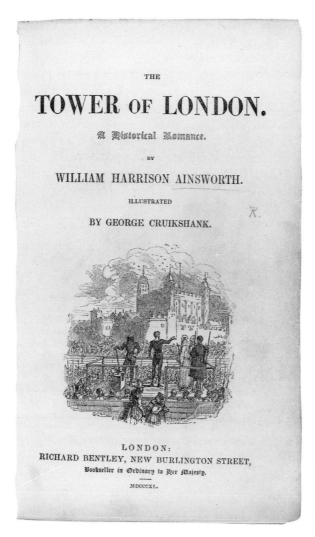

THE

# TOWER OF LONDON.

A Historical Romance.

BY

WILLIAM HARRISON AINSWORTH.

ILLUSTRATED

BY GEORGE CRUIKSHANK.

LONDON:
RICHARD BENTLEY, NEW BURLINGTON STREET,
Bookseller in Ordinary to Her Majesty.

MDCCCXL.

10 Ainsworth's *Tower of London* (1840), part-romance, part-guidebook, gave a further boost to mass tourism.

It was not necessary to share Howitt's radical politics to agree with him that royal palaces might be considered to some extent 'public property'.[39] It would be much harder to make the case for buildings such as country houses, which were obviously private property, and the property of a class highly jealous of its rights in this respect. Yet the intensity of popular identification with the Olden Time and the success of the Victorian culture industry in propagandizing for a national heritage meant that even these private homes fell to a surprising extent into the imaginative and also the physical possession of the Victorian public.

## Mansions of the Olden Time

The relics of the Olden Time that were most numerous and conspicuous on the English landscape were the country mansions of the gentry
and aristocracy: it was, after all, a great part of the Olden Time's
appeal to the Victorians that its art and money poured not into
religion or battle but into domestic life. So many hundreds of country
houses were built in the sixteenth and early seventeenth centuries that
despite the stuccoing and classicizing destructiveness of the intervening
period there were still Tudor and Stuart mansions scattered liberally all
over the country. Many had been virtually deserted by their owners,
leaving them prey to deterioration or alternative use – as farmhouses,
brewhouses, stables and worse, as in the sad case of the semi-ruin
of Kirby Hall, Northamptonshire, described indignantly by Samuel
Carter Hall in the mid-1840s:

> a farmer occupies a suite of rooms, the decorations of which would
> excite astonishment and admiration in a London Club-house; farm-
> servants sleep surrounded by exquisite carvings; one room in
> the south side of the Quadrangle, decorated with a fine old fire-
> place . . . served, at the time of the artist's visit, the purpose of a
> dog-kennel; and an elegant Chapel, constructed by Inigo Jones,
> is entered with difficulty through piles of lumber and heaps of
> rubbish.[40]

Fortunately for nineteenth-century taste, it was the smaller manor
houses that had been the most likely to disappear, to make way
for more commodious Georgian homes, or to suffer farmers' and
labourers' occupation in the village while the big house was erected
on a more elevated site. Larger buildings, including nearly all of the
huge 'prodigy houses' erected competitively by Elizabethan courtiers,
were too great an asset to throw away. Instead, owners of great Olden
Time houses – such as Knole, Haddon Hall, Temple Newsam,
Wollaton and Hardwick – preserved these old fossils, out of pride or
sentiment, but used the surplus cash yielded by the great Georgian
agricultural revolution to build themselves more comfortable and
fashionable residences. The eighteenth- and early nineteenth-century
Dukes of Rutland and Devonshire lived at Belvoir and Chatsworth
while nearby Haddon and Hardwick mouldered quietly away, enlivened occasionally by a shooting party, otherwise kept up only adequately by a skeleton staff. The Meynells, who inherited sprawling
Temple Newsam in 1834, left it 'neglected and ill kept' for several
generations, preferring their Staffordshire home of Hoar Cross.[41] Lord

Middleton, the owner of Wollaton Hall outside Nottingham, had no fewer than four other seats, including a second in the same county, and either let his Elizabethan white elephant to *nouveaux-riches* tenants or shut it up entirely.[42]

However disused and neglected, these mansions of the Olden Time were still private property, and the property, too, of that class most notoriously jealous of its property rights. In the first half of the nineteenth century, when tensions were high between aristocracy and people, those rights became more heavily freighted still. Was the crowd outside the country-house gates friend or foe? Was the rich man inside them a patriot or a tyrant? So long as these questions were still being asked it would not be easy for the nation to develop an aesthetic or historical interest in the mansions of the aristocracy. During the Reform riots of 1831, a mob burnt down the Duke of Newcastle's mansion in the centre of Nottingham; country houses became targets for demonstrations by roving bands of Chartists, if never on the same scale as was later the case in Ireland; and as late as 1844, one Ultra-Tory MP, John Tollemache, commissioned from the architect Anthony Salvin a working medieval castle at Peckforton in Cheshire, perhaps in the same spirit of defiance of modernity as had moved George III in the shadow of the French Revolution.[43]

There may not have been much overlap between the composition of the Chartist crowds and the audience for the culture industry's efforts to construct a national heritage, but the idea of heritage was nevertheless enmeshed by such social tensions. Accordingly, the culture industry's approach to the real, existing mansions of the Olden Time – as opposed to their depictions in Scott and Ainsworth, however thinly fictionalized – was at first hesitant. Hampton Court and the Tower of London were one thing, Haddon and Knole another.

Medieval ruins were much more easily dealt with. They were just as likely to be private property as habitable buildings – everything in Britain was private property, a shocked Henry James noted when visiting in the 1870s[44] – but for a variety of reasons their owners were not so concerned to enforce their property rights over them. As already seen, ruined abbeys had been the object of polite tourism from quite early on. Gilpin and others had pronounced judgement on them in the 'court of Taste'. Originally Church property, they already had a national air to them. The scholarly antiquarianism of the early nineteenth century sanctified them further. Castles, too, had their transcendental qualities magnified by élite medievalism. It is interesting, however, that Scott tended to set his romances in ruined castles,

which had been deprived of their domestic character.[45] His greatest
Olden Time novel, *Kenilworth*, was set in one of the few ruined
mansions of the country, where only the gatehouse was habitable.
Ainsworth, though keen to anglicize the continental romance by
setting it in 'an old English manorial residence' and indeed 'wishing to
describe, somewhat minutely . . . an ancient Hall with which I was
acquainted', did not name Cuckfield Hall, the model for *Rookwood*
(1834), and did not feel free until much later to fix his novels in
identifiable private homes.[46]

In the 1820s and 1830s, popular antiquarians, too, when they wrote
about buildings chose most often to write about medieval secular
and ecclesiastical ruins.[47] Among other reasons, they knew that their
audience would have relatively free access to these sites. Tintern and
Fountains remained favourite subjects, but others, comparatively
neglected previously, rose to prominence because of their proximity
to towns. Netley Abbey outside Southampton, for instance, became a
highly popular sightseeing and picnic spot in the 1830s, its appeal lying
'not so much in any architectural magnificence of which it has
to boast,' said the *Penny Magazine*, 'as in the singular loveliness of
the spot'.[48] A decade later, in R. H. Barham's classic spoof of élite
medievalism, *The Ingoldsby Legends*, a gentlemanly visitor to Netley
declared himself 'exceedingly angry, and very much scandalized/
Finding these beautiful ruins so Vandalized' by 'All the World and his
wife' dancing and drinking tea on this holy ground. He blamed the
owner for not policing his property more strictly.[49]

Mounting enthusiasm for the Olden Time in the 1830s could not
forever be confined to imaginary or fragmentary settings when so
many splendidly well-preserved sites were in reality available. Two
works published at the end of the decade marked something of a
breakthrough.[50]

The first volume of Joseph Nash's drawings of *Mansions of England
in the Olden Time* appeared in 1839, to be followed over the next ten
years by three more volumes, gaining progressively in accuracy and
sensitivity (partly due, once again, to technological improvements in
pictorial reproduction). Nash's lithographs were not issued separately
or in parts, but only in these four large and expensive volumes, which
were themselves not reprinted until 1869.[51] But their influence on
popular knowledge and taste was enormous. They unleashed a body of
immensely potent images of life and art in the Olden Time which
became the standard way of visualizing this most highly valued period
in English history. Immediately upon publication in book form they
were copied in woodcuts carried by the popular weekly *Saturday*

11 Netley Abbey, a popular early Victorian picnicking spot (as depicted in the *Penny Magazine*, 13 April 1833).

*Magazine*, principal rival to Charles Knight's *Penny Magazine*.[52] They were subsequently reproduced in other people's books, plagiarized and embroidered upon for a century or more; only since the 1960s have they been no longer accepted as sufficiently accurate or balanced to appear even in children's books.[53]

Significantly, this pioneering work was published by a man crossing over from élite to popular culture. Joseph Nash had been trained as an architect and architectural draughtsman by Augustus Pugin, father of

# THE
# Saturday Magazine.

No. 642.   JULY   2ND, 1842.   { PRICE
{ ONE PENNY.

THE HALL, WOLLATON
*From* NASH's *Mansions of England in the Olden Time.   Third Series.*

12   Nash's *Mansions of England in the Olden Time* (1839–49) were first popularized in cheap woodcut versions on the cover of the *Saturday Magazine*. The hall at Wollaton, from the issue of 2 July 1842.

the famous Gothicist, and most of his early work was high-quality illustrations of Gothic details for prestigious architectural publications. But Nash's own imagination, and perhaps his sense of the way public opinion was drifting, could not be contained within the bounds of High Gothic austerity. He showed an early preference for the architecture of the Olden Time and developed a distinctive style of peopling his finely detailed buildings with figures contemporary to the buildings they inhabited, authentically costumed and going about their daily lives, providing ample doses of historical and literary association, costume, manners and social history with the art and architecture. Nash was not the only artist of his time to deviate from architectural purism in this way. George Cattermole, another architectural draughtsman who put aside his Gothic work in the 1830s to concentrate on watercolours of Olden Time scenes, followed a similar line of development, inspired initially by his work illustrating an edition of Scott; his *Wanderers Entertained*, exhibited in the same year of 1839, became a standard image of Olden Time virtue, widely distributed as an engraving under the title *Old English Hospitality*. But Nash's intimacy and sentimentality went much further. In 1838 he had already gone overboard in a volume of plates nominally illustrating the *Architecture of the Middle Ages*, but which frankly degenerated into a celebration of what architects snobbily called 'Cinque Cento', that is, the exuberant Elizabethan: impure, Nash admitted to his Gothicist audience, but so imaginative, so fanciful![54] The *Mansions of England in the Olden Time* was a natural sequel.

These hundred or so plates were a revelation to a public that had never before had so full an opportunity to visualize the actual physical settings of their Scott and Ainsworth romances, the buildings in which their history scenes took place. Indeed, few architectural specialists would have seen or for that matter known of many of the houses Nash depicted. He had travelled painstakingly all over the country to ferret out obscure Olden Time details, making initial drawings on the spot, and then transferring them to the lithographer's stone in order to transmit his personal experience direct to the viewer. The intimacy of Nash's drawings is derived not only from his use of the new lithotinting process (also employed by Cattermole), which imported painterly effects of texture and shading into mass-produced works, and from the attention to detail with which the domestic life of the Olden Time is portrayed, but also from his deliberate effort to put himself into his audience's romantic shoes:

> In producing a set of views of the picturesque architecture of the mansions of England, the artist's object has been to present them in

a new and attractive light . . . glowing with the genial warmth of
their fire-sides, and enlivened with the presence of their inmates
and guests, enjoying the recreations and pastimes, or celebrating the
festivals, of our ancestors . . . in attempting this the artist has
endeavoured to place himself in the position of a visitor to these
ancient edifices, whose fancy peoples the deserted halls, stripped of
all movable ornaments and looking damp and cheerless, with the
family and household of the 'old English gentleman' surrounded by
their everyday comforts, sharing the more rare and courteous
hospitalities offered to the guests, or partaking of the boisterous
merriment of Christmas gambols.[55]

Here Nash has neatly summed up the content of his plates. Most
showed interiors, the upper two-thirds of the frame filled to bursting
with frantic Elizabethan ornament, the bottom normally occupied by
some domestic scene: laughing cavaliers courting their richly brocaded
ladies, children and pets frolicking on carpets flowing down a long
gallery, a lonely maid with a book in her lap or idly strumming a lute.
Viewed through half-closed eyes, these might – designedly – be scenes
of warmth and comfort from an over-stuffed Victorian parlour. Then
there are views signalling the idiosyncracies of the Olden Time:
Roundheads and Cavaliers engaging in sword-play on the staircase at
Aston Hall; tilting at the quintain outside the picturesque gabled front
of Compton Wynyates; a dramatic moon and torch-lit scene of a
travelling party approaching Hardwick; a game of 'Hoodman blind' –
the blindman's buff of the Olden Time – in the great hall at
Athelhampton; Henry VIII himself processing through a gateway into
the courtyard of Hever Castle, and later drawing Anne Boleyn into a
nook in the long gallery above. Most imitated of all are a few
portrayals of bacchanalian revels in the great halls of Penshurst,
Haddon and Ightham Mote, where everything that the Victorians
most loved about the Olden Time could be set on a single stage: the
importance of hospitality and the sense of social connection between
all ranks, the surfeit of food and noise and high spirits, more than a
hint of illicit wildness, which the viewer could perhaps enjoy only
vicariously.
   Nash's method of animating his buildings with these social-
historical details was not popular at the time (nor has it been since)
with architectural purists. To their eyes his technique pandered to a
philistine audience who required historical and literary associations to
interest them in buildings whose formal properties they were incapable of appreciating.[56] But the criticism confuses both genres and

audiences. Nash's plates were not the successor to the country-house views of the eighteenth century, for which the classical detail of the houses was the *raison d'être*. They were, rather, the successor to the history paintings of the 1820s and 1830s, for which incident and sentiment were central – and the successor, too, to purely literary realizations of the Olden Time, which had no visual component whatsoever. Seen from this angle, Nash's *Mansions* were great architectural steps forward. If anything they indulge in some Piranesian licence, exaggerating and fantasizing with details of plasterwork and timbering that were not quite prominent enough. They trained the early Victorian eye to love Elizabethan superabundance, just as Gilpin had trained the late Georgian to appreciate the tamer pleasures of the Picturesque. They confirmed what the popular audience wanted to believe, that the mansions of the Olden Time, far from being crude and gloomy as polite taste insisted, had before recent neglect 'realised every necessary comfort in their day, while they were a hundredfold more artistic and interesting than the cold formal mansions of the Georgian era'.[57] Above all, they invited ordinary readers to seek out the Olden Time with which they were already familiar, not only in books and heavily stylized history paintings, but in actual buildings, still intact in much the same state as Nash depicted them.

The usefulness of literary and historical associations in persuading the English that these aristocratic mansions were indeed part of their own tradition is clearer in a second work, the first volume of which appeared on the heels of Nash's. This was William Howitt's *Visits to Remarkable Places*, published by Longman in 1840; a second volume appeared in 1842. Whereas Nash had probably been unfamiliar to most readers before the *Mansions*, Howitt and his wife Mary had been an established part of the culture industry for a decade, principally as imitators of and propagandists for Romantic poetry in the annuals, magazines and their own cheap compilations. They had gained an immense popularity, not only at home, but in the United States, where their simplicity and egalitarianism won them more friends than their Romantic heroes could claim; one scholar has suggested that by the late 1830s Mary Howitt was the Americans' favourite living foreign poet.[58]

The Howitts were the foremost early Victorian proponents of 'culture' as a national patrimony that had to be reclaimed from aristocratic exclusiveness for the whole of the people. 'Culture' to them meant the unappropriated English landscape and the great deeds done upon it by men and women who had sprung from the people, especially poets and patriots. Like Cobbett, they were champions of

14  Nash's *Mansions of England in the Olden Time* (1839–49): Roundheads and Cavaliers at Aston Hall.

13a and b ( *facing page*)  Nash's *Mansions of England in the Olden Time* (1839–49): scenes of domesticity (*top*, the gallery over the hall at Knole; *bottom*, Speke Hall).

15–18 Nash's *Mansions of England in the Olden Time* (1839–49): *above*, tilting at the quintain outside Compton Wynyates . . .

. . . moonlit mystery at Hardwick Hall . . .

. . . Hoodman blind in the great hall of Athelhampton . . .

. . . Henry VIII arriving at Hever Castle.

'traditional' rural life as they imagined it had existed before the recent over-enrichment of the aristocracy – peasant cultivation, native games and sports, free and frank relations between the classes. Unlike Cobbett, they were also unambiguous moderns with a simple optimism about the ability of the present generation to claim its patrimony that undoubtedly stemmed from their youthful Quakerism. As writers themselves, they were naturally proudest of modern literature, for its humane evocations of natural beauty (Wordsworth and Southey) and of ancient liberty (Scott above all), necessary antidotes to the grim materialism that accompanied modern prosperity. But neither were they blind to the advantages of prosperity in disseminating culture, and in the late 1830s and the 1840s they were particularly enamoured of steam for bringing the delights of nature and history to the people (or, rather, vice versa).[59]

The influence of steam-driven mobility was already apparent in Howitt's two-volume *Rural Life of England* (1838), a Cobbettite paean to traditional England and a critique of modern social and cultural immiseration. *Rural Life* had included accounts of Howitt's visits to scenes from Byron's life and other spots near his own native Nottingham, including Hardwick and Annesley Halls and Newstead Abbey, and it closed with an appeal to his readers to vary their life of labour with pilgrimages of their own. *Visits to Remarkable Places* aimed to facilitate such pilgrimages. It began the work of drawing up a literary and historical map of England for the new age of mass tourism. Importantly, this map followed the shifting balance of population and concentrated upon the Midlands and the North, where, Howitt claimed, the great poets had recognized that the history and beauty of the land was concentrated: 'southward, tradition becomes more faint'.[60] Scenes associated with the work of Shakespeare, Wordsworth and Scott predominate, though the seventeenth-century struggles for liberty provide a significant counterpoint, and a search for reminiscences of Rousseau's brief stay in Staffordshire in 1766–7 forms a curious coda.

Howitt's animus against the aristocracy of his own time was closely connected to an admiration for the aristocracy of the Olden Time, and pilgrimages to castles and country houses of the Tudor and Elizabethan periods are central to the two volumes of *Visits*.[61] 'Our country houses, and especially the older ones, are in themselves an inestimable national treasure', he had written in *Rural Life*, the radical democrat originating a line of 'national heritage' thinking, now often derided as an aristocratic plot.[62] In part this had to do with associations. The leadership of the aristocracy in the Olden Time had sanctified their houses as places of poetry and liberty; visitors to Penshurst Place in Kent, home of the Sidneys, poets and liberators, 'know that they will . . . tread the same ground, and gaze on the same scenes as these patriots and heroes'.[63] But the houses themselves were also legible records of social history, 'the very construction of them' testifying to the quality of life in the Olden Time:

> ample courts . . . rambling and extensive offices that once were necessary to the jolly establishment of the age . . . vast kitchens . . . great halls, where scores of rude revellers have feasted in returning from battle, or the chase . . . tapestried chambers . . . the very closets and bowers of the ladies themselves . . . the antique chapel, and the library . . . But the armoury and the great gallery – these are the places in which a flood of historic light pours in upon you, and the spirit of the past is made so palpable, that you forget your real existence in this utilitarian century.[64]

This again may be architectural writing insufficiently aesthetic for modern tastes, but in its own time it was a sound recipe for stimulating a popular taste for antiquities.

In the early 1840s, when both Chartism and anti-Corn Law sentiment were in the air to heighten tension between aristocracy and people, it probably required a radical egalitarian such as Howitt to sanction popular admiration of old country houses. In the succeeding decades, especially after political pressure eased in the late 1840s, his example and that of Joseph Nash were taken up by all branches of the culture industry in a swelling stream of prints, magazine articles, topographical writings and, as the railway network extended, guidebooks and handbooks. The *Penny Magazine*, which had gingerly avoided country houses for most of the 1830s, suddenly in 1839 unleashed a series that embraced Knole, Belvoir, Wilton, Blenheim, Chatsworth and Hampden House (home of the Parliamentarian hero), and was notably delirious about the Olden Time Knole and censorious about the super-aristocratic Chatsworth.[65]

Samuel Carter Hall, with his nose for a marketable commodity, launched a frank imitation of Nash's series in 1843, *The Baronial Halls, Picturesque Edifices, and Ancient Churches of England*. Issued in parts to capture a larger audience, it offered lithotints, very much in the Nash style, of drawings – almost exclusively of 'baronial halls', despite the catch-all title – by nearly all the leading architectural and landscape painters of the day. These were accompanied by Hall's commentary, pointing out the literary and historical associations of the houses illustrated and highlighting details for potential visitors, thus combining the functions of the Nash and Howitt volumes. Hall was very conscious of his market. He began his series with Cobham in Kent, whose 'proximity to the Metropolis . . . supplies a sufficient motive for the selection'. Like Howitt, he otherwise gave special attention to houses near the great concentrations of population in the Midlands and North, especially in Warwickshire and Cheshire. Coming as they do from many different hands, the plates are of varying quality and content; many of them set their houses in modern rather than historic dress, and none go to Nash's lengths of fantasy and extravagance. Still, Hall's vigorous text encourages his readers strongly to venture out in search of these vestiges of the Olden Time, a part of their history that was fast falling victim to the depredations of time and ignorance.[66] Hall followed up this success with a diverse series of articles on country houses in his *Art Journal*, co-written with his friend Llewellynn Jewitt, and despite the *Journal's* limited readership, like Nash and Howitt's works, the Hall and Jewitt essays became a resource for all sorts of later uses. Jewitt's lyrical tour of Haddon Hall was still in use as a guide-book to that house at the time of the First World War.[67]

Mansions of the Olden Time were regularly featured in magazines that had a wider circulation than the *Art Journal*, and especially in the abundantly illustrated Christmas numbers, which by the 1850s had taken over from the annuals as the most highly prized sources of illustration and reading matter. The *Illustrated London News* was the most famous and successful of these magazines, and its Christmas issues were regularly stuffed with engravings of Olden Time scenes from famous history paintings, of 'moated granges' and 'picturesque old houses', both real and imagined. Similar features ran in the specialized leisure-interest magazines that popped up in this period, titles like *Once A Week*, *Good Words* and *The Leisure Hour*, though the more religiously oriented magazines, for example the last-named, were inclined to disapprove of the Olden Time because of its sensuality and grotesquerie.[68] Magazines aimed specifically at a radical working-class audience were, in contrast, eager to play up the alien and the out-landish. When *Reynolds's Miscellany* wanted to depict Christmas in the Olden Time, it rendered even more disorderly and chaotic one of Nash's extreme scenes of seasonal revels in the great hall of Haddon.[69] The superstitious and bloodthirsty events such magazines required were more easily set in the Middle Ages – the Gothicism of the 'Gothic' never vanished – but the mansions of the Olden Time continued to serve for sensationalist radicals as symbols of the 'older and merrier days' against which the modern aristocracy could be judged severely.[70] Publications that did not have this specific political

19  Pushing the Olden Time over the top: this further elaboration on Nash's depiction of Christmas at Haddon Hall (*see p. 34*), already a plagiarism when it first appeared in 1859, was then reprinted by the radical *Reynolds's Miscellany* on 25 May 1867.

motive would be more likely to dwell upon the literary and historical associations that linked aristocracy and people into a common story, of which these houses were a living record.

Two pairs of houses, one pair in Kent and the other in Derbyshire, illustrate the range and intensity of popular identifications with the mansions of the Olden Time – and of later times, too.

Knole, nestled in a fold of its great oak-strewn park alongside the town of Sevenoaks in Kent, had already won a kind of appreciation in Horace Walpole's day. The core of this huge rambling assemblage is late fifteenth century, but the west front, which the visitor sights when approaching from across the park, was added by Henry VIII, and nearly the whole of the rest of the exterior and the interior remain as remodelled by Thomas Sackville, 1st Earl of Dorset, between 1603 and 1608. Walpole liked the symmetry and simplicity of the west front.[71] Victorian visitors would have climbed one of the nearby knolls to get a view of the whole, which presents a highly picturesque silhouette of turrets, pinnacles, battlements and cupolas. The riches

20   Knole in its deer park (*Penny Magazine*, 16 February 1839).

inside are so varied and splendid that, again, there is something for every generation. The polite Georgian visitor goggled at the Louis-Quatorze sumptuousness of the King's Room, all gold and silver and ebony, other staterooms decorated in the baroque late seventeenth- and early eighteenth-century style, and the wonderful collection of Reynolds portraits, including the famous likeness of Dr Johnson admired by Fanny Burney. The Victorians marvelled instead that the rest of the interior had *not* been altered after 1608, preserving an unparalleled collection of Elizabethan and Jacobean furnishings, 'numerous relics of ancient magnificence', in the words of an 1839 guidebook, 'which afford a pleasing illustration of the domestic decorations, manners and customs of our ancestors'.[72]

As a house of 'modern' wonders to the eighteenth-century traveller, Knole, though close to London, was not particularly remarkable; as a living relic of the Olden Time, however, it was practically unique. It lacked historical associations – after Henry VIII's occupation it fell into the hands of the Sackvilles, who never distinguished themselves as patrons or soldiers in the way the Victorians would have liked – but its value as a record of social history in the Olden Time gradually percolated into the wider public's consciousness. At the beginning of the nineteenth century, it was already attracting hundreds of visitors a year;[73] unmentioned in a county guide of 1810, it earned a passing tribute in a new edition twelve years later;[74] in 1819 it acquired its first guidebook; and in the full flood of Olden Time sentiment in the 1830s its preeminence was finally acknowledged. Sketchers and painters flocked to what Frith called 'that delightful hunting-ground for artists' to copy authentic details of the Jacobean furniture, especially the unique 'Knole settee', the panelling, plasterwork and enormous marble overmantels, as well as the less authentic portraits of great religious reformers, poets and statesmen that crammed the Brown Gallery and the Poet's Parlour.[75] Nash offered seven views of Knole, more than of any other house. More diffusely, Knole must have evoked visions of the Olden Time for thousands of visitors, much like that reported by the writer for the *Penny Magazine* when he stepped into the Jacobean great hall:

at once [it] makes us centuries older: we not only think of, but feel with, the past. The loneliness seems suddenly to be broken, the bustle of countless attendants going in and out begins, the tables groan with the profusion of the feast, bright jewels and still brighter eyes begin to sparkle, gorgeous vestments and sacerdotal robes mingle together, the solemn strains of music peal forth – it is some high festival! Alas! of our imagination only, as we are soon convinced by the gentle hint of the domestic at our elbow, which we obey, and move forwards.[76]

So persuasive and enduring was this fantasy that it was plagiarized by a highly respectable antiquarian writer introducing Knole to the readers of the *The Leisure Hour* fifty years later.[77]

Many visitors to Knole would also have visited the complementary delights of Penshurst Place, which the *Penny Magazine* writer claimed to have glimpsed from a path in Knole Park, though it lay some miles off. Smaller and plainer than Knole, Penshurst had many of the same qualities – a rolling park of oaks, well-preserved rooms and furnishings of the Olden Time – and best of all literary and historical associations that sent Victorian commentators scrambling for their superlatives. Medieval at its core – the great hall dates from the mid-fourteenth century – Penshurst's fame derived from the Sidney family who were granted it in 1552, remodelled much of the exterior, accumulated its gems of art and furnishings, and whose political and literary doings won them places in the Victorian pantheon. Essentially deserted from the early eighteenth century, it had, unlike Knole, little to attract Georgian visitors and as late as the 1830s was threatened by a

21   Penshurst, framed by its oaks (*Penny Magazine*, 17 June 1843).

picturesque Gothic makeover which might have destroyed all of the authentic Gothic features. The 2nd Lord De L'Isle who inherited in 1851 fell into step with the latest thinking on Gothic authenticity and preserved Penshurst very much as it is today.[78]

What Lord De L'Isle was able to preserve was the best late medieval great hall remaining in England and a suite of rooms with important Elizabethan portraits and furnishings. Victorians delighted in the fact that the primitive hall, with an open fire in its centre vented through a hole in the timbered ceiling, was apparently still in use in its original state in the days of the Sidneys. Howitt had been irritated to discover that the 1st Lord De L'Isle had allowed an over-civilized cupola to cover the famous vent when he visited in September 1838 and was pleased when De L'Isle agreed to remove it. Shortly thereafter Nash made it the setting of one of his Yuletide orgies. Howitt was more impressed by the Elizabethan state rooms and the new suite in Elizabethan style added by the 1st Lord: 'All is England, and English of the right date, which is rarer still.'[79]

What really earned Howitt's awe, however, was that this was the home of the Sidneys, the noblest family in England:

> But it is by a far higher nobility than that of ancient descent, or martial or political power, that the name of Sidney arrests the admiration of Englishmen. It is one of our great watchwords of liberty. It is one of the household words of English veneration. It is a name hallowed by some of our proudest historical and literary associations; identified in the very staple of our minds with a sense of high principle, magnanimity of sentiment, and generous and heroic devotion to the cause of our country and of man.[80]

Not only did the Sidneys supply, in the shape of Sir Philip, one of Shakespeare's contemporaries and near-rivals, a soldier for Protestantism and a great English poet, but also his sister, Lady Pembroke, poet and patroness, his brother, Lord Leicester, diplomat and versifier, and his grand-nephew Algernon, the republican martyr. Around this family orbited practically the full complement of Elizabethan and Jacobean poets for whom Penshurst was a place of frequent resort, and Ben Jonson had hymned the home and his hosts in terms that delighted the Victorians.

> Thou art not, Penshurst, built to envious show
> Of touch, or marble; nor canst boast a row
> Of polish'd pillars, or a roofe of gold.

In contrast to statelier piles, Penshurst's wealth lay in human qualities of domesticity and hospitality – 'their lords have built, but thy lord dwells' – and Jonson descanted lovingly upon the rich fare dispensed liberally in that smoky great hall.[81] What capped the moral value of Penshurst to the Victorians was that Walpole had so thoroughly disapproved of the Sidneys: 'Frivolous and lax in mind and practice,' sniffed Charles Knight of Walpole, 'cold, flippant, heartless; of all men least fitted to appreciate or even understand the lofty poetic seriousness of Sir Philip's character.' The feelings elicited by the visitor's familiarity with the lives and writings of the Sidneys would more than make up for some of the decay and destruction that had beset Penshurst in Walpole's time. A mere stroll in the park, thought Charles Knight, with stops at Sidney's Oak and Sacharissa's Walk, would establish the right frame of mind for viewing what was left of Olden Time Penshurst, especially the Sidney portraits and rooms associated with Queen Elizabeth's visits, and of course the 'striking and interesting' hall.[82]

Further north, on the fringe of Derbyshire's Peak District, a house often compared – sometimes confused – with Penshurst attracted equal if not greater attention. Like Penshurst, Haddon has a medieval heart and much Elizabethan dressing, especially in the interiors. Also like Penshurst, it was virtually abandoned by the Dukes of Rutland throughout the period in which it might otherwise have been 'improved', and thus survived to enjoyed a Victorian revival as the Middle Ages and the Olden Time gained in prestige. Haddon's great hall dates from the fourteenth century, but its modern appearance is Elizabethan, with panelling, gallery and long table that more perfectly summoned up the approved images of revelry and hospitality than any other. Scott borrowed from it for both medieval and Elizabethan romances, Cattermole painted it often, Nash's plate of it was his most frequently copied and it became a hackneyed feature of Royal Academy and watercolour exhibitions in mid-nineteenth century London.[83]

Apart from the hall, Haddon's greatest fame attached to a piece of romance, probably spurious, but one which, as Henry James said, simply had to be invented to encapsulate the house's powerful emotional appeal. In 1558, Dorothy, the last of the Vernons, the family that had held Haddon since 1170, was thought to have eloped in highly romantic circumstances with young John Manners, the first of the family that has owned Haddon ever since. The route of the elopement lovingly traced by generations of guides, through the house, out of 'a little dusky door opening from a turret', across the Jacobean south terrace, down some steps to the river and over a

22   A tourist party at Haddon Hall, drawn by Thomas Allom and published in S.C. Hall's *Baronial Halls of England* (1845–6).

humpback bridge, was practically invented to show off the Olden Time highlights of the place and certainly had nothing to do with any real elopement, as most of the features were constructed by John Manners when he had come into possession of the estate long after the marriage.[84] But this kind of invention was petty compared to the liberties taken by subsequent recreations. Arthur Sullivan's Savoy opera *Haddon Hall* (1892) transported the action to the time of the Civil War, 'in order to provide a comic element out of the Puritan in the Commonwealth'; there followed a popular novel, *Dorothy Vernon of Haddon Hall* and, finally, a silent movie starring Mary Pickford and Douglas Fairbanks.[85] But there was plenty of Victorian writing about Haddon that used the Vernon elopement story fairly, as James himself did, to help the reader or visitor leap the gap between the Haddon that is and the Haddon that was, using all that could be experienced in the present to summon up 'the private life of the past'.[86] Even so high-minded an architectural critic as Sir Nikolaus Pevsner admitted that he 'would indeed be hard put to it if he were asked to define

23   Dorothy Vernon's doorway, drawn by George Cattermole for S. Rayner's *History and Antiquities of Haddon Hall* (1836) and later reprinted in cheap tourist souvenirs.

24   The romantic approach to Chatsworth (*Penny Magazine*, 17 September 1839).

what in the sensations of a first visit to Haddon Hall is due to aesthetic
and what to extraneous values'.[87]

Almost adjacent to the Haddon estate lies the last of this quartet of
English mansions, and the only one with few Olden Time associations, which is what makes it useful as a comparison. Chatsworth, the
house and park of the Dukes of Devonshire, was first built up in the
1550s by Sir William Cavendish and his wife Bess, who was also
responsible for Hardwick Hall – yet another Derbyshire mansion as
much admired by the Victorians as sneered at by Walpole. Later
Cavendishes pulled the Elizabethan house at Chatsworth to pieces and
built the house that now stands there, the main block and gardens
around 1700, an extensive addition early in the nineteenth century,
and grandiose garden buildings designed by Joseph Paxton (later of
Crystal Palace fame) in the 1830s and 1840s. There was very little of
the Olden Time left at the time when it became most of interest.

Writers on Chatsworth made much of two fragments in the grounds, 'Queen Mary's Bower', a little platform where Mary Queen of Scots was thought to have taken the air during periods of confinement at Chatsworth, and the 'Hunting Tower', which had nothing to do with Mary Queen of Scots but was of the right date and so also sometimes named after her. Mrs S. C. Hall pronounced her climb to the Hunting Tower 'the crowning point of our excursion' on a visit in 1852. Equally ludicrously, rooms in the classical block occupying roughly the same spot as Mary's place of confinement became known as the 'Queen of Scots' Rooms', and a tradition was invented that 'they had been preserved, propped up, and built round, from the old house'.[88]

Nothing, however, could disguise the fact that the bulk of the house was 'modern'. It had been in the eighteenth century and was still in the mid-nineteenth century the very height of modern aristocratic luxury. From the florid early eighteenth-century decoration of the Painted Hall and chapel, and the heavily gilded staterooms redecorated by the 6th Duke in the 1820s, to the fabulous collection of Old Master drawings and the impressive display of classical marbles, Chatsworth had everything the polite visitor of the eighteenth century wished for. Victorian observers, however, were puzzled by it. On the one hand, the Duke of Devonshire was splendidly liberal in permitting year-round access to his domains, to such an extent that Chatsworth remained the most visited country house in the land throughout the nineteenth century. The park and the gardens were the greatest attractions: romantic declivities, picturesque views, noble oaks, spectacular fountains and, of course, Paxton's Great Conservatory were picked out for special favour; the very features which the eighteenth century had strained to swallow had now become the cynosure. And it seemed ungrateful to pass up the opportunity to view a house so generously thrown open; but what a house! The *Penny Magazine* was frankly distressed by what it found inside:

> in the decorations of those parts of the mansion which have been left in their original state, the chaster taste of the present day has to lament the employment of artists, who, although fashionable in their time, are now justly condemned for the flutter and gaudiness of their productions.[89]

An American visitor who had just come from Haddon felt 'stunned and wearied by the ever-beginning, never-ending displays of boundless magnificence', much too 'French', 'ostentatious' and 'gaudy' for his liking.[90] Nearly every commentator took the opportunity to compare Chatsworth unfavourably to Haddon. *The Leisure Hour* drew the typical conclusion:

> In Chatsworth we have all that wealth can procure, all that luxury can demand, all that a refined and highly cultivated taste could select. On the other hand, in Haddon Hall we have a revelation of the facts of human history during several consecutive centuries, and that recorded in characters so plain that the simple man may decipher them, and with a little effort of the imagination may re-people the mouldering solitude and recall the daily life of the generations that have passed away. For our part . . . we confess to being far more impressed by the contemplation of Haddon Hall than by the splendours of Chatsworth . . .[91]

In any Victorian competition between taste and history, history would always win out.

The examples of these four houses could be multiplied dozens of times, for there were many houses across the country to rival these four: medieval castles with Olden Time associations, such as Hever near Penshurst, haunted by Henry VIII and two wives, or Warwick, Berkeley, Raby, Arundel; the 'prodigy houses' of the Elizabethan era – Longleat, Burghley, Hatfield and Wollaton – regarded as overblown and indisciplined by architectural writers but vigorously defended by lovers of history and romance;[92] houses lacking what the Victorians considered great beauty but enhanced instead by associations, for example Wilton near Salisbury, linked to Penshurst, and Alnwick Castle in Northumberland, nearly ruined by 'restoration' but still the home of the Percy family. The whole land of England was littered with these historical monuments, with which the Victorian public became steadily more familiar. By the 1870s, they were familiar enough to have acquired a collective noun, 'the stately homes of England', a tag coined by the highly popular annuals' poet Felicia Hemans in a poem first published in 1828, but not widely in use until country houses had sufficiently entered the public consciousness to deserve an epithet.[93]

The label 'stately home' embodied mixed messages of familiarity and distance. On the one hand, the aristocratic mansions of England were homes like any other, private property certainly, but also sites of conventional domesticity in the present as well as the past. Mrs Hemans's poem was entitled 'The Homes of England' and in it she equated the stately home with the cottage home in a characteristically romantic way. On the other hand, 'stateliness' carried a message of otherness and hierarchy. 'Stately' had colloquially meant of high estate, princely or noble, but it could (especially in such sensitive times) also imply aloofness and arrogance. 'Stately home' was thus very slightly oxymoronic. From its earliest uses, it could convey both admiration and criticism. Haddon Hall, for instance, could be 'stately' in the sense of displaying the fine moral and aesthetic qualities of the upper ranks in the Olden Time, but Chatsworth could be less happily 'stately', overpowering present-day observers with its excessive opulence and offensively modern taste.

The tension embedded here points to the limits that might be placed on popular identification with the aristocratic home as a part of the national history, limits that rarely manifested themselves before 1880. 'Stateliness' was tolerable, even admirable to the early and mid-Victorians so long as it was not exercised in an aloof and exclusive way. The Victorian idea of heritage left a goodly space for aristocratic participation in its acknowledgement of past service and achievement. In return, the Victorian aristocracy was expected to reciprocate by showing that it shared or at least accepted the new popular taste for and identification with the prevalent reading of national history. The rich are, of course, different from us – and it did not surprise popular antiquarians when aristocrats failed to jump on their bandwagon – but on the other hand the Victorian balance between real social difference and imagined national cohesion could never have functioned if the aristocracy had not in so many ways made the effort expected of them. This dictum applies to the idea of heritage and the place for the English country house in it as much as to better-known points of potential conflict in politics and religion, which were also compromised or sublimated in highly imaginative ways.

Arriving at a tacit agreement on the value of old English mansions was, however, made difficult by aesthetic differences already hinted at between élite and popular culture, and also by the widening disengagement of the landed classes from the arts and aesthetics altogether. In general, rather than seeing eye to eye, owners of stately homes and the potential public for them agreed to disagree on a basis that protected both groups' interests.

As already seen, the Victorian attachment to history and heritage arose out of a dramatic expansion in the market for such cultural commodities as books, pictures, theatre and travel. Aristocratic culture was not necessarily much affected by these changes, particularly male aristocratic culture. Public-school and university education was, indeed, notoriously immune to them, continuing to subsist well into the nineteenth century on the eighteenth-century diet of classical literature and history, albeit mixed with a tincture of sport and piety.

The only English history that was generally studied and discussed in male aristocratic circles was the relatively recent history of diplomacy and high-political manoeuvre that formed what might be called a rule-book for contemporary aristocratic diplomats and politicians. Macaulay's *History of England*, immensely popular especially in upper-middle-class circles from the appearance of its first volume in 1849, essentially picked up where popular history left off, around 1660. As Olive Anderson has shown, historical precedents were widely cited in public discussion of the Crimean War of 1854–6, but in Parliament the illustrations were drawn from the military history of the eighteenth century, while among 'the small shopkeepers, clerks, artisans' and their kin the talk was all about ancient liberty and the decay of aristocratic conduct since the Restoration: two different worlds of history.[94]

The Gothic, of course, had its appeal for those in aristocratic society with intellectual pretensions; there were aristocratic patrons of scholarly antiquarian societies, Gothicist publishing ventures – especially for the Gothic current in the Church of England; and medievalism also supplied a stock of chivalric ideals and poses useful to social leaders but less so to the mass of the citizenry. Yet overall the aristocratic contribution to the Victorian Gothic is pretty marginal compared to the aristocracy's patronage of various classical revivals in the preceding century. Art and architecture were becoming increasingly professionalized businesses, led by practitioners rather than patrons – or indeed by a widening marketplace in which the small number of very wealthy patrons played a diminishing role. The rise of the Gothic therefore reveals little about aristocratic taste, even in the sphere of country-house architecture. Few owners of old houses felt any need or desire to remodel them in Victorian style. Until the 1850s, owners seeking to build new houses tended rather lazily to prefer variations on the old classical model. When, in the 1860s, the Gothic became the predominant country-house mode, the motive force seems to have come not from owners but from architects.[95]

Neither architects nor owners were completely immune to the fad for the Olden Time, and in the early nineteenth-century anarchy of copyism it would be surprising not to find some Olden Time replicas alongside the Byzantine and the Baroque. New 'Tudor' and 'Elizabethan' country houses begin to appear in the 1820s, perhaps prompted by the publication of *Kenilworth* in 1821, and in the 1830s and 1840s when the Olden Time vogue was gathering steam, the style became truly fashionable for a time. A few architects – prominently Anthony Salvin, Edward Blore and William Burn – made it into a speciality, though it was always only one of several stylistic arrows in their quivers.[96] In a few cases, owners adopted the style deliberately to convey broader social and political messages. The antiquary Sir Samuel Rush Meyrick commissioned Blore to design a mixed medieval and Tudor castle at Goodrich Court in Herefordshire in order to house his collection of arms and armour, a purposefully educational display shown to the public by guards 'clothed in the costume of Henry VIII'.[97]

In the 1840s, at the peak of social conflict, some Ultra-Tories made a more comprehensive effort to revive the Olden Time connections between aristocracy and people, making a fetish of the great hall with its communal revelries and hospitality. This 'Young England' group included Lord John Manners, younger son of the Duke of Rutland, who liked to hold *soirées* at Haddon for the local people at which he sang the virtues of the Olden Time and rather preened himself as a paternal aristocrat in the traditional mould.[98] But, unlike popular interest in the Olden Time, this aristocratic fad was a fleeting affectation; 'Young England' was never more than a tiny clique, much mocked by the broader public, including those who admired the Olden Time without seeking to recreate it. As most architects hated the bastard styles between the medieval and the classical, they were more than happy to drop the Elizabethan when their patrons tired of it. Only those elements of the Olden Time that were also found in the Gothic lingered. A curious example is the recurrence of the great hall in purpose-built Victorian country houses. Gothicists felt that the heyday of the great hall had been in their beloved fourteenth century, not later.[99] They urged great halls upon their patrons on stylistic, symbolic and even functional grounds, though only the most utopian – Pugin – imagined that the latter-day aristocracy was genuinely interested in reviving Old English Hospitality.[100] The result was that a few dozen great halls were built in the 1840s and 1850s, which never had any real use at all and soon degenerated into over-large billiards rooms or were used for coat and gun storage.[101]

The bathetic fate of the great hall is nicely symbolic of the aristocracy's true feeling for the Olden Time. They were often cheerfully willing to go along with their architects' enthusiasms or with currents in popular taste, but they rarely took them to their hearts. Most Victorian aristocrats looked upon their country houses, old or new, as homes; they were interested in their functional and financial rather than their historical and sentimental value. The high importance they naturally placed on comfort and convenience meant that they were usually happier with a modern than a historic mansion, with the Victorian Gothic than the medieval Gothic, the *faux* baronial rather

25 A drawing of 1837 for the Great Hall at Scarisbrick Hall, Lancashire, by A.W.N. Pugin (British Architectural Library, RIBA, London).

than the real thing. A few owners went so far as to tear down Elizabethan houses and build neo-Elizabethan houses – with all mod. cons – on their foundations.[102]

These priorities were reflected in those prints and books about country seats aimed at the owners' market; these were careful not to denigrate modern mansions and, in fact, trained the spotlight on whatever was currently the height of fashion.[103] Popular antiquarians reversed these preferences; they were nearly always sorrowful, and sometimes censorious, when they came across a historic house excessively 'improved' for comfort's sake, as Howitt found at Raby Castle:

> It is, in fact, this complete adaptation to modern uses and splendour, which disappoints one in the interior of Raby. The exterior is so fine, so feudal, so antiquely great, that when we step in and find ourselves at once in modern drawing-rooms, with silken couches and gilt cornices, the Nevilles and their times vanish. We forget again that we are at Raby, the castle of the victims of Neville's Cross . . . and feel that we are only in the saloons of the modern Duke of Cleveland.[104]

Worse even than the modernization of a historic building for occupation was neglect of an unused historic building. In this period it was never proposed that anyone but the owners were responsible for the maintainence of historic houses, but, again, that limit on the public interest could only be maintained if the owners fulfilled their responsibility. Popular antiquarians thus felt fully entitled to call the owners to account. Samuel Carter Hall was particularly vocal in cases where he felt owners were not doing their duty; his *Baronial Halls* volumes were explicitly intended – in addition to cashing in on Nash's success – to alert the public to the inroads neglect and decay were making on the nation's stock of historic houses. Speke Hall, near Liverpool, had been 'shamefully neglected' by mercantile owners seeking only profit from letting. Montacute had been deserted by its ancestral owners, who should have had more pride. Many other owners had over-restored and over-upholstered historic interiors in deplorable modern taste.[105] Howitt was equally shocked by the appalling state into which the Lords Northampton had let Compton Wynyates fall, and by the fact that not even the caretaker knew any of the history attaching to the place, so that 'the house, stripped as it was, was obliged to speak for itself'.[106]

Antiquarian policing of this sort was, until the middle of the century, rarely necessary. Owners who did not particularly care for their mansions of the Olden Time were still rich and responsible enough to keep them up to a standard that the public was coming to expect. There were some conspicuous heroes of preservation, such as the 2nd Lord De L'Isle at Penshurst, but on the whole maintenance and increasingly respectful restoration went ahead semi-automatically, as stewards and bailiffs had ample funds and freedom to keep up the nation's architectural heritage.

Owners did not, then, care to make themselves conspicuous champions of their Olden Time mansions. What they did was to go along with a wave of popular sentiment with which, vaguely, they sympathized. If this had meant only keeping in good repair houses their families had maintained for centuries, and restoring more sympathetically houses hit by fire or other calamity, their role would not be deserving of any special notice. But, in fact, public expectations and the owners' response went well beyond this minimal responsibility to preserve. For the Victorian public was by no means content with metaphorical and literary possession of the mansions of England. A wealthier, more mobile, more leisured population could not easily be contained within the covers of a book or the frame of a print. That public wanted physical possession of their mansions of the Olden Time – they wanted to see and to touch, to climb the turret-stair and push aside the arras. The extent to which the owners made that possible is a much more impressive testimony to the tacit pact settled between Victorian aristocracy and people, by no means simply to the former's advantage.

# MIDLAND RAILWAY.

By the liberality of the EARL OF SHREWSBURY AND TALBOT, the
beautiful Grounds of

# ALTON TOWERS

### WILL BE OPENED

## On MONDAY, JUNE 7th, 1869.

ON WHICH DAY

# THE EARL OF SHREWSBURY'S BAND

WILL BE IN ATTENDANCE.

In addition to the usual attractions, there is now a very fine

## DISPLAY OF RHODODENDRONS.

Refreshment Tents, Waiting Rooms, &c., provided for the comfort of the visitors.

## On MONDAY, JUNE 7th, 1869.

# CHEAP EXCURSION TRAINS

Will Run from the undermentioned Stations, to

# ALTON TOWERS,

At the following Fares there and back, INCLUDING ADMISSION
TO THE GARDENS.

| STATIONS. | | First Class. | Cov. Cars. |
|---|---|---|---|
| | a.m. | s.    d. | s.    d. |
| Northampton (Midland Station) | 8  0 | | |
| Wellingboro' | 8  32 | 7  0 | 3  6 |
| Finedon | 8  42 | | |
| Kettering | 8  50 | | |
| Harboro' | 9  15 | 6  0 | 3  0 |
| Kibworth | 9  30 | | |

Children under 3 years of age, Free; above 3 and under 12, Half-fares.

The Return Train will leave Alton at 7 p.m., the same evening,
and the Tickets will be available for returning by this train only.

| STATIONS. | | First Class. | Cov. Cars. |
|---|---|---|---|
| | a.m. | s.    d. | s.    d. |
| Leicester | 10  0 | | |
| Syston | 10  10 | 6  0 | 3  0 |
| Sileby | 10  20 | | |
| Loughborough | 10  33 | | |
| Kegworth | 10  43 | | |
| Nottingham | 10  40 | 5  0 | 2  6 |
| Beeston | 10  48 | | |
| Trent | 11  0 | | |

Children under 3 years of age, Free; above 3 and under 12, Half-fares.

The return Train will leave Alton at 7 0 p.m., the same evening,
and the Tickets will be available for returning by this Train only.

| STATIONS. | | First Class. | Cov. Cars. |
|---|---|---|---|
| | a.m. | s.    d. | s.    d. |
| Birmingham (New Street Station) | 10  10 | | |
| Saltney | 10  15 | 6  0 | 3  0 |
| Castle Bromwich | 10  20 | | |
| Forge Mills | 10  35 | | |
| Wilnecote | 10  50 | 4  0 | 2  0 |
| Tamworth | 10  55 | | |

Children under 3 years of age, Free; above 3 and under 12, Half-fares.

The Return Train will leave Alton at 7 15 p.m., the same evening,
and the Tickets will be available for returning by this Train only.

*Derby, June*, 1869.  **JAMES ALLPORT, General Manager.**

Societies, Schools, Committees, &c., wishing to arrange for Special Trains or
admission to the Gardens for large parties, will please apply to

**JOHN M. COOK, 98, Fleet Street, London,**

Corresponding Agent for the Right Hon. the Earl of Shrewsbury and Talbot.

### ALSO ON SAME DAY FROM FOLLOWING NORTH STAFFORD STATIONS:

| STATIONS. | | First Class. | Cov. Cars. |
|---|---|---|---|
| | a.m. | s.    d. | s.    d. |
| Derby | 11  30 | | |
| Burton | 11  30 | | |
| Eggington | 11  36 | 3  0 | 1  6 |
| Tutbury | 11  46 | | |
| Sudbury | 11  55 | | |
| Uttoxeter | 12  20 | | |

Children under Three years of age, Free; above Three and under Twelve, Half-fares.

The Return Trains for Eggington and Derby will leave Alton at
7 0 p.m., and for Uttoxeter, Sudbury, Tutbury, and Burton at 7 15
p.m., the same evening, and the Tickets will be available for
returning by these trains only.

*Stoke, May*, 1869.  **PERCY MORRIS, General Manager.**

Societies, Schools, Committees, &c., wishing to arrange for Special Trains or
admission to the Gardens for large parties, will please apply to

**JOHN M. COOK, 98, Fleet-street, London,**

Corresponding Agent for the Right Hon. the Earl of Shrewsbury and Talbot.

26   Cheap excursion trains to Alton Towers,
from *Cook's Excursionist and Tourist Advertiser*, 1
June 1869.

## CHAPTER 2

# Hosts and Guests: The Opening of the Country House

A tourist's visit to a country house may have nothing to do with a sense of heritage. It may be motivated by curiosity about the lives (present as well as past) of the rich and famous, a curiosity itself fuelled perhaps by envy, perhaps by deference, perhaps by a more innocent quest for fun. The visitor may be seeking distractions for the children, refuge from the weather, or quite often just a breath of fresh air. All of these motives applied to tourists of the first age of mass country-house visiting, the Victorian period; country-house visiting – while linked to the Victorian idea of heritage – was also a product of more humdrum developments, such as extending leisure and transport facilities.

To complicate matters further, country-house visiting in this period was also enmeshed in a living relationship between aristocracy and people, something that concerns few modern visitors. The opening of the country house to the general public in the nineteenth century was not a commercial transaction, but a cultural and political gesture on the part of both aristocratic hosts and the mass of guests. Investigation into Victorian country-house visiting will therefore reveal something more about the emerging idea of heritage, here hitherto traced principally in print and image, and something about the expanding world of touristic opportunities, of which 'heritage' appreciation was only a part. But it will also touch upon the relationship between aristocracy and people, a relationship that determined to what extent aristocratic culture could be part of a truly national identity.

## The First Age of Mass Visiting

In the eighteenth century, as noted earlier, country-house visiting was common only among a fairly exclusive set and within restricted physical corridors. Then, in the early nineteenth century, some of the same economic and technological developments that caused a revolution in the market for printed matter also transformed the state of travel and tourism.

One seemingly obvious development – urbanization – is nevertheless a prerequisite of the very idea of the rural idyll. A nation that lives in the country has no special reason to holiday there and, in fact, the reverse impulse made the spa town the retreat of choice until the early nineteenth century. By 1851, in contrast, the nation was predominantly urban – in certain areas, very unpleasantly so – and the special kind of rural appreciation that originates from the heart of the city was already in full flower. As early as the 1860s, Londoners were fleeing not just to the suburbs, but to country cottages in the Surrey hills.[1]

The country cottage, of course, was available only to the fairly well-heeled, and, in fact, desired as yet only by the avant-garde. Short holidays in the country were more general – recognizably a mass phenomenon as early as the 1820s. As with mass-market publishing, because tourism did not yet extend as far as the bulk of the working class, social historians have been reluctant to recognize the early existence of mass tourism, but, again, the patterns established by large numbers of people in the lower-middle ranks would have a lasting effect on the culture as a whole. Thus, the stranglehold of Bath and other genteel spas on the watering trade was broken in the early nineteenth century by an influx of new clients seeking cheaper accommodation, which they found at such resorts as Brighton and Leamington. Leamington was already known in the mid-1820s as a favourite resort of London shopkeepers, who could be seen in their hundreds touring neighbouring Warwick Castle. This intrusion on what had been their private preserve struck gentlemanly visitors as comically incongruous and even a little offensive:

> The London cockney, from his two days watering at Leamington, stops his pony-chaise, hired at half-a-crown the hour, and walks Mrs Popkins over the old draw-bridge as peacefully as if it were the threshold of his shop in the Strand . . . What would old Guy say, or the 'noble imp' whose effigy is among the escutcheoned tombs of his fathers, if they could rise through their marble slabs, and be whirled over the draw-bridge in a post-chaise? How indignantly they would listen to the reckoning within their own portcullis, of the rates for chaise or postilion![2]

A generation later, in the 1850s, the week's holiday that had formerly been restricted to the self-employed was beginning to spread to the lesser-salaried men – bank and merchants' clerks, for instance – and some skilled workers. By 1875, a fortnight's paid holiday was enjoyed by clerks in many banks, insurance companies and dock and railway offices. Very large numbers of workers took more-or-less official holidays at Whitsunside and, in the industrial North, during the 'wakes weeks' of summer, though usually without pay.[3]

However, the rarity of paid holidays until the end of the century meant that the really explosive growth in tourism came in the form of the day-trip.[4] Surprisingly, the day-trip was boosted by but not dependent upon the advent of the railway. Day-trippers were already pouring out of the great towns in the 1830s in horse-drawn wagons and brakes. This was how many of the more than 100,000 visitors to Hampton Court made their way in the first year of public opening, 1839, and how as many as 800 people travelled the twelve miles to Chatsworth from Sheffield on an average summer Sunday before the railway arrived in 1849.[5] But there is no question that steam immensely extended the range of the average day-tripper's ambition. The first steam-propelled day-trips went to Gravesend, down the Thames in a steamer, in 1816. There were then already twenty-six boats making the run; by 1833, almost 300,000 trips to Gravesend were made in a year; by 1850, 250,000 in a single month.[6]

Some of these trippers made their way on to the little village of Cobham, in the early 1830s famous for the brasses in its church, its quaint cottages and for the great oaks and Olden Time façade of Cobham Park and Hall, then made more famous still as Tracy Tupman's place of refuge in *Pickwick Papers*. 'Every visitor to Gravesend has either seen or heard of Cobham,' wrote a guidebook in 1864, 'flymen intuitively greet each arrival at pier or station with "Cobham, sir?"' Those unable to afford a fly could catch the Rochester omnibus and walk two miles from the setting-down point at Cobham to the park. Sufficient numbers were willing to navigate this obstacle course to prompt the Countess of Darnley to limit numbers by establishing a strikingly modern ticket system. Visitors were restricted to Fridays between the hours of eleven and four, and asked to equip themselves first with a one-shilling ticket obtainable at the Gravesend bookseller. Even so, hundreds ran the gauntlet each year, and Cobham Hall was already a familiar landmark to thousands of Londoners when S. C. Hall chose it to inaugurate his series of Olden Time views in 1843.[7]

From the 1840s, the railway gradually extended to denizens of all the great towns the same opportunities that Londoners had enjoyed along the Thames since the 1820s. Since country-house owners were as anxious as anyone to secure rail access, most country houses were,

27    Tourists at Cobham Hall, from S.C. Hall's *Baronial Halls of England*, issued in parts from 1843 and in book form in 1845–6.

soon, at least potentially accessible by train, and especially in the Midlands large numbers of great houses were within a day-trip's reach of large masses of people. Sundays were, of course, the natural day for such excursions, though sabbatarian feeling kept many rural attractions closed on Sundays. But other days were more free than is sometimes imagined. The great mercantile houses of Manchester had granted a Saturday half-holiday to their clerks by the mid-1840s, and shop-workers gradually won this right, too, assisted by the early-closing movement in which people such as S.C. Hall played a leading role.[8] Among manual workers, 'Saint Monday' was a widely observed unofficial holiday, especially on hot summer weekends, throughout the century. Easter and Whit Mondays were always national holidays, during which millions of people travelled into the countryside, and the August Bank Holiday Monday was added in 1871.[9] Later in the century, many employers organized or accommodated an annual excursion in the summer, by no means always on a weekend, and as masonic groups, Sunday schools, choirs and friendly societies followed suit, a self-improving working man, shopworker or clerk could enjoy several 'annual excursions' a year.

Travelling on this scale – taking into account day-excursions as well as touring proper – meant that the tourist map of England, first drawn rather sketchily by the Picturesque travellers of the late eighteenth century, was in the mid-nineteenth century redrawn with many of the gaps now filled in. Tourist attention, which had formerly been focused on a few 'honey-pot' areas, for example the Wye Valley, the Lake District, Norfolk and portions of Wales and Scotland, now had a more genuinely national purview. Each centre of population strove to develop and advertise its rural attractions. The county archaeological associations that emerged from the 1840s raised local consciousness of antiquities in one way; more popular were the detailed county guides published by John Murray from 1851, the pioneers in a genre that has culminated in the twentieth century with Pevsner's *Buildings of England* guides, a comprehensive audit of the nation's historic buildings stock. The *Murray's Handbooks*, particularly in their early editions, were refreshingly free of the narrow-gauge antiquarianism that limited the range of later guidebooks, such as the Methuen *Little Guides*. Written by an eclectic variety of amateurs and enthusiasts, they did not dwell obsessively on ancient parish churches and medieval relics to the exclusion of more recent history, as did the *Little Guides*.[10] Instead, they offered a more commonsense and touristic survey of the principal historical and architectural monuments of all periods in each county, paying a good deal of attention to such important details as opening hours and transport arrangements, and not skimping either on the legends and associations that mattered so much to the Victorian tourist. They were not above drawing on popular writing such as that of the Howitts, to the detriment perhaps of their scholarship but rather to the advantage of their sales. Most of the county *Handbooks* went through many editions in the second half of the nineteenth century, selling probably more to residents than to travellers. They quickly spawned cheap imitations, notably a series produced by the Edinburgh publishers A. & C. Black, and from 1860 a popular series of penny guides for a working-class readership published by Abel Heywood, a leading Manchester Radical and newsagent.

Whereas the more intellectually respectable *Little Guides* tell us a good deal about élite taste and scholarship, the *Murray's Handbooks* and their cheaper imitators reveal a wider world of middlebrow – and lower-middlebrow – travel and tourism. In this world country houses loomed very large indeed. Country houses were, after all, the most conspicuous buildings in the rural landscape. Many of them, as already seen, were by the middle of the nineteenth century widely considered to be an integral part of the national history and culture. Even the more modern houses were seats of families with valuable literary and historical associations, or set in parks of great natural beauty and recreational value. Where the *Little Guide* might speak slightingly if at all about the dozens of country houses scattered about the county, conveying praise only in instances of great antiquity or ruin, *Murray's* invariably gives a full architectural and historical description and often a tour of the interior, noting highlights of art and history. Such descriptions did not necessarily imply that the interior was open to the public, or that the exterior was visible from a public right-of-way. But the fact is – and *Murray's* would not have devoted so much print and space in this way were it not so – that the mid-Victorian traveller expected the country house, especially if of great historical interest, to be accessible, particularly when the owner was not in residence.

Most historians who have glanced at this subject have assumed that the country house, open to polite visiting in the eighteenth century, closed its doors to the more numerous tourists of the railway age. Their owners are taken to have been too philistine, too domestic and too consumed with other kinds of social responsibility – religious and philanthropic – to maintain the limited role as custodians of culture played by their fathers and grandfathers.[11] A few recent writers, seeking the origins of late twentieth-century country-house visiting, have cast doubt upon these assumptions, arguing instead that increasing demand meant that houses became progressively more open over the long span between eighteenth-century connoisseurship and twentieth-century heritage industry.[12] Neither view stands up to detailed inspection. Country-house tourism in the mid-nineteenth century represented an unusual peak between the select touring of the Picturesque period and a steady decline from the 1880s. This peak reflects the distinctive relationship between aristocracy and people characteristic of the years between early-Victorian social conflict and late-Victorian agricultural depression. That relationship made possible a coincidence of popular fascination with the mansions of England and aristocratic tolerance: not so much a meeting of minds as a mutually agreeable exchange of hospitality and admiration.

Something like a hundred houses around England can be described as 'show-houses', advertised in the guidebooks as open on specific days of the week or at any time in the absence of the family. Most of these would be on a beaten track, with sufficient tourist demand to require formal recognition. The Midlands was for this reason exceptionally well represented (just as the London–Bath route had been in the eighteenth century). Eaton Hall, Alton Towers, Chatsworth, Hardwick and Haddon, Newstead Abbey, Belvoir and Warwick

# REGULATIONS

FOR VIEWING

# WOBURN ABBEY.

---

**The days for viewing WOBURN ABBEY are altered from Mondays to Fridays, from Eleven till Four between Lady Day and Michaelmas, and from Eleven till Three between Michaelmas and Lady Day.**

---

Persons desirous of viewing it to apply to MR. BENNETT, at the Park Farm Office, on Fridays, between Ten and Three in Summer, and between Ten and Two in Winter, for Two TICKETS, (one for the Abbey and one for the Gardens) and to enter their names and residences in a book kept there, and also in a book kept in the waiting-room at the Abbey.

The TICKETS to be dated on the day they are issued, and to serve only for that day.

A TICKET will not admit more than six persons.

Persons having TICKETS to present them at the Abbey, and wait in the WAITING-ROOM till the person appointed to go round with them is ready to do so.

Persons having with them Sticks, Whips, Parasols, or Umbrellas to leave them whilst viewing the Abbey, in the waiting-room.

The TICKET for the Gardens to be delivered, on entering them, to the Gardener.

No persons will be allowed to take with them any collation or refreshments, to take in the Abbey, the Gardens, or the Park.

28 A Victorian 'show-house': regulations for viewing Woburn Abbey, 1850s.

Castles were all powerful magnets for tourists from that thick belt of population between Manchester and Birmingham, each clocking up tens of thousands of visitors a year in the 1870s.

In more remote spots, hundreds more houses were probably view-able on personal application, much as in the old days, and in the mid-nineteenth century it was comparatively rare for a house to be absolutely closed. In those rare cases, as when a historic house was allowed to fall into neglect, popular antiquarians felt justified in expressing considerable indignation. Ashburnham Place, in Sussex, was a particular source of grievance, the more so as its famous relics of Charles I,

> given to his attendant John Ashburnham, and by one of his succes-sors 'bequeathed to the parish forever', 'to be exhibited as great curiosities', have been removed from the church, where they were long preserved, to Ashburnham House – where, together with other collections of great interest, they are entirely inaccessible to the public.[13]

The Ashburnhams' only defence was that 'Lady Ashburnham was hustled and nearly knocked down her own stairs by the crowd of sight-seers'.[14] Mrs Wren of Wroxall Abbey, Warwickshire, 'resolutely closes the doors, not only of the mansion but of the adjacent chapel,' complained S. C. Hall, 'and her discourtesy is consequently a proverb in the neighbourhood'. He looked forward to the house passing to her more obliging heir, but the estate was subsequently sold to a Liverpool merchant, who tore down the old house and built a modern Gothic-Tudor hybrid in its place.[15] Mrs Wren was really quite unusual, and among owners of Olden Time mansions she was very nearly unique. A few classical houses that had been standbys of the eighteenth-century circuit – Stowe, West Wycombe, Holkham – were closed to the public for various reasons in the nineteenth century without arousing much notice one way or the other. To close a medieval or Olden Time mansion was practically unthinkable. 'An Earl of War-wick who would make his whole castle his own in the spirit of an inhospitable curmudgeon, who would shut out all eyes but his own from the feast within those walls, is a being so opposed to every English tradition that it is difficult to realise him', concluded the *Daily Telegraph* in 1871 – and this from a paper that at the time was a bulwark of the Liberal party.[16]

What motivated owners to maintain their stately homes as show-houses? It is fair to say that intense personal identification with their houses' history and fabric was not a prominent factor. Given that

aristocratic culture lagged some way behind popular culture in reverence for the Olden Time and its associations, and that owners tended
to take a functional view of their houses, in a buoyant agricultural
economy it was easy enough to maintain the mansions of the Olden
Time with a skeleton staff, without going so far as to live in them.
Such unmodernized houses as Haddon Hall or Compton Wynyates
were familiar family possessions, but not usually cherished homes.

An extreme case was Dunster Castle, then a principally Jacobean
house near Minehead in Somerset, with fine seventeenth-century
plasterwork and wood carving and a famous Van Dyck portrait
of Oliver Cromwell. 'The owner, an inveterate Batchelor, lives in
London, and hardly ever comes here', noted a neighbouring landowner's wife, on a tourist's visit in 1845:

> Two old maiden sisters live in the house − in great seclusion − and
> the stables containing stalls for 20 or 30 horses are quite empty −
> and not a dog in the kennel, where there was formerly a pack of
> hounds. The old servants, coachmen    grooms − huntsmen −
> gamekeepers etc. are retained, but have nothing to do, and about 20
> idle people dine together every day in the Hall.[17]

It was only after this bachelor and his brother died that, in 1867, the
house passed to G. F. Luttrell, who resumed residence, closed the
castle, and commissioned extensive modernization by Anthony Salvin.

Haddon, Compton Wynyates and Dunster may have been unusual
in being accessible to tourists for the whole year, but many other
houses were used only for fixed periods a year, outside of which
tourism could proceed unencumbered.[18] As the most common seasonal use was for hunting − in late autumn and winter − the peak
tourist season might be hardly disturbed. In County Durham, for
instance, the Vanes were known to inhabit Raby Castle for a fixed
six-to-eight-week period. At other times, an omnibus conveyed visitors from the railway station at Staindrop, and those who could afford
their own carriage enjoyed the marvellous privilege of setting down
actually inside the enormous Great Hall, wheels and hooves echoing
among the rafters, the whole brilliantly illumined by two roaring fires
and gas lighting as well.[19] Nearby Lumley Castle ran on the same
schedule. The Lumleys resided only for part of the summer, 'when the
visit is of the nature of a picnic, for the accommodation is not of the
most luxurious kind'. At other times, 'the castle is a favourite rendez-
vous for holiday makers', from the local gentry who held their archery
meetings there to 'vans . . . full of pitmen and operatives from the
neighbouring towns, eager to exchange their native smoke and coal-

dust for a brief sniff of the sweet-scented Lumley air'.[20] Naworth
Castle, in Cumberland, was used for most of the nineteenth century
purely as a shooting lodge, and so rarely that it was effectively open to
the public year round. When Naworth's heir George Howard made a
visit on his honeymoon in October 1864, his bride was surprised to
find the place something of a resort. 'The visitors to the castle are
rather a nuisance,' she wrote to her mother, adding with remarkable
aplomb, 'but they don't come into our sitting room.'[21] Nor was the
pattern very different closer to London. When Lord Ronald Gower
launched himself on a tour of his favourite old houses in 1872, starting
from London on August Bank Holiday Monday, he did not find a
house in occupation until he reached Castle Ashby in Northamptonshire; most were left to servants and tourists.[22] His first stop was at
Hatfield House, within easy reach of the London crowds, normally
open only at midweek and only in the Parliamentary season, to
accommodate weekend house parties. But an exception was made for
the Whitsun and August Bank Holidays, when the family took refuge
with a picnic in a closed wood while the masses 'swarmed in the Park,
and were all day conducted in parties through the House'.[23]

   In fact, perhaps half the show-houses were open when the family
*was* in residence. In these cases the family had to make way for the
tourists, rather than vice versa. At Blenheim, Lord Alfred Churchill
complained that he had to retire to his bedroom for the two hours
three days a week when druggets were laid down in the state rooms
for visitors.[24] When Lord Harry Vane inherited Battle Abbey in 1857,
he was amazed to discover that tourists – eight hundred a day –

> came and peered through the window of the study . . . till they
> fairly stared him out of countenance, and drove him from the
> room . . . Others glued their faces with equal persistence to the
> panes of the Duchess's sitting-room windows; but there they met
> their match, for being roused to great indignation, she resolved to
> try the power of the human eye upon them in her turn, especially
> as she possessed the additional advantage of wearing a large pair of
> spectacles. Armed with these powerful auxiliaries she stared stead-
> fastly at the invaders, and rising very slowly from her chair, without
> averting her eyes, moved gradually, step by step, across the
> room . . . long before she had reached the window the whole party
> had fled.

Similar experiences were recorded at Lowther Castle in the Lake
District and at Holkham in Norfolk, where one noble guest was once
surprised in his dressing-room by a large party of visitors.[25]

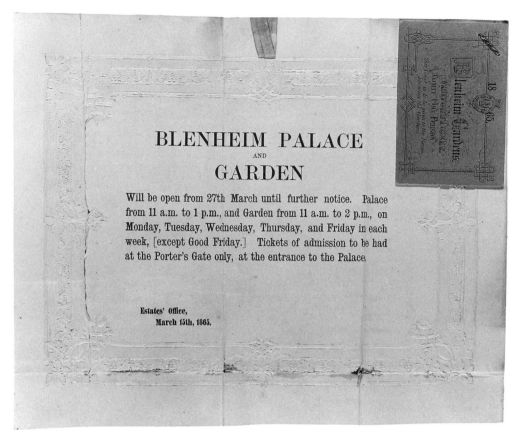

**BLENHEIM PALACE**
AND
**GARDEN**

Will be open from 27th March until further notice. Palace from 11 a.m. to 1 p.m., and Garden from 11 a.m. to 2 p.m., on Monday, Tuesday, Wednesday, Thursday, and Friday in each week, [except Good Friday.] Tickets of admission to be had at the Porter's Gate only, at the entrance to the Palace.

Estates' Office,
March 15th, 1865.

29   Show-houses were often open even when the family was in residence: regulations for viewing Blenheim Palace and Garden, with separate Visitor's Ticket for palace and garden attached (1865).

Given what has been written – fully justifiably – about the growing domesticity of the Victorian aristocracy, and the ease with which they could now travel back and forth between town and country, the willingness to keep open main residences to tourists must be evidence of some strong and overriding sense of public responsibility. It seems clear that owners of historic houses saw it as their role to cater to popular interest in medieval and Olden Time antiquities, even if they did not themselves quite share in it. Far from conflicting with their moral and philanthropic responsibilities, making provision for country-house visiting was part of those responsibilities. This is a marked shift from attitudes earlier in the century. In and after the Napoleonic era, many landlords had abandoned their own cultural indulgences in order to devote themselves to projects of moral and economic regeneration, to salvage their economic position and to enhance social discipline and cohesion. In the 1820s, the idea that anyone would want to visit the mansions of the Olden Time – and that owners had a responsibility to let them – would still have seemed bizarre. In the 1830s and 1840s tourism and the culture industry combined to develop a taste for such things, more among the lower than the higher classes. If, at first, owners were slow to cater to this taste, by the mid-Victorian years they were doing so *nolens volens*. In this sphere, as in many others, the social tensions of the 1830s and 1840s had caused the aristocracy to adjust their relationship to the people. Discipline and punishment were not enough; improvement and inclusiveness had to be embraced, if only superficially.[26] Some noblemen became slum-visitors, mechanics'-institute preachers, even Christian Socialists. But it was easier and more pleasant to throw open the gates of the park, for the local infants' school annual outing and bunfeast, for public strolls through the woods or boating on the lake, for country-house tourism. Country-house visiting was thus part of the largely tacit compromise settled upon pragmatically after Reform and Chartism, by which aristocratic owners were left unmolested in enjoyment of many of their past privileges so long as they appeared to exercise those privileges in a more generous and less exclusive way.

Hosts and guests naturally interpreted this relationship in different ways. Owners were bound to see the accessibility of their homes principally as an act of pure benevolence, carrying little cultural or political significance, and the visitors as docile and grateful recipients, rather than cultural actors in their own right. Unlike the servants, who either complained about the dirtiness and thievery of visitors or identified with their enthusiasm, owners ritually marvelled at the neatness and order of the throngs.[27] 'The cheap excursion trains enchant me,' wrote Lady Granville to her nephew Lord Carlisle after a high-summer visit to Castle Howard, 'They sit about with their baskets of provisions as if it were the Bois de Boulogne, and the Methodists' schools sing hymns beautifully.'[28] After a successful Cook's tour of Belvoir, the Duke of Rutland congratulated himself on being such a good judge of character.[29] The 6th Duke of Devonshire claimed to adore the summertime invasion of Chatsworth but, then, he was a rather lonely bachelor – while the 7th Duke, somewhat more typically, fled from it.[30]

As with other such mid-Victorian compromises, public access to country houses and parks could be interpreted in different ways by different sections of the political spectrum. A Liberal paper such as the *Daily Telegraph* might emphasize duty and reciprocity rather than pure

benevolence. 'England is full of unwritten obligations,' it pointed out
in the leader quoted earlier, 'and men are obligated to do suit and
service that no antiquary has ever laid down.'[31] The more conservative
*Times* was bound to see the same phenomenon differently:

> The British public has much to be thankful for . . . Wherever they
> go they have, within an easy drive, some great place, with park,
> gardens, very fine oak trees, natural curiosities, and some fine
> pictures. A moderate gratuity to the servants will often purchase for
> them as much pleasure as the noble or gentle owner has in a year
> for enormous expenditure. He only goes down, perhaps, to bleed
> money at every pore, to scold, to give orders, to entertain, and
> convert his house into an hotel, with the privilege of paying all the
> bills. The public, a chartered libertine, steps in and enjoys a glimpse
> of Paradise – as much as is good for any of us – at the moderate cost
> of a shilling a head for a party of five, perhaps . . . A Fifth Monarchy
> man of the sternest Communist type used to admit that there was
> one good in our gentry – they made the country picturesque. The
> truth is, England would be naked without them.[32]

And in fact Radicals could be found even at this early date defending
access to country houses as an important public benefit.[33] For much
the same reasons, Whig and Tory owners were equally represented in
the show-house ranks. So long as relative political peace reigned
between aristocracy and people, this system functioned smoothly and
practically without comment. In the words of Thomas Cook – who,
of course, had a vested interest, but was also a genuine product of the
autodidact radical culture of the Midlands:

> the visits paid by large numbers of excursionists to . . . great houses
> thrown open to them by their rich owners, did an immense amount
> of social good, and gave rise to the growth of pleasant feeling
> between the benefited and the benefactors.[34]

The unwritten obligation to throw historic houses open to visitors
was only one of a cluster of ways in which country houses were
becoming more and not less public in this period. Though Gilbert
Scott's fancy that the great hall could once again become a community
centre was never likely to be realized, he was certainly right to see that
country houses and their parks had developed new local uses: as places
for scientific and antiquarian meetings, training grounds for the Volunteer force, sites for school treats and outings, and, later in the
century, for mass political rallies. Many of these functions were aimed
at the immediate locality, the rural community centred around the

great estate, and so are not strictly relevant to our search for a national identity or heritage. But in the railway age the line between the local and the regional was becoming blurred, and country houses near great towns could attract huge crowds to what might previously have been small-scale local activities. A crowd of twenty to thirty thousand assembled for a fête at Londesborough Park in July 1869 ostensibly intended to benefit the 2,500 Volunteers of the East Riding of Yorkshire. The annual Foal Show at Welbeck in Nottinghamshire drew 20,000 visitors on an occasion when Lord Kitchener was present. Family celebrations at Chatsworth often drew curiosity seekers from Sheffield and Derby and further afield still.[35]

The most common act of public-spiritedness, and the one that was probably enjoyed by the greatest number of people, was the throwing open of the park for picnics, excursions and general recreation. In mid-Victorian conditions of overcrowding and limited public space, the availability of private parks and gardens was of no small value, a benefit often overlooked when the paucity of public parks before the 1870s is considered.[36] This oversight applies not only to historians, but also to some contemporaries, including Tennyson, who once asked rhetorically:

> Why should not these great Sirs
> Give up their parks some dozen times a year,
> To let the people breathe?

This reproach might have had some merit in 1847, when Tennyson first proffered it,[37] but a generation later popular antiquaries were eager to refute it. 'The poet cannot be aware,' wrote Hall and Jewitt, 'that a very large number of the "parks" of the nobility and gentry of England are "thrown up" not a "dozen times" but a hundred times in every year.'[38]

Most big cities had at least one great estate open to public recreation within ready rail access by the 1850s. South Londoners had Knole to enjoy every day of the year; North Londoners could choose between Cassiobury, Grove Park and Hatfield; West Londoners made much use of Cliveden for boating and picnicking. Dunham Massey was 'a perfect paradise for Manchester picnickers and pleasure-seekers'.[39] When the railway from Manchester made scenic Alderley Edge accessible in 1843, there was a kind of bidding war between the de Traffords and the Stanleys over who could provide the best facilities for visitors to their estates, the de Traffords triumphing by offering not only walks, seats and wells for the excursionists, but also a great banquet for 143 railway directors.[40]

Again, not coincidentally, the Midlands were particularly blessed with private parks open on a liberal basis. Trentham gardens were very widely enjoyed in the Potteries, as were, somewhat further afield, the grounds of Alton Towers and Enville Hall. The Black Country had Hagley, 'the resort of excursionists every Sunday'.[41] On three days a week, including Saturdays, the public was free to wander through the famous 'Dukeries', the congeries of immense estates in north Nottinghamshire, including great chunks of Sherwood Forest. The principal owners – the dukes of Portland and Newcastle and Earl Manvers – extended an extra facility to local innkeepers, giving them keys to the various estate gates so that their guests could take their carriages along the private ways on these open days. Many of the open parks were attached to eighteenth-century houses of little interest to the tourist trade, so access could be liberally granted without threatening the privacy of the home. At the same time, granting access to park or grounds gave owners who lacked the desirable historic houses an opportunity to be a part of this mutual-benefit system.

## Varieties of Visiting: Historic Shrines and Show-places

So far mid-Victorian country-house visiting has been looked at from the point of view of the owners: who gave access and why. It remains now to ask who the visitors were, and why they went. The answers follow closely the profile traced of the popular market for Olden Time writing and illustration, but with the added complication that stately homes and parks played those multiple roles noted above, local and recreational as well as cultural in the narrow sense; that is, country-house visiting testifies both to the mid-Victorian idea of heritage and the mid-Victorian relationship between aristocracy and people, overlapping but not identical subjects. The large number of houses open and their varying appeal, as well as the scarcity of reliable evidence, makes it difficult to generalize about audiences, though in what follows some use has been made of visitors' books to put numbers and social type to different houses' constituencies.

Starting from the top of the social ladder, it is clear that polite visiting along eighteenth-century lines continued throughout the nineteenth century. Classical architecture remained of some limited professional and aesthetic interest at least until mid-century, as the touring notebooks of the landscape architect J.C. Loudon indicate.[42] Thereafter people had little good to say about classical architecture so they tended to say nothing at all. More durable at least in polite circles was the appeal of the great art collections. Within the exclusive ambit of the art world, cosmopolitan tastes resisted nationalism and medievalism well into the late nineteenth century; Ruskin's influence on behalf of the early Renaissance was not decisive until the 1870s at the earliest.[43] Catalogues of private collections drawn up by the German art historians J.D. Passavant and G.F. Waagen spelled out what treasures were where, and Waagen's descriptions were often dutifully repeated in the *Murray's Guides*. Consequently the treasure-houses on the old London-to-Bath route, with their classical statuary, their Claudes and Carraccis, retained their appeal for a limited band of art lovers, though not on anything like the scale of the Olden Time houses or even of these same houses a century before. A visitor to Wiltshire in the 1860s could see the pictures at Longford Castle on Tuesdays or Fridays, at Stourhead on Mondays, at Wardour Castle on Mondays or Fridays, at Wilton on Wednesdays or Fridays, and what was left of the pictures after a recent sale at Corsham Court on most weekdays. Wilton, once the most visited house in England, was already in the 1820s reduced to a few dozen parties a season, some of them complaining 'of how ill the House is shown, the Maid who used to show it not having had sense enough to pull the Blinds up during the time that People were looking at the Pictures'.[44] Wardour Castle, despite its name, an austere Palladian mansion and famed for its collections, was similarly drawing no more than one or two hundred visitors a year in the 1840s and fewer in the 1860s. By then it had probably been overtaken as a tourist attraction by the Old Castle in its grounds, a mainly Elizabethan ruin where visitors could see 'the deep marks where the balls struck the masonry' during Civil War bombardment.[45] Even Blenheim, among the most visited of all country houses in the eighteenth and twentieth centuries, was less popular in the nineteenth, though this had much to do with the truculence of the owners. It was only shown between 11 a.m. and 1 p.m. on weekdays to 'small parties under the influence of a real love of art', for a one-shilling fee, though the park remained freely open 'to conciliate the goodwill of the *profanum vulgus*'.[46] All of these houses suffered from the disapproval that Victorian guidebook writers felt bound to cast upon classical architecture. Blenheim was regularly described as 'heavy though imposing'. Of Petworth, granted by *Murray's* to be 'a resort of art pilgrims from all parts of Europe', 'it cannot be said that the house possesses the slightest architectural attraction. The part towards the park resembles a strip from an indifferent London terrace.'[47]

The more popular show-houses fell into two categories, historic shrines and excursion centres. The former, houses of medieval and Olden Time origin and preferably with romantic historical associa-

30   The most popular show-house of the Victorian age: Warwick Castle, in a cheap lithotint by J.D.
Harding (1844).

tions, grew predictably in popularity as the history craze developed.
Knole, visited by over five hundred people a year at the beginning of
the century, had multiplied those numbers ten times by the late 1860s.
The army officers and clerical gentlemen of the earlier period had in
the meantime been swamped by thousands of family and school
parties, mostly from London and its Kentish suburbs, and larger groups
such as the Croydon Volunteer Fire Brigade and the Waterloo Road
Bible Christian Sunday School. A thriving inn and hotel trade grew
up in Sevenoaks on the strength of Knole's attractions.[48]
  Warwick Castle followed the same trajectory at a more rapid pace.
It was not much visited before 1815, but in peacetime and with help
from Sir Walter Scott it soon proved irresistible to the sojourners of
neighbouring Leamington Spa. The façade of gentlemanly visiting
could not long be maintained in the face of the thousands of shopkeepers and clerks who were pouring in from Leamington and Birmingham by the mid-1820s. There were at least six thousand visitors
in 1825–6; the tea that had been served to polite visitors on silver trays
by liveried servants was discontinued, reportedly when it was discov-

ered that 'local tradesmen's wives were availing themselves of a free tea each week'. When the Earl of Warwick's housekeeper died in 1834, she was said to have left £30,000 earned from tourists' tips.[49] Honeymooning couples were supposed to be particularly partial to the romantic castle on the Avon. So were Americans, who were turning up in their hundreds by the 1840s, attracted not only by Shakespeare country but also by specific recommendations of Warwick by Washington Irving and Nathaniel Hawthorne. When Harriet Beecher Stowe made the obligatory visit in 1853, she found the castle so infested with tourists that she considered it had become 'a public museum and pleasure-grounds for the use of the people'.[50] As with Sevenoaks and Knole, Hastings and Battle Abbey, the innkeepers of Leamington credited Warwick Castle with transforming their town's prospects, despite the rival claims of the spa.[51] T. Cooke & Son, the Warwick publisher, sold a range of tourist paraphernalia not far short of modern offerings, including guidebooks, photographs, album views, stereoscopic slides, illustrated books and prints. When the castle was swept by fire in 1871, Cooke's rushed out new 'before' and 'after' views.[52] Nearby, at Kenilworth, Henry James had to run a gauntlet of 'a row of ancient peddlers outside the castle wall, hawking twopenny pamphlets and photographs'.[53] A similar touristic apparatus could be found at Haddon Hall, open every day; by the 1880s it was the first stop on a Cook's tour of Europe for Americans.[54]

Of course, not all of the mansions of the Olden Time attracted the crowds that poured through Knole or Warwick or Haddon. But it is striking how many of them were open to inspection and, even in comparatively remote locations, became objects of pilgrimage for people in the vicinity. Burghley House near Stamford was drawing over two thousand visitors annually in the 1850s, including school parties and outings of fairly humble people from Wisbech, Peterborough, Oakham, Leicester and Melton.[55] Local people visited Temple Newsam near Leeds, though probably not in very large numbers as it was normally open only on Thursdays; even so, in a fine summer month like June 1868, over one thousand people might take advantage of more liberal arrangements.[56] Compton Wynyates was notoriously inaccessible — it had to be reached in its dell on foot — but already in 1839 Howitt found that a visitors' book had been instituted, 'for even this most retired mansion, by its peculiar style, and traditions belonging to it, has begun to draw the attention of the curious'.[57]

The explicit attraction of all these Olden Time houses was not that they were aristocratic residences but that they were part of the common heritage. It is worth insisting on this, because contemporaries

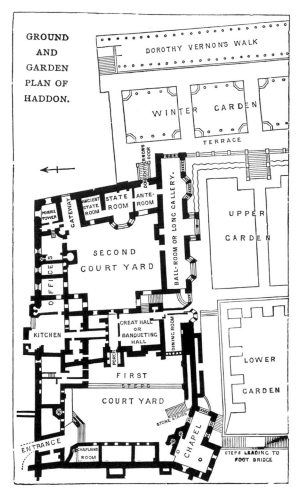

31 Haddon Hall had several rival guidebooks in the nineteenth century. Llewellynn Jewitt's included a floor-plan and room-by-room description and appeared in several forms: as an article in the *Art Journal*, as a chapter in Jewitt and Hall's *Stately Homes of England* (1874), and as a pamphlet on sale locally as late as the First World War.

who wanted to flatter aristocratic owners or their own superior taste sometimes said otherwise. One American visitor in 1877 thought that 'the English people who visit [show-houses] do so chiefly to see the state in which majesty and nobility live; to look at the grand furniture, the gilded cornices, and other splendors of the apartments, with little or no interest in architectural or historic associations'.[58] In this case, the author was keen to assert the great cultural sensitivity of Americans, much as Henry James was wont to do. Others, especially rank-and-file Tories making obeisance to their masters, made the reverse point, assuring the aristocracy of popular interest in their present-day affairs and perquisites.[59]

There is little direct evidence of tourists' motives one way or the other, but the public record of tourist activity – guidebooks and leisure-oriented material in the popular press, for instance – lays down the same criteria that we have already seen in the literary and pictorial representation of country houses. Tourists were encouraged to like baronial halls owned still by the founding families, because the family continuity was another form of connection to the Olden Time and because ancestral houses were better preserved. But they were emphatically *not* supposed to like houses that had been modernized, either by restoration or up-to-date furnishing, even if this betokened continued family residence. Perfectly preserved houses like Knole were the beau ideal, but bare shells like Haddon where dreams could be spun and the past recreated in the mind's eye were preferable to displays of modern opulence. Neither offered much in the way of 'lifestyles of the rich and famous' – that would raise potentially divisive questions about aristocracy and people, which in this period were usually left alone.

Perhaps Charles Knight's zeal for intellectual improvement caused him to expect too much from country-house tourists, but his reasons for visiting ancient halls were nevertheless typical of those cited in the popular literature:

> the weather-beaten walls, and the dusty family records, would alike furnish matter which the wand of fancy might transform into vivid and speaking realities. The different parts of the building would recal [sic] and illustrate the varying phases of public and domestic life; the embattled towers would tell of those ruder times when the feudal chief might have to call around him his retainers and tenants, and prepare against the approach of some hostile band; the huge halls and capacious kitchens, of ancient state and hospitality; the graceful bay-windows, of the growth of elegance and security; while all would display the progress of architectural skill and taste. How distinctly, too, would the apartments and their garniture record the shifting habits of social life – changing slowly and almost imperceptibly from year to year, but showing so vast a difference between the present time and that when the foundations of the house were laid, it may be some four or five centuries ago! And then in the fortunes of its owners – often the mighty, the famous, the unhappy – how impressive a story might be read! To most who visit these ancient halls some such thoughts occur . . .[60]

Somewhat closer to the horse's mouth, expressing proper deference but also indicating a depth of historical feeling that should not be slighted, is this rare testimony from a working man thanking Lord

Salisbury for permitting a Club and Institute Union excursion to Hatfield House and park in July 1870:

> The Timber at Hatfield, including Old Mulberry Trees, rivitted with Iron, – Queen Elizabeth's Oak and her Picture in the Freshness of Youth, – that of the Old Marchioness of Salisbury, who was burned to death, and a good Sketch-likeness of yourself, struck me to be among the best of the many associations with Hatfield, which I saw.[61]

Modern opulence was more of a positive factor in the other type of popular show-house, the excursion centre. These were houses which lacked historical or romantic associations but attracted very large numbers of tourists simply because they had space and facilities to accommodate them, valuable commodities in mid-Victorian conditions of touristic under-development. Not many owners were ready or able to contemplate this degree of self-sacrifice. Large houses were expensive enough to run as residences without taking on the extra expense of mass tourism and accepting the extensive invasions of privacy. A handful of very rich owners could and did accept this responsibility however, conscious of the good it did to the reputation of their class. Most owners of houses open to the public had little to do with the tourist arrangements, which were considered *infra dig.* and best left to stewards and housekeepers, usually confined in any case to periods when the family was not in residence. But the owners of these super show-houses took a proprietary pride and sometimes a close personal interest in fulfilling this unusual responsibility.

The Marquess of Westminster, as the richest man in England, was the leading candidate for the job, and successive Westminsters took up the challenge with alacrity. The 1st Marquess spent a small fortune rebuilding his undistinguished classical house near Chester, Eaton Hall, into what Pevsner has described as a 'spectacular Gothic mansion . . . with its delicate battlements, pinnacles, iron tracery, and plaster fan-vaults' between 1803 and 1825. He filled it with sumptuous furnishings and art treasures and threw it open to the public each year from May until October. By the early 1840s, three or four thousand people a year from Manchester and Liverpool as well as closer to home were taking the opportunity, including a sizeable number of Americans travelling down from the port at Liverpool on their way to London.[62] The 2nd Marquess, trying to keep pace with the fashion for Gothic authenticity, spent another large sum remodelling the house between 1845 and 1854 before throwing it open once again. Now the house was open four days a week, June to August only, by means of an

32  Eaton Hall re-
opens to the public
after renovations:
announcement in
the *Chester Courant*,
10 May 1854.

### Local News.
*(Continued from our sixth page.)*

EATON HALL.—We have authority to state that this magnificent mansion, the seat of the Marquis of West-minster, which has for several years been undergoing alterations and improvements, will be re-opened, by his Lordship's kindness, for the inspection of visitors, on the 5th of June next. Eaton Hall may be seen this summer in the months of June, July, and August, on Mondays, Tuesdays, and Wednesdays, between the hours of ten and four, by separate tickets, for House or Gardens, to be procured in Chester at the Royal and Albion Hotels, or of Messrs. Prichard, Roberts, and Co., booksellers, Bridge-street Row; at Pulford, from the master of the School; and at Aldford, from the landlord of the Talbot Inn. Foreigners and travellers will be admitted also on Thursdays in the same months. Parties who desire to visit the gardens *only*, will be admitted with their tickets by the Lodge, at Eccleston Village.

elaborate ticket system differentiating between locals and travellers, small parties and large, house and garden admissions. Ostensibly in order to obviate the need for tipping, a fee was charged on a sliding scale according to size of party, from over one shilling a head to under three pence for large excursion parties. The proceeds paid the four men who showed house and garden and the surplus went to local charities. Neither the new house or the new system seems to have met with approval, and numbers fell off somewhat to about two thousand a year.[63] *Murray's* deemed the renovated house 'a mistake'.[64]

The 3rd Marquess (and 1st Duke) tried again. Between 1870 and 1883 he spent £600,000 transforming Eaton to a design by Alfred Waterhouse that followed the latest fashion, striving not for Gothic authenticity but sheer spectacle, creating a 'Wagnerian palace' of breathtaking variety and lavishness. Third time lucky. Twelve thousand visitors crammed into Eaton in the three summer months of the first opening season, and although the gardener confidently expected numbers to fall off after the novelty had passed, he was proved wrong. By 1891, seventeen thousand visitors a year were passing through the Eaton lodges, mostly in groups, including large numbers of 'cheap excursionists' at threepence each. They came by rail from all the great cities of the North and Midlands, by steamboat down the Dee, by public brake and tramway from Chester or by private carriage through the wooded park, to enjoy the freedom of the park, to goggle at the modern stained glass, mosaics and paintings, to picnic or purchase light refreshments at two separate sites, and to endure twenty-eight tunes played by the carillon in the 183-foot clock-tower – one of the last remnants of this fantasy still standing at Eaton. The scale and splendour were part of the show, but nobody would have confused this Victorian Disneyland with a true baronial hall.[65] *Baedeker's Great Britain* probably spoke for many of the thousands when it opined, cautiously, that Eaton's 'sylvan beauties . . . and the well-timbered park with its herds of deer, will make the excursion pleasant even to those who have little taste for the triumphs of modern luxury'.[66]

In the Midlands, especially, great estate-owners vied with each other to provide facilities for excursionists. There was a bit of political needle between the high Whig Duke of Devonshire and the high Tory Duke of Rutland to see who could reach new heights of hospitality. Whig Chatsworth, as we know, was already attracting thousands of trippers in wagons from Sheffield before the railway arrived from Derby in 1849. The house was open six days a week – 'we do not allow anything to come up to Chatsworth', bragged Joseph Paxton, the Duke's agent – and the park and grounds seven days, the Duke overruling a protest from his gardeners against having to do Sunday duty. Once the railway reached nearby Rowsley in June 1849, the Duke made immediate arrangements with Thomas Cook for summer excursion trains, and within weeks parties were arriving in their thousands from Derby, Sheffield, Bradford, Leeds and as far afield as Birmingham and Leicester. It says something about the flexibility of summer excursion-taking that these large groups were normally scheduled for Wednesdays and Fridays, never weekends, when the casual trade alone could boost the numbers up to 2,000 a day. By the end of the century, Chatsworth claimed to entertain 80,000 visitors a season, the most-visited private house in England before the First World War.[67] The Duke of Rutland strove mightily to match Chatsworth's record. Cook's first stately-home excursion was a road trip to Belvoir from Leicester in August 1848. Rutland prided himself on keeping Belvoir park absolutely open – 'park palings, lodges, bolts, bars, and locks are unknown', Jewitt and Hall wrote in the 1870s, 'for miles in extent, and from every side, the public may wander on foot, or drive, through the estate and up to the very doors'. Or through the doors: more rooms were said to be open to the public inside Belvoir Castle than in any stately home in the kingdom.[68]

The attractions of Chatsworth and Belvoir, like those of Eaton, were not primarily indoors, however, and they had little to do with history or even with aristocracy. As noted earlier, Chatsworth's modernity, inside and out, was viewed with great suspicion by popular writers, and tourists may well have felt some of the same uneasiness.

## A DAY AT CHATSWORTH.

### BY MRS. S. C. HALL.

#### THE ILLUSTRATIONS BY F. W. FAIRHOLT, F.S.A.

ERBYSHIRE is so entirely an English stronghold of interest and scenery, that it merits and repays the attention of all who, residing in our rich Prairie counties, scarcely can imagine its variety, sublimity, and extreme loveliness. The hills, without approaching to the height or dignity of mountains, mimic Alpine scenery to perfection, in gaunt or fantastic peaks; while the exquisitely toned woods, the dales, the folded "bluffs," the winding rivers, the wide moors, the ancient castles, the venerable mansions, the mysterious caverns, the hollows filled with tufts of trees, the brawling gulleys,—the lonely villages, surprising the traveller at some unexpected turn of a defile or rocky pass—the carts, laden with shining ore, the troops of miners with their safety lamps and quaint costume—the beautiful spars—very jewels of geology—the bubbling health-springs—are so many varied sources of deep and exciting interest.

Who would not visit the sweet hamlet of Hathersage, resting in the bosom of the hills, —to seek out, in its green church-yard, the grave of Robin Hood's own bow-bearer, "brave Little John?" Who would not covet the repose of nature in Hope Dale, rich in all sylvan graces, through which generous Derwent bountifully flows? Who would not climb to where the castle of the Peverils frowned, for ages, from the rocky heights —proud, bold, and stern? Who, once having seen, would not long again to wander in Monsal Dale, the very Tempé of Derbyshire, where the foaming Wye seems to change its nature, and expands in silver sheets of living water to the loving meadows which slope to meet the kisses it bestows.

The antiquary may feed his very soul in Derbyshire. And it is never a profitless retrospect—this looking back into the past; it tends to a higher appreciation of the liberty and prosperity we actually enjoy; it deepens our interest in the beauties of nature, outliving as they do the changing thoughts and habits of the "peopled desert;" it elevates us to the threshold of that Immortality which rises above all decay.

Bounding rivers intersect the county as if they had studied how to beautify it best. The Dove rises a little distance south of Buxton, and flowing generally through rocky channels, presents us with a miniature copy of the Gap of Dunloe. The Vale of the Dove is one of the sweetest of English valleys; and the capricious character of the river adds to its charm: sometimes it inclines to the south, then to the east; then rushing from the pyramidal mountain of Thorp Cloud, it goes westward, until it reaches the vale of Uttoxeter,—when, again turning to the east, it flows beneath the bold hill which displays the ruins of Tutbury Castle. Tutbury! one of the prisons of the unfortunate Mary of Scotland. The Wye becomes near Bakewell a tributary stream to increase the beauty of the queenly Derwent. After it has added the animation of river life to the magnificence of Chatsworth, the pleasant vale of Darley is brightened by these united streams; and on they go until their channel is ingulphed between lofty rocks, which in their recesses enclose the romantic scenery of Matlock Dale—where

" * * * All his force lost,
Gentle and still, a deep and silent stream
He scarcely seems to move ; o'er him the boughs
Bend their green foliage, shivering with the wind,
And dip into his surface."

We are so little proud of the beauties of England, that the foreigner only hears of Derbyshire as the casket which contains the rich

THE ENTRANCE GATES.

familiar title of "The Palace of the Peak." It was the object of our pilgrimage; and we recalled

jewel of CHATSWORTH. The setting is worthy of the gem. It ranks foremost among the proudly beautiful of English mansions; and merits its

the history of the nobles of its House.

The family of Cavendish is one of our oldest

THE BRIDGE ACROSS THE DERWENT.

descents; it may be traced lineally from Robert de Gernon, who entered England with the Con-

queror, and whose descendant, Roger Gernon, of Grimston, in Suffolk, marrying the daughter and

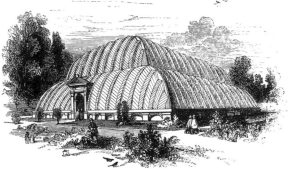

THE GREAT CONSERVATORY.

sole heiress of John Potton, Lord of Cavendish in that county, in the reign of Edward II., gave the name of that estate as a surname to his chil-

dren, which they ever after bore. The study of the law seems to have been for a long period the means of according position and celebrity to the

33    The guidebook highlights of Chatsworth were modern wonders, such as the fountains and conservatories, and fragments of the Olden Time, but not the hyper-aristocratic interiors. In this tour by Mrs S. C. Hall, the visit to the Elizabethan Hunting Tower was described as 'the crowning point of our excursion'. Illustrated by F. W. Fairholt, Mrs Hall's description appeared in the *Art Journal*, January 1852.

family, Sir William Cavendish, in whose person all the estates conjoined, was Privy Councillor to Henry VIII., Edward VI., and Queen Mary; he had been Gentleman-Usher to Wolsey; and after the fall of the great Cardinal, was retained in the service of Henry VIII. He accumulated much wealth, but chiefly by his third and last marriage with Elizabeth, then the wealthy widow of Robert Barley, Esq., at whose instigation he sold his estates in other parts of England, to purchase lands in Derbyshire, where her great property lay. Hardwick Hall was her paternal estate, but Sir William began to build another residence at Chatsworth, which he did not live to finish. Ultimately, she became the wife of George Talbot, Earl of Shrewsbury; she was one of the most remarkable women of her time—the foundress of the two noble houses of Devonshire and Newcastle. Her second son, William, by the death of his elder brother in 1616, became possessed of his large estates, and after being created Baron Cavendish, of Hardwick, was, in 1618, created Earl of Devonshire. It was happily said of him, "his learning operated on his conduct, but was seldom shown in his discourse." His son, the third Earl, was 'a zealous loyalist; like his father remarkable for his cultivated taste and learning which was perfected under the superintendence of the famous Hobbes, of Malmesbury. His eldest son, William, was the first Duke of Devonshire; he was the friend of Lord Russell, and one of the few who fearlessly came forth to testify to his honour on his memorable trial. Wearied of courts, he retired to Chatsworth, which at that time was a quadrangular building, with turrets in the Elizabethan taste; and then, "as if his mind rose upon the depression of his fortune," says Dr. Kennett, "he first projected the now glorious pile of Chatsworth;" he pulled down the south side of "that good old seat," and rebuilt it on a plan "so fair and august, that it looked like a model only of what might be done in after ages." After seven years, he added the other sides, "yet the building was his least charge, if regard be had to his gardens, water-works, statues, pictures, and other the finest pieces of Art and nature that could be obtained abroad or at home." He was highly honoured with the favour and confidence of King William III. and his successor Queen Anne. Dying in 1707, his son William, who was Lord Lieutenant of Ireland, spent the latter part of his life at Chatsworth, dying there in 1755. It is now the favourite country residence of his great grandson, the sixth Duke and ninth Earl of Devonshire—his seats being Chatsworth House and Hardwick Hall, Derbyshire; Bolton Abbey, Yorkshire; Chiswick House, Middlesex; Lismore Castle, Waterford; and Devonshire House in London.

We would avoid the semblance of adulation in speaking of the Duke of Devonshire; but it is impossible to write of him without praise—as, in Ireland as well as in England, the best of landlords, the truest of men, and the most perfect of gentlemen—one who has made and retained more friends and fewer enemies than fall to the lot of most persons—gentle or simple; one whose rank, high as it is among the highest, is but "the guinea stamp."

His tastes are evidenced at Chatsworth; they are of the purest and happiest order;—and are to be found in the adornments of his rooms, the shelves of his library, the glorious Art-riches of his galleries, and the rare and beautiful exotic marvels of his gardens and conservatories.

Charles Cotton in his poem descriptive of the "Wonders of the Peak," thus wrote, two centuries ago, of the then Earl of Devonshire; and surely no language can apply with greater force or truth to the Duke who is the descendant of that Earl, and now the master of princely Chatsworth :—

"But that which crowns all this, and does impart
A lustre far beyond the pow'r of Art,
Is the great Owner; He, whose noble mind
For such a Fortune only was design'd.
Whose bounties, as the Ocean's bosom wide
Flow in a constant, unexhausted tide
Of Hospitality, and free access,
Liberal Condescension, cheerfulness,
Honour and Truth, as ev'ry of them strove
At once to captivate Respect and Love:
And with such order all perform'd, and grace,
As rivet wonder to the stately place."

Although by the courtesy of the Duke carriages are permitted to drive from the railway terminus at Rowsley, to the pretty and pleasant

THE HUNTING TOWER.

inn at Edensor, by a road which passes directly under the house, the stranger should receive his first impressions of Chatsworth from one of the

THE ENTRANCE HALL.

surrounding heights. It is impossible to convey a just idea of its breadth and dignity; the platform upon which it stands is a fitting base for such

a structure; the trees, that at intervals relieve and enliven the vast space, are of every rich variety, the terraces nearly twelve hundred feet in extent—"the emperor fountain" throwing its jet two hundred and seventy feet into the air, far over-topping the noble avenue of majestic trees ot which it forms the centre. The dancing fountain, the great cascade, even the smaller fountains (wonderful objects any where, except here, where there are so many more wonderful) sparkle through the foliage; while all is backed by magnificent hanging woods, and the high lands of Derbyshire, extending from the hills of Matlock to Stoney Middleton. And the foreground of the picture is, in its way, equally beautiful; the expansive view, the meadows now broken into green hills and mimic valleys, the groups of fallow deer, and herds of cattle, reposing beneath the shade of widespreading chesnuts, or the stately beech —all is harmony to perfection; nothing is wanting to complete the fascination of the whole. The enlarged and cultivated minds which conceived these vast yet minute arrangements, did not consider minor details as unimportant: every tree, and brake, and bush; every ornament, every path, is exactly in its right place, and seems to have ever been there. Nothing however great, or however small, has escaped consideration; there are no bewildering effects, such as are frequently seen in large domains, and which render it difficult to recall what at the time may have been much admired; all is arranged with the dignity of order; all, however graceful, is substantial; the ornamentations, sometimes elaborate, never descend into prettiness; the character of the scenery has been borne in mind, and its beauty never outraged by extravagance. All is in harmony with the character which Nature in her most generous mood gave to the hills and

# NOTICE.

TAKEN from the Conservatory, at Chatsworth, on the night of the 2nd of December, 1843, by some person who, probably not aware of its value, was merely desirous of a relic of the occasion,

A SMALL

# BROWN CRYSTAL.

Whoever will return it to Mr. Paxton, shall receive *by post* the sum of Five Pounds.

J. GOODWIN, PRINTER, BAKEWELL.

34   Even the well-behaved tourists at Chatsworth had their little weaknesses, as this polite notice of December 1843 suggests.

There was little to see there of historical interest, as at Belvoir, 'built at the worst of all known architectural periods' (that is, the recent past), though art-lovers could glut themselves.[69] The modern magnificence was stunning in both places, but all parties agreed it was unwise to dwell on this aspect. Most visitors to Chatsworth did go round the rooms, waiting patiently in pens to be taken around fifty at a time by housemaids, and did so 'in the most orderly, quiet manner', Paxton claimed, 'awe-struck with the magnificence of the scene before them'. But if guidebook and press accounts are anything to go by, the true marvels of Victorian Chatsworth were outdoors and as much technological as aesthetic: Paxton's Great Conservatory, acclaimed as 'the wonder of Chatsworth', 'the leading feature of the place' with its tropical foliage, birds and aquarium, and the amazing waterworks, which included the highest gravity-driven fountain in the world and a metal tree that spouted water at a gardener's touch. 'Chatsworth seems like a brilliant episode from the "Arabian Night's Entertainments", rather than the English residence of an English duke', wrote Thomas Cook's representative in 1867, selling the delights of the new direct rail line from Manchester.[70]

Much the same could be said for Alton Towers, another great Midlands show-place. Most observers agreed that this monstrous modern Gothic pile was politically as well as architecturally incorrect – 'a vast, dreary, ill-connected series of galleries and towers', just what one would expect from a Popish peer, was *Murray's* particularly bigoted description – and few seemed to regret the sale of the collections and furnishings in the 1850s, least of all Joseph Paxton, who picked up some of the choicest pieces for Chatsworth.[71] What thousands of visitors came to enjoy were the famous landscape features, the fountains, conservatories, picturesque cottages for shelter and refreshment, and 'the Modern Stonehenge', 'an imitation "Druidic" circle formed of stones of about nine tons in weight each'. These *al fresco* attractions rendered Alton Towers 'a kind of earthly paradise', the 'Staffordshire Elysium'.[72] At Welbeck, in the Dukeries, the house – Palladian, 'dignified but not very individual' – was not open at all, but the real draw for thousands of excursionists from Nottingham and Leicester was the bizarre gas-lit underground rooms and passages excavated by the 5th Duke of Portland, including the 160-foot-long picture gallery, the mile-and-a-half-long carriage tunnel towards Worksop, and the miniature railway connecting underground kitchen with underground dining room.[73]

One final Midlands show-place, practically uniquely, combined the two roles of historic shrine and place of popular entertainment. Aston Hall, near the centre of Birmingham, is a grand though relatively plain Jacobean house built for the Holte family between 1618 and 1635. It acquired 'undying interest' for posterity through its associations with Charles I, who took refuge at Aston *en route* to the relief of Banbury in October 1642; in the next year, the townspeople of Birmingham besieged the Royalist forces in the hall and cannonading left marks still visible two hundred years later. The missing ornament on the Great Staircase lopped off by a Parliamentary cannon-ball was a great point of interest to Victorian visitors, and Joseph Nash portrayed the scene – Roundhead and Cavalier fencing up the shattered staircase – in *Mansions of England in the Olden Time*.

The male line of the Holtes failed in the late eighteenth century, and the estate passed to a firm of Warwick bankers in 1817. In the normal course of events the hall would have found a private purchaser, but the city of Birmingham had begun to encroach worryingly

35    Aston Hall, turned into a place of public resort from 1857, with the miniature Crystal Palace added
to the west front, at left.

on Aston, and the hall seemed fated for demolition until a working
men's committee intervened in 1857 and offered to buy the house and
a small amount of parkland for conversion into a people's park, a
transaction completed with financial help from Birmingham magnates
at the cost of £35,000.

A canny decision was made to restore 'to their original and pristine
state' the intact Jacobean features – the Great Hall, that famous
staircase, one of the finest long galleries in England, and some of the
private apartments, the latter lent further glamour when used by
Queen Victoria on a visit to inaugurate the hall in June 1858. An
amazing Olden Time miscellany was lodged in these rooms: 'a chair
which belonged to a branch of the Shakespeare family', bronzes of
Charles I at Edgehill and Queen Henrietta at Stratford, modern
furnishings designed for Queen Victoria with Tudor and Elizabethan
royal embellishments, busts and portraits of Shakespeare, Jonson,
Cromwell, Bunyan, Newton, Elizabeth, Mary Queen of Scots,
Raleigh, Lady Sidney and Leicester, suits of armour, (new) stained-
glass windows with the Holte arms, (old) Holte family portraits, and a
cabinet of Charles I's, which, over the years, lost many of its lion-
headed handles to marauding visitors. Revealingly, the eighteenth-
century rooms were ripped out and refitted to house a museum of

36 Advertisement for Christmas revels of the Olden Time staged at Aston Hall in 1859.

37   Aston Hall as a municipal museum: the Great Hall in 1874.

curiosities deemed more likely to attract paying visitors. A tableau of
Eskimo life was displayed in the chapel, the Neo-classical library was
transformed into a stalactite cave and in the small dining room were
placed waxworks of a Chinese street scene with a barber shaving his
customer's head. A miniature 'Crystal Palace', 136 feet long, was
erected along the west front; historically accurate tableaux and recreations were staged; acrobats and balloonists plied their trades in the
park. Such a mixture of Olden Time heritage and popular recreation
was irresistible, and over 100,000 visitors paid their penny admission in
the first year, nearly putting Aston on a par with Hampton Court and
the Tower. Incredibly, through a combination of fiscal mismanage-
ment, accident and fraud, the Aston Hall Company went bust, and in
1864 the Birmingham Corporation – always a pioneer in municipal
enterprise – took over hall and park and ran it as a public service with
much the same attractions.[74]

Aston Hall thereby became the first municipally owned country
house in default only of a private purchaser, and well ahead of its time;
Birmingham's example was not followed until Manchester bought the

Heaton Park estate from the Earl of Wilton in 1902.[75] Nevertheless, the fate of Aston was taken as an ominous warning by an aristocracy naturally suspicious of public bodies buying up private property. The growing identification of large masses of people with a national history vested in private buildings, and their increasing habit of traipsing through such buildings as if they were 'Liberty Halls', was only tolerable so long as private ownership was completely unquestioned. The Victorian compromise depended on that formula of private wealth directed to public ends. The very existence of a publically owned country house was threatening to this formula; even a public contribution to a private house was shunned as admitting a public *locus standi*. When in 1854 John Ruskin proposed to the Society of Antiquaries that it establish a Conservation Fund to protect ancient buildings 'from the ravages of time or negligence', it was objected that this might infringe the rights and necessities of private owners. Why should not the Society's President, Earl Stanhope, be completely free to alter his mansion at Chevening to provide for modern comforts, asked one critic, 'notwithstanding a gable here or an old stack of chimneys there might have to be removed'? The Fund was established, but Ruskin was practically the only donor to it, and it made only a few small contributions to church buildings.[76]

Until the middle of the nineteenth century, private owners were too proud and too rich to either need or want any public role, and there were few occasions for the question even to arise. When the Duke of Buckingham went bankrupt in the ominous year of 1848, the contents of Stowe were auctioned off in a great sale much enjoyed by the public, which flocked to it in specially laid-on omnibuses, and also by the radical press. Not many tears were shed for the fabulous eighteenth-century house or even for its famous landscaped park, though the 'mighty wreck of historical, national, and poetical associations' was impressive all the same. One popular journal made much of the sale, 'like a worthless bauble at a Jew-auction', of a 'lock of silken hair' taken from the exhumed body of Henry VIII's sister Mary.[77] But there was no question of selling Stowe; the house was simply closed to the public and left to rot, essentially unmaintained, until after the First World War. It was an unsatisfactory outcome, but the only one tolerable to the honour and pocket of the family. Fortunately few such disasters had to be contemplated during the last golden age of British agriculture, the 1850s and 1860s. But in 1871 a peculiar situation did arise that revealed the fragility of the Victorian compromise, and the mare's-nest of complications in which the Victorian aristocracy had involved themselves by permitting their homes to be taken up as national symbols. As a portent of worse to come once aristocratic power began to collapse in the agricultural depression, the Warwick Castle fire and its aftermath serves as a telling coda to the story of the first period of mass country-house visiting.

In the early morning of Sunday, 3 December 1871, servants at Warwick Castle were awakened by the sound of shattering glass to find that a fire had broken out in Lady Warwick's dressing room. Most of the family were absent in London and the main water supply had been cut off, so it took some time to marshal firefighting capacity and the fire spread rapidly. Two small Greville children and their governess had to be hustled out over a roof by the house-steward (a scene depicted later in the London illustrated newspapers). Fire engines from Warwick, Leamington, Coventry and Birmingham eventually arrived and worked through the day until the blaze was finally quenched around three in the afternoon. From the outside, the destruction appeared very extensive; some hasty commentators said total. Only after some weeks, when the architect Anthony Salvin made a complete survey, did it become clear that the ancient parts of the castle had been hardly touched at all: the family wing where the fire broke out was naturally removed at some distance from the tourist-infested state-rooms. The principal loss was that of the great hall with its seventeenth-century panelling, suits of armour and historical furnishings.

Still, as belted earls went, the Earl of Warwick was not a rich man. His friends knew that he would never be able to restore the castle to its former glories, except perhaps over a very long span of time. Friends of the town and county of Warwick were panicked at the thought of losing this great tourist magnet for some time, perhaps permanently. So Lord Leigh, Lord Lieutenant of the county, took the unusual step of launching a public appeal for funds to help in the restoration. A Warwick Castle Restoration Fund was established in London under the chairmanship of Sir Coutts Lindsay. Satellite funds sprang up within weeks in Warwick, Leamington, Coventry, Rugby, Birmingham and as far afield as New York City.

The restoration appeal was a most delicate business. It had to be conducted entirely without reference to Lord Warwick, in order to protect his honour, and yet it had to be conducted in such a way that he could accept whatever sum was raised, also to protect his honour. The proper balance of power had to be carefully maintained, the definition of hosts and guests kept clear. It had to be intimated that a public subscription was practically Lord Warwick's *due*, just recognition of his generosity in maintaining this great national monument at

38  A national monument at risk: rescuing the contents from the Warwick Castle fire, as portrayed by
the *Illustrated London News*, 9 December 1871.

ruinous personal expense. The public was only showing proper gratitude to him for having shared his private property so liberally in the
past. Once the castle was restored, the Earl could resume his former
role as host – or not, as was his right. This was the burden of a *Times*
leader published on 21 December (and widely reprinted in the provincial press) to pave the way for the appeal, launched formally the next
day. It was a matter of chivalry, of 'knightly service', *The Times*
concluded, to respond generously to one who had served us all
chivalrously in the past:

> If there should happen to be among us any survivors of the good
> old stock exhausting themselves to keep up a monument of England
> as it used to be, some of us may be thankful for the opportunity to
> allow ourselves not unworthy of the country we have the good
> fortune to live in.[78]

Alas for *The Times* and the Earl of Warwick, chivalric appeals registered only with those of the chivalric classes. If Lord Leigh had been
content to do a quiet whip-round among his peers and intimates, the

restoration fund might have been quickly and safely achieved. But a public appeal in response to a 'national calamity', as the fire was generally regarded, set off different resonances in different ears, and the London committee immediately lost control of its interpretation.

John Ruskin fired off the first broadside. He was, everyone knew, the best friend a castle could have, but he was for genuine castles, not mock ones, castles that were 'national memorials', not aristocratic mansions. He thought a public subscription to help Lord Warwick restore his private apartments disgusting in the presence of so much genuine homelessness and destitution. 'If a noble family cannot rebuild their own castle, in God's name let them live in the nearest ditch till they can.' Behind this effusion of disgust at modern aristocracy lay a barely disguised disgust at the popular idea of heritage that was complicit with it. 'By all means', he sneered,

> let the public subscribe to build a spick-and-span new Warwick Castle; let the pictures be touched up, and exhibited by gaslight; let the family live in the back rooms, and let there be a *table d'hote* in the great hall at two and six every day, 2s 6d a head, and let us have Guy's bowl for a dinner-bell.[79]

In Birmingham, more conventional Radicals were offended by Ruskin's gibe at vulgar tourism, but their conscience was pricked by his tirade against subsidy of the aristocracy. In the aftermath of the Second Reform Act of 1867, agitation was picking up against the political privileges of the monarchy and aristocracy and the mid-Victorian regard for the stately home was no longer so unproblematic. The popular view that aristocratic homes were part of the national heritage could and did now slide into the explicitly Radical view that aristocratic property was part of the national heritage, *wrongly appropriated*.[80] 'All sorts of wild speculation as to the future of the Castle is afloat,' wrote a neighbouring landowner, C. N. Newdegate, to Lord Warwick, who remained in London, reportedly unable to face the sight of the steaming ruin, 'some seem to think it will virtually become something like Aston Hall . . . others doubt, how far it will when restored be really your own house'. John Jaffray, proprietor of the *Birmingham Daily Post* and organizer of the local appeal, lent some substance to these speculations by asserting that Lord Warwick was 'rather the steward than the owner of a place which belongs to English history, and therefore to all English people'. Jaffray had launched the appeal 'not with the view of relieving Lord Warwick in any way from the responsibility attaching to every man, but of aiding in restoring and preserving a monument of English life, and a famous landmark of

English history . . . his action had been guided by a desire to restore that part which was in effect, if not in fact, public property'.[81] These were loaded words, but they were inescapable in the circumstances. Even such a respectable Liberal newspaper as the *Telegraph*, also stung by Ruskin's criticism, subtly reversed the roles of host and guest laid out by *The Times*:

> The beauty of the building, the grace it exemplified, the thoughts it suggested belonged to any humble excursionist with a soul as closely as to the noble proprietor himself . . . there was a Warwick Castle in people's thoughts, built on the basis of the Castle by the Avon – the building re-filled by men and women of old – the building that was seen by the dead – the building that brought back days of real baronial power – the actual stones laid cunningly on one another in Warwickshire serving as mute remembrances of many a page in 'our rough island story'.

Far from restoring to Lord Warwick his personal property in gratitude for its loan, by launching the fund the people are 'restoring in a sense a piece of national property, and entrusting it again to Lord Warwick as before'.[82]

Lord Warwick was helpless in the face of this metaphorical reconstruction of his home. Coutts Lindsay told him to keep his distance from the whole affair and issued a public statement on behalf of the London committee saying what should not have had to be said – that the appeal was not a commercial contract, neither a reward for past services nor a promise of services in the future, and that the fund when collected would be offered to Lord Warwick completely *ex gratia* and with no strings attached. Lord Warwick's friends 'would deeply regret that any action of theirs should expose the unstained and sensitive honour of their friend to the small artillery of newspaper correspondents'.[83]

The matter almost rested there; unfortunately, Lord Warwick's own actions exposed him to continued artillery fire. At a time when he was supposed to be in London, in deep mourning and virtual penury, it was reported in the press that he and a large party had been shooting on the Warwick Castle estate over Christmas. This turned out to be false – the Earl was not himself present – but members of his family *had* been indulging in the seasonal shoot and the details of the huge bag of game had been leaked to the press. Such a tangible reminder of the daily routine of the upper classes left a sour taste in many mouths. The gross contrast with the plight of the agricultural labourer, then being agitated by fledgling agricultural trade unionists near the War-

wick Castle estate, further exacerbated the situation – not coincidentally, as both urban radicalism and rural trade unionism had been
stirred up by the political changes since 1867.[84] Coutts Lindsay was
frantic about the bad press, and passed on a message to the Earl via
Lord Somers: 'Pray don't let your game be counted except privately
by yourself, so that it *cannot* be put in the papers . . . the *papers are*
important at the present moment. Nothing that one *does* signifies, it is
what is said that signifies.'[85]

It was immensely disagreeable to be put in such a situation, but
thereafter the scandal passed over. The appeal raised £9,000, paid over
to the Earl in June, and Salvin quickly completed his restorations.
Tourists were soon flowing through the castle again, to the immense
relief of the innkeepers of Warwick and Leamington, and the fire
became in the way of these things a point of interest for tourists. 'The
hold baronial 'all,' rattled off the guide in showing around a party of
Americans a few years later, 'this is the 'all that was destroyed by fire;
hancient harmor; Guy of Warwick's 'elmet; hetruskin vawses . . .'[86]

Had the economic and political situation remained smooth and
unchanging, the Warwick Castle affair might have passed into
memory without any further significance. Few stately-home owners
needed or solicited any financial contribution from the public that
came to view their homes. At this point only three or four houses in
the kingdom even charged an entrance fee, and they did so principally
to obviate tipping.[87] But politics and economics changed, and so did
the culture and its feelings about the stately home. In the generation
after the Warwick Castle fire, the growth of a more assertive democracy and the creeping impoverishment of the landed élite gradually
broke up the compromise by which the people had been allowed to
cherish the mansions of England. An aristocracy on the defensive was
tempted to withdraw its compliance. And a democracy on the attack
was tempted to withdraw its affection – not only its tourist trade, but
its very inclusion of the aristocratic home in the changing definition of
national heritage.

PART II
_____

# *Fortresses of Barbarism, 1867–1914*

'The Stately Homes of England! How beautiful they stand –
As Mrs. Hemans rightly sang – o'er all the pleasant land!
But Westminster, my noble friend, things are not what they seem.
Say is this Budget solid fact, or but a horrid dream?'

'The Merry Homes of England! Yes, Devonshire, oh! *Very!*
I wonder Harcourt makes two bites at his financial cherry.
Why not try Henry George's dodge, a sweeping Single Tax
Of Twenty Shillings in the Pound? He's only got to "ax".'

'The Free, Fair Homes of England! Fair, Westminster, *and* free!
We charge the British Public nought when they drop in to see.
A Briton's home's his Castle. But *our* Castles are *his* home,
In a sort of way, on a holiday, whene'er he likes to come!' . . .

'The Ancient Homes of England! Ah! Devonshire, old chum,
I fear me that an Ancient Home is but an Ancient Hum
To poky, proletariat prigs who, fired with ravenous greeds,
Would pry into long pedigree, and question title-deeds.'

'Yes, Westminster, I know they would. To records Anglo-Saxon,
Plantagenet and Tudor, they (with aim to pop a tax on)
Would turn and search, and cry, with their accustomed incivility,
"Ah! if there are Old Nobblers, 'tis our blooming Old Nobility!" '

— 'Depressed Dukes: A Dirge for Two Voices!'
(*Punch*, 30 June 1894, 303)

## CHAPTER 3

# Philistines, Barbarians and Aesthetes

The late Victorian years are now generally regarded as the fateful period during which Britain stepped back from modernity, preferring to fantasize about the national past and the rural idyll rather than to face the realities of urban and industrial democracy. The assumption is that before this 'counter-revolution of values' the dominant Victorian value was the 'industrial spirit' – bourgeois, modern, anti-historical and anti-aristocratic – an assumption that this book has sought to modify: Victorian culture was modern, but certainly not anti-historical and not deeply anti-aristocratic.[1]

What follows will suggest that, taken as a whole, English culture became less interested in history and more hostile to the aristocracy *after* 1870; there was a counter-revolution of values in attitudes to heritage, but it was one that questioned the relevance of the national past and devalued the contributions of the aristocracy. The present chapter considers the late Victorian development of three themes, all present in embryo in the Warwick Castle affair of 1871–2.

First, commercialized leisure and culture on an unprecedented scale would overwhelm the historical and literary frameworks within which mass culture had been contained in its fledgling stages. For all his snobbery, Ruskin had been right to surmise that cultural consumption had become a big business by the 1870s, hardly compatible any longer with didacticism of any kind, much less the spiritual messages he had in mind. Commerce, urbanization, mass consumption and mass leisure would generate new national identities with which ideas of heritage would find it hard to compete.

Second, the economic and political power of the landed aristocracy suffered some crushing blows, which made it difficult for the owners of the mansions of England to play a role in the defence of 'heritage' or 'culture', assuming that they even desired such a role. In a deep agricultural depression that lasted a generation, one, two, many Earls of Warwick were created. Though most of the greatest landlords weathered this depression with remarkable resilience, they did so only by reining in their public responsibilities as stately-home and estate owners, or even by abandoning these responsibilities altogether. A class which had never had more than a loosely benevolent connection to ideas of heritage was neither able nor willing to defend those ideas when under attack by a rampant modernity.

Third, between the mass audience and the old élite, both increasingly estranged from ideas of heritage, lay an aesthetic minority for whom heritage *did* become more important, more intense, almost a religion. Their idea of heritage was a protest *against* the dominant spirit of the age. Artists and intellectuals, who earlier in the century had catered to a mass audience thirsty for cultural and historical education, now found themselves bypassed as that audience grew larger and more independent. Those aesthetes who would not or could not serve the new democratic tastes turned to a smaller and more discriminating audience of professional and educated people like themselves. In these milieux the idea of heritage became more important, but it also became less social, less popular, less national; it acquired a new tone and fixed on different objects. Ruskin's highly aesthetic and rather ethereal vocabulary, which was hardly comprehensible in 1871, would become a more familiar way of speaking about historical buildings in the years that followed. It would retain the Victorian admiration for the Olden Time, but shift the focus of admiration from social life to art, and seek to protect this aesthetic heritage from the grubby threats posed to it by the material concerns of the present-day democracy.

In these late Victorian and Edwardian years, *some* people's idea of what was the national heritage grew sharper and more intense, but also narrower and more refined, aiming not so much to integrate the nation as to re-stratify it. It is this aesthetic minority's copious writings and furious activities in defence of their idea of heritage that provide the evidence for an anti-modern turn in these years.

## The Philistines: Modernizing the Nation

The unusually widespread and absorbing interest in the national past and its physical vestiges that prevailed in the middle third of the nineteenth century had rested on very historically specific foundations. Until the 1870s, those foundations seemed secure. The general illustrated magazines, with their potted national histories, domestic travelogues and picturesque Olden Time illustrations, enjoyed the peak of their prosperity and creativity in the 1860s. The publication in 1874 of

J. R. Green's *Short History of the English People*, strongly streaked with populism and with an enthusiasm for the ructions of the Olden Time that puzzled Green's fellow-medievalists, marked, in Roy Strong's view, 'the last time that serious history was also popular literature'.[2] The crowds at Royal Academy Summer Exhibitions – still dominated by realistic history painting, including those unavoidable views of Haddon Hall in the Olden Time – were at their largest in 1879, when 391,197 visitors paid their shillings; thereafter, a slow rot set in.[3] Probably also – though this is harder to quantify – both the number of Olden Time mansions open to the public and the size of that public were reaching a zenith in the 1870s, benevolently tolerated by an aristocracy still at a height of power and prosperity unparalleled in Europe.[4]

But if the mass-culture industry was still, a generation later, operating on models and playing themes established in the 1830s, it could not continue to do so indefinitely. What had seemed to contemporaries a remarkably homogeneous, rather cosy and tight-knit milieu of mass-market producers – journalists, illustrators, engravers and painters – catering to a remarkably heterogeneous social constituency, began to show signs of strain and break-up in the 1870s. Cultural critics, such as John Ruskin and Matthew Arnold – neither of whom had had much taste even for the jolly superficialities of the Olden Time – expressed mounting alarm at the further deterioration in literary and aesthetic values that they saw around them. While Ruskin prescribed as antidote a more profound dose of historical consciousness and Arnold a different mixture of what he called 'sweetness and light' (roughly, beauty and idealism), they were agreed on denouncing the great mass of their countrymen as philistines.

Any account of the changing definition of national heritage – and of the changing position of heritage in the larger bundle of national identities – must give as much consideration to this majority 'philistinism' as to the 'aestheticism' of the cultural minority that developed in reaction to it. It was, after all, as Ruskin and Arnold appreciated, the philistinism of the majority that prevented the British State from acting as a setter of national norms and standards in culture as the French, German and Italian states were able to do. While the effect of national philistinism in preventing State sponsorship of modernism (avant-garde ideas about art, design and industry) has been exhaustively discussed, its equally powerful effect in blocking State protection of the heritage has hardly been noticed, giving an unbalanced impression of the impact of *laissez-faire* on British modernity.[5]

Roughly speaking, what lay behind late Victorian 'philistinism' and

the decline of historical consciousness was only a further intensification of the democratizing forces that in their weaker forms had created
the Victorian idea of heritage in the first place. This process can be
seen at work in the growth of the reading public. In the last third of
the century, new technologies were being harnessed, new levels of
prosperity attained, and, partly due to the nationalization of education,
the size of the literate public was again rapidly extended. 'By 1900,'
Richard Altick concluded in the 1950s, 'the English reading public
had attained substantially the size and character it possesses today.'[6]
One immediate effect of this expansion on the culture world was a
marked tendency towards segmentation, that is, towards the emergence of specialized products aimed at narrow, single-interest markets
rather than at a broad swathe of the whole reading public. It was
no longer possible to capture the whole spectrum from shopgirl to
clubman with a single cultural idiom.

In the short term, segmentation might expand the audience for high
art and historical matter, and yet its proportional share of a rapidly
expanding culture market might be shrinking, sapping its claim to
contribute to a 'national identity'. Thus the *Magazine of Art*, founded
in 1878, reached a wider audience than the *Art Journal* had ever
attained, but it and rival magazines purveying a diet of high-art
reproductions and museum news took on a more exclusive tone,
while their kind of material vanished from those general illustrated
magazines that survived.[7]

For general magazines to survive in a diversifying and segmenting
market, they needed to diversify their content, and this marginalized
the hitherto central historical material of earlier Victorian periodicals.
Some movement in this direction was already evident in mid-
Victorian miscellanies such as *Cassell's Magazine*, which eschewed the
sobrieties of a Charles Knight, or even the lengthy serials and political
tirades of popular journalism, in favour of a grape-shot of anecdotes,
curiosities, interviews with celebrities and jokes.[8] *Cassell's* was
immensely successful commercially, but its example was not widely
taken up until the 1890s, often seen as the watershed for commercial
publishing. These years saw the rise of the Newnes, Harmsworth and
Pearson publishing empires, spearheaded by light, snappy, self-
consciously 'modern' and consumer-oriented titles – *Tit-Bits*, *Pearson's
Weekly* and *Answers* – some of which topped a million in circulation.
Harmsworth extended this formula to the daily newspaper in launching the *Daily Mail* in 1896.

The same tendencies to diversify, lighten, shorten and modernize
the content of reading-matter can be detected among the smaller but

also growing middle-class public. Contemporaries spoke of a 'New Journalism' in which crime, gossip, investigative reporting and the 'human interest story' were revolutionizing formerly respectable corners of the publishing world. Arnold and Ruskin were, already in the 1870s, complaining about the popularity in their own circles of the 'smart', newsy *Daily Telegraph*. W. T. Stead's crusading paper, the *Pall Mall Gazette*, took the process a step further in the 1880s. After leaving the *Gazette* Stead had an even greater success in the 1890s with the *Review of Reviews*, which as its title suggests was largely composed of snippets from other journals, augmented by Stead's interviews, opinion polls and populist editorializing. Harmsworth, Pearson and Newnes had their successes in this market, too; *The Strand Magazine*, for instance, adopting in disguised form many of the popularization techniques of its downmarket stablemates. The New Journalism had a counterpart in the New Novel, though it was not so-called at the time. The dominance of the heavy, conventional novel of fashion – three volumes of convoluted plot set either in high society or in historical dress (or both) – was breaking up. Shorter, single-volume novels with a greater diversity of subject-matter and a more modern, realistic, 'smart' and 'clever' tone were more popular with middle-class readers in the 1890s and particularly after 1901, when social leaders at the new Edwardian Court began to set a different tone themselves.[9] Scott, Dickens and Ainsworth alone among earlier nineteenth-century authors retained their popularity, but were now seen as modern classics, taking on an air of worthiness as they joined the high Victorian poets in the schoolroom.[10]

For a number of reasons it is as difficult to generalize about the content as about the form of the late Victorian reading world: it was too diverse, for one thing; for another, segmentation meant that the superficiality of the mass market was counter-balanced by the growth and intensification of all special interests, including high art, history and heritage. But while historians have dwelt upon the cultivated élites' mounting reaction to democratization in this period, and especially upon their growing reverence for the high art of the national past, the culture as a whole was clearly veering away from the same interests, in art and history and the older sense of 'Englishness'. These things came to be frozen together in the public mind into an unpleasant package which, as Raymond Williams has noted, began to be labelled pejoratively as 'culture' in the 1870s – despite or because of the simultaneous efforts of Arnoldites and Ruskinians to turn 'culture' into a new religion.[11]

Rejecting the collectivism, historical interests and aesthetics of 'culture' (or of 'heritage', a later usage),[12] turn-of-the-century society turned instead to embrace the values of individuality, modernity and the world of goods. New national identities were under construction. These currents swept through all classes and cut across them; although anti-modern reactions tended to be concentrated in the more edu-cated classes, the effects of modernity themselves were well-diffused. It would be wrong to conclude, with Martin Wiener, that the nation's élites, the 'shapers of middle- and upper-class opinion', were in this period hiving themselves off from 'the sources of dynamism in existing society' and promoting 'a change in collective self-image from that of a still-young and innovative nation to one ancient and peculiarly stable'. Some were – but many others, especially the nation's political leaders, had perforce and often by choice to remain close to those 'sources of dynamism'.[13]

Certainly, the earlier sense of Englishness carefully constructed by the Victorians as an antidote to aristocratic cosmopolitanism was under direct attack in all sections of society by a democratic kind of cosmopolitanism made possible by the communications revolution. If foreign travel was not yet generally familiar, the contents of foreign cultures were. The inventions of telegraphy, photography and steam travel caused a hail of titbits, news items and pictures from foreign parts to rain down upon England's green and pleasant land, to be eagerly soaked up by mass-circulation journals and newspapers looking for just this sort of miscellaneous information. The domestic travel and topography that filled so many earlier Victorian pages was, by the end of the century, almost completely displaced by exotica about the most distant parts of the globe. The setting for serial fiction likewise tended to shift from English history or high society to foreign parts, notably in the vogue for stories of adventure, exploration and conquest. Technology was responsible only in part; imperialism naturally played an important role; so did the freer flow of consumer goods around the world, a movement to which free-trading Britain was uniquely susceptible. Insofar as politicians sought to inculcate ideas of nationality – often with support for imperial ventures as their goal – the nation in question was less likely to be England than Britain or, more loosely still, the British Empire. Since 'Britain' did not exist before 1707 (or even 1801), it was a nation necessarily less historical, with less of a heritage, though highly relevant to the present.[14] School-books, which for most of the nineteenth century had inculcated an English (never British) history symbolized by men of culture and learning, became, at the end of the century, more conscious of their military and imperial responsibilities, and the new British history began to focus on its explorers and conquerors: Drake, Wolfe, Clive and, especially, Marlborough and Nelson.[15]

History in general was marginalized by all of these late-century trends. Here again the inherent newsiness of telegraphy and present-mindedness of photography were potent corrosives of the feel for the past that had been characteristic of the mid-Victorian culture industry, with its sketch-books, engraver's tools and romantic imagination. Widening prosperity and consumerism provided other distractions. All of these things, and the very phenomenon of cultural diversification, stimulated a popular taste for 'smartness' and 'modernity' into which the Olden Time fitted uncomfortably, if at all. As with the lingering taste for Dickens and Scott, that section of the public for whom Old England retained a fascination had now to do so in defiance of 'smartness', and to accept the flavour of earnestness and didacticism that now adhered to 'old things'. For the majority, as Jose Harris has put it, 'the unique dominance of the present time' in late Victorian and Edwardian Britain 'seemed to many people at the time like a quantum leap into a new era of human existence', ruled by economic growth, science, reason and evolution. Social change, which had been accepted and absorbed by earlier Victorians through analogies with the past, now required less justification and seemed to have its own logic and momentum.[16]

The same shift of emphasis away from Englishness and history was even evident to some degree in developments in travel and tourism, which (until foreign travel became more general) should have had the countervailing effect of shoring up popular identification with the national past. There was a dramatic expansion in leisure time and particularly in tourism in the late nineteenth century, just as there was in the market for print. The excursion trade received a famous fillip with the enactment in 1871 of Sir John Lubbock's Bank Holidays Act, making universal the traditional Boxing Day, Easter Monday and Whit Monday holidays (in addition to Christmas and Good Friday), and adding a wholly new holiday on the first Monday in August, dubbed 'Saint Lubbock's Day' by the *Daily Telegraph*. More important in the longer term was the real growth in earnings in the 1880s and 1890s, which relaxed the national puritanism to a great degree and caused first the Saturday half-holiday and later the week-long annual holiday to spread to large numbers of manual workers. By the end of the century, clerical workers were normally in receipt of a fortnight's *paid* holiday, in many cases rising to three weeks after long service.[17]

Notoriously, the favoured holiday site for most of these new urban tourists was not the countryside but the city-by-the-sea, the seaside resort. Here individuality, modernity and the world of goods were more widely available than at home, in the form of a freer sexual atmosphere, plenty of cheap consumables and a positive frenzy of gaslights, steel piers and towers, amusement arcades and music halls. It was not only the new mass market that was attracted by the seaside; the middle and upper-middle-class market grew, too, though channelled away from the crowded traditional resorts towards new sites in Wales, the West Country and East Anglia, where entrepreneurs were laying on tennis courts and golf courses to attract this upmarket clientele.[18] The richest stratum also went to the seaside, but abroad, to Biarritz or Nice or Venice, attracting much comment from advocates of Englishness who accused the rich of abandoning their native culture for foreign frivolity.[19]

Travel into the countryside benefited from the dramatic expansion and commercialization of leisure, too, but, as the advocates of high culture invariably complained, this meant principally the taking of urban pleasures into a rural setting. In the middle of the century, excursionism had been channelled by such organizations as Thomas Cook's along well-controlled and often educational lines. Growing demand dissolved these controls from the 1870s onwards. The Midland Railway set a precedent in 1872, by providing third-class carriages on all trains, which by the end of that decade made almost every train an excursion train. The full extension of the national railway network opened up the whole of the countryside, and rural stations became starting-points for the exploration of lanes and public footpaths by ramblers and (from the 1880s) cyclists.[20] Hitherto 'unspoilt' tracts of countryside near major population centres filled up with ramblers, topers and 'bean-feasters'.[21]

As with the persisting audience for Victorian classics, the serious, heritage-oriented tourism of the earlier Victorian period also survived, but as a smaller, better-defined part of the whole leisure market, carrying a heavier and sometimes discouraging cultural load. The domestic guidebook market splintered in reflection of this trend; there was no longer much demand for the *Murray's* handbooks, with their promiscuous mix of anecdote, history, architecture, archaeology and topography. When the English county series was finally completed with the publication of Warwickshire in 1899, sales were already flagging; the series was shortly thereafter sold off to Edward Stanford and no new editions were published. In *Murray's* place had sprung up, on the one hand, a whole host of cheaper and flashier regional guides, such as those published by Ward & Lock, pitched at the more elevated end of the seaside trade seeking picturesque day-trips away from the resorts. They dispensed with all but a minimum of historical and artistic content, concentrating instead on the mechanics of tourism: hotels, transport, excursions, resort attractions. On the other hand, Methuen began to issue in 1897 a new county series, the famous *Little Guides*, for the serious architectural tourist. Sober and scholarly, aesthetically sectarian, organized alphabetically so as to deter all but the most systematic traveller, the *Little Guides* were nevertheless the architectural oracle for at least three generations of connoisseurs, until Pevsner's *Buildings of England* began to appear after the Second World War. Between these two extremes, the middle ground of *Murray's* had fallen away, though to some extent it was filled by the single-volume *Baedeker's Great Britain*, first published in 1887, which tried to combine history, aesthetics and day-to-day tourist concerns, inevitably in highly abbreviated form.[22]

The weakening of the Victorian idea of heritage would alone, therefore, have weakened the place of the 'mansions of the Olden Time' in the national heart. But modernity was also working against the country house in other, more direct ways. The stately-home-owning class, which had never been closely attached to ideas of heritage and which was equally affected by the wave of material present-mindedness sweeping through all classes, also had unique economic and political challenges to confront in the late Victorian decades. Far from driving aristocrats to cherish their houses more dearly as cultural objects, these pressures forced many owners to consider their houses as disposable assets – and to dispose of them.

## The Barbarians: Privatizing the Country House

In his catalogue of the enemies of 'culture', Matthew Arnold deemed the aristocratic class – whom he dubbed 'barbarians' – to be just as culpable as the ignorant populace and the materialistic philistines:

> One has often wondered whether upon the whole earth there is anything so unintelligent, so unapt to perceive how the world is really going, as an ordinary young Englishman of our upper class. Ideas he has not, and neither has he that seriousness of our middle class which is, as I have often said, the great strength of this class, and may become its salvation.

In place of ideas and seriousness, Arnold thought, the British aristocrat had only a stubborn obsession with individual liberty (which forestalled his subscribing to any canons of truth or beauty), an excessive valuation of outward appearances (which blinded him to spiritual goodness) and a love of field-sports.[23]

As Arnold appreciated – and as we have seen in the aristocracy's relative detachment from the Victorian idea of heritage – these traits had already been evident for at least a generation or two by 1870. Broadly speaking, in order to marshal their resources and protect their economic and political power, British aristocrats in the early to mid-nineteenth century had gradually abdicated positions of cultural patronage which were too expensive, too unproductive and too conspicuous. The Gothicism of 'Young England' – an unusual late effort to knit together the social fabric by means of cultural as well as moral and economic leadership – was a dismal failure, and the experiment was not repeated in the 1850s and 1860s.

This process of cultural detachment was, if anything, accelerated by the new and more direct challenges to their economic and political power that great landlords had to face from the 1870s onwards. Mere economic survival became the prime imperative in most landlords' consciousness, further driving any lingering historical or aesthetic impulses into the background.

The most immediate and unmistakable challenge to the position of the landed aristocracy was posed by the great agricultural depression which set in after 1874. Improvements in steam transport triggered a flood of cheap corn from abroad, principally from the Americas, and grain prices in Britain tumbled by almost 50 per cent. Reinforced by an international price deflation in all kinds of produce, these low prices prevailed until the late 1890s. Agricultural labourers and tenant farmers suffered most from the price collapse, while the impact on landowners was highly variable. Landowners who were reliant on the monocultural grain estates of the south and east, especially those on heavy clay soils into which a lot of investment had been poured in the preceding decades, were hit the hardest. Gross income on many estates in these areas fell by more than half. Landowners in the north and west, with a greater stake in dairying and livestock, escaped comparatively unscathed. Great landowners with diverse portfolios – different kinds of estate (including rapidly appreciating urban and mineral-rich land) and non-agricultural investments – were better able to ride out even a twenty-year depression than the less well-endowed gentry; but no landowner was unaffected. Only a handful could expect their assets to appreciate, as non-landed assets were doing. The high levels of debt incurred in the preceding generation, which by keeping the land profitable had seemed prudent at the time, now rendered precarious the position of some of the most substantial landowners.[24] Contemporaries were justified in perceiving a general crisis of agricultural landownership.

This crisis undoubtedly put pressure on landlords to view all their assets in a more grimly material light and to maximize their value, regardless of the cultural consequences. In general, the effect was to preserve land at the expense of houses and especially of their contents. Landownership had always been the basis of the aristocracy's social and political power, as well as of its fortunes. It would take many decades of agricultural depression for owners to see that land was undergoing an irreversible decline in profitability and status. Furthermore, complicated legal mechanisms had been devised over preceding generations to keep estates together, notably the collection of practices known as strict settlement, which limited the owner's ability to sell land against the interests of his heirs. There were consequently few major land sales in the depression's early years. As the depression deepened, the land market collapsed and sale became difficult anyway. To give owners more flexibility, the Settled Land Act of 1882 loosened some of the restrictions on sale, but its function was principally to tidy up land-ownership rather than to redistribute it. Landowners used the Act to lop off smaller, isolated acreages, the better to fall back on their core estates.

The 1882 Act made the sale of settled land easier, but it forbade the sale of settled mansion houses. This provision did not reflect any sensitivity about the country house – as one historian of strict settle-ment has put it, 'the house itself was of no concern' – but was inserted to ensure that only outlying parts of estates, and not the core, might be sold.[25] Large country houses were ruinously expensive to maintain, and their costs could make the difference between profit or loss on the estate. One contemporary estimate put the staff needs alone of the smaller country house at £2,600 a year, representing the wages of fifty-eight men, all but six of whom would be engaged in essential maintenance (i.e. not employed as household servants). Heating, light-ing and care of the fabric obviously mounted with the age and size of a house.[26] Such burdens militated against family sentiment and a concern for national history. Consequently, many owners – including some great aristocrats who were not under any immediate pressure – took steps to realize the value of their houses or at least to minimize their cost, whatever the cultural consequences.

Where houses were legally saleable and where buyers could be found, houses were sold, apparently regardless of their antiquity. The problem was that buyers were not thick on the ground; old wealth already had too many houses, and new wealth might prefer to build new homes, fully equipped with modern comforts. A few eccentric American plutocrats, seeking instant cachet, might oblige. William Waldorf Astor did so twice, relieving the Duke of Westminster of his classical box and extensive gardens at Cliveden, on the Thames, in 1893, and purchasing one of Nash's Mansions, Hever Castle, in Kent, from country gentleman E. G. Meade-Waldo in 1903.[27] Some native plutocrats – figures from the 'beerage', for instance, brewers with new titles – might be similarly interested. The head of the Guinness empire tried to purchase cavernous Tottenham House (and its Savernake Forest estate) from the financially desperate Marquess of Ailesbury in 1892, but was temporarily frustrated by the Settled Land Act and then by the Marquess's death in 1894; the heir halted the sale.

Houses within easy reach of London – such as Cliveden and Hever – were easier to sell. The Guinnesses finally settled on Elveden Hall in Suffolk. The mustard magnate Jeremiah Colman purchased Gatton Park, an early Victorian house in Surrey much esteemed by the guidebooks for its Marble Hall patterned after the Corsini Chapel in Rome, from Lord Monson in 1889. In Suffolk, after many failed attempts, the Gages finally sold Hengrave Hall to the cotton king John Wood in 1897. Lord Westmorland unloaded Apethorpe Hall near Peterborough to Leonard Brassey, grandson of the great railway contractor Thomas Brassey, in 1904. Lord Carrington, a particularly unsentimental (and successful) speculator, sold off his desirable Wycombe Abbey, near the metropolis (the first of many country houses to become a boarding school), buying a farmhouse nearby to safeguard his local interest and acquiring a Tudor mansion in Wales from a cousin to serve as the family's country seat.[28] Such institutional sales as that of Wycombe Abbey were still a rarity, except for some houses completely gobbled up by urban sprawl which were turned to urban or suburban uses. The plain classical blocks of Camden Place, Chislehurst, and Eltham Lodge, near Woolwich, were the first of many country houses to be adopted by golf clubs, in 1894 and 1906 respectively.[29]

Houses that could not be sold might still be turned to profit. The Strickland family, owners of Sizergh Castle in Westmorland, sold not a house but a room – the famous Inlaid Chamber, immortalized by Nash's depiction in the *Mansions*, bought as an Olden Time gem by the Victoria and Albert Museum in 1891. The parks of houses in urban and industrial areas could be developed for housing or minerals, the house simply shuttered up and left to rot. As early as 1846, the earls of Dudley had abandoned Himley Hall as too close to their eponymous urban district and moved further out to Witley Court,

39   The Inlaid Chamber at Sizergh Castle, as depicted by Joseph Nash in *Mansions of England in the Olden Time* (*above*) and as reconstructed, with the original panelling, at the Victoria & Albert Museum from 1891 (*below*).

bought a few years previously for just this purpose. Nearby, the earls of Dartmouth, feeling the breath of Black Countrymen on their necks at Sandwell Hall in West Bromwich, purchased a new estate not far off at Patshull in 1848 and gradually relocated there over the next few decades, leaving Sandwell to be mined, though the house was not abandoned until the First World War.[30] Lord Middleton already had so many other houses that he had no qualms about stripping his great Elizabethan mansion, Wollaton Hall, near Nottingham, of its valuable parkland. It was left to Lady Middleton to bemoan its fate with a sentimental elegy that neatly sidestepped her family's role:

> Sad are things many! Sad is the gradual creep of the city down to the park walls . . . Sad is the nighness of the local colliery, which it was left to the last generation to plant in the pretty village itself; and whose smouldering pit-bank generates sulphur fumes which will surely in time do to death the noblest trees.[31]

Houses in more salubrious climes could be let, for their proximity to the metropolis or for their sport, or both, or to men who wanted a temporary country house without the expense of purchase or new construction. Nash's Mansions were particularly popular for this purpose: Broughton Castle, essentially deserted since 1824, was let in the 1880s; Wollaton Hall also found tenants; Montacute was let sporadically by the Phelips family, including to Lord Curzon, a connoisseur of country houses of all eras. The Lyttons let Knebworth and the Cholmondeleys, who had returned to their Cheshire seat, failed to find a buyer for Houghton Hall, their Palladian palace in Norfolk, but found a series of tenants from 1883. Battle Abbey in Sussex, a Victorian country house incorporating medieval monastic ruins, was taken by the American banker M.P. Grace, who installed bathrooms and electric lighting and severely restricted the tourist trade to the ruins.

Otherwise, large country houses – whatever their antiquity – that did not have any immediate material value and were not needed for residence or estate administration, were viewed as dormant assets that (consistent with the law and with aristocratic conservatism) should be kept, but (consistent with aristocratic prudence) at a minimum expense. The Duke of Devonshire's Palladian villa at Chiswick, which had become unpleasantly suburbanized, was stripped of its fixtures and let as a lunatic asylum. Temple Newsam, the highly picturesque Tudor and Jacobean house near Leeds, its stonework under immediate threat from 'the poisonous fumes from Leeds chimneys', was shored up cheaply by its ancestral owners with 'duplicates made in cast iron', until the family was finally able to unload their burden by sale in

1904.[32] The Marquess of Ailesbury who inherited in 1894, and who had fought his young nephew's attempt to sell Savernake Forest to the Guinnesses, tried to make the best of the estate by selling off much of the live game, exploiting the rest by letting the shooting, and vacating the mansion house for a smaller house on the estate.[33]

What had motivated the family's opposition to the sale of Savernake Forest was that this *was* the family's core estate; its loss would mean the loss of all landed income and position.[34] For the same reasons, most families held on tenaciously to their principal seat, even if lesser seats were sold or let or abandoned. Yet, as some of the instances already cited suggest, when the definition of 'principal seat' was unclear, *which* seat was retained had much more to do with the state of the land market than any sentimental or cultural attachment to specific houses. Middleton would not, otherwise, have abandoned Wollaton, the one house he owned which connoisseurs recognized as a unique treasure. Indeed, as F. M. L. Thompson has shown, owners in this period sank a great deal of money into the modernization of their remaining houses, a gesture of faith in country life and country residence, though not in history or heritage. In the 1880s and 1890s, at least, extensive use was made of an 1870 Act which permitted loans on settled estates to raise money for the modernization of mansion houses, as well as of the 1882 Settled Land Act for the same purpose.[35]

As a result, the old country houses that were retained became much more clearly *homes* than they had been before. Electric lighting, oil-fired central heating, lifts and modern kitchens all made their appearance. In one extreme case, Compton Wynyates, the Tudor gem owned by the Marquesses of Northampton that had been empty since 1770 (except for the growing number of tourists tramping through its rooms), was reoccupied by the family in 1884, repanelled and refurnished; 'it is as a home most of all, though it was so unlike one sixty years ago, that the house strikes you', wrote a visitor in 1903.[36] Rosalind and George Howard gave Naworth Castle, in Cumberland, an equally extensive refurbishment in the 1880s, after years of neglect and use only as a rather uncomfortable shooting box.[37] The greater 'homeliness' of country houses and the more careful use of surplus houses, such as Compton Wynyates and Naworth Castle, would alone have impeded country-house tourism, even if broader social and political considerations were not involved.[38]

Economic difficulties had a rather different impact on the owner's relationship to his movable treasures than on land or houses. For one thing, there was a far livelier market in fine art, antique furnishings, rare books and manuscripts than in land or country houses; these commodities were unaffected by the agricultural depression, they were coveted by people of new as much as of old wealth, and the rich American and German markets were wide open to objects that could be easily exported. Furthermore, because the contents of houses were not strictly speaking necessary for landed position, the relaxations on sale of these 'heirlooms' made possible by the Settled Land Act of 1882 (and a subsequent Act of 1884) were more complete and the effect more immediate.[39]

Beginning in 1882, and then almost every year until the outbreak of the First World War, there were enormous public auctions or well-publicized private sales of famous country-house collections. The series got off to a good start in the summer of 1882, when the Duke of Hamilton netted about half a million pounds from the sale of Old Masters, rare books (including William Beckford's library), glass, enamel and furnishings. Contemporaries were aware that the Hamilton Palace sale − 'the most remarkable in the artistic history of the present century' − inaugurated a new era; the great Stowe sale of 1848 had yielded only about £75,000.[40] The Duke of Marlborough was not far in the rear, offering books and manuscripts, enamels, Old Master drawings and Old Master paintings in a chain of private and public sales throughout 1886. Thereafter sales became so commonplace that only the high points can be mentioned: the emptying of Stourhead in 1883; the piecemeal dismemberment of the Earl of Crawford's great library at Haigh Hall, from 1887; the sale in 1892 of the famous Althorp library to Mrs John Rylands, who donated it the University of Manchester; the sales of the books and manuscripts at Ashburnham Place in Sussex in 1897 and 1898; and a cascade of sales after 1909, when the political and economic situation of great landowners sharply worsened again.[41]

Quite apart from their greater frequency and visibility − owners often preferred public auctions as they increased the yield − these sales of *virtù* engaged national attention and opinion in a way that country-house sales did not, because they opened questions of public policy. Art objects were movable and could be exported; Britain was a free-trade nation and raised few barriers to exports and imports; and for all its wealth, Britain alone could not compete at auction against all other wealth-holders of the Old and New Worlds combined. Consequently, much of the art sold from country houses in this period went abroad. At first, the Parisian dealers − often acting for Rothschilds − were to the fore, competing at the Hamilton and Blenheim sales; from around 1900, the American plutocrats began to intervene more forcefully, and English aristocrats benefited from some delirious auctions. In the last

# Fifth Portion.

## CATALOGUE

OF

THE COLLECTION OF

# PICTURES,

## Works of Art,

AND

## DECORATIVE OBJECTS,

THE PROPERTY OF HIS GRACE

# THE DUKE OF HAMILTON, K.T.:

WHICH

## Will be Sold by Auction, by

### Messrs. CHRISTIE, MANSON & WOODS,

AT THEIR GREAT ROOMS,

8 KING STREET, ST. JAMES'S SQUARE,

On SATURDAY, JULY 15,

And MONDAY, JULY 17, 1882,

And following days,

AT ONE O'CLOCK PRECISELY.

———∞◦⦂◦∞———

Each Portion may be publicly viewed Three Days preceding.

Catalogues of the whole Collection, Five Shillings each; by post, Five Shillings and Sixpence.

Catalogues of each Portion, One Shilling each.

Illustrated Catalogues of the whole Collection, Price Twenty-one Shillings each, may be had at Messrs. CHRISTIE, MANSON and WOODS' Offices, 8 *King Street, St. James's Square, S.W.*

40   Everything must go: catalogue from the huge Hamilton Palace sale of 1882, 'the most remarkable in the artistic history of the present century'.

year before the First World War, 'the most lavish in all the recorded
annals of art history', Henry Clay Frick and Henry Huntington
duelled for Gainsboroughs on offer from Lord Radnor and Lord
Bessborough; P.A.B. Widener paid over $1 million for a Rembrandt
and a Raphael; and J.P. Morgan bought a set of precious tapestries
from Knole for $325,000.[42] In addition, foreign governments – with a
tradition of nationalist art history and cultural *dirigisme* still alien to the
British – went prospecting for their national treasures and paid handsomely to recapture them. The German government plucked relevant
manuscripts from the Hamilton Palace sale, for instance, and the
Italian and French governments negotiated privately for 'their' manuscripts at Ashburnham Place. Such exports inevitably raised questions
about British intervention. Were the treasures filched on the Grand
Tour of the eighteenth century part of the British national heritage?
Was there even such a thing as the British national heritage?

These questions were raised first and most sharply in connection
with European art treasures simply because these treasures were threatened with export, whereas British art and architecture – inevitably of
less interest to foreigners, and in the latter case not so readily saleable
– were not.[43] Even though books were often the first contents of a
country house to be sold (their absence could be rendered less conspicuous), there was comparatively little anxiety aroused by the sale of
English books, because they went for smaller sums and were more
likely to stay in the country (as in the case of the Althorp library).[44] In
these circumstances, even British government interventions – purchases by the National Gallery, for instance – were bound to focus on
non-British objects. The Gallery picked up a dozen Old Masters at the
Hamilton Palace sale – spending a mere £21,719 out of the £400,000
realized on art – and, controversially, negotiated privately with the
Duke of Marlborough to buy another dozen from Blenheim.

The continental origins of these commodities made it very difficult
for fine-art connoisseurs to present them as objects of national heritage
deserving of State purchase. But the difficulties went much deeper
than this; there were enduring British traditions of free trade and
*laissez-faire* to contend with, and, in the 1880s, the trend of 'philistine'
public opinion was moving away from public recognition of heritage
in any form, least of all in the form of aristocratic property. This was
the worst possible moment for connoisseurs to seek to forge a national
heritage policy on a French, German or Italian model. The National
Gallery's annual purchase-grant therefore remained stuck at a pitiful
£5,000, and the special Treasury grants that had made possible the
Hamilton Palace and Blenheim purchases – and extended to the

purchase of three portraits from Longford Castle in 1890 – remained few and far between.[45] In response, connoisseurs sought to mobilize public opinion and public funds in support of the national galleries by forming the National Art-Collections Fund in 1903, but this was of course only a fallback position necessitated by the failure to develop a national policy.

If the cosmopolitan taste imported by the liveliness of the art market in the years before the Great War hardly touched public opinion, it could not but affect the barbarians of the aristocracy. Owners began to cast a newly interested eye on canvases and furnishings that had been adorning their rooms for generations without attracting much notice. Unlike houses, which were an all-or-nothing proposition, works of art could be sold off one-by-one – indeed, the flagship sales notwith-standing, most were – and family interest tended to build up over time. This interest could also prove profitable. When, in 1889 the 5th Earl of Radnor succeeded to Longford Castle with its fabulous Old Master collection, including some celebrated Holbeins, the new Lady Radnor took an interest in the pictures and their provenance. Her father-in-law had, in response to her queries,

> always replied that 'there was not a single record', and that *he* had no idea where one of them came from, and did not think that anybody else had . . . my husband, knowing that I was fond of 'poking about' among old records, said to me that, provided that I put things back in their places, I might do what I liked in the Muniment Room.

The result of these researches was a full catalogue raisonné published in 1909. Lady Radnor's pleasantly innocent account of her project makes no mention of the sales that began with the National Gallery purchase of 1890, though she does acknowledge the involvement in her private researches of a battery of 'experts', led by two successive Keepers of the National Portrait Gallery, Barclay Squire of the British Museum and the *Daily Telegraph*'s art critic Sir Claude Phillips. Prod-ded by such external stimuli, the most sluggish of philistine aristocrats might be expected to take more of an interest in Old Masters than had his recent predecessors.[46]

The agricultural depression had a differential effect, therefore, on the landed classes' attitudes to their land, their country houses and their art treasures. Land was still cherished as the foundation of social and political power, but had now to be parcelled up and traded more brutishly than before. Houses had also to be viewed more hard-headedly, to be used properly as homes or to be reserved as dormant assets; the result was to discourage the 'valuation' of them by others as cultural and historical objects. Art treasures, on the other hand, could be valued – as assets – and 'valued' – as art objects. The interest of the wider culture in country houses, as heritage objects, had to be repulsed to preserve the houses' utility. The interest of the wider culture in art was to be invited, as raising the art objects' value, but it proved easier to stimulate the interest of foreign millionaires than of poorer fellow citizens. Aristocratic philistinism was, in different measures, intensified and somewhat moderated, but in the latter case moderated at odds with public opinion.

The tendency to view the country house more exclusively as a private home for private use was not simply a product of crude economic necessity; it was also encouraged by political pressures and the general run of landed culture. Political as well as economic pressures encouraged owners to withdraw from the public sphere and, to the extent that they remained public figures, to portray their houses as the (admittedly rather splendid) private homes of the public man. The country house was repositioned simply as the centre of modern country life.

For the more marginal landowners, a return to closer agricultural management was necessary, and the squire's house had to be portrayed as the focus of a serious agricultural community.[47] Not only for squires, but also for great aristocrats, country sports and occupations proved an enjoyable alternative to hard work. Here they were in tune rather than in conflict with modernity. Hunting, shooting and fishing were leisure pursuits popular with the professional and commercial middle classes as much as with the landed gentry. The fully extended rail network, and later the motor car, made it possible to combine these rural pursuits with urban residence. The younger generation could enjoy a 'traditional' country life without its responsibilities. A frivolous but also glamorous and politically uncomplicated image was being cultivated for the aristocracy. Young Lord Rocksavage, one of the wealthiest and also 'the most beautiful of all the young men of his day', set the tone by 'driving a red Mercedes around the country houses of England'.[48]

So successful was this formula of modern country life that even the continental nobilities, long more urbanized and self-consciously cultivated than their English counterparts, sought to emulate it. For the first time in history, Dominic Lieven has noted, 'the English aristocracy became a model for others to follow, not only in politics or agricultural improvement but also in style and habits of leisure'. Riding, racing, fox-hunting, *battue*-shooting and luxurious rural domesticity were all the rage on estates from the Channel to the Urals.[49] The spread of these fashions was facilitated by the flood of uprooted English landowners on to the Continent – in temporary exile from shuttered country houses or on holiday in Biarritz or Central European spas. This lifestyle was given decisive cachet by its wholehearted endorsement by the Prince of Wales – Edward VII from 1901 – whose Marlborough House Set both publicized and popularized the new ideals of aristocratic 'smartness'.

In these circles, country houses were prized not for their transcendental aesthetic or historic value, but for their luxuriousness as homes, their convenience for hospitality, their usefulness as bases for country sports. Bernard Shaw satirized this kind of country house as Horseback Hall, 'a prison for horses with an annex for the ladies and gentlemen who . . . gave nine-tenths of their lives to them'.[50] In this world art and culture were not only marginal – 'confined as far as possible to a world of their own which young men who took the ballroom floor were expected to avoid', as the novelist Douglas Goldring complained – but positively 'boring', that ultimate adjective of philistine dismissal which first made its appearance in Elinor Glyn's society novel, *Visits of Elizabeth* (1900).[51] Glyn had the opportunity to practise what she preached, when her lover Lord Curzon handed over the Elizabethan mansion of Montacute which he had leased from the owners, for her to decorate in her own very imitable style, with tiger skins and mauve carpets.[52] In a not dissimilar spirit, the rather more venerable Tory leader Lord Salisbury delighted in adapting Hatfield House to suit his needs, whether that meant slashing through tapestry to make a door, or nailing a tray for letters through the veneer of a table. 'Welcome to Hatfield', he greeted a prospective daughter-in-law, 'its other name is Gaza, the capital of Philistia.' He prided himself on keeping Hatfield up-to-date, installing what was probably the first country-house telephone.[53]

The image of the country house as home – a stylish, up-to-the-minute, and yet very personal home – was greatly preferable to most owners than the loose talk about 'national property' that arose during the Warwick Castle affair. It attracted the support and admiration of a large middle-class public, keen on 'smartness' and domesticity, yet kept the country house firmly in the private sphere, the aristocrat's analogue to the terraced house or cottage. If the aristocratic 'cottage' was inconveniently large and expensive, that could be justified, too, as necessary to support the hospitality and recreational pursuits provided by the best hosts.

There was also an allowable political angle to these exclusive functions. Tory journalists began to speak of the 'country-house system', by which they meant the growing use of country houses for political entertainment, made possible by the extension of the railway system. Landed politicians had done business only with their peers in the extended country-house parties of earlier periods. Now professional men – academics, lawyers and scientists – could mix over long weekends with the nation's traditional political leaders and thus, by osmosis, modernity and the middle class would seep into political life. The grandeur of the country house was justified on this basis, that it helped prepare the professional ruling class to rule.[54]

T. H. S. Escott, writing at the turn of the century, recast the whole historical development of the country house in this light. To Escott, country-house hospitality through the ages meant not so much paternal care for the community or even patronage of arts and literature, but rather the growth of the political house-party. This began in Chaucer's day – when country houses operated as 'chambers of commerce', transmitting merchants' views to the Court – and culminated in Escott's own day in the mushrooming of suburban hospitality by new men of wealth, in purpose-built as well as comfortably modernized old houses: 'There has been a change of scene, but not of spirit or method. Nowhere are the old traditions preserved more faithfully than beneath the new roofs.' Antiquity was here an incidental, almost an impediment, to the country-house story.[55] The same biases appear in the many country-house profiles that pop up in end-of-the-century journalism: the 'celebrities' who lived therein were the cynosure, the legends and traditions simply embellishment, and accompanying photographs (substituting for the old Nash realizations) lent a slick, modern gloss.[56]

Those owners who departed from their peers' barbarism and grew to appreciate their houses as works of art were still careful to keep their devotions private. These were the people of Heartbreak House, in Bernard Shaw's cosmology separate from and subordinate to the barbarians of Horseback Hall. Many were women, tending quietly to the family heritage while their husbands did the dirty work of stripping and selling, as in the cases of Lady Middleton at Wollaton, Lady Radnor at Longford Castle or Lady Sackville at Knole.[57] The few noblemen and women who openly embraced *la vie bohème*, consorting with artists or dabbling in the arts themselves, had to accept virtual ostracism from society as a result. Sir Coutts Lindsay, the patron of the Warwick Castle restoration appeal, was a decidedly odd bird who affected artists' dress – caps and capes, the occasional bits of armour – and, worse, artists' mores – he acknowledged his illegitimate children and travelled in a *menage à trois* with his fellow aristocrat-aesthetes, Lord and Lady Somers.[58] In the same circles moved George and Rosalind Howard, heirs to Castle Howard and Naworth. George cared really only for his art, and not at all for society; he wore old clothes and always travelled third-class on trains, including the disreputable Underground. Rosalind was more directly defiant of her peers, refusing invitations to country-house weekends and devoting her life to Naworth and to a series of Radical causes.[59]

One circle of noble aesthetes, in which women also played an unusually assertive role, was unabashedly devoted to the junction of high art and high society. These were the famous 'Souls', so-called for their passionate introspectiveness. Numbering only two or three dozen, linked by breeding, blood, marriage and carnal connection, the Souls revolved loosely around their (Tory) political leaders, George Curzon and Arthur Balfour, but their real distinctiveness was cultural or stylistic and not political. They were emotionally over-wrought, sexually permissive, intellectually ambitious and highly sensitive to aesthetics.[60] They were also, in consequence, shunned by the bulk of their peers. 'We considered that the heads of historic houses who read serious works, encouraged scientists and the like very, very dull and they had only the scantiest contact with us', admitted a repentant Lady Warwick, jewel of the Marlborough House Set, many years later.[61] The Souls were happy enough in their isolation, where their heterodoxy went unnoticed, but they could not be the model aristocrats they fancied themselves.

The Souls' devotion to their country houses was therefore passionate but relatively uncontagious. Their houses were modern and historic – they included Clouds,[62] the most innovative late Victorian country house, Hewell Grange, a deliberate copy of Olden Time Montacute on the outside (and outrageously High Renaissance inside),[63] and also the likes of Belvoir and Haddon – but whether modern or historic, all the Souls' homes were furnished and rebuilt to a high pitch of tastefulness, which could include careful restoration of historic buildings. Departing from the Ruskinian goal of preserving historic buildings as evidences of the national past, however, the Souls' restorations aimed at integrating the beauties of history into a modern residence: 'to use what has survived for the creation of beauty and comfortable habitation by modern families', in the words of Curzon's friend Martin Conway, who bought Allington Castle in Kent for this purpose in 1903.[64] Curzon himself was more idealistic; inspired by Conway, he bought several manor houses and castles for restoration and ultimately presented them to the nation. But Curzon was practically unique, and viewed suspiciously by many of his peers.[65] And even Curzon could stumble: it was he who delivered the Olden Time mansion of Montacute into the hands of Elinor Glyn and her famous tiger skins. After all, the Souls' sense of history was personal, not national. John Manners, son of the Soulful Lady Granby, fell in love with Haddon Hall as a schoolboy around the turn of the century. With his sister Diana he ferreted around local farmhouses and the antique shops of Sheffield, Manchester and Derby, searching for appropriate oak furniture with which to refurnish the hall, picking up in the process some of its original contents. By 1912 he had formed the plan of converting Haddon back into a family residence – the first of his family so to view it for hundreds of years.[66] Haddon would eventually join the vast majority of show-houses progressively withdrawn from public view in the years after 1880.

Even the more aesthetic aristocrats, therefore, did little to swim against the tide, a tide that was withdrawing the country house from the sphere of heritage, and for that matter diverting the nation's attention from the very idea of heritage. And yet the period after 1880 is also thought of today as the seedbed of the modern understanding of 'Englishness', a national identity that today seems supersaturated with feeling for heritage and particularly for the aristocratic contribution. Accounts of the late twentieth-century 'heritage industry' and the web of conservation organizations and legislative provisions invariably look back to these Victorian and Edwardian years for the roots of a semi-sacred and socially deferential concept of the national past. This is not absolutely a chimera; but it refers to a minority that was in those years narrow and embattled.

## The Aesthetes: Refining the Olden Time

A philistine public and a barbaric aristocracy were deserting the Victorian idea of heritage for the blandishments of modernity: where did this leave the community of writers, artists and designers who had shaped and profited from that idea? The explosive growth of the culture market in the late nineteenth century had, in fact, a confusing, cross-cutting effect. On the one hand, the culture as a whole seemed an increasingly unpleasant place – shallow and jejune, but also crowded and cacophonous – provoking the jeremiads of Ruskin and Arnold. On the other hand, in such an enlarged cultural sphere, it was possible for the first time for some creative artists to make a living by narrowing their pitch – by doing art for art's sake, and letting the philistines go hang. For these lucky few, it was possible to develop an idea of heritage that was *more* aesthetic and discriminating. At the same time as the general public was drifting away from the Victorian idea of heritage as insufficiently modern and progressive, these aesthetes were taking the view that the Victorian idea of heritage had been *too* modern and progressive, too concerned with the uses of the past in the present, insufficiently appreciative of the remoteness and strangeness of the past.[67] This was the diagnosis of the Arts and Crafts movement and it produced a new vision of the national past that can loosely be called the Arts and Crafts idea of heritage.

The Arts and Crafts idea of heritage differed from the earlier Victorian idea, but it did not mark a clean break. The artists and designers who developed the Arts and Crafts style were themselves products of the mid-Victorian culture industry and many of them retained their youthful affection for the Olden Time of Nash and Cattermole, Scott and Ainsworth, which they nevertheless outgrew. Their critique only emerged slowly and haltingly, as they achieved some economic independence from the mass-culture market, and then deepened as they acquired a fuller sense of independence, a self-awareness as an avant-garde.

Independence first became possible because of the maturation of the popular culture market in the 1850s and 1860s. As already noted, the market boomed and general illustrated magazines flourished, but the market also began to segment, making room for more specialized, even eccentric tastes. Sporadically from the 1850s, small groups of creative artists mustered the confidence to deviate from the dominant values of early Victorian taste. Artists and architects were in the vanguard of this rebellion, because Victorian taste had been so much more literary than pictorial. The vogue for paintings that told stories, conveyed morals and copied scenes from history on the basis of scholarly reconstruction had left little scope for the artistic imagination. The copyism and utilitarianism prevailing in architecture put similar restraints on the architect's freedom to decorate and design. The Gothicists at least had the passion of piety on their side, but this particular emotional expression – stemming from an increasingly illiberal religion, at that – appealed less and less to a slowly secularizing professional and artistic class.

Ruskin's calls in the 1850s for a new attitude to art thus fell on well-prepared ground, at least among artists and architects. If his precise doctrines were rather too sibylline to attract proper disciples, nevertheless he had an immense influence in propagating general principles: the greater emphasis on visual qualities of colour and texture, the cultivation of the critical eye and the application of common standards across all the arts, and especially the insistence on authenticity – not copyism, but the free and honest expression of the creative spirit.

Ruskin was of his time as well as against it. In some respects, notably in his attitude to history, he selected and exaggerated rather than repudiating elements in contemporary taste. He shared in the cult of the Olden Time, and especially admired its morals; he had high words of praise for the simplicity and nobility of the work of George Cattermole and other popular Olden Time painters of the 1830s and 1840s. What he disliked about the Olden Time was its formal and visual values – too undisciplined, hybridized, excessively grandiose and 'picturesque' – and in rebellion against them he roved backwards in time, finding in the late Middle Ages and especially in French and Italian Gothic an architectural model. Not that Ruskin recommended copyism even here: his Gothic was a pure foundation upon which modern architects ought to build and innovate.

The Pre-Raphaelite painters, who came together in the early 1850s partly under Ruskin's inspiration, followed their master's historical move backwards. They espoused the cause of the early Italian Renaissance – the Trecento and Quattrocento – as a kind of return to basics, away from the flowery exuberance of Raphael and his successors, towards some primitive principles of painting through which pure spirituality could be conveyed without betraying either the medium or the message. As subsequent critics have often complained, both the Pre-Raphaelites' moralism and, ultimately, their style marked no very abrupt break from the dominant academic styles. Some, notoriously J. E. Millais, soon slipped back into a mode that hardly differentiated him from the history and genre painters, though others, such as Burne-Jones and Rossetti, continued to wear the cloak of bohemianism and also stuck to their medievalism against the lure of Olden Time themes.

The Pre-Raphaelite influence was evident in the younger generation of history painters, for whom dramatic set-pieces of heroism and opulence were replaced by more intimate scenes of romantic longing, domestic vice and virtue, and greater whimsy. Literary references may have still predominated, but in the 1860s and 1870s they were more likely to be to Shakespeare than to Scott – Lear and his daughters, the sprites of *A Midsummer Night's Dream*, Romeo courting Juliet, rather than knights with broadswords and bucklers, or cavaliers quaffing from goblets.

Pre-Raphaelite influences made their impact on architects, as well, though with different consequences for their historical orientation.

The taste constraining architectural creativity in the 1850s was not popular but élite, not Olden Time pomp but Gothic heaviness. The only real design work available to the leading architectural practices came from government (still havering between classicism and Gothic), country-house building (now dominated by Goths), and church building (completely Gothic). The search for a lighter, sweeter, less formal style – paralleling the Pre-Raphaelites' plunge backward into the Quattrocento and earlier – sent younger architects forward into the same period, from the thirteenth and fourteenth into the fifteenth century. Perpendicular and early Tudor styles, long deplored as corrupt and even Protestant by strict Gothicists, became briefly fashionable. The humble styles and materials of the English vernacular tradition, as it emerged in fifteenth-century conditions of prosperity for the 'middling sort', were explored: the black-and-white patterning of lath-and-plaster construction, the Tudor use of brick, the loosening of Gothic formality before the advent of classical formality in the mid-sixteenth century were all attractive.

Young painters and architects attracted by these vaguely Ruskinian ideas mixed together in the 1850s, heeding Ruskin's call for a greater unity in the arts. The architectural apprentices William Morris and Philip Webb, who met in the Gothic practice of George Edmund Street, struck up a friendship with the Pre-Raphaelite painters Dante Gabriel Rossetti and Edward Burne-Jones around 1855. By 1861 they had set up what today would be called a multi-media design practice, the basis for the famous Morris & Co. Rossetti's Pre-Raphaelitism was also a catalyst for the move away from Gothic by Richard Norman Shaw, another student of Street's, and his partner from 1863, W. E. Nesfield.[68]

What drew these men together was not only a common style of art, but also a common style of life, which separated them from the older generation and from most of contemporary society, as well. Their high seriousness about their art and an emotional informality about life drew them away from the demand-driven professionalism of painting and especially architecture, closer to a bohemianism hitherto associated more closely with actors. They made no effort to hide their essential irreligiousness, and the way in which their art was taking the place of conventional piety as a channel for feeling. Sexual mores correspondingly relaxed; Nesfield was a well-known womanizer, and his friend Edward Godwin eloped with Ellen Terry – an actress, no less. Nesfield's office felt like 'the studio of an artist rather than the business room of a professional man' – which might have spelled financial death a decade earlier.[69]

The reason why the younger architects' departures from Gothic orthodoxy and social formality did not doom them was that new sources of patronage were opening up among sections of the professional middle classes, whose own attitudes were more flexible. Without this the departure from Gothic might have remained a figment of the imaginations of Nesfield and Shaw. Most important of all was the growing popularity, sparked by the facilities offered by the railway but also by the cult of the Olden Time, of residence in the countryside. Artists themselves led the way; as early as the 1840s, a genuine artist's colony had sprung up in the Kentish countryside around Penshurst, where the great patron William Wells entertained all the leading history painters at Redleaf, and where Lord De L'Isle was undertaking careful restorations at Penshurst Place itself. This whole strip of immediately exurban Kent and Surrey was particularly rich in great Olden Time shrines – in addition to Penshurst, Knole, Hever and Ightham Mote all lay within a short drive – and, of later significance to the young architects, in humbler vernacular architecture of the same period, brick farmhouses and distinctive tile-hung cottages. Into some of these smaller houses artists were moving by the 1850s, 'among the earliest commuters and weekenders'. James Hook and Richard Redgrave were the pioneers, buying country retreats at Abinger, in Surrey, in 1853 and 1856; in 1861 they were joined by the watercolourist Myles Birket Foster, who moved to nearby Witley, building himself a new – but old-seeming (half-timbered, lead-paned) – house for the purpose and decorating it with Pre-Raphaelite pictures and stained glass. By that time, an artists' colony had also sprung up around Cranbrook in Kent, which included Thomas Webster, Frederic Hardy and the history painter J. E. Horsley.[70]

Horsley, famous for his depiction of *Rent Day at Haddon Hall* (1836), was the source of Norman Shaw's first important commission, a Tudor vernacular facelift of the Georgian brick-box farmhouse he had bought at Willesley, one mile north of Cranbrook, in 1864. Shaw had been preparing himself for such a commission for some years. He had sketched both Penshurst Place and its cottages, made a tour of Sussex vernacular architecture with Nesfield, and with Nesfield sketched one of the smaller of Nash's Mansions, Ockwells, in September 1864.

Accordingly, he turned Horsley's plain box into an architect's fantasy upon this kind of 'Old English' style, adding a hipped gable to the flat roof, placing casement windows under the eaves, hanging the plain brick walls with Kentish tiles, spewing soft colours all around. Inside he replaced the decorous Georgian entryway with a great hall. Nor-

41    A Norman Shaw hall (Merrist Wood, Surrey, 1875–7): Shaw's halls, unlike Pugin's or Scott's, were working halls in which families actually lived and played.

man Shaw's great halls, at least in their early form, speak eloquently of
the shifts in emphasis from high Victorian Olden Timery. The useless
great halls of Pugin and Gilbert Scott had been grandiose gestures by
great landowners and their architects towards the ideal of cross-class
communication and patronage. Shaw's intention at Willesley was
more earnest and also more purposefully intimate and domestic. The
Horsleys prided themselves on their genuine hospitality – not of
course towards dependants and servants, but towards family friends
and relatives. They did not want a showcase, but a working hall which
would foster conviviality and cosiness in a simple, honest, small-scale
setting. So Shaw set to work equipping this not-so-great hall with an
inglenook fireplace, heavy but comfortable settles and rush-seated
angle chairs, all designed of a piece with the room and in conjunction
with the craftsmen who made the furnishings, in approved Ruskinian
mode.[71]

The Horsley commission marks the public debut of Shaw and
Nesfield's 'Old English' style, which would crop up with increasing
frequency around the south of England in the 1870s and 1880s. Shaw
was a highly individual artist, who soon moved beyond his own style,
and who later came to regret his association with the English vernacular revival; but it was not anyway his invention alone.[72] It tapped into
a growing interest among the aesthetically inclined middle classes in a
smaller-scale, more domestic, a simpler and more wholesome version
of the Olden Time, suited to an independent artistic and professional
community rather than to the harmonious unity of masters and servants that the early Victorian public had sought.

Already in the 1860s there were signs of tension between this
minority's newly aestheticized vision of the Olden Time and the
wider public for whom the Olden Time was becoming old hat. The
opportunities for lampoon or jest thus created might fix simply on
artiness itself, at a time when the general public was getting less arty,
or on the artist's precious, quasi-religious devotion to his art, but it
could also fix on the specifically backward-looking aspects of the
artistic vision. Earlier, popular appropriations of the Olden Time had
not been susceptible to this kind of criticism, but the more self-
indulgent and privatized visions of the Pre-Raphaelites were. *Punch*,
never reluctant to play on popular philistinism, made a speciality of
this theme in the 1860s.

One episode attracted a deal of attention. A handful of young
history painters known as the St John's Wood Clique, after their
London residence, had grafted some Pre-Raphaelite poses on to quite
conventional Olden Time themes. In the summer of 1866, three of

42   The St John's Wood Clique at Hever Castle, summer 1866: (left to right) Philip Calderon, W. F. Yeames, David Wynfield.

the Clique – Philip Calderon, William Yeames and David Wynfield – determined on a rural idyll in the Kentish countryside and were delighted to be able to rent Hever Castle, a small fortified house long disused as a residence by its landed owners. Over three harmless months they set themselves up as lords of the manor, drinking, painting, philosophizing, entertaining such members of the Clique as Stacy Marks and other friends, and generally soaking up Hever's atmosphere, a delicious compound of late medieval fortification and Olden Time atmosphere – one of Nash's Mansions and associated with not one but two of Henry VIII's wives. But they made the mistake of inviting *Punch*'s F. C. Burnand. Soon enough, their little fantasy was pretty devastatingly lampooned in the pages of *Punch* and then widely reprinted in Burnand's collection of *Happy Thoughts*. Rats and damp and fake nostalgia are the keynotes at 'Bovor Castle':

Here, in mediaeval times assembled pilgrims, retainers, falconers, barons, knights, ladies, mitred abbots, pages, dogs in leashes, and good-looking young men coming of age on the steps. 'By my halidome! gadso!' quoth the shorter of the two knights, over whose fair head some twenty-five summers had shed their something or other, I forget what now. Ah, I wish I'd lived then. On thinking it over, why? Chiefly I think because they said 'By my halidome,' and 'zooks' and 'the merry maskins', and, generally, because it was 'the olden time'. Ours will be the olden time one of these days.

The men of the Clique are toiling away at a five-act drama about Anne Boleyn and Henry VIII, entitled 'Bovor'; 'a grand historical picture for next year's Academy . . . "Bovor Castle in the Olden Time" . . . portraying Anne Boleyn playing on the dulcimer to Henry the Eighth'; and an article on 'Henry the Eighth and Medievalism', in fact about Bovor. And yet these foolish romantics cannot tell a bastion from a barbican, or decide whether the principal room is the chapel, the refectory, the armoury or the hall.[73] This was the treatment meted out to fairly mainstream figures, who took it in good part; it was not unlike the ribbing given Gothicism by the *Ingoldsby Legends* a genera-tion earlier, but now ridicule was aimed at respectable figures in the art world as part of a general campaign of depreciation against aesthetic style and the artistic imagination.

Burnand and his *Punch* colleague George du Maurier kept up their jovial barrage throughout the 1870s.[74] Towards the end of the decade, they shifted their targets slightly, aiming at the more extreme urban aestheticism of James Whistler and Oscar Wilde, next to whose excesses of formal experimentation and sexual ambiguity Ruskinian historicism seemed positively normal, and Ruskin obliged the con-servative public by berating Whistler for immorality and frivolity, leading to a famous law-suit in 1878. But the Ruskin–Whistler con-frontation hardly rendered Ruskinism respectable simply by revealing something worse; it merely lowered the whole artistic community further in popular estimation.[75]

At the same time, some artists were indeed retreating further into an 'Old English' rural idyll, to escape both the jeering philistinism of *Punch* (or worse) and the shocking cosmopolitanism and effeminacy of the Wildes and Whistlers. Artists' colonies were spreading further afield. William Morris and Rossetti had already strayed into Oxford-shire in 1871, when they took a tenancy on Kelmscott Manor, 'a beautiful and strangely naif house,' Morris described it, 'Elizabethan in appearance though much later in date, as in that out of the way corner people built Gothic till the beginning or middle of last century.'[76] Some American artists, led by Frank Millet, John Singer Sargent,

Alfred Parsons and Edwin Abbey, were the first to discover the Cotswolds, with its own vernacular in honey-coloured stone and thatch. A search for Olden Time models was again the immediate stimulus; Millet had been painting 'Puritan peasants' and Burne-Jones suggested Broadway as a source of appropriate backgrounds. Millet bought a small Queen Anne house there in 1884, and set about restoring the ruined priory that lay at the foot of its garden, while Parsons reconstructed the garden. Mrs Comyns Carr, who visited in 1888, thought that as Americans they were likely to take 'a greater interest in the old buildings . . . than mere English philistines might have done'.[77] Limpsfield, on the Surrey–Kent borders, was another centre by the 1890s, drawing assorted Fabians, and later the novelist Ford Madox Ford and the art and travel writer E. V. Lucas.[78]

For those artists most alienated from contemporary society, the countryside did acquire a talismanic significance, offering a point around which utopias could be erected. William Morris and Philip Webb were already drawing conclusions about the ideality of the Old English countryside in the early 1860s, with which people like Shaw and Nesfield – for all their fascination with the Old English – would not have concurred. At this time Warington Taylor, later manager of Morris & Co., could posit the Old English countryside as 'essentially' English, as opposed both to overgrown English cities and the élite cosmopolitanism of the Goths, who

> seek to make impression by 'stately' (q[uer]y pretentious?) Buildings
> – sensation! – all that is huge coarse in Gothic they seize – but they
> have no feeling for the poetry of that very insular characteristic
> 'littleness of English nature', everything English, except stock-
> jobbing London or cotton Manchester, is essentially small, and of a
> homely farmhouse kind of poetry . . . Above all things nationality is
> the greatest social trait, English Gothic is small as our landscape is
> small, it is sweet picturesque homely, farmyardish, Japanese, social,
> domestic – French is aspiring, grand straining after the extraordinary
> all very well in France but is wrong here.[79]

The expressions of alienation were Ruskinian and not unusual, but the association of Englishness with the 'homely farmhouse kind of poetry' was new.

Morris's radicalism, which deepened into socialism in the 1880s, took the association a step further. Increasingly horrified by urban and industrial capitalism, he sought in the honest craftsmanship of the English countryside an antidote which, he thought, could be revived and diffused throughout the nation whose essence it was. Accordingly he and his fellows in Morris & Co. set about rediscovering the arts and crafts which had last flourished in the fifteenth century, but which had been progressively smothered by professionalization (which among other things brought in classicism, the professional architect's abstraction), urbanization and industrialization.

The Arts and Crafts movement, of which Morris became a mainstay, attracted many people who did not have Morris's specific political motives. For scholarly antiquarians, the Arts and Crafts' seriousness about the artistic qualities of objects and buildings was attractive, and offered an escape route from the confining political and religious context in which scholarly Gothicism had initially emerged. By the turn of the century, scholarly forums such as the Victoria County History and the Society of Antiquaries had taken on a pronounced Arts and Crafts flavour.[80] Others were drawn in by the revolutionary stylistic break with Victorian elaboration and clutter. Arts and Crafts has thus been viewed as a precursor of Modernism, for its emphasis on simplicity and the link between form and function, and even for the tendency of its simple patterns to spill over into pure abstraction. But there is no doubt that the powerful social and political charge brought to the movement by Morris gave it a conspicuously alienated, anti-modern flavour. It attracted to its ranks not only radicals and socialists, liberals and moderns, but many people whose temperament was frankly Tory and who saw in the Old English countryside a model not of egalitarian craftsmanship but of organic hierarchy – values repudiated by the modern Conservative party as much as by the Liberals.

Thus by the end of the century a new narrative of English history was established, not so much by antiquarians and historians, or by journalists and novelists, but by artists and designers, which grew out of and at the same time offered an alternative to the high Victorian narrative. The Olden Time was still admired, but now for rather different reasons than those put forward by the likes of Charles Knight and Harrison Ainsworth. Not patriotic heroism, conspicuous consumption, economic growth and mutuality between the classes, but homeliness, craftsmanship, simplicity and honesty were the qualities sought after. These were first to be found in the fifteenth century, when the higher domestic virtues were finally able to struggle out of poverty and barbarism. They were located less – some would say not at all – in the tiltyards, the great halls and the long galleries of the aristocracy, but at the humbler hearths of the skilled craftsman, the farmer and the petty merchant. The village, not the big house, was the essential unit of community.

As commercial capitalism rumbled on to the scene in the sixteenth century, this community of plain folk was already being riven by class division, some merchants growing too great and separated from the countryside, some farmers immiserated into peasants and craftsmen into early proletarians. 'Liberty' – which earlier Victorians thought had thrived under Elizabeth and been defended heroically by Hampden and Pym – was already threatened by the Tudors and, besides, was now held to consist not so much in 'rights' as in 'community'. The arts admired were not the patriotic poetry of Sidney and Spenser, which, for all their vernacular origins, were too civilized and Court-bound.

Only the crafts, especially domestic architecture and furnishing, being part of daily life, could reflect the virtue of the old organic community. These, too, were already under threat in the sixteenth century. Henry VIII and Elizabeth imported foreign fashion in the form of classicism, which was clumsily grafted on to the good old English style, and some craftsmen got so far above themselves as to be known as 'architects' and to be recognized as individual creators, ripped out of their proper communal context. Only in rural back-waters, such as Morris thought he had found at Kelmscott, did the old vernacular style persist until the seventeenth century and later. Christopher Wren, in this narrative, wins some limited applause for turning élite taste back to vernacular influences after the excessive classicizing of Inigo Jones; but Wren's plain brick houses, pitched roofs and tall chimneys enjoy only a moment in fashion before the hated super-aristocratic classicism of the Palladians, and later Robert Adam and his ilk, returns for good in the mid-eighteenth century.[81]

This interpretation of English history embodies a different relation-ship between past and present than had the earlier Victorian idea of heritage. Whereas Nash and Howitt had celebrated their own culture for its rediscovery of old English virtues, playing heavily on analogies between past and present, the Arts and Crafts idea of heritage counterposed past to present, generally to the past's benefit. It adopted a semi-religious attitude to the relics of the past, which had an authenticity and a humanity that contemporary manufacture had lost. While the more optimistic of the Arts and Crafts world, like William Morris himself, hoped to recapture some of these qualities by devising a new modern style and new modes of craftsmanship, indeed an entire reconstruction of society, for others the temptation to lapse into cultural pessimism or retreat and a swooning adoration of the 'pastness' of the past was too strong.

The Arts and Crafts vision was narrower, too, in privileging the

South of England over the Midlands and North (where Howitt's heart had lain). The North was too crude and blustery for the lovers of 'littleness', of sweet cottages and farmyards.[82] Only in the cultivated South had skill and domesticity and the spirit of independence thrived among the common people, allowing them to throw off paternalism and patronage. As later critics pointed out, this was a rather perverse conclusion to draw, as enclosure and the tyranny of the great estate were nowhere more predominant than in the South, but it was perhaps an inevitable conclusion for an avant-garde so heavily concentrated around the metropolis.[83]

The Arts and Crafts community blamed aristocracy, past and present, for much of the world's ills, and this further distinguished them from the Victorian cult of the Olden Time. Whereas even a radical such as Howitt had celebrated the big house as a conduit for culture flowing between city and country, for his late Victorian successors the conduit had become an effluent pipe, pumping the poisons of urban life – capitalist exploitation, courtly affectation, foreignness and, more recently, mass production and modern technology – into the Old English countryside. This analysis led to a consistent denigration of large country houses of all periods, as symbolic of a distancing from the plain, small house that was both social and stylistic. 'State and grandeur have become irksome to us, and are even despised,' wrote J. J. Stevenson in an early manifesto for the new sensibility, 'no doubt because so frequently the sign of power which has departed . . . Comfort and convenience are all that are insisted on . . . [Domestic architecture] should be more pleasing than impressive, more beautiful than grand, characterised by refinement rather than by state.'[84] 'Palace' had now become a dirty word. Palaces were 'grand or gloomy', 'huge and ugly', endless chains of 'lofty, comfortless, sarcophagus-like saloons'.[85]

Classical houses – still, after all, the vast majority of country houses – bore the brunt. Earlier Victorian writers had passed over them diplomatically, or shunted them aside as 'cold or proud', but now real scorn could be aimed against them. Castle Howard was a favourite target. A popular guide to *Our Own Country* of the early 1880s, presumably as yet untouched by pure Arts and Crafts thinking, called it 'a little repellent', reflecting 'the "pomposity" of the 18th century . . . rather dreary and monotonous'.[86] 'The soul that loves not the Renaissance must resent the intrusion of any modern classical building amidst the quiet pastoral scenery of this part of the East Riding', complained another authority on historic houses in 1891, regretting that Castle Howard was neither a 'feudal castle' nor a 'stately *home*'.[87]

Castle Howard attracted special distaste for its size as well as its baroque style. But the smaller, more numerous classical houses – some of them quite plain – were also dismissed contemptuously. The *Little Guides* that began to appear in 1897 and became the standard architectural handbooks of their generation tended to ignore classical architecture entirely, giving exhaustive coverage of secular and domestic architecture before the sixteenth century but petering out rapidly after that. Their more opinionated contributors were not above applying epithets such as 'wretched' and 'rubbish' to plain Georgian work.[88]

More novel was the occasional extension of this language to the grander mansions of the Olden Time as well, including some specimens that Nash had elevated as ideals. 'It is not, as a rule, in the greatest mansions, the vast piles erected by the great nobles of the Court, that we find such artistic qualities, but most often in the smaller manor-houses of knights and squires,' asserted a leading Ruskinian antiquary, P. H. Ditchfield:

> Most of our great houses and manor-houses sprang up in the great Elizabethan building epoch . . . The great noblemen and gentlemen of the Court were filled with the desire for extravagant display, and built such clumsy piles as Wollaton and Burghley House, importing French and German artisans to load them with bastard Renaissance detail. Some of these vast structures are not very admirable with their distorted gables, their chaotic proportions, and their crazy imitations of classic orders. But the typical Elizabethan mansion, whose builder's means or good taste would not permit of such a profusion of these architectural luxuries, is unequalled in its combination of stateliness with homeliness, in its expression of the manner of life of the class for which it was built. And in the humbler manors and farm-houses the latter idea is even more perfectly expressed . . .[89]

Romantic Hatfield House, with its sentimental Elizabethan associations, was now more interesting for its 'delightful old gardens, groves and avenues' than for its Olden Time collections, and 'depressing' Warwick Castle, 'where the visitors steal the writing paper, and the hideous ornaments are dwelt on with pride by the solemn *cicerone*', was 'terrible'.[90]

Much closer attention was paid to the smaller of Nash's Mansions and a flood of writing begins to open up in the 1880s, bringing to light hundreds of little gems that Nash, with his more catholic tastes, had overlooked. Fortunately for the metropolitan bourgeoisie, small manor houses in vernacular styles and materials were scattered thickly

43   Ockwells in the 1880s, photographed by Allan Fea in its neglected state.

in the Kent and Surrey exurban belt. That miniature Tudor castle, Hever, was already a cynosure in the late 1860s; somewhat later, the antiquarian writer Allan Fea drew attention to the sad state of Ockwells, the earliest of Nash's Mansions, which Pevsner has called 'the most refined and the most sophisticated timber-framed mansion in England'. It is almost entirely mid-fifteenth century in construction and decoration. Having 'degenerated into a barn', it was about to be sold as a farm building when Fea appealed in the *Standard* for a saviour; Sir Edward Barry, who came forward, was able miraculously to replace Ockwells' missing medieval stained glass and ultimately to restore the entire manor as a home.[91] Ockwells was only one of dozens of small manor houses and 'picturesque old houses', mostly in the Home Counties and the Cotswolds, that Fea brought to light for a discriminating audience in the late 1880s and 1890s.[92] In Manchester and Liverpool, arty types – thinner on the ground – similarly took up the cause of the humble black-and-white buildings that dotted the nearby countryside. Here, too, one of Nash's earliest Mansions – Little Moreton Hall, begun in the late fifteenth century – and a remarkable medieval house entirely too early for Nash - Stokesay Castle, begun in the 1270s – were particularly treasured.[93]

Small manor houses of this type had been deserted long ago by landowners, grown too rich and grand for these homely English dwellings. Their subsequent use as farmhouses, deplorable from the point of view of the fabric, nevertheless preserved an air of plainness and humility which the new taste valued. Mrs Dale, the farmer's wife who showed off Little Moreton Hall to antiquarians, was a popular figure even though she charged one shilling for photography; the plain meal of home-made cheese and butter that she served was just right, and best of all she bore the same name as the fifteenth-century carpenter who, unusually for a craftsman, had left his name on the window frames of the hall.[94] Humble folk like the Dales would not and could not ruin their houses by modernization, as aristocrats were wont to do. 'Fashion decrees the downfall of old houses,' complained Ditchfield,

> and the old weather-beaten pile that had sheltered the family for generations, and was of good old English design with nothing foreign or strange about it, was compelled to give place to a new-fangled dwelling-place which was neither beautiful nor comfortable.

Perversely, Ditchfield also railed against aristocrats who did keep their old houses but made them comfortable:

> Old panelled rooms and the ancient floor-timbers understand not the latest experiments in electric lighting, and yield themselves to the flames with scarce a struggle. Our forefathers were content with hangings to keep out the draughts and open fireplaces to keep them warm. They were a hardy race, and feared not a touch or breath of cold. Their degenerate sons must have an elaborate heating apparatus, which again distresses the old timbers of the house and fires their hearts of oak.[95]

The centrist *Spectator* was equally displeased with contemporary aristocratic mores — 'a wealthy landlord finds the house which suited his fathers too small for his pride or his hospitality' — and Fea, who was not above crawling to the aristocracy when he needed them, could also be gloomy about their evident lack of 'interest or pride' in their ancestral homes and long lineage.[96] The old landed élite had laid down its custodianship of the heritage. That responsibility, suitably refined to suit bourgeois lifestyles and sensibilities, would have to be taken up by a new class — if it was to be taken up at all.

To what extent was this responsibility taken up? To what extent did the Arts and Crafts idea of heritage spread more widely in the middle and upper classes and in the culture at large? Writers on the Arts and

Crafts tend to exaggerate its influence – the subtlety, novelty and sheer excitement of the movement are impressive and distracting, causing historians to magnify its impact. It should be possible instead to specify more carefully what groups did take up the Arts and Crafts' idea of heritage, when, and with what consequences for the care and preservation of 'Old England'.

Something of a peak was reached around the end of the century. What had begun as a secret vice of artists and architects in the 1860s and 1870s had blossomed by then into a bourgeois fashion. In reminiscing about his early travels of the mid-1880s, Fea could still pose as a pioneer, proud of having discovered the Cotswolds before the tourists, spinning yarns of his battles through hedges and gates to attain the grail of an old moated grange, of penetrating to Canons Ashby 'in a sort of makeshift train that travelled once a week along discarded grass-grown metals'. By the turn of the century, however, he was selling the countryside to a wider audience, opening up 'a new field for the speculative restorer' and realizing 'the profitable possibilities of marketable Tudor and Stuart buildings, especially with historical associations'.[97] The rush to the country was on.

Fea was not alone in appreciating the commercial possibilities of the growing fashion for country life within sections of the urban and suburban middle classes. Publishers Edward Hudson and George Newnes brought out the first issue of *Country Life Illustrated* – soon simply *Country Life* – in January 1897, 'directed', its historian tells us, 'at readers who might well be members of a Surrey golf club'. In some respects, for instance its coverage of field sports and natural history, *Country Life* resembled an older, established magazine of the true gentry, *The Field*, but its aesthetic interest in small old country houses betrayed a different constituency. 'Country Homes and Gardens Old and New' was a regular feature from the first issue, adorned with an aesthetic motif supplied by the Arts and Crafts designer Walter Crane. These profiles of individual country houses were mostly written by H. Avray Tipping, younger son of a Kentish squire who had consciously turned against his peers' preoccupations with racing and dancing and devoted himself to cultural pursuits, including the extensive restoration in the 1890s of a late medieval manor house and garden in Monmouthshire. New technology – the production of half-tone photography on high-speed presses – made possible extensive views, handsomely captured by Charles Latham, which were later collected and issued in book form. (The same technology gave a boost to arts magazines in general, such as the Arts and Crafts inspired *Studio*, from 1893, and *Connoisseur*, from 1901.) These profiles interacted subtly

## COVNTRY HOMES

### OCKWELLS MANOR, BERKSHIRE,

#### THE SEAT OF
#### MR. BARRY, J.P., F.S.A.

THOUGH possessing no such romantic association as casts the great spell over the venerable walls of Haddon, the ancient manor house of Ockwells, or Ockholt, near Bray, on the Thames, scarcely yields to it in architectural interest or old-world charm. Here is no intrusion of modern things, little trace of the classic taste which appeared even in the days of Henry VII., nothing at all to spoil the charm of a genuine mediæval dwelling-place or of its goodly, beautiful interior. Small wonder, we think, in this lovely part of England, that the half-legendary Vicar of Bray should have held through storm and shine to his post, and have declared

" That whatsoever king shall reign
    I'll be the Vicar of Bray."

It is but a walk of some two miles through the water-meadows from the gateway of the Jesus Hospital to the old house of Ockwells, and, as we see its ancient timber front, enriched beyond almost any of its compeers, rising above the hedgerows, we bethink us that it is something of a phenomenon that this quaint dwelling of wood should have kinship with another famous timber mansion standing far away—with the venerable hall of Speke by the Mersey.

It was a member of the old house of Norreys, or Norris, of Speke, one Richard de Norreys, holding the sinecure office of "cook" to Eleanor of Provence, Queen of Henry III., that received the manor of Ockholt, or Ockwells, in Berkshire, at a fee farm rent of forty shillings, in 1267. Here the King is said to have had a hunting-lodge within easy reach of the Royal Castle of Windsor. What manner of house stood at Ockholt, to use the old name, in 1267, we have no means of knowing, but it is fair to surmise that it was moated for protection, that it was also mostly built of timber, and, perhaps, that it looked not wholly unlike the structure we depict. More than a century after Richard Norreys, the "cook," had re-

ceived the manor in fee, it fell to John Norreys, second son by his second marriage of Sir Henry Norreys of Speke. This John must be regarded as the real founder of the great line of the Berkshire house of Norreys, which gave many notable men to the State. John's half-brother, William, was the great-grandfather of another John Norreys, who established a second family of the name at Fyfield, also in Berkshire. The great-grandson of John whom we have described as the "founder" of his family upon the acres by the Thames, was the builder of Ockwells Manor House. He also bore the favourite name of John, and was a very important man in his time, standing high in the favour of the Court, and having the ability to steer his ship adroitly amid the shoals and in the strong and troubled currents of the Wars of the Roses. He was First Usher to the Chamber in the reign of Henry VI., Squire of the Body to the King, Master of the Royal Wardrobe, Sheriff of Oxfordshire and Berkshire in 1442 and 1457, and Squire of the Body to Edward IV., being afterwards knighted.

So important a man must needs have an important house, well fitted to receive his guests, and so it came that Ockwells was built. Few people realise what it was to raise in those days so glorious a house. There was something in the operation analogous to the building of a ship—the same need for seasoned oak, the same labour with saw and adze, the same pegging of joint and tenon, and so the structure rose complete and solid. There was superadded the fine craft of the carver, the loving labour of the man who fashioned the cusped window frames, the magnificent barge-boards, and the finials. Then came the glass-stainer, with his splendid blazonry, to flood the rooms with colour, and the tapestry, often from distant looms, and the ladies in their bower working at fair embroideries for the adornment of the abode.

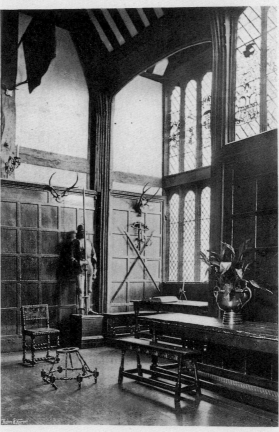

Copyright                    THE RECESS.                    "COUNTRY LIFE."

44   Ockwells in 1904, restored and featured (along with many other manor houses) in *Country Life*'s weekly 'Country Homes and Gardens Old and New' column.

with similarly photographed small advertisements for country houses for sale. *Country Life* could not have survived without the financial support of Knight Frank & Rutley, a firm of estate agents founded in 1896 to market country homes, who ran their first full-page advertisement in the magazine in August 1898.

Building on this commercial interest, Tipping saw it his job gently to develop his audience's aesthetic tastes, playing on the fashion for the cottage and small manor house, but testing and broadening it all the while.[98] In this he was encouraged by the architectural profession, which had become disenchanted with the Arts and Crafts' emphasis on the anonymous craftsman. Kind words were even found for Castle Howard.[99] But it is fair to say that *Country Life*'s chief impact, at least up to the First World War, lay more in diffusing the small-manor-house taste than in developing new and more catholic tastes.[100]

There was more to the rush to the country than the small-manor-house fashion. A more general turn against the excesses of urbanism and a hankering for rural rhythms can be detected in the 1890s. The German architect Hermann Muthesius, posted to the London embassy between 1896 and 1903, found 'a very active movement towards a closer contact with nature'. Saturday-to-Monday, or 'weekending' in the country, had spread from high society to a broader stratum of the professional and commercial middle classes. Old houses adapted for modern use and modern houses built in an Arts and Crafts influenced style could be found all over Kent, Surrey and the southern and eastern coasts, used at weekends and by the family in summer, while the head of the household commuted into the metropolis. For those who could not afford or abide genuine country life, suburban gardens and weekend golf proved popular substitutes, while country tourism of the kind pioneered by Allan Fea, by rail and on foot, opened up dramatically. In London's leading shops, like Heal's, Arts and Crafts style fabrics and furnishings, 'simple, genuine and unobtrusively well-made' could be found 'at extremely reasonable prices', indicating to Muthesius that 'Ruskin's reassessment of artistic values has also spread to wider circles'.[101]

And yet by the time Muthesius had ended his sojourn, these fashions were already on the ebb. The 1904 book in which he documented and praised the 'English style', *The English House*, was published in Germany – where it helped to popularize new ideals of honesty and simplicity in modern design – but not in Britain; it was not translated into English until 1979. In Edwardian England, bourgeois taste did not develop along the modernist lines Muthesius advocated, but neither did it fester into the deadening nostalgia of the

Arts and Crafts purists; it did not develop at all. Aestheticism of most kinds went out of fashion. Many of the institutions of the Arts and Crafts movement, and the publications that had promoted it among amateurs, had folded by 1907.[102] 'The arts do not at this moment express the final intelligence of the country', concluded the erstwhile Arts and Crafts architect Reginald Blomfield. National energies were focused on science and commerce, and the arts 'are not at present regarded as worthy of serious and sustained attention'. Not only Blomfield, but also Norman Shaw and Lutyens accordingly steered between the extremes of continental modernism and Arts and Crafts aestheticism, aiming at the plain, classical and more international style that they thought better suited to a masculine and imperial nation.[103]

Insofar as Arts and Crafts influences lingered, they did so by adapting openly to the demands of English taste and modern living. Some rural and historical motifs appeared in urban settings: half-timbering and tile-hanging filtered into London suburbs; golf and gardening became national obsessions. While only artists and their fashionable imitators were likely to take up permanent residence in the countryside, and to romanticize it as a living utopia, a larger proportion of an increasingly mobile, prosperous and urban population was interested in the countryside as a place of occasional resort for health and leisure. In the Edwardian years, the advent of the motor-car gave rural tourism a new fillip. The most popular country travel writer, J.J. Hissey, had in the 1890s made his name with nostalgic tours through the Old English countryside on the box-seat of a coach, a protest against the hustle-and-bustle of the railway; but he could not resist the lure of the motor. After 1906, his travelogues blended the romance of olde-worlde inns, moated manor houses and sturdy, plain-speaking yeomen with the romance of the internal-combustion engine. 'The motor car has restored us our heritage of the road', he claimed.[104]

If so, it was a heritage unrecognized by the Arts and Crafts movement. Aesthetes of the next generation would become so horrified by the urban adaptations of the Arts and Crafts that they would turn against the style altogether.[105] In the meantime, those who were unwilling to follow Blomfield in adapting themselves to modern materialism were forced to retreat further from urban life to maintain the purity of their vision. C.R. Ashbee and his Guild of Handicraft were among the first to emigrate to the Cotswolds, leaving 'Babylon' (London) for Chipping Campden in 1902.[106] There, Muthesius complained, they worshipped 'the ideal of handicraft naked and unadorned', further separating themselves from a public understandably 'scornful of such demonstrations'.[107]

By progressively narrowing and spiritualizing its idea of heritage, therefore, the Arts and Crafts movement had indeed cut itself off from the 'sources of dynamism' in society. Its influence in shaping either bourgeois taste or public policy was correspondingly restricted. Its impact on artists and architects was more direct, but this at a time when public opinion of those creative professions was low and dropping. Where the movement intersected with independent trends favouring rural leisure and suburban living some of its motifs left their trace, but these degraded gestures towards art and history were deplored by true aesthetes. These limits on the purchase of the Arts and Crafts' idea of heritage – indeed any idea of heritage – were all too evident when political claims upon aristocratic property were made in the period when the Arts and Crafts movement was at its zenith; and it will be seen to what a limited extent those claims were couched in cultural terms – to what a paltry extent aristocratic property could be defined as 'national heritage' before the First World War. Who and what were the 'dominant classes' and the 'dominant values' should then be perfectly clear.

## CHAPTER 4

# Philistines vs. Barbarians: Popular Politics and the Failure of Preservation

Nearly every government in Europe developed a national heritage policy in the latter part of the nineteenth century, to protect by legislation and the funding of voluntary action those national monuments, historic buildings and works of art that might otherwise be threatened by rapid social and economic change. By contrast with the German, French and Italian governments, to take some appropriate comparisons, British government action was slow and partial. Gerard Baldwin Brown, an art historian and advocate of preservation who surveyed the practice of all European countries at the turn of the century, concluded that the British did less and spent less in this field than any of its rivals. Baldwin Brown dismissed the argument – still popular among cultural historians today – that central government intervention to preserve the national heritage was unnecessary in Britain because of the voluntary efforts of private owners and local government; in effect, that concern for the national heritage was so generalized in Britain that compulsion was unnecessary. This argument may have applied to education and religion, he granted, but there was no evidence of widely diffused heritage consciousness in British society that might explain central government inactivity. To the contrary; on the Continent, it had been rising standards of taste and education that had led to government intervention to protect art and buildings, whereas in Britain, national utilitarianism lay at the root of aesthetic *laissez-faire*.[1]

If Baldwin Brown's conclusions were true of the national heritage generally, they must have applied all the more forcefully to that portion of the national heritage represented by aristocratic property. The late nineteenth century was a time of mounting attack on aristocratic privilege and property as the British political system became more democratic and the mid-Victorian compromise – whereby aristocratic privilege had been retained, yet exercised responsibly – broke down. If ideas of national heritage had been as well diffused in Britain as Baldwin Brown felt they were in France or Italy, then the historically valued parts of the aristocratic legacy might have been protected from this onslaught: kept in private hands with public tolerance or even subsidy, conveyed to voluntary associations or local government, or taken over directly by central government. This did not happen; the forces discussed in the previous chapter made that impossible. Heritage consciousness was a declining force in the culture; there was wider evidence of it in the 1870s than in the 1900s, when Baldwin Brown was writing. Warwick Castle was practically appropriated as a national monument in 1872, but such an outcome was less likely a generation later, as the story of Tattershall Castle will illustrate. Popular pressure for central government intervention manifested itself in many spheres in this period, but not for the protection of the cultural heritage. Nor were the owners of threatened cultural property likely to seek such protection. Their own philistinism – greatly strengthened by economic adversity – made it difficult for them to view their possessions as aesthetically valuable. Political adversity only further stiffened their resistance. They defended their private property against all public claims, economic and cultural; in opposing taxation and expropriation, they opposed, too, any suggestion that their homes and contents could be considered in any sense national property. Faced with these powerful forces, the efforts of an aesthetic minority to preserve selected bits of aristocratic property for the nation look comparatively puny.[2]

## Radicalism and Heritage, 1867–1885

Overtly anti-aristocratic politics, which had been confined to disempowered extra-Parliamentary radical groups earlier in the century, became a powerful feature in party politics after the Second Reform Act of 1867. This Act itself greatly reduced one of the principal privileges of the landed élite – direct influence over the electorate – by reducing the number of small constituencies where 'deference' to the landowner had thrived and could be policed. Further heavy blows were struck by the Ballot Act of 1872 – rendering voting secret – and the Third Reform and Redistribution Acts of the mid-1880s – essentially completing the process of democratizing the electorate. Most of the other gross political privileges of the land had been eliminated long before: corruption and patronage in government had been severely pared back by the 1830s, access to the civil service and ancient universities made more meritocratic in the 1850s. Radical attention after 1867 consequently focused on the economic benefits that the land still enjoyed in law, especially in the field of taxation. As the agricultural depression bit very early on in this process, landlords felt Radical attacks on their economic 'privileges' more than usually perverse – why savage agriculture just as it was falling to its knees? – but an anti-aristocratic politics could have few other targets in the 1870s and 1880s. Besides, Radicals did not accept the landlords' identification of their own interests with agriculture's – for one thing, there were tenants' and labourers' interests to take into account; for another, many rural landlords were holders of great urban freeholds as well, which were appreciating far more rapidly than rural holdings were declining.

At first, the Radical critique of aristocratic landownership was a compound of an older, romantic vision – which drew on the Victorian idea of heritage – and a newer, more brutally materialist analysis. The traditional Radical view was that aristocratic possessions – not just land, but also vestiges of the national history like ancient monuments and works of art – had been wrongly wrested from the people by means of political privilege. Those privileges had now been brought to an end, but full restitution would entail some new disposition of these ill-gotten gains. The classic late Victorian exposition of this old Radical analysis was *Our Old Nobility*, serialized in the *Echo* and published in book form in 1879. Its author was Howard Evans, associated with both Birmingham Radicalism and the agricultural labourers' movement, a true follower of Cobbett and Howitt who valued the Olden Time as an age of culture and virtue and excoriated the corrupt and exclusive aristocracy of the post-Civil War period. Evans was particularly scathing about the Earl of Warwick, who had accepted public money to rebuild his castle, 'as if it were a hospital or a charity-school', and yet still expected visitors to 'to give half a dozen tips to different domestics before you can see all that is to be seen in this historic pile'.[3]

Evans's historically minded radicalism was, however, beginning to give way to a newer kind, which Evans worriedly associated with socialism.[4] This more materialist perspective cared less for these supposed 'national' possessions. It viewed land, houses, and chattels as wealth – much as their owners were now disposed to view them – which should be subject to equal taxation. The national benefit would lie not so much in reclaiming historical remnants as in converting them into revenue, for expenditure on worthy objects such as schools, municipal services, national defence, and – most importantly – tax relief for poorer citizens.[5]

The landlords' response might have been to draw on the traditional argument themselves, and to show how in preceding generations they had, in fact, served as custodians of the nation's history by preserving the countryside, ancient monuments, historic buildings and great works of art for the people's benefit. So prevalent is this argument today, in the late twentieth century, that we are inclined to exaggerate the significance of a few aristocrats who did make it in the late nineteenth century; but, as the Warwick Castle affair amply demonstrated, it was a brave and exceptional landlord who was willing to abandon his freedom of action in this way. Quite apart from the dishonour incurred by truckling to popular pressure, the economic pressures of the agricultural depression made it difficult to play the role of the 'good custodian'. Admitting a public interest in the disposition of one's house and chattels would directly limit their pecuniary value – if not lead down a slippery slope to virtual nationalization, the spectre of Aston Hall that had been waved in the face of the Earl of Warwick. Consequently the tendency of most landlords was to resist the argument about historical possessions altogether, with charges of spoliation and socialism and a defence of private property. In any case, the most potent arguments against them were the redistributive arguments, aimed at 'equalizing' taxation, and against these the only effective rejoinder was the same claim of private property reinforced by the needs of agriculture. Culture and history – what today would be called heritage – were again at a discount.

The first struggles, immediately after the Second Reform Act and the election of a more interventionist Liberal government in 1868, were fought on the traditional ground; they represented the culmination of a decades-long struggle for some statutory recognition of the Victorian idea of heritage, even if only lip-service was paid in the form of permissive legislation. Antiquarians had long wanted Parliament to take an interest in national history, first of all by ordering its own records – for which a Public Record Office was authorized in 1838 – and then by inventorying, if not regulating, historical records in private hands. The new Liberal government finally established a Historical Manuscripts Commission in 1869, to be administered from the Public Record Office, which would seek to catalogue private holdings purely on a voluntary basis. Even this mild, permissive gesture drew down a storm of criticism, the great collector Sir Thomas Phillipps denouncing it as 'an arbitrary interference with the rights of Private

Property'. It was an antiquary, Thomas Kerslake, who voiced the worst fears of the owners most baldly:

> In these days, when 'Compulsory Purchase'... has ... openly declared itself as one of the most active motive forces of the State – there may be a particular significance in the portentous eyes of a Royal Commission specially directed to that class of private property which exists in the form of ancient manuscripts. Something it is, indeed, under the present aspect of the political atmosphere, that the Noblemen and Gentlemen of England are asked voluntarily to produce their most precious heirlooms, and often the most costly of their moveable property ... to be examined and inventoried by the agents of a Government deeply pledged to the principle of expediency – confiscation: to place them indeed under the surveillance of the central power of the State.[6]

This was clearly overkill; Gladstone's government, itself dominated by landlords (though not a representative selection of them), was hardly likely to target the 'Noblemen and Gentlemen of England' for the confiscation of their most valuable heirlooms. On the contrary, the Historical Manuscripts Commission found itself welcomed by many landlords who wished to take advantage of its cataloguing and preservation service in order to enhance the value of their manuscripts. It was only when *compulsory* interference was threatened – which did savour of confiscation – that real opposition was put up, which helps to explain both why the Historical Manuscripts Commission's voluntary services advanced smoothly for some decades, but also why no enhancement of its powers was contemplated for forty years.

Compulsion was threatened on a second front later in the term of the same government. The antiquarian and Liberal MP Sir John Lubbock – the 'Saint Lubbock' of the Bank Holidays Act – introduced in 1873 the first of a series of bills aimed at preserving 'national monuments' – by which he meant principally prehistoric remains, such as the circle of stones at Avebury which he had himself purchased in 1872 in order to prevent its destruction. Prehistoric remains were a fairly safe starting-point: they were most in danger (being hardest to identify as monuments), the least expensive to maintain, most beloved of scholarly antiquarians (for whom the older the better), and, lacking any modern use, the least like 'private property'. But landowners were not fooled, and they succeeded in shuffling this and the subsequent bills proposed nearly annually by Lubbock into various Parliamentary lay-bys. After 1874, when a Tory government was in place, they were relatively safe. It was not necessary to argue, as it had been under Liberal auspices, that landlords were good custodians for national property; the view could be re-stated that landlords' property was simply their own and not the public's. As the Attorney-General put it in throwing out Lubbock's bill of 1877:

> perhaps it would be contended some day that because the public had been allowed to enjoy parks which private individuals had thrown open the owners ought to be restrained if they wished to close them ... Why should they not equally provide for preserva-tion of the mediaeval monuments – of those old abbeys and castles which were quite as interesting as the Druidical remains? And why should they stop even there? Why not impose restrictions on the owners of pictures or statues which might be of great national interest? If the owner of the 'Three Marys' or of Gainsborough's 'Blue Boy' proposed to send it out of the country, were they to prevent him, on the ground that the matter was one of national concern?[7]

When the Liberals returned in 1880, government backing swung around and Lubbock finally achieved some success with the Protec-tion of Ancient Monuments Act in 1882. Like the Historical Manu-scripts Commission, however, the machinery put into place by this Act was entirely voluntary. A single Inspector of Ancient Monuments was appointed, a job placed in the safe hands of General Augustus Pitt-Rivers, a Tory MP, great landowner, and a model 'good custo-dian' who provided public recreation grounds and free access to the medieval remains on his Dorset estate. Fifty ancient monuments were 'scheduled' – which entitled the inspector to examine and to care for them, *if the owner agreed*. At first owners hesitated to agree, worried that registration of an ancient monument might restrict their ability to sell the land on which it sat. Lubbock himself wavered over registering his stones at Avebury for precisely this reason. In the end, many owners came to the same conclusion as they had done in the case of historical manuscripts – that State inspection and preservation, if vol-untary, could enhance the value of their holdings. Even so, Pitt-Rivers only succeeded in registering half of the fifty monuments in the nearly twenty years of his inspectorate, though by adding to the original schedule he was able to bring his total up to forty-four.[8] Nearly all those resisting scheduling were large landowners from the peerage and gentry, whereas smaller landowners, clergymen and widows figure prominently among the compliant.[9] And again, with owners worried about the slippery slope to compulsion, no serious enhancement of the 1882 powers was contemplated until just before the First World War. Pitt-Rivers himself deprecated any extension of public control, contending that 'the majority of the owners take an interest in their *own* monuments as family possessions'.[10] The story of ancient monuments legislation up until about 1910 is a story of successful landed opposition to national claims.

Over the same period, roughly from the mid-1860s to the early 1880s, landlords were also subjected to a series of court cases, partly inspired by a traditional Radical concern for the people's heritage, challenging their enclosure – in effect, appropriation – of common land. Spearheaded by the Commons Preservation Society (CPS), founded in July 1865 by a knot of Liberal and Radical lawyers and MPs, these cases gradually re-established the public claim to patches of waste and green near the older villages that had been cavalierly infringed on by landlords too generous in their interpretation of their manorial rights. This work was particularly useful in securing some open space in the scattered villages that had now been welded together in the metropolis. Because it relied on highly technical and exhausting points of law, it did not lead to any climactic political confrontation between aristocratic and popular rights. Attempts to override existing law by statute in favour of a public interest in open space were fairly easily seen off by the House of Lords.[11] Some manorial lords, especially in London, were able to negotiate pretty compensation packages in return for the surrender of legally suspect rights. But the constant tattoo of court cases that the CPS was able to mount again raised cries of 'confiscation' and contributed to a crude defensiveness about their property among substantial landowners. The atmosphere was further heated by the CPS's chosen tactic of mounting midnight raids against illegal fences and gates on common lands. In one case, the CPS arranged for a special train carrying 120 navvies to descend on Lord Brownlow's Ashridge estate, to dismantle iron railings on Berkhamsted Common between the hours of midnight and 6 a.m., and thus to trigger a suit for trespass by Lord Brownlow which ultimately led to the restoration of common rights.[12]

The CPS brought together Radical land reformers with an ideological animus against the aristocracy and the more moderate and respectable Liberal gentlemen, interested in the healthful and civilizing effects of open space on the working masses. Some of these latter gentlemen were touched by a tincture of Ruskinism, an enhanced appreciation for nature helping to fill the gulf in the Liberal tradition left by the fading of genuine religious faith. Leslie Stephen founded a walking club of such Liberal gentlemen, the Sunday Tramps, in 1879.

But the touch of Ruskin was very light. A heightened emotional response to the outdoors was a diluted and more manly version of the truly Ruskinian turn from religion to art made by the openly unconventional. It also intersected with hygienic concerns and with the growing demand by urban populations for extended recreational facilities.[13]

In contrast, the purer Ruskinian project of preserving historic works of art and architecture attracted only meagre support in this period, and virtually none at all from politically mainstream opinion. The Society for the Protection of Ancient Buildings, founded by William Morris and some of his Arts and Crafts associates in March 1877, was largely a club of artists and architects. On occasion it used a forthright language of national heritage – 'I think our ancient historical Monuments are national property', wrote William Morris to *The Times* in June 1877 – but this reflected the marginality not only of its aesthetics but also of its politics (which were a mixture of romantic socialism and romantic conservatism). The SPAB remained a painfully small pressure group throughout its early history, with 372 members in 1880 and still only 443 in 1910.[14] While influential among architectural specialists – for instance, in preventing over-restoration of ruined or dilapidated buildings, to preserve their authentic historic texture – it cannot be said to have much influenced the public's idea of what constituted a historic building and to what extent it should be protected.[15] Government viewed the SPAB as a suspicious fringe organization, and when its chairman sought to join the Ancient Monuments Inspectorate's advisory board in 1912, he was rejected – by a sympathetic official – as 'an extremist – or as some might say a faddist'.[16] The SPAB's influence throughout this period was much greater on the Continent, where public and expert opinion, as well as government, already accepted the idea of a national heritage and was keen to accept guidance on how to preserve it.[17]

## Radicalism against Heritage, 1885–1905

The political challenges in the years immediately after 1867 still bore the flavour of the old Radicalism, making national claims to aristocratic property on historical and sentimental grounds. But in the 1880s and 1890s the old Radicalism was progressively supplanted by the new, and its threats were more worrying, because more destructive, aimed not so much at preserving national assets for the nation as at dissolving and redistributing aristocratic property through taxation. Here Gladstone's propertied variety of Liberalism was at first proof against redistributive Radicalism, but after 1880 Gladstone, too, was under mounting pressure. A range of tax privileges from which the land allegedly benefited came under scrutiny.[18]

Some were relatively minor. One small but annoying privilege was derived from the practice of levying local rates on the rental value of a house. The largest country houses – Blenheim was often cited as an example – were normally deemed to be unlettable, to have a low or nil rental value, and therefore to be unrateable as well. But this anomaly would only apply to the truly elephantine houses, and as already seen more and more country houses were, in fact, found to be lettable, presumably incurring rates. A survey made by the Knole estate in 1883 found that a sample of large country houses – including Belvoir, Cobham and Hatfield – all carried a rateable value of between £500 and £750, with a similar value assigned to their parks.[19]

More serious were the exemptions from which aristocratic fortunes benefited in the assessment of death duties. Of the two main death duties, the probate duty on personal wealth was levied at 3 per cent, the succession duty on land at only 1 per cent (raised to $1\frac{1}{2}$ per cent in 1888).[20] Furthermore, personalty under settlement was not liable to *any* duty, because the possessors – who were unable to realize the value of these 'heirlooms' by sale – were not deemed to benefit from it. By a similar line of reasoning, land – whether or not under settlement – was valued for succession duty at its nominal value over the lifetime of its possessor, only a small portion of its capital value. Since something between half and two-thirds of landed property (along with associated houses and chattels) was under settlement at any one time, these exemptions amounted to an impressive privilege essentially reserved to the landed élite.[21] For instance, when the 7th Duke of Devonshire died in 1891, his successor had to pay only £357 in duty on Chatsworth, its treasures and park. On his enormous agricultural estates, he had to pay a good deal more – about £40,000 – but this still represented only about a 2 per cent charge on an estate valued for duty purposes at just over £2 million, half its capital value.[22]

In their defence, landowners pointed to the benefits of the existing system – including settlement – in keeping together large and efficient estates with sufficient capital to maintain investment levels through occasional slumps. They argued that the entire burden of local taxation – the rates – fell ultimately on landed property, thus entitling it to relief from imperial taxation. They were mystified why anyone, at the depth of the agricultural depression, would want to increase the tax burden on the land.

Yet that was the clear direction in which public finance was heading. In 1886, during Gladstone's brief third ministry, the Radicals successfully forced through a resolution calling for the imposition of rates on owners as well as tenants and for a proper valuation of country houses (i.e. by setting rateable value at a small fixed per- centage of sale rather than letting value). Joseph Chamberlain, replying in the debate for the government, was sympathetic to the resolution, but also worried about the trend towards viewing country houses simply as big houses. He had never seen Blenheim himself – he had heard that it was something of a 'white elephant' – but on the other hand there was historical value as well as material value which such a tax might affect adversely:

> it would lead to the destruction of many of the most splendid historical places in the country, and of many very old and inter- esting country houses which, as now maintained, were part of the tradition and the glory of the country, but which could only be maintained if a reasonable valuation were placed upon them.

Chamberlain, with the rest of the government, still voted for the resolution. The Tory spokesman Arthur Balfour – who certainly had visited Blenheim and probably cared more for such houses than Chamberlain – was nevertheless reluctant to acknowledge any 'value' in them at all. In opposing the resolution, he tried to play down their interest:

> Whatever crimes a landlord may have committed, those crimes have been amply atoned by the possession of the big country house . . . Is there a man so abandoned, so idiotic, so utterly lost to the first glimmerings of self-interest that he would deliberately be saddled with one of these gigantic structures without the estate of which it forms part? . . . The man whom you tax can only avoid the tax by throwing up his country house . . . if he does not do that, the only thing which prevents him is the fact that it is his home in which he was brought up. Round that home many sentiments have crystallized. It is the home in which he and his family have lived, perhaps, for generations; it is those sentiments – and those senti- ments alone – which induce him to retain that home.[23]

The country house escaped the application of this resolution as Gladstone's government was not long-lived. But with the Liberals in opposition, the Radical drum-beat against the land rolled and rolled again. The taxation of ground rents and land values – in effect, capital taxes – was now being agitated. When Gladstone was returned to office a final time in 1892, and even more when he retired in Lord

Rosebery's favour early in 1894, the Radical pressure on financial policy became irresistible. In order to meet unprecedented calls on government expenditure and to stave off Radical demands for more thorough-going financial reform, the Liberal Chancellor of the Exchequer Sir William Harcourt introduced in his 1894 budget a consolidated death duty, Estate Duty, to fall on realty as well as personalty, settled as well as free, and to increase progressively with the size of the estate up to a maximum of 8 per cent on fortunes of more than £1 million.

In many ways Harcourt's new Estate Duty was framed so as to cushion its impact on the landed interest. Property was to be assessed at nearer capital value, but the capital value of agricultural land and country houses had never been lower. Settled personalty – heirlooms – and realty were to be taxed, but, at most, only once in the course of a settlement – perhaps every two or three generations – and settled estates would only pay an extra 1 per cent in Settlement Estate Duty to compensate for the intervening successions at which no tax at all was payable. In the course of the budget debate, Harcourt also agreed to fix the valuation of agricultural land and country houses at a maximum of twenty-five years' purchase – twenty-five times their depressed lettable value. All in all, Harcourt – himself the heir presumptive to a massive landed estate in Oxfordshire – considered that he had met the demands of Radical finance in a way that was fair and unconvulsive to agricultural landowners, while at the same time allowing him to tap real millionaires in order to relieve middling taxpayers.[24]

That was not, of course, how most landlords saw it. They were not Liberals, and certainly not Liberal cabinet ministers familiar with the exigencies of Radical finance. The standard response was anger at confiscation – the progressive element of the Estate Duty, with its unusually high marginal rate of 8 per cent, was the greatest novelty – or, at best, a kind of wounded sulkiness, a feeling that the nation should have appreciated better the land's past services, especially now that agriculture was down on its luck. But when this feeling was expressed in public, as it was by the Lincolnshire squire Henry Chaplin in the House of Commons and the great Duke of Devonshire in the Lords, the scornful Radical response shocked them further still.

Devonshire took the highest profile, speaking out not only in Parliament but also in a public appearance at Buxton, near the Chatsworth estate, in June. Here he mixed pathos with veiled threats, regretting that the impact of the death duties must be a substantial curtailment of his family's traditional benevolence. Their roles not only

**DEPRESSED DUKES.**

*Duke of D-v-nsh-re.* "If this Budget passes, I don't know *how* I'm going to keep up Chatsworth!"

*Duke of W-stm-nst-r.* "If you come to that, we may consider ourselves lucky if we can keep a Tomb over our Heads!"

45 'Depressed Dukes': *Punch* (30 June 1894) joins in the chorus of fun poked at the Duke of Devonshire after his ill-advised threat to close Chatsworth.

as agricultural and domestic employers, but also as philanthropists, local patrons, and custodians of amenity and heritage were threatened:

> I do not contend that it is a necessity that I or my family or my successors should be in a position to keep up great places like Chatsworth, or Hardwick, or Bolton Abbey, or Lismore, in Ireland. I do not contend that it is a necessity that we should be placed in a position where we can enjoy the luxury of striving to be surrounded by a contented and prosperous tenantry and people. I do not contend that it is a necessity for us that we should have the privilege of aiding in every good and charitable work in every part of the counties with which we are connected. These things have been a pride and a pleasure to my predecessors and to myself; but they are not necessities.

These 'luxuries', public benefits all, would be inexorably extinguished by 'democratic finance'.[25]

At Buxton, such sentiments were bound to be met with sympathy. Elsewhere they were met with some ridicule: benevolence was no longer a sufficient substitute for equality under the law. From the ultra-democratic *Reynolds's Newspaper*, strong language was perhaps to be expected:

> The Duke of Devonshire, one of the wealthiest landgrabbers in the world, is suffering from a fit of melancholia because Sir William Harcourt's Budget provides that landlords shall in future pay taxes like other people . . . Was ever such a thing heard of? How on earth is the fabulously-rich Duke of Devonshire to find money for his race-course orgies, and his country house parties, and the other resources of idling luxury if he pays his taxes?[26]

At a public meeting in Rotherham the next week, John Morley, if anything a rather Gladstonian member of the cabinet, took the opportunity to make the same point more sweetly:

> if the wealthy man pays less than his share the poor man will have to pay more than his share in order to make up the deficiency. Ah, but the Duke of Devonshire ['Oh!' from the crowd] said the other day . . . 'If this graduated taxation is imposed upon us I am sorry to say there will have to be a withdrawal of subscriptions from benevolent objects. ['Oh!'] These great palaces and pleasure grounds to which we freely admit' – and that is quite true – 'the public, we shall have to starve the maintenance of those palaces and pleasure grounds, and the public will be deprived of pleasure.' [A voice –

'We could get on without them' – followed by general laughter.]
My friend says we should get on without them. I dare say we
should . . . it is you and I who have been keeping up the pleasure
grounds. If the Duke pays so much less than his proper share in
order to perform these public duties you and I have to pay so much
more. I repeat that it is we who keep up Chatsworth.[27]

Devonshire had unwisely opened up a debate which country-house
owners had, largely successfully, kept closed after the Aston Hall and
Warwick Castle affairs. Were the great country houses, their grounds
and collections part of a 'national heritage'? If so, and their owners
were unable to maintain them, should not the nation take responsibility for them? Devonshire had hoped that, faced with these choices, his
opponents would prefer to return to the old system of private ownership and voluntary benevolence, supported where necessary by tax
concessions. He was surprised by the degree to which anti-aristocratic
feeling now made this impossible.

Other alternatives were canvassed instead, nearly all horrifying to
owners. The more philistine Radical voices were happy to see the
great houses and collections broken up: what benefit had they conveyed to the mass of the people, locked up behind closed doors? The
Quaker banker and Durham MP Sir Joseph Pease 'objected that his
constituents should be taxed extra in order that somebody else might
see a collection of pictures which was only to be seen in a private
house'.[28] *Reynolds's* opposed even the purchase of aristocratic art by
the National Gallery, on the grounds that the Gallery was closed on
Sundays and therefore of no use to the mass of the workers. In any
case, *Reynolds's* said dismissively, 'the working classes of Great Britain
at this moment want bread, not pictures'.[29] More cultivated Liberals
argued that the break-up of art collections was likely to benefit rather
than harm the public, by disseminating ownership. Harcourt, for one,
'found that very few persons had ever seen some of the most famous
pictures until they went to Christie's,' and 'imagined that the knowledge of pictures was not retarded, but was accelerated, by the sale and
redistribution and re-arrangement of pictures which took place from
time to time'.[30]

The Radical *Daily Chronicle* took a different tack, which will be
familiar to the modern reader, though from an unfamiliar political
position:

Of course, if the Duke and his friends propose to fight and evade
the death duties, the State will have to meet them in the same spirit.
If it were necessary, we should be ready to appoint commissioners

to guard the woods and forests of great estates from being cut down or curtailed by landlords who do not immediately see their way to the payment of the duties.

But, the *Chronicle* went on, why not make an accommodation with those, like the Duke of Devonshire, who *had* been good custodians, and render their role public?

> He has spent money freely, so that the joys of Chatsworth may be fairly divided between himself and the people of his county, and indeed of England. He has, in a word, regarded himself as a bailiff rather than as an unqualified owner. The question arises whether the Budget might not contain a provision for emphasising and enlarging this aspect of the landlord's position in the State. It might be possible to offer his heirs an alternative. Supposing they desire to sell that portion of his property which has been freely open to the public view. 'Very well,' says the council or the municipality, 'you may take your historic residence on condition that you reserve it permanently for limited use by the people. In return, we will remit you a portion of the estate duty, and you will consider yourself the trustee of your historic house rather than its sole owner.' . . . he and his like could still be the lords of their Chatsworths; the people would simply acquire something of a vested interest in half a dozen of England's lordliest pleasure-houses.[31]

Fortunately for the delicate hearts of the landowners of England, few of them read the *Daily Chronicle*. Half a century later, when all other escape-routes had been stopped up, owners might turn to such accommodations, but in 1894 they were the Radical alternative, and any owner showing the slightest glimmer of interest in them would have been shunned as a traitor to his class.

The difficulty posed for owners by such questions was evident in discussion of possible exemption from the new death duties once their passage appeared inevitable. Teams of Tory lawyers tried to extract from Harcourt amendments that would exempt special classes of works of art from duty, until sold. All but one – which exempted works of art bequeathed to public bodies – were successfully resisted.[32] Interestingly, few great owners participated in these debates. One reason may have been a desire to distance themselves from the extravagant claims made by Tory backbenchers about the degree of public access to private collections. One lawyer claimed that 'fully 99 per cent. of the great collections throughout the length and breadth of the Kingdom were open to the public'. George Wyndham, one of the

Souls, thought great country houses were virtually 'local museums', the equivalent of the public museums that every small French or Italian town possessed, and that without them English philistinism would be immeasurably worse. Such arguments – apart from being based on false premisses[33] – gave hostages to fortune. If they yielded tax concessions, they might well better the economic position of great owners; if they served as precedent for public claims of the kind envisioned by the *Daily Chronicle*, then the saleability of works of art was threatened and the economic position of the owners made graver still.[34]

When the Tories returned to office in 1895, they faced the same dilemma themselves. The new Chancellor, Sir Michael Hicks Beach, came under pressure from the owners of country-house collections – notably Victoria Sackville-West, chatelaine of Knole – for some exemption from the death duty on heirlooms.[35] Attention was again focused on works of art because they, unlike houses and parks, were valuable, both to the owner and to the taxman.[36] Hicks Beach's solution was to propose a general exemption for settled heirlooms that were deemed by the Treasury to be of 'national or historic interest'. Like the pre-1894 death duty concessions for land and settled personalty, the exemption would by definition apply only to aristocratic property. The proposal again stirred up Liberal demands for public compensation. A young Welsh firebrand named David Lloyd George tried to limit the exemption to collections that 'have been accessible during the lifetime of their late possessor to public view and inspection under reasonable conditions, and where such property is'. Hicks Beach squirmed; he saw some justice in the suggestion; however he feared it might be 'an intolerable hardship'. Lord Cranborne, heir to Hatfield, squashed any such suggestion flat. 'Though nearly every owner of curiosities was most anxious to show them to the public, anything like a specific direction to do so in an Act of Parliament would be open to great objection.' Other Liberals again expressed the view that art sales were, in the end, the best way to ensure the dissemination of taste. They were outraged at such 'class legislation', making (as Harcourt saw it) 'an enormous present to the richest millionaires in the country'. The exemption as written conveyed no public benefit: 'for the first time they were giving exemption to private individuals who kept up these collections for their own use.'[37] In the end, of course, the government majority got its way, and in application, the exemption was applied even more specifically to country-house owners than had been originally proposed, taking in not only the most important artistic and historical objects, but also 'pictures which though of moderate artistic merit, directly illustrate the history of a county or of a county family of historical importance'.[38]

The threat of death duties can be seen, therefore, to have raised the same ambiguous questions in aristocratic minds that the market for fine art engendered. Art collections – but not houses or land – came to be more highly valued by their owners, yet it was unclear whether the value attached was aesthetic or material. Aesthetic value could be recognized and advertised so long as such display did not affect material value. After 1894, death duties were often cited by owners as the sad pretext for the sale of some chattels, in order to preserve the rest. It was the same Victoria Sackville-West who had pressed Hicks-Beach so hard for heirloom protection who also negotiated with J. P. Morgan the sale of selected Knole heirlooms. Taxation made sales necessary, she said, to keep together the main bulk of the collection; but these monies also made possible the installation of electric light and 'very expensive' central heating, the purchase of one of the first country-house motor-cars, and generally making Knole, as she bragged privately, 'the most comfortable large house in England, uniting the beauties of Windsor Castle with the comforts of the Ritz'.[39]

The death duty debates revealed not only aristocratic doubts about the idea of heritage, but more generally the indifference of politicians of all stripes to such considerations. With Liberals increasingly bent on fiscal expropriation and Tories bent on fending it off, the pressure for historic preservation by legislation actually slackened between the 1880s and the 1900s. The old Radicalism which valued the aristocratic heritage and wished to preserve it for the people had lost much of its punch. The new Radicalism was more interested in the taxation of land values and urban social problems. Aesthetic lobbies such as the SPAB were no substitute. Ruskin and Morris became heroes of the socialist movement, but that, too, exerted a negligible influence on policy – some would say on politics – before the First World War. The Tory governments in power for most of the years between 1885 and 1905 shrugged off occasional suggestions that they should take compulsory powers to protect ancient monuments. They agreed to extend their power to care for prehistoric monuments voluntarily registered by private owners to medieval buildings as well, but they did not replace the single inspector of such monuments, General Pitt-Rivers, when he died in 1900. Instead a minor civil servant in the Office of Works took on the job as 'a labour of love' in his spare time and annual leave. Only a single English medieval building was regis-tered by a private owner.[40]

Nor did local authorities, to which central government preferred to leave such tasks, leap into the breach. The SPAB prodded Leeds Corporation about the fate of the Kirkstall Abbey ruins outside the town, which were falling into disrepair due to the indifference of their owner, Lady Cardigan. The Corporation showed insufficient zeal until a private purchaser, the entrepreneur J. T. North, came forward and presented the ruins to the city at his own expense. They were opened to the public in 1895. The acquisition of Kirkstall Abbey has been taken as evidence that 'the tastes and attitudes of London-based [SPAB] spread to provincial centers'.[41] But Kirkstall Abbey was an isolated case. Few historic buildings were acquired by local authorities before the First World War. Tamworth bought its Olden Time castle, in the centre of town, in 1897, and Bolton accepted Hall-in-th'-Wood, an Elizabethan timber-framed house, from Lord Leverhulme in 1900. In most of the handful of other cases, historic buildings were acquired less for their own interest than as incidentals in the purchase of a park or other open space, or as a container for libraries and museums.[42]

A more explicit case of historic preservation was Worcestershire County Council's attempt to lease Harvington Hall, a middling-sized Elizabethan brick house famed for its priest holes and Tudor wall paintings, to prevent its owner from ruining it. But, admitted the council's chairman, 'to take a house of that kind and to put it in repair frightened us at once, and the whole thing fell through, and the place is now falling rapidly into ruins'.[43] These isolated instances may testify more to the persistence of older Radical valuations of the Olden Time, especially in the Midlands, than to the presence of SPAB's kind of motives, but in either case they are slender reeds upon which to rest an argument for widespread heritage consciousness.[44]

The typical local authority's true priorities are revealed in the instance of Heaton Park. Manchester was delighted to buy this recently suburbanized estate from the Earl of Wilton in 1902. It paid the massive sum of £230,000 for 623 acres, which it subsequently equipped with a boating lake, tennis courts and two golf courses. But what to do with the boring classical country house in its centre? The structure, it was thought, might be used to house some of the Corporation's accumulated curios, but the contents, fixtures and fittings were auctioned off, and 'many family portraits and large pieces of furniture' virtually given away. Fletcher Moss, the lone art-lover on the City Council (whose own taste ran to the small manor house), tried to staunch the flow, but to no avail: 'my colleagues', he sighed, 'would not trouble about it. They look upon me as merely an antiquary, that is one who is afflicted with a harmless form of lunacy'.[45] This house, which the official guidebook to the park described as 'of little interest to the student of architecture or to the historian', is now characterized by the *Buildings of England* as 'one of the finest [of its period] in the country'. Had Heaton been a small half-timbered manor house, the outcome might have been different – but perhaps not, as the same Corporation later came to possess a number of fine specimens of this type which it left 'decaying, neglected, pulled down, or beyond repair'.[46] Nor did the London County Council do much in 1894 to save Jacobean Bromley Palace, sold by the London School Board to house-breakers for £250 to clear space for new school buildings; only one room was salvaged by the effort of Arts and Crafts antiquarians and re-erected in the Victoria and Albert Museum.[47] The fact is that Moss was right – historic architecture was still considered a mild folly, while schools and parks and open spaces for urban recreation were rapidly becoming a social priority.

The failure of either central or local government to intervene directly to salvage historic buildings was one of the motive forces behind the formation of a new preservationist organization in January 1895. The Commons Preservation Society activists Octavia Hill and Robert Hunter had the idea as early as 1884 to set up a charitable trust that could hold land and buildings in the public interest, as they had found local authorities incapable of holding property simply to preserve it. A charitable trust had a further attraction in that it could gain support from people who saw a charity as a stop-gap for government action, and also from those who were frightened by confiscatory Radicalism but could swallow private philanthropy for the public good. The National Trust for Places of Historic Interest or Natural Beauty as finally established ten years later was therefore able to embrace a wider range of interests than had the CPS. Its early membership included SPAB types with a passion for late medieval architecture and those more concerned with the healthful effects of open space, Radicals and Socialists pressing for State action and Liberal landowners seeking to do good privately. Its first chairman was the moderate Duke of Westminster, and by including representatives of other artistic and scholarly bodies on its council, it was able to extend its reach still further, involving a few Tory peers who were art-gallery trustees, such as Lord Crawford (one of the omnipresent Lindsay family) and Lord Plymouth, whose wife was a leading Soul and who became the Trust's chairman in 1913.[48]

The Trust was therefore a much broader church than earlier preservationist bodies like the CPS or the SPAB, despite their shared roots. Its leadership actively supported efforts to extend State control over open space and historic buildings, but its public image was more gentle and philanthropic, accepting gifts and buying by public sub-scription land and buildings of exceptional beauty or historic impor-tance.[49] It acquired about sixty separate properties before the First World War, with concentrations in the Lake District and the Surrey hills. It also took on a few small historic buildings which the SPAB, unequipped to own property, pressed upon it – mostly small medieval buildings, but including one Tudor manor house and farm, Barrington Court in Somerset, for which it had received a bequest and which it let out to a tenant.

Through its well-publicized appeals, its consensual tone and methods and its focus on romantic beauty spots, the Trust won a fair amount of public support before the war. Yet even this philanthropic approach to open-space preservation remained the commitment of a small minority, carrying a whiff of heterodoxy in respectable society. Fewer than five hundred donors paid annual subscriptions, the usual cast of artists, philanthropists and reformers. To make a comparison of which contemporaries were aware, the National Art-Collections Fund, buying conventional art for the national galleries, was founded eight years after the Trust but by 1914 had recruited nearly treble its membership. The Fund also attracted far more backing from aristo-crats, eager to sell their art but not to abandon their land or homes.[50] Landowners' love of the countryside was still overwhelmingly ex-pressed through agriculture, fishing, shooting and hunting, activities that co-existed unhappily with public enjoyment of open spaces. At a time when most landowners were retrenching on their public obliga-tions and defending the integrity of private ownership, few had time or money to waste on open-space philanthropy.[51]

Despite its philanthropic methods, the National Trust was associated in many landowners' minds with Radical attacks on the great estates. Most landlords were more concerned to halt that break-up than to assist in it, however indirectly, by putting land into quasi-public ownership.[52] Although the public was more interested in the National Trust's open spaces than in the historic buildings cherished by the SPAB, even this interest was limited, as politicians understood, and certainly dwarfed by public hostility to landlordism. Destruction was a far more potent force than preservation. This was to be amply illus-trated in the years after the National Trust's foundation, when a final political assault on aristocratic property was made and pres-ervationism's inability to salvage any of that property for cultural use was again made embarrassingly clear.

## Crisis of the Aristocracy, 1905–1914

The first years of the new century were not kind to the great landowners, even before the Liberals came to power in December 1905 and promptly won a landslide victory in the election of January 1906. The aged Queen Victoria's death early in 1901 drew a symbolic line under the old era as surely as did the advent of a new century. The new king, Edward VII, presided over many gaudy scenes of conspicuous consumption which gave a tonic to high society and lent new glamour to deference, but this did not always wear well with a people grumbling over landowners' tax privileges and mounting evidence of urban degeneration. A debate began over whether landowners of all kinds – the mere gentry as well as the great aristocrats and plutocrats – had not become selfish, effeminate and cosmopolitan. Even those who blamed depression and taxation for the crisis had to admit that the traditional structures of rural society had broken down irretrievably.[53] Novels and plays questioning the aristocracy's morals, their patriotism and their taste, which had formerly been the province of priggish bourgeois or ultra-democrats, began to trickle into the mainstream. Popular authors such as H. G. Wells and Bernard Shaw questioned whether country-house life deserved the indulgence and privilege granted it by modern society.[54] One interpretation might be that the servants were wreaking their revenge; Wells, at least, was the grandson of the head gardener at Penshurst Place, his father had been under-gardener at nearby Redleaf when artists gathered there in the 1840s, and his mother served as a lady's maid at Uppark in Sussex.[55] But the critique was not limited to low-born Fabians. The highly respectable John Galsworthy launched in a series of novels what Charles Masterman described as a 'rather fierce indictment . . . an impeachment of the country house and conventional life of successful England . . . its satisfaction, its docility, its absence of high purpose and adventure.'[56]

Within the Liberal party, Radical ideas about the taxation of land values and social reform were no longer confined to marginal, faintly plebeian figures. A younger generation – the so-called New Liberals – had embraced these ideas and cloaked them in philosophical respectability, and in some social respectability as well; among the New Liberals were guiltily puritanical gentlemen like C. P. Trevelyan, heir to a baronetcy and 20,000 acres in Northumberland centred on Wallington Hall. The party leadership was still broadly Gladstonian and not hostile to large landownership *per se*, but no leading Liberal could avoid adopting the language of expropriation and redistribution when the subject of land came up. The colourless Prime Minister, Sir Henry Campbell-Bannerman, gave a hint of what was to come at a pre-election rally in the Albert Hall in December 1905. 'We desire to develop our own undeveloped estate in this country,' he declared, 'we wish to make the land less of a pleasure-ground for the rich and more of a treasure-house for the nation.'[57]

What was to come came quickly. Campbell-Bannerman's retirement in 1908 to make way for H. H. Asquith, the first non-landed prime minister in the nation's history, opened the door wide to Radical finance. The 'People's Budget' introduced in the next year by David Lloyd George, and finally enacted in 1910 after a year's bloody struggle with the Peers (and two general elections), aimed both substantial and symbolic blows at the land. Substantially, a range of new and largely unavoidable taxes on the land were imposed. The taxation of land values – capital taxes on land, not only on death and not only on the income derived – entered in the form of a 20 per cent tax on the 'unearned increment' of land (the rise in property values not due to development or investment) each time it was transfered by inheritance or sale. A 10 per cent tax on enhanced values at the transfer or renewal of a leasehold and a small annual tax on undeveloped land were also imposed, to catch more of the 'unearned increment' between freehold transfers. In order to implement these land taxes, the budget also set afoot a great national land valuation, a general inquisition into the ownership and value of land which raised fears of nationalization and provided more ammunition for anti-aristocratic campaigns to come. If Lloyd George had had his way, he would also have put an end to the avoidance of death duties by settled estates, levying the full duties at each succession, but this provision was blocked in Cabinet, ironically by Lewis Harcourt, son of the graduated death duties' progenitor. Instead, the extra Settlement Estate Duty meant to catch some of the lost tax was doubled, though it was still commonly avoided.[58] These were the chief taxes aimed specifically at the land; other taxes levied on the rich – higher rates on unearned income, a super-tax of sixpence in the pound on incomes over £5,000, a new top rate of 15 per cent for the death duties – also hit landowners disproportionately.

Symbolically, Lloyd George made explicit that the goal of the new taxes was to end the passive enjoyment of appreciating property values by 'idle' landowners, rural and urban. Personally he did not care whether this led to the break-up of estates or to their more efficient development and taxation, but many of his rural followers did expect a cascade of land sales to the benefit of tenant farmers and small-holders. In the rhetorical battle royal that followed, Lloyd George hammered away at the landed élite's parasitism and uselessness for modern purposes. The Chancellor's speech at Limehouse in July 1909 before a crowd of four thousand put the wind up his cooler colleagues as well as its direct targets, the great landowners. Not only was the class as a whole written off as lazy, selfish and heartless, but individual landowners were named and pilloried. The Duke of Northumberland had extorted inflated sums from a poor county council desperate for land for schools. The Duke of Westminster had confiscated the profits of his successful tenants by means of 'reversion taxes'. 'Oh, these dukes – (loud laughter) – how they harass us! (More laughter.)' The credit which wealthy dukes had claimed in 1894 for their benevolence – dubious then – was now brutally repudiated.[59]

When, in the autumn, the Tories rose to the bait and prepared to block the budget in the Lords, the indictment could legitimately broaden to challenge the remaining political as well as economic power of the peerage. At Newcastle in October, Lloyd George asked:

> Should 500 men, ordinary men, chosen accidentally from among the unemployed, override the judgement – the deliberate judgement – of millions of people who are engaged in the industry which makes the wealth of the country?

The victory that the Liberals ultimately achieved over the Tory aristocracy was therefore a political as well as an economic victory – it resulted in the passage not only of the People's Budget in 1910 but also of the Parliament Act, removing the Lords' veto, in 1911. It may have been a pyrrhic victory, frightening off many of the Liberals' milder supporters and even laying the groundwork for the future collapse of the party, but it established Lloyd George as the most visible member of the government and the great estates as the principal bogy of modern Liberalism.

To keep the initiative against moderate cabinet rivals, Lloyd George decided to take the war from Westminster into the Tories' rural heartlands immediately after the contest with the Lords had concluded. In the spring of 1912, he organized a group of New Liberals to launch a private inquiry into social conditions in the countryside. The bulk of the work was done by the reforming industrialist Seebohm Rowntree, whose family trust funded the inquiry, but both the chairman, Arthur Acland, and the secretary, C. R. Buxton, were upright scions of great landowning families. Rowntree was specifically instructed to dig up some sensational stuff on aristocratic luxury: 'to select a few parishes where the wages of the Agricultural Labourer are low and his housing bad, but where the landlord lives in a fine house and keeps up a great style.' Fed thus by Rowntree's muckraking, Lloyd George launched his freelance Land Campaign with a speech at Bedford in October 1913, which accused 'Landlord Parliaments' since the sixteenth century of confiscating the labourer's 'heritage' – a material heritage, of course, not a cultural one.

> He has been converted from a contented, well-fed, independent peasant to a hopeless, underpaid, landless drudge on the soil. His wages are less to-day in proportion to their purchasing capacity than they were in the reign of Henry the Seventh.[60]

The result was a package of government proposals for a new Ministry of Lands and Forests, a tutelary genius for rural society that would guarantee security of tenure for farmers and minimum wages for labourers, expedite land sales and the development of rural industries, and begin acquiring land itself for housing and development purposes. To these proposals were added in the 1914 Budget more tax increases and, finally, an end to death-duty avoidance for settled estates. Liberal fortunes among the rural electorate rose immediately, thereby regaining some of the ground lost in the wearying struggles of 1909–11. The outbreak of war in August 1914 called a temporary halt to the full package of rural reorganization, but the Liberals had by then already committed themselves to pulling apart the traditional rural hierarchy.[61]

The effect on the Liberal intelligentsia of this sharp anti-aristocratic turn in politics was hardly to make it more nostalgic for the English countryside, as has sometimes been alleged. Instead, a social conscience began to infiltrate and give an edge to formerly anodyne celebrations of rural beauty. In a 1904 tourist's description of Sussex, as apolitical a figure as E. V. Lucas felt bound to mention the feeble pulse of Arundel and Petworth, the one 'under the shadow of Rome and the Duke [of Norfolk] . . . still medieval and curiously foreign', the other 'with the great house and its traditions at the top of the town like a weight on the forehead'. Picturesque they might be, offering 'the authentic thrill' of feudalism, but they were also 'a little oppressive . . . I should not like to make Petworth my home, but as a place of pilgrimage, it is almost unique'. A decade later, these hints were taken up and magnified by polemicists. The fire-breathing F. E. Green thought Lucas had just caught a glimpse of the 'physical and spiritual decay' experienced by ordinary people in conditions of rural tyranny. A little further inquiry would reveal much worse, and tourism in these circumstances was frankly offensive. 'If you feel so disposed you can come here and experience the authentic thrill of a past age', but the picturesqueness was only skin deep. Even at Chipping Campden in the Cotswolds,

> the country home of the Arts and Crafts Guild, a place where men, animated by high ideals, possessed minds astir with the spirit of modernity . . . the infusion of men from London and Glasgow with democratic ideals has failed to cause more than a ripple in this stagnant pool of mediaevalism.[62]

The Arts and Crafts movement had not been devoid of a social conscience, of course, but the New Liberalism shifted attention from an aesthetic crisis to a material crisis in the countryside. Working in parallel with Lloyd George's Land Campaign, radical historians – J. L. and Barbara Hammond, R. H. Tawney – were pioneering a new rural history which saw the enclosures of the sixteenth to the nineteenth centuries as a historic caesura, permanently cutting off the Old English countryside from the present, demanding redress for the injustice to the rural labourer but permitting no simple return via rural nostalgia.[63] Those Liberals who loved the countryside for its natural beauty found it difficult to come to terms with this transformation. In his highly influential survey of *The Condition of England* (1909), Charles Masterman pondered worriedly about the value of a countryside deprived of its peasantry:

> The beauty of continental landscape . . . is the beauty of 'peasants' country': the beauty that is provided by security and close cultivation, excited wherever the peasant is assured that he will reap what he has sown. The beauty of the English landscape is the beauty of 'landlords' country' – the open woods, the large grass fields and wide hedges, the ample demesnes, which signify a country given up less to industry than to opulence and dignified ease . . . The typical English countryside is that of great avenues leading to residences which lack no comfort, broad parks, stretches of private land, sparsely cultivated, but convenient for hunting, shooting, and a kind of stately splendour.

The English countryside had, in short, been redesigned in the land-lord's image. Now the landlords had themselves turned their backs on the countryside, preferring the incredibly bland and superficial lures of high society or the 'scramble and smash and shriek' of the motor car. This left parts of the countryside still beautiful, but a social nullity; the beauty did not, as the Arts and Crafts movement had felt, emanate from the remnants of traditional society, but rather from a hateful feudalism. Its owners did not appreciate it, and neither – understand-ably – did the working masses who had been swept away to make it possible.[64]

On the Tory side, the response to the land campaign was not much more conducive to rural nostalgia. It was once thought that Lloyd George drove the Tory peers back into a romantic defence of tradi-tional rural values, a gang of backwoodsmen, the 'Diehards', fighting valiantly to the last ditch. But it is now more common – and only sensible – to consider the pre-war Tory party in the light of its interwar success at modernization. The mainstream of the Tory party tried to play down their party's special relationship with agriculture. Agriculturalists had to turn to their own pressure groups to argue their case – first, the Central Landowners' Association, founded in 1906, and later also the Land Defence League and the Land Union. Faced with the threats of land nationalization or the splintering of estates into smallholdings, the CLA quickly adopted the position that landlords should lead the break-up of great estates themselves, to ensure an orderly transition to the farmers and to retain a role for the landed élite as super-farmers.[65] As for the Diehards, it has been shown that they were not impoverished squires at all, but prosperous landowners also improvising skilfully a defence of their property and their business that could thrive in the modern world. Far from falling back on a dream-world of rural paternalism, they – like typical landowners – took a grimly practical approach to the crisis of aristocracy, diversify-ing their holdings beyond agriculture, selling estates where they could, modernizing estates where they could not or would not sell, buying new estates in the Empire, and fighting the Liberals' tax and constitu-tional proposals tooth and nail.[66]

The pragmatic approach adopted by more moderate Tories as well as Diehards – sloughing off politically and economically vulnerable estates – was smoothed by a not-entirely coincidental upturn in the land market from around 1910. After a generation of retrenchment and streamlining, agriculture was recovering and more tenants were in a position to purchase their land. Eager to diversify out of land, owners were in a position to sell. The Duke of Bedford led a virtual stampede by selling his entire Thorney estate to his tenants in 1909. In the next five years, 800,000 acres to a value of £20 million changed hands. Whether this was simply a sound fiscal strategy or reflective of a more amorphous 'declining confidence' in country life, the result was to reinforce the aristocrat's hardheaded attitude towards his family assets that had begun to form in the 1880s and 1890s.[67]

The fine-art market also went into high gear. Both the millionaires'

market for Old Masters, English portraiture and fine French furniture
and a newer, nearly mass market for lesser 'antiques' prospered in the
atmosphere of insecurity and social change. Throughout the nineteenth century, the cult of the Olden Time had lent a certain prestige
to pseudo-Elizabethan arts and crafts, the style not authenticity being
the great *desideratum*; now the real thing was on offer and eagerly
sought-after. Whether this represented a demand-fuelled Arts and
Crafts consciousness of the unique qualities of age, or an acute marketing ploy by historic owners and their agents, 'Old England' was
everywhere on sale in the years before the war. The housebreaker
made his appearance, dismantling manor houses bit by bit and selling
their contents, fixtures and even semi-structural features such as stair-
cases, in urban auction-rooms. Entire London town houses were
purchased by the dealers Lenygon and Owen Grant in 1909 to display
their current stock, and Avray Tipping was commissioned to write a
history of one of them as a high-class advertising brochure.[68] Rumours
began to circulate of American millionaires, not content with English
country life, buying whole manor houses and transplanting them in

46  Max Beerbohm's view of the art market in high gear before the First World War: 'Further
Economies in the Library of Chatsworth: The Duke, having disposed disadvantageously of his sofa,
sleeps where the Caxtons stood (Spring, 1914).' The volumes serving as pillow include titles such as
*Smiles on Self-Help* and *The Beggars' Opera*.

pieces to the New World. They were all untrue – pointing again to some clever publicity, or some strategic alarmism, or both.

All of this put advocates of historic preservation in a spin. The Liberals were distracting attention from the aesthetic value of the countryside by posing its social problematic more sharply. Country-men among the Liberals, such as Masterman, felt guilty about their admiration for 'landlords' country'. The Tories were gradually distancing themselves from 'landlords' country' and the landlords themselves were trying to dump whatever responsibilities they had left. The market for country houses, works of art and amenity land was whirring dangerously back into action. The effect was to heighten the rhetoric and emotions of the fledgling heritage lobby, but not necessarily to enhance its standing in society at large, or its political effectiveness.

Perhaps the most famous of all hymns to the Old English country-side, Kenneth Grahame's *The Wind in the Willows*, published in October 1908, projected its amazing fantasy of the organic community as a despairing *cri de coeur* over the current crisis – a conjuncture that subsequent generations of readers have not, of course, necessarily appreciated. As a younger man, Grahame had been closely enmeshed with the aesthetic and the Arts and Crafts movements, but as he aged his alienation from modern life had grown and he had become embittered. A pistol wound from a deranged Socialist, who broke into his office at the Bank of England and shot him at random in November 1903, aggravated his mood. *The Wind in the Willows* establishes an ideal rural community dominated by gentlemen (Rat, Mole, Badger, Otter) but threatened both from without, by the railway and the Radical mob (stoats and weasels), and from within, by its irresponsible aristocrat (Toad of Toad Hall, a composite of various Thamesside country houses), happy to bleed Toad Hall dry to pay for his high life and especially for his motor car. Although the gentlemen fend off the mob and bring Toad to heel, the ideal world can never be reclaimed, as the linchpin – the great landowner – is gone for good. 'Of course Toad never really reformed,' wrote Grahame in a private letter, 'he was by nature incapable of it. But the subject is a painful one to pursue.' Recent attempts notwithstanding, *The Wind in the Willows* can have no sequel: the village community, Grahame knew, was irretrievable.[69]

Sentiments of alarm and despair manifested themselves in all quarters of the art- and history-loving communities, but they did not spread rapidly through public opinion, which if anything had grown more hostile to artiness and rural nostalgia. The amenity societies that had developed from the Arts and Crafts and open-space movements – the SPAB and the National Trust – were caught in the doldrums.[70] Many of the institutions of the Arts and Crafts movement chose this moment to fall apart. Looking back gloomily on the hopes he had had in the 1870s and 1880s, of the promise then held out by the Romantic movement, the Oxford movement, the Arts and Crafts movement, the Soul George Wyndham wrote to his mother in autumn 1907, 'there are now no movements: only stagnation. We live in a phase of indolent mediocrity.'[71] The rising cause among left-wing intellectuals – Fabianism – was determinedly urban and industrial in its concerns, while retaining some of the aesthetic impulses (especially in music and drama) it inherited from its Arts and Crafts roots.[72] For Bernard Shaw and H. G. Wells, an admiration for the art of the past warred with a consciousness of the social good to be achieved by smashing up the old order. It is doubtful, for instance, whether Shaw's appeal at the annual meeting of the National Art-Collections Fund did more good or harm, when he scorned any recourse 'in the ordinary timid and quiet way to the culture of the rich classes':

> I think it would be much better for us to call the rich classes very sternly to book: to make them understand that if they will fill the country with magnificent buildings and monuments, and with magnificent pictures and statues, so that whenever a citizen turned he could see triumphs of Art provided for him as the result of self-culture on the highest plane, then their incomes may be defended as a good national investment; but that if they persist in dishonestly treating their money as their own without regard to the public, and endow nothing but week-end hotels, where they may be seen from Friday to Tuesday in evening dress, eating dinners in the evening instead of the middle of the day . . . then there is in reserve that alternative method of dealing with them which is represented in history by the guillotine.[73]

Within the Liberal party, there was some concern about the effect of its economic policies on high culture in the countryside, particularly among such well-born New Liberals as Masterman and Trevelyan, but the picture was very confused. The government spoke a language of national interest and the public good, but nearly always in connection with material interests and material goods. Local and central government were given more powers to acquire land and plan land-use, but cultural and amenity uses were hardly considered in such legislation. The 1909 Housing and Town Planning Act made no provision for rural authorities at all and only scant consideration was given to the acquisition of cultural assets by urban authorities; as before, powers were confined to museums and open space.[74] In the People's Budget, the only concession made to heritage interests was an extension of the death-duty exemption for chattels of historic or artistic importance from settled to free estates, as much an act of justice to non-aristocratic property as a broadening of the national interest in works of art. One aesthetic Liberal peer, Lord Beauchamp, complained that this concession had gone virtually unnoticed in debate.[75] As preservationists pointed out incessantly, every other European country – with better-established statist and academic traditions – was taking the opportunity to define and control the national heritage in countryside, works of art and historic buildings.[76] The Liberals did not at first feel disposed to make any such effort. The Inspectorate of Ancient Monuments was left vacant, as it had been since 1900. The Office of Works, the nearest thing (and not very near) to a Ministry of Fine Arts, had had a tradition of resisting any extension of its powers in this sphere.

Instead, individual ministers with cultural concerns took initiatives. Masterman appealed to 'the suburban and professional people' to shake off their own attraction to the materialism and superficiality of high society and stake an independent claim to their heritage: he was seeking some external stimulus which he did not get. At the Board of Education, another patrician Radical, C. P. Trevelyan, tried to encourage these aspirations by developing a sense of heritage in the school curriculum. A circular issued to heads of secondary schools recommended:

> It is far more important that pupils should leave school with their eye trained to observe the historical remains which are to be found in almost every part of England, than that they should attempt to remember the whole of the political history, much of which they cannot understand.

Field trips for schoolchildren were organized to medieval castles and ecclesiastical monuments, and the London County Council organized a conference on the teaching of history which emphasized the teaching of local history by reference to ancient monuments.[77]

The Office of Works did come under scholarly pressure at least to monitor the effects that Liberal fiscal policy was having on the nation's stock of ancient monuments. Scholarly bodies, such as the Society of Antiquaries, which had hitherto remained studiously aloof from the promotion of legislation, were concerned about the swelling market for land, buildings and parts of buildings. They were also by now affected by the dilute version of the Arts and Crafts ethos that had trickled down into the antiquarian milieu. These scholarly bodies proposed initially that a national audit of historical monuments be undertaken, similar to the survey of historical manuscripts that an earlier Liberal government had set afoot in 1869. In 1908 government agreed to the appointment of a Royal Commission on Historical Monuments, to be chaired by the Liberal peer Lord Burghclere, but to include antiquaries and interested Tory peers, such as Lords Crawford and Plymouth. The Commission was charged with drawing up a list and description of monuments and buildings of historical interest dating from before 1700, and it went about its work thoroughly but cautiously. Despite this modesty, the Commission found its access impeded by 'fear of Government control'. As the Commission's Secretary explained to a Parliamentary inquiry,

> we are able to get over it by saying that we have no power over the monuments that we see; that our enquiry is merely a national stocktaking, and that the nation wishes to know what it has in the way of monuments, and there our functions cease. But practically at every house we visit we have to explain that we are not connected with taxation of land values.[78]

Its first report, on Hertfordshire (chosen because the Victoria County History had already done much work on this county), was issued to muted public interest in October 1910. The report was a work of sober scholarship, dry and descriptive, in which by specific *diktat* 'all flamboyancy of language was to be avoided'. The sole concession to the public imagination, the insertion of 'small illustrations and plans . . . after the fashion of those well known advertisements of houses to be let or sold which appear weekly in the 'Country Life' newspaper', was nearly rejected on financial grounds.[79]

The work of the Royal Commission for the first time gave some official status to historic buildings as an object of public interest. It stimulated Lewis Harcourt, the First Commissioner of Works, to apply to the Treasury to fill the Inspectorate of Ancient Monuments, and in March 1910 – after a decade's vacancy – the appointment was made of C. R. Peers, Secretary to the Society of Antiquaries and an assistant commissioner in the Hertfordshire inquiry. The Hertfordshire report sought to give a further boost to activity by deploring the state of many of the monuments it surveyed, noting that the work of the Royal Commission would probably not be completed for another twenty years, and hinting at the need for legislative intervention to prevent further decay in the interim. Peers seconded this recommendation when he reported officially on his first year's activities in March 1911.[80] However, neither Harcourt nor his successor at the head of the Office of Works, Lord Beauchamp, took any further action, and there was no sign of legislative activity until the long-awaited external stimulus appeared in the autumn of 1911, the Tattershall Castle affair.

Tattershall Castle is an unusual brick keep, dating from the mid-fifteenth century, which looms alarmingly out of the Lincolnshire Fens in a remote location. Not quite a castle but not yet a country house, Tattershall had retained something of the character of a residence but was not convertible to modern residential purposes; it had not been lived in since 1693, had become semi-ruinous and was sold by Lord Fortescue early in 1910 to a speculator, T. H. Hooley, as an incidental to an agricultural estate. The estate was useful, the castle not, but it had a special appeal to antiquarians: it was both a medieval castle and a great manor house; it was fifteenth century, thus not High Gothic but not contaminated with the foreign Renaissance either; for Goths and patriots of all stripes, there was the added attraction that Pugin had modelled the fireplaces in the Houses of Parliament on its set of four chimneypieces. Whereas thirty years earlier, its historic value might have counted for naught against its low economic value, in the early twentieth century the antiques market bid to bring the two values together. The castle was offered separately in 1910 to a former Mayor of Nottingham, Albert Ball, as 'an interesting speculation' priced at £1,125. Ball in turn offered it for £2,000 to the National Trust – contending that 'the land, with the custodian's house and the bricks of the Castle, was worth £2,000 to an ordinary speculator, quite apart from any question of historic value' – but the Trust, after some dithering, declined. Ball concluded their negotiations, 'I have had a very considerable sum offered for the mantelpieces, and I am sure I should get more for them if I break them up, which is my intention unless I dispose of [the castle]'. This appears to have been a bluff, for, seeing no opportunity for profit, Ball withdrew from the purchase and by May 1911 the castle was in the hands of Hooley's creditor, the Capital & Counties Bank. After unsuccessfully offering the castle again to the Trust – now for £3,000 – the bank finally began to realize its value by selling the chimneypieces separately to an art dealer, who planned to rip them out, transport them down to London and then export them to America.

Early in September, a Lincolnshire antiquarian, Colonel Knollys, discovered the chimneypieces 'in actual process of being prised out . . . We know not whether to some millionaire's hotch-potch of curios in America or to some dealer's warehouse in England.' He and

**THE WRECKERS' WORK AT TATTERSHALL CASTLE**
The gaping masonry hole in the Castle walls where one of the mantelpieces was originally fixed.

47   The passion of the Tattershall chimneypieces: reported missing in September 1911.

Canon Rawnsley of the National Trust kicked up a fuss in *The Times*, appealing to benefactors to come forward and save the precious relics. The chief effect of this was to draw out of the woodwork various unsavoury intermediaries offering the chimneypieces and the castle to the Trust at ever higher prices. As the antiquarians' rhetoric escalated, so did the price, reaching £5,000 for castle and chimneypieces together by 14 September. The Trust was shocked to discover that the castle was worth far more to private buyers, in pieces, than to the general public, as a heritage object, intact. Its appeal for £4,800 raised the princely sum of £600, £500 of which came from a single donor, and the campaign was abandoned. It was at this point that the chimneypieces, badly damaged by their removal, were loaded on to steam-wagons by contractors – heckled by 'indignant spectators' – and carried by road down to London, where they were stored awaiting the dealer's instructions. At the same time the bank quietly sold the castle to yet another dealer for £2,250, reportedly also for export to America.

As soon as press discussion of the affair died down, Lord Curzon began to take an interest. He rather prided himself as a trustee for the public in such matters, and as a shrewd businessman, as well. In late October he took the train up to Tattershall, looked around and immediately made an offer for the castle; within a few days, the castle was his at a cost of £2,750, leaving the dealer with £500 profit for a few weeks' work. Appealing privately to his wealthy friends, he then began to raise money to buy back the chimneypieces, and with help principally from Lord Iveagh, Lord Brownlow, Alfred Shuttleworth, Archibald Weigall and Walter Morrison, he was able by May 1912 to conclude the deal at £5,155, a neat profit of some thousands of pounds for the dealers through whose hands the chimneypieces had passed. Thus, a package which the National Trust had declined for £2,000 a few years earlier had been acquired for £8,000. The chimneypieces were restored with much ceremony in June 1912 and, reconstructed sensitively by the SPAB's William Weir, the whole

48   Tattershall Castle restored by Lord Curzon, here acting as tour guide (centre, with hand raised).

castle was opened to the public in June 1914; it was ultimately conveyed to the National Trust in Curzon's will.[81]

Though it is sometimes portrayed as a moment of national revelation, the halt on the road to Philistia, the Tattershall Castle affair's real import was profoundly mixed.[82] *The Times*'s correspondents did indeed report the passion of the Tattershall chimneypieces with implicitly religious imagery, 'the victims . . . prostrate on the ground', hauled over 'a rough road', stowed 'in an obscure yard behind a London public house', then miraculously resurrected and restored by near-divine intervention. For some aesthetic Tories, the chimneypieces could now be hailed as a national treasure; their loss 'must needs wring the heart of any Englishman who in these days, when so much that is honoured is being overthrown, prizes the monumental record of a nobler time', as Colonel Knollys bitterly observed.[83] But by the same token, the hearts of other Englishmen – who were in fact doing the overthrowing – must needs be colder to what they did not see as a nobler time. *The Times*'s Liberal counterparts were relatively unimpressed by the whole business: 'And so the relics must go,' philosophized the *Westminster Gazette* after the National Trust appeal collapsed, 'We do not know that very much regret need be occasioned by this result.'[84] And Tory papers such as the *Standard*, catering to a more conventional middle-class audience, hardly mentioned the affair at all, preferring to lend space to the campaign for more suburban post-offices.[85] It was the depth of public indifference – evident in the paltry response to the Trust's appeal – that was most fully revealed by what preservationists called the 'Tattershall Vandalism'.

For scholars and preservationists at the SPAB and National Trust, already committed to the national importance of castles and mantel-pieces, the lesson of the Vandalism was clear: public opinion and private greed had both to be combatted by legislation. 'We ought,' wrote the Trust's Robert Hunter to Rawnsley in the midst of the scandal, 'to bend our energies to getting an alteration in the law which shall prevent this sort of thing in future.' A conference of interested bodies was called in December 1911, and it was agreed that Lord Eversley of the CPS[86] would introduce a bill in the new year's session to equip the Office of Works with an advisory board of antiquaries, which could give prudent advice on the protection and compulsory purchase of ancient monuments.[87]

In scholarly meetings and even in the pages of *The Times*, preservationism could be discussed as a technical matter and kept out of politics. Once it entered wider debate in Parliament, however, the emerging consensus among scholarly and amenity groups hit stormy waters. Liberals had to decide whether they (and their voters) cared enough about castles to extend legislative protection – or perhaps whether legislative control over historic buildings was worthwhile simply as a stroke against the landowners, as the *Westminster Gazette* seemed to conclude in its coverage of the Vandalism.[88] Tories had to decide whether they cared enough about castles to accept the infringements on private property – and more strokes against the land – that such legislation would entail.

Not the one but a little shower of bills was introduced in the months following the Vandalism. They ranged from Eversley's consensus bill, relying heavily on the probity of the experts, to a bill prepared by the Office of Works, which gave more autonomy to that body, to a sweeping measure of public control introduced by the New Liberal Noel Buxton.[89] They were all referred to a joint Select Committee of the two houses, where a wider spectrum of opinion still was canvassed and more mutual suspicion was fostered.

On the one hand, the scholars and preservationists propounded their official line about the sanctity of ancient buildings and the need to prevent any meddling with them, even the repair of a tower or the knocking down of an interior wall – to the horror of the peers on the committee, dwellers in such buildings. The scholars wanted the Office of Works, properly advised, to have the power to 'schedule' important buildings and then to prevent alterations, restorations or sales of scheduled buildings without first entitling the State to purchase them. On the other hand, a phalanx of these peers, led by the Duke of Rutland and the Marquess of Salisbury, put up a stiff resistance to what Rutland called 'the artistic element in the country', and 'those who are concerned in preserving for the benefit of themselves places, pictures, and articles of artistic value at the expense of the owners thereof'. Rutland blamed 'recent legislation and the fear of future legislation' for sales such as that of Tattershall, denounced the 'system of meddling with and spying into every one's private affairs which is just now in vogue' and rejected any attempt to extend this system 'under the cloak of the preservation of ancient monuments'. It was, he fumed, 'a piece of massive impudence . . . Fancy my not being allowed to make a necessary alteration at Haddon without first obtaining the leave of some inspector . . . !'[90] Unbeknownst to Rutland's auditors, 'necessary alterations' were indeed afoot, as his heir had recently hatched a plan to convert Haddon from tourist resort to private home. Rutland and Salisbury's alarm at the extension of Liberal legislation to their doorsteps was echoed from other quarters, normally preservationist but also politically conservative: the architectural historians J. A. Gotch and Reginald Blomfield, for instance, who worried that 'a tendency to sentimentalism' about old buildings was more dangerous than vandalism.[91]

Between these two extremes Lord Beauchamp, the First Commissioner of Works, tried to steer some bill – any bill – through both Houses. All of the acknowledged 'experts', and now some of his own civil servants (led by Peers, the expert-turned-Inspector), were urging him to take compulsory powers of preservation and/or purchase over any number of monuments identified as of national importance by the Royal Commission on Historical Monuments. Few of his Liberal colleagues in either House were much interested in this cause one way or the other; Beauchamp himself was highly unusual, as a Liberal landowner, as an aesthetic aristocrat and as a homosexual of tender sensibility so much mistrusted by some of his peers that his brother-in-law the Duke of Westminster would later hound him out of the country. As for the Tories, Rutland and Salisbury were successfully making the equation between legislation for ancient monuments and other acts of Liberal confiscation. Beauchamp's difficulty was exemplified by the ambivalent position of Lord Curzon.

As the private protector of Tattershall Castle, Curzon fancied himself as the champion of ancient buildings, castles, country houses, manor houses, bridges, market crosses, cottages, barns – the lot. He claimed to regard them as 'part of the heritage of the nation, because every citizen feels an interest in them', and owners as 'in a broad sense . . . trustees to the nation at large'. He rebuked Beauchamp for not taking the subject as seriously as it deserved. But, as a prominent Tory, he was unable and unwilling to join the Liberal drive to State control. He believed implicitly – blindly – in the good faith of private owners. He was happy for the State to play an educational role, scheduling and thus publicizing ancient monuments, but he opposed the compulsory purchase of ancient monuments, defended the owner's right to resist scheduling, and opposed any regulation at all of 'dwelling-houses' such as Tattershall (thanks to his restoration) was about to become. In this way he assisted Rutland and Salisbury's dismantling of the government bill, while inveighing all the while against the 'indifference, carelessness, vandalism, and the heedless utilitarianism of our day'.[92]

The resulting Ancient Monuments Act 1913 did little more than confirm and accelerate the laborious 'stocktaking' function of the Royal Commission. It established an advisory board to the Office of Works which could schedule ancient and historical monuments even if the Royal Commission had not yet reported on them. But the impact of this scheduling was minimal. Owners were required to give notice of their intention to demolish or alter scheduled monuments, but they did not then have to receive permission from the Office of Works to do so. If government wished to prevent demolition or alteration, or to stop neglect, it could issue a Preservation Order temporarily extending government protection; that Preservation Order had then to be confirmed by Parliament and compensation be paid to the owner that was tantamount to purchase at full market value. Dwelling-houses – including all country houses and intact castles of any age – were absolutely excluded from the working of the Act.

Like the Tattershall Vandalism that preceded it, the 1913 Act was a highly ambiguous achievement for historic preservation. On the one hand, it established the principle of a national interest in all historic buildings – not just prehistoric monuments – and provided an official foothold for experts and antiquaries in the form of the advisory board and the Office of Works' Inspectorate. Forced to choose between the destruction of historical buildings and some kind of legislative interference, some Tory aesthetes were now ready to choose the latter. On the other hand, the Act was besmirched by its association with confiscatory legislation. Some of the proposals mooted in 1912–13 were the most draconian of any enacted before the 1960s. As with the Liberal Ancient Monuments Act of 1882, the 1913 Act was followed by two decades of quiescence. No new bill of any kind was introduced in the Commons before 1930. No real advance in the control of historic buildings was seriously considered until a Socialist government came to power after the Second World War. The surviving elements of compulsion in the 1913 Act – such as Preservation Orders – became dead letters.

It is doubtful, therefore, whether the panic over the fate of the built heritage triggered by Liberal anti-landlordism advanced or retarded the spread of ideas of heritage. Some aesthetes in both parties, as well as the antiquarian establishment, now saw the need for the public to take over those responsibilities for the heritage that were formerly the province of private owners. But did either the public or private owners recognize the same need? For the public, the net effect of the Edwardian crisis may well have been further to advance hostility to high – and especially aristocratic – culture in all its aspects. One of the shrewder advocates of preservation, Gerard Baldwin Brown, objected to 'the perfervid zeal of some eloquent lovers of monuments' as distancing their cause from the general public; he and Hunter had tried in vain to prevent Rawnsley's 'perfervid zeal' from queering the

pitch at the time of the Tattershall Vandalism. 'The ordinary citizen,'
Brown appreciated, 'held up to obloquy as a utilitarian, has stiffened
his back and tries to keep the champion of amenity at a distance.'[93] For
landowners, the defence of private property and the protection of
material assets from expropriation became the all-important consideration. They welcomed the attention of an aesthetic minority, willing to
bid up the prices of assets for sale, but not the claims made on behalf
of the majority to some transcendental 'national' value. By 1914, ideas
of heritage had certainly been refined, but not very well diffused, and
the progress made towards preserving the heritage thus defined was
very limited indeed.

49   Title page to W. T. Stead's 'The Splendid Paupers', the Christmas 1894 number of the *Review of Reviews*: Ping Ying Yaloo, the Mandarin millionaire, supplants the Duke of Devonshire at Chatsworth.

CHAPTER 5

# 'Splendid Paupers': The Closing of the Country House

At Christmas 1894, the popular journalist W. T. Stead published as a special number of his monthly, *The Review of Reviews*, a fable of his own writing entitled 'The Splendid Paupers: A Tale of the Coming Plutocracy'. Like his previous Christmas annuals, 'The Splendid Paupers' sought to synthesize some of the key events of the preceding year into a parable about the condition of England that reflected Stead's idiosyncratic world-view. In Stead's judgement, 1894 had been the year of 'death duties, bimetallism, agricultural depression, and the war in the Orient', and what these added up to in his imagination was a tale of the downfall of the landed aristocracy and its replacement by a plutocracy compounded of American scientists, Jewish manufacturers and Chinese financiers.

Although on the surface 'The Splendid Paupers' appears to be a straightforwardly reactionary tale of virtuous but penurious Old England swamped by corrupt and super-rich aliens, Stead's peculiar brand of mid-Victorian Radicalism – in 1894 already rather dated – gave it some interesting twists. The heroes are Edward Wilkes, a Radical who comes to see the virtues of the landed aristocracy, and his wife Lady Aenid Belsover, heiress to an impoverished estate but also a liberated woman who cycles and studies the social question. Together they transform Lady Aenid's collapsing estate into 'a self-protecting cooperative association that would have all the benefits of socialism and all the advantages of feudalism'. Stead explicitly treats this resolution as a restoration of the Olden Time: 'We shall bring it back,' exults Lady Aenid, 'the masques and music and all the bright revelry of the Elizabethan age.' But, reminds Wilkes, 'it will be in the future as it has been in the past; not by isolation, nor by insistence on caste distinctions, but rather by the hearty union between the English democracy and its natural leaders.'[1]

Consistent with this celebration of the Olden Time, the physical symbols of virtue in 'The Splendid Paupers' are two mansions of England in Derbyshire: a barely disguised Bolsover Castle, the Elizabethan house destroyed (like the Olden Time itself) by the cannon of the Civil War, and Haddon Hall, 'that flower of English history and romance'.[2] Literally and emblematically they stand on either side of Chatsworth, which in some ways stood as a symbol of what had gone wrong with the English aristocracy, and in 'The Splendid Paupers' is bought up, walled off and converted into a Chinese palace by Ping Ying Yaloo, the soulless Mandarin millionaire. The fate of Chatsworth introduces a subsidiary theme of the book, an echo of the Duke of Devonshire's complaint against the Harcourt death duties that they were choking off what charity and benevolence remained possible to the aristocracy after the agricultural depression – and, specifically, the generosity with which owners had thrown open their stately homes to visits by the general public.

After criticism from the Radical press, Stead admitted that – like some of the participants in the death duties debates – he had exaggerated the extent of *noblesse oblige* as currently practised, but explained that his purpose had been to rouse the aristocracy to do its duty 'by a picture of their order as it ought to be'.[3] In the spirit of social science that was another aspect of his complicated personality, he then launched an enquiry in the *Review of Reviews* into the status of the country house, asking his readers and correspondents two questions:

> 1.   Has the agricultural depression produced in your neighbourhood any change in the way in which the country houses of the landed aristocracy have been kept up?

> 2.   Do the landed proprietors in your neighbourhood permit the public access to their parks, picture galleries, treasure-houses, etc., regarding themselves, in short, as if they held them as trustees for the public?[4]

The results of this enquiry, which he published over several months in the *Review*, gave a mixed and not ultimately very optimistic picture.[5] Had Stead lived to repeat his experiment twenty years later – in fact he went down with the Titanic in 1912 – he would have found the results gloomier still.

Stead's survey, and the array of sources employed in chapter 2 to show how the country house opened to the masses before the agricultural depression, can together give a more complete picture of how far and why the country house closed during and after the depression.

ALNWICK.

EATON.

In Liquidation. **THE** *NOVEMBER 25th, 1905.*

# BRITISH ARISTOCRACY

## CATALOGUE OF

# CASTLES, ESTATES

### AND OTHER EFFECTS.

## To be Sold by Private Treaty

WITH IMMEDIATE POSSESSION OR FOR FUTURE DELIVERY.

# GLOGOUL & FAULMANN,

### ESTATE AGENTS,

## PALL MALL, S.W.

CHATSWORTH.

WARWICK

WHAT WE ARE COMING TO: A SALE CATALOGUE OF A.D. 1905.

50 Frontispiece to 'The Splendid Paupers': W.T. Stead's dismal forecast of the fate of the stately homes of England, looking forward ten years from 1894.

They will illustrate vividly and concretely how the mid-Victorian
consensus over the national and historical significance of the country
house splintered and gave way under political and economic pressures.
Country-house visiting did not come to an end by 1914, but its
prevalence and meaning changed: like ideas of heritage generally,
country-house visiting became more refined and aesthetic, but also
more controversial. The closure of houses could provoke bitterness,
sometimes violence; the houses that remained open made a more
pointed statement to a better-defined audience.

## Restriction, Riot and Resentment

There is little doubt that country-house visiting was at an historic peak
in the 1870s, just as the agricultural depression began to bite. The
mobility given by railways, new opportunities for leisure given at least
to the middling classes by improved living standards, and the determination of owners to demonstrate benevolence combined to maintain
both demand and supply. The railway was, of course, also enhancing
the country house's value to its owner – for weekending, or sporadic
year-round rather than purely seasonal use – but this does not seem to
have restricted visitors' access yet. As owners were using the railway to
holiday further afield – Scotland, the Continent – 'the finest places in
England', one noble aesthete noted in 1872, 'are left to solitude,
tourists, and the charge of a housekeeper.'[6]

Nevertheless, the sheer scale of tourism at the great show-houses –
some dozen of which were drawing over 10,000 visitors a year, and
probably dozens more with similar numbers admitted to parks and
gardens[7] – was already proving a financial and logistical burden. When
the 6th Duke of Devonshire died in 1858, his more retiring heir
reversed an earlier decision to close Chatsworth to the public, but was
anxious to find a way to simplify and economize the opening, perhaps
by contracting the management to his head gardeners, funding the
extra staff wages from tips; certainly, urged Sarah Paxton, his agent's
wife, 'I should never think of the Duke being charged with any
expence in showing the [gardens] again – and the same thing to apply
to the House.'[8]

The shy but proud 7th Duke would not, however, stoop to charging the tourists. Of all the country houses then open to the public,
only a handful had adopted that course, partly (as at Eaton) to manage
the numbers, with the proceeds donated to charity. Yet twenty-five
years later, when the agricultural depression was in full swing, the 7th
Duke of Devonshire and others in similar situations were forced to

consider following suit. At the end of an exhausting summer marshalling tourists in 1883, the Head Gardener Thomas Speed circularized his colleagues at other great houses to ask what arrangements they made for controlling numbers and expenses.

The answers he received – mostly from the servants of enormously wealthy peers – show a system under strain but not yet cracking. Blenheim, Eaton, Alton Towers and the Marquess of Exeter's Elizabethan prodigy house, Burghley, all charged a shilling a head.[9] Eaton gave reduced rates to excursionists and visitors pleading poverty. Other custodians had not yet moved to charging, but were evidently casting about, like Speed, for some excuse to do so. To Lord Stamford's pleasure gardens at Enville Hall, Staffordshire, large crowds were flocking for a stroll through the vast conservatory, around the lake and amongst the Gothick follies, cascades and fountains – said to be visible from Wolverhampton – that dotted the grounds. A deal of management was required, said the gardener:

51   A system under strain: George Du Maurier satirizes late-Victorian country-house visiting, servants and visitors equally at a loss.

PROFESSIONAL BEAUTIES OF THE PAST

HOUSEKEEPER (*showing visitors over historic mansion*). — "This is the portrait of Queen Catherine of Medici — sister to the *Venus* of that name. . . ."

I place a man at the entrance and he admits all who come. We do not allow any bottles or baskets to be taken in the grounds. They can be left at the gate. All parties are requested not to walk on the grass. I have a few men about the grounds just to see that parties are behaving themselves . . . We do not allow any pic-nics or any games to be carried on inside the grounds only to walk quietly round.[10]

At Belvoir,

the increased facilities offered by Railways bring a great invasion of visitors and I am sorry to say that no regulations exist to meet such circumstances . . . Should the Duke take up his residence at the Castle in the summer time he would find it annoying to have people all over the place.

A nominal charge of twopence had been attached to the gardens, but 'people are at liberty to take or leave these tickets'.[11] Woburn, too, had tickets as a means of control – they were compulsory, but free.[12]

In the end, Speed and his master, agent Gilson Martin, decided against charging. They did try to tighten up the regulations, so as to keep the size of parties down and exclude school parties altogether; there were no Sunday openings as there had been in the 6th Duke's time; but in other respects, a visitor reported in 1891, it remained the show-house it had been fifty years before:

It is odd to read in old books how the visitor was led, precisely as he is still led, from the ducal gates to the porch of the entrance-hall, and how he was then requested to tarry a while, until the house-keeper had been persuaded either to offer her services to the stranger or find a capable deputy for the task of cicerone.[13]

Picnicking in the park was still permitted, and the American million-aire Andrew Carnegie found 'crowds of Manchester and Birmingham workers' there, goggling at sights that Carnegie himself felt were 'too modern'.[14]

Possibly Speed was dissuaded from charging by the advice he received from his old friend Stevens, Head Gardener at Trentham, the Duke of Sutherland's estate in Staffordshire. Until 1877, the gardens had been shown free of charge, but then the Duke on a visit to his sister the Duchess of Westminster learned about the charging system at Eaton, which he promptly installed at Trentham, 'with the result,' said Stevens, that the charging cut off almost entirely the respectable labouring classes from seeing the gardens – and only a comparatively few people came to see the gardens after it was known that a charge was being made – except in large bodies. The representatives of these large parties generally came to me as a deputation – to make terms which they could meet – and if they could not see the gardens at a *small* rate per head – they could not pay and merely went to the Park. Parsons, and other good people, taking an interest in various charitable societies, used to besiege me, begging admission for a poor school – choir – teachers – etc. etc. – and altogether the plan of charging was a nuisance and made no money for which it was worth while sacrificing a noble Duke's repute for generosity and good feeling towards the masses.

This year we have *returned* to the *old lines* again . . . and no poor respectable body need now peer through the garden gates, longing for a peep inside which his means cannot commend.

Those who could afford it left a contribution which in any case 'pays all expenses incurred in showing the gardens'. Then, as an after-thought, the Duke of Sutherland's gardener tipped the Duke of Devonshire a wink:

Of course, if a nobleman likes to set up a penny or a shilling peep show – he has a perfect right to do so – But after all the 'penny a peep' dodge cannot be good for our good old aristocracy even although it be covered by the graceful idea of '*money devoted to the use of Hospitals*' – and my advice to you is not to promote the plan of having people in gold buttons to show your gardens . . . as to the interests of our good old families – I need not coach you in what direction their interests lay – but certainly not in taking money over the turnstyle . . . I have added this postscript of *opinion* for **your** *enlightenment*!!! As living in the Hills as *you do* – you may not be able to recognize those delicate undercurrents of human feeling in the masses . . .

Message received. There was to be no charging at Chatsworth, only, as at Trentham, tips to servants and gardeners – so that the 8th Duke was still in a position of advantage when, in 1894, he claimed a right to tax relief in return for his benevolence.[15]

The dukes of Westminster and Sutherland had in fact several good reasons to keep their gates as open as possible – they were both rich beyond the dreams of avarice; they had many houses and did not have to live at Trentham or Chatsworth in the summer; and, in 1883, they

were both still Liberals, pledged politically to maintaining good relations with nearby urban electorates. Rich Tories such as the Duke of
Rutland could preserve traditional hospitality at Haddon and Belvoir,
but poorer Tories – in the 1880s, the great bulk of country-house
owners – had less reason and ability to accommodate hordes of
trippers, or indeed any visitors at all. Already by 1883, the neo-Gothic
monstrosity at Alton Towers had closed, though the more popular
gardens remained open, and one of the most celebrated of all show-
places, the Olden Time shrine at Knole, had also been closed by its
hard-hit master, Lord Sackville – with fateful and particularly revealing
consequences.

For decades, access to Knole had been particularly generous, as the
estate was almost in abeyance. The male line of the Sackvilles had died
out in 1843 and the last Duke of Dorset's co-heiresses, both married
to other peers, left their Knole estate pretty much to the tourists until
the 1860s. In 1864, to secure the estate's future, the younger sister,
Countess De La Warr, accepted in her own right the new peerage of
Buckhurst which was to pass with the Sackville estates to a younger
son. When her husband died in 1869, the eldest son naturally inherited
as 6th Earl De La Warr, seated at nearby Buckhurst Park, and when
the old Countess died in 1870, the second son accordingly inherited as
2nd Lord Buckhurst, seated at Knole. Alas for best-laid plans, only
three years later the 6th Earl De La Warr died childless, giving his
brother Buckhurst the chance to re-amalgamate titles and estates,
manifestly against their mother's desire. At this point the three other
brothers stepped in; all felt they had a moral and legal right to inherit,
and all had some expectations – Mortimer as the next senior in age,
Lionel as the childless Mortimer's heir presumptive and William as the
only one of the younger brothers with heirs of his own. After a
vicious legal tussle that reached the House of Lords and was not finally
decided until 1877, Mortimer was confirmed in the Knole and other
Sackville estates, but not in the Buckhurst title; in 1876 he was
compensated for this, too, with the new creation of the Barony of
Sackville.[16]

Knole itself suffered badly from this internecine struggle. Buckhurst
had, during his brief tenancy, sold off bits and pieces of its contents,
which Mortimer then tried to retrieve. He had also kept the house
open in the 1873 season, when his tenancy was already disputed.
Mortimer won occupancy of the house in the autumn of that year,
and re-opened to the public as normal in 1874; but, for one reason or
another, he was discontented. It may have been out of a desire to
enjoy fully the fruits for which he had struggled; it may have been

resentment at the lordly way in which Buckhurst had pretended to carry on the Knole tradition;[17] or it may have been (as many contemporaries claimed) that Mortimer was just a particularly sour and stuck-up old Tory who hated the dirty and ungrateful *canaille*. From whatever motive, he shut up the house in October 1874 and refused thereafter to show it to tourists. His publicly stated reason was a simple defence of private property:

> people strayed away from their parties, broke into our rooms, tore the fringe off the chairs and couches, and did all manner of things, whereupon I felt obliged to shut up the place; and then the 'row' began.[18]

And what a row![19] At first, resentment at Sackville's high-handedness was muted and confined to Sevenoaks, the thriving market town that bordered Knole Park and which had learned to depend on the hordes of visitors from London and nearby spas. If the house was closed, the park still remained open and probably much of the tourist trade survived, though Sackville's brooding presence was not very welcoming. The antiquarian Allan Fea remembered, years later, a visit to Knole Park at about this time, when

> in wandering around the immense extent of [Knole's] outer walls, I ventured to trespass through a courtyard entrance, and while gazing, rapture-bound, upon the endless gable ends and mullioned windows, a casement in one of the latter flew open, and his Sackville lordship himself stood there shaking his fist and demanding an immediate exit. This I made in double quick time, for the first Sackville Baron had a feudal manner that was almost suggestive of dangling from the battlements . . .[20]

One by one, Sackville stopped up the little privileges that helped to grease relations between a town and its chief landowner. The keys to private gates which had been traditionally held by tradesmen and local eminences were withdrawn; Sackville drew the Local Board into litigation over drainage; the public's right to stray from the footpaths on to lesser tracks around the park was brought to an end.[21]

Finally, open warfare was joined in the summer of 1883, when Sackville shut off the main right-of-way, a bridle-path through the park, as well. At first the pretext was a customary one, the protection of the deer in the mating season, but when in the autumn he was politely requested by the Local Board to re-open the bridle-path Sackville replied that the public had been abusing its privileges by roaming about the park, 'frightening the deer, and defying the keepers', and that he had decided to bar them absolutely.[22] At this stage, a whole host of resentments against Sackville poured out. Nearly every inhabitant of Sevenoaks was discommoded by the deprivation of eastwards access out of the town across Knole Park. The shopkeepers, publicans and other tradesmen were nearly in despair at the loss of tourist custom. 'The churlishness of the Lord of Knole,' wrote the popular antiquarian Edward Walford in a local Radical paper,

> is injuring the town of Sevenoaks, which has no trade or manufac-
> tures to fall back upon. Its inns and hotels are only half full, and lack
> those customers who used to come over on pleasure parties from
> Tunbridge Wells and Maidstone. Its shopkeepers have been obliged
> to reduce their stock-in-trade; and the very local 'Guide' itself has
> been allowed to go out of print. In fact, the quiet town of
> Sevenoaks is in a very fair way to decay, thanks to the shutting up
> of Knole.[23]

Discontent was not confined to local Radicals and interested parties. Sackville had further isolated himself with a deliberate piece of rude-ness to 'a gentleman of high university and literary standing', refusing him permission to view a portrait of Dr Johnson for scholarly pur-poses; this churlish behaviour bothered even Tory papers, who approved his exclusion of the 'ill-bred cockneys of the lower orders', but wondered 'why should Lord Sackville punish all the upper and middle classes on account of [their] misdeeds'. Some days later, at Sevenoaks's traditional Bonfire Night procession, the locals pro-nounced their verdict with

> a *representation* of the Bridle path through Knole Park, with a rough
> drawing of Knole House, surmounted by a pig [and] a cleverly
> sketched portrait, over which were the words, 'Dr. Johnson', and
> underneath, 'Lent from Knole House' . . . placed back to back in a
> van . . .[24]

Matters rested there over the winter, but antagonism burst out again with renewed vigour in the spring. Sackville's selfishness now became nearly a national issue. Anti-aristocratic feeling was at one of its occasional peaks, as the Third Reform Act – enfranchising large portions of the rural population – passed through both Houses of Parliament against stiff Tory opposition. Sevenoaks stood to gain more new voters than virtually any other district in the county, and a town already narrowly balanced between the two parties looked set to go Liberal. Hoping to make some party capital out of the Knole Park issue, Sevenoaks Liberals agitated against the issue on the Local Board and then – in association with the Commons Preservation Society – called a public meeting for the evening of 18 June 1884 to assert the public's right-of-way through the park. This meeting, chaired by Major German, a magistrate and leading Sevenoaks Liberal, attracted a crowd of over five hundred to a marquee erected behind the Rose and Crown public house. A Knole servant present testified later that the language used against his master was 'worse than you would hear in the slums of London'. The CPS speaker urged upon the assembled townsmen the Society's favoured direct-action tactics, and German was reported to have agreed that the public had a right to remove the posts and chains blocking the bridle-path as a means of testing the legality of the right-of-way. With this encouragement, the crowd rose when the meeting adjourned, swept through Sevenoaks, swelling to some thousand or more, and closed in on the gate in question, breaking the chains and pulling up the posts. The mob then moved through the park to the front entrance of the house, where the posts and chains were deposited. Unsure what move to make next, the protesters milled about outside the house, hammering on the knocker, singing the National Anthem and 'Rule Britannia' and allegedly shouting, 'Bring him out, and let's hang him!' Eventually they moved on to knock down another gate, then returned to town, and ended the evening outside Maywood, Major German's house, not to hang but to serenade him.[25]

The 'Knole Disturbances' reverberated in one way or another throughout the summer. A second mob gathered on the next night and destroyed another fence in the park, and on the third night shouts of 'Bring him out and murder him!' were again reported by Sackville on his front doorstep. County police were then posted in Sevenoaks and the violence subsided. Sackville was by now thoroughly shaken – 'We certainly cannot live here under the present conditions', he admitted – but he was not driven by events to learn diplomacy. He gave a widely reprinted interview excoriating the Liberal Home Secretary, Sir William Harcourt, for denying him Metropolitan Police protection and for declining to prosecute Major German for inciting to riot.[26] He initiated his own civil action against German and contested the claim to the right-of-way. In the end, however, he had to concede the latter. The whole town celebrated at their next Bonfire Night procession:

Placed on a car was a coffin, which was also turfed, the representation of a headstone bearing the following inscription – 'In memory of the Knole Park Obstructions removed June 18th, 1884, taken to Knole House, and there left to be for ever with the Lorde.' The representation of the footstone bare the letters K.P.O. (Knole Park Obstruction) and skull and cross-bones . . . Two of the most prominent characters in the procession were 'The Priest' . . . and the 'Evil One' . . . 'The Priest' and the 'Evil one' mounted the funereal car, and arranged themselves one each side of the coffin, amid bursts of laughter from the on-lookers.[27]

But of course Sackville was not obliged to re-open the house, and its doors remained barred to the public until after his death in 1888.

The Knole Disturbances were fully discussed in the London papers. They clearly demonstrated how much landed power and privilege rested on such informal arrangements as public access to houses and parks, and, therefore, how power and privilege could be challenged when such courtesies could not or would not be sustained. If the landlords failed to act as 'trustees' for their land and treasures, then the people would have to reclaim them. The journalist Walford had made this claim explicit:

> Like its neighbour and only rival, Penshurst, it belongs to the history of our country – in other words, to Englishmen in general. Its present legal owner is Lord Sackville; but, like the owners of other entailed estates, he is only a trustee.

Other Radicals unearthed an old grievance against the Knole estate, that it had been left by its owners in the Olden Time to the benefit of the 'poor of Surrey', but then arbitrarily granted by James I to his favourite Thomas Sackville.[28] On the other side, while some of the society papers cheered Sackville on for resisting 'agitators' and their 'poisonous and revolutionary doctrines',[29] responsible Tories uneasily distanced themselves from their reckless peer. Tory leaders stood aloof from his vendetta against Harcourt: 'In a small country with thirty million inhabitants,' concluded the *Sevenoaks Chronicle*, a Conservative organ, 'the owner of uncultivated land five miles in circumference, must recognise his duties to the community as well as to himself.' His conduct was contrasted with that of Lord Stanhope of nearby Chevening, who had negotiated reasonably about rights-of-way and opened Chevening gardens to the public in the summer.[30]

The Knole Disturbances were extraordinary, largely due to Sackville's extraordinary incivility. But the tension between local populations, used to enjoying parks, grounds and houses as their own, and landlords with declining funds of money and patience to underpin these practices was increasingly widespread. Particularly in the south-

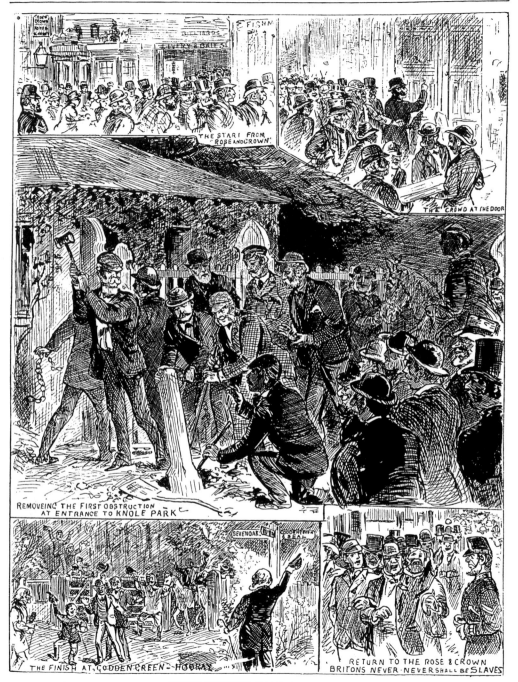

REMOVING OBSTRUCTIONS AT KNOLE PARK   *See page 7.)*

52   The 'Knole Disturbances' illustrated by the *Penny Pictorial News*, 28 June 1884.

east of England, where ramblers and trippers were everywhere and landed hardship worst, public access to country houses and parks became a fraught issue in the 1880s and 1890s. Stead found in his 1895 survey that relations had almost completely broken down in this part of the world:

> The landed proprietors in this neighbourhood prevent public access to their parks, treasure-houses, historical buildings, collections of art and curios, in a general way . . . it cannot be said that any one acts generally as if he considered himself trustee for the public . . . [Herts.]

> They permit access to parks only where public right of way exists . . . The idea of *noblesse oblige* is . . . a fiction practically . . . Trespassers are warned in all directions, and old footpaths are constantly in danger of being closed . . . [Kent]

> On the whole, the landed proprietors act as trustees, who do not wish to surfeit the beneficiaries of the trust with too much of their good things, and the average beanfeaster from London and other large towns seems bent on showing that even the narrow limits of privilege he enjoys in that direction you indicate are too much for him . . . [Sussex]

> To the public as such, no, thank goodness . . . [Hants.][31]

Many of these correspondents felt that restriction of access was quite justified, given the misbehaviour of the humble tourist and the vastly increased numbers made possible by rail travel. But the problem cannot be reduced to one of crowd-management: bigger issues were at stake and deeper emotions evoked. Organizations such as the CPS and Radical ramblers such as Howard Evans practically encouraged trespassing as a point of principle.[32] Landlords responded with acerbity. George Vansittart of Bisham Abbey on the Thames used to police his many miles of woods personally to warn off trippers, on whom he vented his 'peppery and ill-controlled temper'.[33] On the same stretch of the river in 1893, at Cliveden, William Waldorf Astor banned boating parties from landing, erected a stone wall topped with broken glass around his property and earned the epithet 'Walled-Off Astor' from annoyed locals. Ten years later he gave Hever Castle exactly the same treatment 'to mask from public gaze a castle which was historic but long had been a farmhouse to which any courteous stranger might be admitted', and worse:

> He built on to it and altered it and had costly sham antiques made

and then enclosed the whole within high walls and huge electri-cally-operated gates so that when his motor car came, the door opened silently and closed smoothly and swiftly almost upon the back of the car as it entered.[34]

In the North, Stead's correspondents generally agreed, the relatively light impact of the depression on an economy not based on grain eased matters somewhat; access was 'very generous'. However, ticket systems had been introduced to control numbers – as at Alnwick – and many woods had been closed for game preservation and nature con-servation purposes. Whereas parks remained open, houses were gener-ally closed and historical ruins open only for a fee. Furthermore, as George Rowell of Newcastle shrewdly commented, 'The owners of all these places *act* as if they were trustees for the public, but whether they consider themselves as such is another question.'[35]

Public access to country houses and parks was, as earlier in the century, most widely enjoyed in the Midlands. Places such as Trentham, Sandon, Alton Towers, Warwick Castle, Stoneleigh Abbey, Belvoir, Haddon, Chatsworth, Hardwick, Bolsover, Burghley and the Nottinghamshire Dukeries of Welbeck, Thoresby, Clumber and Rufford all remained virtual playgrounds for the masses. But even here ominous signs of change were springing up. In Warwickshire, one correspondent felt there were

> few instances where the public are allowed into the parks of this county . . . It has been the other way about, as public roads across many estates have been closed up, and there has been a continual enclosing of land belonging to the public by the landed proprietors.

In Nottinghamshire, Newstead Abbey, mecca for thousands in the 1860s, was now open only on the most restricted basis and Lord Middleton's Wollaton Park outside Nottingham 'is not open to the public to walk in as it should be'.[36]

Whether the public has access to a park is sometimes quite debat-able – one of Stead's readers wrote that Sir Clifford Constable 'tried to stop access to the beauties of the Greta, but I have gone there whenever I chose'[37] – and the thinness of the evidence makes it hard to quantify. It is easier to be more precise about access to houses, and here the picture is unambiguous. Of the hundred or so houses publi-cized as open to the public in the 1860s and 1870s, about half were closed by 1914, and of those two-thirds before 1900. Whereas in earlier days foreigners often remarked on the openness of country houses, in 1904 the German diplomat Muthesius warned,

> The curious traveller who imagines that by journeying across England he will be able to see the much celebrated English country-houses in their dozens will usually be in for a rude disappointment . . . Special arrangements are necessary if one is to make its acquaintance, as well as good connections to break the spell of its privacy.[38]

All kinds of houses were affected: those of the very rich (Blenheim, Hever, Woburn), those of the comparatively poor (Knebworth, Tottenham Park, Sizergh Castle), houses of the Olden Time (Raby Castle, Speke Hall, Compton Wynyates) and of modern times (Lowther Castle, Alton Towers, The Deepdene), and of course many eighteenth-century houses that were no longer of much interest anyway (Kedleston, West Wycombe, Audley End, etc.). In some cases, a thriving tourist trade was suddenly blighted by a closure, as at Sevenoaks, or Woodstock at Blenheim gates, found by some American tourists just before the First World War to be

> a village of brooding silence, for the shutting of the palace to visitors and its practical disuse of late years has stopped the stream of travel, and all this seems largely to have done away, for the time, with the prosperity of the place.[39]

What specific factors led to these closures is harder to specify. One factor it is possible to reject. The advent of the plutocrat, Stead's great bugbear, affected relatively few. Astor's bad behaviour at Cliveden and Hever attracted a lot of attention – Stead's especially, for Astor had bought the *Pall Mall Gazette* at about the same time he bought Cliveden, and immediately swept away many of the achievements of its former editor, one W. T. Stead – but it is hard to find further examples; only a few cases where plutocrats rented houses from penurious owners and, naturally, no longer admitted the public.[40]

Otherwise, the full gamut of considerations came into play. Hard-pressed owners shed houses in ways that made public visiting difficult or pointless, by letting or stripping them. Some famous collections – the pictures at Leigh Court and Belvedere, the armour at Goodrich Court, the fixtures at Sizergh Castle – were sold. Owners shedding surplus houses re-appropriated remaining ones as homes. Probably, in many cases less publicized than that of Knole, suppressed bitterness against the public came into it. A generational effect was almost certainly operating. Old men upheld the family traditions; when their sons inherited, modern concerns – the fast life, the Smart Set, defiance of the Radicals – supervened. At Belvoir, the ancient 7th Duke of

Rutland kept alive until his death in 1906 the fantasies of Merrie England that had entertained him as Lord John Manners in the 1840s. His granddaughter, Lady Diana Cooper, remembered:

> He loved his tourists. They represented to him England and liberty and the feudal system, and were a link between the nobility and the people. The house was open to them three times a week and on all bank holidays. They would arrive in four-in-hand charabancs from all over the country. Bedrooms and one drawing-room, one study and a dining-room were excluded from their tour. Otherwise, from morning to dark, armies of sightseers tramped through that welcoming house . . . the atmosphere – the smell – was asphyxiating . . . they all brought picnics too and were encouraged to eat and sleep and take their boots off and comb their hair in the garden, on the terraces, all about and everywhere. They paid no admittance . . .

As soon as the 8th Duke inherited, however, 'the old order began to change'. Bathrooms, hot water and heating were installed. Though married to a Lindsay, the new Duke was 'frankly philistine'; he knew about dry-fly fishing but 'very little about the possessions which he inherited'.[41] Visiting continued for a time, but a fee was imposed to improve the clientele, and after the First World War the 9th Duke closed both Belvoir *and* Haddon to tourists. The turn of the generations also changed conditions at mighty Chatsworth, where the forty-year-old 9th Duke inherited in 1908 and wound up the tourist attractions his three predecessors had cultivated for nearly a century. Only very sporadic visiting – and for periods none at all – was possible at Chatsworth until after the Second World War.[42]

Where visiting was permitted to continue, it did so generally on a new basis, consistent with the altered relations between aristocracy and people established towards the end of the century. There was closer regulation and some friction even at those great playgrounds that remained open. In many places numbers were deliberately restricted and a more respectable clientele courted. Everywhere, a visit to a country house took on a more pointed political and social meaning.

## Tourism Refined

The growth of population, the spread of wealth, the expansion of leisure time and the advent of cheap rail-travel should have increased greatly the extent of country-house visiting. The constricted supply of open houses should have put more pressure on those that remained open – and did, in particular ways. Enjoyment of country-house parks

and gardens and ramblers' use of public footpaths undoubtedly intensified from the 1880s onwards, leading on occasion to conflicts over
rights-of-way, especially in the south-east. Fewer of the great show-
houses than of the great parks remained open, however, and where
owners continued to invite thousands of trippers to view their homes
and collections, strains showed.

As the Chatsworth enquiry of 1883 suggests, the great show-places
were anxious to regulate tourism more closely, but not necessarily to
discourage it. Though Chatsworth refrained, most of the more popular houses were charging some kind of regular entrance fee by the turn
of the century. At Eaton, the pioneer of such schemes, efforts were
made to ensure that fees did not discourage the poorer class of tripper.
Discounts on the one shilling fee were offered to excursionists, free
open-days were offered and the visiting schedule was well publicized
in the Cheshire and Lancashire press. Over a thousand visitors could
turn up on Whit Mondays and August Bank Holidays and an annual
peak of some 24,000 visitors was reached in 1901. Yet even Eaton –
purposely maintained by the Duke of Westminster as a place of public
resort – could be affected by the greater ease of use afforded the owner
by the railway. It often happened that the Duke chose to linger at
Eaton through June and postpone the opening season until later in the
summer, and this could cut annual attendances in half. The visiting
peaks came in 1899–1901 after the death of the 1st Duke and before
the marriage of the 2nd Duke. After that date, visiting was again prone
to interruption by the 2nd Duke's unpredictable pattern of summer
residence, falling to around 10,000 just before the war.[43] At Haddon,
a fee was introduced for the first time around the turn of the century
but deliberately pitched low at fourpence, which was thought not to
discourage the working man.[44]

Higher fees were sometimes imposed, not merely to regulate and to
subsidize visiting, but openly to restrict it. Whether intentional or no,
this may have been the effect at Berkeley Castle – widely visited in the
1850s, virtually unknown fifty years later[45] – at Eastnor Castle and at
Penshurst, all of which introduced a one-shilling charge. At Ightham
Mote, a two-shilling fee was almost certainly expected to discourage
casual visitors, and two shillings was charged at Burghley for special
days, when the respectable visitor could view in peace. At Burghley,
the effect both of fees and limits on open days was to reduce visitor
numbers from a peak of nearly four thousand annually in the 1890s to
around two thousand in 1913.[46] Most clearly, upon the death of the
unpleasant Mortimer, 1st Lord Sackville, in 1888, the heirs to Knole

decided to re-open to the public, but only on a basis compatible with their own residence. The house was thereafter shown normally only on a few afternoons a week, at a two-shilling fee. Whereas before the Disturbances the house and park had attracted large family and school parties, predominantly from London, now the clientele was more local, more artistic, travelling in small parties and more often making their plans far in advance. Numbers fell from around 10,000, their pre-Disturbances peak, to 3,500 in 1890 and below 2,000 after 1900.[47]

At Castle Howard, the imperious Rosalind, Lady Carlisle, decided in 1909 to vet personally all applications from parties to view the house, substantially modifying the open-door policy formerly maintained by her husband:

> Last summer I found that these parties made a great deal of work in the house, & as I am not sure that the viewing of the house is of any particular educational advantage to the People, I do not want to make their application a mere matter of form . . . a request to see the house must be granted as a favour, & each case considered on its merits . . . In this way excursionists will learn that the house is not open as a matter of right, but a privilege.[48]

And this from one of the few remaining Liberal partisans among the aristocracy.

It is difficult to say anything certain about the meanings and motives of the visitors who continued to flock to the great show-places that were open to them. Many of them were presumably enjoying a day out in the open air, with historical and educational sidelights, just as they always had, regardless of any political or social implications. Still, it is striking how observers' descriptions of the great crowds at places like Eaton, Chatsworth, the Dukeries or Hatfield take on a sharper tone later in the century. In mid-Victorian days, when all parties were striving to give the appearance of consensus, comment was nearly unanimous on how well-behaved and grateful the throngs of visitors were. By the closing decades of the century, 'the mob' had arrived. Mortimer Sackville complained of the damage done to Knole's priceless interiors and his cheerleaders in the press sneered at the presumption of 'ill-bred cockneys of the lower orders, the "Arries and Arrietts" of the east end'.[49] Many of Stead's correspondents in the 'Splendid Paupers' survey defended country-house closures by pointing to the toll taken by tourists. The owner of Farnley Hall, home to a unique collection of Turners, declared himself hospitable to 'true lovers of art' but not 'mere curiosity-mongers' and 'idlers':

Much has been suffered from the lawless incursions of visitors, who handle the china, test the chairs, and inspect the carpets, but never glance at a picture.[50]

Such complaints no doubt contained a grain of truth. But the way in which they multiplied in the 1880s – coincident with a shift in the political mood but not with an increase in tourist numbers – implies that social tension was partly to blame. Tension was, of course, a two-way street; some visitors were no doubt taking their envy and anger out on the fabric of aristocratic wealth. Two tourists at Chatsworth in July 1889 proudly recorded themselves in the visitors' book as a 'Socialist' and a 'Radical'.[51] Less articulate malcontents showed off in different ways. In Elinor Glyn's fictional *Visits of Elizabeth*, the house-keeper of historic Retby is driven to tears by the disrespect of the Bank Holiday crowds. 'Oh, my lady,' she said, 'they treats us as if we was *ruins*.'[52] And some American tourists found at Welbeck just before the war a veritable playlet of class struggle involving

> hordes of English visitors; almost all men – 'trippers' from Leeds, Sheffield and such nearby cities, it being a Saturday afternoon – with the wives left at home ... They go through with a careless swaggering, with a sort of admiring contempt in which the con-tempt is stronger than the admiration – and a certain furtive jeal-ousy is evidently, with many, stronger than either ... a number of the men pluck garden flowers and baldly make a show of them, and in the great underground rooms we notice that some of them, from bravado and contempt, sit down and sprawl in valuable chairs not supposed to be even touched ... it was interesting to hear a quiet Englishman, looking with disapproval on all this, say: 'I would rather have laws made by a crazy duke than by a workingman's member of parliament.'[53]

But by 1914 fewer and fewer working men were interested in being herded through such aristocratic follies as the underground rooms at Welbeck, and fewer owners were willing to show them: the Welbeck tour itself ended with the outbreak of war and has never resumed. When *The Times*, always ready to look on the bright side of country-house life, tried in 1913 to revive Stead's argument that generous access was given to most parks and houses, its own correspondents cut the ground from under it – owners wrote in to complain about touristic vandalism, ramblers demanded not country-house tours but public footpaths.[54]

For some owners, and probably for many visitors, country-house tourism became an explicitly political act, a demonstration of faith in the bonds uniting aristocracy and people at a time when they were under attack. Naturally, the political significance of the country house was now almost exclusively Tory. The Duke of Rutland used the freedom of Belvoir and Haddon to oppose the legislative protection of ancient monuments, and the Duke of Devonshire turned Chatsworth into a political counter against the progressive death duties.

Lord Salisbury, a rising figure in the Tory party in the 1870s and its effective leader from 1881, was one of the few great owners to make his house more rather than less public in this period. House and park were open in midweek from Easter to the beginning of August, closed on weekends when Salisbury and his house-parties came up from town, but open on Bank Holidays.[55] In addition to many individual tourists, dozens of parties of one hundred or more each were accommodated, with teas and marquees provided for a small charge. These parties often hailed from groups with Tory attachments: Sunday schools, Church of England bodies, branches of the Primrose League or the Tory party itself. A group of Conservative working men came from as far as Huddersfield, 'the first excursion to Hatfield ever planned from . . . the North of England'. Sometimes these politicized visits could lead to trouble. On August Bank Holiday 1887, a Tory group was camped in the park combustibly alongside a party from the Welsh Sunday School Union and 'a youth . . . ascended a van in the vicinity of the Marquee in which the Conservative meeting was held, and harangued, by way of amusement, his friends therefrom'; scuffles ensued and were deplored in the newspapers.[56] Belvoir and Welbeck were used by their Tory owners in similar ways – the gardener at Belvoir complained of a visit of five thousand Sheffield Conservatives 'who gave us a great deal of work and finally presented me with a Penknife!' – and many parks which had never been open to the public were now put to use for Conservative fêtes and open-air meetings.[57] On a smaller scale, a knot of Tory councillors and their friends formed the York Tourist Society to tour country houses and parks around the north of England in the 1870s and 1880s – by no means the innocent enterprise it has been depicted, but larded with pointed insults at Liberal teetotalism and pointed praise for the benevolence of their aristocratic hosts.[58]

The great show-houses were most affected by the gross economic and political changes of the end of the century because they were as likely to be symbols of aristocratic wealth and privilege as of art or history. Places such as Chatsworth, Blenheim, Belvoir and Eaton were very ostentatious and very expensive to keep up, thus difficult for both owners and public. Large but historical houses such as Knole and Haddon remained interesting and, often, accessible, but to a smaller, paying public. Houses that were both modest and historical, especially those that fit well into the Arts and Crafts narrative of English history, were in the best position of all. Not so susceptible to viewing because of their size, they were nevertheless sought out by the select band of Arts and Crafts influenced tourists, who might be armed with a *Little Guide*, or the somewhat larger audience inspired by the writing of Allan Fea or J. J. Hissey. Aesthetically minded ramblers, cyclists and, in the new century, motorists wormed their way into the countryside from the 1880s and, if they were now more likely to be attracted by villages than by palaces, still worshipped the manor house as the village's spiritual core. The Cotswold villages with their honey-coloured cottages and vernacular manor houses were among the first to be discovered, having been colonized by Americans and artists in the early 1880s. By 1890, further afield, Dunster in Somerset had become a 'show place'. Earlier in the century, Dunster's castle had been open and its family portraits and Olden Time associations had been the chief attraction; now the castle was closed, and

> the little yarn market, having remained for more than a century, deserted and useless, must now have a large annual value as a source of aesthetic gratification and historical instruction to a constant stream of sightseers from just those districts where woollen yarn is at present made and sold, and where antiquity and beauty are not.[59]

To judge from the volume of visitors to the castle gardens, open as the castle was not for a fee of fourpence, and to the nearby ruins of Cleeve Abbey (one shilling), the Dunster tourist trade doubled in each decade from the 1880s to the 1900s.[60]

Just over the county border in Wiltshire, South Wraxall Manor House enjoyed a similar popularity. Unusually for a house of its size, South Wraxall was open to the public from 1854, having been deserted by its owners in 1817 and subsequently used as a school. In the 1870s the few visitors were mostly graduates of that school revisiting their old haunts. But in the 1880s and 1890s, this small manor house with its beamed hall of the fifteenth century and its flamboyantly Elizabethan upstairs rooms took on a new interest. It was featured in the *Art Journal* in 1883, visited by parties of architects and archaeologists in 1887, guides were published in 1880 and 1893, and in 1904 it received the ultimate accolade of a *Country Life* profile. Whereas a mere 150 visitors recorded their names in 1883 (including

53  The cult of the small manor house: South Wraxall Manor, featured in *Country Life*.

George Wardle and Philip Webb, both Arts and Crafts men), by the
turn of the century custom had topped one thousand a year.[61]

Surprisingly, the general boost which Ruskin and the Arts and
Crafts gave to the appreciation of fine art among sections of the upper
middle classes does not seem to have stimulated commensurate interest
in country-house art collections. In *Jude the Obscure*, Hardy sends Jude
Fawley and Sue Bridehead off on a half-holiday to view the pictures
at Wardour Castle. Jude has a roughly Pre-Raphaelite sensibility, Sue
a more advanced (though shallow) revulsion against the crudities of
the Olden Time and a sneaking admiration for the refinements of the
eighteenth century; Jude genuflects before the devotional pictures of
Del Sarto, Spagnoletto and Carlo Dolci, Sue strikes poses in front of
Lelys and Reynoldses. But they must have been virtually alone in the
Wardour gallery. Barely a hundred people a year visited in the 1880s
and 1890s, while the ruins of the old castle in the grounds which Sue
contemned – 'Gothic ruins – and I hate Gothic!' – drew over five

FLUNKYANA

(A Visit to the Portrait-Gallery of Brabazon Towers.)

"Pardon me! But you have passed over that picture in the corner. An old Dutch master, I think."
"Oh, *that!* 'The Burgermaster' it's called. By Rembrank, I b'lieve. It ain't nothing much. Only a work of hart. *Not one of the family, you know!*"

54    The select band of fine-art connoisseurs: George Du Maurier views those visitors who *do* know better than the servants.

hundred in the 1880s, over one thousand by 1900.[62] Wilton House, equally famed for its pictures and sculpture, had as many as a thousand visitors a year in the late 1860s but numbers fell back to around four hundred in the 1880s and were hardly more at the turn of the century.[63] A partial exception to this desuetude of the noble art galleries was Petworth House in Sussex, with its starry collection of Turners hymned by Ruskin. It, too, was only attracting several hundred visitors a year in the 1880s, but over the next few decades climbed towards the respectable levels established by Knole, reaching almost three thousand by 1910.[64]

The fact is that a catholic taste in art – extending to an appreciation of the eighteenth century such as Sue Bridehead affected – was still a very rare quality. Appreciation of such classical houses as Wardour Castle, Wilton and Petworth in their own right was rarer still. The Arts and Crafts movement may have heightened some people's aesthetic sensibility, but it did so in selective ways, which continued to ignore or condemn the majority of great country houses. Visitors dutifully filing through rooms of classical proportion – rooms as celebrated today as Inigo Jones's Double Cube at Wilton – were often chafing to get out; 'one feels incessantly the Emersonian eagerness to get to the windows,' admitted one writer on Wilton, and E. V. Lucas found his attention wandering from the guide at Petworth 'to the deer on the vast lawn that extends from the windows to the lake – the lake that Turner painted and fished in'.[65] A party of antiquarians on a visit to the 'unusually complete small manor-house built around 1510' at Water Eaton found themselves lured into nearby Blenheim – clearly nothing like as powerful an attraction – and got out again as quickly as possible, turning 'with relief' to the beautiful gardens.[66] Such people had fallen in love with the country, but not by any means with the country house, generically speaking.

It is no paradox, then, to say that while appreciation of the countryside was burgeoning before the First World War – as an open space for healthful recreation for masses of ramblers and cyclists, as the historic and aesthetic soul of the nation for the Arts and Crafts-minded – country-house visiting was on the wane. Many houses were closing; others were regulating and restricting their visitors; others were losing whatever fashionable interest they had retained from earlier in the century. The closing of the English country house was only partly a matter of demand – changing taste in architecture, history and art. More decisive was the declining ability or inclination of country-house owners to regard this particular aspect of *noblesse oblige*. Owners simply did not see cultural leadership as an obvious solution to their growing political and economic problems; it did not come naturally to the modern aristocrat, it seemed a waste of time and money or, worse, a dangerous concession to a ravening mob. It could have been otherwise: with sufficient will or under sufficient duress, the aristocracy could have taken a cultural lead and worked to place their houses at the centre of an emerging sense of rural heritage – as so many have sought to do since the Second World War. Instead of meeting the invasion of the mob with defiance or retreat, a practical embrace was conceivable – as the Earl of Warwick demonstrated.

In the 1870s, penury and opportunity had forced the 4th Earl of Warwick to accept that the public enjoyment of Warwick Castle –

and public support for its rebuilding – had effectively transformed it
from a private house into a national icon. In the following decades, he
and his son turned that loss to their advantage. Abandoning any real
claim that the castle was their private residence, they converted it
gradually into a commercial tourist attraction that gave them both the
strong local position and the profit that agriculture could no longer
provide; it also helped to shore up the sagging reputation of their
Olden Time colossus. Long before the First World War, Warwick
Castle – not Longleat or Beaulieu or Woburn – had become the
pioneer of the 'stately home business'.

As might be expected, this transformation was sly and unheralded,
in the two-faced manner of Lord Warwick's handling of the 1872
appeal: honour was preserved but the cash was banked. For some years
after the restoration, visiting to the castle had resumed on its former
casual basis; the castle was open for most of the peak tourist season and
visitors were shown around at odd intervals in large parties by a
servant, who was compensated by tips. In the spring of 1885, however
– not long after the Knole Disturbances had died down – the castle
failed to open as usual. Nearby Leamington Spa, nearly as dependent
upon the castle trade as Sevenoaks had been on Knole, grew restless as
the peak tourist periods of Easter and Whitsun passed without any
communication from the castle. Early in July the Leamington Town
Council wrote respectfully to the Earl of Warwick regretting the
closure, pointing to its effect on the trade of Leamington, and tentatively hoping that 'your Lordship can see your way to re-open the
castle to visitors'. The same sentiments were voiced in the town of
Warwick itself, where the 'disappointment of those who have travelled some distance to visit the Castle has been intense [and] the trade
of the town has suffered'.[67]

What Warwick and Leamington did not know is that the Earl and
his agent Captain Fosbery had closed the castle temporarily only to
plot 'a complete change in the system of showing it'. Aware that these
changes might provoke some local dissatisfaction – and perhaps with
an eye to Lord Sackville's poor tactics – Fosbery may even have
delayed the reopening to underscore the dependence of the locality on
the castle; certainly he thought it important that Leamington 'should
realise how important a factor in the prosperity of the Town is the
influx of Visitors to the Castle'. Only when impatience had burst into
public print did Lord Warwick announce the imminent reopening on
a new, as yet unspecified basis. This reassurance was good enough to
quash the topic entirely in the local press, even though another month
passed and the August Bank Holiday trade was lost before the new

system was revealed and the castle reopened to the public on 10 August.[68]

What Fosbery and the Earl had done was to professionalize the showing of the castle. Pensioning off the servant who had hitherto been charged with introducing visitors, Fosbery had approached the Corps of Commissionaires – an association formed in 1859 to retrain pensioned soldiers as messengers and porters – and hired three of their men as full-time guides, one to show the gardens and two to show the castle. Their wages were to be funded not by tips but by one-shilling admission tickets, sold from an office on Mill Street (Fosbery had also considered opening an agency in Leamington). Regular hours of ten to four were established and, although allowance was made for occasional closings to suit the family, in practice the castle was now open year round, from 1 January to 31 December, a schedule that has been maintained with startlingly few exceptions ever since.[69]

The new system was greeted with gratifyingly little dissent. One correspondent in the chief Liberal paper in Birmingham complained that a shilling was too high a fee for working men and their families, recommended instead sixpence (and less for large parties) as charged at Burghley, Hardwick and elsewhere, or the good old system of tipping at discretion as at Chatsworth and Haddon. To this, however, a correspondent in Birmingham's leading Tory paper retorted that the system was hardly excluding anyone – 'I never saw such a rush of sightseers as there has been since the new regulation was put in force'. Fosbery confirmed this impression to the Earl in private:

> the public have taken very kindly to the new order of things and neither have numbers fallen off – for I had them counted this time last year – nor has the payment been found to exclude working people, a great many of whom have been since the reopening.

The system of continuous viewing was a success and the commissionaires 'were kept moving the whole of the time the Castle was open'. All in all, he concluded, he was surprised 'that a change of this nature has caused so little adverse remark'. After the first weeks, there was no more comment in the press. Over seven hundred visitors paid their shillings in the first four days – as Fosbery said, maintaining the previous year's levels – almost eight thousand by the end of the year and about twenty thousand in the first full year of operation in 1886. This put Warwick Castle in the league of Eaton and perhaps exceeded only by Chatsworth, the difference being that Warwick's tourist trade turned a profit, whereas Eaton's benefited charity (after the guides' expenses were paid) and Chatsworth's was a dead loss.[70]

It is not clear what precisely were the Earl's motives in instituting this reorganization. Control and security were probably a factor, as the groups shown around by a single old servant were getting too large. Limitation of numbers and safeguarding of a private residence were not in question, however. To the contrary, the effect of the new system was to maintain and ultimately increase numbers, as the fixed schedule became known and well-publicized. As at Eaton, over a thousand visitors might show up on peak days like Easter Monday, Whit Monday and August Bank Holiday, and annual volume crept up to twenty-five thousand by 1889 – by which time the staff of commissionaires had been increased to five – and to a peak of forty thousand by 1905.[71]

Protecting his reputation, the Earl would not admit even in private to his friends the reasons for the move, passing it off as 'the greatest annoyance'.[72] But it seems pretty obvious that money lay at the root, and that Lord Warwick was now reconciled to serving actually as the public's trustee rather than as the private owner of Warwick Castle by the assurance that the castle could in this way be a source of profit rather than expense. If the old Earl could never quite admit to seeing it this way, his son, who succeeded as 5th Earl in December 1893, was from a different mould. A sportsman and sometime politician, he cared little for the castle and his Warwickshire estates, preferring to live at his wife's family seat, Easton Lodge in Essex, from where he had been elected MP for Colchester before succeeding to the title. He regarded the castle show as a bit of a laugh and kept on his watch-chain a half-sovereign that an American tourist had once given him as a tip, mistaking him for a commissionaire.[73] His wife Daisy had been a celebrated society beauty and lover of the Prince of Wales, known for her extravagance of views and manners. (It was she, Stead claimed bizarrely, who coined the phrase 'The Splendid Paupers' in an 'auto-telepathic interview' with him.[74]) But after her husband succeeded, she made an equally flamboyant conversion to socialism and thereafter spoke openly of Warwick Castle as public property, 'a national rather than a private heirloom'. She never considered it as a home, viewing it as a museum with a 'depressing likeness' to Holloway Prison, and her son the 6th Earl followed suit, favouring instead a fishing lodge on the river in the park.[75]

Under the 5th Earl, the castle began to take on many of the attributes associated with the commercialized stately home of the late twentieth century. In 1893 the castle staged a pageant, the first of its kind on a grand scale, mobilizing large numbers of local craftsmen and amateur actors to stage a professionally produced historical play in the castle grounds. Aimed to celebrate the millenary of the foundation of the Kingdom of Mercia by Queen Ethelfleda, 'when [the pageant] was worked out, the central figure became in reality, not Queen Ethelfleda, but Queen Elizabeth', and the climax of the show was a splendid Olden Time tableau showing Elizabeth's ceremonial arrival, some revels (a bit-part played by a seven-year-old William Shakespeare) and her departure down the Avon on a red-canopied barge.[76] The experiment was tried again on a more magnificent scale in the summer of 1906, scripted by the professional pageant-master Louis Parker and drawing thirty thousand visitors from all over the country.[77]

As the tourist trade mounted, Warwick Castle became more and more frankly a commercial property for its owners. In the early years of the new scheme, the tourist account showed a profit of about £600–700 on takings of over £1,000, after commissionaires' wages and other opening expenses were paid. In 1899, the castle and its estate were incorporated as a limited company, a hedge against death duties, which became common among large landowners after 1894, but which also permitted the Earl to charge other expenses against the takings before tax: upkeep of the garden and gardeners' wages, some shooting and fishing expenses. Under cover of the second pageant, the admission fee was doubled to two shillings in 1906, and although this temporarily depressed tourist volume – from forty thousand in 1905 to twenty-six thousand in 1913 – it boosted income from £2,100 to £2,666. By this last full season before the war, the tourist account was now paying not only for opening expenses, gardens and electricity, but also for a large portion of the servants' wage-bill and still leaving a profit of over £1,000.[78]

Not many country-house owners were in a position to emulate the Warwicks' example. Warwick Castle had distinctive advantages in its geographical situation at the 'Heart of England', its proximity to a spa town long accustomed to visitors, and to the mushrooming tourist attractions of Kenilworth and Stratford. It had historical attractions for medievalists and Olden Time enthusiasts, fine art and armour, Shakespearean associations, and – despite its gaudiness, grossness and bluster – some Arts and Crafts appeal due to the beauty of its setting and Ruskin's admiration. Its sheer size suited it to mass tourism. But what was truly unique about it was its owners' choice of a populist, commercial path. In contrast, the owners of Chatsworth and Alton Towers, Blenheim and Woburn, Raby and Newstead responded to the same kind of financial and logistical pressures by going into retreat. They were soon to be followed by the owners of Haddon and Belvoir, Eaton, Berkeley and Lumley. All over England, the 'splendid paupers' were closing their doors.

# PART III

## *White Elephants, 1914–1939*

The Stately Homes of England,
How beautiful they stand,
To prove the upper classes
Have still the upper hand;
Though the fact that they have to be rebuilt
And frequently mortgaged to the hilt
Is inclined to take the gilt
Off the gingerbread,
And certainly damps the fun
Of the eldest son –
But still we won't be beaten,
We'll scrimp and scrape and save,
The playing fields of Eton
Have made us frightfully brave –
And though if the Van Dycks have to go
And we pawn the Bechstein Grand
We'll stand
By the Stately Homes of England . . .

The Stately Homes of England
We proudly represent,
We only keep them up for Americans to rent.
Though the pipes that supply the bathroom burst
And the lavatory makes you fear the worst,
It was used by Charles the First
Quite informally,
And later by George the Fourth
On a journey north.

The State Apartments keep their
Historical renown,
It's wiser not to sleep there
In case they tumble down;
But still if they ever catch on fire
Which, with any luck, they might
We'll fight
For the Stately Homes of England.

      — Noël Coward, 'The Stately
      Homes of England' (1938)

# Land without Lords: The Nadir of the Country House

> The class which strangled the aristocracy . . . has been haunted ever since by the ghost of its victim . . . it has come into power consequent on the Industrial Revolution and Reform Bills and the Death Duties. But it has never been able to build itself an appropriate home, and when it asserts that an Englishman's home is his castle, it reveals the precise nature of its failure. We who belong to it still copy the past . . . The castles and the great mansions are gone, we have to live in semi-detached villas instead . . . Our minds still hanker after the feudal stronghold which we condemned as uninhabitable.[1]

With these words, published in 1939, E. M. Forster caught perfectly the tone of disappointment – mingled here with a liberal dose of self-disgust – with which intellectuals then and since have approached the middle classes between the wars. The intellectuals' indictment of their own class went something like this. The English middle classes, unlike their revolutionary counterparts on the Continent, were unable to claim a thumping victory over their aristocracy, unable to construct a 'home' – an identity – of their own. England was suspended between its own feudal past and everyone else's modern future. The result was muddle, mediocrity and – in the view perpetuated by cultural critics of our own time – a national identity hopelessly in thrall to nostalgia. The old world was dying, messily; the new could not be born.

England did undoubtedly diverge from its continental counterparts between the wars, but most people at the time would have disagreed with Forster's pessimistic interpretation. It was not necessary then, nor is it necessary now to treat this divergence as abnormal or in the long term anti-modern. England did not break with its past in the abrupt way desired by revolutionaries and the *avant garde*, but neither did it become the past's prisoner. This complex and commercial society – conservative *and* modern – loosened its bonds to tradition in less dramatic but equally powerful ways. Its aristocracy had been carefully harmonizing itself with modernity for generations, throwing off the trappings of feudalism and accepting successive reformulations of its remaining power. Now that its landed power-base was threatened by urbanization, agricultural depression and fiscal policy, it was prepared to abandon much of its land – and with the land its rationale as the traditional governing class – even to accept a degree of social invisibility in order to retain its accumulated fortunes, where necessary in bankable (non-landed) form.

The withdrawal of the aristocracy from the land paved the way for the reappropriation of the countryside by urban society. This urge to identify with the countryside, to represent urbanity and modernity by analogy with the rural past, was of course nothing new. It had featured prominently in the early Victorians' self-description when England was the 'Workshop of the World'. It had been partially obscured later in the nineteenth century by the climacteric of urbanization and by unusual political tension between aristocracy and people, which rendered ownership of the countryside (literal as well as spiritual) problematic.

England's passage beyond the peak of urbanization – in advance of other countries – and its resolution of the aristocratic problem made possible a resolution of the 'ownership' problem. After the First World War, as political conflict between aristocracy and people died down, the countryside became more available for reconnection with a national identity. This was convenient for a nation shying away from the modernism of the avant-garde, from what was seen as the gigantism and extremism plaguing France, Germany, Russia and in some ways America, too. A much larger social constituency now discovered the England of the Arts and Crafts movement – the small, homely, farmyard country. Out went the philistine bombast and ambition of the Edwardians and, abroad, of the Dictators; in came modesty, simplicity, privacy, the primacy of the domestic. Out went the clamour and collectivism of urban life; in came the quiet and contemplation of the country cottage.[2]

These images resonated because they caught the tone of England's peculiar, conservative modernity between the wars. They were not particularly loaded with fear, guilt or longing; on the contrary, to many they stood for a great feeling of liberation and self-expression. As we shall see, the 'ghost' of the aristocracy became just at this moment a figure of fun rather than dread. At the same time, the countryside became a playground and an imaginative space in which urban society could reconstruct itself on new lines. In the process, the Arts and Crafts vision was warped and shifted out of all recognition. Intellectuals complained bitterly that the 'real' countryside – the one they had discovered before the war – was being destroyed. The interwar bourgeoisie was not enough in thrall to the past: it had taken what it could use, what it liked from the Old English countryside, and thrown away the 'genuine', much in the style of the Victorian cult of the Olden Time.

The erasure of the aristocracy from the Old English countryside was something at which Arts and Crafts intellectuals had themselves connived and of which they could not honestly complain. Yet some would be so disturbed at the distortion of their dream by a swollen, consuming and unaesthetic middle class that they would come to regret the passing of the old order – and, as Forster's entire *oeuvre* testifies, feel the blood on their own hands.

In the meantime, the urban rediscovery of the countryside contributed inexorably to that old order's total disintegration. The great estates were breaking up and the country houses coming down. The stately homes of England, which had been sites of common history for the Victorians and political footballs for the Edwardians, were now largely obstacles to the urban middle classes' occupation of the countryside. 'The stately homes of England make good photographs, and create the illusion of a connection with the Elizabethans', mused Lady Chatterley in D. H. Lawrence's novel of 1928; 'Now they are pulling down the stately homes, the Georgian halls are going . . . This is history. One England blots out another.'[3]

## The Modern Countryside

Whether or not the flood of land sales immediately before the war can be taken as evidence of an irreversible loss of aristocratic confidence, the effect of war and its aftermath was to set the current flowing firmly in that direction. In retrospect, it is hard to say whether Lloyd George's wartime coalition or the Tory governments that eventually succeeded him contributed more to bringing down the landed élite. War brought new levels of taxation and expanded governmental responsibilities, undermining both landed fortunes and traditional governing practices. But after Lloyd George's fall and the break-up of the old Liberal party, the Tories under Bonar Law and Baldwin took over the centre ground from their former enemies and aimed to satisfy a broader spectrum of middle-class opinion.

Their former allies in the aristocracy suffered the most. The top level of death duties, for instance, was doubled from 1914 levels to 50 per cent only after the Armistice, and most of the higher levels were raised again by the Tories in 1925.[4] Subsidies and controls designed in war to guarantee food production had given agriculture a brief boost of confidence, but these guarantees were swept away in the 'Great Betrayal' of 1921, and the Tories subsequently left agriculture to the tender mercies of a depressed free market. The collapse of Liberalism may have relieved pressure for the transfer of land from great landlords to a smallholding peasantry, but the new Toryism was positioning itself as champion of a property-owning democracy. This stance implied a food policy that favoured urban consumers and an agricultural policy that encouraged the transfer of land to substantial owner-occupiers.[5] Nor were the Tories anxious any longer to be associated politically with the aristocracy. Led successively by a Glasgow iron-merchant, the son of a Worcestershire ironmaster and the son of a Birmingham screw-manufacturer, at least in public image the Tory party was now portraying itself as the moderate heir of urban Liberalism.

Small wonder, then, that so many large landowners took the hint and sold off their estates in medium-sized chunks to their former tenants. The greatest aristocrats had been quietly diversifying out of land for years and were now joined by owners of all sizes, including many of the smaller gentry who had impoverished themselves earlier by hanging on through the long depression. The proportion of English and Welsh agricultural land held by owner-occupiers rose from 11 per cent in 1914 to 37 per cent by 1927. These transfers still left most land in large estates, but the suddenness and scale of the change – especially in 1919–21 – made a tremendous psychological impact. Headlines like 'England Changing Hands' – this from *The Times*, which preferred the old hands – conveyed a sense of the national inheritance passing, not between generations but between classes.

While the greatest aristocrats could still remain afloat by selling off outlying estates, and others could reduce their main estate, about one-fifth of all landowners fell out of the caste altogether by selling the whole of their heartland.[6] In extreme cases, entire counties were transformed. A third of the great estates of Derbyshire were broken up by 1930.[7] In the famous Dukeries, enormous tracts of Nottinghamshire owned originally by a small set of dukes, owners had resisted the exploitation of underlying coal deposits to preserve their agricultural estates, their traditional way of life and, they said, rural amenity. These inhibitions were suddenly lost after 1918. Mineral rights were let out gaily, the district rapidly became 'uninhabitable', and by 1939 all but one of the major landowners had vacated their premises.[8]

Elsewhere, where break-up was more piecemeal, ownership of the countryside was still losing its special aura of exclusivity and near-feudal control. Even where ownership remained in concentrated hands, the renewed depression that set in after 1921 forced landlords to abandon the visible symbols and guarantors of that exclusivity. Porters and gamekeepers were laid off, walls and fences neglected, trespassers were not prosecuted. Signs of demoralization among the old owners were everywhere.

Into this vacuum moved new owners, inexorably if not trium-phantly. Apart from the farmers who bought the agricultural land, insignificant in numbers, most of these new owners were middle-class urbanites seeking to move out of overcrowded towns. Britain had reached its urban peak before the First World War, in advance of other countries, and it was now past it, also in advance of other countries. Its pressure-cooker cities began to let off steam by growing extensively rather than intensively, spilling into the emptying country-side. Sometimes this process of suburbanization was a matter of social policy – the London County Council decreed a height limitation on city-centre building and began to build 'cottage estates' outside its own boundaries – but everywhere it was a matter of social choice, as the environmental advantages of suburban life became clear. The choice was made easier and more widely available by the spread of family limitation which brought the ownership of a new home in the suburbs within reach of the lower middle class. Gradually the cities flowed out into the country; the number of houses in England increased by 30 per cent in interwar decades when the population increased by only 10 per cent.

Suburban life was city life in the country: not so much *rus in urbe* as *urbs in rure*. The suburb had transport links to the city, depended upon its employment opportunities and still looked to its cultural facilities. It was laid out like a village with a high street, often a 'green', semi-detached or detached 'cottages', and large gardens – and named like a village: the suburb itself preferably suffixed 'Park', its arteries dubbed Gardens, Drive, Rise or Way in preference to Street or Road, its villas given individual cottagey names like Meadowside or Woodsview. But the 'village' life sought by the suburbanite was nothing like traditional country life. It had no lord and no peasants. It had its own pursuits – tennis, golf, croquet – that were not urban but were not rural, either. The suburb's most conspicuous non-residential building was a cinema, not a church; in Greater London, few suburbs were even provided with a church.[9]

Along with the villagey layout and nomenclature went a villagey style for the façades and interior decoration of the suburban home: half-timbering, gables, tiles and diamond-paned 'leaded' windows outdoors; oak beams, panelling, chunky tables and chairs, even big Tudor overmantels indoors. In adopting this style, the suburbanite was following the example of the prewar aesthetes who had identified in the Tudor yeoman's house a historical model for independent middle-class domesticity. Like that aesthetic minority, the suburbanite saw in the Tudor cottage style a symbol of independence – spacious self-sufficiency, property ownership, the integrity of the family unit, the potential for self-expression through interior decoration.[10] These traits were all the more important as a counterpoint to the cramped, rented, unindividuated urban accommodation that upwardly mobile subur-banites would recently have vacated.[11]

Unlike the aesthete, however, and rather more like the Victorian admirers of the Olden Time, the suburbanite only needed his Tudor villa to *look* genuine; that is, he cared neither for a modernist adapta-tion of the vernacular (as sought by the Arts and Crafts pioneers) nor for real historicity. For the aesthetic minority, *Country Life* had before the war nurtured a cult of the Old English countryside and the true Tudor house. For the suburban mass between the wars, a fleet of imitation magazines sprang up – with titles such as *Town and Country* or *Country Illustrated* – in which authenticity and history went for naught. Just as Knight Frank & Rutley, the estate agent that made *Country Life* possible, had spotted the market for 'real' history and rurality, so a host of estate developers – whose advertisements sus-tained the new 'town and country' magazines – had identified a much larger market for modern comfort in a rural setting.[12] The 'new old houses' featured in these magazines were prized particularly for the combination of old-world appearance and modern technology. The fake-Tudor exteriors were important, but so were the modern kitchens, filled with labour-saving devices for the servantless housewife, gas-fired heating systems and electric appliances like the radio for which the houses were specially designed. Genuinely old houses almost by definition could not qualify. As *Country Life* complained in 1930, 'the general public have as yet only got as far as appreciating "quaintness" for its own sake'; it anticipated 'a long up-hill fight' before an 'appreciation for the subtle harmonies of time and texture' would be attained.[13]

Beyond the literal ownership of the urbanized countryside represented by suburbia, the interwar middle classes also took symbolic
ownership of the whole of the country by travelling and exploring it.
Here, too, Britain was hardly unique, and not even in the vanguard,
for its unusual concentration of rural landownership before the First
World War had limited the exploitation of the countryside for urban
leisure purposes that had already become a familiar feature of German
and American culture.[14]

Excursions into the countryside had long been a popular form of
recreation, especially after the advent of the railway, but had been
limited by the scarcity of leisure time and the need to negotiate access.
Those limits relaxed on all fronts in the early twentieth century. While
the prevalence of paid holidays among the working classes did not
appreciably increase between the wars, as workers preferred income to
leisure in times that were for them economically insecure, they did
extend dramatically among the swelling middle classes. The postwar
relaxation of religious inhibitions against hedonistic indulgence –
which probably had never much bothered the working population –
undoubtedly contributed to an air of liberation sweeping through the
middling ranks. For those with means, the motor car in particular
represented the ideal vehicle with which to satisfy this newfound
'appetite for change and excitement', the lust to travel and explore.

55   Motor cars and motor-buses open up the countryside: a motorized party of American lawyers visit
Sulgrave Manor, George Washington's ancestral home, in July 1924.

The less prosperous made do with the bicycle – of which there were
ten million by 1930 – or with shanks's pony; either, in conjunction
with the railway and the new motor-coach network, made accessible
the most remote corners of the English countryside.[15] Always a place
of resort and refuge, that countryside now became something more –
the national playground.

Rural touring was, like the suburb, fundamentally about making the
countryside comfortable for townspeople. The extension of the road
(as also the electricity) network spoke unambiguously of the presence
of the town in the country. Residential build-up alongside new roads
– what came to be known as ribbon development – made that
presence more emphatic still. Beyond the built-up areas, motor roads
were widely regarded by vested rural interests as a foreign (i.e. urban)
intrusion. To tour the countryside often meant, much to the annoyance of 'true' countrymen, picnicking on the verge – in large parties,
in casual city dress, equipped not only with huge hampers but also
sometimes with gramophones to make an *al fresco* dance-hall. In
villages across the land, tourist facilities sprang up – teashops, bed and
breakfast accommodation, garages and petrol stations, half-timbered
'road-houses' – that had, before the war, been evident in a few honey-
pot sites near London, such as the Cotswolds. At those well-
established sites, something like congestion was experienced. The
Shakespeare Festival at Stratford, for instance, held regularly since
1879, attracted fourteen thousand visitors in 1904 but 200,000 by
1938.[16] The private owner of Stonehenge had begun to charge admission in 1901, when fewer than four thousand visitors paid; by 1930,
now under public auspices, the numbers had soared to 100,000 per
annum.[17]

For these thousands of people fanning out into open country, often
for the first time, the country did in fact seem to be 'open'. The
breakup of the great estates and the decay of estate maintenance meant
that fewer obstacles were being offered. This comparative freedom
surely made the countryside a less forbidding and politically loaded
place. Though deliberate trespassing continued, especially on northern
moorland, much more trespassing was committed on private property
with only innocent pleasure intended and certainly without owners
registering the fact.

When owners did notice, their embittered comments betrayed a
good deal of impotence. At the virtually unstaffed Castle Howard
estate in the late 1930s, the furious agent regularly confronted parties
of cyclists, motorists and motor-coach tourists picnicking and playing
games in the private park. One party brought in hundreds of school-

# PARTICULARS AS TO ADMISSION TO CASTLE HOWARD

The interior of Castle Howard is open to the Public on Wednesdays, Thursdays and Saturdays between the hours of 1 and 5 p.m. and on Bank Holidays (excepting Good Friday) from 10 a.m. to 5 p.m. The charge for admission is One Shilling per head.

Visitors may not walk down to the Castle unless they wish to see through the house on the appointed days. They are reminded that Castle Howard Park is private property and they are requested :—

Not to leave litter or broken glass about.

Not to allow dogs to run loose in the Park.

Not to swing on the boughs of trees nor pick the wild flowers, ferns or shrubs in the Park.

Not to bathe in the lake nor play games in the Park without first obtaining permission from the Agent.

All vehicles must be left by the side of the public road or near the obelisk.

Parties numbering more than twenty who wish to see through the Castle, must apply by letter, before coming, to the Agent, Estate Office, Castle Howard, York.

56 Vain attempts by the Castle Howard estate to preserve the privacy of the park, *c.*1938.

children from Hull, another erected a tent as a refreshments pavilion, and on one Sunday sixty motors were counted parked on the private road. These culprits' surprised excuses were variously that they 'were doing no harm . . . the road was not fenced in . . . he had a perfect right . . . thought it was a public park'. What could be done? Alarming notices were already liberally posted about the place. Clearly there were insufficient groundsmen to patrol the roads.[18] Even the well-heeled Duke of Marlborough found it difficult to grapple with such incursions. Blenheim Park, which was open to the public, was subject to various depredations that seem more hostile than careless: 'Fair Rosamund's Well' was stopped up with clay (cutting off the water supply to the palace), notice boards had been hacked down and saplings felled, iron fencing was thrown into the lake, the private gardens broken into and flowers stolen.[19]

Millions of urban English people were thus taking an almost physical possession of the countryside in succession to its traditional owners, the aristocracy. What did they make of it? That is, what images of the countryside did they bring and take away, and how did these images impinge on their sense of self, on their own 'English-ness'? Historians have tended to extrapolate generalizations about national identity from alarmist tracts and intellectuals' pronouncements that were written precisely *against* such popular appropriation of the countryside and in favour of its sacred preservation. Yet these expressions of horror at what was happening to the countryside are evidence that a national identity carefully tended by anxious intellectuals on a basis of preservation was being decisively repudiated.

While it is far too easy to interpret the articulate and purposeful literary writing on rural England, it is more difficult to penetrate the thoughts and feelings of casual tourists.[20] But they did have their own 'literature' through which can be glimpsed an understanding of 'national identity' quite different from that of the intellectuals. An avalanche of printed matter on the English countryside was produced in the 1920s and 1930s to cater to the rural tourist, most of it naturally preoccupied with logistical information and simple descriptions. A slightly more ambitious genre also made an appearance, combining the functions of travel guide and philosophizer on Englishness, of which by far the most popular was H. V. Morton's *In Search of England*, first published in 1927 and then in twenty-three editions in the next decade.

Morton's travel pieces were too serious for the *Daily Express* in which they first appeared – his editor would have preferred more populist stuff like 'Searching for the Perfect Seaside Landlady' – but they gradually built up a large following, especially in book form.[21] Morton took a frankly paternalistic view of his readership and saw his role as educating the aspiring masses to some eternal truths about the traditions and healthfulness of the countryside. Yet he was no reactionary – he gladly deserted the *Express* for the left-wing *Daily Herald* – and stressed what the countryside had to offer to a 'virile and progressive nation . . . which can keep pace with the modern industrial world'. Predictably his 'England' was a relatively liberated and democratic version of the Arts and Crafts countryside, in which the village is the crucial unit, popular customs and crafts its most picturesque aspects, and 'a contented and flourishing peasantry' the principal object of his solicitude. Only at the very end of the book does the question of the landlord class even arise; its imminent demise is accepted; what remains is the ordinary rhythm of village life – which *is* England. Tourism is seen as a wholly positive phenomenon, educational and civilizing, and he has only good things to say about the many fresh-faced shopgirls and hikers he meets on his travels. The tone throughout is bluff and optimistic, sentimental but not soppy and positively fizzing with sexual energy, alternately wolfish and chivalrous. Morton's 'search' is an adventure, not an elegy.[22]

As the *Express* editor complained, Morton's writing made room for a deal of historical and archaeological detail and betrayed a genuine feeling for the past. His nearest rival for popularity as a guide to England was even breezier and more present-minded. Personally an arch-Tory and a self-confessed snob, priding himself on his aristocratic connections, S. P. B. Mais – dubbed in BBC advertising 'the Modern Columbus' – was careful to keep these prejudices from limiting the appeal of his broadcasts and journalism. Mais first came to wide public notice as the organizer for railway companies of mass rambles in the South of England in the early 1930s. His rambling guides sold in the hundreds of thousands and he reached a wider audience still with broadcasts, beginning with seventeen journeys in 1932 under the title 'The Unknown Island'. Shrewdly in touch with his audience of 'lonely clerks and typists and little shopkeepers', he denied himself rural nostalgia, snob appeal or even Morton's improving messages, and homed in on the *Wanderlust* that fuelled the rambling craze. His journalism and still more his broadcasts convey a keen sense of the physical challenges and stimuli of walking. Weather, terrain, panoramas and the unexpected personal encounters are dominant. When history peeps in, it takes Gothic forms: ruined castles, ghostly presences, craggy battlefields. Mais managed occasionally to insert some self-conscious plugs for 'feudalism', asserting his own status as a 'character', but the overall effect was that of an Everyman, striding over rough, wet ground in rather too much of a hurry.[23] And his was the dominant style of broadcasting 'in search of England' between the wars.[24]

Mais's naturalistic approach to the countryside gained further popularity in the 1930s by the spread of the rambling fad to new social strata. 'Hiking' took off among the working classes, especially in the large industrial towns of the North that were ringed by vast tracts of privately owned moorland. To some extent this was a matter of slowly improving living standards, at least for those in employment. It was also a deliberate political statement from a better-organized labour movement, absorbing some of the anti-aristocratic feeling of pre-war radicalism. The Peak District became for a while in the mid-1930s a battleground between teams of working-class hikers, defending their right to hike, and the dukes of Norfolk and Devonshire's gamekeepers, defending their grouse.[25] Hiking was also, less politically, an

57   Hiking in the Lake District, c.1941: by this date, respectful rambling had degenerated into hiking, a more youthful and adventurous activity, often defiant about private-property rights.

assertion of a modern style; hikers modelled themselves after the German *Wandervögel*, a prewar movement that made a connection between youth, health, nature and equality, but without that movement's élitism and ultra-patriotic overtones. Hikers dressed in the khaki uniform familiar on the Continent, open-necked shirts, shorts, berets and ankle socks. They walked in teams, across long distances, interested exclusively in challenging terrain and the health-giving effects of athletic exercise, linking together cross-country journeys with overnight stays in purpose-designed hostels. The Youth Hostels Association was founded in 1929 to cater to this new demand and by 1939 it had opened nearly 400 hostels, providing over half a million 'overnights' a year (at a shilling each for bed and breakfast).[26] With the hiker we have come very far indeed from the Arts and Crafts vision of the Old English countryside; the hiker's 'essential' England was wild, bare, open and timeless.[27]

To those intellectuals and aesthetes who had been reared on the ideals of the Arts and Crafts movement, the modern generation's approach to the countryside seemed fundamentally destructive, material and anti-historical. Those who had been Liberals, who had cherished dreams of diffusing spiritual values among the masses, were especially crushed. H. J. Massingham, for instance, a crusading Radical before the war, found himself turning to 'a Conservatism of a much older tradition' in the 1920s. He left London and went to live deep in the Cotswolds, immersing himself in the Tudor vernacular and dreaming of self-sufficient farming communities, ending up writing regularly on farming for the country gentleman's organ, *The Field*.[28] His books hymning the bygone English countryside are often cited as evidences of interwar rural nostalgia, yet purer protests against the spirit of the age would be hard to find. His friend J. C. Squire went through a similar if less violent disillusionment. As late as 1918, he had contested a university seat in Parliament for the Labour party, but in the course of the 1920s he fell into a deepening sulk about the destruction of beauty in England. By the early 1930s he had abandoned entirely 'the great democracy of England, in whom I have no faith at all'. He put his faith instead in small cliques of right-minded people, such as gathered around his literary magazine, the *London Mercury*, and his Architecture Club, 'rather inward-looking coterie affairs with little effect on outside opinion', as the more ambitious Clough Williams-Ellis described them.[29] The historian G. M. Trevelyan, a one-time supporter of Lloyd George's Land Campaign, also found himself simultaneously less hopeful about democratic politics and more concerned with the decline of spiritual values as

represented by the traditional countryside. 'Modern man needs to
have his imagination kept in touch with the past and its spiritual and
aesthetic values,' he wrote in a 1929 tract, *Must England's Beauty
Perish?* Alas, he concluded later, 'those of us who care for preservation
of natural beauty are still outnumbered and overborne'.[30]

The collapse of liberalism made it easier for aesthetes concerned
with preserving the countryside to come together, but their loss of
connection to modern politics deprived them of influence on
Williams-Ellis's 'outside opinion'. The old preservationist organizations like the SPAB and the National Trust became embattled and
sclerotic in the 1920s. Under a new Chairman, John Bailey, the Trust
made a conscious decision to eschew 'work of a "militant" character'
and concentrate on 'its functions as a holding body';[31] it continued to
accumulate bits and pieces of 'beauty-spot' countryside and the occasional medieval building. This policy gave it a reputation as 'England's
executor', to draw again on Clough Williams-Ellis's ready stock of
criticism, 'a museum in which are preserved here and there carefully
selected and ticketed specimens of what England *was*'.[32] Though its
membership inched up in the 1920s, gathering in the scattered
remnant, it had almost no public visibility. 'There are many who
connect the National Trust merely with an occasional paragraph in the
newspaper telling of another beauty spot being saved for the nation',
complained one member as late as 1939; 'What the Trust is, or how
it came into being, does not interest them.'[33] Often its supporters
could not even get its name right.[34] Compared to other cultural
lobbies, like the National Art-Collections Fund, with a stylish, go-
ahead image, the Trust – and the causes of rural and historic preservation in general – appeared fogeyish and narrowly antiquarian.
Whenever the Trust went to government for aid, it was always
rebuked with the rapid growth of the NA-CF and told to go out and
connect better with the general public.[35]

Government, ever sensitive to the true hierarchy of public concerns, was not very sympathetic to the preservationist lobby, especially
in the 1920s when money was tight and *laissez-faire* the dominant
ideology. Any momentum established before the war by the Liberal
preservation legislation was completely dissipated by the war itself. In
the last days of the Lloyd George coalition, the Office of Works tried
to recapture that momentum by appointing a committee under its
prewar minister Lord Beauchamp to consider a further extension of
the Ancient Monuments Acts. Beauchamp's report, issued in 1921,
combined its chairman's liberalism with the preservationist experts'
professional interests, asserting a national claim on ancient monuments

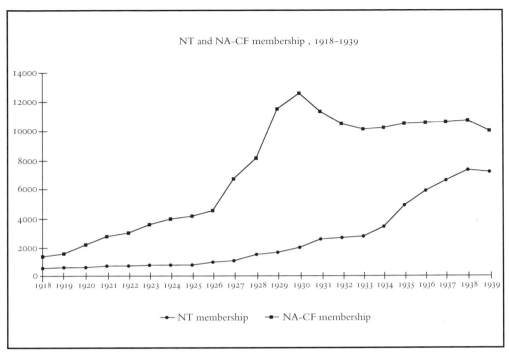

NT and NA-CF membership , 1918-1939

—•— NT membership      —■— NA-CF membership

58   The widening gap in membership between the National Trust (NT) and the National Art-Collections Fund (NA-CF), finally checked in the 1930s by more effective publicity on behalf of the Trust.

'apart from, and in some respects superior to, the interests of the legal owners'. Beauchamp recommended enactment of the powers over historic houses that had been excised by aristocratic critics in 1913. Some of the force behind his argument came from an older Arts and Crafts outlook, laying emphasis on cottages in villages, 'a national asset of high importance' and an 'influence on contemporary architecture', but the crisis of the great estate was now also entering his thinking:

> the old country houses and manor houses, are undoubtedly of first rate importance, and should be included in any scheme of protection. The upkeep of a large country house is likely to be an ever growing burden. The State should be prepared to recognise the services of an owner who maintains on account of its historic and artistic value a structure which is ill suited for modern requirements.

Beauchamp proposed tax reliefs and maintenance grants for historic houses in return for an extension of preservationist control:

the owner's freedom of usage and amenities may of necessity be limited. Part of the house may in fact become little more than a museum. Rooms may be maintained in an unuseable condition as examples of by-gone social manners or as things of beauty. Such limitations should be taken into account in assessing the value of the house for rating, taxation, and death duties.[36]

However, these arguments, reflecting the growing catholicity of taste among the experts as well as Beauchamp's consciousness of a crisis of aristocratic property, cut no ice with politicians in touch with public opinion. Lord Crawford, the First Commissioner of Works, decided to bury the report. For all his own personal attachment to historic architecture, Crawford was as yet unwilling to admit a public interest, 'so grave an inroad upon private rights and the development of property'.[37] The officials at the Office of Works were beside themselves with frustration, but with the fall of Lloyd George in 1922, their slimmest hopes disappeared; the Treasury was horrified at the thought of 'all manner of ugly, inconvenient and antiquated houses' falling into public hands. It considered Ancient Monuments expenditures 'entirely a luxury' and flatly refused 'to waste its resources on schemes which, however desirable from the aesthetic point of view, do not enrich the country or add to its commercial equipment'. The Office of Works tried to backpedal by disclaiming any interest in large houses; 'we have mainly in view the possibility of an interesting old cottage being offered which would be best preserved by being kept habitable', protested one civil servant meekly to the Treasury in 1925. But the issue was just about dead by then. Reluctantly, the Permanent Secretary, Sir Lionel Earle, who had signed the Beauchamp Report, concluded, 'public feeling would lie against us at this moment if we were to fight the Treasury'. And yet, he noted, 'we certainly have less powers in this matter, I think, than any other country in Europe, with the exception of the Balkan States and Turkey'.[38]

The powers proposed by Beauchamp and the Office of Works were comparatively puny, representing hardly more than a limited acceptance by the government of the executor's function of the National Trust, purchasing isolated buildings threatened by destruction and perhaps aiding from a small fund those owners incapable of maintaining their historic buildings. Interwar governments balked even at this much, fearing public indifference or hostility, and themselves lacking any conception of State responsibility for the national heritage. This was true of the most aesthetic Tories, such as Crawford or Lord Curzon, who, when he died in 1925, left Tattershall and Bodiam

Castles not to the Office of Works but to the National Trust (which was not entirely sure it could afford to accept them).

The broader task of preserving not only this or that bit of Old England but the basic fabric of the countryside was well beyond Tory abilities or ambitions. Stanley Baldwin has inexplicably gained a reputation as the man most responsible for fixing national identity firmly in the rural past.[39] He certainly did cater to a middle-class yearning for a quieter, less conflictual, less urban tone in politics, and – at least in the mid-1920s – he made political capital by contrasting his broad, common-sense 'middle England' to an alien proletarian militancy represented by Bolshevism abroad and the General Strike at home.[40] In doing so, Baldwin steered England through a period of tremendous social and economic change while preserving at the top the façade of reassuring continuity that was adopted at the grass-roots in the suburban cottage and 'village green'. Like the suburbanite, he was careful *not* to allow rural nostalgia to gum up the works of modern society. Unlike French and German politicians he had no peasants to protect, so he could establish in Britain a policy that endures today of tolerating protracted agricultural shrinkage. Baldwin presided over a massive roadbuilding and electrification programme that shredded the countryside. He detached his party and also his own portrayals of the English character from its aristocratic past, playing up a gentle, modest, domesticated, cottage-loving image that fitted neatly with established trends within the middle class.[41]

For all this, he won not plaudits but persistent criticism from the true preservationists. Their horror of the half-timbered suburban villa was echoed by their indignation with this country-lover who would not lift a finger to save the country. 'He must have approved our aims, but couldn't be bothered,' wrote Clough Williams-Ellis much later.[42] At the time, he mocked Baldwin's 'yards and yards of sob-stuff about the beauties of the countryside', while *Country Life* went further, denouncing his kind of 'hypocrisy' and 'stupidity'.[43] Those who were Conservatives were just about able to admit the political advantages of having a man like Baldwin at the helm, but they were no more at ease with the modern England he was preparing for them: This 'land of small-holders, frugal, parsimonious, and intensely conservative,' wrote Charles Harper, one of the leading interwar writers on the rural heritage, will be 'a countering influence to the insincerity of Liberalism and the poison of unsocial Socialism: but *what* a country it will be! A land of fierce uncultivated individualism, without ideals, except of a cheese-paring frugality.'[44]

## Desertion, Demolition, Disuse

A countryside filling up with cottages had less and less room for the big house. This was a social and cultural fact as much as a physical one. Of course, landlords who sold off their entire estates had to dispose of their main residence with the land, and live in town or buy a smaller house elsewhere in the country where they had no historic connection. J. M. Lee's study of the disintegration of the Cheshire élite found that much of its social life had already transferred to the metropolis by the First World War – the Cheshire Society of London was founded in 1914 – and it had collapsed completely fifteen years later – the Knutsford County Assembly, traditional focal point of gentry socializing, held its last dance in December 1930. In its place grew up a new rural élite, composed mostly of well-off commuters, who considered themselves above the normal run of suburbia, but whose 'country life' was modern and revolved around decidedly non-traditional pursuits such as motoring, golf and polo.[45] The Cheshire gentry's fate was shared by the élites of other counties contiguous to great cities – Berkshire, Surrey, Warwickshire, Staffordshire, Derbyshire – where *nouveaux riches* could be found to take on houses unwanted by their traditional owners.[46] Deeper in the countryside, there were not these substitutes for county society, and a different kind of county leadership emerged with a different agenda, dictated by the needs of smaller landowners, labourers and rural industry.[47]

Desertion of the countryside was not only a matter of necessity and temptation, for it affected the grandees, too, who were not forced off the land but abdicated voluntarily, indicating a deeper estrangement from traditional roles. The Duke of Sutherland, whose family had dwelt in Shropshire and Staffordshire since the seventeenth century, deserted Trentham before the war as too urbanized but after the war sold his other local base, Lilleshall, in favour of London residence and a country house at Sutton Place in Surrey, 'nearer London where I could enjoy the beauty and peace of the countryside and yet be able to travel to and from London with ease'.[48] Two landlords of the Dukeries, who took their money and ran, decamped to smaller country houses in Wiltshire and Yorkshire: Lord Savile sold Rufford Abbey to Albert Ball, the speculator of Tattershall, who dispersed the contents but failed to find a buyer for the house and let it fall into ruin; the Duke of Newcastle was also unable to find a buyer for Clumber, sold off its contents – some oak panelling wound up in the new County Council chambers in Nottingham – and then sold the fabric of the house for scrap. Piquantly, 300,000 hand-made eighteenth-century bricks were picked up to face a new church on a slum-clearance estate in Sheffield.[49] Many of the richest aristocrats sold off the whole of their estates and their traditional seats, simply because they could find better investments. The whole of the Bridgewater estate was sold off and £3.3 million in proceeds invested in equities. Even the Duke of Devonshire, who retained not one but several core estates and four large country houses, was by the 1920s earning more from stock dividends than from agriculture.[50]

Such desertions cast doubt on the claim – made nowadays both by admirers of the aristocracy and, oddly, by its critics – that

> by the inter-war years, it was preservation rather than destruction that most took the aristocracy's attention in rural affairs. As a landowning élite in the process of territorial abdication, they could no longer control the countryside. But they could present themselves instead as the guardians of its beauty and its amenities.[51]

Beauty and amenity in the high-cultural sense had long been alien concepts in landed society. They had played some role in the maintenance of a neat and ordered landed estate before the agricultural depression. But now beauty and amenity were expensive luxuries in a time when most landlords were seeking to economize on their remaining holdings. As the general secretary of the land agents' society wrote in 1933, 'amenity preservation' had become 'a matter of very minor importance' to landlords. 'So the Halls empty, and the roads are filled!'[52]

Furthermore, after the assaults of the 1910s and the betrayals of the 1920s, landlords as a class felt wounded and shunned by modern society and were reluctant to 'present' themselves as anything in public. They were, said *Country Life*, 'disheartened, not to say cowed . . . They have got it into their heads that they are not popular with the majority and will not be listened to. Many are as frightened as mice.'[53] It was no easy task – nor necessarily seen as a desirable one – to pick up new leadership roles just as they were being forced to abdicate their old ones.

True lovers of beauty and amenity in the countryside were in fact rather bitter about the complete abdication of the landed élite from its rural responsibilities. Christopher Hussey, the squire's son who succeeded Avray Tipping as chief architectural writer for *Country Life*, blamed second only after Lloyd George 'the "fashionable" . . . decadent element' among landowners, 'apt to think mainly of the superficial advantages of their position . . . [yet] this is the type of person who is gradually succeeding to the famous estates of the country'. Sport had become the opium of the upper classes, indicating 'some structural defect in the society which over-indulges it'. Hussey hoped for 'a *risorgimento* of the squires', but he was too intelligent to expect it.[54] Another defender of an ideal landed class against the real one, Ralph Nevill, was more pessimistic:

> many a landowner, having had to exchange his luxurious mansion for a small London flat, sits bewailing that Radical legislation is ruining the country – by which, of course, he means him- self . . . To-day the vast majority of those living even in houses of historic interest appear ready to sell or let their residence without the least feeling of regret, provided they can secure advantageous terms.[55]

Both Hussey and Nevill saw that, if the aristocracy was giving a cultural lead anywhere, it was in the metropolis. Landowners who had sold up and moved to town, or took advantage of the motor to use their country houses only for weekend entertainments, now had the opportunity to pursue a new public role as 'personalities', modernizing once again the public image developed before the war by portions of the 'smart set'. If stripped of associations with political power and social tyranny, titles and fortunes could be employed as assets to compete for public attention with theatrical impresarios and film-stars. Gossip columns in mass-circulation papers were filled with stories of aristocratic cocktail parties, fancy-dress dances, practical jokes, jolly japes and stunts, mostly the doing of a sexually liberated younger generation referred to collectively as the 'Bright Young People' – or, as Hussey preferred to call them, 'the decadent youth'.

The Bright Young People may have been leaders of a kind, but they had little to do with culture, history or rural amenity, and they disgusted those few who *were* slaving to preserve some fig-leaves of aristocratic dignity in the countryside. Lord Crawford for one was sickened by the antics of these most visible of interwar aristocrats:

> the vile social columns of the *Mail* and *Mirror* and *Express* describe day by day the extravagance and vulgarities of the smart London set – a positive disgrace . . . The Sunday papers describing the doings and witticisms of the smart set provide the Socialists with their most telling arguments when they denounce the idle rich . . .[56]

Crawford took some comfort in the fact that 'the heroes and heroines of this tittle-tattle from the cocktail parties and night clubs are all second-rate people', often indeed *déclassés*, but he was not much more impressed by the taste of the first-rate people.[57]

Insofar as culture and history remained concerns of the aristocracy, few could afford any longer to attach these qualities to large country houses. Not only were big houses ruinous to maintain, heat and staff in straitened times, but they were just not consistent with modern standards of good taste and comfort. Lord Crawford himself granted that, were it not for the presence of his beloved art and book collections, Haigh Hall would be 'uninhabitable'. Many owners both of town and country palaces laid them down with relief. Lord Lansdowne confided to Crawford after selling Lansdowne House to London property developers that 'for the first time in his life he realised what real comfort was', 'installed in the small comfortable house in Brook Street'.[58] The Duke of Portland's heir, one of the last owners to stick to the Dukeries, nevertheless announced publicly that he 'prefers not to be burdened with residence in a palatial mansion' like Welbeck Abbey, and he had built for himself a new, smaller house in the old house's grounds.[59]

Potential buyers felt the same way. It was almost impossible to sell a big house, no matter how historical, and therefore the connection between cultural and financial value, established tenuously before the war in sales to Americans and plutocrats, broke down. Landlords considered themselves lucky if they were able to divest themselves of historic houses for the price of the land they sat upon. Such was the fate of some of Nash's larger Mansions, traditionally the most prized houses in the land. The heir of the Ingrams, Edward Wood, sold Temple Newsam and its six-hundred-acre park to Leeds Corporation on very easy terms in 1922. Nottingham Corporation acquired both Wollaton Hall and Newstead Abbey, the former in 1924 from Lord Middleton for the price of its eight-hundred-acre park (upon most of which houses were built), the latter in 1931 free as a gift from Sir Julien Cahn (only after the National Trust had declined it). Cheshire County Council refused the gift of Crewe Hall, but Lord Crewe arranged to transfer it along with most of his estates to the Duchy of Lancaster.[60] Bramshill in Hampshire, described by Hussey as one of 'the five supreme houses in England intact with all its wonderful things', was one of the few to find a private buyer, the plutocrat Lord Brocket.[61] Another of Nash's Mansions, Bramall Hall in Cheshire, was about to be demolished when a local businessman stepped in and bought it for a song.[62] Others were advertised to let – great Knole itself in 1921, Levens Hall in Lancashire in 1928.[63] Montacute, which had been let off and on for years, failed to sell at auction in 1929 and was only saved from dereliction by the intervention of Ernest Cook – nicely, an heir of Thomas Cook the stately-home excursionist. Cook

conveyed it to the National Trust, which accepted its first major
country house with some reluctance, alarmed by the potential maintenance costs.[64]

This kind of holding operation could be mounted for a few of the
greatest Olden Time mansions, but it was neither possible nor desirable in the case of the vast majority of large country houses now
surplus to requirements. Hundreds of them were demolished; by one
estimate, 7 per cent of the total stock of country houses. Nearly all of
these were houses in the classical style, long criticized as ugly and
foreign, now doubly damned as big and draughty.[65] *The Field* advised
owners to demolish houses that, twenty years ago 'emblems of justi-
fiable family pride', were to-day 'incubuses sitting heavily upon
impoverished acres which can no longer support them . . . It may be
taken practically for granted that the vast mansions of Vanbrugh, Inigo
Jones, Wyatt and others can never again be supported by their land.'
In a bizarre twist of history, owners were now urged to reinhabit the
'small and beautiful manor houses' abandoned by their ancestors in the
eighteenth century.[66] Alternatively, if eighteenth- and nineteenth-
century wings had been added to an older core, the house could be
cut down to size to reduce costs.[67]

Short of demolition, white elephants might be converted to some
remunerative use. When this occurred, sentimentality was rarely an
issue, more a grim determination to exploit all available assets to their
fullest. The real giants could be put to institutional use. In 1919 it was
proposed – abortively – to turn Warwick Castle into a hostel for
wealthy American girls.[68] Stowe's four hundred rooms were successfully converted in 1922 for use as a boys' public school. Horace
Walpole's Strawberry Hill became a Roman Catholic teacher-training
college. Maxstoke Castle made a better hotel than a private home,
thought *Country Life*.[69] A number of country houses in the Peak
District were converted into youth hostels for hikers. Some developers
had hopes that conversion of country houses into flats might be
economical. This was to be the fate of Newstead Abbey before Sir
Julien Cahn rescued it from its owners. But flat-buyers seemed to
prefer purpose-built blocks, which were cheaper and usually better
equipped.[70] As the years wore on, owners grew giddy – or desperate
– with the possibilities. Patrick Balfour recommended, only half in
jest, that instead of selling off their houses for use as hotels, owners
should 'continue to have your friends down, but let them come as
paying instead of as free guests . . . We really must get more tough
about money. All this false delicacy is absurd'.[71] A land agent proposed
that country houses would make good civic centres for garden cities.[72]

59   Stowe opens for business as a school: the headmaster receiving boys, May 1923.

In 1936 the Earl of Dudley converted the ruins of Dudley Castle into a zoo.[73]

Inevitably, the combination of owners' detachment from their historic roots and the disintegration of many old houses further reduced the stock of stately homes open to public visitation. Of the Victorian open houses, about half had been closed by 1914; close to three-quarters were closed by the early 1930s.[74] Nearly all of the great show-houses that had attracted thousands in the nineteenth century were now closed, including Woburn, Eaton, Haddon, Lumley, Berkeley, Cobham, Belvoir, Alnwick, the Dukeries' parks and marvels, Newstead Abbey (until its donation to the local authority) and Blenheim Palace. Many owners of lesser attractions who had prided themselves on their accessibility also quietly withdrew.

Outright sales account for few of these closures; as in the case of Stowe, the house had been closed long before it was sold. More often, especially among the younger generation, it was a matter of the owner no longer feeling a sense of responsibility to the public or, for that matter, a sense of pride in the house. The Dukes of Bedford and Westminster could afford to live at Woburn and Eaton, but chose not

60    The ruins and grounds of Dudley Castle redeployed as a zoo, from 1936.

to, and at the same time countermanded their longstanding visiting arrangements. Others were determined to live properly in their homes and repelled the public for that reason. The last Earl of Berkeley, having sold his London estate for £2 million, undertook extensive modernizations at Berkeley Castle including installation of a marble bathroom in the American style. In any case he would have discontinued visiting: 'I loathe humanity', he kindly informed his second wife.[75] Blenheim was also modernized and closed; when H. V. Morton walked through the park in May 1939, no one he met knew or cared anything about the palace and its history. Appreciation was confined to the likes of the seven hundred revellers who attended a floodlit ball there some months later, with 'rivers of champagne', which the dandy Chips Channon found 'gay, young, brilliant, in short, perfection'.[76]

Owing either to fatalism or lack of interest, country-house closures no longer attracted the cries of protest that arose earlier over Knole or Warwick Castle. An exception was made for the most shocking closure of all, that of Haddon Hall, probably apart from Knole and

Penshurst the most beloved house in England. Lord Granby, the heir to Haddon, had nurtured a desire to reinhabit it since his youth. His father deeded it to him outright in 1921 and he began tastefully to modernize it: all the old fixtures and fittings were preserved, but renewed, electricity and running water were introduced and tennis courts installed. In the early stages of the building work, visiting continued unimpeded and in fact Granby posted placards and notice-boards to attract motor-charabanc tourists. He had also raised the ticket price, by his own admission to help subsidize the building work.

Then early in 1925, as the work neared completion, Granby began to pull Haddon out of the public sphere. First he closed off the footpaths through Haddon park, complaining that the charabanc parties 'left litter about, and behaved like so many worthy people of a certain class behaved themselves when out on holiday'. The local authority took him to court, claiming that the closed footpaths were public rights-of-way, an action which ended in a compromise whereby outlying paths remained open but those closest to the hall were closed; locals grumbled that peace had been purchased 'at too great a price', but there seemed no legal alternative. The hall remained open for the time.[77] In May 1925 Granby succeeded as Duke of Rutland and assumed all the family estates; the next month, just after the Whitsun crowds had reached their peak, a small fire broke out in the public tearooms, it was said because the furious boiling of hundreds of teas had overheated the chimneys. Little damage was done, but Haddon Hall was closed to the public.[78] In January 1926 Rutland went so far as to remove the old bell from the local parish church and install it at Haddon (he offered the parish church a new substitute). The house remained closed that summer and early in the next summer of 1927 the Duke and Duchess finally entered into residence. Thereafter the house was closed to the public except for a one-day opening each year to benefit local charities.[79] By the time S. P. B. Mais tramped by in early 1932, the hall was 'not only closed to the public but even (which strikes me as unnecessary) shut off from their view by newly-planted shrubs'. Permission to take photographs was refused. One hundred years of popular admiration was thus repudiated.[80]

At the lowest point between the wars, the stock of privately owned country houses open to the public was down to about two dozen, although this number included a hard core of Olden Time favourites: Hardwick, Hatfield, Ightham Mote, Knole, Penshurst, Burghley, Compton Wynyates and Warwick Castle. Other houses were opened fitfully, according to owners' whims or movements. Chatsworth, once the most visited house in England, now admitted the public only at

# THE HADDON HALL FOOTPATHS AGREEMENT.

## WHAT HAS BEEN GAINED AND WHAT LOST.

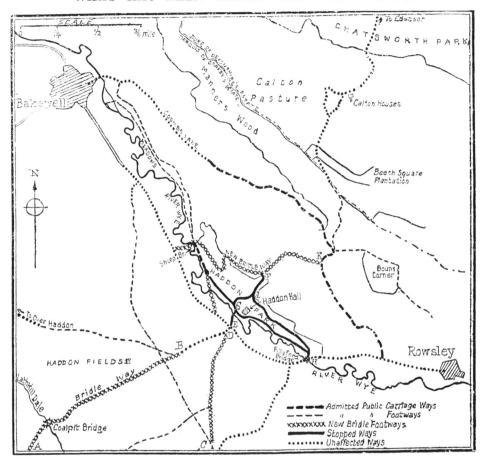

The map given herewith makes clear what has been lost and what gained in the Haddon Hall footpaths litigation which was settled between the parties concerned on Monday. Put in the simplest terms, walkers may read the map thus: those ways which are indicated by a continuous line are now stopped; those indicated by any other markings may be walked on.

It will be observed that there are four other markings employed. The thick discontinuous lines are the ways which are admitted to be public carriage ways; the thin discontinuous lines are the ways admitted to be public footways. The ways indicated by crosses are those which the Marquis of Granby is conceding to the public—ways which have not existed before. The well-known public routes which are unaffected by the action are indicated by dotted lines.

The following is the explanation of the capital letters placed here and there on the map. A to B and C to D are ways which were stopped by order of justices in 1799 and are now re-dedicated. E to F was also stopped by order of justices in 1799, and by the settlement arrived at on Monday that stoppage is maintained. Of G to H, part was stopped by order of justices in 1813, and the settlement leaves the stoppage absolute over the whole distance. I to H was admitted by the urban and the rural district councils to be a private way, and remains so. F to K was stopped by order of justices in 1799 and is now rededicated.

Both parties feel that the settlement is a satisfactory one. The defendants' taxed costs will be paid by the Marquis of Granby.

61   Defending the rights of ramblers on the Haddon Hall estate: the concessions extracted by Bakewell District Council from the Marquess of Granby, illustrated in the *Manchester Guardian*, 19 March 1925.

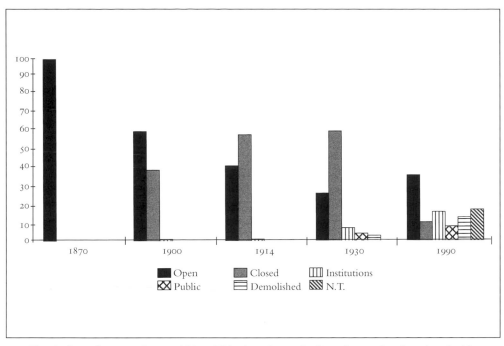

62   The decline of country-house visiting. This chart shows the fate of a sample of one hundred houses that were open to the public in 1870. Until the Second World War, the trend was for open houses to close but remain in private ownership. Relatively few were demolished, institutionalized or acquired by public bodies or the National Trust until after the war. (The chart does not take into account a few houses that were not open to the public in 1870 but did open between the wars, nor the large number that opened for the first time after 1945.)

midweek through a limited Whitsun to August Bank Holiday season, which in some years was further limited by arbitrary closings. Alnwick and Arundel Castles, where the families were only occasionally in residence, also posed stumbling blocks to the hopeful visitor. Americans, who were visiting England in greater numbers and eager to see the exotic stately homes, found this unpredictability highly irritating. The Parker family, touring in the summer of 1930, saw Penshurst, Compton Wynyates, Warwick Castle, Little Moreton Hall and Stokesay Castle, but were turned away from Haddon (open only one day in the year), Alnwick (closed unexpectedly), Raby ('All I could do was to climb a wall and take a picture'), Welbeck ('the Duke could not afford the necessary servants') and Belvoir (open erratically).[81]

Nearly all open houses found the numbers of visitors declining. Even when Chatsworth was open for its full summer season, it only averaged 11,000 visitors a year, about 10 per cent of its peak levels.[82]

Knole declined from around three thousand a year before the war to one thousand in the 1920s, and Petworth more gently from the same levels to around 2,500 in seasons when it was open between the wars.[83] Castle Howard slid from 3,500 in the 1920s to around two thousand in the 1930s.[84] These figures must be considered in a context of explosive growth for countryside tourism. Admissions to the Office of Works' ancient monuments – prehistoric sites such as Stonehenge, ruined abbeys and castles – nearly doubled in five years between 1925 and 1930, while the incalculable flow through picturesque villages and scenic countryside probably grew more rapidly.[85] The quality of the visiting experience was also in decay. Visitors to neglected and uninhabited homes noticed 'the cheerlessness of the state rooms (and particularly the dust at Knole)', 'the smell of dry rot combining with damp and dirt' at Compton Wynyates, 'the silken brocades and carpets sadly faded in places because the family are poor' at Burghley.[86]

From the owners' point of view, the precariousness of country-house visiting was all to the good. Rationing visitors to only occasional glimpses of their houses preserved their privacy and restored the status of the visit as a gracious privilege, rather than the right it had been in danger of becoming. It repelled the casual tourists who thronged the modern countryside and admitted only the decorous, the well-heeled and the deferential. Opening for a few shillings to benefit charity on one day a year, the course adopted at Haddon, was a useful way to cultivate this impression. The National Art-Collections Fund began in 1920 to organize special excursions for its members to country-house collections, and these 'treats' came to contribute substantially to the NA–CF's elevated tone as well as to its coffers.[87] More ambitiously, from 1927 the Queen's Institute for District Nursing organized for its own benefit a series of charity openings of gardens around the country. By tapping into the national craze for gardening, the programme – still thriving today as the National Gardens Scheme – made an instant success, showing 400 gardens in its first year, over 1,000 gardens to 250,000 visitors annually in the 1930s. A large proportion of these came on day-trips from seaside resorts, and the scheme was thus concentrated on the South Coast. Far more people glimpsed the outside of country houses while inspecting their gardens than visited houses for their own sake.[88]

The success of these schemes points to ways in which the country house might have been a real attraction, at least to sections of the public, had the owners been so inclined. Art appreciation and gardening were uncontroversial hobbies with growing followings.

Beyond them, the pressure of countryside tourism was such that a huge audience was hanging about at the big house's gates, waiting to be invited in for a curious look. On Haddon's rare open days, thousands might show up; journalists marvelled at the novel sight of hundreds of motor cars parked in the fields around.[89] Charity day at Eastnor Castle could draw over five thousand on a single afternoon.[90] Publicly owned houses like Newstead and Temple Newsam which were open regularly near population centres did a booming trade.[91]

As always, the Earl of Warwick showed the way it could be done by a private owner. The tentative commercialization undertaken by the 5th Earl gave way to a wholehearted tourist industry under the 6th Earl from 1924. At its interwar peak in 1930, Warwick Castle was clocking up over eighty thousand visitors a year. The decline experienced at Warwick as at many tourist attractions in the trough of the slump after 1930 was vigorously combatted by special arrangements with travel bureaux and tour groups, aggressive advertising and efforts to attract film deals from Hollywood. The Earl saw not only his house as a set but himself as a star, and for a time was under contract with MGM. 'They said I was not the type,' he commented when released, 'we will see about that.'[92] By this time, the Earl was covering the castle upkeep and staff expenses with tourist takings and also withdrawing large sums from the tourist account to support his playboy lifestyle. The castle itself was kept in tiptop shape; later he claimed to have spent £100,000 from interwar tourist income on refurbishment and improvement.[93]

Few noblemen had a house like the Earl of Warwick's, but more important was the fact that few noblemen had his entrepreneurial approach to the paying public. Country-house owners were not yet ready to regard the public as a potential ally or support. They were still in retreat, in debt, in a sulk or in confusion. They felt, in Christopher Hussey's words, 'as a class, mistrusted by the majority of the politically minded among the people, and singled out to make heavier contributions to the national exchequer than other persons, or, indeed, than their incomes could economically bear.'[94] They were reluctant even to make the tentative overtures to modern tastes required by such as the Queen's Institute scheme; organizers of the scheme in its early days found it difficult to get owners to commit to regular annual openings, so anxious were they that the public would somehow take unfair advantage.[95] Perhaps they were right to feel anxious. In these years of desertion, demolition and disuse, the public image of the country house was at an historic low. Disrespect, even derision were more in evidence than the guilty conscience detected by Forster.

## A Ghostly Presence

The general public's near-total indifference to the fate of the country house in the 1920s and 1930s – callous and inexplicably philistine as it may seem today – is fully intelligible in its proper context. There was, first of all, little concept of 'the country house'. There were instead 'mansions of the Olden Time', which had been prized as much for their historical associations as for their architectural qualities. That fashion had long been fading from its Victorian peak. The Ruskinian concerns which the Arts and Crafts movement had promoted also had no category of 'the country house', but only a set of aesthetic criteria which favoured smaller, handcrafted domestic buildings. That fashion, too, felt a little dusty by the 1920s. Furthermore, strict limits had been placed on the sense of a 'national heritage' in buildings. The presumption of *laissez-faire* in all things had been undermined somewhat by prewar Liberalism's broader interpretation of public interests, including in culture, but Liberalism's subsequent collapse left a vacuum. The Tory attitude to the cultural heritage was to leave it to private owners and private philanthropy. Private owners, who had begun to see some value in national claims to their movable art treasures, still vigorously resisted any claim to their useful land and buildings. Thus the pervasive sense in the interwar years that the aristocracy had become superannuated – or at least redundant to country life – also attached to their large private homes. Not only the philistine public, but also many connoisseurs of art and architecture were content to leave owners to dispose of their old houses as they saw fit.

The larger houses of the eighteenth and nineteenth centuries had been so consistently depreciated from all quarters that they had become almost completely emptied of meaning.[96] They resembled 'hotels or hydros rather than private residences,' wrote one correspondent to *The Times*, 'the mania [for adding wings] being an outlet for energy nowadays devoted to business or else to the wider usefulness of improving dwellings on the estate.'[97] Another writer condemned as 'foolish' the idea that 'because these buildings are old, they are necessarily beautiful': 'with their innumerable bedrooms, endless corridors, and servants' offices', they would be better off broken up, and their lovely materials – 'lichen-coloured slates, rose-red tiles, wainscot panelling, bricks, and beams' – re-used in smaller homes.[98] Clough Williams-Ellis, in calling for preservation of 'the honest-to-God Stately Homes of England', stressed the need to cut them off in the public mind from 'the considerable tail of merely large or

pretentious houses'.[99] G. M. Trevelyan granted that an empty palace
was 'a somewhat melancholy affair', difficult to insinuate into the
public's affection: 'It was meant for daily life, and . . . modern conditions render the life of "great families" no longer possible in these
surroundings.'[100]

When one of these enormous white elephants fell to the wreckers'
ball, then, it was often more a subject of curiosity or hilarity than of
mourning. One of the first victims after the Armistice was the vast
Hamilton Palace, which had been gradually emptied of its contents
since 1882 and by 1919 had been engirdled and undermined by the
Lanarkshire coalfield. Avray Tipping, writing in *Country Life*, accepted
'its condemnation by general consent'. 'The exaggerated grandeur of
the great magnate of a century ago makes no appeal', he understood,
though his own sentiments pulled him in a different direction. 'The
house has the air of drawing back into itself, yearly more ugly and
solitary, as the new conditions close in upon it,' agreed Lady Margaret
Sackville, in the same pages,

> some old houses adapt themselves graciously and beautifully
> compromise as it were . . . *this* house with its melancholy grounds
> has neither loveliness nor charm . . . who could love this grey pile,
> wrought as it is in that spirit of barren pomp which placed empty
> urns and bleakly worded epitaphs on tombs?[101]

The projected demolition in 1922 of the equally pompous Stowe
elicited the same philosophic response: 'It has outlived its purpose.'[102]
*The Times* commented bitterly that contemporary taste preferred
Stowe in ruins to Stowe intact, 'imposing in its ruined, almost wild,
grandeur'.[103]

Smaller houses from the same period did not attract much more
sympathy. Eighteenth-century houses were discarded as 'unhomely'
and alien to the English countryside. When Nuthall Temple, a
Palladian villa outside Nottingham, was put up for sale, not even
preservationists could muster much enthusiasm. 'The style of Nuthall
Temple is very distinctive,' grudged *The Times*, 'but the practical
common sense of English landowners never favoured the experiment
of building houses in that manner for this country.' Nuthall 'lacked
only one thing – Architecture', agreed *Country Life*. Only after the
Temple was sold to the housebreakers did *Country Life* come to regret
its earlier dismissal.[104] The people of Nottingham had no such regrets.
They were entertained by the sight of its spectacular demolition on
the afternoon of 31 July 1929, when a property developer and a
local journalist sprinkled the shell with paraffin and petrol and made

a bonfire of it. 'Impressive Scene' ran next day's headline in the *Nottingham Evening News*.[105]

Older houses were likely to be granted more historical and aesthetic value, but did not win much more public sympathy when endangered. Time and time again in these years, the National Trust failed to raise sufficient funds on appeal to save some old manor house. The SPAB tried to get the Trust to help it save Eastbury Manor House, a gem of an Elizabethan manor house in Barking, but an appeal 'met with very slight response'. Only the intervention of a few wealthy guarantors made it possible to repair Eastbury sufficiently to let it to an ex-servicemen's group as a clubhouse.[106] Swakeleys, another manor house threatened by metropolitan development, was also the subject of a failed appeal and was saved in the same way, let to the Foreign Office for use as a staff clubhouse.[107] At this time, the Trust was finding it difficult to scrape together even the £2,000 needed to pay death duties on its gifts from Lord Curzon, Bodiam and Tattershall Castles. In contrast, when it appealed for funds to save an open space in the Greater London area, Ashridge Park, it raised over £40,000 in a matter of weeks.[108]

A large number of country houses threatened by suburban development in this way were acquired by local authorities, continuing the trend established before the war. As before, the houses often came as unwelcome baggage with a property desired for its recreational value. Eastbury, which was eventually taken on by Barking District Council, was chiefly of interest for its bowling greens and tennis courts. Most of the growing suburban London councils acquired parks in this way, with the houses very much an afterthought. In one case, Broomfield House in Palmers Green, an unpleasantly classical house, was half-timbered to make it more acceptable to the ratepayers.[109] Kenwood was added to Hampstead Heath for its 'woodland joys, sylvan beauties, shady dells, leafy delights, umbrageous spaces', not for its Adam house that was described in the guidebook as 'massive rather than elegant'; the house would have been omitted entirely from the bargain had not Lord Iveagh bought it and donated it free of charge to the London County Council to house his bequest of pictures.[110] Another Palladian villa, Chiswick House, was spared Nuthall Temple's fate for the value of its walks and gardens, so long 'screened off . . . from the public eye'.[111]

Around England, country houses acquired with parks were used as dumping-grounds for the local authorities' museum collections, without much regard for matching contents to setting. A survey in 1928 found that 20 per cent of local authority museums were housed

# NUTHALL TEMPLE BURNED.

## NOVEL DEMOLITION PLAN CARRIED OUT.

## IMPRESSIVE SCENE

## DESTRUCTION OF NOTED LOCAL LANDMARK.

AT 2.30 to-day Mr. J. H. Brough, of Beeston, and a "Nottingham Evening News" reporter set fire to Nuthall Temple.

The whole of the west wing was sprinkled with paraffin and petrol, and then lighted brands were thrown at the foot of this historic pile, without protest from the village constable or any of the spectators.

Within three-quarters of an hour the west wall crumbled and fell with a roar like a thunder-clap, which must have been heard for a mile or so away.

The flames had eaten away large wooden supports which had been erected in the foundations, and when these began to drop out the 400 odd tons of masonry began to bulge and crack.

### A Wonderful Sight.

The few spectators who stood near the building at the beginning had to beat a hurried retreat as the fire became unbearably fierce, and when the shout had gone up that the great wall was coming down, there was a general stampede.

Fortunately, none of the huge stones flew off at a tangent and only a few of them rolled to the feet of the nearest watcher.

It was a wonderful sight, though to many who would have preferred to see the Temple preserved it must have been mingled with regret.

Mr. Brough, who purchased the shell of the temple, is slowly demolishing it and the idea of burning away the foundations occured to him some time ago.

What took only a few minutes to demolish by fire might have taken by the pick and shovel method a month or two.

All that now remains of the west wing is a black and dusty ruin.

63   A developer and a reporter complete the demolition of Nuthall Temple (*Nottingham Evening News*, 1 August 1929).

in former country mansions, especially in the Northern industrial towns, 'where the corporation have taken the opportunity of acquiring both a house for a museum, etc., and a recreation ground. Such mansions, however, are often ill-adapted for museum purposes'. Of the 507 local museums in Britain, only sixteen were 'interesting historical buildings furnished so as to present the appearance of an inhabited house of the period', and these were mostly town-houses.[112]

A few conspicuous exceptions could be found in the North and the Midlands, where the popular attachment to mansions of the Olden Time seems to have persisted, or at least where a greatly diminished aristocracy no longer posed a threat. Some of the grandest of these historical houses now fell into public hands. Following the example set by Birmingham's Aston Hall, Burnley's Towneley Hall and Bolton's Hall-in-th'-Wood, Chorley acquired the seventeenth-century Astley Hall in 1922, Leeds bought Temple Newsam in the same year, and Nottingham took on both Wollaton Hall in 1924 and Byron's Newstead Abbey in 1931. Wollaton Hall attracted an unusual degree of praise for its architectural value – 'beauty of outline is not sacrificed to massive solidity' – but here, too, the first priority was the land, which Nottingham Corporation coveted for suburban development and recreational use. Advocates of the purchase could not disguise a note of sweet revenge as 'a Paradise behind locked gates' was claimed for 'the sweated and imprisoned denizens of filthy little streets'.[113] Temple Newsam was also taken seriously by its public purchasers; a scholarly guidebook was commissioned which noted the building's affinities to two other municipalized stately homes, Aston and Wollaton.[114] Still, when a country-house lover from the National Trust visited in 1937, he could not help contrasting the 'gardens really well kept up by Corporation' with the 'usual lack of taste' inside the house.[115]

Few people can have shared the view that even these Olden Time mansions were part of a common heritage, fewer still that that heritage was worth preserving as integral to modern identity. Old country houses were more frequently represented as relics of a past standing in the way of, or at least at a distance from modern life. The gates of Hatfield were shut, Arnold Bennett said accusatorily to Lord David Cecil at a party in 1930, 'shut away from life'. 'But open on Thursdays', rejoined Cecil; 'I don't want to go on Thursdays', Bennett grunted.[116] Houses were demolished to make way for things people really wanted – houses, roads, parks – or converted to modern uses – hospitals, schools, blocks of flats, hotels. Either they retained their traditional and social meanings, in which case they were ultimately doomed, or they lost them and became mere shells for modern uses, leaving behind only a dim spectre of power departed.

Raymond Williams detected something of this in the emergence of the country-house murder mystery, in which country houses became sites of abstract terror and suspense, their distance from the modern city useful for the artificial purposes of the genre.[117] Alison Light's recent analysis of the country-house murder between the wars goes further. She suggests that the 'tuft-hunting' murder mystery was really an Edwardian phenomenon, reflecting an old-fashioned deference to the 'smart set' and the heroes of clubland. The popular murder mysteries between the wars, like Agatha Christie's, modernized the *mise-en-scène* for a more suburban and female audience. Christie's country houses, while useful for the purposes described by Williams, were deliberately populated not by landed families of ancient lineage but by *nouveaux riches*, mixing cocktails, dancing to the gramophone, subject to domestic and emotional foibles that were familiar to her readership and which gave her plots their verisimilitude. While her parvenus may derive a *frisson* from having taken the places of the old aristocracy, they wish neither to imitate them nor particularly to summon up their ghosts.[118]

The country-house ghost is a presence in interwar culture, but his presence – it is rarely her presence – is, inevitably, rather insubstantial. In the nineteenth century ghosts had been given their rightful place in country-house history. Walter Scott popularized the ghost of Littlecote, in Wiltshire, which preserved the memory of a real sixteenth-century infanticide, and ghosts of Mary Queen of Scots and other Olden Time heroes were common features of houses of the right period. In the period of aristocratic decline, however, ghosts began to take on a less historical – and also less serious – complexion. Oscar Wilde was the pioneer: in 'The Canterville Ghost' (1887), the ancestral ghost is cheerfully greeted and later mocked by the Americans who have bought Canterville Chase; he has pillows thrown at him, Rising Sun Lubricator rubbed on his creaking chains and a placard hung round his neck advertising 'Ye Onlie True and Originale Spooke – Beware of Ye Imitationes'. These indignities are really the central feature of the story, which then screeches to a suddenly conventional ending, as the ghost passes Canterville Chase on to the American heroine, who conveniently marries a duke and restores the house to native hands.[119]

Wilde's story was updated and linked to the Tattershall Castle fiasco in a 1932 *Punch* story by Eric Keown, later made into a popular film, *The Ghost Goes West*. In the film version Glourie Castle is not only

64   In the film of *The Ghost Goes West* (1936), Glourie Castle is exported to Florida and equipped with palm trees and a gondola in the moat, as 'sort of a European touch'.

bought up but exported by the Americans, resituated at Sunnymede, 'the little wonder city of Florida', surrounded by palm trees and a moat with a gondola as 'sort of a European touch'. Again the ghost befriends the American heroine and facilitates her marriage to the last of the Glouries which will return the castle to its native soil. But in the original *Punch* version, the ghost's honour is redeemed by saving his American purchaser from gangsters; in this less romantic version, meant for domestic consumption, the stately home, Moat Place, is abandoned to America forever. Both the Canterville and the Glourie ghosts vanish once their castles are secured. Certainly if the ghosts had not interceded, the castles would have been lost, for efforts to stoke up national pride by decrying the export of antiquities were invariably a flop, as had been the case with Tattershall.[120]

It is also significant that Americans feature in these ghost stories – not only as symbols of the New World, but as symbols of the New World susceptible to the romance of the old. Americans were widely held to be more interested in such things than 'the dull kind of Englishman who seems to know nothing about the history of his own country'.[121] The natives in *The Ghost Goes West* – they are Scottish, not English – care only about getting their money's worth out of the castle's laird, while the heroine guesses that 'every American has a hankering for this kind of romance and beauty and peacefulness'. Noël Coward's 'Stately Homes of England' (1938) offers an enticing array of spooks as well as historical associations 'for Americans to rent'. *Punch* sent up the prosaic indifference of the younger sort of Englishman with a 1932 cartoon set in a country house converted into a hostel: 'Do you hike?', asks the unfazed hiker on meeting the family ghost. 'No,' replies the indignant ghost, 'I walk.'[122]

If to most of the country 'the stately homes of England' had become something of a joke, there were always a few who took them deadly seriously, for whom the holocaust of houses was a great

65   The modern hiker (in the familiar uniform) meets the Olden Time ghost in *Punch*, 6 July 1932.

[Several ancestral houses in the country are being converted into hikers' hostels.]
*Holiday-maker (meeting the Family Ghost).* " Do you hike? "
*Ghost (haughtily).* " No, I walk. "

tragedy. Little clusters of aristocratic aesthetes continued to nurture their devotions privately, if anything more explicitly now in defiance of the democratic world. If they could afford to, they restored and beautified their own homes for personal enjoyment, as the 9th Duke of Rutland did at Haddon. Lord Crawford's clan, the Lindsays, were again conspicuous: Rutland's mother, Violet Lindsay, was an influence on her son as well as on her daughter, Lady Anglesey, who restored Beaudesert in Staffordshire; Violet's brother Harry restored Sutton Courtenay in Berkshire. Another circle gathered around Vita Sackville-West, daughter of the Lady Sackville who had lavished so much money on Knole. Sackville-West and her husband Harold Nicolson restored first Long Barn, a small Tudor house in Kent, and then nearby Sissinghurst, more substantial fragments of an Elizabethan castle.[123]

Sackville-West elaborated some of her ideas about old country houses and their value in the modern world in a short novel, *The Heir*, published in 1922. She tells the story of a moated Tudor house, loosely based on Groombridge Place in Kent, which is inherited by Peregrine Chase, a conventional and humourless insurance broker from Wolverhampton. Initially blind to the house's charms, he consigns it to an auction-house, but while awaiting the estate's break-up he is gradually drawn into its spell. The climax comes with the day of the sale, as 'the London motors' arrive, bringing Americans, Brazilians, speculators and developers. Chase has a vision: 'The house unveiled, prostituted; yes, it was like seeing one's mistress in a slave-market.' He buys in the house and, though all the land is sold, the house is saved. His status as a landowner has been sacrificed, a sympathetic cottager has lost his home to a hotel proprietor (for conversion into a tea-room), but what does this matter, when 'this beauty, this pride' has been rescued from such a rape? Part racial mysticism, part aesthetic delirium, *The Heir* does summon up the beauties of a Tudor manor house as seen through an Arts and Crafts sensibility, but it also opposes those beauties rigidly to the whole of the human world, saving only the ancient family and its retainers.[124]

In real life, Sackville-West's family pride was vested in Knole, which she as a daughter was barred from inheriting. That pride was infectious enough to inspire probably the best-known country-house novel of the interwar period, Virginia Woolf's *Orlando* (1928), a fantasia on Knole and its endurance through the ages. Woolf, like many liberal intellectuals, had been hostile enough to aristocrats and their cultural illiteracy before the war, holding Arnold's view of the 'fortresses of barbarism'. Now, though she did not abandon her liberalism, she shared the disappointment of liberals in the drift of modernity and for a time revelled in Vita's fantasy of an aristocracy that was really a cultural élite, a saving remnant untouched by the tide of materialism, the eternal patrons of the literary class. Now, if her head knew still that the owners of these houses had typically been crass and dull, her heart could feel that these country houses were in fact 'little fortresses of civilization, where you could read books, act plays, make laws, meet your neighbours, and talk with strangers from abroad'.[125]

If the future of the country house depended on a romantic love affair with the aristocracy, then it was surely doomed. Yet in the 1920s at least there was almost no general defence of the country house possible that did not rest on a defence of the landed élite, present as well as past. Politically, the break-up of the great estates was the culmination of a long and broadly desirable process, and there seemed no public-interest grounds on which to oppose it. Landowners themselves could think of none that were not backward-looking defences of their traditional roles. Aesthetically, the most active defenders of culture had been reared in an Arts and Crafts tradition, which condemned post-Restoration architecture, and they had little sympathy for the bulk of country houses facing destruction. Sackville-West did not extend her loyalties beyond Knole and Groombridge to the large Georgian house.[126] The few who did were considered footmen to the rich.[127]

To address the full gravity of the threat, and to annex a substantial section of public opinion to a solution, would require a great breach with late Victorian canons both of politics and of taste. Those breaches were made tentatively and with mixed success only in the 1930s; they are the subject of the next chapter.

66 Lord Gerald Wellesley, aesthete and architect (and later Duke of Wellington), designed his own town house in a highly polished Regency style: Wellesley's drawing-room at 11, Titchfield Terrace, from a *Country Life* profile by his former housemate Christopher Hussey, 11 April 1931. (*See pp. 286–7.*)

## CHAPTER 7

# Brideshead Rehabilitated: Georgian Salvage in the 1930s

The decay, dismemberment and invasion of the old English country-side in the 1920s threw its aesthetic and intellectual advocates into considerable confusion. Some, like H. J. Massingham and J. C. Squire, recoiled into what Clough Williams-Ellis called their 'private paradises', deep retreats into the backwoods or embittered nostalgia; others responded quite differently. Joining in a general revulsion against all things Victorian, they pronounced the countryside of the Arts and Crafts movement dead and gone. Old enemies, the aristocracy, had been declawed; old heroes, the peasantry, had disappeared. All that were left were hordes of mock-Tudor yeomen marauding around the countryside, yet another reason to consider the Arts and Crafts movement a failure.

The anti-Victorian reaction of the 1930s made possible, for the first time since the 1830s, a movement in favour of the Georgian, an aesthetic that had been so long damned as alien and exclusive. This Georgian revival went in many different directions. At one extreme, it could be rehabilitated as a clean, efficient, almost avant-garde style, one which had shaped the 'ordinary' countryside of twentieth-century England – so beloved of contemporaries – and was therefore compatible with modern standards of taste and leisure. But at another extreme, the Georgian could be prized precisely for its aloofness from modern life, its elegance, civility and grandeur contrasting sharply with the glutinous sentimentality and domesticity of bourgeois suburbia.

For both these varieties of neo-Georgian, the fate of the country house and its estate became matters of great concern. They united uncomfortably in the years just before the Second World War in a concerted attempt to rehabilitate the large country house as a symbol of English art and greatness. The National Trust's Country House Scheme, launched in 1936, was the culmination of this campaign.

Perhaps this scheme laid the foundations for the postwar revival of the country house. But if so, it lay on shaky foundations. In the 1930s, while the Georgian revival in general scored significant successes, its country-house campaign was too explicitly aimed against popular tastes and aspirations and was its least successful venture. The public was not yet ready to embrace such a symbol of conspicuous 'taste' and social inequality, and – just as important – owners were not yet ready to embrace the public.

## Order in the Countryside

From its origins, the Arts and Crafts movement had been bedevilled by the gulf that lay between the country as it was and the country as it should be. The Arts and Crafts ideal was the kind of traditional village life that had flourished in the fifteenth and sixteenth centuries, but which since then had been progressively overlaid and stifled by the aesthetic formality and social tyranny of the great estate. This history made it difficult for such countryside lovers as Charles Masterman to enjoy typical countryside – 'landlords' country' – without guilt. It also tended to confine the active preservationist efforts of Arts and Crafts bodies like the SPAB and, to a lesser extent, the National Trust to rescuing remaining fragments of the 'unspoilt' prelapsarian past: historic buildings from ancient times to the Middle Ages and Tudor and Stuart periods, romantic, uncultivated beauty spots in the Lake District and upland regions.

The collapse of the old order after 1918 began to peel away some of these inhibitions. First, it became clear that all of rural England – not only the beauty spots and historic buildings – was now subject to spoilage by speculative development and urban incursion. Second, the breakup of the great estates, while it removed a source of hope – the heroic peasant – also de-fanged a traditional enemy – the despotic lord. Cautiously, a more catholic view of the English countryside emerged among aesthetes and intellectuals, one that could embrace ordinary landscape as well as the village and the 'ancient building'. Just at a time when the bulk of England was absorbing a version of the Arts and Crafts vision – coming to appreciate the littleness and homeliness of the cottage and the village – intellectuals were finding a way to love the great estate and to defend it as a public good.

The earliest advocates of 'landlords' country' on this modern basis were, unsurprisingly, progressive offspring of the Liberal squirearchy, who had inherited their parents' love of open space and wished now to preserve it for public benefit. Clough Williams-Ellis, for instance, had inherited one of his family's Welsh properties, 'a rambling old Carolean Plas . . . set in a wildly romantic little estate amongst the Welsh mountains that had been held by my family for over four centuries', and his care in tending and restoring it developed his appreciation for landlordship. On the other hand, his Bohemian life as an architect and husband of the socialist writer Amabel Strachey persuaded him that the landlord's function had to be carried on in future by more democratic hands. Masterman's dear friend Reginald Bray, squire of Shere, considered himself a custodian not only for his estate-workers but also for the growing numbers of ramblers and weekenders who were descending on his part of Surrey; he worked closely with local authorities to preserve amenity land from development, and designed specially discreet holiday cabins for visitors, who included Williams-Ellis and George Trevelyan. The Trevelyan brothers, Charles and George, developed the same kind of appreciation on their family's Wallington estate in Northumberland, which Charles sought to inject into the Labour party, while George (as we have seen) worked on Baldwin. George's friend Edward Hilton Young drew his love of humanized nature from his Liberal baronet father and from the family mansion at Formosa Fishery, across the Thames from Cliveden; he stuck with the Liberals until 1926 when, fleeing from socialism, he, too, took on the task of expanding Baldwin's ambitions for the countryside.[1]

Men like these – the last fragments of the Liberal gentry – would have been an isolated and derisory force had they not been strengthened at the end of the 1920s by a broader and more modern element also discovering hitherto unsuspected virtue in the great estate. A younger generation of planning-oriented intellectuals was then reacting against the chaotic individualism of their Victorian parents. These planners disliked the haphazard and inefficient way in which the countryside was being carved up, but they also disliked Victorian aesthetics – including the Arts and Crafts – which they saw as fussy, disordered and excessively individualistic. To them, broad acres of well-cultivated and well-tended countryside presented a refreshingly modern, efficient and ordered contrast to the backward muddle that was 'Old England', with its ramshackle cottages, crooked lanes, ruins and earthworks. Theirs was a new idea of heritage, one which dwelt upon the lingering utility of the historically constructed countryside – for agriculture, recreation, education – rather than upon some more spiritual notion of the uniqueness and wholesomeness of the past. These ideas lay behind the formation in 1926 of the Council for the Preservation of Rural England, which ranged together planners (nota-

67   The Council for the Preservation of Rural England (CPRE) campaigns for an ordered countryside: neat (*not* cluttered and 'picturesque') villages, as at Lechlade, and well-cultivated fields.

bly, the CPRE's founder, Patrick Abercrombie), modern-minded intellectuals, some liberal landowners and the older amenity societies, scrambling to keep up with the new wave.[2]

After half a century of pretty consistent denigration by liberal intellectuals, the amenity functions of the great estate were once again represented as potentially social rather than anti-social. Turning on its head the Arts and Crafts argument about the effect of enclosure on rural England, Abercrombie maintained that the monopolization of the land by great landowners

> gave a richness to the country . . . Whether this was sound on social lines or no, it increased the efficiency of farming and altered the general appearance of the countryside, at the same time taming its wildness . . . This park-like effect of the country was evidently the result of a desire to irradiate the influences of the private garden and park on the surrounding country.[3]

G. M. Trevelyan was more specific. In the 'South-English landscape'

> we have what we may call the marriage of man's work and nature's in perfect harmony. It reached its culminating point of perfection in the reign of George III, with the last enclosures, the great planta-

tions of woodland estates and parks round the country seats, and the building in great profusion of substantial but beautiful farms, farmbuildings and cottages harmonious with the landscape.[4]

Williams-Ellis also praised the 'general sense of order and beauty' so evident in the eighteenth and not in the nineteenth century. What had gone wrong was that landlords had tried to keep this beauty to themselves, making of the country 'a Private Paradise', driving the people into urban ugliness, and thereby – when democracy finally came – digging their own grave.[5]

Along with this breach with Arts and Crafts values came a breach with Arts and Crafts methods of preservation. The traditional strategy adopted by groups such as the SPAB and the National Trust had been to draw public attention to isolated monuments or beauty spots threatened by development and call for their preservation, either by State purchase or by charitable appeal. This strategy had been appropriate when the scale of the threat was more limited, but also appropriate to an aesthetic which placed the highest value on individual pieces of human craftsmanship – a cottage, a cathedral, a ruined castle. The new preservationism which saw value in the basic structure of the countryside also had to adopt a basic, structural means of saving it. The landlord class had to be replaced with some equally powerful and pervasive public authority that could maintain land in its pristine state and bend it to public benefit. 'The difficult game is to find substitutes for the old aristocracy – not to be called that name', as George Trevelyan once wrote to Hilton Young.[6]

Trevelyan and Young might have spoken like this because at heart they yearned to see the old aristocracy reinstated, but others used the same language with different intent, insisting that the aristocracy not only could but *should* be replaced by a public authority. In the CPRE and cognate circles were planners and socialists who considered private landownership to be fundamentally unsound. The considerable social and aesthetic achievements of the great estate had been built upon the selfish concerns of a small clique, which could not possibly encompass the range of interests in the countryside present in modern society. New forces had to be intruded into the great estate to ensure that it continued to produce food efficiently, maintain beauty and amenity for public enjoyment, and, where necessary, make way for careful, planned development of roads, pylons and new building. Opinions differed whether landlords should be guided to these ends by planning controls – as Abercrombie advocated – or whether their estates should be taken over completely by land nationalization.

Debate over such questions was a purely academic matter in the first years of the CPRE. What a few liberal landowners and professors of town planning felt paled into insignificance next to the powerful interests content with a *laissez-faire* approach to rural development. Worse still, the general public did not yet see the fate of the country-side as a problem; it seemed hardly touched, if anything vastly under-used. When intellectuals came forward to 'preserve' the countryside, they were interpreted as preserving from the public rather than for it.

The advent of a Labour government in 1929 promised to open up new challenges and also new opportunities for countryside preserva-tion, however. Labour came to power pledged to renew the pre-war Liberal tax programme by further raising death duties and by again pursuing a capital tax on the value of land. For the first time, it became urgent to determine what Labour's countryside policy was. Had it inherited Liberalism's unconcern with the aesthetic and social consequences of estate breakup, or was it prepared to take responsibil-ity for the consequences of its tax proposals with a programme of rural preservation? If so, which countryside was it to preserve?

The auguries were mixed. On the one hand, the older generation of the Labour party had been reared on Ruskin and Morris's idealiza-tion of the old and cottagey; they had been reinforced after 1918 by the defection of certain likeminded New Liberals, so that, for instance, both Charles and Noël Buxton, promoters of strong preservationist legislation in 1913, were sitting as Labour MPs in 1929. When George Lansbury was appointed in 1929 to head the Office of Works, home of official Arts and Crafts preservationism, Noël Buxton wrote to him to remind him of this long-neglected cause, 'the question of better preservation of ancient buildings. It is a scandal that priceless monu-ments should be destroyed; the State should prevent it as in other countries'.[7] Lansbury was heard to mutter some reminiscence of his work alongside William Morris to save Bow's fifteenth-century parish church.[8]

But no one paid much attention to the maunderings of these old men. Even the experts at the Office of Works, who had preserved so effectively the government's little stock of ancient buildings, felt that this line of intervention had run its course. Despite the growing numbers of tourists passing through the turnstiles of its ruined castles and abbeys, the Office understood that no modern government, striv-ing for efficiency and development in straitened times, could afford to spend more money on 'Old England'. Any extension of government powers would have to be 'tackled from the point of view of town and regional planning . . . what can be called "country planning"'.[9]

This cause had one important advocate, the new Prime Minister, Ramsay MacDonald. MacDonald had a long history of affection for nature, and especially for the wilder parts of his native Scotland; he is said to have come to appreciate the amenity functions of the land-owner when, during his first brief premiership in 1924, he was shocked by the expense necessary to put into order the estate at Chequers Court, which had been donated to the nation in 1917 as the Prime Minister's country residence.[10] This experience concentrated his mind on the need to couple future tax increases with a positive policy towards the countryside, and he supported the CPRE from its incep-tion. In addition to the lip-service which Baldwin had paid, MacDonald made a point of meeting with the CPRE shortly after taking office and almost immediately set several lines of policy devel-opment afoot. One was the appointment of an inter-departmental committee to consider the establishment of national parks, which would place large tracts of unspoilt countryside not in public owner-ship but under special planning bodies to preserve amenity and access. A second – prompted by Edward Hilton Young's Rural Amenities bills, advanced sympathetically from the Conservative backbenches – was the drafting of a new general planning act which would extend urban powers to regulate building and development to rural authori-ties as well. A third was the strengthening of State powers over historic buildings and ancient monuments, though this, as the Office of Works granted, was likely to be effected under the planning rubric.[11]

The opening up of these opportunities for countryside preservation in 1929–30 attracted a good deal of attention beyond the narrow circles of planners and aesthetes. The BBC, which had hitherto steered clear of a subject it considered marginal and politically controversial, began for a time to broadcast on behalf of 'saving the countryside', lending a soapbox to the likes of Lady Trevelyan, Clough Williams-Ellis, Mr and Mrs J. C. Squire and, most frequently, C. R. Ashbee, speaking for the CPRE. This campaign began shortly before Labour came to power, at the instance of Hilda Matheson, the BBC's Direc-tor of Talks, but it reached its peak in 1930 when MacDonald's initiatives had established a framework for public discussion. The new language of efficiency and public interest was much in evidence. Matheson insisted on keeping her campaign distinct from those

> people who were out of touch and out of sympathy with all modern life, including wider roads, motoring, charabancs, new and better houses, and all housing schemes . . . our task is not to hold up

and obstruct progress, oppose all building schemes and road building, etc., but to get everyone concerned to realise the importance
of having these things reasonably and with forethought and taste.

Great emphasis was placed on country planning and the national parks
idea, and reactionary, anti-urban sentiments were weeded out of an
audience-reaction programme, 'What the Listener Thinks'.[12]

When Labour's fiscal policy of taxing the land materialized in 1930
– the top rate of death duties went back up to fifty per cent and a
Land Valuation Bill was announced – a few landowners also came out
in favour of the State taking over their agricultural and amenity
functions. Almost by definition, they were highly unusual in that they
had essentially given up on private landownership. The Marquess of
Lothian, for instance, a Christian Scientist and one of the few remaining Liberal peers, acknowledged 'the complete destruction of the old
territorial position', and went so far as to call it 'a good thing from the
national point of view', provided the State stepped in at the same time
'to discharge the functions of the landlord in a better way than the
average landlord ever did'.[13] The Duke of Montrose, a Scottish
Nationalist then in the process of selling off his estates, also called on
the government to take over the business of landownership, and for
landlords

> to get the unpleasant business over as quickly as possible, and then
> settle down under the new condition of affairs. If in doing this
> landowners can feel that something is being achieved to preserve
> the beauties, amenities and health of Old England, there will be less
> cause to grumble . . .[14]

His heir would later transfer the family's base of operations to
Rhodesia.

The sense of a final crisis that Lothian and Montrose had did not
spread far in the landowning community, and the peak of the threat
seemed to pass in 1931, when the Labour government fell apart and
was succeeded by a National Coalition, MacDonald still at its head but
Baldwin in control at his side. Nevertheless, the initiatives that
MacDonald had set in train proceeded in modified form, and the fate
of the different policy approaches to countryside preservation reveals
much about the limits on a sense of national heritage in the countryside in the 1930s. As the Office of Works had recognized, an extension of historic preservation was out of the question. The minor
Ancient Monuments Act 1931 conveyed no substantive powers
beyond those enacted in 1913, and the national parks idea, which

threatened to impose national planning upon local authorities, also ran into the sand.

What remained was the general planning bill, extending urban authorities' powers over land use to rural authorities as well. This Town and Country Planning Bill was now in the friendly hands of Edward Hilton Young, appointed to the Ministry of Health within whose ambit planning matters lay. But here the landed interest, confidence regained with the fall of Labour, mounted a successful rearguard action to sabotage planning controls over their land. *Country Life*, which supported the CPRE in putting amenity and historical concerns over property rights in this case, was very bitter about the outcome:

> Certainly there can never have been a precedent for a Government Bill being dismembered in such a manner by its own nominal supporters, or of a measure being largely made nugatory by the very class of citizen whose interests it was framed to further. For, although landowners have been the principal opponents of the Bill in Committee, their interests in the long run are bound up with the ideal of applying forethought to the inevitable development of the countryside . . . for better or worse, the local authority is replacing the paternal government of the squire, and, instead of burying their heads in the sand, it is up to the more intelligent classes of countrymen to get themselves elected to the local authority and cause those much abused bodies to act as befits them.[15]

The Act in its final form omitted most compulsory powers over rural land, giving local authorities the power only to make agreements with owners to set land aside for amenity use. There was little incentive provided for local authorities to take these initiatives, and the rural authorities empowered to act were the smaller, poorer lower-tier authorities – district councils, rather than county councils. Ordinary agricultural land was excluded altogether from the workings of the Act.[16] The ease with which MacDonald's early good intentions were nullified points not only to landowners' continuing hostility to the idea of a national heritage in their land, but also, as John Sheail has said, to the public's continuing lack of interest in the same idea.[17] 'Public opinion seems not to want beauty', concluded one MP, 'On the contrary, it seems to want passionately about a dozen things which are totally incompatible with beauty.'[18]

In one small but perhaps significant detail, the 1932 Act did extend public control over aristocratic property, despite resistance. At the instance of the Office of Works, a clause was inserted into the planning bill giving local authorities some powers over intact historic houses that the Office itself had been seeking in vain since before 1913. Those powers had been excised from the 1913 Ancient Monuments Act by Lord Salisbury's vigilance, and now in 1932 his son, Lord Cranborne, took up the cudgels against a similar provision, though one less dangerous because confined to lethargic and penny-pinching local authorities. 'The whole principle of liberty is infringed', protested Cranborne in a letter to *The Times*. 'It used to be said that an Englishman's house was his castle. It seems that this is no longer true in a town-planned area.'[19]

*Country Life* tried to dissuade him from pursuing his point, arguing that the clause was not aimed against old families like the Cecils. 'The twentieth is, alas! not the seventeenth century. Many of the houses affected may not not be in the loving hands of educated ancestral owners.'[20] Cranborne would not give it up and harried Hilton Young about it for some months. Prompted by the Office of Works, Young stood up to Cranborne and refused to abandon the clause. But it was made clear that the powers were only intended for limited use in towns, 'in the prevention of such things as the insertion of unsuitable shop fronts into ancient buildings, and the destruction of the character of interesting streets', and that no new claim about the national heritage was being made.[21] In the event, the powers were used hardly at all.[22] Local authorities' universal reluctance to incur expense to preserve historic buildings was then cited by ministers as evidence that public opinion was not yet behind the cause. From this point of view, the clause may have done more harm than good.[23]

The whole structure of the 1932 planning system worked in this way. The unwillingness of local authorities to use their voluntary powers demonstrated implicitly the weakness of public support for countryside preservation. The few exceptions – for instance, the work of Surrey and London County Councils to preserve open space for recreational use in areas of intense suburbanization – suggest that public opinion could only be mobilized behind the most immediately utilitarian and unhistorical amenities. All of the trends in the 1930s ran against appeals based on tradition or pure aesthetics. It was not only government budgets that were tight, but household budgets, too. The popularity of hiking and cycling in these years testifies to extending leisure preferences in the working classes, but also to a tightening of the belt among the middle classes. All classes felt virtuous indulging in recreation that was healthy and spartan and contributed to national efficiency. Similar feelings probably lay behind the surge in attendance at museums of science and technology, at a time when art galleries were experiencing falling numbers.[24]

These considerations prompted adjustments in the arguments made for countryside preservation after the crisis of 1929–31. The tendency already evident before 1929 to emphasize the modern, recreational and 'ordinary' properties of the countryside over the historical qualities of Old England grew more pronounced. After Hilda Matheson left the BBC in 1931, it toned down its countryside campaign.[25] Although it continued to broadcast on rural crafts and customs, a favourite theme, it was more cautious about aiming preservationist propaganda at the urban audience, anxious about 'appearing to moralise and to be grandmotherly'. Matheson's successor Lionel Fielden replaced the angry voices of J. C. Squire and C. R. Ashbee with the more emollient tones of the chatty journalist Howard Marshall, whose autumn 1933 series 'Vanishing England' called for sensible compromises in the use of the land, and was still criticized for 'romanticism'. At the same time Fielden was repulsing as 'bilge' overtures from preservationists seeking to save historic architecture in London. A planned series in 1935 on 'places worth seeing from the historic point of view' metamorphosed into a less contentious set of holiday ideas reflecting modern ideas of rural leisure: sailing, climbing, hiking, cycling and caravanning.[26]

A new burst of literature about the 'beauty of Britain', which is sometimes cited as evidence of mounting nostalgia and antimodernism in the 1930s, betokens instead this same swerve away from an historical account of the Old English countryside towards a modernized version.[27] The publisher B. T. Batsford, long a repository of Arts and Crafts taste, now salted its list with books that emphasized the visual and geographical qualities of English landscape rather than the historical and artistic features that had hitherto been foremost. One disgruntled Batsford author, H. J. Massingham, complained of this 'descriptive and topographical account . . . from the point of view of the detached, appreciative, aesthetic connoisseur' that it left out the social dimension of the English landscape, the contribution of the craftsman-peasant. But this social emptiness helped to enhance the appeal of the countryside for urban consumers who had been put off by sterile Victorian debates over landlord and peasant.[28]

Although the National Government continued to turn a deaf ear, preservationist organizations found they were able to attract more public support by taking up this less sentimental, planning-oriented approach. The CPRE, after fruitless flings before 1931 against the advance of roads and electricity pylons, scored successes in the early

## PYLONS AND THE COUNTRYSIDE: A NEW FOREST SCHEME

HE NEW FOREST.—A view from the outskirts of the village of Godshill in the New Forest, looking towards Godshill Enclosure, showing a stretch of the land upon which the Central ...ity Board propose to erect pylons for grid lines.   The proposals are meeting with the most determined opposition from the authorities concerned with the preservation of the Forest, and a mass meeting of protest is to be held at Brockenhurst by the New Forest Association to-day.

68    By the time of the New Forest electrification scheme, 1932, preservationists were scoring successes against roads and pylons by taking a less absolutist stance and striking compromises.

1930s by negotiating with local authorities over the ordered placement of these modern features on the English countryside.[29] The National Trust, happy for many years with a minuscule membership and a self-image as an aesthetic lobby, also began to remodel itself as an 'amenity society', concerned with countryside planning, national parks and mass leisure. It took on professional fundraisers, made deals with motoring organizations and the Youth Hostels Association, publicized its work through films and radio broadcasts, and found its membership growing robustly from just one thousand in 1929 to almost three thousand in 1934 and about seven thousand by the outbreak of the Second World War.[30] This infusion of numbers and funds gave it renewed confidence in its traditional work of historic preservation and beauty-spot rescue, but it also set up a tension, between a modern, outdoorsy public and a leadership committed to historical and artistic connoisseurship, that continues to this day.

The effect of this new orientation on the great estate was to develop further appreciation of the consciously landscaped nature of ordinary countryside, and the need to invest in its maintenance, but also to deepen pessimism about the willingness or ability of the old order to sustain it. Planners spoke ever more admiringly of the 'ordinary, quiet, agricultural and pastoral country which interests the modern generation', and they called for local authorities to intervene in its preservation. A few practical experiments, such as the piecing together of the London Green Belt, showed how it was possible to transfer landlords' responsibility for amenity to public bodies. Other county councils were encouraged to follow suit and to buy up gems of eighteenth-century landscape design for use as public gardens.[31] Clough Williams-Ellis, whose first call in 1928 for public control of amenity land had seemed highly quixotic, was able to gather a team of eminent public figures to argue for the same cause in 1937. John Maynard Keynes scorned the private charity of a group such as the National Trust and demanded a more expansive interpretation of the State's cultural functions. C. E. M. Joad denounced governing-class barbarism, compared it to the sane happiness of 'the hikers, the Scouts, the Guides and the campers', and demanded for the people 'such opportunities of access to their heritage as are not incompatible with its maintenance', ultimately by 'compulsory purchase of land now in private hands'. Even A. G. Street, the farmer's friend,

> who [had] long hated the very idea of land nationalization, [had] come to the conclusion that such a step in the near future is the only one which will ensure that our children's children will be able to enjoy a sufficiency of unspoilt countryside.[32]

Some ideological modernists went further, arguing that admiration for the eighteenth-century landscape tradition – even if shared by the masses – was still too confining. A close study of Georgian landscape design would show that 'among the impulses which have contributed to the formation of the beauty we know to-day that of preservation had no place'. Armed with this lesson, the countryside designer should concentrate on making new landscapes for new purposes: 'intensive cultivation' of Dorset meadows, the afforestation with conifers of the Sussex Downs, relandscaping on modern design principles 'to make the countryside available to the masses instead of to the few'.[33]

Present-day critics of the 'heritage industry' echo this demand. Preservation of anything – even ordinary countryside – is felt to stifle contemporary creativity and to embody an anti-democratic longing for a lost arcadia. Probably anyone with a distinctive aesthetic theory or preference can be accused of undemocratic thinking – including the modernists who had their own agenda for the countryside. Planning-minded preservationists were undoubtedly reacting in some ways against the clamour and clutter of modern life, seeking to impose upon it some Olympian order and sense. But their call to order was not sounding the retreat. In reacting against the taste for Old England and praising the eighteenth-century landscape, they were identifying a historical model for modern shifts in taste, away from the cottage and the parish church out into open country, away from the slow accretions of time towards conscious design. It was paradoxical, admitted one writer on planning, but a study of eighteenth-century aesthetics could actually liberate you from history.[34] By prising open the angry fist of tradition which the Arts and Crafts movement had formed to beat upon modernity, the study of the Georgian helped some intellectuals to estimate better the requirements of modern England and more realistically to imagine its future.

Like other appropriations of the stuff of history for modern purposes, the planners' admiration for Georgian countryside was highly selective. They had little interest in supporting the traditional owners of that countryside, in shoring up the social structure upon which it had been built, or in a broader valuation of Georgian culture. Country houses featured remarkably rarely in their assessments of the countryside.[35] Modernists were interested in Georgian architecture for its contribution to urban planning and design, but they found no redeeming value in the Georgian country house.[36] It represented too many of those aspects of élite culture in the eighteenth century that were *not* adaptable to modern purposes. Its size necessitated a large staff of domestic servants and its collections rested on a tradition of aristocratic connoisseurship. Its interior decoration could embody elements of simple elegance that chimed with avant-garde taste, but that was again as much a town-house as a country-house phenomenon; Georgian country houses were too full of the accumulated *omnium gatherum* of centuries to be properly spare and simple.[37]

For these reasons, it was more difficult to rehabilitate the Georgian country house than the Georgian countryside in the public's eye, more difficult to claim as a national heritage the aristocrat's house as well as his land. Lonely advocates of country-house preservation had an uphill struggle in the 1930s. Their task was made no easier by the continuing resistance of owners, nor by the fact that for some the Georgian country house became in the 1930s a symbol of defiance rather than accommodation to modernity.

## The Rule of Taste from George V to George VI

By the time of the Great War, a generational rebellion against the Arts and Crafts aesthetic was long overdue; once the war had shattered lingering ideals and illusions, élite culture was ripe for a change in taste. The Arts and Crafts movement had never completely broken from its Victorian roots, and despite abortive attempts before the First World War it had never fully developed its own, modern identity. By 1914, both the mock-Tudor and the real Tudor were beginning to seem very ancient fashions indeed. Already before then, architects such as Norman Shaw and his followers Blomfield and Lutyens had sickened of the Little Englishness of the Arts and Crafts, and begun to search for something grander, more stately, and, as Blomfield saw it, something more befitting a world power and its capital.

After the war, the architects' tentative Georgianism spread to new quarters in élite culture. The eighteenth century had many attractions and many uses for the survivors of the Great War. First and foremost, it was anti-Victorian: the eighteenth century lay like an oasis of civilization between the crudity and half-primitiveness of the Olden Time and the gross materialism and imitativeness of the Victorians themselves. For aesthetes disappointed by the Arts and Crafts' lapse into rural nostalgia, the eighteenth century was on the one hand conceived as quintessentially urban and cosmopolitan – a time when London was linked to Paris and Rome and Venice in a European network of élite sensibility – and also aesthetically fresh, bright and contemporary, a potential model for a more successful modern style. Its architectural forms and design principles were simple, dignified and plain, but also rested on a considerable body of intellectual and aesthetic tradition, thus both accessible and (where convenient) remote.

The ubiquitousness of the Georgian revival in élite culture between the wars can easily mislead. One cultural historian goes so far as to claim for it a 'hegemony', establishing 'a new identity for "England", a new meaning to "being English", in the world at large'.[38] Yet of course what made the Georgian style so acceptable to polite society was its clear opposition to the old meanings and identities widespread in the world at large, as the Arts and Crafts aesthetic trickled down to the masses. By embracing the Georgian, the younger generation could simultaneously reject the feeble, romantic aestheticism of their elders *and* the mean, fussy Englishness of bourgeois suburbia. It was just as likely to offer a route out of England, or at least out of the grubby reach of most Englishmen, as to provide a model for a new kind of Englishness.

In high society, the Georgian was simply a new style adopted without much concern for its aesthetic or historical implications, though it did mark an aesthetic advance in these circles. The further decay of rural society, the washing up in London of many old families with money but with loosening ties to the land, caused a reaction against the philistinism and jolly ruralism of prewar years. Country sports, huge country-house parties, the raffishness of the Edwardian Court were out; dances and cocktail parties, the refurbishment and

69   Between the wars, town houses filled up with inherited furnishings decanted from the countryside: the informal collection in Anthony Prinsep's house, 1935.

redesign of town-house interiors, a certain stylishness and perky knowingness were in. These qualities typified the world of the Bright Young People in 1920s London. Naturally it helped that there were plenty of genuine Georgian materials at hand. Fashionable London had never deserted its Georgian town houses in the West End, and since the 1880s these had gradually filled with country-house contents, including much eighteenth-century continental art and English furniture, a process renewed after 1918 by 'England changing hands' and the revival of the art market. These settings and antiques provided backdrops for the new creations of the fashionable interior decorators who flourished in the 1920s and 1930s.[39]

High-fashion Georgianism did not necessarily have anything more to do with history – with the real eighteenth-century – than mock-Tudor had to do with real Tudor. It was adopted for its contemporary value and in fact for its parallels with a stylish modernism, flushing out the 'sham mediaevalism and sham folklorism of the early nineteen hundreds', as *House and Garden* (a stablemate of *Vogue*) said in 1923; 'The spirit of Wren has ousted the spirit of pseudo-peasant art . . . Dignity, symmetry, fine proportion are coming into their own again.' Having climbed from 'the beastly slough in which Ruskin contrived to plunge it . . . that bog of details and features . . . sham Gothicism, pseudo-peasantry and quaintness', English architecture and design finally had the chance to forge a modern style like that blooming on the Continent.[40] Fashion might take inspiration from the past, but its nature was to create something of the moment.

Overlapping with fashionable Georgianism was a connoisseur's Georgianism. This, too, rose with the tide of the European art market since the 1880s, as an international community of fine art collectors, dealers and scholars coalesced, greased with American and German money. The interest in fine art of the Renaissance extended to the seventeenth- and eighteenth-century paintings which Grand Tourists had collected and which now filled the auction houses, and even to eighteenth-century English portraiture. Connoisseurship found a wider urban audience, which considered art-appreciation and gallery-going to be urbane and stylish, as evidenced by the growth of London gallery attendances and the activities of the National Art-Collections Fund; membership of the latter had crawled up to almost 1,500 by the outbreak of war but then grew nearly tenfold in the course of the 1920s.[41]

Fashion and connoisseurship in turn fuelled a scholarly renaissance in the art and architecture of the eighteenth century. Beginning with Geoffrey Scott's philosophical disquisition on the 'architecture of humanism' – that is, the European Renaissance – and A. E. Richardson's survey of the classical style in eighteenth- and nineteenth-century Britain, both published in 1914, an appreciation and understanding of a variety of eighteenth-century styles – from Baroque elaboration to the delicacy of the Adam brothers – unfolded tentatively in the 1920s. Architects who had been consistently reviled for a century enjoyed, one by one, mild revaluations: the unknown Sir John Soane, the foreign and feminine Robert Adam, the ponderous Vanbrugh and his accomplice Hawksmoor. Most interestingly, Sir Christopher Wren, who had served as a transitional figure for those such as Blomfield who gradually broke away from the Arts and Crafts, now appeared in quite a different light. The Wren of the small, vernacular, yet plain and geometrical country house, a model for the architectural 'Wrenaissance' of Blomfield and Lutyens, gave way to the Wren of monumental urban architecture: noble City churches, big town-planning schemes like Greenwich, public buildings for ritual, civic and national uses. This shift of emphasis reflects the cultural position of the scholarly renaissance, which was then closer to élite taste than it is today, and in the 1920s decidedly urban, cosmopolitan and often linked to fine art connoisseurship.[42]

What of the country house in the Georgian revival? Because of the revival's urban and cosmpolitan orientation, the English country house figured only marginally.[43] Material interests were vested in the refurbishment and decoration of the town house. Aesthetes luxuriated in European connoisseurship and its urban network. County society had broken down, and what had once been a short London Season had now extended into an almost year-round calendar. Scholarship was aesthetically and often economically dependent on élite taste. Both the more nostalgic and the more modernist admirers of the Georgian thus found their concerns focused on urban architecture. Preservationist targets of the interwar years ranged from the City churches to Kensington Square to Waterloo Bridge to Carlton House Terrace. Blomfield differentiated explicitly between the London squares and 'a country mansion in some remote place off the beaten track. In the former case the public, to whom the buildings had long been familiar objects, forming some concrete and definite part of the life of the people, had a sort of vested interest.'[44] (Blomfield's implicit definition of 'the public' – one that had a vested interest in Kensington Square – is itself revealing.) Others, more genuinely dedicated to the Georgian than Blomfield, still confined their defence largely to Georgian London; this was true of the Georgian Group, founded by an odd assortment of literary men, genteel aesthetes and modern architects in 1937.[45]

However, in the general revaluation of taste there were bound to be a few with reasons to extend their loyalties to the Georgian country house. Two groups – not always easily distinguishable – can be discerned; one passionate for the Georgian country house as a symbol of a bygone world into which they wished to retreat, and thus relatively unconcerned with proselytizing for it, the other, in contrast, keen to add the Georgian country house to the approved historical sequence so that the country-house tradition could at last be fully acknowledged by society at large. Both groups found their impulses – whether to retreat or to diffuse – enflamed in the early 1930s by the apparently decisive political and economic turmoil of those years.

The first group is more conspicuous, notorious for the choler and colour of its opinions, though less promising for the future of the country house. They came from among the Bright Young People, the scrum of young aristocrats, would-be aristocrats and well-born aes-

thetes who lit up the gossip columns of the middlebrow press in the
1920s. Though fundamentally modern and urban, that milieu had
harshly satirical and extreme elements that were finely balanced
between celebration of and disgust with the chaos of modern life, a
balance that gave an edge to Evelyn Waugh's early novels, *Decline and
Fall* (1928) and *Vile Bodies* (1930). As Martin Green and Humphrey
Carpenter have pointed out, Waugh and his circle were thrown off-
balance by the national crisis of 1929–31, experienced a revulsion from
the compromises and struggles of their own time and fell back thereafter on to an absolute and orderly aesthetic that they identified with
the eighteenth-century landed élite.[46]

Waugh's search for 'taste' was at first predicated mostly on vague
antitheses to the Little Englishness of his parents and social inferiors. In
a much-quoted passage from *Labels* (1930), Waugh paraded the gallery
of pet hates, many of them pet loves of his father, the publisher Arthur
Waugh:

> The detestation of 'quaintness' and 'picturesque bits' which is felt by
> every decently constituted Englishman, is, after all, a very insular
> prejudice. It has developed naturally in self-defence against arts and
> crafts, and the preservation of rural England, and the preservation of
> ancient monuments, and the transplantation of Tudor cottages, and
> the collection of pewter and old oak, and the reformed public
> houses, and the Ye Olde Inne and the Kynde Dragone and Ye
> Cheshire Cheese, Broadway, Stratford-on-Avon, folk-dancing,
> Nativity plays, reformed dress, free love in a cottage, glee singing,
> the Lyric, Hammersmith, Belloc, Ditchling, Wessex-worship, vil-
> lage signs, local customs, heraldry, madrigals, wassail, regional cook-
> ery, Devonshire teas, letters to *The Times* about saving timbered
> alms-houses from destruction, the preservation of the Welsh lan-
> guage, etc. It is inevitable that English taste, confronted with all
> these frightful menaces to its integrity, should have adopted an
> uncompromising attitude to anything the least tainted with ye
> oldeness.[47]

After an uneasy search for newness in the 1920s, Waugh took
consolation in a more tasteful past that he found in Georgian country
life. He began to consort with the aesthetic kind of noblewoman,
among them Lord Beauchamp's daughters Ladies Mary and Dorothy
Lygon, and motored with them around the countryside in search of
Georgian country houses. Ultimately he married one such lady –
Laura Herbert, niece of the Earl of Carnarvon – and '[set] himself up
as a squire' at Piers Court in Gloucestershire, a mixed bag of Georgian

façade, Elizabethan structure, Robert Adam chimneypiece and Victorian furniture. In this setting he could idealize and conflate the living aristocracy – represented only by his select group – and the Georgian aristocracy – represented only by the paragons of taste among them. This progress can be traced in his next spate of novels, rising (or descending) from *A Handful of Dust* (1934), which, like the earlier works, mocks the aristocracy for eccentricity and anachronism but also clings to these characteristics for security in a mad world, to the frankly elegiac *Brideshead Revisited* (1945), where 'Brideshead' – an amalgam of the Baroque wonder Castle Howard and the Lygons' house at Madresfield – stands purely for the true and the good.

Much of this fantasy stems from Waugh's inner life, precipitated by personal disappointments among the Bright Young People, but it was a potent fantasy made more potent by his literary talent. Nor was it unique to him; his friend John Betjeman could claim to have discovered it earlier. Also reacting against a bourgeois Arts and Crafts upbringing – his father manufactured fancy 'hand-crafted' household wares for the upper-middle classes – Betjeman turned as early as his school days against the 'officially approved' Tudor manor houses and thatched cottages and instead 'sought out eighteenth-century buildings', developing 'a respect for the system of hereditary landowning'.[48] His Georgianism co-existed, as it did for others, with a search for a tasteful modern architecture until he, too, abandoned that quest in favour of nostalgia. His half-serious tract of 1933, *Ghastly Good Taste*, finds him in mid-turn. In what is mostly a denunciation of all buildings postdating the mid-nineteenth century, he objects even to the contemporary fashion for urban Georgianism – which he feels has already been sentimentalised into 'quaint old-world artiness' – and holds up for admiration the 'hard and reasonable architecture' of the classical country house. Somewhat half-heartedly, he admits that these houses – perfect for their own times – are unsuitable for modern purposes and calls for a new architecture meeting new needs as well. But the whole work is addressed to the squire of today sitting in the library of his Georgian country house, embattled by death duties, petrol stations, speculative villas and his own compromises with the modern world, and the implicit message is that civilization persists only here. 'Preservation of the countryside is but an ineffective compromise.' Only the real thing – the original article – will do.[49]

Betjeman had to earn his living in the 1930s as an architectural journalist, so never retreated as far into the backwoods – psychologically or geographically – as Waugh. His more exposed position also made him a more effective propagandist for his aesthetic and he prodded forwards a number of his likeminded friends. It was he who instigated Osbert Lancaster to write his influential series of handbooks satirizing bad English architecture – a lengthy elaboration on *Ghastly Good Taste* – and he commissioned others to write for the series of county guidebooks for motor tourists that he edited for the Shell oil company from 1934.[50] Yet even Betjeman's ingenious preaching rested on some unrealistic assumptions that limited his effect; his enthusiasms remained very much a private joke and were discovered by a popular audience only after the Second World War. Like Waugh, Betjeman enjoyed his aristocratic friends' company and patronage too much, making unwarranted generalizations about their class's virtue, past and present. The *Shell Guides* were well ahead of their time in their promotion of the Georgian and even more *outré* styles, but they were too far ahead; their jokey, cliquey tone and frequent lapses into snobbishness make entertaining reading today, but they were hardly influential in their own time. Betjeman's sympathies were clearly more with owners and their houses than with the tourist: 'I have mentioned farms and country houses wherever they are worth looking at,' he muses in the *Shell Guide to Devon*,

> but I do not suggest that you should drive up in a motor-car and demand to see the house, be it farm or mansion. If you have not applied to see the house beforehand, drive slowly past and look longingly at it. Some tenants and proprietors gladly show their houses to visitors; others, and we can hardly blame them, are inclined to be short.[51]

The *Shell Guides* often promote the attractions of great country houses, whether or not they could be viewed by the *hoi polloi*, and in a myriad little ways make the tourist feel like an irritant in an otherwise well-ordered countryside.

Writing of this kind valued the eighteenth century too highly and the twentieth century not highly enough. It delighted in the discovery of an era of taste but doubted its applicability to a modern democratic society, as the sad tale of decline since the Regency testified. A belief in an objective standard of beauty, governed by rules to be upheld by an élite of taste-makers, had existed in Britain in the eighteenth century, argued John Steegmann in *The Rule of Taste from George I to George IV* (1936). Unlike in France or Italy, it had not existed before – when the mansions of the great had been 'massive, ponderous and barbaric' – or since – when democracy and individualism had dispersed the élite, overturned rules and substituted more accessible literary values for the finer aesthetic ones.[52] If some fragments of taste had survived the holocaust of democracy, they could only be appreciated properly by those who had imbibed them with their mothers' milk – a small and shrinking hereditary caste – or by the artists who had been supported historically by their patronage. This position was therefore too exclusive socially and aesthetically to trigger a more general revaluation of the English country house.

For an adaptation of the Georgian fashion better suited to saving the country house, we have to turn to a second group, who knew both the real aristocracy and the full stock of country houses rather better. In the main, these were the more aesthetic children of the squirearchy and aristocracy, who rebelled against their parents' philistinism or Victorian tastes and came to love the remaining classical houses of their friends and neighbours. At Eton and Oxford during and just after the First World War, a number of these landed Georgians appeared. Christopher Hussey, heir presumptive to Scotney Castle in Kent, and Ralph Dutton, heir to the Hinton Ampner estate in Hampshire, formed a friendship at Eton during the war based on a mutual appreciation of art and architecture, especially that of the early eighteenth century, 'Culture's palmiest days' as Hussey put it to Dutton in 1918.[53] Both went to Oxford, where Dutton formed the Uffizi Society, devoted to Renaissance art, with, among others, Angus Holden and Lord David Cecil.[54]

Hussey and Dutton – like their close friends, the slightly older Sitwell brothers, Osbert and Sacheverell – set out consciously in the early 1920s to explore the buried classical traditions of their forebears. Hussey had the easiest time of it, for his parents and grandparents had kept up artistic interests, albeit in a Victorian idiom, and in the course of the 1920s Hussey developed a theory about the picturesque tradition in English landscape and architecture which formed a kind of bridge between his parents' taste and his own emerging Georgianism.[55] Dutton and the Sitwells had to break free from unsympathetic forebears. In Dutton's case, an ambitious Victorian grandfather had obscured what Dutton saw as a lapidary Georgian house at Hinton Ampner with a hideous Tudor makeover and gloomy interior decor. His father had then compounded the problem during the agricultural depression with a combination of strict economy in decoration and gradual modernization for comfort. As Dutton matured, accumulating a fine collection of art and furniture in his London flat, his horror at Hinton Ampner increased, but it was not until his father's death in 1935 that he was able to restore the house to its former glories. Aware that his father would have been appalled by the taste and expense involved, he spent the rest of his life stripping away the Victorian accretions to expose what was left of the Georgian house and augmenting it with neo-Georgian additions designed by his friend Lord Gerald Wellesley.[56] Sacheverell Sitwell was fortunate to inherit a subsidiary family house, the classical Weston Hall in Northamptonshire, as early as 1923, but his elder brother Osbert had to wait another twenty years to wrest the main house, rambling Renishaw Hall, from the eccentric Sir George. In the meantime, the Sitwells decorated their town house in Carlyle Square in the neo-Baroque and, with Lord Gerald Wellesley, Christopher Hussey and likeminded friends, in 1924 founded the Magnasco Society, to cherish the Italian collections of eighteenth-century Grand Tourists.[57]

At first, these isolated admirers in the 1920s felt that theirs were devotions of filial piety, a piety owed not even in most cases to their immediate forebears but to a family tradition buried for a hundred years. The little clubs they formed and the thin volumes they wrote were aimed at most at winning over a few of their Old Etonian and Oxonian confreres, who – if they liked architecture at all – were still mostly fixated upon the Tudor and Jacobean. But their responsibilities for real houses – as owners rather than mere guests – forced them over time to consider carefully how their private passions might be generalized, converted into a public responsibility to be taken up by their less sensitive peers and by a wider community.

Christopher Hussey was the first to make more ambitious efforts, through his position at *Country Life*. In 1920, fresh from Oxford, he had been shrewdly enlisted by Avray Tipping to help continue *Country Life*'s long-running series of country-house profiles. Tipping had already moved some distance from his and the magazine's Arts and Crafts roots by publishing respectful, if unpassionate, articles on classical houses before the war, but in Hussey he had found an almost unique figure who could cater honestly to the readership's old-fashioned tastes but also strike a spark for the Georgian. This Hussey was able to some extent to do. To judge from the magazine's correspondence columns, the ancient building, the dilapidated cottage, the ruined manor house were still the main objects of readers' solicitude, but they got used to reading in the weekly country-house slot – beside profiles of Tudor manor houses – paeans of praise to unfamiliar Georgian names and places. And by weaving together Georgian country houses with Georgian antiques and works of art and neo-Georgian modern architecture in other parts of the magazine, *Country Life* was also able to freshen up its image and readership, aligning itself with the latest currents in fashion and connoisseurship. His potent combination of interests and talents rapidly made Hussey a dominant force at *Country Life*, and by 1933 he was its editor.

In his early writings Hussey was concerned not so much to replace an Arts and Crafts aesthetic with a Georgian one, as to heal the breach between the two by constructing a continuous landed tradition uninterrupted in the eighteenth century. He held an almost racial view of the landowning class as the nation's natural leaders, rooted in the English soil and responsible for a series of aesthetic forms each appropriate to its time and place. He regretted the social effect of enclosure, but he did not – as would the Arts and Crafts dogmatist Massingham – see it as an artistic disaster; neither did he see it as a displacement of barbarism by civilization. Each tradition could be admired for its own virtues, and the unifying thread was the leadership and patronage of squires and nobles in the countryside. There was an almost modernistic detachment about this view – beauty, he wrote in 1924, 'consists in meeting a natural requirement completely' – which made it possible for him to admire equally different historical phases and also to search for a new style for his own day.[58] But the most important thing for him was the role of the landowner in making possible all of these styles, so that when later he turned against modernism, what kept him going was his belief in the continuous tradition of rural art under landed patronage. When John Murray asked him to write on the 'decadence of English Country Homes' for the *Quarterly Review*, he produced not an elegy on decline but a call for squirearchical revival in the interests of the nation and concluded:

> our country houses, and those of the old families who still live in them, represent symbolically and actually the continuity of life . . . Continuity of traditions has made England the most free and leisured nation of the world.[59]

Later in the 1920s, Hussey's emphasis slipped gradually from the role of the landed élite to the aesthetic achievements for which they were responsible. His own serious study of aesthetics may have been partly responsible; in *The Picturesque* (1927) he delineated what he saw as a peculiarly English style of harmonizing art with nature, which was always vital but reached a peak of theoretical sophistication and practical scope in the landscape designs of the late eighteenth century. He was also clearly influenced by the crisis of 1929–31. This influence worked in two ways. On the one hand, he grew increasingly unhappy with the mechanical and utilitarian way in which modernists approached questions of design, which he thought inimical to the native tradition of harmonizing art with nature. On the other hand, he saw in the countryside planning movement an opportunity to preserve the best of that tradition for all time – an opportunity that required making an appeal not to squires but to the public.[60] As they entered the 1930s, therefore, Hussey and his friends became more and more active in an effort, first, to define what they saw as a continuous country-house tradition, and then to secure its inclusion under the countryside planning rubric. Saving ordinary countryside because it was healthy and useful and orderly was not enough; a national heritage in rural art and architecture had to be saved as well.

The first necessity was to establish the country house generically as a characteristic piece of English art. It is easy to forget how novel a definition this was. In the nineteenth century, the 'stately home' had been a social rather than an aesthetic category; it contained the houses of nobility, and deference was paid to it because deference was paid to that class. Aesthetically, the Victorians had recognized 'the mansions of the Olden Time' and later 'the manor houses of England', but these categories excluded the majority of 'stately homes' built in unhappy styles and sizes. Tipping's profiles of houses in *Country Life* had through the 1920s grown gradually more catholic, but as late as the mid-1920s earlier prejudices against classical houses lingered. Hussey himself could lapse into the most exaggerated lyricism about Elizabethan and Jacobean architecture – 'That; that, was England!' – and corresponding doubts about the styles that followed – 'the refinement and affectation of the French and the drawling boorishness of the Puritans were soon to unite in putting an end to Merry England'.[61]

Dogma was now put aside in favour of a broader tradition which embraced all of the country houses under threat, classical houses like Chatsworth and Petworth with great art collections as well as the more famous Olden Time mansions like Knole, Penshurst and Haddon. The expensive, fully illustrated collections of country-house articles that *Country Life* had been issuing before the war had specialized in the approved pre-Civil War styles; a new series begun in the 1920s aimed at complete coverage since the Middle Ages, including the shunned Baroque (1926) and late Georgian (1928) periods. Hussey started to experiment with cheaper, more popular compilations aimed at motorists and other tourists, beginning in 1928 with *The Old Homes of Britain*, a guide to the south of England, and county guides to the houses of Kent and Dorset edited by his colleague Arthur Oswald in 1933 and 1935. He also had a hand in infiltrating country-house books into the Batsford *British Heritage* and *English Life* series, culminating in 1935 with Ralph Dutton's *The English Country House* – foreword by

Osbert Sitwell – which for decades reigned as the definitive work on the subject.[62]

A number of linked themes were elaborated in these works, which aimed at establishing the English country house as a distinctive and valuable creation. One fundamental theme was in some ways the easiest to argue – that the 'country home' was the basic building block of English national life. Familiar since the dawn of the Arts and Crafts movement, this argument would in the 1930s have been widely accepted by aesthetes, suburbanites and outdoors enthusiasts of all stripes. More difficult was the further step towards accepting the 'country house' – that is, the landowner's large house – as emblematic of the 'country home'. The Arts and Crafts movement had accepted the manor as an integral part of what Dutton called the 'traditional village group' – including church, rectory and cottages – but argued that the manor had become overblown and, after the Civil War, had all too often been deserted by the great landowners for their isolated mansion in the walled-off park. This social removal was accompanied by an aesthetic removal, the retreat from national to cosmopolitan styles. Dutton, for one, was not very well able to counter these arguments. He echoed the conventional view that 'no more excellent houses have been built in this country than during the middle-Tudor period', and that, of post-Civil War architects, only Wren had been able to devise 'a second vernacular as appropriate and delightful as that which had flourished with the Tudors'. All he could do was to plaster on to this conventional account his new appreciation for the Georgian, 'a halcyon period of taste', cultured and cosmopolitan but admittedly not very English.[63]

Hussey's solution to this little local difficulty was to shift attention from specific social and aesthetic periods to what linked them, that is, the very fact of continuity of ownership by old landed families. He attempted head-on a defence of the landowning class on a variety of social, economic and aesthetic grounds. Annexing the old arguments for the great landowners' centrality to modern agriculture, and the newer arguments for great landowners' contribution to landscape maintenance and amenity, he argued also that in the country house the great landowners had contributed 'a national possession to which there is no parallel in the world'. Other nations had their châteaux and Schlosses, but these were dead shells because unlived in and uncared for. Only England had a surviving aristocracy caring for its great houses, 'history still alive and present among us'.[64]

Victorian writers such as Charles Knight had made the 'living history' argument before, but confined it to periods of history that interested them – essentially, the Olden Time – and, because the aristocracy was not then threatened as a class, had no need to broaden the defence. Thereafter, Victorians searching for their national art and history tended not to locate it among the aristocracy. Even in *Country Life* the argument for the country house as a generic epitome of national art and history hardly appeared before the crisis of 1929–31 seemed to demand it. Now, however, it became a regular theme. In some hands it acquired more specific characteristics, though finding qualities that persisted from the sixteenth to the nineteenth centuries required considerable powers of imagination. Highly abstract ideas about Englishness were developed to be located in 'the country house': individuality, fitness, moderation, reticence. Robert Byron, an architectural writer in Betjeman's circle, claimed in 1932 that 'these houses accumulate tradition or idiosyncracy till it becomes almost physically oppressive . . . their way of life has permitted a cultivation of the individual, of his freaks and virtues alike, unknown outside England'.[65] In the same year, in *Country Life*, Byron spoke of 'the pervasive English sense of fitness':

> It is precisely this sense of fitness which distinguishes English design in all fields from that of other countries and which is at the same time so hard to define . . . The plethoric satisfaction to be obtained from the best English work, whether on palace or teaspoon, derives from the faculty of the design to assume the beholder's physical presence into itself, to take his measure and, as it were, to fall into a reciprocal state of affection with him.[66]

This 'fitness' – sometimes expressed as 'reticence' or 'moderation' – which was thought to have protected English architecture from the extremes of continental Rococo and modernism had its own problems. To Georgian enthusiasts, it smacked of Arts and Crafts 'littleness' and 'homeliness'. It was too dogmatic for Hussey and tended to exclude English extremities that he approved of – Vanbrugh's monumentalism, for instance, or some rather good copies of continental art. 'It is very difficult to resist the conclusion that nationality in the arts is very largely an illusion', insisted a leader in *Country Life*. 'We may feel that in our domestic architecture in the past it is possible to detect a certain English quality of reticence.' But it put an unacceptable damper on creativity to insist upon this reticence, more so to insist on the 'reticence' of specific styles, or architects such as Wren.[67]

Hussey preferred to rely on the generic argument for the country house – the very continuity of ownership – than on any specific qualities. For him, the variety and peculiarity of country-house archi-

. . KENT

Xii.—IGHTHAM MOTE.  THE " MOATED GRANGE " OF ROMANCE.

70   Ightham Mote, from the first of the popular *Country Life* guidebooks aimed at motorists, 1928.

tecture and collections were what made them unique and unreproducible and therefore worth saving *en masse*. The slow accretions of time built up a palimpsest which a *parvenu* or a modern could not create from scratch, 'the dear jumble of a home' that he found at his own Scotney.[68] This approach made possible the most catholic of country-house tastes. For example, Christopher Hobhouse, a friend of Betjeman's who compiled the *Shell Guide to Derbyshire*, was one of the first writers to praise Chatsworth and Haddon equally, finding in the former a unifying ribbon of taste, 'the history of a single family', and in the latter a similar 'discontinuous continuity'.[69] This kind of appraisal required two leaps of faith – an aesthetic tolerance and an acceptance of the cultural importance of the landed élite – neither of which were easy to make in the 1930s, but Hussey was persuaded that both were necessary if the full range of country houses were to be recognized as part of the national heritage.

Arguments for the country house as part of the national heritage, however persuasive aesthetically, had to overcome the indifference or outright hostility of two important groups, the taxpaying public and the owners of the houses. Hussey and his friends felt this acutely in the crisis of 1929–31, when the threats to landowners and their houses appeared particularly grave, and the 'solutions' advanced by the countryside planners sometimes seemed worse than useless. *Country Life* intervened aggressively – if not very effectively – in the public debate over the future of the countryside, taking a special (nearly unique) interest in the future of the country house.

Among owners, *Country Life* preached vigorously for a sense of trusteeship or stewardship in the country house. The weakest link in the continuity of ownership was of course the present. Owners may have laboured to create and preserve this unique cultural heritage in past centuries, but in the 1930s they were everywhere demolishing it, selling it off or shutting it up. Hussey maintained that owners were only responding to economic exigency and political hostility. Their real desire was to nurture beauty and amenity for national benefit. Resuscitating the claim made (with more grounds) by W. T. Stead in the 1890s, Hussey held that country houses had 'always' been open to the public for their enjoyment and instruction. Their owners were 'public benefactors' who deserved praise and support. 'In many cases it is the inherited public spirit and pride of history alone that keep the owners of great houses from exploiting their estates to their own profit.' A few conspicuous examples were regularly cited – one *Country Life* leader was revealingly entitled 'Such as Knole', and the cases of Chatsworth, Hardwick, Burghley and Penshurst were also raised.[70]

But Hussey was, of course, aware that these cases were rarer than they had once been. *Country Life* proselytized vigorously for country-house visiting in these years, among owners and among the public. It spoke optimistically of 'a renewed interest in our old country homes' among the latter and the eagerness with which opportunities such as the Queen's Institute garden openings were taken up.[71] In 1934, Ralph Dutton and Angus Holden published the first national listing of *English Country Houses Open to the Public*. By scraping together about thirty-five privately owned and twenty-five publicly owned houses and some buildings that were either not country houses or not open to the public, they were able to list about seventy properties. The privately owned houses were mostly open only on a very restricted basis.[72] By contrast, when Dutton and Holden compiled a companion volume of French châteaux open to the public, their 'selective, rather than exhaustive' list of seventy properties included fifty-eight privately owned châteaux, twenty-two of which were open every day of the year, and this list represented only a third of the privately owned châteaux actually open to the public.[73] The point of their efforts, clearly, was rather to propagandize for country-house opening than to document it.

Among the public, when countryside planners were looking to planning mechanisms or outright nationalization to save the Georgian countryside, *Country Life* endorsed the extension of planning – against the wishes of many owners – but argued distinctively for an additional programme of death-duty exemptions and maintenance grants to help owners meet the obligations of the plan. Owners had 'always' opened their houses to the public, but could no longer afford to do so. If historic houses and parks were exempted from death duties, or even dealt out subsidies by the Office of Works, they would gladly accept a degree of public access as an acceptable 'servitude' (as the tax-lawyers called it) in return.[74]

Coherent and persuasive as this package of tax reliefs, maintenance grants and public access may look today – it is roughly the system that has grown up since the early 1950s – it depended in the 1930s on a sleight of hand. The public might possibly be interested in country houses, and certainly was interested in their amenity lands: but interested enough to pay the owners to maintain them? Owners were certainly interested in tax reliefs and maintenance grants for their houses and parks: but interested enough to tolerate the public tramping through them?

In the early 1930s, there was little sign of an affirmative answer on either side. The Labour government was completely unwilling to consider tax exemptions for a rich and feared section of the community, though death duty exemption was granted in 1931 for lands given to the National Trust; in fact, a new tax on land values (one penny in the pound) was imposed in the same budget.[75] The National Government that succeeded it dropped some of the more draconian land tax ideas but was no more responsive to proposals for exemptions; neither were owners moved. A few more houses opened to the public in the early 1930s, but these were mostly rare cases where the owners had failed to let their houses and yet were unwilling to demolish.[76] *The Field*, the squire's organ, which had hitherto shown little interest in the cultural properties of country houses, proved eager to join *Country Life*'s campaign for tax exemptions but less eager to consider public access: its assumed alternative was still demolition.[77] When, a few years later, the National Trust jumped on *Country Life*'s bandwagon and attempted to organize owners behind just this combination of 'servitudes' and 'reliefs', the limits of owners' and public's enthusiasm for a national heritage in the country house became all too clear.

## Saving the Country House

Philip Kerr, Liberal statesman, philosopher of empire and Christian Scientist, succeeded his cousin somewhat unexpectedly as 11th Marquess of Lothian in March 1930. In addition to the title, his inheritance comprised a raft of estates and country houses in England and Scotland and a death duties' bill for a quarter of a million pounds, which, as a Liberal, he viewed as his just deserts but also as a problem for agriculture and rural society. His political response has already been alluded to; he pressed Lloyd George to move towards a system of State control over and support for agriculture. Practically, he began to divest himself of his assets to pay the bills and streamline the estate. Fernichirst Castle was let to the Scottish Youth Hostels Association, Newbattle Abbey established as an independent adult education college, and treasures from Newbattle and the Jacobean house, Blickling, in Norfolk, were sold at auction in New York in January 1932. Reserving the Monteviot (Roxburghshire) and Melbourne Hall (Derbyshire) estates for his successors, he then bent his mind to the fate of Blickling, one of the greatest surviving Olden Time houses, which had been shut up for years. Characteristically, he thought of Blickling not as a personal but as a social problem: were these great houses and estates of public benefit? if so, how could they be preserved and used?[78]

Instinctively, he answered the first question in the affirmative, but he did not have fixed views on the second question. He was not a man of strong aesthetic impulses, nor did he have a particular attachment to country houses, either his own or others'. As his friend Herbert Baker observed, 'perhaps he inherited so many mansions that, where he had not spent his youth, he could feel no especial affection for the intimate associations of any one of them . . . he always seemed to be a restless spirit with no abiding resting-place'.[79] Country houses had been for him places where civilized discourse and socially conscious politicking could take place, and these were the uses to which he put Blickling in his lifetime: meetings of the Round Table (his circle of thinkers on imperial questions), discussions on India, Africa, Liberalism and unemployment, concerts, pageants and a place of retreat where Stanley Baldwin could gird his loins for the abdication crisis of 1936.[80]

Early in 1934, Lothian asked his Round Table friend, MacLeod Matheson, who had recently become Secretary of the National Trust, whether the Trust might not take up the country-house question. Matheson was one of a new generation of leadership at the Trust. The first generation of Ruskinian zealots had long passed; the interim leaders of the 1920s, who had kept the Trust going quietly as a small holding body for beauty spots and buildings, were retiring; a quite different group – some landlords, some Liberals, mostly positive men of affairs, all keen to find a place for the Trust and its artistic heritage in the State's unfolding plans for countryside planning – was taking over. Matheson was the Trust's first fully professional Secretary. Its Chairman from 1932 was the Marquess of Zetland, a disciple of Lord Curzon and like him a rare Tory grandee with powerful historical and artistic interests. Its leading committees were headed by two Liberals, well-known in public life, the historian G. M. Trevelyan (Chairman of the Estates Committee from 1928) and the 3rd Viscount Esher (Chairman of the Finance and General Purposes Committee from 1935). All of these men were casting about for ways the Trust might intervene more decisively and extensively in preserving rural amenity. They were helped in this by a stabilization of the Trust's finances, owing to the prudent policy of the 1920s and the influx of membership on the outdoors boom of the early 1930s.

Matheson invited Lothian to float some ideas about country houses at the Trust's Annual General Meeting in July 1934. This he did, after consulting with *Country Life*, in a manner both ambitious in its proposals and vague in its general intentions. 'The country houses of Britain, with their gardens, parks, pictures, furniture, and their peculiar architectural charm,' he suggested, 'represented a treasure of quiet beauty which was not only specially characteristic of our land but quite unrivalled in any other.' As he had argued with regard to agriculture in 1931, a government that legitimately taxed landowners to death had a responsibility to step in and preserve the landowners' legacy. On the how and why of preservation, Lothian was rather indiscriminate. He proposed that the Trust be enabled to take on country houses with adequate tax-exempt endowments to modernize them, and let them out to new tenants 'who would respect and preserve, so far as they could, the tradition of beauty they enshrined' (presumably he had Blickling in mind). In some cases, he suggested, the most appropriate tenants would be the old owners, perpetuating their old traditions in a new status as semi-public servants. But he went further: why should not the government exempt from taxes all of the great houses that remained in private hands, just as they already exempted from death duties the historical and artistic contents of those houses? *Country Life* had furnished him readily enough with a list of 600–700 such houses; could not the Royal Commission on Historical Monuments do a quick survey of country houses (extending its remit past 1714 through the Georgian period) and draw up a schedule of houses, tax-exempt so long as they were preserved with their park and contents? 'This would tend to mean that even where the abhorred shears of taxation compelled an ancient family to sell its property, the dwelling and its contents would tend to pass into the hands of those who would appreciate them and keep them intact.'[81]

Lothian's kite was ambiguous enough to trigger a revealing array of reactions. The principal reaction was silence: the National Trust was a small and exclusive society whose meetings were never reported in the middlebrow press. Among the minority who worried about the future of the countryside, different strands were plucked from Lothian's speech. Chuter Ede, Labour Chairman of Surrey County Council and a pioneer in preserving open space for public use, welcomed what he saw as a classic planning agreement, trading tax exemptions for 'limited, but well-defined rights of public access' to 'the worthiest inspiration of nature and the gardener's art'.[82] *Country Life* naturally played up the cultural treasures of house and contents rather than the Ruskinian delights of parks and gardens, and recommended owners to extend public visiting rights to their home, as a necessary prelude to future tax concessions. It pointed to the model of the French château-owners' society, La Demeure Historique, 'the most aristocratic Trades Union in the world', which raised funds from tourists' admission fees and, by 'capitalising generosity into the more impressive guise of a national service', had earned public recognition of the fact that 'they are trustees for the nation of some of its more glorious possessions'.[83]

Owners of country houses had a quite different reaction to Lothian's speech. Their hopes raised by the demise of the Labour government and its land-tax plans, they seized on Lothian's talk of tax exemptions to re-open the case for the old order in rural society. *The Field* detected the turning of the tide in proposals from 'a member of the Radical left wing of the Liberal Party' that recognized the benevolence and self-denial of the landed élite. Speaking cavalierly (and inaccurately) on a subject that had never previously interested it, *The Field* asserted that over a hundred historic houses were opened to the public completely voluntarily and welcomed the prospect of some long overdue financial recognition of this fact.[84] Others took up the call for sweeping tax exemptions for agriculture. The problem of rural society was not one of houses – these were only symbols, and not very valuable ones at that – but of land, 'the foundations of the house' and the landed way of life, 'which, apart from sentiment, affords employment and leadership in [its] neighbourhood'.[85] Most owners looked down their noses at *Country Life*'s quisling notion of a trade union in the public service; they resented the suggestion that they had fallen as far as the French nobility. The Duke of Rutland, scenting a threat to Haddon, was '*entirely* against the formation of any such society . . . If the Government of the day want to protect some ancient building, let them do so by providing the owner with the necessary money, and only if the owner is agreeable'.[86] Surprisingly, *Country Life* let itself be drawn into this line of reasoning. It did not dwell upon its tourism ideas and for a time joined the calls for sweeping tax exemptions on agriculture to revive private landownership.[87]

If landowners were hoping that the National Government might look more favourably on these arguments than had Labour, they were fooling themselves. When Zetland approached the Chancellor of the Exchequer, Neville Chamberlain, with Lothian's bag of ideas, Chamberlain was privately dismissive; Zetland's proposals were 'unacceptable and would probably be quite ineffective'. The Treasury was implacably opposed to tax reliefs for private citizens and predicted a public outcry if private houses were subsidized in this way just because they were 'historic'. Nor was the Treasury interested in taking over ownership of houses and estates, as Lothian himself had hoped. At the time of Zetland's overture, it was grappling unhappily with an offer from Sir Charles Trevelyan of the house and estate at Wallington in Northumberland, which Trevelyan was offering as a gift to the nation if some public use could be found for it. No government department showed any interest in this gift, even as an investment. At most, the Treasury was willing to consider legal changes that might make it easier for the Trust to accept gifts such as Wallington, free of estate duty, to spare the State the embarrassment.[88]

Chamberlain, however, was willing to look at the question in a different way, influenced by the countryside planning approach. He agreed with the Treasury's objection to private benefits, but was willing to consider concessions to the Trust if private owners submitted themselves to closer public control.[89] Both he and Sir William Ormsby-Gore, the head of the Office of Works, took *Country Life*'s brief for the country house seriously. But if the country house really was a national heritage, they felt, it required national planning, not some hole-and-corner, case-by-case negotiation with the National

Trust. At the Trust's next annual meeting, in July 1935, Ormsby-Gore
accepted that the

> wonderful houses in their beautiful parks, houses which still con-
> tained the accumulation by many generations of successive
> occupiers of the utmost historic and artistic interest in almost every
> county, was a unique heritage of Britain. No other country could
> match possessions like Penshurst, Knole, Bramshill, Hatfield, and
> Blickling.

But did the public recognize this fact? The Trust had only a few
thousand members, he pointed out, a fraction the size of the National
Art-Collections Fund. And did owners accept their new status as
curators of the national heritage? Before the government could act,
the Trust and owners had first to work together to rally public
opinion and cement a new relationship.[90]

Chamberlain then presented the Trust with two schemes. Scheme 1
would implement legal changes allowing the Trust to accept houses
without payment of death duties, and even to lease them back to their
formers owners. Under this scheme, owners

> would have sacrificed the pride of ancestral ownership, but would
> have acquired instead the security of tenure subject only to good
> behaviour, payment of a reasonable rent, and a reasonable allowance
> of access to the public, and be rid of the burden and anxiety of
> maintenance and death duty liabilities.

Scheme 2 involved the formation of an owners' association – perhaps
under Trust auspices – which would demonstrate their willingness to
submit to visiting and a degree of public control. The two schemes
were linked; the Trust and the owners could not have the first
without the second.[91]

Conservative elements within the Trust – its lawyers and members
of the Finance Committee, possibly even Zetland – were now won-
dering what Lothian had got them into.[92] A gradual scheme whereby
the Treasury made selective Trust acquisitions feasible – Blickling,
Wallington and a few others that were on the cards – was one thing,
but now that scheme was dependent upon the co-operation of the
entire class of country-house owners, recalcitrant and suspicious, very
different from the likes of Lord Lothian. However, the more ambitious elements – Matheson, Esher (now chairing the Finance Committee), Lothian – did their best to follow the government's
suggestions.

They were reinforced by a new face, that of another Liberal peer,

Lord Methuen, who had recently inherited his title and Corsham
Court in Wiltshire. Methuen was a painter and Francophile who had
independently developed an enthusiasm for La Demeure Historique
and its system of public visiting. Corsham Court had long been open
to the public for two days a week for viewing of its art collection, and
though Methuen acknowledged that this custom was little known
even in the immediate vicinity, he believed in its potential. As early as
1933 he had tried to interest the Land Agents' Society in organized
country-house tourism, and after Lothian's appeal he began to talk it
up more widely among his friends. 'The great thing is to get the
papers enthusiastic over this scheme', his mother advised him, 'so it
can be widely advertised and will help to steam up the public.' Alas,
she granted sadly, 'It is hard to get people in your position keen . . .
they are *so* Conservative – but as you say – have patience'. By late
1935 he had made contact with Lothian, introduced him to the
baronesse de la Boullerie, daughter of Demeure Historique's founder,
and persuaded him of the necessity for such a scheme in England.[93]
Therefore, when Lothian heard of the Treasury's conditions, he
pressed the Trust hard to respond on the Demeure Historique model:

> The *Demeure Historique* advertises the chateaux and houses and
> organises char-a-banc tours and uses its revenues to make grants for
> the restoration or repair of selected houses which are falling into
> ruins. The core of the whole system, however, is the tourist
> industry. I see no reason why once prejudice against intrusion into
> privacy is broken down in this country a very considerable income
> should not be made available to the owners of ancient houses in the
> same way. I should imagine that a good many thousand people
> every year, both foreign and British, would spend part of their
> summer holidays in visiting houses as they now do in visiting
> cathedrals and natural beauty spots.[94]

In the light of their experiences of the previous year, both the Trust
and *Country Life* were still sceptical of owners' willingness to participate, but Chamberlain's ultimatum had given them little choice, and
Matheson had already started to assemble what later became the
Trust's Country Houses Committee. On Lothian's suggestion, he
recruited Methuen, and Methuen in turn roped in a reluctant
Christopher Hussey. Selected owners of houses on *Country Life*'s list
were circularized in January 1936 and asked to attend a private
meeting at the House of Lords in late February, to be followed by a
public reception for the duc de Noailles and other members of La
Demeure Historique.[95]

The meeting was carefully stage-managed. Zetland chaired, summarized the Trust's discussions with government and explained that reliefs would only follow 'a quid pro quo – i.e. *access*', which would require the formation of a new branch of the National Trust composed of private owners. Then Lothian spoke, warmly congratulating Zetland on his achievements thus far, and seconding the idea of an association. It was not a large meeting and only a few owners chimed in – Salisbury of Hatfield, Ancaster of Grimsthorpe, Bath of Longleat, Lytton of Knebworth, Harewood of Harewood, Miss Fox-Talbot of Lacock Abbey. Most had previous experience of tourism. The tone was decidedly muted; Ancaster thought the tourist trade was 'an untapped source of wealth', which the Queen's Institute Gardens Scheme had only hinted at, but his house was not open, whereas Lord Lytton – who opened Knebworth every day – thought the contribution of tourism was negligible. Salisbury's private opinion was that Matheson was 'under a complete illusion as to the amount of money which could be collected on these lines' and, like most owners, he was holding out for substantial tax reliefs, but he had been coached beforehand by Matheson to agree that a committee should be formed as a short-term measure. On this slender encouragement, it was agreed that the Trust should set up a committee, a few names were proposed for its membership and Zetland was able to announce the formation of the committee at the public reception the next day.[96]

The committee as established was not at all a committee of owners, much less a representative committee, but rather a country-house pressure group within the National Trust. Only a few owners not previously involved with the Trust – Lord Salisbury, Lord Brocket, Lord Carlisle – were recruited and they played a fairly token role. More important were the country-house enthusiasts within the Trust, notably Lord Esher, chairman of the committee for twenty-five years, who moved the Trust to take this part of its work more seriously, and the penumbra of experts and aesthetes already engaged in country-house propaganda, for whom this represented the first practical exercise in preservationism and a point where information and ideas could be accumulated.[97]

The linchpin proved to be the committee's full-time Secretary, the young James Lees-Milne, hired in March 1936. Lees-Milne had been recommended to the Trust by Vita Sackville-West, who had heard of the opening from her friend Hilda Matheson, MacLeod's sister and lately instigator of the BBC's countryside campaign. A fringe figure in Betjeman's circle with raw architectural passions, Lees-Milne was a fervent Georgian in reaction against his father's Little English Arts and

Crafts tastes as well as the pervasive philistinism of the age. He had looked on with horror as his father, a Worcestershire squire, had razed Georgian estate cottages and replaced them with half-timbered fakes, only slightly more authentic than suburban villas, and thrown the elegant Georgian furnishings on to a bonfire, putting in their place 'medieval' tables and chests that he had antiqued himself by burying them in the ground for six months. Young Lees-Milne's moment of epiphany came as an Oxford undergraduate, at a country-house party at Rousham in Oxfordshire, where his host entertained the carousers by shooting off the private parts of classical statues with a rifle:

> The experience was a turning point in my life. It brought home to me how passionately I cared for architecture and the continuity of history, of which it was the mouthpiece. Those Rococco rooms at Rousham, with their delicate furniture, and portraits of bewigged, beribboned ancestors, were living, palpable children to me. They and the man-fashioned landscape outside were the England that mattered . . . That evening I made a vow . . . that I would devote my energies and abilities, such as they were, to preserving the country houses of England.[98]

In some ways, then, Lees-Milne was the ideal candidate for this post. With Christopher Hussey, Ralph Dutton, Lord Gerald Wellesley and others he brought together the tiny community of country-house lovers with an existing preservationist body, equipped with some funds and statutory powers, the National Trust. On the other hand, his vision of England was marginal and sectarian – what he liked was not really distinctively English, but an eighteenth-century England that was tied to classical taste on the Continent (and even more a Catholic, Baroque taste that hardly existed in England). His loyalties were thus to the houses first, the owners second, the Trust third – and the rest of the country a distant fourth. What allowed Lees-Milne to triumph over these limitations were his personal qualities: a certain sinuous charm, a tactful hypocrisy, flares of real industry and ingenuity, whatever was necessary to gull owners and public into saving the houses he (and generally not they) so loved. He was perfectly partnered by Esher, who was much more at home with a changing England, and who was able to channel these illicit passions for a vanished world towards practical and acceptable ends.

Esher and Lees-Milne's task – persuading owners to save their own houses, in order to persuade the government of the feasibility of the overall project – proved every bit as difficult as the auguries of early 1936 had suggested. A sub-committee of Hussey, Wellesley, the architect W. A. Forsyth and Sir Charles Peers (former Chief Inspector of Ancient Monuments) drew up a tighter list of about 230 first-class country houses, and their owners were informed of the Trust's scheme in a circular clumsily drafted by MacLeod Matheson. As responses came in, Lees-Milne opened correspondence with sympathetic owners and in many cases journeyed into the countryside to meet the owners *in situ* and look over their houses, beginning an absorbing business that would occupy him for thirty years. While Lees-Milne thereby learned much about houses (many hitherto unknown, even to *Country Life*), and educated his own taste, what he learned about the owners was not very encouraging.

The average owner was curtly dismissive of Scheme 2, the self-help association upon which government insisted. 'Nearly every owner who has replied to this Memorandum,' Lees-Milne reported in October 1936, 'has shown undisguised and bitter disappointment over this Scheme.' Their hopes had been raised by talk of sweeping tax exemptions and they now saw themselves asked to sacrifice their own privacy and limited funds to an unproved tourist trade. Only the very poorest and most desperate were interested in this option, hoping for subsidy from their richer fellows and the Trust.[99] Others showed their lack of fellow-feeling for their class. 'I fully understand the merits of the arrangement for owners of these houses who are at the last gasp,' wrote Lord Salisbury, but as to others, 'Why in the world should they come into the Scheme?' There was only 'the charitable motive . . . and nothing more', and in his view this 'seems to destroy the Scheme root and branch'.[100] Kind words from a member of the Country Houses Committee!

Those who already opened their houses saw no particular reason to contribute a portion of their meagre takings to anyone else, and were not keen to attract any more visitors than they already had. Mrs Roper of Forde Abbey complained of the 'considerable trouble' involved in opening: 'The public require continual supervision in the gardens as well as in the house.' Lord Harewood 'is put to enormous expense by char-a-bancs in the upkeep of his drives . . . he is often under the necessity of turning a surplus number of visitors away'. Of these owners, only Mrs Whitmore Jones of Chastleton and Lord Bath of Longleat – both on the American route through the Cotswolds to Bath – thought that tourism was really profitable. Those who did not open entertained a variety of fears about doing so. Lord Burnham thought that 'once the Public had been allowed into a House, they would look upon it as a legal obligation and become tiresome'. Lord Ilchester felt Holland House would become impossible to live in, and fretted about burglary. C. R. N. Bishop of Shipton Hall wanted to exclude 'undesirable looking people'. One prominent land agent argued that it was impossible to combine tourist and residential functions: 'Gardens lend themselves to be seen by the Public but not private houses.'[101] Owners liked the cachet of occasional charitable openings and did not want to enter into a business. Several saw general opening as the final bargaining chip, which should only be given up when significant tax reliefs were on the table.[102]

Almost immediately, therefore, Scheme 2 was proved impracticable. The Committee focused its energies instead on a limited version of Scheme 1, by which the Trust itself would take over properties, hoping that some tax concessions could still be squeezed from the Treasury, even though the owners had failed to do their required part. Here, too, however, Lees-Milne encountered disappointment or, at best, indifference. Whereas only the very poor had been interested in Scheme 2, only the very rich were even eligible for Scheme 1. Because the government was offering no subsidy, for the Trust to take on a house and estate the owner had to contribute a large endowment to maintain the fabric in perpetuity while he and his heirs remained in possession as tenants. The advantage to the owner, as Chamberlain had said, was that future tranches of death duty were avoided and the cares of maintenance transferred to the Trust. But the rich owners who could afford such an arrangement had their own private 'trusts', in the form of settlements, estate companies and the like. Lord Harewood confided to Lothian, what he had tactfully refrained from saying at the initial meeting of owners, that his lawyers were just as adept at death duty avoidance as the Trust (Lothian was interested, and received a little tutorial).[103] Besides, Harewood and people like him still enjoyed the status and business of landownership; they were not ready to give up. If they had heirs, the heirs often exerted pressure to retain future discretion over the estate. Finally, not many owners saw a reason to put their remaining assets to the service of country-house preservation. 'I think the Mansion-House here, as on many other estates, is the least attractive part of the estate,' wrote one Scottish laird to a member of the Committee in 1938, 'it is too big, requires too large a staff, and is not the type of house I would choose to live in, if I were deprived of the other benefits [of landownership].'[104]

However, there were a few owners more attached to their houses than to their heirs or their own independence who were willing to proceed, and the committee went forward on this basis; it no longer pretended to be an owners' committee, but worked purely to establish a collection of country houses under the umbrella of the National

Trust. Given the Trust's precarious situation and most owners' lack of interest, this was quite enough to take on. It involved promoting a bill in Parliament to enable owners to transfer their houses to the National Trust with an endowment and a leaseback arrangement, and an amendment to the 1937 Budget exempting the endowment and lease-hold from tax liability. After a year or two, it emerged that houses already in a private trust – i.e. a settlement – were almost impossible to transfer to the public trust. Lord Esher then promoted yet another bill, in the Lords, to make it easier for life tenants of settled estates to hand over to the Trust.

The storm aroused by this bill indicated yet again how tenacious owners were of their private rights, and also how low on their list of priorities preserving the house was. In the Lords' debates, peers objected to settled land being conveyed against the future interests of the heirs simply to support a house, 'charming as it may be'. 'The tenant for life,' opined the Lord Chancellor, 'is in the position, as I see it, of having a white elephant, and not an income with which he could live in the house in any useful manner.' All the arguments used for nearly a century to put the class interests of unborn heirs over the 'national interests' in the historic and artistic heritage were being trotted out again, observed Lord Crawford, who had been listening to them for forty years. But the combined efforts of Esher, Zetland, Lothian, Methuen and Crawford were inadequate against the silent majority of peers. The bill went into a Select Committee and emerged amended so as to fortify heirs' ability to dictate terms over the lease but also, mourned Esher, so as to limit the Trust's ability to accept settled property. The Trust's failure in the Lords was to haunt it for years to come.[105]

All that remained was to find some owners willing and able to take advantage of the new scheme! Lees-Milne toured the country visiting houses, but early interest invariably melted away when the owners discovered the limited financial advantages of the scheme. The scheme's first firm offers nearly all stemmed from acts of philanthropy by high-minded owners. The Liberal MP Sir Geoffrey Mander gave Wightwick Manor, not a historic house at all but a fifty-year-old gem of Arts and Crafts historicism, which the Trust would only take on because of Mander's generous endowment. Methuen offered Corsham Court, Lothian offered Blickling, Sir Charles Trevelyan offered Wallington. The fact that these early offers came from Liberals or even Socialists was itself chilling. Lord Bath advised the Trust not to publicise Trevelyan's offer 'if we do not wish to make [the] majority of owners suspicious'.[106] Apart from Wightwick, the only offer that could be accepted before the war came from the desired rarity, an extremely rich landlord without immediate heirs, Sir Henry Hoare of Stourhead in Wiltshire. Stourhead's historic value had been much reduced by a catastrophic fire in 1902, but it was acceptable for its collections and its remarkable Georgian landscape garden.[107] Other-wise, the scheme had to subsist on dreams. The greatest of these dreams was Knole, held by a sympathetic owner but like Cinderella seemingly unobtainable through a curtain of thorns: the poverty of the estate, the complexity of the settlement, the ambiguity of the tax status.

On the superficial level the National Trust's Country Houses Scheme was a failure in these early years. Owners were unwilling to participate and sometimes openly denunciatory. No amount of *Country Life* propaganda could disguise the fact that most owners saw themselves as trustees for their heirs, not for the public. The public responded in kind. Chamberlain's offer of a place within the country-side planning rubric was rebuffed, and thereafter no government funding was forthcoming; even the Trust received only the most meagre death-duty exemptions. Despite the ceaseless flow of propa-ganda in favour of country-house visiting and the country-house heritage, neither the Trust's committee nor *Country Life* really believed that the cause of the historic house was yet popular.[108] When they collaborated in an exhibition of *British Country Life Through the Centuries* in London in summer 1937, to aid the Country House Scheme – and also to educate the public in the beauties of the Georgian country house – it was, wrote Lees-Milne glumly to Methuen, a damp squib, with only four hundred paying visitors in its first week, despite a big send-off.[109]

However, the scheme did bring discussion of the country house, its status and its fate, into public life in a way it had not been just a few years earlier when Hussey was almost alone in promoting it. Weighty figures like Zetland, Lothian and Methuen – even if untypical of the landed class – had public platforms that the experts and aesthetes had not, and the scheme pulled them into activity: Methuen, for instance, had been neither a subscriber to *Country Life* nor a member of the National Trust before he was recruited by Lothian in the autumn of 1935. Methuen's influence secured a fifteen-minute broadcast on the scheme over the BBC's West of England service in July 1938, which attracted two thousand letters of enquiry from the general public, although Lees-Milne regretted that the press was 'not particularly interested'.[110] A newsreel film was produced in the *March of Time* series which, while pretty scathing about 'the tradition and snobbery of the

71  Lord Methuen (bottom step, centre, facing camera) entertains château-owners from France and Belgium at Corsham Court in July 1938. Part of a campaign to publicize the National Trust's Country Houses Scheme, the visit, Methuen complained, 'seems to have received no publicity whatever'.

English country house', backed the Trust's scheme for providing 'a new interest for tourists'.[111] There were at last debates in both Houses of Parliament in the late 1930s in which the future of the country house was at least considered, if not dealt with. A Tory backbencher's motion in February 1937, calling on the government to incorporate historic preservation into its countryside planning programme, gave Geoffrey Mander an opportunity to plug the scheme, though discussion of this motion tended to drift from historic houses to questions of landscape and town planning, the acceptable faces of the Georgian fashion, or, worse, to drift further to 'ancient buildings' and 'our beautiful old villages'.[112] Government's stock response was to urge the National Trust to educate public opinion in its direction. In the meantime, civil servants concluded, 'there was nothing to be done'; there was no money to be spent, 'if Housing, Milk for Mothers and a cancer scheme are to have priority (and it seems difficult to avoid the conclusion that they should)'; and, in any case, 'it is necessary to remember that the countryside is not the preserve of the wealthy and leisured classes', so that government was right to stimulate new building development in the countryside rather than to dwell on the preservation of the old.[113]

Nevertheless, the country house was at least present on the list of objects in the countryside to be preserved, if not at the top of that list. The rhetoric of planning had established a political context within which the rural heritage could be considered, and the rhetoric of Georgianism had established an aesthetic context within which most country houses could be included. Now they were being brought together, however uncomfortably. The Socialist Chuter Ede spoke eagerly in Parliament of 'national heritages' which have 'up to the moment largely been in the occupation of one class, and the majority of people have had few opportunities for seeing them', but now 'will be available for the country as a whole'.[114] The Tory Zetland wrote in a different tone in the *Sunday Times* of the country house as 'part of the spiritual and aesthetic heritage of the nation, imbuing it with reverence and educating its taste'. It was already 'cherished not only by those few privileged to possess such homes to-day, but unquestionably by most sections of the British public', to whom generous access was accorded.[115] In between, the Liberal Methuen temporized: most owners recognized their national role by opening their houses, but they needed to court a sceptical public further, by 'considerably extended privileges' which showed that country houses had a 'useful purpose'.[116]

The cross-party nature of this campaign should not mislead: Ede, Zetland, even Methuen represented tiny minorities in their respective parties. Furthermore, though they were at least agreed that the country house represented a national heritage, they had significantly different ideas of how country houses should be owned, visited and appreciated. They had still to convert the public, persuading them to divert significant national resources to historic preservation of any kind, and the owners, by luring them into the scheme. It would take a further social and political cataclysm to effect those conversions, but in the late 1930s Britain was on the verge of just such a cataclysm, and change came more quickly than anyone would have predicted. In 1929, when the 2nd Lord Montagu of Beaulieu died, leaving the Palace House and Beaulieu Abbey to his three-year-old son, he chose as his epitaph, 'He loved Beaulieu, deeming his possession of it a sacred trust to be handed on to his successors in a like manner'. In the hands of the 3rd Lord after the Second World War, that private trust became something quite different, a playground for the million, and hundreds of other country houses and estates followed suit or went further still, realizing the public trust that Lothian had vaguely invented in 1934.

# PART IV

## *Open Houses, 1939–1974*

The Englishman's home is his castle they say,
Be it never so splendid and stately.
The family seat must be saved from decay
Though built and embellished ornately.
Aid is due to the heirs of great houses of England
Where rain drips through many a dome,
> Where stone work is shaky
> Where turrets are crumbling,
> Where stucco is flaky
> And chimneys are tumbling –
> Though their means are restricted
> They won't be evicted,
For the Englishman's castle's his home.

For national monuments, Treasury alms,
For palaces scheduled historic,
For Blenheim and Cliveden and Hatfield and Glamis,
For Arundel, Walmer and Warwick.
If owners throw open great houses of England
The State tax-relief may adjust –
> A council will earmark
> As national heirlooms
> The dower-house, the deer-park,
> The State-rooms, the spare rooms,
> The portraits, the panels
> The plate and enamels,
For the Englishman's castle's a Trust.

This realm might have lost every family seat
If maintenance had not been granted,
For mansions historic with contents complete
Could be sold overseas, and transplanted.
But the State will take over great houses of England,
With half-crown set teas on the lawn
    And owner caretakers
    Will be reinstated
    When halls and broad acres
    Have been designated,
    Retained on condition
    Of public admission
The Englishman's castle's in pawn.

—'Sagittarius' [Olga Katzin],
'The Englishman's Castle',
*New Statesman*, 1 July 1950

## CHAPTER 8

# The Country House and the Welfare State

Evelyn Waugh's fantasy about the English country house as a place of essential good beset in the 1930s by the contemporary evils of material greed and philistinism, reached its apotheosis in early 1946 with the publication of *Brideshead Revisited*. Brideshead, a loose amalgam of Castle Howard and Madresfield Court in Worcestershire (where Waugh had spent many a happy weekend with his friends the Lygon sisters), comes to stand also for Waugh's bourgeois hero Charles Ryder as an oasis of peace and patronage in the increasingly corrupt and unsettled interwar world. The beginning and end of the novel reveal what has become of Brideshead since 1939: 'The place had been marked for destruction before the army came to it', the estate laid out for a suburban housing tract, but it has instead suffered a worse fate – desecration rather than destruction. Unfeeling clerks and beastly soldiers had been accommodated in the ground floor rooms of the house and defaced what fixtures had not been boarded up. The grand fountain had been turned into a rubbish bin for sandwich crusts and half-smoked cigarettes. Roads had been slashed through hedges and balustrades. Ryder's unit is expected to turn the park into an assault course and a mortar range. What remains of the ancestral family, Ryder's protectors, is huddled in a few upstairs rooms. Downstairs, the coming generation is triumphant, the 'Young England' of postwar socialism symbolized for Ryder by his adjutant Hooper, classless, featureless, half-educated, mean and ignorant: the future. 'The age of Hooper' – what Waugh elsewhere called 'the Hooper-Attlee terror' – had begun; civilization, as embodied in Brideshead, had fallen.[1]

But just as Waugh's romanticism wildly inflated the virtues of Brideshead, so his taste for the grotesque exaggerated the hostility of Hooper. The war did indeed lay the country house low; wartime uses often led to desecration of the kind described, and the austerity both of war and peace continued to reveal what had been appreciated already in the 1930s, that large country houses had little future as private homes. Yet wartime collectivism at the same time strengthened the hand of those countryside planners who wished to protect rural England from the random depredations of roads, pylons and bungalows. A new realism on the part of owners allowed the country house to be considered as part of that planned countryside. And an interesting convergence of taste between historically conscious aesthetes and modernist planners drew renewed attention to the special claims of the country house. Hooper would prove more careful, more magnanimous, and – in Waugh's terms – more 'civilized' than Waugh himself could ever admit.

## Old Houses in the New Jerusalem

Whereas the First World War undermined the country house chiefly by sapping its landed foundations, the Second World War had a more direct and devastating impact. Private property was no longer so sacrosanct and owners themselves cared less for the integrity of their houses; it was widely acknowledged even before war broke out that any large buildings in the countryside, unexposed to urban bombing, would be requisitioned to accommodate evacuees and army operations. Instead of seeking to dodge wartime use altogether, farsighted owners struck private bargains to secure relatively friendly uses. One of the most favoured alternatives was use by girls' schools, from which soldiers would be kept well away: Chatsworth accommodated Penrhos College, Longleat a girls' school from Bath and Castle Howard Queen Margaret's School, Scarborough. Boys' schools were only marginally less desirable, and Blenheim had a 'good war' billeting Malvern College. Government departments were also highly desirable evacuees. The 11th Duke of Bedford persuaded the government to take on Woburn Abbey in early 1939 for intelligence work and was able to confine the spies to the east wing and some outbuildings (applying also a 'no smoking' rule). Alas, after the Duke's death in August 1940, his heir the 12th Duke, something of a crypto-Nazi, was ordered to keep clear of the Abbey and the whole of the estate was taken over, left in a terrible mess for the 13th Duke to retrieve when he inherited in 1953. Blenheim had better luck when it took in MI5 after Malvern College returned home. Three country houses in Northamptonshire were used to store treasures from national art collections and archives, as were West Wycombe, Mentmore, Compton Wynyates, Montacute, Muncaster and Sudeley Castles, Haddon, Belvoir and Clandon.

72    The boys of Malvern College bed down in the Long Library at Blenheim Palace.

At the other extreme, the worst fates befell those houses that, like Brideshead, had to accommodate troops. Unlike the custodians of public schools and national collections, troops had neither familiarity with nor interest in the delicate fitments of country houses. Panelling, fireplaces, fountains and balustrades suffered accordingly. Jury-rigged heating systems led to fires, such as a disastrous one at Castle Howard that destroyed much of the central block, including the paintings in the great dome. Sometimes damage was more purposeful: grave-robbing airmen broke into the mausoleum at Blickling in search of jewellery; the conservatories at Alton Towers absorbed 'friendly fire' from trigger-happy machine-gunners; Kedleston's doors lost their ormolu rosettes. Owners considered themselves lucky if their billeted soldiers were non-ambulatory, as at Corsham and Ragley, both used as military hospitals.[2]

The collateral damage inflicted by wartime requisitioning was far greater and more extensive than any direct hits by enemy action. Of major country houses, only Holland House in the centre of London, Mount Edgcumbe on Plymouth harbour, Sandling Park in Kent and Appuldurcombe in the Isle of Wight incurred serious bomb damage. The fact that so much damage was self-inflicted has attracted bitter recriminations since, but at the time only from an outraged few like Waugh, or James Lees-Milne surveying the ruins for the National Trust. Most contemporaries were quietly philosophic: the occupying troops because they had no reason to feel otherwise, but owners, too, because the war was effecting a complete sea change in their attitudes to their homes.[3] Older owners, who often remained in residence, eating, living and sleeping in a room or two, with only a few servants, while the troops caroused downstairs, might feel resentment or anger. But younger owners, in particular, experienced their displacement as a blessed relief. The white elephants had been taken off their hands. Financial liabilities vanished in a flash. The advantages of living in a cottage or flat, unaffected by servant, fuel and building material short-ages, were manifest. Many would have military responsibilities any-way, but even those who remained behind to supervise agricultural work often felt this was as easily achieved from a snug billet in the stable-block or an entrance lodge as from the big house.

Neither the difficulties of life in the big house nor the disenchant-ment was relieved much in the immediate postwar years. The persist-ence of rationing meant that fuel and building materials were still in short supply. The building licence system, introduced in wartime to regulate repairs and new building, was only gradually phased out. Even when owners were compensated for 'dilapidations' incurred during wartime use, they were not necessarily allowed to spend the money to put their houses to rights. For instance in 1945 the National Trust was granted £450 to reinstate Aylsham Old Hall after six years of billeting troops, but it was only permitted to spend £100 of that sum immediately and a mere £10 per annum thereafter – 'which means', as James Lees-Milne noted, 'that no one can quite possibly inhabit large houses after troops have been billeted in them'.[4] Building licences were required – and not always granted – even to demolish dilapidated houses. In one celebrated case as late as 1953, servants of the Duke of Bedford were fined for their role in the partial demolition of Woburn Abbey.[5]

But it was not only sheer economic austerity that seemed to doom the big house. Changing social conditions also hardened owners' hearts against it. The servant problem after the war was a matter not so much of labour shortage as of a change in attitudes: domestic service was now widely perceived as unseemly in a modern age, and rural domestic service, remote from urban entertainments, was deemed the lowest of the low. Tax rates, which had naturally soared to spectacular heights to pay for the war, remained high to pay for the peace, but also as a deliberate social policy. Large incomes – at levels necessary to live in a mansion – were out of fashion. With marginal rates pushing towards 100 per cent, it was virtually impossible to keep an income above £5,000 a year, and one big house alone could easily eat up that sum. The Duke of Northumberland, for example, paid 70 per cent of his £130,000 rent roll on income tax and surtax in 1949. After paying necessary estate expenses, he was left with £2,600 to live on – not a bad sum for a normal householder, but Alnwick Castle cost £7,000 a year to run, Syon House another £4,000.[6] The surplus had to come out of capital.

Then there were taxes directly on capital, principally death duties. The top rate had gone up from 50 per cent to 65 per cent during the war and the favoured path of escape since the settled land exemptions had been cancelled – the formation of estate companies – had been blocked. Death duties could still be evaded by handing over the estate to the heir well before death. But the hand-over was often fumbled, particularly after 1946 when the point at which hand-over had to be completed was extended from three to five years before death. Two of the most punishing death-duty levies resulted from such fumbles: the 11th Duke of Devonshire inherited in 1952, four months too early to avoid £2.5 million in duties, and the 13th Duke of Bedford was made liable to £4.5 million in duties by a matter of weeks only in 1953. The dutiable value of country houses was of course pathetically low, but when they were stuffed with art – as were Chatsworth and Woburn – they represented yet another painful liability to the integrity of the landed estate on which they sat. To tradition-minded owners, and particularly their legally minded trustees, these brute sums tolled the death-knell for life in the big house. Where the house threatened the capital values of the estate, the house had to go.[7]

Because aristocratic wealth and confidence revived in the 1950s and 1960s, it has been easy to overlook the very low ebb of the 1940s. Owners have frequently been acclaimed for their devotion to their homes, their determination to soldier on, the great sacrifices they made to cling to country residence.[8] This was simply not the case in

73   In the immediate aftermath of war, many country-house owners felt private ownership to be more of a burden than a privilege, as *Punch* slyly suggests, 22 January 1947.

*"This is my last warning, Charles. If you do not mend your ways I shall leave the estate to you instead of to the National Trust."*

the 1940s; whether willingly or grudgingly, hardly any owner felt in that decade that there was a future in country-house life. Houses viewed today as triumphant symbols of aristocratic continuity — particularly the larger houses of the eighteenth century — were slated for abandonment in the 1940s. Neither the 10th nor the 11th Dukes of Devonshire had any intention of living at Chatsworth; for some years, the 11th Duke tried to palm Chatsworth off on to the government in partial payment of death duties, and it was only in the mid-1950s, with recovery well under way, that he decided to keep Chatsworth and abandon Hardwick instead. The 13th Duke of Bedford felt 'there was no future for the aristocracy in England', and had been unmoved by the partial demolition of Woburn in 1953. Only gradually did he come to see Woburn as an asset rather than a debit, and it took him many years to persuade his trustees of this. The trustees of Castle Howard hoped to unload the house on to the school that had occupied it in wartime, and it was not until 1951 that George Howard decided not to sell, and only in 1953 that he actually moved back into the house. The Earl of Leicester was bitterly disappointed that the terms of his settlement prevented his disposing of Holkham.[9] Attachment to the older houses was greater — and not always because they were smaller. There were no plans to abandon Hatfield, Burghley or Penshurst, but these houses of the Olden Time formed only a small portion of the whole, and for those who had before the war been laboriously building up the notion of a unified country-house tradition, the declining attachment to country-house life among the owners was a vexing difficulty.

The National Trust's Country Houses Scheme both benefited and suffered from these circumstances. On the one hand, higher tax rates undoubtedly magnified the financial advantages of handing over a house and capital endowment to the Trust in return for continued residence. On the other hand, continued residence was no longer seen as so desirable or worthy of substantial capital sacrifices. As one assessment put it in 1943:

> To-day many owners are little attracted by a scheme which may make it easier for their children and grandchildren to live on in the old family home, subject to restrictions. They are uneasily aware that the coming generations will probably want to live in a small house or flat and have a larger surplus to spend as their tastes and inclinations may direct.[10]

For the first eighteen months of the war, there was no movement either way. Lees-Milne was in the army and the country-house side of

74    The National Trust staff in their wartime billet at West Wycombe Park, c.1940.

the Trust's work ground to a halt. In late 1941 Lees-Milne was discharged on health grounds and permitted to return to the Trust's staff, which had been evacuated to West Wycombe Park in Buckinghamshire. As his celebrated diaries so entertainingly recount, he spent the rest of the war chugging about the country by rail or on rationed petrol, trying to cajole his friends and his friends' friends to hand over their rotting or deserted houses to the Trust. A few important houses finally began to come in – Wallington and Blickling, whose transfer had been afoot before the war; Hatchlands was offered by the architect H. S. Goodhart-Rendel; Cliveden, the Astor mansion with its wonderful gardens perched over the Thames, was accepted more for its setting and the handsome endowment than the architectural merits of the house. But most of the houses entering the scheme were smaller and second rate.

The results were so disappointing that in early 1942 Lord Esher began agitating for relaxed financial standards. 'I hear on all sides that we ask too much', he reported; owners were simply not willing to fork out large endowments. Lees-Milne agreed: 'The Country Houses scheme was after all first conceived by owners for their own benefit as well as of their historic houses.'[11] Over the objections of the accountants, the endowment standard was reduced, so that only basic structural maintenance (and not improvement or modernization) would be covered. So eager were the scheme's managers to catch one big fish that they even agreed to supply part of the endowment for Knole out of the Trust's own meagre reserves. Other concessions were made to owners to induce them under the umbrella. At Knole and Petworth, the valuable contents remained the property of the owners while the crumbling fabric went to the Trust for maintenance. Public access conditions were relaxed and considerable autonomy over the management of the house and estate was conceded to the owners of Cliveden, West Wycombe and Knole.[12]

Although progress was made on these and other negotiations, such that two dozen houses were in Trust hands by the end of the war, the Trust's leadership was losing confidence in the long-term viability of the scheme. Too few owners wished to reside, fewer still to endow their houses, and thus at a time of mass desertion the Trust would be unable to save more than a handful of houses, and not necessarily the most important ones, either. By 1944, the list of first-class houses that owners wished to abandon but would not or could not endow was an impressive one: it included Lumley and Naworth Castles, Audley End, Lyme Park, Osterley, Althorp, Mount Edgcumbe, Burton Agnes and Rousham. By then it had been accepted – by Lees-Milne, by the Trust's secretary MacLeod Matheson, by the Trust's most aesthetic grandee Lord Esher – that its country-house work could not continue without direct subvention by government, and that would require a substantial re-orientation away from a scheme protecting the interests of residential owners and towards public interests and non-residential uses.[13]

If so many important country houses were up for grabs, then the attitude of the public and of government became all-important. Here there were some signs of hope, although not necessarily signs that the National Trust or *Country Life* would at first recognize. Unlike the chaos in the countryside unleashed by the First World War, the paralysis of private landownership wrought by the Second World War met with a very much more positive and coherent public response. Opinion is divided as to whether this response emanated from intellectuals and élite politicians, whose interest in physical planning had been mounting in the 1930s and who were determined not to repeat the mistakes of the 1920s, or whether it reflects a genuinely popular enthusiasm for a new era in town and country planning. Whatever the source, the signs of a new departure are unmistakable. The First World War had been succeeded by a messy land-grab, in which land sales and abandonment by traditional owners was met by a disorganized repossession of the land by ramblers, motorists, property developers and suburban home-owners; the boundaries between town and country had been blurred, and the traditional shape of the landscape had in many places been scarred and disfigured out of recognition. In the 1940s, there was a powerful desire not to let this happen again: public control of some kind had to be imposed on the ownership and use of the land. When contemporaries spoke in the 1940s of 'building a New Jerusalem', they meant this literally – not only remaking society on more equitable social and economic lines, but also controlling more deliberately the physical appearance of the English landscape.

So far as the countryside went, the physical appearance that was apparently desired was some return to the traditional shape of the land before uncontrolled development and suburbanization had begun to eat into it between the wars. In this way, the war undoubtedly triggered a revived idealization of the traditional landscape and of agriculture in particular. This does not mean, however, as is sometimes too readily assumed, that the identity of ordinary town dwellers became more wrapped up in a rural fantasy.[14] In fact the idealized agricultural landscape was in many ways more distant from their lived experience: it was a place designed not for them but for countrymen, an educational and touristic asset to be visited by the mass of English people, but not inhabited by them. The interwar hiker or motorist or suburbanite had yearned to take possession of the countryside, to wreak revenge on the recently dispossessed landlord. The new attitude saw the countryside as something different from the town, to be cordoned off and separated from it, to enable it to fulfil its separate destiny, appreciated by the mass from a remove. In the shift from a declining Liberalism to a rising Labourism, from a nervous middle-class identity to a more confident popular identity, old neuroses about the countryside were being shaken off and a cooler approach both to country *and* town could be contemplated. For the flip side of this new rural preservationism was a new urbanism, a desire to use physical planning to enhance the urban living experience which was, after all, the experience of the average citizen. If the country was to be saved from desecration and incursion, the city had to be made more liveable: its own cultural assets had to be built up, its housing stock renewed and vastly expanded, its distinctive delights and satisfactions recognized. New towns had to be designed from scratch; they were the inevitable corollary of cordoning off national parks and agricultural reserves. If there was a new idealization of the countryside, there was also a new idealization of the city, in the end a far more powerful force.

What did this mean in practice? During the war, a series of government reports – physical planning's equivalent to the welfare state's Beveridge Report – established a national consensus as to how town and country were to be planned after the war. The Scott Report of September 1942 established the need to plan town and country separately, the former for housing and employment, the latter for agriculture and open space. Although Scott was undeniably romantic about agriculture's contribution to the economy and to the appearance of the land, it did emphasize that the land was a 'national estate' aimed at satisfying the needs of the whole of the population, which was mostly made up of town dwellers. This collectivist approach to the countryside was given fiscal bite by the Uthwatt Report, which finally cut through the Gordian Knot of private property rights by recommending that the State should nationalize not the land but the right to develop the land. In short, together the Scott and Uthwatt reports recommended that landowners be confined to their most important public function – agriculture – and that they be stripped of the rights to sell off or develop their land that they had used so irresponsibly between the wars. The system was broadly implemented by the postwar Labour government in the Town and Country Planning Act of 1947.[15]

Perhaps surprisingly, an influential strand of landed opinion responded warmly to these ideas. Landowners who had been but a few years earlier inveighing against the weak 1932 Planning Act as confiscatory and un-English now saw the division of labour proposed by Scott and Uthwatt as the salvation of any recognizable landed class. As early as 1941 'an amorphous and confidential body' came together to 'administer a little common sense to the Tory Party' on topics such as the future of the land, a body that included the historian G. M. Young and the self-appointed peers' tribune Lord Salisbury.[16] This group accepted the inevitability of central planning as preferable to nationalization, and wished only to gain maximum control over agriculture for farmer-landowners. Income reinvested in the land was to be untaxed, although there was some doubt as to how much 'pocket money' landowners might be allowed to retain for the 'upkeep of house and demesne'.

Young saw this rededication to agriculture as the salvation of the landed gentry, and regretted bitterly that the Tories had allowed themselves to be distracted from this mission. Since the 1880s, landowners' ties to the people had lost their functional element, had become merely 'traditional'. Today, 'four-fifths of our electorate live in urban areas'. What need did they have for an aristocracy? 'Now, having dismissed the [traditional] argument as inapplicable, we have to see what grounds we have for the alternative argument of utility, *as it can be presented to that electorate*.' Young embraced Scott and Uthwatt wholeheartedly – indeed, he edited the bestselling Penguin digest of the reports, offering the exchange of development rights for an agricultural revival as 'a good bargain between Town and Country', one which would put an end to land speculation in the country and at the same time allow the town to 'own itself'.[17] This became a popular argument among landed opinion-shapers, including the traditionally conservative Country Landowners' Association.[18] Predictably, *Country Life* endorsed the argument – Christopher Hussey had been making it almost alone for nearly twenty years – but amazingly so did writers in *The Field*, in the 1930s the mouthpiece of diehard anti-planners.[19]

There was here, then, the germ of a national consensus on the future of the countryside. Landowners who found themselves backed into a corner, stripped of their income, their acres imperilled, began to see the way clear to a revived role as professional farmers in a countryside planned and ordered in the national interest. Agricultural stewardship became once again a matter not only of class but of national honour for the traditional landed classes. When in 1943 Sir Richard Acland, one of the few remaining left-wing landlords, donated to the National Trust his 17,000-acre estate in Somerset and Devon, he was widely decried as a bolter.[20] The very existence of the landed class depended on fulfilling, not abandoning the agricultural role.

But the future of the country house in these new arrangements remained unclear. In so many cases it was proving a liability to the privately owned estate. Owners were finding houses impossible to maintain and were deserting in droves. Their newfound identity as professional farmers did not sit well with the old grandeur and state. Many owners preferred to abandon rather than to draw the State into their private living arrangements. While a few owners of the most historic houses – the Duke of Norfolk at Arundel, the Earl of Pembroke at Wilton – began to show an interest in *Country Life*'s old scheme for State-subsidized tourism, the typical owner was more cautious. 'The future of the great houses is by no means a simple question', wrote a leading landowners' representative, R. G. Proby, in April 1942:

Some, such as Arundel and Wilton, are of such historic and architectural importance that they *must* at all costs be preserved, but there are many Victorian barracks which I think might well be demolished without great harm being done. I doubt myself if it will be possible in the future, except in very exceptional circumstances, for the owners to live all over them . . . in many cases a nice middle course might be found, i.e., the owner could live in comfort in a wing, with the power of throwing the state rooms open on important occasions.[21]

Even at the National Trust, some of the less aesthetic leaders felt that the value of the ordinary country house was not so high as to be worth incurring State intervention. Both Lord Zetland and R. C. Norman had crossed swords with Lord Esher earlier in the war, arguing against him that State and Trust alike should confine their attentions to the very best houses, respecting the remainder as private property. As Norman said of the great majority of ordinary country houses, 'Perhaps it doesn't matter much what their fate is'.[22]

If owners were uncertain what place the new consensus might have for the country house, the public was still more doubtful. The question was now one of 'utility', in G. M. Young's words, as it could be presented to the urban electorate. During the war there was growing hostility to the maintenance of country-house privileges even on the restricted basis envisaged by Proby. Granted, there was no longer the gleeful lust for destruction of the country house that was evident between the wars. The case of Wentworth Woodhouse – whose grounds were strip-mined for coal right up to Lord Fitzwilliam's doorstep, it was said vindictively – was exceptional.[23] If nothing else, restrictions on new building lent old buildings an enhanced utility, and there was a dawning appreciation of eighteenth-century country houses as art objects.

The fabric of the old country house was therefore gaining some respect; but there remained widespread suspicion of the privileged lifestyle that was carried on inside. One sign of this was mounting public dissatisfaction with the National Trust's Country Houses Scheme. Largely invisible before the war, the scheme now came under scrutiny in popular newspapers, as more houses entered it and public sensitivity to the disposition of property increased. A friend of the Trust wrote in November 1943 to warn of

the widespread and growing criticism of the country houses scheme . . . Briefly, the criticism is that the country houses scheme is a funk hole for death duty dodgers, and that the public has got by far the worst of the bargain inasmuch as it merely has the promise of some unknown amount of access – presumably, however, occa-

sional and limited – in some unknown future . . . It seems to me
that the only possible justification for allowing owners of estates and
houses to present them to the Trust, but to go on living there and
for their successors to have the right to continue living there, is for
the public to get something pretty substantial in return. After all, the
Trust is supposed to hold properties for the benefit of *the Nation.*

MacLeod Matheson took this seriously enough to seek to plant a
favourable article in some left-wing popular paper like the *Daily
Herald.* But the limits of the Trust's network were revealed by the fact
that this plan degenerated into yet another puff piece in *The Times,* a
prime instance of preaching to the converted.[24]

When the next mention of the scheme arose in the popular press,
it came not from the Trust's mouthpieces but again from its critics.
The *Sunday Pictorial,* forerunner of the *Sunday Mirror,* lambasted the
Trust for accepting Gunby Hall with only limited public access provision. When Lees-Milne remonstrated with the *Pictorial*'s editor, he
got a good lesson in public attitudes: the editor 'expressed much
ignorance about the Trust and aesthetic matters generally', thought
Blenheim 'too ugly for words', and 'was surprised that the Trust
should want to own any eighteenth-century buildings'. However, he
was genial enough and invited Lees-Milne to contribute a follow-up
piece.[25] The invitation was at length accepted, yet again the response
to Lees-Milne's defence of the country house offered an unpleasant
lesson in popular feeling. Readers who accepted Lees-Milne's invitation to suggest ways of preserving country houses were nearly unanimous in their view that 'the coming social changes' made continued
residence impossible and undesirable. Instead they put forward a host
of alternative uses: 'a café cum dance hall' (as one reader reported had
been successfully attempted at a castle in Denmark), 'a good beer
house with dancing room etc. and café Continental style', 'Eventide
homes for workers . . . Nurses, Teachers, Welfare Workers', or adoption by factories for use as 'holiday centre, sanitarium, hostel or
convalescent home'.[26] A report on the postwar future of the National
Trust secured from a public-relations firm in early 1944 came to a
slightly more elevated conclusion. If country houses were to be
preserved, they had to be re-used in ways consistent with the 'radical
social and economic changes that are proceeding in all parts of the
world'. The report recommended their adaptation as 'centres for
drama, art, or similar cultural activities':

> Such centres, however, would have to be planned very broadly,
> operating as festivals with a minimum of instruction, for as a people

we are inclined to avoid anything which is blatantly educational . . . These proposals do appear to break away from the
original purpose of the Trust, namely, to maintain country houses
intact. The houses are, however, intended for the benefit of the
public, and, in order to be of such benefit and because of social and
economic changes, that original purpose is likely to have to be
modified.[27]

By the end of the war, even long-standing advocates of the country
house as a living art treasure, such as the Trust or *Country Life*, had
come reluctantly to accept that extensive preservation on the old basis
was not possible. Owners were either not able to live in their houses
or unwilling to pay the price, and the public was certainly unwilling
to pay that price for them. On the other hand, the public seemed
moderately supportive of country-house preservation on a new,
socially expanded basis. Accordingly, much effort began to be channelled into finding 'alternative uses' for country houses. As early as
February 1943, the National Trust put its name behind an appeal to
find new uses for country houses after the war, although it was
worried that this amounted to an admission of defeat for its own
scheme.[28] By the time of its Annual Report in autumn 1944, that
admission had effectively been made.[29] Although the Trust knew that
some houses would continue to trickle into its scheme, it now understood that a wider solution to the country-house problem depended
on alternative use. In December 1944 the Country Houses Committee
accepted Lees-Milne's proposal to approach the government for aid in
accepting houses for alternative use, including leaseback to the government for its own departments.[30] If the choice was between a
'friendly' use, respectful of the house's tradition and decoration, an
'unfriendly' use requiring extensive renovation, and demolition, then
energies were best expended on encouraging the friendliest possible
uses.

Alternative use of a country house was generally considered to be
friendly if it perpetuated the residential function on a new basis, or
drew attention to the aesthetic qualities, or – best of all – both. Lord
Methuen was particularly keen on the use of country houses as
residential colleges:

in the past these large country houses may have performed a useful
role, anyhow to their owners, and they were obviously built for a
certain purpose which has now ceased to exist. Therefore if they are
to remain in existence a new function for them must be found. You
can only have a few country house museums. But there is no saying

how many educational particularly adult educational establishments this country will or at any rate should have if it is to provide a crying need. What better background could be provided than by many of these country houses with their well planned settings, where such men as Brown and Repton and others have given their best.[31]

Other uses considered desirable by connoisseurs were local arts centres (mini-Glyndebournes), homes for distressed gentlefolk and residential training centres for the professions.

The vague public feeling that alternative use was the best possible fate for country houses was crystallized by the actual fate of houses after the war ended. The expected cascade of demolitions did ensue in the late 1940s and early 1950s; by one count, whereas only twenty-eight country houses had been lost during the war, seventy-eight were demolished in the five years to 1950, and – with the relaxation of building controls – no fewer than 204 in the five years to 1955, the peak period of demolition in the twentieth century.[32] This represented a greater loss than had been incurred between the wars. More striking still was the sudden burst of activity after 1945 in country house sales.

75   Country houses for sale: the Countess of Abingdon lurking outside the tent as the contents of Highcliffe Castle go under the hammer, July 1949; the house itself was destined for alternative use as a seminary.

Although it is more difficult to monitor sale than demolition, one statistical sample suggests that twice as many houses were sold after the war as demolished. Of these sales, the vast majority involved change of use from private homes to institutions, and the vast majority of these took place in the immediate postwar years, to 1950, when the pent-up demand for schools, colleges, hospitals and other such institutions was released.[33] The plain fact is that the building licence system, which favoured the recycling of old buildings over the construction of new ones, certainly saved more country houses than the National Trust ever did.

Most of these salvages would have constituted 'unfriendly' use, but there were many successes to report. Lord Methuen leased part of Corsham Court to the Bath Academy of Art, with whom he cohabited happily for the rest of his life. The City of Bath was encouraged to convert two other neighbouring country houses for educational purposes. After a long struggle, the highly important Gosfield Hall in Essex was bought by a charity for use as a residential nursing home. Government agencies purchased dozens of country houses as residential training centres, including several for agricultural purposes. The Duke of Portland shared Welbeck Abbey with an Army preparatory boarding school and Bramshill, one of Nash's Mansions of the Olden Time, was purchased by the Home Office for use as a police training college. The scheme for distressed gentlefolks materialized in the form of the Mutual Households Association, which purchased several country houses in the 1950s and operated them successfully on a commercial basis. In the same period Christopher Buxton started up his 'Period and Country Houses' business to convert country houses into tasteful modern flats.

These adaptations were by no means limited to artistically inferior or ordinary houses. Of the 320 houses agreed by the National Trust and the Ministry of Works in 1939 to be the best privately owned country houses in England and Wales, about 10 per cent had been abandoned and another 10 per cent institutionalized by 1952. Many more were just in limbo; James Lees-Milne estimated that fewer than half of the 320 were actually inhabited. Relatively few had been demolished, in part because the new planning authorities had been given powers under the 1947 Act to obstruct the demolition of the best historic buildings, but in other respects the fate of the best houses was not much rosier than the fate of the average houses.[34]

These melancholy outcomes certainly did not satisfy the ardent aesthetes at *Country Life* and the National Trust, who had been slaving on behalf of the living country house for over a decade. They had faced facts at the end of the war and accepted alternative use as a miserable minimum goal, but the cruel reality of demolition and alteration after the war was almost too much to bear. Combined with the shocking Socialist victory of July 1945 and the harsh, fuelless winter of 1946/7, the remorseless dismantling of centuries of country-house civilization pointed to a future hardly worth living. Lees-Milne was frankly disgusted by the tenants of the New Jerusalem now lodging in his beloved country houses. At Killerton, the Aclands had installed 'the Workers' Transport Company, people smelling of disin-fectant, a working woman singing out of tune'. Attingham Park, which he had worked very hard to win for the Trust, was let to the Shropshire County Council for use as an adult education college to be run by G. M. Trevelyan's Socialist nephew George.

> A little folk-dancing, some social economy and Fabianism for the miners and their wives. We felt quite sick from the nonsense of it all. At a time when this country is supposed to be bankrupt they spend (our) money on semi-education of the lower classes who will merely learn from it to be dissatisfied.[35]

A more lighthearted but still tart protest trod the boards of the West End stage in December 1949, when both nationalization and the conversion of country houses were at a peak. Alan Melville's *Castle in the Air* portrayed the comic plight of the Earl of Locharne, unable in postwar conditions to keep up his stately home with its forty-eight-bedroom Victorian wing. As in earlier satires, the castle is Scottish (safely distanced) and haunted (though in this case the ghost cannot even muster an on-stage presence), and salvation arrives in the familiar form of an American heiress. But the position has deteriorated from *The Canterville Ghost* or *The Ghost Goes West*. The Earl cannot hope to save his castle for himself; all he wants is to stop the National Coal Board from requisitioning it as a holiday hostel for miners and their families:

> You know what they'll do – take the place for five years – pack it with thousands of miners with millions of children – and hand it back when they've done with it, encrusted in soot and with a bill for five years' rates and taxes. Well, they're damned well not going to get it!

The outcome is not marriage and triumphant continuity, but outright sale to the Yankee, who is no longer the worst fate; as the curtain falls, the Earl pockets his £120,000 in cash and embarks on a long cruise to Cuba with his secretary. *Castle in the Air* packed them in for three hundred performances, helped along by publicity from a ridiculous attempt by the National Coal Board to get the play banned, lending some force to the cynical gibes against the Socialists with which the play is peppered. For a comedy, the tone is prounouncedly bitter and resigned.[36]

The general acceptance of alternative use – willing or reluctant – posed the question of whether a preservation body like the National Trust had any role at all to play in the postwar world. If the government was to control land use by planning, create national parks and channel country houses into alternative use, what was there left for the National Trust to do? There were prominent people at the Trust who were ready to throw in the towel, hand over the whole operation to the government.[37] But the pillars of the Country Houses Committee (now strategically renamed the Historic Buildings Committee), especially the ebullient Lord Esher, were pragmatically searching for a new role. Perhaps the Trust could not expect to hold for their owners the hundreds of country houses Lothian had hoped to bring into the scheme; perhaps alternative use was the future for most; but might there not still be a place in the New Jerusalem for some country-house museums, a collection of the very finest houses – those neither their owners nor the Trust could afford to maintain on their own – the Chatsworths and Haddons and Penshursts and Knoles? Surely as *their* owners gave up the ghost in the postwar years, the government could not let them die, or hand them over to adult education colleges. And if they were to be nationalized as museums for the benefit of the semi-educated masses, might not the National Trust be the agency to administer them? It was to this role – country-house museum-keeper to Socialist Britain – that the National Trust gradually turned after July 1945.[38]

## Nationalizing the Country House?

The prospects for interesting the postwar Labour Government in a collection of country-house museums were not as dim as the wartime and immediate postwar fate of most houses might suggest. The Labour government, busy with interventions in so many spheres, was not shortchanging culture. The Arts Council was one product of the wartime consensus that benefited from steadily mounting grant support after the war; so was the Third Programme on the BBC. A national opera house and, at least in theory, a national theatre were established, the latter owing much to the efforts of Lord Esher. Many liberal intellectuals like Esher – or J. M. Keynes, first Chairman of the Arts Council and the Covent Garden Opera Trust, or Harold Nicolson, who found himself joining both the Labour Party and the Trust's Historic Buildings Committee – busied themselves in these postwar years by embedding as many fragments of the old culture as they could gather together in the fabric of the new Socialist commonwealth.[39]

Already during the war, historic buildings had been acknowledged as appropriate objects of government solicitude. The combination of relaxed property rights and extending planning legislation made it possible to do in 1944 what had been impossible a few years earlier, to lump in inhabited buildings with the ruined ancient monuments to which government action had long been confined. The German bombing raids on historic towns and the extension of artistic education during the war had also excited popular attachment to the traditional townscapes that were now threatened. Shortly after the Ministry of Town and Country Planning was set up in 1943, therefore, it was empowered to draw up a national inventory of historic buildings – the famous 'listing' process – and in 1947 Labour's planning legislation allowed the Ministry to control the alteration or demolition of listed buildings, up to the point of compulsory purchase. The National Buildings Record (later National Monuments Record) was also established during the war, to keep a central supply of photographs and drawings of historic buildings. The Royal Commission on Historical Monuments had its hoary prohibition on studying post-1714 buildings lifted. The Ministry of Works, custodian of the State's ancient monuments, could now reasonably look to the day when it might be empowered to hold habitable buildings as well.[40]

Because of the impact of bombing and redevelopment, but also because of the nation's renewed urban identity, most of this attention was devoted to towns. Architects, planners, politicians and thousands of citizens debated how much of the historic fabric should be incorporated into rebuilt and redeveloped cities. The listing process began in the towns. Perhaps the most influential work of architectural history published at this time was John Summerson's *Georgian London* (1945), through which the Georgian fad of the 1930s, put firmly in an urban planning context, finally reached a popular audience. When Summerson gave an important lecture on the future of historic preservationism in 1947, he assumed that this future would be almost entirely a matter of urban reconstruction.[41]

Yet the planning consensus, differentiating firmly between town and country, was a two-pronged fork: urban identity was to be separated from rural identity, and even if for most city-dwelling Britons that rural identity was of less personal and pressing interest, still it was there to be staked out and explored. What had for centuries been 'landlords' country', and which more recently had become a muddied field trampled upon by would-be peasants and yeomen from the towns, could now be easily appreciated for the first time *as* 'landlords' country', without any of the old prejudice or sentimentality. The aristocracy was no longer a threat, Arts and Crafts yearnings for 'village' or 'peasant England' had ebbed away and aristocratic culture could be studied with some detachment and indeed an awareness of long neglect.

The collapse of private ownership made the subject literally more accessible, too. Landowners were decanting their collections of manuscripts into the county record offices that were springing up around the country (sometimes, as at Delapré Abbey in Northamptonshire, in recycled country houses).[42] Their gates and doors were off their hinges. John Summerson recalled that when, as an architectural student in the 1920s, he had tried to sketch country houses, he had been warned off by footmen; at Blickling, they threatened to call the police.[13] After 1945, there were no footmen left, and owners seemed pathetically grateful for any outside interest. Scholars were free to discover this unknown country. Nikolaus Pevsner began his national catalogue of historic buildings, the famous *Buildings of England* series, immediately after the war and was gratified to find country houses almost universally accessible. At the same time he commissioned Summerson to contribute a volume on early modern British architecture to his *Pelican History of Art* series, and Summerson – hitherto exclusively an urban historian – found his curiosity piqued by the great country houses. *Architecture in Britain, 1530 to 1830*, first published in 1953, is still the standard work; it drew attention to the large Elizabethan mansions, which Summerson called 'prodigy houses', and treated them as part of a continuous tradition that included the post-Civil War houses in classical styles, an argument confined to the *Country Life* circle before the war.

In these postwar years, many other scholars travelled the same country-house circuit: Rupert Gunnis documented holdings of sculpture, Howard Colvin laid the foundations for his great dictionary of British architects, numerous art historians (some working for the auction houses) spied out unknown paintings, and H. J. Habakkuk, Lawrence Stone, David Spring and F. M. L. Thompson began to unveil the aristocracy's social history.[44] There were occasional awkwardnesses as the scholars entered Sleeping Beauty's castle.

Summerson had an odd encounter with the 'Hogarthian' owner of Deene Park, which he visited for his Pelican book.

> The old baronet . . . asked about my wife: who was she before we married. I replied that her father was a civil engineer, the family background was wool. There was a pause. 'My wife', said the baronet, 'is descended from St Luke.'[45]

Stone was anxious not to violate his own liberal conscience by kowtowing too much to the aristocracy, but he found himself uncharacteristically knotting his Christ Church tie for country-house visits.[46]

The scholarly work was swelled by a new wave of writing from *Country Life* and related circles. Christopher Hussey resumed his work on a complete catalogue raisonné of country houses with volumes on the eighteenth century. Vita Sackville-West's *English Country Houses* (1941) and Sacheverell Sitwell's *British Architects and Craftsmen* (1945) were both much reprinted after the war. John Piper continued the *Shell Guide* series that John Betjeman had started before the war, and the two men collaborated in an unsuccessful attempt to revive the *Murray's Guide* series on a more architecturally serious basis. James Lees-Milne launched his writing career with *The Age of Adam* (1947), 'nostalgic reflections', as he declared defiantly in the preface, 'upon that earlier, less progressive age, when politics was a game, society an art and art religion'.[47] Despite the occasional self-indulgence, however, aesthetically motivated work such as Lees-Milne's was enriched by intermingling with the high intellectual standards of the new scholarship.[48]

This convergence of scholars, mostly of bourgeois backgrounds and with Liberal or left-wing politics, and right-wing aesthetic gents such as Hussey, Lees-Milne and Sitwell was, like the encounters of scholars and owners, not without its discomforts. Evelyn Waugh and John Betjeman may have aspired to be squires, but Pevsner and Summerson had no such leanings. Their new-found enthusiasm for the country house drew criticism from younger colleagues who felt they were betraying modernism and urbanism.[49] Against this, Pevsner and Summerson argued that, unlike the aesthetes, they could separate the houses from the vanished way of life they had once embodied. Summerson distinguished between right-wing preservationists, 'to whom the preservation of buildings meant the preservation of values threatened by the advance of democracy', and 'that kind of interest in the social and economic history of man which belongs to the political left', which saw architecture as 'a witness of phases of human life in the past'. He defended his own position acerbically in a radio broadcast in July 1950:

> In this century I suppose we are being sufficiently objective and realistic to separate the values out. We do realise that the country house life of the eighteenth century is not likely to appear again but that there are certain values in these houses which make them worth preserving in themselves.[50]

And there was the extraordinary neglect of country houses among the last several generations of scholars to make up for.

The audience for both kinds of work, the scholarly and the aesthetic, was not confined to the readers of heavy tomes. Thanks largely to the efforts of Geoffrey Grigson, the BBC made an effort to elevate the tone of its countryside programming to reflect the new cultural history being written. Between the wars radio had steered clear of a controversial aristocracy, preferring what Grigson scorned as the 'slop and glow' of peasant life, but now a more objective and cosmopolitan approach was deemed appropriate, on the Home Service as well as the Third Programme. Pevsner, Summerson and Betjeman were frequent broadcasters. The most popular of all was Brian Vesey-Fitzgerald, who specialized in intelligent leisure-oriented programmes, such as 'There and Back' or 'Let's Go', aimed at revealing the cultural as well as physical pleasure of rural tourism.[51] This trend was greatly accelerated when country-house tourism took off in the 1950s, but it was already well under way by the late 1940s, when the West of England Service especially built up a reputation for 'excellent talks about archaeology, about local history, local architecture and topography'.[52] Beyond this, there were stirrings of interest elsewhere: adult education courses on the country house in the houses that were now accommodating colleges; charities such as the Pilgrim Trust turning their efforts to the preservation of historic buildings; the slow recovery of country-house visiting in conditions of petrol rationing and labour shortages. Promoters of the country house were, after all, building up from a very low ebb. As one educator put it in 1949:

> in view of the dearth of educational material existing on the houses, the scarcity of good books on English architecture giving any description of the houses, the prevalence of (in some instances) completely uneducated guides, and foolish little books sold on the houses; one is forced to realize that the educational opportunities have hardly been grasped.[53]

So it would take some time to overcome the accumulated prejudices of preceding generations against aristocratic culture, even as an 'objective' part of the national history. The most that can be said is that in the late 1940s academic experts were coming to share the opinion, formerly confined to aristocratic and pseudo-aristocratic connoisseurs of the English country house, that such houses were works of art and historical documents. Given ingrained prejudices (especially among the older generation), the pressing national need for greater social and economic equality and, above all, the lingering association of country houses with their still unpopular owners, what chance was there of persuading a Labour government to spend precious money on preserving *any* of the stately homes of England? The answer to this question after 1945 rested in the hands of two men, one a Tory grandee, the other a Socialist politician.

The Tory grandee was the 28th Earl of Crawford, who succeeded Zetland as Chairman of the National Trust in the autumn of 1945. Crawford's appointment was a welcome tonic to the Trust and especially to its work on behalf of the 'living' country house. As the senior representative of the Lindsay family, Crawford was uniquely qualified to represent an aristocracy with pretensions to cultural stewardship. He was also extremely charming, assiduous in persuasion, commanding in argument, but not too 'grand' in manner. Whereas Zetland had been inclined to struggle against the Socialist current, and Esher perhaps too ready to swim with it, Crawford was – as Lees-Milne soon saw, to his delight – up to the task of defending the National Trust's traditional activities inside a Labour-governed Britain. Under Crawford's leadership, there was no longer any talk of handing over country houses to the State; the question was how the State could be used to extend the Trust's ownership of country houses.

The Socialist politician upon whom Crawford levelled his sights was the new Chancellor of the Exchequer, Hugh Dalton. From a privileged background himself, Dalton was both a convinced egalitarian and a highly skilled economic technician, probably the most serious Socialist ever to occupy 11 Downing Street (and thus, in Lees-Milne's universe, 'Mephistophelean'). Among Dalton's immediate plans in the autumn of 1945 was a Budget that would attack great concentrations of wealth, including landownership, and to this end not only did he maintain wartime levels of income tax and surtax, but he screwed the top rate of death duty up further, from 65 per cent to 75 per cent. Aware of the chaos in the countryside unleashed by previous doses of capital taxation administered by left-wing governments in 1894, 1910–14 and 1929–31, Dalton determined also to have a complementary plan for the land and other assets thus liquidated. He knew that Labour's planning legislation would not permit the kind of speculative development that had ensued between the wars, but he wanted to provide a positive alternative, a means by which the State might turn land sales in payment of death duty to public benefit.[54]

For this purpose, he dreamed up in the autumn of 1945 what became in the 1946 Budget the National Land Fund. From the beginning he intended to endow this Fund handsomely from the sale of surplus war stores, 'to be spent on real estate only, e.g. in promoting National Parks, in aiding National Trust' and in accepting land directly from owners as part payment of death-duty bills. Triumphing over determined Treasury resistance to this idea, Dalton won Cabinet approval for an immense dowry of £50 million – the annual interest of which alone represented about four times the Arts Council budget – to be applied to virtually any land acquisition that the Chancellor might feel was in the public interest.[55] As Dalton explained to the nation in his Budget broadcast in April 1946:

> This money will be used to buy some of the best of our still unspoiled open country, and stretches of coast, to be preserved for ever, not for the enjoyment of a few private land-owners, but as a playground and a national possession for all our people. I want the young people in particular to have free access to all the most beautiful parts of Britain. I want to help the Ramblers Associations and the Youth Hostels Associations and the National Trust in the fine work they are doing.[56]

Dalton's rhetoric made clear two things: first, that Dalton had a very high opinion of the National Trust, which he saw as doing the public's business in a semi-nationalized fashion (he had once described it as 'a typically British example of Practical Socialism in action'); and second, that his personal idea of the public's business in the countryside was that of the interwar Left, happy young people tramping across the moors (once out of office, he accepted the presidency of the Ramblers' Association). With characteristic optimism, Lord Crawford seized on the first of these facts and sought to circumvent the second. After years of awkward and unsuccessful efforts to interest Labour politicians in aiding the Trust's work, and equally unsuccessful attempts to persuade the Ministry of Works that the Trust was a worthy custodian of historic buildings,[57] a direct overture was made to Dalton in February 1946 – before anyone knew of the NLF plan – through Professor R. S. T. Chorley, a Trust insider who had recently failed by fifteen votes to win election as Labour MP for Northwich.

Chorley told Dalton that the Trust's chief problem lay in the country-house sphere. Owners were no longer willing to endow their houses in order to live in them; 'No-one can produce these sums of money except the State.' Could the State provide endowments for houses to be passed to the Trust, or could it offer a direct grant to the Trust which might then be used as endowment?[58]

Dalton was not particularly concerned about the fate of the country house (on his single recorded visit to one – Longleat – he was patently bored by the accumulated treasures of the Thynne family and bursting to get out to explore the surrounding landscape[59]), but he was pleased at this overture just at the time when privately he had been preparing a scheme to pass land to the Trust. He offered an immediate cash donation, in the form of a pound-for-pound matching contribution to the Trust's Jubilee Appeal (already under way and already flagging), and the assurance that the Trust would be a special beneficiary of NLF bounty.[60] In Parliament he offered an additional tribute, while announcing the matching grant. The Trust's work, he said, was 'of great national importance . . . I hope it will be continued on the same broad lines as in the past and on a larger scale'.[61] There remained the problem that Dalton's idea of the Trust's work and the Trust's idea of the Trust's work were about a generation apart. 'Dalton has a weak-ness for land', sighed R. C. Norman, whereas the Trust's weakness was for (and in) country houses. However, Crawford was content with the gains already made: the enormous potential of the NLF, the official benison extended to the Trust's very existence, not to mention the useful matching pounds that began to roll in that summer. So long as the Trust was not required to take on too much revenue-draining open space, such as the Bala estate in North Wales, which Dalton was pressing on them, then the whole *démarche* might still have a splendid future.[62]

Some Trust leaders worried that this entanglement with govern-ment would threaten the Trust's independence and thus its future; but the reverse was probably the case. In 1946 the Trust found itself at a very low ebb indeed. The response to its Jubilee Appeal was disappointing; people had little ready money and were disinclined to give what they had to private charities. At a press conference that summer, Lees-Milne detected 'an atmosphere of hostility, boredom, and criticism on the part of the Press that we were out of touch with the public'.[63] Paradoxically, only government could at that stage estab-lish the Trust's independence. Dalton's assurance that the Trust had a defined place in the postwar world, as a semi-nationalized custodian of land and buildings in the public interest, pointed a way forward.

NOTICE
THIS BUILDING
IS NOW
NATIONAL
TRUST
PROPERTY

WILLS.

*"You realize, I suppose, that this makes us Civil Servants."*

76  After Hugh Dalton's embrace in 1946, the National Trust began to be seen as a public institution, or just another nationalized industry (*Punch*, 14 May 1947).

National Trust membership jumped from under eight thousand to over twelve thousand in 1946. At a time when its longstanding rival the National Art-Collections Fund found its membership stagnating, the Trust was embarked on an extended period of slow but steady growth, but this was requiring a reorientation away from the interests of private landowners towards the interests of the public. Crawford invited Mrs Dalton and a backbench Labour MP to join the Trust's Executive. Lees-Milne was now devoting much more attention to the public opening and presentation of country houses than to the court-ing of owners. Most new houses, their contents and endowment funds, it was more or less accepted, would have to come via govern-ment. After all, now that the NLF existed to take houses in payment of death duty, why would any owner pass to the Trust for nothing what he could get death-duty credit for from the Treasury?[64]

As soon as the creation of the NLF broke the deadlock, the Trust busied itself with clearing the backlog of first-class houses that it had been offered but proved unable to accept for lack of funds.[65] In 1947 Cotehele in Cornwall became the first house transferred to the Trust after being accepted by the National Land Fund in payment of death duties. This pre-Civil War house, so perfectly intact in furnishings, hangings and ambience (because unoccupied since 1667) that Lees-Milne dubbed it the 'Knole of the West', was a popular first acquisition; 'It would have been a great pity if it had been lost' was Dalton's dry verdict.[66] Ham House, of similar vintage and preservation but immediately accessible to London trippers, was acquired at about the same time. Since Ham's owners, the Tollemache family, were not then in debt for death duties and in any case did not want to sell to government, the National Land Fund could not be used, and a complicated arrangement was required whereby the Trust took ownership of house and grounds and the Victoria and Albert Museum bought the contents and administered the collection. For the same reasons, Osterley Park, Lord Jersey's magnificent Adam mansion on the western fringe of London, came to the Trust with an endowment partly funded by local authority purchase of estate land and central government purchase of the contents.

The cases of Ham and Osterley reinforced the Trust's argument that it had a special role to play in cajoling owners to nationalize their houses, even if continued residence was no longer in question. But now that the government was in the country-house business, its own agencies were clamouring for a bigger slice of the pie. The Victoria and Albert Museum, which had been collecting individual rooms of country houses since acquiring the Inlaid Chamber of Sizergh Castle in 1891, was now itching (under an aggressive new director, Sir Leigh Ashton) to acquire some complete houses with collections as satellite museums. In 1947 it won the right to administer Apsley House, the Duke of Wellington's town house ('No. 1 London') which had been handed over to the State, and then a share in the management of Ham and Osterley. At the same time, the Ministry of Works was putting its case. As custodian of the State's ancient monuments, it felt that any historic buildings falling into State care should become its responsibility.

When in autumn 1946 the National Trust brought up the case of Audley End, one of Nash's Mansions with Adam interiors near Cambridge, the Ministry of Works staked its claim. The trustees for Lord

*"It's a toss-up whether it goes to the National Trust or the Ministry of Works."*

77  By 1948, the Ministry of Works and the National Trust were competing for ownership of country houses abandoned by their owners, as observed by the cartoonist Michael ffolkes.

Braybrooke had paid their death duties but were now willing to sell outright to government. In this case, the Ministry suggested to the Treasury, where the owner was happy to sell direct to the State, there was no need for the semi-nationalized custodianship of the Trust; full nationalization was possible: 'One or two country houses of this supreme quality ought, we think, to be available for full inspection by the public.' Audley End could not only become 'the country house counterpart of a Royal Palace like Hampton Court or Holyrood House, but, through the teachers who used it, would contribute to broadening the cultural horizon of the nation at large to an even greater extent than they do'. Ultimately this argument was accepted; the Treasury paid for Audley End and the Ministry of Works operated it as a museum, with various national museums taking responsibility for maintaining the contents that Lord Braybrooke left on extended loan.[67]

As a result of Dalton's initiative, therefore, government had by the end of 1947 slipped into the ownership of a small but growing collection of country houses, both through endowing the National Trust and in its own right. In addition to Cotehele, Ham, Osterley and Audley End, there were also Speke Hall and Lyme Park, National Trust acquisitions made possible by arrangements with local authorities in Liverpool and Stockport. Under the influence of their own scholars at the national museums and the Ancient Monuments service, ministers could now be heard advocating the educational value of great houses intact with their collections (but not with their owners). Dalton himself, who had no previous history of interest in country houses, made a personal commitment to push through Audley End. 'I say straight away,' his colleague the Minister of Education granted in recommending the Ham House purchase to the Commons,

> that I believe that it is to the benefit of the country that the nation should own these places and that they should be used specifically for educational purposes . . . if we can come up to London for the Cup, occasionally we might come up to see something really of national value. I would like to see the development of a taste for this sort of thing, with a desire on the part of the people from the Midlands to go to a place like Ham House in order to discover something worth while.[68]

Such an argument was possible now because Dalton had separated houses from owners, and had more or less forced the National Trust (insofar as it was to receive public funds) to follow suit. Most country houses were still destined for alternative use. But, reconceptualized as national museums, a sample of the very best country houses was now deemed a worthy target of public expenditure. As 1948 dawned, a new tranche of country houses seemed fated to fall into public ownership; leading the pack was Harewood House, home of the Princess Royal, which she and her son Lord Harewood were offering in payment of death duties and upon which the Ministry of Works had fixed its beady eye.[69]

At this point, however, a trick of fate intervened. In November 1947 Dalton had committed a rare indiscretion, leaking some trivial details of his next budget to a reporter minutes before the budget speech, and had been forced to resign. His successor Sir Stafford Cripps, while from a minor landowning family and reputed to care about rural amenities, in fact had much less vivid a view of the State's expanding role in the culture as a whole than had Dalton. Lees-Milne noted bitterly that he 'had only once been to the opera, and that was in Russia'.[70] Cripps was prepared to continue Dalton's policy of using the NLF to pass land and houses on to the National Trust; in fact he wished to use the NLF not only to accept houses in payment of death duty but also to make direct purchases. But he was confused by the competitive clamour for houses from various governmental bodies, and concerned too at the *ad hoc* way in which public expenditure on acquisitions was made. He wanted reassurance that a 'considered selection' of house-museums was being made and the best means of administering them applied.[71] Accordingly he commissioned a committee of inquiry into the whole question in June 1948. The issue of how to preserve 'a good cross section of the beautiful or historic houses in the country' was left 'quite flexible': museums, 'public or social purposes', but also semi-nationalized homes. On the suggestion of his civil servants, he agreed that 'we should not rule out arrangements by which the owner or his family would continue to live in the house, or part of it, on condition that suitable arrangements are made for public access'. All this was to be mulled over by the committee. As we shall see, by leaving open the question of subsidy for private residence Cripps was storing up trouble.[72]

A career civil servant, Sir Ernest Gowers, was appointed to head the inquiry. Other members were selected as experts on technical matters – the art historian Anthony Blunt, the architect W. H. Ansell – or as representatives of political opinion – the trade unionist Jack Little and Lady Anderson, wife of the wartime Chancellor Sir John Anderson – or as regional representatives – the Scottish jurist J. D. Imrie and the Welsh archaeologist Cyril Fox.[73] No one knew what to expect from this committee, not even ministers. Herbert Morrison complained that it included no obvious defenders of the public interest and feared it would degenerate into a scheme 'to relieve the idle rich at the expense of the taxpayer'.[74] At the other extreme, owners, suspicious of government commissions, thought its purpose was to nationalize the National Trust (Lady Anderson herself thought this at first). In between, the Trust was wary but immediately set about wooing the members, particularly Lady Anderson, assiduously cultivated by James Lees-Milne, who knew her slightly, and Anthony Blunt, a sympathetic expert who had serendipitously just joined the Trust's Historic Buildings Committee. Lees-Milne also began lining up friendly owners to testify before the inquiry.[75]

The committee took testimony throughout 1949 and into 1950. It heard from all sides: owners such as Lord Sackville of Knole and Sir John Dashwood of West Wycombe, who had entered the Trust's Scheme; owners such as the dukes of Marlborough and Devonshire, the marquesses of Salisbury and Bath, who had opened their houses to the public; local authorities and educational bodies; aesthetic enthusiasts for the country house like Christopher Hussey and the Duke of Wellington; landowners' organizations; a variety of government agencies.[76] All those who queued up to testify impressed upon the committee the cultural significance of the country house with its contents and setting. Where they differed was on how it might best be preserved. Landowners and their representatives, including Hussey, took the opportunity to reopen the case for private residence, made possible by tax reliefs on land and buildings as well as cash subsidies.[77] The Ministry of Works argued that it should take over from the National Trust the responsibility for holding publicly owned houses and that it should also be given funds to subsidize private owners, in return for public access.[78]

The National Trust fretted for some time over the form its submission should take. The danger was that, if the Trust stuck to the museum policy as pursued by Dalton, the Ministry of Works would be able to argue that a fully public body should be entrusted with these fully public buildings, as it had done successfully in the case of Audley End.[79] So the Trust turned back to its own Country Houses Scheme. Quietly conceding to the Ministry of Works the custodianship of 'Museums, Schools and Institutions to which it feels entitled', the Trust claimed for itself the distinctive task of holding houses still inhabited by their families but supported by the State. 'It is when the family remains,' Esher argued,

> that our custody is superior to the Ministry of Works, and as many families should be retained as possible, as it is only they who can maintain the 'country house' atmosphere and who also make the best custodians.[80]

To this end, the Trust urged that the NLF be used in future to transfer into its hands houses and contents *with the families in situ*, as had already been negotiated successfully and cheaply at places such as Knole and West Wycombe. It also asked for an annual State grant to help endow and maintain such properties.[81]

The committee reported in June 1950. Like many government reports of this period, it set the terms of future debate on its subject. Unlike many government reports of this period, however, it repudiated existing policy and thus put a stop to the policy of nationalization pursued by Dalton. Yet its own recommendations marked such a novel departure that they, too, would prove politically void.

*Doles for Dukes*

To most people's surprise, and some people's delight, the Gowers Report enthusiastically endorsed *Country Life*'s line on the future of the English country house. Its most widely quoted words, in fact, came from Christopher Hussey's confrère, the Duke of Wellington: 'the English country house is the greatest contribution made by England to the visual arts . . . an association of beauty, of art and of nature – the achievement often of centuries of effort – which is irreplaceable, and has seldom, if ever, been equalled in the history of civilisation.' It was not a matter of a few jewels – the whole array of country houses was in question, some two thousand by one count – nor of preserving houses as museums – the way of life which underpinned the country house's special identity as a home had to be preserved, too. For this purpose, neither alternative use for the many nor public ownership of the few was appropriate. Nothing less than country-house life had to be restored to health, and for this a sweeping range of tax reductions and exemptions was required – income-tax reliefs and death-duty exemption not only on houses and contents but also on endowment capital – as well as supplementary grants to be disbursed by new Historic Buildings Councils. In return, the public would get the permanent preservation of its national heritage, in some cases with rights of access for educational or tourist purposes.[82]

These findings came at a propitious juncture for the private ownership of country houses. The postwar boom in alternative uses was passing; the choice was now more clearly between private ownership or demolition for all but the few that were passing into public ownership. In the next year, Labour would lose power and the Conservatives would begin to restore owners' freedom of action, including the right to develop their land for profit. At the same time, the more entrepreneurial owners were beginning to explore the possibilities of country-house tourism: the first widespread opening of privately owned houses to the public took place during the summer of 1950, and the number of open houses would double in the summer of 1951, as part of a tourism offensive for the Festival of Britain. In the long run, therefore, the Report had working for it powerful forces in politics and society, but it was also ahead of its time, the first official statement of the high cultural significance of the country house and of the need to maintain it in ancestral hands.[83] It gave a powerful impetus to arguments long advanced by *Country Life* and the more romantic elements in the National Trust – indeed it made them more romantic, as Lees-Milne, after years of pragmatic compromise, re-emerged as a passionate defender of houses' owners against government and even against the National Trust.[84] But the Report was also working *against* the established policy and social attitudes of the preceding decade.

As even *The Times* recognized, the Gowers Report would be very difficult for a Labour government to swallow.[85] The first reaction of leading ministers was in fact to choke. Cripps, who in later years was mythologized as the Report's great patron, said immediately that

> the method of solving the problem is politically quite impossible. It amounts to creating 2,000 pensioner families in perpetuity who – whatever their qualities and their way of life – are to be kept by the State in large houses with gardens etc. This, I am certain, would make the whole proposition quite hopeless. We must devise a better way.[86]

In this he was reinforced by Hugh Dalton, back in Cabinet as Planning Minister:

> The national interest is in the houses, contents and amenity lands; not in their present owners. I would like to see it made much easier for such houses, etc., to pass into possession of the National Trust and other public bodies.[87]

When, shortly thereafter, Cripps, in ill health, was replaced by Hugh Gaitskell, he added to the chorus of unanimity.

> I do not like the idea of creating the privileged class of owner occupiers – i.e. a sort of bribe to induce people to live in these houses . . . I am not opposed *a outrance* [*sic*] to measures to enable more of these houses to be kept in better repair – but I should like this done in the main by edging more of them into the National Trust or similar schemes.[88]

These ministers attempted to maintain existing government policy, which was to preserve country houses only in public or semi-public ownership. But the Gowers Report had effectively shifted the terrain of debate. Before the Report, National Trust ownership was the *least* nationalized form of preservation being contemplated; now, it was the *most* nationalized form conceivable. Maintenance grants to private owners in return for public access were on the table, a less nationalized alternative; and the Report's central recommendation, tax reliefs, represented a completely privatized approach to country-house preservation.[89]

The latter option ministers rejected definitively. The Inland Revenue had costed it at £10 million a year, but it was objectionable on principle. Though an activist civil servant at the Treasury, E. W. Playfair, devoted himself aggressively to advocating this positive response to the Gowers Report, Gaitskell remained implacable. Only with great reluctance would he accept any subsidy at all to private owners, and tax reliefs were out of the question.[90] Support for country houses would have to be confined to a handful of the most important, and not to the full two thousand, as a matter of politics as well as economy.

Two legislative responses crystallized in the course of 1951. First, renewed efforts were to be made to entice land, houses and contents into the National Trust's scheme, on the basis of continuing private *occupation* but semi-public *ownership*. This was to be achieved by a number of means: use of the NLF to acquire contents as well as land and buildings; wider use of the NLF to pass country houses on to the National Trust and local authorities; extended tax concessions to the National Trust, to induce owners to enter its scheme voluntarily. Second, the Ministry of Works, through advisory Historic Buildings Councils for England, Wales and Scotland, was to be empowered to offer maintenance grants to the National Trust and to private owners. These grants were to come attached with powerful servitudes: the public were to have access to grant-aided houses; the Ministry of Works was to have first right of purchase when grant-aided houses went on to the market; private owners were to be subject to stringent means tests and required to contribute to all grant-aided works. The Cabinet approved legislation along these lines in April 1951, accepting Gaitskell's argument that its policy

> should not be to encourage the continued private ownership of these houses at the expense of the general taxpayer . . . but rather that these houses were part of the national heritage and that from that angle the Government were taking over partial responsibility for them.[91]

Labour did not get a chance to implement its plan. It lost the October 1951 General Election and Gaitskell made way for R. A. Butler. The new Minister of Works was David Eccles, a member of the Georgian Group and well-known collector of eighteenth-century art and antiques. To Lord Crawford's amazement, Eccles was temperamentally opposed to any legislation on country houses at all.[92] His gut reaction to Labour's proposals was that they were part of the whole Socialist apparatus of planning, which he and his colleagues were pledged to dismantle. Semi-nationalization was not much better than nationalization *tout court*. He was even opposed to the existing 'negative' controls on the demolition of listed buildings. Nor was he much attracted to the full Gowers package of tax reliefs: tax reliefs must be applied across the board, as part of mainline Tory economic policy, and not targeted sentimentally on a privileged class of museum-keepers. 'We cannot choose to live as our ancestors and it is unhealthy to try too hard to do so,' he maintained, 'the nation is finished which prefers to be a curator of monuments rather than the creator of something new.'[93] In this opinion the new Planning Minister, Harold Macmillan, concurred. He was no more interested in planning the past than he was in planning the future:

> the fact must be faced that the mode of life for which these notable houses stood was doomed. A small number of their owners, particularly the older ones, would no doubt continue heroically to resist the process of social evolution for as long as possible but the burden of taxation and the difficulty of obtaining domestic staff had irreparably undermined their whole basis. All that the Government could hope to do, therefore, would be to preserve, in whatever way might be most suitable, a small selection of these houses as symbols of a former civilisation.

Although Lord Salisbury launched a campaign to persuade his colleagues that the Gowers proposals would be a good place to begin a policy of tax cuts, it was Macmillan's view – in fact, his words – which the Cabinet eventually endorsed.[94]

It took them a long time to get around to it. Historic buildings were much lower on the Tory than on the Labour agenda, and Chancellor Butler clearly felt his money was better spent elsewhere. But the delay in producing *any* governmental response to the Gowers Report was registering in public opinion. For the first time ever, the press – prominently, the provincial Tory press – began to agitate in favour of country-house preservation. The details of Labour's bill had leaked out and it became something of a lowest-common-denominator rallying point. In the autumn of 1952, the National Trust publicized in its Annual Report the increasing numbers of houses fated for demolition and attracted an unusually high level of press comment. Support for the custodianship of country houses both by the National Trust and by private owners, as part of the nation's artistic and historical heritage, was now seen as an area of all-party consensus on which the Tory Government should act.[95] Another wave of publicity accompanied backbench motions in the winter and spring of 1953 by Arthur Colegate in the Commons and Lord Methuen in the Lords.[96] Eccles again expressed himself against 'turning ourselves into a nation of subsidised museum keepers' but finally he announced in February 1953 that the Cabinet had approved a scaled-down version of the Labour plan. This 'limited salvage operation of a few of the very best houses' was the most to which the Treasury would consent.[97]

The legislation that emerged in 1953 was very much Labour's plan, but with less money. Labour had already in the Finance Act 1951 exempted from death duty the contents of historic houses bequeathed to the National Trust. The Tories now added a provision in the Finance Act 1953 for the acceptance of contents in payment of death duty, through the National Land Fund. At the same time, R. A. Butler promised to release £100,000 a year for five years from the National Land Fund – a small fraction of the amount envisaged by Labour – to fund such acquisitions of houses and contents by the Ministry of Works, with the assumption that most would be passed to the National Trust. Eccles also piloted through Parliament the Historic Buildings and Ancient Monuments Act. This established Historic Buildings Councils for England, Wales and Scotland, which were to advise the Ministry of Works on the payment of maintenance grants to owners of historic houses. Butler equipped the HBCs with £250,000 a year to begin with, about half the sum provisionally allotted by Gaitskell.[98] Some of this money would be used to support National Trust houses and the hope was that the National Trust would in general serve as agent for the HBCs in policing the administration of grants to private owners.[99]

The machinery erected in 1953 has been widely hailed as a success; it is still, in essentials, the system that operates for the preservation of historic buildings today. However modest, it had something for everybody. First, the composition of the Historic Buildings Council for England was carefully balanced. The mistake made in appointing the Gowers Committee was not repeated; most members were not 'neutrals', capable of being swayed in one direction, but were strong advocates of the various positions that had all to be taken into account. The exception to this rule was the full-time chairman, Sir Alan 'Tommy' Lascelles, a courtier who knew landed society but had no strong feelings for or knowledge of art or architecture. Eccles told him he had been selected because 'you know nothing about architects, and . . . you have not got long hair'.[100] The National Trust and *Country Life* points of view were represented in the persons of Christopher Hussey and the Earl of Euston, who were both asked to resign their positions on National Trust committees. The political Left was represented by Labour MP Chuter Ede, an open-space man, and the trade unionist Dorothy Elliot, who was also seen as a representative of 'the point of view of sections of the general public who have an interest in visits to historic houses'. The political Right was represented by W. M. F. Vane, MP, a landowner who knew the ins-and-outs of landed finance. There were two architectural experts with high levels of technical knowledge devoid of sentimentality, W. G. Holford and John Summerson. And there were, finally, an owner, Lady Radnor, and a technical expert on artistic contents, Sir James Mann.[101] Lord Crawford was desperately disappointed; he had hoped for a council of 'experts', by which he meant aesthetes: Lees-Milne, Hussey, Goodhart-Rendel, Rupert Gunnis, Ralph Dutton, Lionel Brett (Esher's architect-heir) and the Duke of Wellington were his unrealistic slate.[102] He was lucky to be ignored; such a claque could never have kept the Council afloat politically. As it was, the initial team remained virtually intact, with remarkably few changes, through the first decade of the Council's work.

That work was also well balanced. The main lines of Labour's quasi-nationalization policy were continued. The National Land Fund was used to transfer some very important houses together with their contents into National Trust hands: the highlights were the Marquess of Bristol's bizarre Georgian folly Ickworth House with its rich collections; the contents of Petworth, which had been held back by the owner when the house entered the Trust's scheme in 1947; and three wonderful post-Civil War ensembles, Saltram Park in Devon, Beningbrough Hall near York and Dyrham Park near Bristol. The biggest catch was Hardwick Hall, probably the best preserved Elizabethan prodigy house in existence, which came in 1958 when the Duke of Devonshire finally settled his death-duty bill, preferring to give up Hardwick and a half dozen of the treasures of Chatsworth, while retaining Chatsworth itself, which he was now running commercially as a tourist attraction.

In addition to these new transfers, grants from the Historic Buildings Council helped further to stabilize the National Trust's country-house holdings by repairing houses and providing annual maintenance stipends for houses that were under-endowed, such as Knole, Lyme Park, Beningbrough and Saltram. In all about 20 per cent of the HBC's grant monies went to the Trust. With this kind of assistance, the number of houses held by the Trust grew from forty-two in 1950 to seventy-five in 1960 and their physical state improved markedly. There were no further outright nationalizations – houses were not taken on unless the National Trust would accept them, sometimes in association with a local authority as had already been attempted at Attingham, Lyme and Speke; but two houses – the popular Olden Time house Cobham Hall in Kent and Rushton Hall in Northamptonshire – were acquired and let for use as a girls' school and a school for blind children respectively. Although alternative uses of this kind became more difficult to find in the 1950s, the HBC did establish a Historic Buildings Bureau to match houses it could not buy with potential users, and some important houses, such as Wardour Castle in Wiltshire and Staunton Harold in Leicestershire, were saved in this way.[103]

The novel departure of the HBC was, however, the granting of public monies to private owners. A higher proportion of funds went to private owners than Dalton and Gaitskell or indeed Eccles and Macmillan intended, as owners' fortunes picked up in the 1950s, alternative uses melted away, and many houses were resumed as homes. In the first twenty years of the Council's work, about 25 per cent of its cash went to 230 privately owned country houses, somewhat more than went to the National Trust. Castle Howard and Ragley Hall each received well in excess of £100,000 over this period and more than a hundred houses received more than £10,000. The Council tried valiantly to hold owners to the servitudes that protected the public interest. The policy was that grant-aided houses must be open to the public on at least one day a week in the summer, the details to be advertised in one of the commercial country-house tourist guides that began to be published in the 1950s. Only a few owners of very small houses were able to wriggle out of this stipulation; a few owners rejected a grant rather than accept opening, notably the Marquess of Cholmondeley at Houghton Hall, so rich he hardly required public funds.[104]

The Cholmondeley case involved another servitude, which the Council found it more difficult to enforce: the means test. Nearly all owners were required to contribute at least half of the cost of the proposed repairs, but it was difficult to determine which owners should contribute more than half, and which owners were so rich that they should not get a grant at all. In this period of high marginal tax-rates, the wealthiest man in England did not have a high income; on the other hand, the 1950s and 1960s were a period of soaring land prices during which many landowners became multi-millionaires. An income means test was therefore meaningless; a capital means test would disqualify most applicants. Lascelles had the difficult task of meeting applicants and their agents, often with Willie Vane the land expert, and negotiating a fair division of expenditure. In most cases, some middle ground was found, usually the fifty-fifty split. Only a few dramatic cases on the extremes revealed the fundamental illogicality of the system.

At one extreme, some owners were just too rich in capital to receive public funds – the dukes of Westminster and Sutherland were privately mentioned. At another extreme, some buildings were too important to be denied public funds – Blenheim Palace, for instance, no matter how wealthy the Duke of Marlborough might be.[105] A particularly difficult case arose in 1963. The Marquess of Hertford had reoccupied Ragley Hall and opened it to the public. He applied for a grant and was offered £30,000 – a large sum to the HBC, but deemed inadequate by the forceful Marquess. As a public-relations professional, he knew how to work the system; he called a press conference, threatened to demolish the house if he was not given more grant, and generally caused trouble until the grant was jacked up to over £100,000.[106] So much for the means test. Nor did the Council have much luck applying another servitude – sanctions on houses that passed to new owners. Informally, the public-access requirement was deemed to lapse when a grantee died, though often his heir would be in the queue for a new grant; furthermore, it proved impossible to impose any conditions when owners sold grant-aided houses. A few grant-aided houses have in this way shrugged off the public's servitudes over the years and reverted to complete privacy.[107]

The application of servitudes, even if not wholly successful, shows how careful the Council was to appease potential public opposition. The fact is that grants to private owners remained controversial in the first decade or so of the Council's work. The Gowers Report had shifted the terms of political debate but it had not erased overnight deep-seated prejudices against aristocratic owners. Periodically throughout the 1950s and 1960s the Beaverbrook press would launch a campaign against what it sneered at as 'doles for dukes'.[108] 'The Beaver hates the aristocracy' was David Eccles's diagnosis, while Lord Antrim at the National Trust blamed the campaign on Beaverbrook's pique at once having had to pay admission to a Trust property; but there is reason to think that some of Beaverbrook's readers shared his antipathy.[109] The HBC kept a very low profile, its work regularly noticed only in friendly élite papers, such as The Times and the Daily Telegraph.[110] Its supporters were noticeably defensive about its work.[111] Parliament kept a firm lid on its expenditure; the initial £250,000 a year for all three councils had been increased to £350,000 in the second year, but after some later increments the budget of the English Council was subject to a Treasury 'ration' and throughout the early 1960s was frozen at £400,000, a cut in real terms.[112]

No one dared to raise the issue of further implementation of the Gowers Report. The National Trust was now so deeply implicated in the system that it deplored any further agitation on behalf of owners,

## More than 4,000,000 sale every day

# OPINION

## NOW THE DUKES GO ON THE DOLE

*The stately homes of England,*
*How beautiful they stand,*
*To prove the upper classes*
*Have still the upper hand . . .*

WHEN Noël Coward wrote those lines the stately homes of England were more numerous and more flourishing than today.

Their owners kept them going by their own resources. In order to do so, " they had disposed of . . . rows and rows of Gainsboroughs and Lawrences, some sporting prints of Aunt Florence's, some of which were rather rude."

Now it seems that their Gainsboroughs, their Lawrences, and the sporting prints of their Aunt Florence's must have dried up. And their resources also.

They are calling on the taxpayer to keep them going.

### At home—on Sundays

WHO hastens to answer this call? The Socialists hasten. And the Tories hasten. They go hand in hand to the rescue of these unfortunate gentlemen.

They propose to distribute £250,000 a year towards the upkeep of these houses. They propose to pay £10,000 a year to the staffs who will administer that fund.

And all they ask in return is that the owners will allow others to view the splendours—at a price—on one or two days of the week.

### Opposites meet

HERE is a most extraordinary state of affairs. On the one hand the Socialists, bitter opposers of privilege and inherited wealth. On the other the Tories, the advocates of enterprise.

They join hands to bolster up those who wish to exist on the fruits of privilege, inheritance, and lack of enterprise.

They offer a dole to the Duke of Devonshire, for the maintenance of Chatsworth House; to the Duke of Marlborough, for the maintenance of Blenheim Palace; to the Earl of Derby, for the maintenance of Knowsley Hall. So that up and down the country noblemen may continue to live where their fathers and their grandfathers lived.

### Keep going or get out

THE British people are only interested in preserving a few historic houses. They have no interest at all in preserving the owners.

The way to deal with this question is to leave the owners to bear the burden of stateliness.

If they are not sufficiently resourceful to do so, then they must be prepared to sell their stately homes to the nation.

And in every case the nation must decide whether the stately home is something desirable, or whether it is something which should be allowed to fall into ruin.

78 'Now the Dukes go on the dole': the Historic Buildings and Ancient Monuments Act as seen by the Beaverbrook press (*Daily Express*, 19 June 1953).

to the disgust of James Lees-Milne, who had left the Trust's full-time employ shortly after publication of the Gowers Report.[113] The only additional tax concession in the twenty years after 1953 actually had the effect of breaking up country-house collections, a 1956 provision for payment of death duties in works of art separate from their houses (adopted in order to permit the Duke of Devonshire to hand over some Chatsworth treasures but not the house). When in 1957 the Duke of Norfolk cheekily sought to win death-duty exemption for Arundel Castle and its estate, on the grounds that it was the official residence of the Hereditary Earl Marshal, his bill was slapped down with equal vehemence by Tory MPs defending economy and Labour MPs defending the tax system; even the *Daily Telegraph* granted that the opposition had the better part of the debate.[114]

The modesty of the 1953 system and its low visibility in public cast some doubt on the value of the Gowers Report to the cause of historic preservation in general and even to the cause of the country house specifically.[115] In the late 1940s, the preservation of historic buildings in town and country had won an unprecedented place in national life. The impact of war and the extension of the planning system had drawn particular attention to the appearance of old towns and villages. As a result, planning legislation and the listing system extended government powers over land and buildings so far that British conservation legislation – long the laggard in Europe – was now in the lead. Dalton, at least, had seemed to know what to do with these powers. Cripps was less engaged; he let the initiative slip and set up an alternative power centre, the Gowers Committee, which embraced the very specific aesthetic interests and policy agenda of country-house lovers. Its report coincided with a period of declining public enthusiasm for physical planning. The historic preservation system that resulted was therefore very largely confined to the country house, with correspondingly small amounts of money and a low level of public interest. For some years the Historic Buildings Council allowed itself to be persuaded that it was *illegal* for it to give grants to town or village groups, at a time when old town centres were subject to wholesale redevelopment. Even its modernist members saw an opportunity to salvage *one* manageable portion of the architectural heritage, the country house, and were content to let the bulk of the Council's meagre funds go that way.[116] The weak protests of some urban-oriented activists in the Georgian Group went unregarded.[117] Only when public opinion revolted against redevelopment and forced urban conservation on to the political agenda in the mid-1960s would it be possible to increase dramatically the scale of the HBC's funds and work. A Country House Council could never win wide public support in the 1950s and early 1960s, but a true Historic Buildings Council did just that in the late 1960s and 1970s.

So the Gowers Report, by turning the preservationist apparatus to the task of saving country houses, limited the popular appeal of that apparatus. It also narrowed the scope for saving country houses. The Gowers Report argued decisively against courses being adopted in the late 1940s — the development of alternative uses and the acquisition by public authorities of country-house museums. Gowers pressed instead for the preservation of the traditional country-house ensemble: house, collections, gardens, park and estate, with the ancestral owners *in situ*. Such a policy proved politically impossible, to Conservatives as much as Socialists. The amount of money government was willing to spend on propping up private owners would prove decidedly limited. These qualms restricted the scope of country-house preservation, scaled well back from the plans put forward by Dalton and Gaitskell. The aristocracy could not be saved by government; it would have to save itself. As it happens, the social and economic trends of the 1950s and 1960s permitted the aristocracy to do just that. The Welfare State had not been so hostile to the country house as Waugh had feared, but it could not save it; affluence — among both owners and their potential public — could.

# HISTORIC HOUSES
# AND CASTLES
## IN GREAT BRITAIN AND IRELAND

1961 EDITION          AN INDEX PUBLICATION          PRICE 3/6

79  Taking advantage of extending education and wealth, and no longer fearing accusations of snobbery, the stately-home business began to court a public that 'knew about art': the cover of the 1961 edition of the bestselling country-house guide pitches to the discriminating cultural consumer. (*See p. 387.*)

## CHAPTER 9

# The Country House and the Affluent Society

A scant fifteen years after the publication of *Brideshead Revisited*, Waugh lightly edited it for re-publication and concluded that his elegy for the English country house had been 'a panegyric preached over an empty coffin'. No one in the spring of 1944, he wrote in 1959, could have possibly foreseen 'the present cult of the English country house':

> Brideshead today would be open to trippers, its treasures rearranged by expert hands and the fabric better maintained than it was by Lord Marchmain. And the English aristocracy has maintained its identity to a degree that then seemed impossible. The advance of Hooper has been held up at several points.[1]

No one since, writing about the present state of the country house, has been able to resist quoting Waugh, but there are several strands to his observation that need disentangling. Like the earlier panegyric, the second thoughts, too, are overstated. The advance of Hooper had plainly been held up in the material sense: the public appropriation of private landed wealth was not only halted but thrown into reverse; aristocratic fortunes were not only preserved, but rebuilt; and aristocratic identity was in this way maintained. But what effect would this material revival have on the advance of the philistine Hooper in matters aesthetic? Aristocratic identity in the cultural sphere had for generations been closer to Hooper than Waugh could admit. Now Hooper was learning, haltingly, to respect the country house; owners had to undergo a learning experience as well. The 'cult' of the country house as 'our chief national artistic achievement' – Waugh's words, echoing Gowers's – was still in the 1960s a matter for a relatively select band of initiates. The health of country houses depended rather more on private wealth than public enthusiasm. When public hostility to private wealth revived again in the late 1960s and early 1970s, the country house would again appear to be in crisis.

*Aristocratic Revival*

The seeds of the postwar revival were laid in the darkest days of the 1940s, when landowners' leaders began to refashion a socially responsible image for their class as providers of the nation's food. While this image had always been part of the repertoire of aristocratic self-defence, it had lost credibility since the 1880s, as landowners variously sold, let or ran down their estates, and as the tenant farmer took over more of the obviously productive functions. During and after the Second World War, however, owners were galvanized into winning back many of these functions from their tenants. Early efforts to rehabilitate the landowner were largely a propaganda campaign against the threat of land nationalization or a break-up of the great estates, such as followed the First World War and seemed threatened by Dalton's 1946 Budget, the 1947 Agriculture Act and the 1948 capital levy. But it soon became apparent that land nationalization was not on the cards and that government was going to work with rather than against farmers. The decision to keep farms together was signalled by the 1949 Agriculture Act which granted a 45 per cent rebate of death duties levied on agricultural land. And postwar agricultural policy under both Labour and the Conservatives was to extend government support for producer prices which led to something like a 10 per cent improvement in real earnings for farmers in the decade after the war.[2]

So landowners became farmers again. Probably fewer owners sold after the Second World War than after the First.[3] While there were some partial sales to pay death duties, to fund estate improvements elsewhere and to consolidate holdings, most great estates held together remarkably well. As late as 1980 about half the families who had owned great estates in 1880 still held great estates, though usually with reduced acreage. Even at the lower end of the aristocratic scale, among the landed gentry, whereas a third of families may have already lost all their land in 1937, the proportion remained under half by 1952 and thereafter landownership held steady; half of all the historic gentry families still held (again, normally reduced) estates in the 1970s.[4] The contrast with the aftermath of the First World War, or with the dire predictions of 1945, is crucial.

Furthermore, to take full advantage of tax concessions, owners not only retained their estates, they resumed control of them. High marginal tax rates meant that rental income was derisory, even if rents could be increased to reflect higher agricultural profits. But a whole host of income tax and surtax rebates was available in the 1950s to the working farmer who ploughed his profits back into repairs, maintenance and capital expenditure. The 1958 Agriculture Act also gave landowners more power over tenancies. Accordingly, accountants advised owners to take their farms back from tenants and cultivate them personally or through estate offices. Many owners, especially younger ones, did take farms in hand; the practice of handing over estates to the heir to avoid death duties, increasingly widespread despite the 45 per cent abatement, helped to accelerate this generational change. By becoming farmers, younger owners could keep more of their income for themselves and improve and prettify their homes and estates in the process. An air of prosperity began to return to long-neglected houses, parks and farms, and a renewed commitment to country life was widely evident.[5]

Taking farms in hand was not only good for the owners' pocketbook, it was good for their public image, too. Even if only one of a dozen farms was run by the owner, he could appear as a 'farmer' rather than as a 'landowner', a worker rather than a drone. The Royal Agricultural College, Cirencester, became a more common destination for heirs straight out of public school than clubland and society balls – or at least a more common termtime destination. Though still a great landowners' oligarchy, the Country Landowners' Association emerged in the 1950 and 1960s as the leading mouthpiece for *farmers*, part of the corporatist complex of State and industry that was said to be modernizing the British economy.[6] The modernization of the aristocratic image was further shored up by other adaptations owners had to make to survive in the modern world. The huge staffs of servants that had, in many cases, been maintained right up to 1939 melted away, replaced by labour-saving devices ranging from modern kitchens to oil-fired central heating. Landowners also took up other professions than farming, which could be carried on as a commuter alongside the estate business.[7]

Yet the real turnaround in aristocratic fortunes stemmed not from such cosmetic modernizations but rather from other forces that owners were less keen to have identified.[8] The market value of owners' capital assets simply soared in the 1950s and 1960s. Land was the key. Among the least discussed Tory denationalizations of the 1950s was the denationalization of development rights, begun by Macmillan in 1953–4 and completed by Henry Brooke in 1959. This 'apotheosis of the free market/*laissez-faire* approach [to real property] in the post-war period' set off a property boom in the early 1960s.[9] The negative effects of the boom were blamed almost entirely on urban speculators and developers, but rural landowners were quiet beneficiaries. Denationalization of development rights, combined with weakened planning controls and an intense demand for new private housing made it possible for landowners to sell off small bits of their estates for enormous capital sums. 'To-day', wrote one enthusiast ill-advisedly, 'the owner of a 5,000 acre estate is a millionaire.'[10] That was in 1965. Prices surged again in the early 1970s, literally exponentially, so that the same owner would be a multi-millionaire by 1975.

Of course, the traditional view was that these capital values were entirely illusory, as estates had always been run out of income and their acreage conserved, but in the new income-poor world, to be capital-rich was the only definition of 'rich' that there was. And owners recognized this by selling small parcels of land strategically in order to improve the rest of their tax-sheltered agricultural estate.[11] The result was that, far from being 'preservationist', landlords in the 1950s and 1960s were taking a more commercial approach to their land. The remnants of the planning system ensured that development was fairly ordered and respectful of amenity, but after the hiatus of the 1940s owners were much more pro-development.[12] Those who were modernizing their estates agriculturally were also putting economic gains ahead of amenity considerations, such as hedgerow protection or the maintenance of traditional tenancies and farming methods.[13]

The same reviving effect on a smaller scale was registered by the dramatic appreciation of other capital assets, stocks and shares but also works of art. Stafford Cripps had commissioned a report from Lord Waverley on stemming the export of works of art at the same time as he commissioned Gowers to consider country houses. The system that resulted did not hamper the art market; in some ways, it greased it, as export licences were denied only where national collections could match the selling price. Once credit was decontrolled in the 1950s, the art market resumed its prewar activity with an intensity built up over a decade of forced abstinence. The highest prices were paid for modern French paintings not prominent in country-house collections, but the general boom benefited Old Masters, too, and also for the first time the kind of seventeenth-century painting acquired by so many eighteenth-century owners on their Grand Tours.[14]

Since the 1880s appreciating values had been causing owners to take more of an interest in their collections, but now that interest tended to be thorough and even professional. Youngsters from landowning families were to be found employed in auction houses, galleries and museums, and their fathers acted as auctioneers' county representatives. As with land, however, 'appreciation' worked in two ways: owners valued their collections aesthetically but also as working assets. To the distress of connoisseurs, owners could now sell off bits and pieces of collections and reap large chunks of capital to pay tax bills or to sink into the landed estate. After 1956 they could also offer works of art in direct payment of death duties and, given the tax advantages to holding land as well as traditional aristocratic attitudes, owners often preferred to offer art rather than land. 'One can replace pictures, never land', observed the artistic 5th Earl of Lichfield.[15] A further inducement to do so was the innovation of the 'douceur', which wrote off 25 per cent of duties owing on previously exempted works of art when they were offered in payment of fresh duties.[16] Thus, the massive Devonshire death-duty bill was finally paid off by offering Hardwick and its contents and by cherrypicking half a dozen of Chatsworth's greatest treasures. The settlement was followed by an unseemly struggle over which museums would get the treasures, and a more muted criticism of the Duke for attacking the integrity of the Chatsworth collection.[17] Later the Duke raised an endowment fund of £2.5 million for Chatsworth by selling a couple of paintings – 'not his best' – and duplicates from his library on the open market.[18] However, as with the land boom, such was the scale of the art boom that few sales at this high level were necessary; despite a very active art market, scares about exports of the artistic heritage were comparatively rare before the 1970s.[19]

What impact did the aristocratic revival have on the position of the country house? The answer is not necessarily a positive one. Unlike land and pictures, houses had at first little obvious material value. The wave of sales in the late 1940s brought little fresh capital, only a relief from further expenditure on repair and maintenance. When the institutional market collapsed at the end of the decade, owners had to choose between demolition, desertion or reoccupation. Many chose the first two options. The early to mid-1950s were the peak years of country-house demolition this century. One extreme estimate has it that one thousand houses were demolished in the decade to 1955. A more systematic survey has suggested that around 8 per cent of the national stock of country houses was lost between 1945 and 1960, probably fewer than five hundred houses (depending on the estimate of the national stock).[20] As we have seen, the very finest houses were largely exempt, national publicity and planning control providing some protection, but many famous houses were still lost, including parts of Woburn Abbey, the bulk of Bowood, Eaton and Rufford, the whole of Panshanger and all but the shell of Lowther Castle.

The fact that land sales were down but house demolitions up from interwar levels suggests that demolishing owners were repudiating the country house to husband the land. A modern agricultural estate

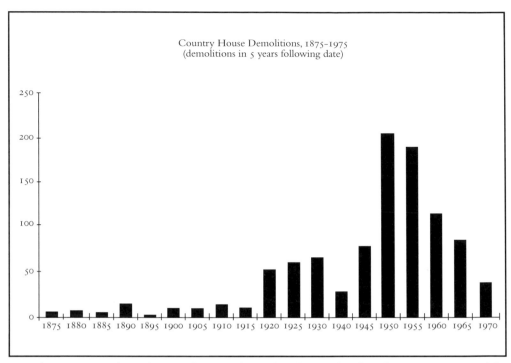

Country House Demolitions, 1875-1975
(demolitions in 5 years following date)

80    The 1950s were the peak years of country-house demolition. This chart shows one estimate of the number of country houses demolished in each five-year period between 1875 and 1975 (1875–9 through 1970–4). Statistics taken from Mark Girouard, 'Country House Crisis?', *Architectural Review*, October 1974, 243–4.

simply could not survive with too large a house sucking money out of it. J. M. Robinson's 1985 survey celebrated the nearly two hundred new country houses built since the war, mostly by old families, but chose not to emphasize the fact that almost half of these new houses were built to replace old ones, while most of the rest represented new work on old houses that substituted modern convenience for historic character.[21] Beyond these numbers there were many more houses that were demolished or abandoned and not replaced, the estate being run instead from a farmhouse or estate office, and large numbers of houses that were 'altered' – that is, partly demolished – to make them more economical. These strategies were advocated not only by desponding older owners, and not only by agents and trustees (who always put the land first), but also by a younger generation impatient with the grand old house and desiring to make a fresh start on a modern basis. The unhappy fact is that the majority of families who still owned country

81 Eaton Hall, in process of almost total demolition from 1961.

82 Lowther Castle: only the shell remains.

houses in 1945 left them in the decades afterwards – both poor families and rich ones, those who were losing and those who were retaining their land.

Sale, abandonment, demolition – what about owners who did choose to live in their houses after the war? Clemenson has estimated that in 1980 about a quarter of all country houses were still inhabited by their historic families, so many – but not most – families owning houses in 1945 must have returned to them.[22] It took some time to screw up courage and/or the necessary funds to reinhabit the bigger places: Castle Howard was empty until 1953, Woburn Abbey until 1955, Ragley and Berkeley Castle until 1956, Chatsworth until 1959. Often there was a strong sense of family tradition behind the decision to reoccupy, and sometimes a passionate dedication to the house and its contents. George Howard stopped his trustees from dismantling Castle Howard as soon as he returned from the war and was always determined to live there – and to be buried in the mausoleum, where no Howard had been buried for two hundred years.[23] Thomas Cottrell-Dormer had been yearning for years to return to Rousham, his dreamy family home in North Oxfordshire, and seized an opportunity when his long-lease tenants vacated in 1945. Humphrey Fitzroy Newdegate took on Arbury Hall in 1950 and fought a fierce battle to prevent the National Coal Board from undermining it. The aesthete Roger Hesketh devoted his retirement to restoring Meols Hall and fitting it up with fragments from demolished houses.[24] There were still a few owners willing to provide the large endowment now required to ensure a house's preservation by the National Trust in perpetuity, although the supply of these petered out at the end of the 1950s. 'Dear Dyrham, we love it – it's a person – but an exacting one', sighed Cecily Blathwayt of Dyrham Park, ultimately handed over to the Trust in 1961.[25]

However, the traditional attachment was normally to the house as centre of the estate rather than in its own right. A sympathetic scientific survey of private estates in the mid-1950s spoke of 'the mystery of unity binding house and lands', in which unity the land, not the house, was the binding force:

> Without its lands the house loses some, if not all, of its residential enchantment, although it is the same house, no whit diminished in size or splendour. Divested of land, it becomes a place out of keeping with itself, incongruous, an emblem of greatness in a lesser world.[26]

This, the continuing centrality of the land in aristocratic life, was why the National Trust found it difficult to keep in residence families who had also handed over their estates as endowment for the house; why so many owners said they would prefer to abandon their houses entirely than hand the estates over with them; why so many heirs opposed their parents' decisions to hand over.[27] Conversely, it was also why many owners reinhabited their houses, however inconvenient, in the 1950s: to re-establish the estate.

Once installed in their historic homes, of course, owners tried to make the best of them. Reluctant residents found themselves enchanted, sucked into an enterprise they had barely understood before. There is no doubt that the younger generation of owners was more alive to the aesthetic value of their homes than had been their parents, although the children sometimes forget this fact themselves in hymning the country house tradition. Lady Victoria Leatham, whose father the 6th Marquess of Exeter inherited Burghley in 1956, writes enthusiastically of her family's sense of duty:

> over 300 years . . . [my] descendants have felt that it was important, where possible, to keep the collections intact, and whenever funds allowed, to go on embellishing the house as best they could . . . In view of the years of effort and the affection shown to the house, I think this generation has no right to turn its back on a pre-eminent part of England's heritage.

But by her own testimony elsewhere, her predecessors had been personally responsible for laying the great house as low as she found it: the 3rd Marquess had been 'a true hedonist' whose vast debts led to a three-day sale of contents at Christie's in 1885, and after the brief tenure of the 4th Marquess, the 5th Marquess had ignored the house in order to tend to his shooting, hunting and riding and to pay for a ridiculously grand lifestyle, maintaining thirty indoor servants in the Slump and eleven as late as 1941;[28] examples could be multiplied.[29] The point is that owners who took an interest in their houses after the war were, despite what they said about family tradition, in reality mostly starting from scratch.

The reoccupation of the country house proceeded cautiously. A single suite of rooms would be put in order and used as a base for expansion, when money allowed for restoration and redecoration. Where more than one suite was available, the surplus could be let as flats to bring in extra income, as at Longleat, Goodwood, Wroxton Abbey, Kedleston, Brocket, Sherborne Castle and Stoneleigh Abbey. Sometimes the stable block could be converted into a residence, a favourite recourse when the main house was too derelict or let to institutional tenants. Then the task of bringing the house back to life was embarked upon. Excitement about this daunting task mounted as funds grew. For the first time since before the First World War, aristocratic wives had ready cash to put into decoration. Decorating fashion had long emanated from town houses (and recently from the *nouveaux riches*), but now the country house was back on top. The firm of Colefax & Fowler became famous for its country-house style that was not a pastiche of old styles but a new vision of expensive comfort in the country. Neatness and simplicity replaced the old clutter, modern chintzes swept away fusty Victorian relics. *House and Garden*, as directed by a divorced Duchess of Westminster, became a propaganda organ for such new country-house styles. Controversially, even the National Trust (which John Fowler advised on restoration)

83   Arundel Park, built on a quasi-Palladian plan in the grounds of Arundel Castle by Claud Phillimore for the Duchess of Norfolk to provide a private family residence after the castle was opened to the public, 1958–62. The interior (here, the drawing-room) was decorated by John Fowler, mixing his own confections with genuine eighteenth-century pieces from the castle.

let the modern Colefax & Fowler style trickle into its uninhabited show-rooms.[30]

Adapting country houses to modern life often involved work on a far greater scale than mere decoration: structural repairs (for which Historic Buildings Council grants were available after 1953) were usually necessary and sometimes a more drastic measure, too, 'alteration'. Alteration – partial demolition – was a sensitive issue for reinhabiting owners. It smacked of the bad old days of shabby-genteel philistinism. In the more enlightened 1950s, demolition was reinterpreted as an aesthetic contribution. Victorian and Edwardian wings could be safely discarded in order to 'reveal' the hidden Georgian gem within, an art treasure which was also conveniently scaled for economical residence. The Earl of Derby actually got himself some good publicity by employing the neo-Georgian architect Claud Phillimore, 'the architectural equivalent of John Fowler', to dismantle large portions of Victorian Knowsley in the mid-1950s. The house was still too big and Phillimore built an entirely new ten-bedroom house for Lord Derby in 1963, when the old house was let as a police headquarters. Phillimore also lopped off thirty of the seventy bedrooms at Rudding Park in Yorkshire to make it habitable for the young heir.[31]

On the whole, the low opinion held of Victorian architecture and the newly high opinion of the Georgian allowed such demolitions – which today would be denounced as the height of vandalism – to pass unnoticed, or even attract praise. The post-Gowers consensus among preservationists was that the country house could only be maintained by private owners, and anything the private owner felt he had to do to keep his house 'alive' – including amputation – was tolerated. On occasions there were murmurs that the baby had been thrown out with the bathwater. Frederick Samuels, who had worked with Phillimore on Knowsley, was hired by the Marquess of Lansdowne to 'alter' Bowood in 1955. It soon appeared that these 'alterations' entailed the complete demolition of the main block, the 'Big House', with its Robert Adam rooms and noble porticos, leaving one Adam wing and two ancillary courtyards to be adapted for the owner's apartments and flats. Demolition sales very much on the interwar model were held in mid- to late 1955, and bits and pieces were carted away – the Adam south portico snapped up for £110, the Adam dining room bought for the directors of Lloyd's (it still exists inside Richard Rogers's high-tech headquarters).

Country-house lovers did not know how to react. Quiet persuasion had done nothing to move Lord Lansdowne. He had rejected proposals from friends such as Lord Methuen to salvage some of the Big

84   The 'Big House' at Bowood, demolished 1955; the portico was bought at the demolition sale; the
low-lying range, at left, remains.

House and furtively broke up the Adam south portico after it failed to
sell at auction. He did not even like to hear praise of the Big House
from a supposed ally, Professor Albert Richardson, who blamed the
government for letting it fall. Lansdowne felt that he was doing his
best to save the estate and as much of the house as he needed. But
some preservationists began to wonder about entrusting the whole of
the country house's future to the owners. Lees–Milne wrote to *The
Times* deploring the indifference to Bowood's fate as 'feeble and
shocking'. Methuen retaliated on what he felt was Lansdowne's
deceptive behaviour by leaking details from their private correspondence to the 'Peterborough' column of the *Daily Telegraph*. The listing
authorities, however, aware of the limits to their funds and powers,
sided with Lansdowne: 'a live home was better than a dead
museum'.[32] Certainly the estate is now alive, a thriving business (with
what remains of the Adam stately home open to the public), but more
recently Lord Lansdowne has again been accused of vandalism by
picking out some delicacies from his famous manuscript collection and
selling them at Christie's.[33]

The Bowood affair raised sharply the question of what precisely the status of the country house was in the post-Gowers era – too sharply, which was why preservationists shied away from it. Houses were being lovingly restored, but for what purpose? For the owner's private convenience and pleasure? For the sake of art? For the public's enjoyment? At the beginning of this period, when the Gowers Report was under discussion and the democracy was being courted, owners were often described as 'trustees for the public' and their homes as 'national assets'.[34] Traditionally, owners had been suspicious about language of this sort. Many were still suspicious. A good number supported tax reliefs but not grants, on the grounds that tax reliefs returned owners' private money whereas grants more explicitly intruded a public claim. Landowners' representatives testifying to the Gowers Committee demurred at aid that would convey a *right* of the public to visit their houses.[35]

This argument was as likely to come from the most forward-looking aristocrats as from backwoodsmen. Pioneers of the stately-home business like Lords Warwick, Bath, De L'Isle and Salisbury were all eager to share their homes with the public, but on terms set by themselves, not the State. 'Personally,' wrote Lord Bath in 1952,

> I do not think any of us ought to ask for assistance from the Government other than the total remission of Death Duties on the house itself . . . If, by our own initiative and enterprise, we are unable to maintain our houses during our lifetime, either by open-ing them to the public or other methods, then as a class we have no right to exist . . . it is imperative that nothing is done or appears to be done which may lead the public to think that these houses have ceased to be the absolute property of the owners . . .[36]

Once tax reliefs had been rejected, these owners stood aloof from the grant system as long as they could.[37] If their entrepreneurial energies failed them, they said, they would rather abandon their houses than become State pensioners – effectively what Lansdowne was saying in 1955. Their Tory individualism was typical of their forebears, and had much in common with the attitudes of such Tory ministers as Eccles and Macmillan, who had also disapproved of the grant system as 'too Socialist'.[38]

However, few owners were so principled. Even the principled ones, by arguing for a special category of tax relief, were accepting a public status unthinkable before the war. The Lord Salisbury who argued vigorously for tax reliefs for 'the owner of a national monu-ment' was the same person who, as Lord Cranborne, had torn into the historic-building controls of the 1932 Town and Country Planning Act, insisting that an Englishman's home was his castle.[39] The average owner was more pragmatic still. He did not think of himself as a trustee for the public, but he was able to weigh up the costs and benefits of posing as one. This equation produced different results for each owner, and for each owner the equation could change over time. The balance had shifted in favour of public status as the private viability of the country house had been thrown into doubt in the 1940s, as public appetite grew and hostility dwindled, as a more outward-looking younger generation inherited, as grants became available. On the other hand, the balance could shift back to private status as the financial position improved and country houses became homelier again.

There was no general or co-ordinated response by country-house owners. The Government's unwillingness to implement the Gowers Report meant that no such response was required – the rule was *sauve qui peut*, an old aristocratic principle. It is revealing that when in 1952 Sir Harold Wernher, who had decided to turn his house at Luton Hoo into a museum, tried to organize a 'Historic Homes Association', he was met with a rude rebuff. His idea was to form a united front of owners both to negotiate with government and to promote tourism. A few of the most entrepreneurial owners, including Lords Warwick and Montagu of Beaulieu, backed the scheme, but others were skittish. 'The [organizational] meeting went very well', observed the wealthy Lord Bathurst languidly, 'until right at the end we were told that it would cost us £25 each for membership, whereupon the meeting broke up.'[40] The death blow to the scheme came with a chatty article in the Manchester *Sunday Chronicle* about 'one of the oddest "trade unions" in the world' – quite harmless, really, but injurious enough to noble dignity to trigger the fledgling association's collapse.[41] It would be another twenty years before owners were united enough (or frightened enough) to form such an association.[42]

So the realization of a trusteeship for the public was left to individual owners' consciences and pocketbooks. It was a question of how many felt moved or compelled to share their houses with the public. Fortunately for the public image of the class, divided and nervous, a growing number of owners who had reoccupied their homes decided also in the 1950s and 1960s to share their cultural assets with the public. This group, by successfully pursuing what became known as the 'Stately Home Business', fulfilled the role of trustee for the class as a whole.

## The Stately-Home Business, 1945–1964

Neither the supply nor the demand for country-house visiting was certain in the immediate aftermath of the war. The very few houses that had, genuinely, always been open to the public did struggle to re-open, against the odds of fuel and labour shortages. Burghley attracted 1,700 visitors for an Easter Sunday opening in 1946, a benefit for the Northamptonshire Nursing Association made possible by volunteer help; thereafter it returned gradually to regular opening twice a week in season. At Burghley visiting was simply part of a restoration of prewar pomp; despite complaints about staff shortages, Lord and Lady Exeter gloried in sixteen servants in 1948, and the costs of opening amounted to a mere 2 per cent of their wages bill. Little attempt was made to take the house seriously as a piece of cultural history, and the fabric of house and contents continued gently to rot as it had done since the late nineteenth century.[43] Penshurst might have suffered a similar fate had not a young, go-ahead heir, trained as an accountant, inherited in 1945. The new Lord De L'Isle re-opened in 1946 'on a proper basis' with 'extensive publicity', and due to his energy and the house's proximity to London was drawing 16,000 visitors to a five-day-a-week summer season by 1949.[44] Another new heir, Lord St Levan of St Michael's Mount in Cornwall, also commercialized the casual operation in place before the war and, in his case benefiting from the seaside trade, drew up to twenty thousand visitors a year in the late 1940s.[45] The 5th Marquess of Salisbury, who inherited in 1947, abandoned the attempt to live in the whole of Hatfield House, created a self-contained residence in one wing and threw the state rooms open to fully fledged tourism: 32,000 visited in 1949.[46]

At Warwick Castle, of course, they did not need to overhaul an already highly commercial business. Visiting actually continued throughout the war, daily at least in summer, although many of the treasures had been removed for safekeeping while the Ministry of Supply occupied part of the castle. Amazingly, there were over ten thousand visitors in 1943–4. By 1949–50, numbers were over the prewar peak of 80,000 a year, although since the price of admission remained at 2s. 6d. and labour costs had jumped fourfold, the tourist business was less profitable than it had been in the 1930s. It was not until the early 1950s, when expenses were successfully reined in, that the business returned to a clear surplus and the Earl of Warwick began once again to live off the tourist trade.[47] At Warwick Castle, as now at Penshurst and St Michael's Mount, tourism was maintaining the house, because maintenance (including indoor servants) could be taken out of this business income before tax.[48]

In the late 1940s, these and one or two other hardy perennials were practically alone among private houses open to the public. The National Trust, however, was now opening the houses it had acquired during the war and its experience in arranging houses and attracting visitors began to provide a useful role-model for private owners considering this option. In these postwar years the Trust was trying to refashion itself as a more public body, and the effort necessitated broadening public access to its country houses, against the spirit of the restrictive agreements forced upon them by owners handing over. Lees-Milne made a herculean effort to open Charlecote, Coughton Court, West Wycombe and Lacock Abbey in spring 1946, Cotehele, Blickling and Knole in spring 1947, to name only the most important among the fifty or so historic buildings in his charge.[49] From thirty days a year opening, the norm proposed in the early years of the Country Houses Scheme, the Trust was trying to move to fifty days in 1945 and to one hundred days or more by the mid-1950s.[50]

There were persistent problems with recalcitrant former owners at Knole, Cliveden and West Wycombe. At Knole Lord Sackville had posted a 'dragoness at the gate' and an 'extraordinary *gauleiter* figure with a walking-stick' who were, Lees-Milne feared, 'extremely dicta-torial with the public'. His assistant Robin Fedden agreed: 'the pre-Trust inhabitants of Knole still feel, and sometimes show, that they are doing the public a great favour in admitting them to My Lord's house at all.' Although Lees-Milne secretly sympathized, he was politic enough to know what was in the Trust's best interest and he and Fedden continued to advocate better presentation and more extensive opening, though not too much publicity.[51] Away from London, there were undeniable success stories. In Warwickshire, Charlecote with its long-inaccessible woods quickly became a family playground – like the commercialized Penshurst and Hatfield, it drew around 15,000 visitors in its first season – and Lacock Abbey in Wiltshire was popular early on for its medieval relics, Gothicked house and peaceful village. It was also relatively easy to promote uninhabited Montacute in Somerset.[52] As the Trust acquired more houses with fewer strings attached, as with Cotehele and (in 1954) St Michael's Mount, the growing-pains eased and criticism of its exclusiveness tailed away, though with rising expectations in the 1960s criticism would be renewed.

The surprising successes, even under rationing, of a few private owners and the National Trust in the late 1940s began to attract imitators around 1950. New factors were also then coming into play.

The sale market had died away and owners were coming to terms with continued residence, needing to find tax-free income to maintain their homes. A big drive to promote tourism was under way: to attract foreigners for their hard currency, but also to find an orderly and healthful occupation for the huge numbers of domestic trippers expected as living standards rose, rationing eased and paid holidays became nearly universal. Preparations for the Festival of Britain, which began with the 1950 season the year before the Festival itself, were aimed at both sets of tourists; so were promotions associated with the Coronation in 1953. In the latter year, the availability of repair and maintenance grants from the Historic Buildings Council offered another incentive to open private homes, usually on a more limited basis than for houses seeking tourist income, but still at least once a week in season as expected by the HBC.

The number of houses open to the public therefore rose sharply from around 1950. In that year at least seventy houses were opened, about half of them by the National Trust. In 1950, the first year in which the media took a close look at the stately-home business, the BBC ran regular leisure-oriented radio programmes on country houses, lists of open houses aimed at tourists began to proliferate and a few papers published 'league tables' of the most-visited houses.[53] In 1951 new private entrants pushed up the number of open houses to around 120, and Country Life and the ABC Coach Guide began to publish annual lists of open houses; the coach guide evolved into Historic Houses Castles and Gardens, still published today, which claimed a circulation of 120,000 by 1960.[54] By the mid-1950s, the number of open houses had topped two hundred. It was at this point that the 'stately-home business' became a regular topic of discussion in the media, no longer a curiosity but an established part of leisure and culture.[55] Radio features on country houses open to the public were almost a weekly occurrence.[56]

By the early 1960s, the business had reached a plateau of around three hundred open houses, of which half were private houses, a quarter National Trust houses and the rest institutions or publicly owned houses. Some of the latter were local-authority-owned houses, formerly warehouses for museums that were now being presented for the first time as country houses.[57] The three hundred open houses represented a fairly small proportion of the national stock of country houses, but a fairly large proportion of the large houses with important collections. The major exceptions, important houses that were not open, fell into two categories: houses of the very wealthy and Victorian houses that were not yet highly valued.[58]

As the business gathered pace, the numbers of visitors per house

# Stately Homes of England

*Alnwick*

*Northumberland*

NORTH SEA

*Lancs*
*Hoghton*
*Astley*
*Speke*
*Knowsley*

*Burton Agnes*

*Yorks*

*Bramhall*
*Adlington*
*Haddon Hall*
*Chatsworth*
*Hardwick*

*Gunby Hall*

*Lincs*

*Blickling Hall*

*Speke Hall*

*Attingham Pk.*
*Salop*

*Burghley Ho.*

*Blickling*

*Rockingham*

*Stokesay C.*
*Stoneleigh*
*Warwick C.*
*Charlecote*
*Clapton Ho.*
*Broughton*
*Compton Wynyates*

*Hinchingbrooke*
*Castle Ashby*
*Audley End*

*Charlecote Park*

*Mon.*
*Blenheim Pal.*

*Luton Hoo*
*Ayot St Lawrence*
*Knebworth*
*Hatfield*
*Hughenden Manor*
*W. Wycombe Pk.*
*Cliveden*

*Beeleigh Abbey*

*Buscot Pk.*

*Clevedon*
*Corsham*
*Lacock Abbey*

*Sion Ho.*
*Ham Ho.*

*Longleat*
*Hants*
*Sutton*
*Knole*
*Kent*
*Penshurst*

*Stourhead*
*Wilton*
*Goodwood*
*Parham Pk.*
*Barrington*
*Montacute*
*Arundel*

*Devon*

*Osborne*

*Cotehele*

*Lacock Abbey*
*Knole*

J.HARRIS

IN this year of Festival there is strange irony in the fact that the Stately Homes of England are a sideshow of the Welfare State.

All over the country the Great Houses, marvels of the extravagance of a bygone age, are getting ready to fling open the doors to the tourist trade.

Last year's highest admission fees of 2s. 6d. for places like Blenheim Palace (Winston Churchill's birthplace, which took about £12,500 in 1950) have been raised to a 3s. level

## Britain's true pride

by Wilton, the Earl of Pembroke's home in Wiltshire, opened for the first time this year.

These great houses are written into the fabric of Britain's history. They provide to visitors the real picture of Britain's greatness. Perhaps visitors will go away with the impression that the "Festival sideshow" is greater and more impressive than the main event.

This week Newsmap turns a blind eye on the South Bank and the Battersea Pleasure Gardens, and pinpoints some of the Stately Homes, the showplaces of a nation whose greatness is not dulled by the changing pattern of life.

85   In the year of the Festival of Britain, 1951, the stately-home business took off: here the *Newcastle Journal* notes, somewhat defiantly, the 'strange irony . . . that the Stately Homes of England are a sideshow of the Welfare State' (26 April 1951).

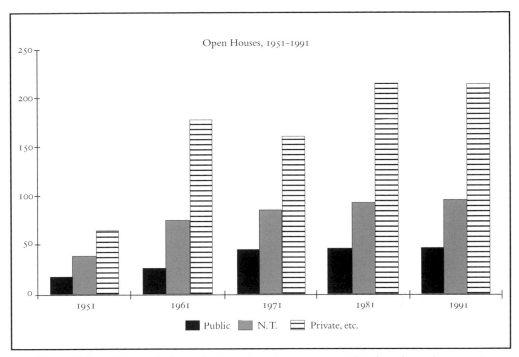

86    The unfolding of the stately-home business since the early 1950s. This chart shows the approximate number of English country houses advertised as open to the public, at ten-year intervals (distinguishing between houses in public ownership, those held by the National Trust, and those in some form of private ownership, including charities and institutions).

grew as well. It is impossible to be precise about global numbers, but in the early 1950s the most popular houses began to pass the 100,000 mark, which not even Warwick Castle had reached before the war and possibly only Chatsworth had attained in the nineteenth century.[59] By 1966 a survey by Lord Montagu of Beaulieu concluded that nine privately owned houses drew more than 100,000 visitors annually, and another twenty-five or so more than 20,000. To the 20,000-plus league could be added about twenty National Trust houses and a few publicly owned houses as well, so that around sixty of the three hundred houses fell into this category.[60]

    These figures point to a phenomenon of great diversity. At the top were fully commercial leisure enterprises seeking to attract as many visitors as possible. Warwick Castle was the true pioneer at this level, but the Marquess of Bath, who opened Longleat on a commercial basis as early as Easter 1949, is usually given credit because he associated himself so personally and actively with the stately-home business

87  Lord Montagu of Beaulieu lending a hand with preparations for the public opening of Beaulieu at Easter 1952: this staged photograph, one of many such gimmicks cooked up by the publicity-conscious peer, appeared in the popular press, in one case captioned: 'It's enough to bring a Peer to his knees.'

in the crucial early years. Lord Bath, who did not live at Longleat even after inheriting in 1946, had had prewar experience in running the Cheddar Caves as a tourist attraction and had tried first to convert Longleat into a luxury hotel for rich foreign tourists. When this failed to win support from the Board of Trade, he converted Longleat into a leisure park for domestic motorists instead, tarring the roads, dredging the lakes, restoring the fountains, installing a cafeteria and souvenir shop and in 1960 a garden centre.[61]

The dynamic young Lord Montagu of Beaulieu, trained in public relations, had also considered converting the Abbey House at Beaulieu into a hotel before opening the estate commercially in Easter 1952, featuring Britain's first motor museum and, later, an exhibition linked to the Coronation. The motor museum was the biggest tourist draw: after a purpose-built motor showroom was opened for the 1959 season, the opening shown live on Southern Television, numbers doubled to over 200,000 a year.[62] The Longleat and Beaulieu precedents were followed to great advantage by the Duke of Bedford when he opened Woburn Abbey commercially at Easter 1955 and lifted to a new level by the Duke's willingness to do anything to promote the enterprise: standing at the gates signing autographs, hosting nudist congresses in the park, inviting media coverage of his family life, doing the twist on Australian television. Bedford and Montagu had become familiar characters in the popular press and on television by the early 1960s, including their double act, singing Noël Coward's 'The Stately Homes of England' on the BBC's *Tonight* programme and promoting the American TV film *The Stately Ghosts of England* shot on their estates in 1964.[63]

Just below this level stood houses that drew large numbers of tourists without much extra promotion: great historic houses in extensive parks, such as Blenheim (benefiting from the Churchill connection as well as the diminishing prejudice against truly stately palaces), Chatsworth, Berkeley Castle, Haddon Hall and Hatfield House. Owners of properties such as these could benefit from the tourist business without having to remodel either themselves or their homes. After all, many had been heavily visited in the nineteenth century with only primitive publicity and facilities; now, with improved transport and better relations between aristocracy and people, the tourists were coming back. Other houses with equal attractions but less well-situated, Castle Howard or the Marquess of Hertford's Ragley, could

88   The Duke of Bedford could stage photographs with the best of them: here he conducts sightseers around Woburn Abbey in 1958.

reach similar levels with attentive promotion. Beneath this level were houses with great potential that drew fewer visitors because their owners were unable or unwilling to do that promotion necessary to offset these disadvantages: the 'gentlemen' or 'amateurs', Montagu called them, as distinct from 'players' like himself. Into this category fell most of the houses in the twenty-thousand-plus league in the 1950s and 1960s.[64]

And beneath them lay the majority of open houses, which attracted relatively few visitors, either because they were too small or because their owners deliberately discouraged tourism. The British Travel Association estimated in 1964 that the average house, including the big operations, drew seven thousand visitors a year.[65] Only about a third of the three hundred houses shown to the public were open six to seven days a week in summer, while a third were open two days a week or less. Many of these latter would be year-round residences, with a ticket-taker's trestle-table placed outside a few days in summer.

89   Most open houses were run on far less professional lines than Beaulieu and Woburn: Giles of the *Sunday Express* pokes fun at the stately home as cottage industry, 28 May 1950.

"Remind me in the morning to put up a notice making it clear the 2s. 6d. trips round the manor do not include bed and breakfast."

An extreme case was that of Lord Walpole, who opened Wolterton on Thursday afternoons in summer only because the Historic Buildings Council required it, and who by carefully minimizing publicity managed to confine his public to forty-six visitors in 1966. The owner of Little Sodbury Manor did even better by 'attracting' thirty-six visitors in his first year of opening, 1956, after which the HBC gave up and allowed him to show only by appointment.[66] But the HBC found that most of its beneficiaries were willing to undertake *some* publicity to attract enough visitors at least to cover the expense of opening.[67] The de Wend-Fenton family opened microscopic Ebberston Hall after receipt of a grant, showed all five of their lived-in rooms and even opened a tearoom in the stables, but the operation was scaled back after babies started to arrive: one party of visitors had had to be shooed away by a nurse from a bedroom in which the mother of the house was giving birth. And Marjorie Mockler built up the summer trade for little Milton Manor House from fifty visitors in 1952 to a couple of thousand in the 1970s.[68]

With such a variety of situations, owners' motives and goals for opening were also bound to be various. But one motive, so often cited by promoters of the country house, can be pretty generally discounted. Few families had a longstanding tradition of 'custodianship' or 'stewardship' of their cultural treasures for the nation. Most had in the past few generations depreciated aesthetic matters. Those who did value their artistic possessions held them 'in trust' not for the nation but for their successors, either as material assets to be hoarded or cultural assets to be shielded from the mob. The 'Curator Earl' Spencer had both a strong sense of family responsibility and a respected position in the art world, but he was shy and abrupt with strangers and highly suspicious of tourists, who were given only limited access to Althorp.[69] The owner of Farnley Hall, Yorkshire, and of its famous collections of Chippendale and Turners, pronounced loftily to Gowers:

> Those who inherit both a Landed Property and a Dwelling House with Cultural Contents are not necessarily endowed with an equally balanced instinct and interest for their dual inheritance. Yet to most there is given a sense of Trusteeship.

He claimed for the Fawkes family 'a long tradition in both wish and practise of past Owners to make it possible for many and diverse sections of the Public to visit Farnley Hall', but his interpretation of this tradition was to admit art societies by appointment and to grant the fullest opportunities to individuals with whom I am acquainted to bring two or three friends who have a special interest to browse to their satisfaction . . . It is essential to rule out parties and individuals who just want a day out and can 'tick off' Farnley Hall as 'Visited' (not seen and felt, and little appreciated).[70]

The most aesthetic sensibilities often felt this most strongly. The architect Duke of Wellington would not countenance visits to Stratfield Saye. When he and James Lees-Milne organized a special opening for National Trust members, they were disappointed with the 'usual ignorant, dreary lot of members' who turned up. Having worked up the idea of trusteeship to win public backing for the National Trust in the 1930s and 1940s, Lees-Milne was now dissatisfied with it in practice: owners lacked the taste to show off their houses properly and people lacked the taste to appreciate them when they were shown well. He recommended that owners turn for advice to a professional man of taste (like himself?), and many owners did so; Rupert Gunnis, the sculpture expert, had a hand in opening and presenting several houses, including Parham, Castle Howard and Arbury.[71]

Even those owners whose families had a real tradition of opening their houses in the past had only a hazy idea of that tradition. There was a vague awareness, stimulated by *Country Life* articles, of the 'polite' visiting of the eighteenth century, but hardly any of the more boisterous mass visiting in the nineteenth century. Lord Herbert, heir to Wilton, was astonished to hear in 1955 the story of a ninety-five-year-old who had seen the acrobat Blondin perform on the tightrope in Wilton park in 1873.[72] The Earl of Warwick chose to view the commercialization of Warwick Castle a few generations earlier as a measure 'to keep [numbers] down and avoid the formation of queues, which gave the house a bad reputation'.[73] In most cases, as at Chatsworth, Burghley and Castle Howard, the 'tradition' of opening the house had worn pretty thin long before 1945.[74] The fact that tradition was so often cited after 1945 is evidence rather that it was then being invented, or reinvented, to veil other motives.

'In house opening money is ninety-nine times out of a hundred the prime motive', Lees-Milne concluded sadly.[75] Probably he was close to the truth. The money motive had long been a central feature of aristocratic culture. But the money motive could take different forms. By definition, owners who opened hailed from that portion of the class that had chosen to reinhabit rather than demolish or desert. They had made a commitment to the house, material or emotional or both, not for the nation but for themselves. In explaining why they opened, owners often stressed continuity, the need to maintain the family trust – 'to preserve what for generations they have kept intact', as the Ashley-Coopers said of St Giles's, Dorset. 'Why', said the Earl of March to himself on being handed Goodwood by his father,

> should the family surrender [to the National Trust] the ultimate control and perhaps even the value of these considerable assets (which in economic terms represented the family's final reserve) just because it was difficult to meet the maintenance and running expenses of the house?[76]

For younger owners such as Lord March, tourism was part of the broader move toward commercialism, one of a series of enterprises undertaken to transform the prospects of the estate. At Goodwood, tourism, forestry, agriculture and leisure services had been organized into separate companies all under family ownership.[77] The Earl of Bradford took a similar approach to Weston Park, commercializing it alongside his fifty farms and forestry enterprise.[78] At Longleat and Beaulieu, tourism played a more important role, generating income that was applied not only to the house but also helped to stimulate other parts of the estate. In the first decade of opening, Lord Bath was able to spend £300,000 to improve the Longleat estate and £80,000 on the house.[79]

For less entrepreneurial owners, opening could be a prophylactic measure to prevent the house draining the agricultural estate. Their goal was to cover as much as possible of the house's running costs. In the era of high marginal tax rates, this goal was achieved by earning enough tourist income to win tax advantages, without seeking to make much of an outright profit. If the tax inspector considered the opening to be a legitimate business, then tourist income could be used to pay many household and estate expenses before being taxed itself.[80] At Wilton in the 1950s, tourist income paid two-thirds of rates and taxes on the house and park, water, lighting, garden maintenance and caretakers' wages (the remaining third being considered personal and not business expense), and the full cost of insurance, fuel oil and gardeners' wages. Once these expenses had been deducted from the tourist income of about £5,000 a year, then a loss of about £1,000 was declared, earning a rebate on personal income tax and contributing further to household expenses.[81] The catch came in satisfying inspectors that opening was a real business. Throughout this period owners complained that the rule was applied unevenly and petitioned for these maintenance claims to be extended to all open houses, regardless of commercial status, on public-interest grounds.[82] It is

impossible to say how many houses did benefit from extended maintenance claims, but private owners among the top third of houses,
open six or seven days a week in season, were clearly seeking either
outright profits or tax advantages.[83]

A final pecuniary motive was the prospect of Historic Buildings
Council grants. These required only minimal opening – one day a
week in summer – and could fund up to half of the structural repairs
even on great houses. This motive certainly figured prominently in
the calculations of many private owners in the bottom third, who only
opened one or two days a week in summer, and also for others. The
wealthy Lord Hertford, for instance, chose to open Ragley more
commercially five days a week (at a loss) but admitted frankly that his
principal motive was 'to obtain . . . enormous grants'.[84] For most
beneficiaries, however, limited opening for grants was the ideal way to
maintain the 'family home' at the centre of the agricultural estate with
the minimum of intrusion.[85]

So much for motives for opening: what about motives for visiting?
What does the success of the stately-home business in the 1950s and
1960s reveal about the wider culture, composed for the most part of
guests rather than hosts? Just as the country-house promoters' view of
opening as cultural stewardship is overblown, so the view of visiting
often put forward by critics, as an imposition by the cultural élite,
must be cut down to size. Certainly, a cultural élite of varying size and
potency had been developing an attachment to the country house out
of a revulsion from democracy and mass culture since the late nineteenth century. For a time, that attachment had been limited by liberal
intellectuals' doubts about the aristocracy and their taste. In the postwar world, however, many liberals, disenchanted with the Welfare
State, were getting less liberal; more aristocrats were acquiring at least
a patina of taste; and appreciation for the fine arts and fine living of the
eighteenth century was creeping back. Not everyone was able to
maintain the scholarly detachment of John Summerson, separating out
the appreciation of art from social values. It would be futile to ignore
a 'neo-romantic' current in high-cultural life in the 1950s and early
1960s, with a country-house element evident in the vogue for John
Piper's paintings of pleasingly decayed mansions and the fashion, at
least among the wealthy, for John Fowler's 'country-house style' in
homes that were not country houses.[86] Sentimental articles on the
stately homes were now appearing in unlikely organs – the *New
Statesman* or the *Manchester Guardian* as well as *The Times* and the *Daily
Telegraph*.[87] The question is, however, what impact this neo-romanticism among the select – far from universal even in those circles – may

have had upon the many? Was it not still a reaction against the main currents in the culture rather than a directing force?[88]

As the last chapter suggested, the political élite at least balked at propping up the country house in any substantial way. The Conservative governments of 1951–64 put a premium on boosting personal consumption after the planning-induced austerity of the late 1940s. Museums and preservation were at a discount. The property boom that so benefited landowners also led to a storm of new house- and office-building in modern styles that transformed the physical face of England. While enough of the planning system remained to preserve Green Belts and much open countryside, it was agriculture rather than culture or tourism that had the upper hand there. Most of the great plans to preserve the countryside went unrealized. A few national parks were created, but with little funding and weak protection.[89] In other words, if there was a powerful élite plan to shape popular attitudes to the countryside, it was Labour's 1940s vision of a complementary modern, productive city and an open, recreational country, and this was weakened by Tory *laissez-faire* in the 1950s. The place where it remained most powerful was at the BBC. The BBC's depiction of the country house was not normally a neo-romantic one of fine art and gracious living, but most often populist and recreational. The provision of tourist facilities by the aristocracy was seen as the rightful modern phase of the country house's long history. On one occasion, when a producer submitted a radio script (about the demolished Clumber House) that was deemed too admiring of tradition, it was sent back with a new message: 'amenity is the great cry of the new ruling class, the urban artisans, and their instrument the National Trust.'[90]

The most powerful forces behind country-house visiting had therefore to be market forces. Strong growth in personal consumption gave families spending-money, leisure and private motor transport. The do-it-yourself motor holiday began to undermine the popularity of the all-in seaside resort. In default of public recreational provision, the beneficiaries were private-sector providers: teashops in the Cotswolds, country inns, the stately-home business and the National Trust. An economist's analysis of National Trust membership, which grew dramatically from 7,000 in 1945 to 100,000 in 1960 and 150,000 in 1964, found that this growth closely correlated with the growth in disposable income, car ownership and leisure time.[91] These were trans-national trends, and historic-house owners benefited elsewhere, too. In France, for instance, the Vieilles Maisons Françaises was established in 1957 to organize the tourist boom in this sector and it soon eclipsed the

90   The consumer boom was the most powerful force behind the stately-home business: private motor-cars fill the lawns at Castle Howard, 1956.

owners' self-help group, La Demeure Historique; by the early 1970s it had twelve thousand owners on its books, a network of departmental committees and subsidies from central government and the French Tourist Office.[92]

For many tourists, therefore, a visit to a stately home was just another day out in the country. Visitors to the most commercialized houses were day-trippers travelling short distances, often from a seaside resort (from which Beaulieu benefited greatly), especially in wet weather. A rare early piece of market research in this sector, done at Beaulieu in 1966, found that these trippers came as much for the leisure attractions – the motor museum, the shopping, the walks – as for the house.[93] But beneath this very commercialized level, a visit to a stately home was obviously something *more* than just another day in the country; it had a special kind of human interest that is not easy to analyse.

The canniest owners carefully cultivated this human interest. They soon grasped that their visitors wanted a nice day trip with tea and souvenirs, but they also wanted to be charmed, impressed and entertained without being stultified by art and history. Promotional material and guided tours were arranged to maximize the human interest in the house's history, contents and present ownership. Scholarly historians were inclined to be contemptuous of the history on offer – John Summerson called it 'a Tussaudesque twilight' peopled solely by 'bad King John, Nell Gwynne, Henry VIII and his wives'[94] – but there is no doubt that this history with a human touch was a draw. A survey of visitors to National Trust houses in 1962 found that 'enjoyment of the visit consisted chiefly in the thrill of direct contact with the past, particularly in thinking about the people who lived in the house'.[95]

Echoes of the Victorian fascination with the romance of the Olden Time can still be heard: Hatfield plugged its Elizabethan associations for all they were worth, showing off the Queen's stocking, her portrait and her oak; at Chastleton, the owner Mrs Whitmore Jones conducted tours wearing the ring worn by Elizabeth's maid of honour

91   Visitors to Castle Howard, 1956, awed but not cowed . . .

in the portrait in the hall; at Wilton, Henry VIII, Sidney, Shakespeare and Van Dyck were given clear precedence in press reports over the patrician finery of Kent and Chippendale.[96] But the postwar public was not so historically blinkered as the Victorians were. It was now possible to find human interest in eighteenth-century grandeur, too: 'how people lived in one of the great country houses' was often stressed in BBC broadcasts, running the gamut from servants and cock-fighting to ice-houses and billiard-tables. When the BBC's North of England Service ran a weekly feature on Sunday outings in summer 1953, it chose four stately homes: Alnwick Castle for its long history, Hardwick House for its Elizabethan interest, and Harewood and Nostell Priory to exemplify 'the age of elegance'.[97]

The past could provide human interest, but so could the present. It is often said that visitors much prefer inhabited houses to 'lifeless museums', and put that way it is hard to deny. This preference is usually reported by owners, who obviously have an interest: even the briskly professional Lord Montagu, in discussing his visitors' survey showing equal interest in the motor museum and the house, admits that the two comments *he* recalls most frequently are, 'You feel like a guest here', and 'We felt that the place was lived in and very much still loved'. Still, it must be true that an inhabited historical house possessed an added attraction, especially now that hostility to the aristocratic lifestyle had subsided.

Again, owners played carefully on this theme. Houses where the owners lived exclusively in self-contained apartments and never in the showrooms were still presented as 'lived-in'. What did this mean to the visitors? Does it attest to what the Australians call 'cultural cringe', awe at the lifestyles of the rich and privileged, or rather an attempt at bringing the grand down to street level? In the 1950s observers saw as much of the latter as the former. A foreign writer considering the stately-home phenomenon at Castle Howard in 1956 thought that visitors clung to the 'homely' and 'practical' as a relief from the oppressiveness of high art:

> 'Look at the exquisite carved cornices!' says the guide. 'Look at the gorgeous anemones in the vase!' echoes a woman to her friend; and in a low voice they continue a private conversation about gardening.[98]

John Summerson felt visitors were 'touched, though inwardly gratified, by the collapse of privilege, and evidences of the descent are eagerly, whisperingly sought'.[99] BBC listener research reported a wide range of reactions: Vita Sackville-West got rave reviews for a broad-

92   . . . in the Great Hall at Castle Howard, an old lady in this party was heard to say, 'I prefer the music-room; it's cosier.'

93   Human interest, and especially 'women's interest': the room where Winston
Churchill was born at Blenheim, with an American tourist trying out the bell-pull,
September 1950.

cast on Knole, communicating both 'deep love' for it as a home and
'nostalgia for the times and conditions that have passed'; a broadcast
on Harewood was most popular for 'descriptions of the work done on
the estate'; listeners to a programme on Alnwick preferred the vivid
historical detail.[100]

One theme which consistently features in visitors' reactions is the
'women's interest'; women were thought to be planning more of the
family outings and to be naturally attracted to a domestic site. It may
also have been felt that women were less 'political' and likely to have
fewer residual resentments against the aristocracy. One of the earliest
television films about stately homes was transmitted on 23 August
1951: *Designed for Women: Visit to a Country House* revolved around a
visit to Hatfield, no doubt inspired by Lady Salisbury's tea party for

journalists in July to advertise the new Sunday openings. 'Do go soon', the film concluded gratifyingly,

> for everything is looking so lovely, and so colourful . . . I spent the most lovely time there . . . I am sure you will, too . . . and now let's hear from Jeanne Heal, who is going to tell us about pearls.[101]

Stately homes were seen as a natural topic for *Woman's Hour* on radio: alternative uses and the Gowers Report were discussed in 1950, spring cleaning at Chatsworth in 1953, three owners were interviewed on separate occasions in 1957 and another in 1958, the smaller manor house was profiled in 1960, country-house holidays in 1962, and weekly country-house items were run throughout the summer of 1963. Women's role in fuelling the stately-home business can also be seen in the growing popularity of the garden in preference to the house. By the mid-1960s, Bodnant, Sheffield Park and Sissinghurst gardens were among the National Trust's most popular properties.[102]

Finally, there was a much smaller but appreciably growing audience for the fine-art qualities and contents of country houses. However modest, this interest was important for the future of the country house. If the stately-home business was only about commercial leisure in the country, then the aristocracy had nothing distinctive to offer and could be supplanted in future. If, however, country houses were taken seriously as part of the 'national heritage' of culture, then the future could be made more secure: public affections could be tied specifically to the country house and more financial support could be extracted. That portion of the public that 'knew about art' had previously known about it mostly through museums and galleries; thus the prewar prominence of the National Art-Collections Fund. With extending education and wealth, that portion was now growing rapidly and was targeted by the stately-home business, which argued that 'art treasures are most advantageously seen *in the surroundings of a house*'.[103] The National Trust, with its older and wealthier membership and many houses unencumbered with family clutter, specialized in presenting its houses as showpieces of art and furniture; so did the central and local authorities that owned country-house museums.[104]

Private owners also cashed in on this market, at first cautiously so as not to frighten away the less refined, later with more confidence. As early as 1952, *Country Life* was pleased to report that scholarly booklets were now available at Hatfield and that in general

> information of the kind offered by F. Anstey's ancestral butler 50 years ago – 'the tapestries in the dining-room are gobbling' – is no longer acceptable to the increasingly enlightened visitors.[105]

Art-fanciers' magazines like *Connoisseur* and *Antique Collector* began in the mid-1950s to run features on private art collections in country houses open to the public, of a kind that had previously been confined to *Country Life*. As Lees-Milne had suggested, scholarly 'men of taste' were invited in to clean up the pictures and arrange the furniture more artistically. Visiting became more like a museum experience; guided tours were abandoned and visitors armed with improved guidebooks made their own way through the house. A quiet convergence between the art public and the country-house public was afoot.

Contemporaries were aware by the early 1960s that serious as well as recreational interest in country houses was growing. The stately-home business was pronounced a success. What the Welfare State had failed to do by legislation, owners and the National Trust had achieved by private enterprise (strategically greased by public subsidy): they had attracted public attention, support, even sympathy to the stately homes of England.

Troubles still lay ahead. The larger public of the 1960s was a better educated, but also more demanding one. In the 1950s, visitors had got used to accepting country houses as more-or-less passive consumers. In the 1960s, they would ask more actively what it was they really wanted from the stately homes. Were they only businesses, or did they have a national function as providers of recreation and education (with corresponding national responsibilities), or were they something even bigger, national symbols? Owners, in turn, had to ask themselves if they really wanted the public on *its* terms. That this debate took place on the culturally unsettled terrain of the 1960s introduced some unpredictable twists.

## Culture, Leisure or Heritage, 1964–1974

For all the growth in rural leisure in the 1950s, interest in the countryside grew more furiously still in the 1960s. To some extent this interest reflected the parallel increases in consumer spending on leisure pursuits that happened to take place in the country. By 1966, there were 12 million motor vehicles, 3 million anglers, 1.5 million family campers and 500,000 sailors in Britain. So it is not surprising that 4 million people visited the Peak District annually, taking advantage of the new M1 motorway, or that many others took the M6 to the Lake District. Nor did anyone at the time find it surprising that the number of visitors to National Trust properties trebled to 3 million a year in the course of the decade (while membership merely doubled to over 200,000). As in the 1950s, these were transnational phenomena of the

**The Stately Homes of SCHWEPPSHIRE**

WETT CHAMBERLAYNE

We have decided to open part of the gardens and visitors are welcome. At the same time we have made it clear that we are not allowing strangers to wander everywhere. We want to share our pleasures with the People (children half price); but we have no intention of imitating some of the more "aristocratic" patrons of stately homes who allow people to amble round on their own. Visitors are welcome between 3.30 and 4.30 except at weekends and holidays unless there is a notice up to the contrary. No dogs are allowed though they may look quietly through the front gates if on a lead. Visitors will be searched for litter before entering, and again, before they leave, for seeds. Cars may drive to the gate but they must be parked inside the manure yard, *backs* to the wall. The dwelling quarters are barricaded off, but visitors are requested not to look at them and are particularly put on their honour not to raise their eyes above the level of the ground floor. And remember: ONE-WAY ONLY: *No Smoking, chewing or snuff:* E PERICOLOSO SPORGERSI: *Tenez la gauche:* GROUND UNDER REPAIR: *Do not Look:* LOOK ROUND AND READ GREAT NATURE'S OPEN BOOK *(Keep Moving):* KEEP OFF: *Do not disturb gardener's boy:* LOW CHATTER ALLOWED HERE: *All cameras will be confiscated here.* The penalties for stealing bulbs or for pulling the communication cord are printed on back of card.

*Written by Stephen Potter ; designed by George Him*

SCHWEPPERVESCENCE LASTS THE WHOLE DRINK THROUGH

94　The commodification of the stately home: this advertisement for Schweppes ran in magazines like the *Economist* as well as *Country Life* as early as 1957, with a cheeky absurdist text and design.

booming Western economy.[106] Also transnational, but with a more
ambiguous relationship to economic growth, was a change in *attitude*
to the countryside. For the 1960s were of course also years of a
heightened consciousness of the 'environment', a new word which
came into non-technical currency in the early 1960s.

Talk of the 'environment' indicated seeds of doubt about the
unfettered modernizations of the preceding decades. 'Environmentalism' had both urban and rural dimensions. On the urban side, it
stemmed from worry about the pace, scale and character of redevelopment, which reached a peak in the early 1960s. Physical change at this
unprecedented level was unsettling enough, but the industrial
building-methods necessary to accomplish it added further ground for
popular suspicion. People began to feel like strangers in a strange land,
and a shoddy land, too, as jerry-built modern architecture stained and
cracked and tottered. One possible response was to hark back to the
small scale and familiar, and attempt to 'conserve' the historic urban
fabric. The grassroots movement for which preservationists had been
hungering since the 1930s finally began to develop, but surprisingly on
urban as much as rural terrain. In the decade after the foundation in
1957 of the Civic Trust, an umbrella group for local 'amenity societies', the number of such societies in Britain shot up from about two
hundred to six hundred, aiming mostly to protect urban and suburban
areas from redevelopment.[107] Another response to urban redevelopment was to turn more fervently to the contrasts of the countryside.
Open nostalgia for a rural arcadia, which for so long had been the
province of an intelligentsia in revolt against mass culture, now began
to infiltrate mass culture itself, as disillusionment with the modern
city and modern processes of development set in. The appetite for
rural pleasures took on pronounced anti-urban and even anti-modern
qualities.

There are reasons to think that 1960s anti-urbanism, while evident
throughout the West, went deeper and cut sharper in Britain than
elsewhere. This was due not to a congenital pastoralism in British
culture, but to something like the reverse: the scale of urban change
and the 'shock of the new' had been much greater in 1950s and 1960s
Britain. In town centres, the dismantling of planning controls and the
resulting property boom – land values doubled in the five years to
1964 – led to feverish and chaotic commercial development, only
halted in London by the new Labour Government's construction
moratorium of November 1964. Outside the centre, public demand
for modern housing led to the construction of 4 million new dwellings

by local authorities. Both commercial and domestic construction was ring-fenced within already urbanized areas by the only part of the planning system that was strictly enforced, the 'green belts' that protected the agricultural countryside from urban sprawl. In conditions of rapid population and traffic growth, this poorly planned and yet concentrated process of redevelopment created a 'pressure-cooker' atmosphere in towns more acute than elsewhere in the West – and led also to a recoil from towns more violent than elsewhere.[108]

The recoil from the modern city naturally delighted old-style preservationists, who had long bemoaned what they saw as a deep-seated materialism and philistinism in mass culture. Yet when the new consciousness came in the 1960s, it came in a populist form with which older, more aesthetic preservationists were not always comfortable. The consumer society was, after all, hardly likely to blame the mess on its own lust for modern shops and homes. Nor, in the 1960s, was much heat yet turned on modern architects and their local-authority clients. Instead, the environmental problems of the 1960s were very largely blamed on *laissez-faire* capitalism, on the private developers who had profited from the property boom and, secondarily, on the private landowners who had kept the countryside to themselves, for pleasure or agriculture. It is not now often remembered that grievances against private landownership were among the factors leading to the election of a Labour Government in 1964 after thirteen years of deregulation. There was even a whiff of renewed anti-aristocratic rhetoric, as Harold Wilson scored easy points off Harold Macmillan's band of ducal cousins and the Earl of Home, who had been reincarnated as plain, old Sir Alec Douglas-Home in order to lead the Tory party to defeat.

The populist streak in 1960s pastoralism made for some odd contradictions and strange bedfellows. Demands for extended rural leisure facilities and improved access to the land sat uneasily with the 'preservation' of the countryside, as the CPRE recognized in changing the word 'preservation' to 'protection' in its title in 1968. For many older preservationists, urban use of the countryside was the problem and private ownership the solution, rather than vice-versa. The more flexible were ready to bridge the contradictions. John Betjeman, jeremiah, became John Betjeman, culture hero, tirading indiscriminately against 'the developers and the grey men', the motorists' lobby, 'the pseudo-progressive professors, the exploded functionalists, and the permanent civil servants'.[109] Even James Lees-Milne made a showing in Betjeman mode, dressing up his old love of squirearchy in environmental language, calling for 'an immediate stop to speculation in land and historic buildings, even to the extent of withholding compensation to owners', and appealing to

> the sanctity of historic buildings and beautiful scenery, and a reverence for nature and wild life – in other words a proper love of one's country. Patriotism in the Kiplingesque sense is rightly out of date . . . [We] love England because of its beautiful buildings and its surviving fields and woods . . .[110]

He called on the National Trust to resume the campaigning language of its founders and lead the struggle against industrial agriculture, pollution and pesticides. Yet at the same time he recognized uneasily that 'love of country' could itself be a threat, as pressure of numbers was ruining many National Trust beauty-spots and stately homes.[111]

Both the National Trust and private landowners thus found themselves in an unaccustomed spotlight in the early 1960s, the object of unusual interest but also of new pressures and criticisms. The Trust, with its peculiar combination of private status and public responsibilities, came under particularly close scrutiny. For a moment in the early 1960s it looked as if it might rise to the challenge. In 1961 the ageing Lord Crawford began to groom as his possible successor the thirty-seven-year-old John Smith, appointing him to succeed Lord Esher as chairman of the Trust's General Purposes Committee. Smith was a Tory banker of landed gentry stock but also 'the only rich, intelligent eccentric left in England'.[112] He was fired by a mission to modernize the National Trust, to improve its internal administration and to shift its public image away from the cautious custodianship of stately homes for elderly visitors and towards environmental causes beloved of the young. Preservation, he maintained in a public address at the Festival Hall in March 1962, was about *creation*:

> creating new opportunities for *people* to do and enjoy and see hundreds of things which they could not enjoy before . . . Our job is to widen life . . . We don't obstruct progress; we *are* progress . . .

The supply of country houses was in any case slackening, and Smith wanted to divert the Trust's energies into new, leisure-oriented directions: the provision of holiday cottages, the revival of the Stratford-on-Avon canal ('traffic-free pleasure to generations of boaters, fishermen, walkers, bird-watchers and other civilised idlers'), more recreational parks such as the Trust had already provided at Clumber in Nottinghamshire, more scope for volunteers in restoration and conservation:

If Town and Country Planning is to pen most of us up in towns, then these are reliefs and pleasures we must have – to live for a brief instant in some piece of England as it all once was.[113]

The biggest departure was not Smith's idea, but became one of his pet projects: Enterprise Neptune, an ambitious public campaign to save nine hundred miles of unspoilt coastline. Over the doubts of the Trust's secretary Jack Rathbone, more comfortable with young men who had grown up in country houses, Smith selected as organizer of Enterprise Neptune the energetic but irascible Commander Conrad Rawnsley, grandson of the Canon Rawnsley whose passion for the Lake District led to the founding of the Trust in 1895.[114]

Yet both Smith and Rawnsley fell foul of the Trust's inertia and, it must be said, the rather different priorities of its old-guard leadership. As early as 1963 Smith was complaining to Crawford that 'we are insufficiently energetic, imaginative or enterprising'. For all the new departures, the Trust's image remained amateurish, complacent and old-fashioned, and as a consequence 'most people think of the Trust as principally concerned with preserving stately homes', a narrow and outdated focus for a countryside organization in the 1960s.[115] Finally, after a climactic row with Rathbone, Smith resigned his leadership position in May 1964, under pressure from Crawford who had become disillusioned with his erstwhile protégé.[116] When Crawford retired as NT chairman in the following year, he was succeeded instead by the Earl of Antrim. Even Antrim's appointment worried the aesthetes at the Trust: Rathbone felt 'the whole tone of the National Trust will be scaled down' and the Earl of Rosse fretted that the twenty-year rule of the 'men of taste' – Crawford and Esher – was at an end.[117] These frictions at the top were paralleled at the local level, where the Trust's 'Representatives', the curators jokingly referred to as 'lilies', and the 'Agents', the land managers or 'hobnail boots', were often pulling in different directions. All of these tensions were kept behind closed doors: that is, until Commander Rawnsley went public with criticisms similar to Smith's in the autumn of 1966.

Enterprise Neptune had by then already done much to improve the Trust's image: it had won a huge amount of free publicity and raised over £700,000, including a big grant from the Labour Government. But Rawnsley was an ambitious man and chafed at constraints which, he imagined, emanated from the 'belted earls' at the helm of the Trust. He was also pretty tactless and his criticisms of the Trust as a feudal institution, 'a protégé of the old landowning class' over-concerned with stately homes, were not only made in private.[118] Finally Antrim gave him his notice in October 1966.

Rawnsley would not go quietly; at a pre-arranged Neptune press conference, he issued a vivid indictment of the Trust as

> an inert and amorphous organization proceeding by the sheer momentum given to it by those who continued to bequeath their wealth and property to it, as often as not to escape death duties.[119]

In the *Observer* a few weeks later, he published a manifesto of concrete proposals to make the Trust more of a leisure-services organization. The Country Houses Scheme had, he claimed, diverted the Trust from the original purposes laid out for it by his grandfather, and also from 'the needs of the people':

> It draws its main support from professional people and the older generation. Should it not provide for the leisure pursuits of the people as a whole?

And he added a specific proposal for the country-house side of the Trust's work that worryingly fingered one of the fissures in the stately-home business:

> Should all the great country houses be shown as museums or should some of them play a more active part in the life of the community? There is little merit in some of the furniture and pictures. Would it not be better to take the best of both and make a few really worthwhile collections, and use the other houses for public assemblies, dances and other activities? Is it really true to have a remote relative of the original donor living in a flat in one wing of a great house makes of the whole a living entity even though the carpets in the public rooms, which are never used, are covered with drugget and the furniture roped off?

To make possible such changes in policy, Rawnsley then launched a campaign among ordinary members of the National Trust to secure constitutional changes that would, he said, democratize what had been (in Antrim's own words) a 'self-perpetuating oligarchy'. These proposals were put forward at an Extraordinary General Meeting of the Trust which attracted 3,500 members to the Central Hall, Westminster, in February 1967.[120]

Rawnsley's proposals were soundly defeated. They were never likely to pass, as Rawnsley's natural constituency was rather in the general public than in the membership, which as he had himself said was still comparatively elderly and conservative. The membership quite liked its 'belted earls' and had little desire for democracy, nor was the blustery Rawnsley a very convincing tribune. If anything, the

Rawnsley affair had the effect of undermining the new image of the Trust projected by Enterprise Neptune. In responding to Rawnsley's charges, Antrim fell into the trap of accepting the dichotomy between access and preservation, between leisure and culture, and put the Trust's work squarely into the latter category:

> The Trust's job is not and will not . . . be to involve itself in the entertainment industry . . . We take over these places to keep them in their natural state, and not to provide holiday camps.[121]

As critics said at the time, and sympathizers granted later, it was foolish to let Rawnsley widen the gulf between leisure and culture in this way: far better to find quiet ways of broadening the Trust's appeal while maintaining 'standards of taste'.[122]

This was in fact the course that the Trust eventually adopted. Having rebuffed Rawnsley's demand for a constitutional inquiry, it set up its own internal inquiry under Sir Henry Benson. No substantial constitutional changes were made and the traditional leadership group of aesthetic landowners remained in place, but the Trust's practices changed. It professionalized its administration, hired a public relations director and a marketing manager, and began strenuously to recruit members, to such an extent that the 1960s pattern of visitor growth outpacing membership growth was reversed in the 1970s. While gently commercializing its stately homes with teashops and boutiques and at the same time expanding its leisure-oriented activities, it found ways to please both lilies and hobnail boots. But some damage to the Trust's image had been done; its low-profile oligarchy had been dragged into the public gaze and accused of putting the exclusive appeal of country houses above more popular outdoors causes. For a time it ran the risk of incurring a government inquisition, as planning minister Richard Crossman was urging unsuccessfully (with covert sympathy from dissidents inside the Trust).[123] In the late 1960s, such risks were still dangerous: when accusations of exclusiveness resurfaced in the 1980s and 1990s, they appeared more marginal, as public opinion was by then more in sympathy with both the National Trust and the country house.[124]

The Rawnsley affair points up the pitfalls of the stately-home business's very successes. A degree of visibility had been achieved, in turbulent cultural conditions, that was not entirely desirable. Private owners came under less direct attack, as their private business touched on the public interest less obviously, but with a Labour Government back in power the threat was always latent. Labour's response to the clamour for rural leisure was on the whole not to undermine private landownership but to make new public initiatives. Its ritualistic attempts to re-nationalize development rights were half-hearted and largely nugatory, while in the taxation sphere it made comparatively few departures. Capital Gains Tax, introduced in 1965 to catch the windfall profits made in the property and stock markets, hardly dented the huge gains made in the long boom, and landowners' representatives did not at the time bother much about it.[125] More positively, Labour's Countryside Act 1968 strengthened the national park system and provided for leisure-oriented 'country parks', which could be joint ventures between local authorities and private owners. The level of funding for rural leisure jumped dramatically. Whereas a private member's bill to add a mere £40,000 to the central government grant for national parks failed under Treasury resistance in 1959, the Countryside Commission set up under the 1968 Act was budgeted at £2 million a year.[126]

Stately-home owners were under less direct pressure to move with the times than was the Trust, but the more acute among them were aware of the potential for trouble and sought to head it off. Montagu of Beaulieu issued a general warning to his peers in 1967:

> We must remove the great prejudice against apparent wealth both at public and private level . . . We must abandon the pretence that the world still owes us a living. We must adopt the attitude and methods of the Impresario. We can all do this with discretion sometimes reinforced with a degree of ruthlessness . . . Unless we can adapt ourselves to the times and conditions in which we live we shall suffer a fate as final, if less dramatic, as the French feudal aristocracy at the end of the eighteenth century. If this happens our great country houses will become as empty and lifeless as many of the Chateaux of the Loire.[127]

Montagu's recommended tools were professional marketing of the stately home and a continuing programme of diversifying attractions to widen the potential audience. In this, he, Bedford and Bath remained in the van, with the addition in the 1960s of miniature railways and lion parks. Before the National Trust, they hired professional public relations and marketing men.

As more of the postwar generation of owners inherited, more stately homes followed the pioneers' lead. New owners in the late 1960s at places like Goodwood, Harewood and Knebworth lifted their operations on to a professional plane and drew in large numbers of tourists. Montagu set up a consulting business which had thirty to forty noble customers by 1972.[128] Where Rupert Gunnis had darted around the country in the 1950s advising nervous owners on how to arrange their furniture for visitors, the Chipperfield circus family played an analogous role in the 1960s setting up animal attractions for the nobility, including the famous lions at Longleat and Woburn and a bird garden at Knebworth. A few enterprising owners – at Knebworth, Burton Constable, Goodwood and Stratfield Saye – went into partnership with the government and opened grant-aided country parks under the 1968 Countryside Act.

In this way, the stately-home business was able to capitalize on the rural leisure boom of the late 1960s, bringing in more income but also – perhaps more importantly – refashioning the stately home's image for a younger, less cultivated, less bourgeois market.[129] A 1968 study of Castle Howard, Tatton and Ragley showed that visitors to these relatively commercialized houses

> had different needs from the earlier public: they wanted a day or half day out, and while the house provided the object of the expedition, it was its amenities and setting that gave the real pleasure.[130]

By catering to these needs, and also by following Montagu's advice and standing less on their dignity, the more commercial owners continued to serve their class by popularizing the image of the aristocrat.

It is striking that, after Harold Wilson's brief rumblings in 1964, the aristocrat and his country house were more often portrayed as glamorous than as sinister or pathetic. Aristocrats had long been treated as celebrities in the gossip columns, but they were now treated *just like* celebrities in other fields – television, film, fashion, non-landed wealth – with whom they also mixed socially. The idea of a 'new aristocracy' – in fact, a blending of old aristocrats with new talent from the pop culture industries – illustrated this phenomenon. Annabel's, the ultra-stylish nightclub, 'gave the impression of a very small country house gone over by a fashionable interior decorator', while, conversely, country houses became venues for pop concerts – Knebworth, most notoriously.[131] The many popular films set in country houses in this period testified not to a fascination with country houses *per se*, but rather to their status as glamorous locations, much like the Riviera or Hollywood (but cheaper). Most people's image of Castle Howard, before its reverent 1980s recreation as Brideshead, was as the set upon which Sophia Loren cavorted in *Lady L* (or, alternatively, as the Kremlin in *The Spy with the Cold Nose*). Chiswick House was used most promiscuously of all, 'not caused by enthusiasm for Palladianism', one critic noted, 'but by its handiness to the A4 and M4', 'an available west London whore' treated as 'a stage-property like Falstaff's laundry basket'.[132] Even a series of journalistic exposés of aristocratic wealth, revealing the extent of the postwar revival, treated the phenomenon as a delightful curiosity, not as a scandal.[133]

Of course, only a selection of the aristocracy was able and willing to go along with the more extreme versions of popularization. Many stately-home owners worried that their showmen peers were going over to the enemy, abandoning what was distinctive about the aristocracy, losing their privacy and freedom of action to the expropriators without gaining any concessions or respect. Lord Antrim may have gone too far in the direction of spurning popular tastes, but Lord Montagu had gone too far in embracing them: he even hinted that he had voted Labour in 1964. Worse, a sequence of countercultural aristocrats was letting down the side by consorting with rock stars and drug addicts.[134]

The average stately-home owner was no longer a fuddy-duddy; as more of the postwar generation succeeded to their houses, acceptance of a semi-public role for the country house spread. The number of open houses actually dipped slightly from a mid-1960s peak, as some new owners found themselves neither needing nor wanting the publicity, but the average owner who remained open in the late 1960s was seeking an increase in his tourist numbers. The number of houses drawing more than twenty thousand visitors a year increased from around sixty in 1967 to around ninety in 1972.[135] A sure sign of growing acceptance of the stately-home business was the formation, after so many false starts, of an owners' association. The British Travel Association, the promoter of foreign tourism with which many of the showmen had long been associated, organized a Historic Houses Committee after a conference of owners in 1965 demonstrated sentiment for a public voice. Government extended its approval by appointing the committee chairman, Hugh Wontner, to the Historic Buildings Council in 1968. After the British Travel Association was remodelled as a semi-public body, the British Tourist Authority, in 1969, a separate Standing Conference for Historic Houses was set up and this in turn metamorphosed into a fully autonomous Historic Houses Association in November 1973, though in its early years it still depended on the BTA for its secretariat.[136] The HHA represented both showmen and less commercial owners, including many who did not yet open their houses at all. Its formation indicated that many more owners were accepting a national role as cultural custodians, feeling for a compromise with a public that they still did not like but which they no longer felt they could ignore.

What these less commercial owners wanted was visiting on a manageable scale, visitors who wanted to see the house and park as they existed in private ownership and did not insist on too many new gimmicks. They had some hope that, if only 1960s populism would die down, gradual educational improvements would train up just such a culturally discriminating and undemanding public, as represented by (for example) the National Trust's membership. Such a public might also be more inclined to extend tax concessions hitherto available only to the more commercialized operations, without extracting further servitudes. What owners were hoping for, in short, was something like what the Gowers Committee had offered: an idea of the country house as a 'national heritage', to be cherished and appreciated by the public, but kept private and not over-exploited. While in the early 1950s neither owners nor public had been ready for this idea, a new generation of owners encouraged by the success of the stately-home business was coming around to it by the early 1970s.

The public, however, was not quite ready. As we have seen, environmentalism and disenchantment with urban modernism were cultivating affection for 'heritage' in promising ways during the 1960s, but as yet little of this affection attached to the country house. The demand was nearly all for better custodianship of the urban heritage. Certainly this was the impulse of the Labour Government. Lord Kennet, the junior planning minister responsible for preservation policy (and, as it happens, the son of the interwar preservationist Sir Edward Hilton Young), praised the country-house showmen for their services to the public but felt public policy must focus on the threat to the urban environment.[137] Important steps were taken to this end: preservation policy was finally transferred from the old Ministry of Works to the urban-oriented planning ministry, Housing and Local Government, in 1966; the Civic Amenities Act 1967 created 'conservation areas', entire districts which could be protected by local authorities; the Town and Country Planning Act 1968 dramatically reduced the demolition of listed buildings, legislation very much aimed against urban developers; and a new role, new members and new funds were found for the Historic Buildings Councils. The HBC for England was gradually remodelled by the appointment of more scholarly experts – including Pevsner and Howard Colvin, though also Hugh Wontner of the HHA and John Cornforth of *Country Life* – and its budget greatly increased as more 'town schemes' were devised and (in 1972) it became the conduit for central government subsidy of conservation areas. Its funds, still rationed to £500,000 in 1965, had by 1973 trebled to £1.5 million with an additional £1 million for conservation areas.[138] By then the traditionally low-profile HBC recognized that its role had been transformed by

> the growing appreciation of the country's architectural heritage by the public and most local authorities and the almost universal demand for the improvement of the environment in general.[139]

Country-house owners may have been ready to have their property conceived as 'heritage', but generally people felt that their 'heritage', the 'environment' most relevant to their own lives and also most at risk, lay in the towns. They had come to accept privately owned stately homes as places of entertainment and relaxation, to some extent as art treasures of national importance, but not yet as some higher, more abstract good requiring special protection independent of use-value. As late as November 1973, Marcus Binney in *Country Life* could warn,

> Few changes in public opinion have been so rapid and at the same time appeared so real and lasting as the growing concern for the preservation of buildings of every kind . . . There is, however, a real danger that one type of building may be left behind – the country house – and this is the more alarming, as it is the only field in which we can claim to have surpassed every other western nation, whether in excellence of architecture, beauty of setting, elegance of interiors, richness of contents, and for the most part, completeness even today.[140]

Public consciousness had come a long way, but it had not yet come to accept the aesthetic programme laid down by *Country Life* in the 1930s and the Gowers Committee in 1950. To attain the higher status in cultural life and the national imagination it enjoys today, the country house had to outlast the populism of the 1960s, endure one more crisis and live to enjoy its greatest triumph.

# Treasure Houses (since 1974)

Marcus Binney's anxiety that public support for preservationism was bypassing the country house may have had some grounds late in 1973, but almost immediately thereafter it became spectacularly baseless – thanks in no small part to the efforts of people like Binney himself. 1974 was a turning-point, and by 1978 Binney could say with reason, 'Never have country houses been more in the limelight than today'.[1] Against a backdrop of rapidly extending and intensifying public concern for the nation's historic fabric – such that by the late 1970s people could talk of a conservation 'mania' and by the early 1980s of a 'heritage industry'[2] – the country house specifically moved to the centre of attention. No longer a poor relation of urban conservation, or even just one of a menu of historic buildings to be preserved, the stately home achieved a special status, widely acknowledged as England's greatest contribution to Western civilization (as the Gowers Report had claimed, less fashionably, in 1950), the purest expression of the national genius. Special tax concessions were granted it, unprecedented lumps of national cash showered upon it, bestselling books written about it; it was flattered by 'country-house' designs in millions of middle-class homes; it provided a setting for fashion shoots, Japanese car advertisements, television series and Hollywood films. Suddenly, it had become a national symbol of sorts, as 'essential' as anything can be in the diversity of late twentieth-century life, and so of course it became the object of a myth – the country house had 'always' enjoyed its contemporary status – the 'tradition' of the country house standing for England had been invented. How can this recent, dramatic enhancement of the country house's status be explained, and how does it fit into the more volatile longer-term history that this book has recounted?

The story of the country house's rise to prominence in and after 1974 is an absorbing one and deserves a book of its own. The year

1974 was important for conservation in general, as it marked the
sudden end of the property boom (after a particularly dizzying spurt
upwards in 1971–3), the onset of inflation, energy shortages, budget
crises, an overall lack of confidence in modern economic development
and a surge in environmental consciousness.[3] These concerns seemed
to crystallize the doubts about modern architecture and urban redevelopment that had been gathering in the 1960s. But, for the country-
house interest in particular, 1974 was also remarkable for the election
of a Labour Government pledged to new capital taxation on a scale
not envisaged since the days of Hugh Dalton. Ever since the late
nineteenth century, the election of left-wing governments with capital
tax proposals had triggered debates about the national stake in the
privately owned heritage. In earlier episodes, government and public
were either heedless of the consequences for art and architecture or, as
in the late 1940s, prepared with an alternative programme of national
provision. In 1974, however, different circumstances obtained. Public
opinion was now highly sensitive to the fate of historic architecture,
but the Labour Government, with a slender majority and deep internal
divisions, was poorly prepared to explain how it could prevent the
break-up of country-house collections. One further novelty appeared
in 1974. Whereas in previous crises the class of country-house owners
was itself divided, voiceless, on the whole reluctant to pose as
defenders of anything 'national', by now sufficient numbers of owners
were accustomed to a public role as custodians of heritage to intervene
directly in the debate.

Labour's concern in 1974 was to capture some portion of the
enormous gains made in capital values over the past twenty years. It
was already committed to replacing death duties with a Capital Transfer Tax (CTT), halting avoidance by taxing the transfer of capital
assets whether in the owner's lifetime ('handing over') or at death, and
incidentally ending the 45 per cent abatement on agricultural land.
In addition, Denis Healey's Green Paper in August 1974 raised the
prospect of a wealth tax that would tap large fortunes even if not
realized or transferred. While CTT would undermine the landed
estates which traditionally maintained country houses, the wealth tax
would hit works of art as well, because the government was disinclined to extend the capital-tax exemptions traditionally enjoyed by
important works of art to the new wealth tax. The ensemble of house,
contents, estate and family which had been kept together since the
1950s not so much by government action as by landed prosperity was
now threatened simultaneously by the economic crisis and by these
new capital taxes.[4]

While some art critics viewed the prospect of a flood of sales with equanimity, landowners, architectural specialists, conservationists and museum interests were horrified. Those who did not oppose capital taxes on principle were still in favour of sweeping exemptions for works of art. Already in the summer of 1974 the Conservative MP Patrick Cormack had formed an all-party group, 'Heritage in Danger', to fight the wealth tax, composed primarily of fellow Tories but decorated also by some Socialist aesthetes lobbying for heritage exemption. And in the autumn of 1974 two events somewhat fortuitously drew attention to the specific problems of the country house.

In the autumn of 1972, the Historic Houses Committee of the British Tourist Authority had commissioned from John Cornforth of *Country Life* a 'wholly independent' study of the economic position of the country house. At that time, the position had not been so pressing but the owners' lobby was concerned about the growing dependence on tourism and wished to explore the case for further tax exemptions. By the time of the report's publication in October 1974, an emergency had developed and Cornforth's report, entitled *Country Houses in Britain: Can They Survive?*, was conveniently ready to marshal all the arguments for sweeping exemptions. Cornforth, unlike his predecessor Christopher Hussey, not a landowner himself, had steeped himself in the problems of the landowners who funded his report and came to the same conclusions that Hussey had drawn in the 1930s and Gowers in 1950. For the country house to survive, the traditional 'way of life' of the landowner had to survive, and for the landowner to survive, extensive State subventions would be necessary. While Cornforth's explicit recommendations stuck to the Gowers agenda of tax exemptions for houses and their contents, implict was an even wider appeal for support of the entire landed estate, drawing on environmental concerns as well as on the traditional defence of squirearchy:

> a country house is, or should be, the centre for a way of life that involves a community ... A dwindling estate means dwindling capital and the disappearance of the way of life that justifies the existence of a house: this is much more important than any matters of aesthetics or preservation law.[5]

At the same time as Cornforth's report, a second, connected presentation of the same case appeared. This was the exhibition at the Victoria and Albert Museum, *The Destruction of the Country House, 1875–1975*, organized by Roy Strong, Marcus Binney and Peter Thornton, which ran from October to December 1974. Inspired by

95   The Hall of Lost Houses at the *Destruction of the Country House* exhibition, Victoria & Albert Museum, autumn 1974.

Cornforth's researches, the *Destruction* exhibition presented many of the same arguments more vividly, in an historical perspective, and to a wider audience. The centrepiece was the 'Hall of Lost Houses', a room artfully constructed to appear as if the wrecker's ball had just hit it, filled with photographs of demolished country houses and haunted by the recorded voice of John Harris intoning the names of these lost seats – an ironic riposte, perhaps, to John Summerson's recorded slogans featured at the MARS Group's exhibition of modern architecture in 1937. The exhibition ended with warnings about the current crisis very much in the Cornforth vein.[6]

Neither the Cornforth report nor the *Destruction* exhibition were at the time the easy, obvious successes they have since appeared. Inevitably they become embroiled in a hot political debate about the tax system, and neutral observers complained about the extreme choices being offered them – philistine confiscation or a dream of squirearchy, brute socialism or brute feudalism.[7] What was immediately significant about both report and exhibition was the much greater public visibility and confidence of the country-house preservation lobby, its ability to intervene in such debates aggressively and successfully. The Historic

Houses Association (into which the British Tourist Authority committee had now evolved) took an unusually high profile in public print as
well as at its own tourist sites in the spring and summer of 1975.
Figures such as Sir Michael Culme-Seymour and his heir Commander
Michael Saunders Watson of Rockingham Castle, the Earl of March
of Goodwood House, the Duke of Buccleuch of Boughton House
(and assorted other houses), made regular and robust defences of the
landowner as custodian of the public interest. The HHA circulated a
petition against the new capital taxes at country houses open to the
public and submitted over one million signatures to Parliament in the
autumn of 1975. The showmen were putting their newly developed
talents to good political use. To dramatize the effect of capital taxation, the Earl of March stripped one of the staterooms at Goodwood
of its pictures and asked tourists to sign the petition if they disliked the
effect.[8] More baldly than ever before, owners were telling the public
that the price of keeping the stately homes open was the retention in
private hands of huge capital assets in land and art.[9]

96   The Earl of March in his artfully disarrayed stateroom at Goodwood, suggesting the effects of
capital taxation on the privately owned heritage.

Out of the *Destruction* exhibition came an allied but subtly different campaign. Marcus Binney, the *Country Life* writer who had been a driving force behind the exhibition, represented a younger and less landed segment of the preservation lobby. For him, country houses were only one part of a much broader historic and environmental heritage under threat in the 1970s. He made no blanket case for landowners, but his researches for the exhibition persuaded him that the owner's attitude was the crucial element in determining the fate of a historic building. 'Problem owners' had to be restrained with further legislative protection of listed buildings, but by the same token conscientious owners had to be encouraged with tax exemptions where necessary.[10]

Binney's approach reflects the way in which a broader, younger and less metropolitan constituency was being mobilized behind the cause of the country house. As part of the publicity campaign for the *Destruction* exhibition, Binney supplied local newspapers up and down the country with photographs and information about country houses under threat in their area. In this way civic amenity societies were linked up to country houses and the local environmental contributions of country estates were underscored – a world away from the genteel, softly-softly approach of the old London-based aesthete circles. The campaign was extended in 1975 by Binney's new pressure group, SAVE Britain's Heritage, founded with the initial goal of policing Britain's participation in European Architectural Heritage Year, to ensure that it was not only a glossy propaganda exercise by the burgeoning Euro-Establishment. The same network of local amenity societies and newspaper contacts was now used to publicize threats to a wider range of historic buildings. Although SAVE counted among its activists other *Country Life* writers such as Simon Jenkins and Mark Girouard, it was never exclusively or even primarily a country-house lobby. Yet Binney had honed his technique on country-house campaigns, his interest in the fate of country houses remained intense and, most importantly, SAVE had made the country-house issue 'safe' for a younger generation of environmental campaigners unimpressed by squirearchy.[11]

The diversity of these campaigns – and especially their media know-how – was important in turning the tide against Labour's capital taxes. To everyone's amazement, the government almost immediately began to back down. In his 1975 budget Denis Healey conceded exemption from Capital Transfer Tax not only for important works of art, as under the old death duties, but also for outstanding buildings and stretches of land. A Select Committee was appointed to consider the wealth tax and, after much damaging criticism was absorbed over the summer of 1975, the tax was quietly dropped at the end of the year. By 1976, the government had adopted an entirely different policy towards heritage property. It now decided to extend exemptions and subsidies much further in return for a nominally greater public stake. A long-standing demand for tax-free endowments was conceded, allowing owners to put assets into maintenance funds that would be free of capital taxes so long as the funds were used to keep up a heritage property open to the public. Furthermore, owners were empowered to vest their houses, collections and estate lands or other assets in charitable trusts which, considered as 'Gifts of Public Benefit', would all be sheltered from CTT. Such charitable trusts, often effectively controlled by the family and allowing for continued family residence, were essentially treated as public bodies; for instance, when works of art were accepted by the government in payment of tax, they could be left *in situ* (and not transferred to a public collection) if the house was part of a private trust.[12] The effect was to create miniature National Trusts, but with the family position better protected, such as the Duke of Norfolk had sought in vain for Arundel Castle in 1957 (and which now exists in the form of Arundel Castle Trustees Ltd).[13]

These concessions to a great extent realized the proposals of the Gowers Report and, more profoundly, realized the vision that *Country Life* had been developing since the 1930s. As country-house advocates pointed out constantly after 1976, it was now a matter of public policy that country houses were accepted as a national heritage, with their traditional owners remaining in possession as custodians or trustees.[14] This formula could work because enough of the public valued the country house, and enough of the owners accepted some public responsibility. Whereas previously only owners who accepted repair grants had to submit to public access, now owners who wished to claim capital-tax exemption for their houses and endowment funds had also to submit to inspection on thirty days a year. The very wealthiest owners who had not sought public assistance previously could be attracted into a system that protected their non-heritage assets from capital taxes. Fifty-six CTT-exempt maintenance funds had been set up by 1992. Not coincidentally, the number of houses open to the public, which had levelled out at around three hundred by 1965, rose after 1975 to the present level of over 350. Traditionally very private (because very wealthy) aristocrats opened their homes: the Earl of Carnarvon at Highclere, the Duke of Buccleuch at Boughton, the Marquess of Cholmondeley at Houghton. In addition, about twenty

owners conveyed their houses to private trusts to provide more permanent protection; these include a number of cases where the family
line has failed, but also others – notably Chatsworth, Arundel and
Harewood – where the family remains *in situ*. In these latter cases the
language of private-public partnership is explicit. A charitable trust
may in spirit still be private, but it avows public goals. The preservation of the house and its collections comes first, the owners' assets,
control and convenience second.

This order of priorities does not come naturally to an aristocratic
owner, thus the limited number of trusts so far created; yet the
precedents were important. Owners were increasingly expected by
public opinion, and indeed by *Country Life*, to act as responsible
custodians. When they sold off pieces of their heritage to protect their
financial position or sustain their lifestyle, they came under heated
criticism from ordinarily friendly quarters, especially after 1979 when
tax rates were lowered so far as to offer little excuse. Heritage lobbyists, who worked so hard to win the fiscal benefits of heritage status,
let these 'renegades' know that they were letting down the side. Even
sales of art organized to endow houses, as at Chatsworth or Castle
Ashby, were viewed as bad publicity.[15]

Even where owners did default on their responsibilities, public
opinion was now prepared to rush into the breach, or so the battered
Labour Government concluded in 1977 when it again faced up to the
country-house lobby. In January of that year the Earl of Rosebery
announced that he would sell off Mentmore, his fantastic Victorian
country house in Buckinghamshire, along with rich collections
of mostly continental art and furnishings accumulated by his
grandmother's Rothschild connections. For years Roy Strong,
Director of the Victoria and Albert Museum, had been trying to
arrange acceptance of Mentmore via the National Land Fund to make
a nineteenth-century branch museum for the V&A, as had been done
with seventeenth-century Ham and eighteenth-century Osterley in
the late 1940s. The deal had foundered on government indifference
and on the Treasury's refusal to spend large sums out of the NLF; the
NLF had, after all, been virtually dormant since the 1960s. A decision
to accept Heveningham Hall, Suffolk, for £300,000 in 1970 had
shocked the Treasury and turned it against further extravagances,
so the government decided to ditch Mentmore and take the
consequences.[16]

Again, it underestimated the change in public feeling about historic
buildings of all kinds, about country houses especially. Considerable
sentiment could now attach even to 'French furniture collected by a

97   The crowds gather for the 'sale of the century' at Mentmore, May 1977.

98   The Earl of Rosebery does a sound-check for Sotheby's, just before the start of the ten-day Mentmore sale.

Jew' housed in a 'hideous lump of stonework'.[17] SAVE swung into action with an instant pamphlet hymning Mentmore's praises, and the art galleries leaped at an opportunity to revive the National Land Fund for art purchases.[18] It proved too late to save Mentmore – the contents were sold in May and the house was later taken on by the Maharishi Mahesh Yogi – but such a failure could not be repeated. An all-party Parliamentary report of June 1978 called for the removal of the National Land Fund from Treasury control, the restitution of the original £50 million given it by Hugh Dalton but stripped away by the Conservatives in 1957, and annual contributions to the Fund so that it could again be used regularly to acquire heritage property for the nation.[19]

By the time the report could be translated into legislation, a Conservative Government was in power. Like the Tories of the early 1950s, the Thatcher Governments after 1979 were constitutionally opposed to public expenditure on heritage as on everything else. In well-publicized statements of the 1980s, Conservative ministers as different as Nicholas Ridley and Michael Heseltine voiced sentiments identical to those of Eccles and Macmillan in the 1950s. The only solution to the country-house problem, they felt, was low taxes; if owners could still not support their houses on their income, they must sell. Consistent with this policy, Heseltine cut the budget for Historic Buildings Council grants in the early 1980s; as for the houses already in public ownership, they had to be squeezed for income. English Heritage was set up in 1984 under Lord Montagu of Beaulieu, charged with making the government's historic buildings and monuments more entrepreneurial and also with administering the HBC grants more efficiently. What chance, then, was there for a huge injection of public money into the National Land Fund to *add* to the national collections?[20]

Yet that was precisely what happened. Quite unlike the experience of the 1950s, when cost-cutting Conservatives pared back the Labour commitment to the national heritage, the Thatcher Government substantially improved on Labour's pledges to the National Land Fund. Two funds were in fact established. One, which would continue to accept heritage property in payment of tax, was kept under political control. The other, launched as the National Heritage Memorial Fund in 1980, was handed over to independent trustees, endowed with a lump sum and an annual budget of over £5 million a year, and empowered to make a much wider range of capital payments than had been possible under the NLF. The new fund could provide cash endowments to the National Trust to enable it to take on unfunded houses, as with Canons Ashby, Belton House and Calke Abbey; it could provide a cash endowment for an independent trust to maintain a house, as at Burton Constable in Yorkshire; it could buy important works of art in the open market or by private treaty, either for deposit in national collections or to be left *in situ* in private houses open to the public; and it could act as an independent but specially positioned lobby for further heritage expenditures, often on a breathtaking scale: at the height of Thatcher's public expenditure squeeze, in February 1985, the NHMF winkled out of the Treasury a £25 million top-up to allow it to purchase Kedleston, the contents and grounds of Weston Park and the furniture at Nostell Priory, mostly for transfer to the National Trust. Since the government tended to find these monies out of other arts or environmental budgets, the effect was to make 'national heritage' the centrepiece of public arts policy in the 1980s.[21]

As potent a force as Thatcherism had to accommodate an intense affinity for 'heritage', and a country-house heritage in particular, that had spread deep and wide in the culture in the 1980s - well beyond public policy. Urban conservationism had not been extinguished, but in important ways was overshadowed by the country-house mania of that decade. This mania manifested itself at many levels. Continued growth in stately-home tourism was one symptom. Despite its own efforts since the Rawnsley affair to diversify its activities and complicate its image, the National Trust became closely identified with the country house in the public mind and benefited from it. Its membership in the 1970s soared well ahead of economic indices. The little gaggle of 1,000 members in the 1920s which had burgeoned into the culture club of 100,000 by 1960 and 200,000 by 1970 had by 1980 become a mass movement of over 1,000,000 − over 2,000,000 by 1990. It had become one of the most powerful non-governmental bodies in Europe. While still, of course, attracting the older and wealthier disproportionately, the practice of country-house visiting had spread very far into the population. A British Market Research Bureau study for Mintel in March 1993 found that a third of the entire adult population had visited a stately home in the last year, more than any other kind of historic site, and another survey suggests the figure may be higher still, perhaps over half of all adults.[22] Country houses have thus gained in popularity among historic sites, at a time when visiting historic sites of all kinds has gained in popularity versus other uses of leisure time.[23]

Tourism growth represents a continuation (though accelerated) of trends evident before the 1970s. More striking has been the appear-

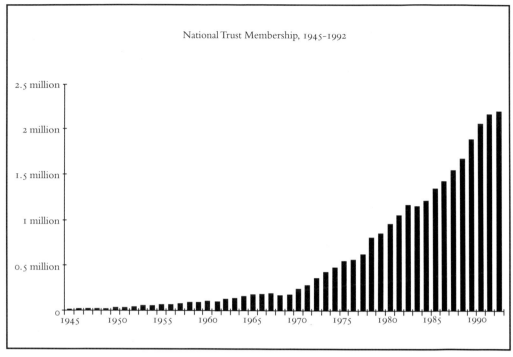

National Trust Membership, 1945-1992

99    The spectacular rise of National Trust membership, 1945–1992.

ance of country houses and their associations in other spheres. In book publishing, the remarkable success of Mark Girouard's *Life in the English Country House* – a scholarly (but not sober) study of aristocratic social history traced through the physical evidences of the houses, published by an academic press in 1978 and selling 65,000 copies in hardcover – spawned many imitators.[24] In television, the lush adaptation of *Brideshead Revisited* in 1976 triggered an avalanche of costume dramas in which the country house was the focus of attention rather than simply the backdrop, as had been the case in the 1960s. Filmmakers followed suit; literary works of the eighteenth to early twentieth century which took the country house for granted (unlike *Brideshead*, which did fetishize it) are now adapted for the screen with country houses dead centre.[25]

Nor has the country-house appeal remained confined to high culture. The idea of the country house as the quintessential English home, which had relatively little purchase through the 1960s upon a modern-minded and technophiliac mass market, gained in currency in the 1970s as the reaction against urban modernism deepened. The

BBC had experimented with a programme about the modern uses of antique furnishings as early as 1965, the year when Arthur Negus's *Going for a Song* first appeared. When James Lees-Milne visited a modest country-house auction in January 1972, he was astonished to discover 'immense crowds', 'the smell of human flesh ghastly', and concluded, with some gratification, that it was owing to the television promotion of the antiques market. *Going for a Song*'s successor, *Antiques Roadshow*, has demonstrated how much further that popularization can reach. A fixture since 1979, it can now reach 13 million people, including, of course, many more homeowners than existed in the 1960s. The precise import of such popularity is hard to pin down – one critic thinks *Antiques Roadshow* is 'a prime example of British snobbery and class prejudice', another more or less the opposite, a force 'to democratize the notion of the collectable, update the notion of the historical' – but the taste that is being 'democratized' is certainly more nostalgic and more aristocratic than the modern modes it has displaced.[26] The same goes for the popularity of the 'country house style', an adaptation of the John Fowler style (itself an adaptation of eighteenth-century styles for the modern aristocrat), which has dominated interior-decoration magazines and middle-market tabloid features since the 1980s. 'Country-house style' is not always explicitly aristocratic – for instance, the popular 'Edwardian Country Lady' look, which began as an illustrated diary and leached into home decoration, is more cottagey than stately – but aristocratic associations tend now to be taken as a positive benefit rather than something slightly embarrassing.[27]

A happy medium can be found in the idolization of squirearchy, not too grand to serve as a model for the urban flat or terrace house, but adequately acred and antique. The cult of the squire has been a feature of publications associated with the Historic Houses Association, the majority of whose members do not have houses open to the public and wish to promote the idea of the country house as a *model* for the nation, not its playground or possession.[28] Getting the voting public to see the stately home as more home-like than stately is obviously beneficial from the point of view of extracting subsidies and tax concessions without the servitudes of access or alternative use.[29] Such a goal is now conceivable, as a mass market grows up viewing the private country house not as a piece of its history to be annexed and explored, still less a target for political expropriation, but as a quintessentially English treasure to be protected, admired and emulated.

★   ★   ★

What is the significance of the preoccupation with the country house at the end of the twentieth century? It is not really the place of a history book to make bold assertions about the present, and certainly not to predict the future, but since the country-house industry today makes assertions about and draws conclusions from history, we can perhaps reciprocate a little and ask what the historical argument advanced in this book suggests about the present.

The past described by contemporary writing about the country house has obviously been carefully manicured to accord with current preoccupations. At an extreme, the past two hundred years have been blurred into a single, unwavering vision of the country house as 'an English arcadia', 'a way of life that has hardly changed', a 'vessel of civilization' carefully constructed by the aristocracy and revered by the people, holding 'a central place . . . in the British national conscious-ness'. These flights of rhetoric were generated, for example, by the *Treasure Houses of Britain* exhibition at the National Gallery in Wash-ington over the winter of 1985/6, an expression of calf-love on the part of the American high-art establishment which rightly drew sharp criticism from British historians.[30]

Nevertheless, subtler versions of the same story pervade the late twentieth-century literature on the national heritage. Thus, eight-eenth-century admiration of the classical 'houses of taste' and nine-teenth-century romanticism about the 'mansions of England' can be run together without dwelling upon the fact that, conversely, the eighteenth century detested older houses (and tore many down), while the nineteenth adored the older houses (and tore the newer ones down). To emphasize this would be to show that the idea of a continuous tradition of 'country houses' hardly existed before the mid-twentieth century, not even among their owners.[31] We are obsessively reminded of Ruskin's passion for old Warwick Castle – perhaps no words about the country house have been more quoted than these:

> it was probably much happier to live in a small house, and have Warwick Castle to be astonished at, than to live in Warwick Castle and have nothing to be astonished at . . . , at all events, it would not make Brunswick Square in the least more pleasantly habitable, to pull Warwick Castle down.[32]

But we are rarely reminded of Ruskin's contempt for the crowds that *were* astonished by Warwick Castle when they visited it, and we are never reminded – the fact has been wholly forgotten – that when it burned down, he was adamantly opposed to the national campaign to rebuild it. To emphasize this would be to point to the yawning gulf between popular and aesthetic ideas about the heritage in the nineteenth century. Nor are we reminded that, for several generations after Ruskin's day, most of his countrymen did in fact feel more comfortable in their small homes to know that the stately homes were being pulled down. To emphasize this would be to appreciate how politically and socially suspect large houses of the aristocracy were until quite recently.[33] As noted at the beginning of this book, even writers who are critical of the 'heritage industry', and consider contemporary Britain's obsession with its aristocratic past to be unhealthy, tend to magnify it. For critics both of the Right and the Left, the disease of snobbery and nostalgia must be made to appear serious enough to require the cure of their potent medicine.[34]

It has been the argument of this book that appeals to some unique and deep-seated English nostalgia for aristocratic country life are not necessary to explain the current country-house fashion. On the contrary, the English experience in the past two hundred years has been notable for an ambivalence towards the aristocratic heritage and a reluctance to take positive steps to preserve it. The continuity of English history does not necessarily entail a clinging to tradition; rather, continuity is only made possible by a constant process of gradual modernization. For this reason a political practice of *laissez-faire* and a highly urbanized and commercialized cultural life have been embraced as much by the aristocracy as by the rest of the nation; only if we fix our attention on clusters of anxious aesthetes and intellectuals do we discover an 'English tradition' of rural nostalgia. It has been other countries, disrupted by revolution and nation-building, that have needed consciously to construct and nurture a 'national heritage' to maintain stability; they cannot afford a too-rapid or unstructured process of modernization.

The pace of environmental change has, however, accelerated throughout the West in the postwar years, and every country has experienced an anti-modern recoil. In this country, changes wrought by modernization had accumulated over a longer period and their pace was still greater than elsewhere as late as the 1960s, when historic town centres were under severest pressure. So Britain *has* experienced a more violent reaction against the modern and in defence of the heritage in the last twenty years – making up for lost time. There have been other short-term factors affecting the shape of Britain's re-engagement with its past.[35] A sharper turn to the political Right in Britain than elsewhere has given additional status to private property and has led to what Patrick Wright has called an 'intensification of private space', a turning inwards towards the private home and away from the collapsing public sphere. Most importantly for the country-house version of the heritage, the mere survival of an aristocracy with much of its land and wealth intact makes an argument for the preservation of private heritage property *possible*, where elsewhere it would be impossible.[36] That aristocracy does not need to have a tradition of preserving and cherishing the heritage; it need only adopt that position *now* to appeal to present-day concerns. Whereas in the past aristocrats routinely demolished their houses and sold off their collections to preserve wealth in the form of estate land, now they can defend the estate land as an essential prop for houses and collections.

Finally, what does the history of the country house and the national heritage suggest about the future?[37] Mostly, it should make us cautious about the durability of the *status quo*. The widespread acceptability today of the 'way of life' understanding of the country house – the acceptance of the private owner's accumulation of property as a key portion of the national heritage – is built not on deep but on shallow foundations. A recent report by the Historic Houses Association, funded by auctioneers, surveyors and accountants, acknowledges this. The exemptions of the 1970s and the tax cuts of the 1980s do not go far enough. While the greatest houses have been reasonably well protected by endowments and charitable trusts, the 'dimmer seats' – the majority of the two thousand family seats still extant in the United Kingdom in the early 1970s – have remained vulnerable; as many as a quarter may have been sold since then. Sales by historic owners have extended to important houses such as Brympton d'Evercy in Somerset and Pitchford Hall in Shropshire; great collections continue to be sold off piecemeal; houses once open to the public are forced to close. The landed 'way of life' is proving too fragile for modern conditions. New tax concessions are called for.[38]

What the report does not add is that aristocratic owners are only continuing their traditional practice of adopting the different survival strategies suited to each new generation. Some are deserting their houses to save the land. Some are deserting their houses *and* land to save their assets. The earls of Warwick may be in advance of this trend as they were in advance of the stately-home business. The 8th Earl, foreseeing no long-term future for a publicly supported but privately owned heritage, moved to Paris in 1975, began to sell off his collections, and in 1978 sold Warwick Castle itself to Madame Tussaud's. While some heritage lobbyists decried him as a bolter, a renegade who had let down the side, sympathizers with the landed class had no choice but to defend his move as in the best interest of his family.[39]

The interests of the landowner and the interests of the nation do not invariably coincide, especially as the nation is a fickle, changeable creature – as it will always be.

This perceived crisis, in the midst of popular support, points to some structural problems in the association of country-house preservation with country-life preservation, the association made by Gowers in 1950, fostered in the 1950s and 1960s by owners, and since the 1970s by government. The fact is that, for all the magnitude of the country-house problem, it is more manageable than the country-life problem. The concentrations of wealth that historically have supported country houses cannot be maintained forever in their historic form. Nor is there a wider framework remaining to fix historic families in their houses or on their estates. Each new generation is again vulnerable not only to tax but to bad decisions (such as to over-invest in Lloyd's), bad fortune (a downturn in the agricultural market), changing values (such as the temptations of city life and professional pursuits). As the HHA report admits, old families are not replaced by 'neo-squires', either. The phalanx of resident families willing to play cultural custodian inevitably shrinks.

Such concerns return us to the other preservation programmes bruited in the 1940s: alternative use, or museumization, or nationalization. Might these not be more effective ways of rooting the country house in the modern economy and in the national affection? Some movement in this direction has been evident recently. We see it in the creation of charitable trusts, which at least to some degree separate the interest of the house from that of the family. We see it in the preservation movement's insistence on the enforcement of listed building controls against 'problem owners' whatever their ancestry.[40] We see it in the National Trust's acceptance that its country houses are *not*, on the whole, still family homes and can be presented in other ways – often to the disgust of their ancestral tenants.[41] We see it in the promotion of alternative uses for houses still in private ownership, such as Kit Martin's adaptations of houses for multiple occupation, or the imaginative new uses by private owners promoted by Marcus Binney: craft workshops at Hatfield House and Parnham, opera at Glyndebourne and Garsington, conferences at Brocket and Castle Ashby, art at Compton Verney.[42] The danger with these half-way measures is that they may still freeze country houses in the illusion of homeliness and limit their ability to evolve.[43]

The French châteaux offer an instructive comparison. English country-house lovers mock them as lifeless shells, lacking the ensemble of house, collection, park, estate and family that is England's gift to

Western civilization; and yet the châteaux may be more permanently secured because owners have been forced by political and economic circumstances to abandon their privacy. Public funds have been available to private owners since the 1840s; in return, there are many more privately owned châteaux open to the public than country houses, nearly all open six or seven days a week, many housing local museums and accommodating local functions and only incidentally providing residence. The long tradition of public attachment to the châteaux has insulated them from the crises and panics that have beset the country house over the last fifty years.[44] While it may be true that the country-house ensemble is England's unique possession, it may also be that the misguided attempt to preserve forever the ensemble is endangering the pieces that make it up. Only diamonds last forever; other treasures, created and valued by humans, must, like humans, evolve to survive.

# NOTES

## Abbreviations

| | |
|---|---|
| *DNB* | *Dictionary of National Biography* |
| *Hansard* | Hansard's Parliamentary Debates |
| HBC | Historic Buildings Council |
| *LJ* | Journals of the House of Lords |
| NA-CF | National Art-Collections Fund |
| *PP* | Parliamentary Papers |
| PRO | Public Record Office, Kew |

## INTRODUCTION

1 Two points of definition should be made here. First, 'country house' is taken to mean a house that when built stood at the centre of a sizeable landed estate, and was therefore originally the property of a large landowner (an 'aristocrat', whether titled or not). Since my topic is the place of the country house in the national heritage, I have focused on historic houses rather than those built in the last two centuries. But of course definitions of what is 'historic' also change, and today even recently built country houses are sometimes counted as 'historic houses'; to that extent I touch on them as well. Second, my subject is the English country house and the English heritage. In matters of national history and heritage, Wales, Scotland and Ireland have different stories, and although I bring those stories in occasionally for comparative purposes, they deserve a full and independent treatment. Where statistics are introduced, figures relate only to England, unless otherwise specified.

## PRELUDE

1 For the now orthodox view of Whig landscape aesthetics as 'about' possession and transformation, see Bermingham, *Landscape and Ideology*. For the adherence of a Tory minority to a more organic view of landscape – as time passed, more self-consciously minoritarian and nostalgic – see Everett, *Tory View of Landscape*.

2 Franklin, 'Liberty of the Park', 142–50; Williamson and Bellamy, *Property and Landscape*, 136–9.

3 Bermingham, *Landscape and Ideology*, esp. 15, but cf. Gainsborough's exception, 29, and also the persistence of the georgic theme in Georgian landscaping, arguing for the reconciliation of 'nature' and 'improvement' in agriculture (Chambers, *Planters of the English Landscape Garden*).

4 Harris, 'Country House Guides', in Summerson, *Concerning Architecture*.

5 Stone and Stone, *An Open Elite?*, 326–7.

6 Moir, *Discovery of Britain*, ch. 5. Cf. the more impressionistic survey of

'the Tour of Norfolk' in Ketton-Cremer, *Norfolk Assembly*, 171–202.

7   Harris, 'Country-House Guides', 61–2; Jackson-Stops, 'Temples of the Arts', 15–16; Fabricant, 'Literature of Domestic Tourism', 256; Tinniswood, *Country-House Visiting*, 88–97; Ousby, *Englishman's England*, 62–87; Colley, *Britons*, 173–7. Something of the same tone is evident in Andrews, *Search for the Picturesque*, though he steers clear of country-house touring and rests his conclusions about landscape tourism on a broader evidentiary base. For particularly extravagant overstatements, see Montagu, *Gilt and the Gingerbread*, 18–19; Kenworthy-Browne, 'Private Houses', 9; M. Saunders Watson's foreword to Sproule and Pollard, *Country House Guide*, 7.

8   Fabricant, 'Literature of Domestic Tourism', claims to have improved on Moir's survey, but her 'new' evidence consists mainly of surprisingly literal textual analyses of some familiar sources. It remains for an eighteenth-century scholar to extract the evidence relating to country-house visiting from estate records in the way that I have started to do for the later period.

9   Moir, *Discovery of Britain*, 80–85; Crook, *Dilemma of Style*, 32.

10  Andrews, *Search for the Picturesque*, 11.

11  Gilpin was born at Scaleby Castle, just outside the Lake District, of an ancient Cumberland landowning family.

12  Franklin, 'Liberty of the Park', 143–7, including the quote from Gilpin in 1786; Andrews, *Search for the Picturesque*, 56–66.

13  See Everett, *Tory View of Landscape*, 103–35, for an attempt to rehabilitate the Picturesque as more socially conscious; also Hemingway, *Landscape Imagery*, 67–75 and *passim*, for an analysis of the Picturesque as gateway to a complex 'naturalism', and n. 24 below on later attempts to marry the Picturesque with agricultural improvement.

14  Hunt, 'Picturesque Mirrors', 181–4, on the anti-historical effects of the Picturesque, is a useful corrective.

15  Burgess, *Essay on the Study of Antiquities*, 2nd edn (1782), i–ii.

16  Hussey, *The Picturesque*, 193–6; Andrews, *Search for the Picturesque*, 48–50; Ousby, *Englishman's England*, 112–26; Hunt, 'Picturesque Mirrors', 171–91. See also Janowitz, *England's Ruins*, on the ahistoricity of the ruin image in the Georgian poem, although at points this argument seems absurdly overdrawn.

17  Everett, *Tory View of Landscape*, 97–100.

18  Colley, *Britons*, 212–5, considers George III's Gothic projects as 'a counterblast to revolution'. Much the same could be said for James and Benjamin Wyatt's Belvoir Castle for the Duke of Rutland.

19  Clark, *Gothic Revival*, 82; Girouard, *Return to Camelot*, 22–4, 44, 49–50.

20  See Newman, *Rise of English Nationalism*, chs 1–2, on aristocratic cosmopolitanism.

21  Girouard, *Victorian Country House*, 52.

22  Reitlinger, *Economics of Taste*, II, 90–93, 98–9.

23  Everett, *Tory View of Landscape*, 167–99. There is of course a huge literature on the political trajectory of Romanticism.

24  See Howkins, 'Turner at Petworth', for a clever illustration of one late attempt to reconcile culture and improvement. Colley, *Britons*, 174–7, makes use of the same example, but seems to hang too much on this and a few other evidences of cultural leadership by the early nineteenth-century aristocracy. Colley's argument about aristocratic resurgence in the Napoleonic era, which is generally persuasive, is weakened by efforts to find it everywhere, even in the most unlikely places.

25  Remarkably little is known about the cultural practices of the early nineteenth-century aristocracy as a whole; there has been little advance

on David Spring's suggestive 'Aristocracy, Social Structure, and Religion', esp. pp. 271–7. Otherwise, much of what has been written on this subject is highly selective and rests on anti-Victorian prejudice: see, e.g., Steegman, *Victorian Taste*, valuable if dated.

CHAPTER 1

1 Colley, *Britons*, 174–7.

2 Ruddick, 'Scott's Northumberland', 25–6.

3 Anderson, *Printed Image*, and Bann, *Clothing of Clio*, the latter placing rather too much emphasis on the diorama dramatized by gas lighting, but usefully drawing attention to 'the ferment in representation which characterised the Europe of the 1820s', p. 25. Also Fox, *Graphic Journalism*, chs 1–2, on the combination of woodcuts with the new technology in mass-circulation journalism.

4 For instance the leading Methodist monthlies of the 1820s and 1830s, the *Methodist Magazine* and *Youth's Instructor*, both drew heavily on the annuals for their copy – another reason why the annuals deserve closer study. See Altick, *English Common Reader*, 117–8.

5 On the emergence of the mass-culture industry generally, there is still nothing to beat Altick, *English Common Reader*, but on the illustrated magazines, especially Knight and the *Penny Magazine*, see now Anderson, *Printed Image*; Fox, *Graphic Journalism*; and, more narrowly, Klancher, *English Reading Audiences*. The annuals still suffer from their reputation as dumping ground for the bin-ends of Romantic poetry. But see A. A. Watts's memoir of his father, *Alaric Watts*.

6 The Howitts have been reasonably well-served by Woodring, *Victorian Samplers*, which is unnecessarily defensive about its subjects' role as popularizers of Romanticism. See also Lee, *Laurels and Rosemary*, a pleasant biography by the Howitts's great-niece.

7 Hall deserves a more extended study than Maas, 'Hall and the Art Journal', and his article in the *DNB*, XXIV, 87–9. His own *Recollections* provide only a discursive starting-point.

8 Goss, *Life and Death of Jewitt*, is again only a starting-point for what could be an interesting life.

9 Fairholt is almost completely unexplored. See his entry in Engen, *Victorian Engravers*, 85–6, and *DNB*, XVIII, 151–2. Only Roy Strong gives him the credit he is due in *And when did you last see?*, 54–5.

10 Ellis, *Ainsworth and his Friends*. For recent disapproving verdicts from literary critics, see Simmons, 'Of Kettledrums', 54–5; Fleishman, *English Historical Novel*, 32–3; Sanders, *Victorian Historical Novel*, 32–4, 39, 46; Rance, *Historical Novel*, 41.

11 Anderson, *Printed Image*, 138.

12 The few literary scholars to comment on this market have viewed it narrowly and unfavourably as reflecting the shopkeeper's fear of the crowd. Klancher, *English Reading Audiences*, 95–6; Rance, *Historical Novel*, 12–14, 38–9. A more broadminded approach is evident in Joyce, *Visions of the People*, 173–8.

13 He was contrasting his romances with the Gothics of Walpole and his generation. Ellis, *Ainsworth and his Friends*, 286–7.

14 On another level, there was a proliferation of popular local history originating in the provinces, as discussed by Joyce, *Visions of the People*, 180–85.

15 Smith, *Nationalist Movements*, 8. On the affinities between the history vogue in France and Britain, see Bann, *Clothing of Clio*. The even greater importance of history in the making of the newly unifying nations (such as Germany and Italy) seems to have escaped historians of Britain; see, e.g., Walker, *German*

*Home Towns*, and Applegate, *Nation of Provincials*, for two English-language treatments of German national identity that give due prominence to history-consciousness. See Wiener, *English Culture*, for the standard view of British history which – in my view, wrongly – sees the early nineteenth century as present-minded and the late nineteenth century as fascinated with the past.

16 Newman, *Rise of English Nationalism*, 109–18, discusses some scholarly precursors of this view in the eighteenth century.

17 Girouard, *Return to Camelot*; see also Wainwright, *Romantic Interior*, esp. 18–24, on élite uses of medieval customs.

18 On antiquarianism, see Piggott, 'Origins of the County Archaeological Societies'; Dorson, *British Folklorists*, chs 1–2; Levine, *Amateur and the Professional*; the medieval historians are splendidly covered by Burrow, *Liberal Descent*.

19 Carter's Gothic engravings appeared in the *Gentleman's Magazine* from 1798 to 1817. His example was taken up commercially by Britton's *Architectural Antiquities of Great Britain* (1805–18) and *Cathedral Antiquities* (1814–35), though Britton was unprepared for the market upheavals of the mid-1820s. See Clark, *Gothic Revival*, 76–80, and Crook, 'John Britton'. On the simultaneous decline of country-house portraiture, see Harris, *Artist and the Country House*, 347.

20 The split had many aspects, of which the scholarly–popular divide was only one (and differences on aristocratic patronage another), but the whole subject deserves further enquiry. For some hints, see Evans, 'Royal Archaeological Institute', Wetherall, 'From Canterbury to Winchester', and the account in the *Journal of the British Archaeological Association*, 1 (1845), i–xv. Levine,

*Amateur and the Professional*, 48–50, considers the split as relatively trivial.

21 See the useful 'Chronology of Ainsworth's Romances' at the front of Axon, *William Harrison Ainsworth*.

22 This is evident from the chronological trend in Roy Strong's list of history paintings in *And when did you last see your father?*; the topics which were predominantly painted before 1840 were Edward III, Richard II, the Wars of the Roses and Edward IV; those predominantly adopted after 1840 included Henry VIII, Thomas More, Jane Grey, Elizabeth and, very markedly so, the Civil War.

23 Briggs, 'Saxons, Normans and Victorians', 12–13.

24 The Olden Time as a theme in Victorian cultural history remains almost completely unexplored. A pioneering start, not taken up since, was made by John Steegman in *Victorian Taste*, ch. 4, 'Architectural Critics and the Olden Time'. Roy Strong's monograph on Victorian history painting, *And when did you last see your father?*, also makes an important contribution. Other works tend to melt the Olden Time into the medieval, e.g. Clark, *Gothic Revival*; Chandler, *A Dream of Order*; Girouard, *Return to Camelot*; Wainwright, *Romantic Interior*; Boos, *History and Community*. Easby, 'Myth of Merrie England', in ibid., puts a nostalgic, medievalist gloss on the Olden Time theme. Literary historians look down on it as 'merely' popular: see the treatment of Ainsworth in n. 10 above, and most strikingly in Chapman, *Sense of the Past*, esp. 81. It is easy to lump the Middle Ages and the Olden Time together, because the Victorians did it themselves, often referring to 'the medieval ages' – only scholarly antiquarians were very precise about labelling – but if we look through the labels we can see marked differences in emphasis and content, as argued

above and further in Mandler, '"In the Olden Time"'.

25 On medievalism's loss of its old political connotations, see Smith, *Gothic Bequest*, 195–6, 201.

26 E.g. in Charles Knight's popular history of 1860, *Old England*, vol. I (to 1485) separates 'royal and baronial' from 'popular' life, but vol. II (principally devoted to the sixteenth and seventeenth centuries) reintegrates the treatment of aristocratic and popular culture, together separated from 'Crown and State'. See also Joyce, *Democratic Subjects*, 32–4, 71–2, for this theme in popular local histories in Lancashire.

27 See, e.g., Dellheim, *Face of the Past*, esp. 55–69, and John Brown's lecture, 'Tours in Yorkshire', in *Tourist Rambles*, 3–9.

28 These popular depictions of Merrie England should be distinguished from expressions of nostalgia (such as actual recreations of old rituals); both were criticisms of upper-class exclusiveness, but the one was popular, modern and egalitarian, the other tended to be aristocratic and paternalist. For excellent studies of nostalgia for Merrie England that still confuse the two categories, see Judge, 'May Day and Merrie England', and Hutton, *Stations of the Sun*, esp. 112–13, 295–7; cf. Mandler, '"In the Olden Time"'.

29 Howitt, *Visits to Remarkable Places*, iii–iv.

30 The context was a defence of Scott's *Kenilworth*. *Penny Magazine*, monthly supplement for July 1835, 289–96.

31 Carlyle quoted by Strong, *And when did you last?*, 31.

32 They did consider themselves more vulnerable to the utilitarian charge that 'culture' of any kind was a luxurious frippery. See, e.g., Howitt's defence in *Visits*, 197–204.

33 'British Artists, No. XXVI. George Cattermole', *Art Journal*, July 1857, 209.

34 Reitlinger, *Economics of Taste*, I, 98–

9, 101; Gillett, *Victorian Art World*, 111–17; Hillier, 'St John's Wood Clique'; Strong, *And when did you last?*, is stronger on the earlier than the later period. Cf. Bann, *Clothing of Clio*, 70–6, on the earlier deviation of French fine art from this tradition, at points unwarrantedly extended to England.

35 On Meyrick, see Strong, *And when did you last?*, 50–3, 56–7; Wainwright, *Romantic Interior*, ch. 9.

36 Ellis, *Ainsworth and his Friends*, 409–20. See also the criticism of limits on public access to Windsor Castle in Knight, *Excursion Companion*, pt VII, 8–11.

37 Report of the Select Committee on National Monuments and Works of Art, *PP* (1841), VI, 525, 543, 557–9, 596. Predictably, even the Parliamentary Radicals on this committee were more concerned with the antiquity of the iron railings around memorials in Westminster Abbey than they were with the popularity of the Olden Time.

38 *The Times*, 28 Sept. 1858.

39 Howitt, *Visits to Remarkable Places*, 234.

40 Hall, *Baronial Halls*, unpag.

41 Sad comments on the state of Temple Newsam by the antiquarian gentlemen Robert Curzon and Ralph Sneyd, 1847 and 1858, in the Sneyd MSS at Keele: a copy kindly shown me by James Lomax of Temple Newsam House.

42 Jacks, *Great Houses of Nottinghamshire*, 179–85.

43 Allibone, *Salvin*, 98–106.

44 Henry James, 'Abbeys and Castles' (1877), in *English Hours*, 140.

45 *The Lay of the Last Minstrel* is set at Branksome Castle, of which only foundations survived in Scott's day. *Marmion* centres on Norham Castle, whose ruins, Scott noted, 'are at present considerable, as well as picturesque'. *The Lady of the Lake*'s topographical interest lies in a lake. *Rokeby* was owned in Scott's time by

a connoisseur of Picturesque landscape who designed there a fine house and grounds, but fortunately for him Scott locates his action at nearby (ruined) Barnard Castle and at Mortham Castle, 'a picturesque tower . . . now converted into a farm-house and offices'. These examples could easily be multiplied. Victorian guidebook writers enjoyed outwitting Scott by making much of his occasional glancing references to intact buildings, like Tamworth Castle which features briefly in *Marmion* and Littlecote Hall, a mere footnote to *Rokeby*. For Scott's pointed comments on the ruins mentioned in his early poems, see Scott, *Poetical Works*, 54–5, 175–6, 381–2, 390, 400.

46   Ellis, *Ainsworth and his Friends*, 230–8. *Guy Fawkes* (1841) has scenes in Ordsall Hall, at the time of writing used only as a school; *The Lancashire Witches* (1848) revolves around Whalley Abbey (mostly ruined) and ends at Hoghton Tower (uninhabited until 1862). In contrast, as noted previously, Ainsworth deliberately set a novel in the Tower of London to raise public consciousness about the place.

47   The *Penny Magazine* had a number of articles on ruins in its early years, but only a few on intact buildings, e.g. Warwick Castle (8 April 1832, 177–8) and Haddon Hall (5 July 1834, 263–4). The same pattern applies to its rival, the *Saturday Magazine*.

48   *Penny Magazine*, 13 April 1833, 137–8.

49   Barham, *Ingoldsby Legends*, 175–6. A similar verdict was rendered in *Murray's, Surrey, Hants. & IOW*, 1858 edn, 204–6.

50   In treating of élite culture, Girouard dates the sudden growth of interest in Elizabethan architecture to a spate of publications some years earlier, in 1833, but much of this professional writing was grudging and often highly critical. As he also notes,

architectural and antiquarian opinion was here being forced by popular opinion, always more enthusiastic about the Elizabethan than were scholars, who tried to keep to a Gothic line. 'Attitudes to Elizabethan Architecture', 21–4.

51   J. Corbet Anderson compiled a reprint with new commentary in 1869–72, published again in four volumes by Henry Sotheran; there were then one-volume reprints of the plates with only minimal commentary in 1906, ed. Charles Holme, and 1912, ed. Reginald Blomfield.

52   The *Saturday Magazine* was an Anglican penny weekly that aimed to match the more utilitarian *Penny Magazine*'s impact upon working-class readers. Despite political differences, their historical content was similar and both developed a pronounced interest in the Olden Time in the late 1830s. The *Saturday Magazine* published by permission three woodcuts from each volume of Nash's *Mansions*, beginning with Ockwells in the issue of 7 March 1840.

53   Probably most illustrations of Tudor and Stuart history in the century between 1839 and the Second World War used Nash's drawings in one form or another; but a close analysis of precisely how they were used would be worth doing. For a few contemporary examples, see Strong's clever analysis of the uses of Nash by W. P. Frith and others, *And when did you last?*, 90–93.

54   Nash, *Architecture of the Middle Ages*. But Nash was already populating his architectural drawings in this style when working for Pugin; see, e.g., Nash, *Series of Views* (1830), where festivities for Henry VIII and Elizabeth are set in Eltham and Croydon palaces.

55   Nash, *Descriptions of the Plates*, I, 1–2.

56   Eastlake, *Gothic Revival*, 239; Steegman, *Artist and the Country House*, 14–15; Ousby, *Englishman's England*, 187; Harris, *Artist and the*

Country House, 347; McClung, 'Country-House Arcadia', 281. In contrast, see Alfred Yockney's praise for Nash's popularizations in his introduction to Holme, *Old English Mansions*, 11.

57 Eastlake, *Gothic Revival*, 238–9.

58 Woodring, *Victorian Samplers*, vii. Her chief rival had been another heroine of the annuals, Felicia Hemans.

59 Lee, *Laurels and Rosemary*, 108–9; Howitt, *Visits to Remarkable Places*, 197–204, 236–7. Of course, the Howitts were highly conscious of the economic value of the culture industry in providing employment to people like themselves.

60 Howitt, *Visits*, 205–7.

61 Howitt was no architectural sectarian, however: he had high praise for Gothic churches and cathedrals, and also recommended visits to eighteenth-century country houses such as Blenheim, Castle Howard and Kedleston, though his own pattern of visits reveals his true preferences.

62 Howitt, *Rural Life*, I, 322–3.

63 Howitt, *Visits*, 27–8.

64 Howitt, *Rural Life*, I, 324–8. For concrete examples, see Howitt's account of Compton Wynyates in *Visits*, 303–26, and Raby and Alnwick Castles in *Visits*, 2nd ser., 252–61, 419–37.

65 *Penny Magazine*, 16 Feb. (Knole), 8 June, 13 July, 17 Aug., 7 Sept. (Chatsworth), 14 Dec. 1839. As Patricia Anderson has noted, by the late 1830s Charles Knight was feeling less bound by the utilitarian strictures of the Society for the Diffusion of Useful Knowledge and the tone of the *Penny Magazine* loosened and warmed up in many respects. Anderson, *Printed Image*, 76–8.

66 Hall, *Baronial Halls*, issued in monthly parts from October 1843; the text collected in two volumes, 1845–6, with details illustrated by F. W. Fairholt; the plates collected in a third volume, 1848. Some of these plates are reprinted in Holme,

*Old English Mansions*. See further Steegman, *Victorian Taste*, 292–4, which unfortunately for the argument at that point of the book postdates the *Baronial Halls* to 1858.

67 The Hall and Jewitt essays were collected into two volumes, *The Stately Homes of England* (1874–6).

68 See, e.g., the *Leisure Hour's* grumpiness about Haddon Hall, 29 Aug. 1874, 552–5, and Hardwick, 1885, 381–6, the latter piece by Paxton Hood, a Nonconformist minister who did however like the political implications of the Olden Time.

69 *Reynolds's Miscellany*, 28 Dec. 1861, 5. The illustration was reproduced by *Reynolds's* from Edward McDermott's *The Merrie Days of England* (1859).

70 E.g. J. F. Smith's immensely popular serial 'Stanfield Hall', serialized in the *London Journal* in 1849, or Margaret Blount's 'Lamia; or, The Dark House of Drerewater', a tale of aristocratic degeneration set in the halfmedieval, half-Tudor Lenyon Hall, serialized in *Reynolds's Miscellany* in 1861; the hall is spine-tinglingly described on 25 May 1861, 353–4. But such examples were duplicated with slight variation in every volume of these magazines.

71 Cf. disapproval of Walpole by E. Walford, 'Knole Park and its Owners', *Kentish Fire*, 3 Nov. 1883, 163.

72 Brady, *Visitor's Guide to Knole*, 95.

73 Five hundred in 1805, by a conservative estimate calculated from visitors' book, 1805–10, Sackville MSS, U269/E19/1.

74 *Cooke's Kent*, 1810 edn, 322; 1822 edn, 281.

75 Strong, *And when did you last?*, 93.

76 'Knowle', *Penny Magazine*, 16 Feb. 1839, 58–9.

77 E. Paxton Hood, 'The Old Homes of England: Knole, the Home of the Sackvilles', *Leisure Hour* (1885), 50–52. Perhaps Hood had no choice but to crib, as Knole was then closed to the public.

78 There is a good account of

Penshurst's nineteenth-century vicis-situdes in Allibone, *George Devey*, 37–41.

79 Howitt, *Visits to Remarkable Places*, 17–18, 20, 22.

80 Ibid., 2.

81 See Raymond Williams's reading of the poem, *To Penshurst* (1616), in *Country and the City*, 27–34.

82 Knight, *Excursion Companion*, pt xv, 18. A similar attack on Walpole can be found in *Murray's, Kent*, 127–30. See also Hall's view in *Baronial Halls*, notably rejecting the Waller associations as too precious and Augustan, and an unusual indictment of the Georgian spoliation of Penshurst in *Bentley's Miscellany*, 26 (1849), 592–9.

83 Scott describes feasts at Haddon in *Ivanhoe* (1819) and *Peveril of the Peak* (1823). The extant hall was not, of course, built by the time of *Ivanhoe* (late twelfth century), though there was a castle at Haddon then. Cattermole did frequently draw Haddon, but it does not feature among his illustrations for Baroness de Calabrella, *Evenings at Haddon Hall* (1846), as is sometimes (naturally enough) assumed. See, instead, the lithographs by S. Rayner after Cattermole's drawings in *Haddon Hall* (1836).

84 Henry James's account of his visit captures the experience of many other mid-Victorian visitors; it can be found in 'Lichfield and Warwick', first published July 1872, repr. *English Hours*, 51–3.

85 *Illustrated London News*, 1 Oct. 1892, 419.

86 See, e.g., *Penny Magazine*, 5 July 1834, 263–4; Rayner, *Haddon Hall* (1836, and in a cheap tourist edition of 1867); G. U., *Visit to Haddon Hall* (1838); T. L. Cuyler, 'A Day at Chatsworth and Haddon', *Godey's Magazine*, Nov. 1844, 231–3; 'Haddon Hall', *Leisure Hour*, 29 Aug. 1874, 552–5; and especially the lengthy treatment given by

Llewellynn Jewitt in Jewitt and Hall, *Stately Homes* (1874), 221–93, the basis for local guides to Haddon in use until the First World War.

87 *Buildings of England, Derbyshire*, 2nd edn, 221.

88 'Chatsworth', *The Mirror of Literature*, 1 Feb. 1834, 66–9; Mrs S. C. Hall, 'A Day at Chatsworth', *Art Journal*, Jan. 1852, 32–3; on the Queen of Scots' Rooms, see the 6th Duke's sensible comments in 1844, showing that he, at least, had no part in sustaining the myth, repr. Devonshire, *The House*, 128–9.

89 *Penny Magazine*, 7 Sept. 1839, 150.

90 T. L. Cuyler, 'A Day at Chatsworth and Haddon', *Godey's Magazine*, Nov. 1844, 232–3.

91 'Chatsworth', *The Leisure Hour*, 5 Sept. 1874, 567–8. See also Edward Rose, 'English Homes. No. xxx. Chatsworth', *Illustrated London News*, 29 Nov. 1892, 550–55.

92 Early editions of *Murray's Handbooks* take pains to rebut the criticisms of Fergusson and others: see, e.g., for Burghley and Hatfield, *Northants and Rutland*, 1878 edn, 98–105.

93 First published in book form in *Records of Woman* (1828).

94 Anderson, 'Political Uses of History'. Aristocratic women, whose reading was not thus shaped by classical and political education, showed more interest in the popular idea of heritage.

95 Girouard, 'Living with the Past'; Franklin, 'Victorian Country House', 400; Girouard, *Victorian Country House*, 15–16.

96 On the neo-Elizabethan style, see Allibone, *Salvin*, 21–52, Girouard, 'Attitudes to Elizabethan Architecture', 21–5, and *Victorian Country House*, 50–54. For some analogues inside the house, see Wainwright, *Romantic Interior*, esp. ch. 8 on Charlecote, where George Lucy began to 'recreate' the Elizabethan interiors (and to 're-edify' the structure) around 1828.

97   See the description in Wainwright, *Romantic Interior*, ch. 9; the quote is from *Murray's, Gloucs. & Herefs.* (1867), 136.

98   See de Calabrella, *Evenings at Haddon Hall*, for what is actually a relatively rare élite exhibition of Olden Time taste, linked to Young England; also an account of a Haddon soirée in *Leicestershire Mercury*, 26 Aug. 1848.

99   See the anti-Elizabethan defence of the medieval great hall in Turner and Parker, *Domestic Architecture in England*, I, 70; III, 19–20.

100  Pugin, *True Principles*, 50–51; Scott, *Remarks on Secular and Domestic Architecture*, 149–52.

101  Girouard, *Victorian Country House*, 43–6; Franklin, *Gentleman's Country House*, 66–9.

102  For example the Keele Hall built by Salvin for Ralph Sneyd, 1856–61 to replace the Keele Hall built for a previous Ralph Sneyd around 1580 (and now itself housing Keele University); or Wroxall Abbey, a 'rather joyless Victorian brick mansion in a style between Late Gothic and Late Tudor', built in 1866 for James Dugdale on the site of the Elizabethan house he had bought from Sir Christopher Wren's descendants. On Sneyd, an antiquarian lover of the Olden Time, see Spring, 'Ralph Sneyd'; on Wroxall, *Buildings of England, Warks.*, 484–5.

103  A good example of a series aimed at the owners' market is J. B. Burke, *A Visitation of the Seats and Arms of the Noblemen and Gentlemen of Great Britain*, 4 vols (1852–5), which has much Olden Time detail but is infatuated with Victorian Gothic.

104  Howitt, *Visits*, 2nd ser., 255–6. Howitt had similar things to say about Alnwick and Lambton castles. On Cobham, see Knight, *Excursion Companion*, pt XV, 22–3. On Warwick Castle, Hall, *Baronial Halls*, unpag.

105  Hall, *Baronial Halls*, unpag.

106  Howitt, *Visits* (1840), 308–10.

CHAPTER 2

1   Marsh, *Back to the Land*, 27–31.

2   The American poet N. P. Willis, 'Loiterings of Travel', in *The Metropolitan*, 17 (Sept.–Dec. 1836), 156–8. See also below, pp. 87–8.

3   Pimlott, *Englishman's Holiday*, 82–4, 116–23, 149–54; 'My Excursion Agent', *All the Year Round*, 7 May 1864, 301–4; Walton, *Seaside Resort*, 5–31.

4   An under-explored topic, but see Delgado, *Annual Outing*, and Walton, *Seaside Resort*, 26–9.

5   Joseph Paxton's testimony to the Commons Select Committee on Public Houses, *PP* (1854), XIV, 172.

6   Pimlott, *Englishman's Holiday*, 77; Lords Select Committee on Carriage of Passengers on the Thames, *PP* (1838), XXIII, 11–12; *Pictorial Guide to Gravesend*, 3–21; Knight, *Excursion Companion*, pt XV, 3–6.

7   'Cobham Hall, Kent', *Penny Magazine*, 2 July 1836, 260–61; Hall, *Baronial Halls*, unpag., Cobham part issued 1 Oct. 1843; *Summer Excursions*, 224–30; Miller, *Jottings of Kent*, 71–4. The Cobham visitors' book begins in 1819, a few years after steamer service was inaugurated; the ticket system was introduced around 1830. Despite repeated efforts to enforce its use, the visitors' book was only laxly kept and is not a reliable guide to numbers, but there was probably a minimum of a few thousand visitors annually in the 1830s. On just four Fridays in August 1833, at least 120 parties – probably over 500 people – passed through the house. Visitors' Book, 1819–(46), Cobham MSS, U565/F/13/1.

8   Manchester's *Half-Holiday Hand-Book*, a twopenny guide to walks and rail excursions for clerks, first appeared in 1846. The *Saturday Half-Holiday Guide to London and the Environs* was not issued until 1868.

9   Pimlott, *Englishman's Holiday*, 82–4, 141–8; Cunningham, *Leisure*, 146–7.

10 The most prolific early *Handbook* writers were G. P. Bevan, a Welsh industrialist, W. E. Flaherty, a printer and popular history writer, and, most prolific of all, R. J. King, essentially a professional local-history and travel-writer, who covered eighteen counties for Murray. Clerics, the bane of the *Little Guides*, were noticeably absent until later. I am very grateful to W. G. Lister Esq., for sharing with me his encyclopedic knowledge of the *Handbooks* and their authors.

11 Montagu, *Gilt and the Gingerbread*, 19; *Historic Houses* (1971), 5–6; Harris, 'Country House Guides', 69–70; Girouard, *Victorian Country House*, 15; Kenworthy-Brown, 'Private Houses', 10; Stone, *An Open Elite?*, 327–8, and 'Public and the Private', 249–50.

12 Tinniswood, *Country-House Visiting*, 137–50, is very good on the rise of mass visiting, but later draws a straight line between mid-nineteenth- and mid-twentieth-century heritage industries; Ousby, *Englishman's England*, 87–91, makes the same argument in a more perfunctory way.

13 *Murray's, Kent and Sussex*, 1863 edn, 344–5. The inaccessibility of the Ashburnham collections again became an issue when the Royal Commission on Historical Manuscripts began to report in the 1870s. See below, pp. 156–7.

14 Nevill, *English Country House Life*, 134.

15 Hall, *Baronial Halls*, unpag.

16 *Daily Telegraph*, 23 Dec. 1871, leader, 4–5.

17 Elizabeth Ernst Journal, 7 Sept. 1845, Ernst of Westcombe MSS, DD/SWD.

18 As Jessica Gerard points out, even modern houses in full residential use were frequently left to a skeleton staff in the London Season. Gerard, *Country House Life*, 36.

19 *Murray's, Durham and Northumberland*, 1864 edn, 59–62; Hall and Jewitt, *Stately Homes*, 2nd ser., 258–

63, including same quote from *Murray's*.

20 Arthur Griffiths, 'Lumley Castle', *Magazine of Art*, Nov. 1880, 1–5.

21 Roberts, *Radical Countess*, 24.

22 Gower, *Reminiscences*, II, 15.

23 Dugdale, *Family Homespun*, 102–3.

24 Lord Alfred Churchill to the *Illustrated London News*, repr. in *The Times*, 27 Oct. 1857, 6.

25 Nevill, *English Country House Life*, 132–6.

26 Burn, *Age of Equipoise*, gives the classic account of this complex process; Hilton, *Age of Atonement*, is the latest word.

27 For some servants' reactions, see Dugdale, *Family Homespun*, 102–3, and Harley, *Gardener at Chatsworth*, 110, 116.

28 Oldfield, *Later Life of Countess Granville*, 161. My thanks to Eeyan Hartley for this reference.

29 Rae, *Business of Travel*, 37–9. This was the 5th Duke. His son, the 6th Duke (from 1857), was a painter and unusually interested in his houses as art objects; he did much to attract public interest to Haddon. See Duchess of Rutland, *Collected Writings*, I, 342–3.

30 See also Sir Joseph Paxton's account of the 'orderly, quiet . . . awe-struck' crowds at Chatsworth, in *PP* (1854), XIV, 173, testimony before Commons Select Committee on Public Houses.

31 *Daily Telegraph*, 23 Dec. 1871, leader, 4–5.

32 *The Times*, 21 Dec. 1871, leader, 7.

33 See, below, pp. 102–6, for further discussion of the Warwick Castle restoration controversy from which much of this commentary derives, for evidence of some Radical positions.

34 'My Excursion Agent', *All the Year Round*, 7 May 1864, 301–4; see also similar sentiments in 1853 by Joseph Sturge and Harriet Beecher Stowe in Stowe, *Sunny Memories*, 175–6.

35 *Yorkshire Gazette*, 29 July 1865, 5; Portland, *Men Women and Things*, 350–51.

36 Bailey, *Leisure and Class*, 27–8, 93–7; Cunningham, *Leisure in the Industrial Revolution*, 81–3, 88–95, 151–7.

37 In *The Princess*.

38 Jewitt and Hall, *Stately Homes*, 1–3, slightly misquoting Tennyson. Escott, *England*, ii, 56–8 assumes that by the late 1870s aristocratic parks were open routinely and the guidebook evidence bears him out.

39 *Murray's, Shropshire, Cheshire and Lancs.*, 1870 edn, 107–8. Also *Half-Holiday Hand-Book* and *Saturday Half-Holiday Guide* for Manchester and London parks.

40 Mitford, *Ladies of Alderley*, 99–100.

41 On Hagley, see *National Sunday League Record*, Aug. 1858, 277–8.

42 A selection from these notebooks has been recently published as Loudon, *In Search of English Gardens*. Similar expressions of polite interest in classical houses can still be found in élite periodicals like the *New Monthly Magazine* in the 1830s.

43 Steegman, *Victorian Taste*, 56–61, 70–74; Hale, *England and the Italian Renaissance*, 111–19, 157–71. On polite visiting to art galleries in aristocratic town houses, see Waterfield, 'Town House as Gallery'.

44 House Money Account, 1822–7, giving account of tips left for servants showing the house, with memorandum from Lord Pembroke to his housekeeper, 6 Jan. 1827: Wilton MSS, A5/37.

45 Wardour Castle Visitors' Book, 1844–1902, Old Castle Visitors' Book, 1879–1904: Wardour Castle MSS, 2667; *Murray's, Wilts., Dorset, Somerset*, 1856 edn, 74, 76–8.

46 'Oxoniensis' in *The Times*, 29 Oct. 1856, 8; Green, *Blenheim*, 199–200.

47 *Murray's, Kent, Sussex*, 1863 edn, 350–55.

48 Visitors' Books, 1805–10, 1852–65, 1866–74: Sackville MSS, E19/1–4. Numbers of dubious accuracy before the late 1860s, after which point the size of parties is meticulously reported.

49 Charles Lines, 'The Story of Opening Houses to the Public', *Historic Houses* (1971), 5–6.

50 Visitors' Books, 1825–6, 1834–9, 1843–61: Warwick Castle MSS, uncatalogued; except for the earliest volume, not reliable records of numbers. Stowe, *Sunny Memories*, 175.

51 'Warwick Castle: Its Past Glory and Present Desolation', *Royal Leamington Spa Courier*, 9 Dec. 1871, 4; 'Leamington and Warwick Castle', ibid., 20 Jan. 1872, 4. The Corporation of Hastings intervened to secure the continued opening of Battle Abbey after it changed hands in 1857. Nevill, *English Country House Life*, 132–3.

52 *Historical and Descriptive Guide to Warwick Castle*, 1877 edn; see also the photographs in Warwick Castle MSS.

53 Henry James, 'In Warwickshire' (1877), repr. in *English Hours*, 124.

54 'Cook's Excursions under Personal Escort. Europe, Season 1889', brochure in Thomas Cook Travel Archive.

55 Visitors' Books, 1837–58, Burghley House; these numbers must represent minima.

56 Visitors' Book, 1844–68, Temple Newsam House; this book was very badly kept and is not a reliable source even for minimum numbers.

57 Howitt, *Visits*, 308.

58 Richard Grant White, 'The Heart of England', *The Galaxy*, July 1877, 118–19.

59 E.g. Burke, *Visitation of the Seats*, i, i–ii; see its citation by Tinniswood, *Country-House Visiting*, 149–50, who also uses the accounts of visits by the York Tourist Society, a body of Tory councillors and their friends.

60 Knight, *Excursion Companion*, pt xiv, 7.

61 George O'Malley Irwin to Lord Salisbury, 9 Aug. 1870: Hatfield MSS, N2.

62 Visitors' Book, 1835–44: Eaton MSS, 962. See also the report by F. L.

Olmsted, the future designer of New York's Central Park, of his visit to Eaton in 1850 while the house was actually under reconstruction: *Walks and Talks*, 137–9.

63 Visitors' Books, 1854–69; 'Rules & Regulations for Shewing the Hall & Gardens', May 1845, with House-Showing Accounts, 1845, 1854–6; House-Showing Accounts, 1858–95: Eaton MSS, 962–3, 958–9.

64 *Murray's, Shropshire, Cheshire and Lancs.*, 1870 edn, 138.

65 *Buildings of England, Cheshire*, 208–9; Girouard, *Victorian Country House*, 2–4; House-Showing Accounts, 1858–95: Eaton MSS, 959; F. Selwood, Eaton Gardener, to [T. Speed, Chatsworth Gardener], 24 Sept. 1883: Chatsworth MSS, AS/890.

66 *Baedeker's Great Britain*, 1887 edn, 278–9.

67 Excursions to Chatsworth amply described by Joseph Paxton to the Commons Select Committee on Public Houses, *PP* (1854), XIV, 172–4, by the Chatsworth gardener Robert Aughtie in his diary, 1848–50, published as Harley, *Gardener at Chatsworth*, and by Revd A. H. Malan, 'Chatsworth', *Pall Mall Magazine*, Feb. 1897, 169–83.

68 Rae, *Business of Travel*, 37–9; Jewitt and Hall, *Stately Homes*, 2nd ser., 2–3, 18; *Historic Houses*, 227–8.

69 *Murray's, Lincs.*, 1890 edn, 13–15.

70 'P', 'Through the Derbyshire Peak District. III. Hassop to Darley', *Cook's Excursionist and Tourist Advertiser*, 27 July 1867, 2–3.

71 *Murray's, Derbys., Notts., Leics. and Staffs.*, 1868 edn, 166–9; Sarah to James Paxton, 5 July 1854: Paxton MSS, 1252.

72 *Stranger's Guide to Alton*, 21–4; Jewitt, *Guide to Alton Towers*, 36–40; *Cook's Excursionist*, 15 May 1869, 3.

73 *Historic Houses*, 6–10.

74 *Official Guide to Aston*, 1858 edn; *Handbook to Aston Hall*, 1871 edn; Aston Hall and Park Co., *Report of the Investigation Committee*; Whitworth Wallis, 'Aston Hall', *English Illustrated Magazine*, Aug. 1889, 776–84; O'Neill, *How Aston Hall and Park Were Saved*; Fairclough, *Grand Old Mansion*, 119–20.

75 Maidstone Corporation had acquired part of sixteenth-century Chillington Manor House as a museum in 1857, but the wings remained in private occupation until purchased 1868–70. Chillington had long been wholly absorbed by the town and was owned by a physician-antiquarian, who, until his death in 1855, used it for his offices and to house his private collection, which was then bequeathed to the Corporation. See *Notes on the History of Chillington*, a reference I owe to Giles Waterfield. A few other municipalities acquired mansions in other ways. Nottingham leased the shell of Nottingham Castle from the Duke of Newcastle in 1878; appropriately, the castle had been burnt by a Nottingham mob agitating for the franchise in 1831. For other early examples as well as the more common post-1918 acquisitions, see below, pp. 170–71 and 256–8.

76 Evans, *History of the Society of Antiquaries*, 310–12.

77 'Stowe', *London Journal*, 9 Sept. 1848, 1–3.

78 *The Times*, 21 Dec. 1871, 7.

79 John Ruskin, letters to the editor, *Daily Telegraph*, 22 Dec. 1871, 5: 25 Dec. 1871, 3.

80 See also below, pp. 156–9, for early and tentative moves after 1867 to recognize the 'national' characteristics of historic property: the first Ancient Monuments bills and the work of the Royal Commission on Historic Manuscripts.

81 C. N. Newdegate to Earl of Warwick, 12 Jan. 1872: Warwick Castle MSS, 631; leader, *Birmingham Daily Post*, 27 Dec. 1871, 4; 'Restoration of Warwick Castle', *Birmingham Daily Post*, 9 Jan. 1872, 6; a similar line to Jaffray's is taken by the more radical *Leamington and Warwickshire Chronicle*, e.g. 23 Dec. 1871, 5; 30 Dec. 1871, 5.

82 Leader, *Daily Telegraph*, 23 Dec. 1871, 4–5.

83 Sir Coutts Lindsay, letter to the editor, *The Times*, 2 Jan. 1872, 4.

84 In fact, Joseph Arch, the founder of the South Warwickshire agricultural labourers' union and later of the national union, was of a family of Warwick Castle estate workers. Horn, *Joseph Arch*, 3.

85 Lord Somers to Earl of Warwick, 29 Jan 1872: Warwick Castle MSS, 631.

86 Richard Grant White, 'The Heart of England', *The Galaxy*, July 1877, 118–19.

87 Cobham, which had charged since around 1830 and Blenheim, which began in 1856, were also seeking to limit numbers; Eaton (1854) and Wilton (c.1870) were raising money for charity. I know of no other houses that charged a prescribed fee before the 1870s.

## CHAPTER 3

1 Wiener, *English Culture*, has become with amazing speed the orthodox view; the coincidence of its publication (1981) with the Thatcherite critique of English backwardness may account for some of its influence, but its view has been endorsed by cultural pessimists on the Left, e.g. many of the contributors to Colls and Dodd, *Englishness* (1986) and Samuel, *Patriotism* (1989), Boyes, *Imagined Village* (1993), and most recently an undergraduate sourcebook, Giles and Middleton, *Writing Englishness*.

2 Strong, *And when did you last?*, 74–5.

3 Gillett, *Victorian Painter's World*, 12–17, 192–4.

4 For some attempts to quantify, see ch. 5.

5 Wiener, *English Culture*, 178–9, gives some examples and adds to them; cf. 70, where political opposition to preservationism is made to seem trivial.

6 Altick, *English Common Reader*, 365.

7 Collins, 'English Art Magazines', 200–4, on the displacement of the general illustrated magazines by specialist publications.

8 Klancher, *English Reading Audiences*, 79–81, considers that this 'bricolage' style typified popular journalism from the beginning, e.g. in Limbird's *Mirror*. This may be true of Limbird and to some extent of Knight, but in ch. 3 I have tried to show patterns in their mosaic that do not exist in *Cassell's* or (*a fortiori*) in late Victorian popular journalism.

9 Cruse, *After the Victorians*, 206–14.

10 Altick, 'From Aldine to Everyman', 181–4; Cruse, *After the Victorians*, 225–36.

11 Williams, *Culture and Society*, 126.

12 One can find occasional usages of the word 'heritage' in something like its modern sense in the nineteenth century, but this usage – referring to physical things belonging to the nation by virtue of their connection to national history – does not become regular until after the First World War. 'National heritage' was a copulation of the 1930s; the first usage I have found is from a *Country Life* leader of 1930.

13 Wiener, *English Culture*, 43.

14 Much of the nation-building that Linda Colley documents in the eighteenth century as culminating in an idea of Britain in the Napoleonic Wars was, I think, undermined by peace and the anti-aristocratic reaction after 1815, but resumed with international aggression in the late 1890s.

15 Chancellor, *History for their Masters*, 70–75. Of the 108 schoolbooks listed by Chancellor as in use in the nineteenth century, only three referred to Britain rather than England in their title (and these three were published in 1874, 1875 and 1904).

16 Cruse, *After the Victorians*, 215–18; Harris, *Private Lives, Public Spirit*, esp. 32–6.

17 Pimlott, *Englishman's Holiday*, 141–52.

18   Walton, *Seaside Resort*, 35–40.

19   Gower, *Reminiscences*, II, 15–17, offers a particularly rich example, since Gower mixed obsessive Italophilia with his fondness for the Olden Time.

20   Pimlott, *Englishman's Holiday*, 164–7.

21   See, e.g., the exploitation of the Cheshire countryside by urban trippers in the 1890s, interestingly described by Lee, *Social Leaders*. Closer attention needs to be paid to mass leisure in the countryside; too often it is assumed, e.g. by Walker, 'Outdoor Movement', that rural leisure remained an élite phenemonon until the First World War.

22   Clifton-Taylor, 'Architectural Touring with the Little Guides', is almost the only serious treatment of domestic guide-books. See below, p. 145, for further comment on the aesthetic politics of the *Little Guides*.

23   Arnold, *Culture and Anarchy*, 45, 63–4.

24   There is much controversy over the extent of indebtedness before the agricultural depression – did a real crisis begin as early as 1830, as David Spring has argued, or even earlier, as suggested by H. J. Habakkuk? But proponents of the late crisis view, such as F. M. L. Thompson and David Cannadine, designate the agricultural depression as the turning-point from which there could be no recovery.

25   Spring, 'Landowners, Lawyers, and Land Law Reform', 54.

26   C. J. Cornish, 'The Cost of Country Houses', *Cornhill Magazine*, n.s., 2 (1897), 474–86.

27   The few other American purchases fall strictly speaking beyond our remit: William Randolph Hearst bought St Donat's Castle in Wales, and sporting estates in Scotland were purchased by a Winans, a Vanderbilt and a Carnegie.

28   Adonis, 'Aristocracy, Agriculture and Liberalism', 876, 883. Habakkuk, *Marriage, Debt, and the Estates System*, 673, gives further examples.

29   'Truly golf has a stately home!' wrote *Country Life*, 'A Palace as Club-House', 16 June 1906, 882, but seems to have muddled up Eltham Lodge and nearby Eltham Palace, a former royal hunting lodge with a fifteenth-century great hall. I owe the reference to Camden Place to an anonymous reader for the Press.

30   Both cases are discussed by Trainor, 'Peers on an Industrial Frontier', 75, 116–7.

31   Jacks, *Great Houses of Nottinghamshire*, 179–85; E. M. Middleton, 'Wollaton Hall', *Pall Mall Magazine*, 22 (Sept.–Dec. 1900), 163–4.

32   S. A. Byles, 'Temple Newsam, and its Art Collection', *Magazine of Art*, 1893, 208–14. As was often the case, the heiresses through whom Temple Newsam passed were more attached to the house than were their husbands, who made the decisions about residence and sale.

33   Thompson, *English Landed Estate*, 314.

34   The family's only other great estate, at Jervaulx Abbey in Yorkshire, had already been sold. For further on the Savernake estate, see Earl of Cardigan, *Wardens of Savernake Forest*, 311–39.

35   Thompson, *English Landed Estate*, 320–21.

36   Revd W. H. Hutton, 'Compton Winyates', *Cornhill Magazine*, n.s., 15 (1903), 135–6. Improvements had already been made from 1867.

37   Surtees, *Artist and the Autocrat*, 118–19.

38   This argument – falsely applied to mid-Victorian houses, as has been shown in ch. 2 – only begins to bite in the 1880s; see ch. 5.

39   Sale of heirlooms – chattels – under the Settled Land Act 1882 required a court order, which sale of land did not, but the monies derived from the sale of heirlooms were thereafter more fully at the disposal of the vendor than the monies derived from the sale of land. Lewin, *Law of Trusts*, 8th edn, 566–7. In other words,

40 'The Hamilton Palace Sale, with Notes on Art Sales Generally', *Arts and Letters*, 1 (Aug.–Sept. 1882), 320–27, 335–42. The author was probably J. Comyns Carr.

41 On book sales, see A. N. L. Munby, 'The Library', in Strong, Binney and Harris, *Destruction of the Country House*, 106–10; on sales of paintings and *objets d'art*, see n. 42, below.

42 Reitlinger, *Economics of Taste*, I, 175–204: II, 136–54; also Cannadine, *Decline and Fall*, 113–15, noting that many of these sales emptied London town houses and not country houses.

43 An exception was the brief vogue for English eighteenth-century portraiture among the American millionaires. More typical was the way in which prices of eighteenth-century English furniture lagged behind eighteenth-century French furniture before 1914. Reitlinger, *Economics of Taste*, I, 191; II, 154.

44 Munby, 'The Library', 108–9.

45 Minihan, *Nationalization of Culture*, 158.

46 Countess-Dowager of Radnor, *From a Great-Grandmother's Armchair*, 176–84.

47 This was urged both by the friends and the enemies of the country gentlemen; see, e.g., 'The Coming Fate of Country Gentlemen', *Spectator*, 9 Sept. 1882, 1160–61, and the debate over 'Where are the Village Gentry?', *Nineteenth Century and After*, 51 (1902), 149–59, 411–28.

48 For this illustration, and the general point about aristocratic detachment from local roots, see the excellent treatment by Lee, *Social Leaders*, 42 and *passim*.

49 Lieven, *Aristocracy in Europe*, 152–8.

50 Shaw, 'Heartbreak House and Horseback Hall', intro. to *Heartbreak House* (1919), 1964 edn, 9.

51 Cruse, *After the Victorians*, 208–14.

52 As reported by Henry Channon in Rhodes James, *Channon Diaries*, 376.

53 Cecil, *Cecils of Hatfield*, 221, 240.

Salisbury's reference to Philistia may not have been generic, but specifically an allusion to Grant Allen's 1884 novel of that title, a spirited quasi-Arnoldian diatribe against aristocratic philistinism.

54 An argument made, e.g., by the *Estates Gazette*, 24 May 1913, 868; see also the young Virginia Stephen's ironic comment on the supposed value of country-house life in Woolf, 'Memoir of Lady Dorothy Nevill', 179.

55 Escott, *Society in the Country House* (1907), *passim*, quote from pp. 484–5. This was a longstanding theme for Escott; cf. his *England* (1879), II, 56–8. Another early and influential conceptualization of the country house in these terms (but with more intellectual content) is W. H. Mallock's *The New Republic*, subtitled 'Culture, Faith and Philosophy in an English Country House' (1877).

56 This paragraph is based on a survey of country-house articles in such late-century publications as the *Graphic*, the *Sketch* (e.g. its series 'Beautiful British Homes'), and the *English Illustrated Magazine* (e.g. 'Historic Homes of England' in the 1890s, which opened with the Duke of Connaught's Bagshot Park, built in the 1870s!). Even the *Illustrated London News*, long a leading exponent of the Olden Time sense of heritage (and a bastion against photography), ran a series on country houses in the late 1880s and early 1890s, pointedly entitled 'English Homes', which skewed the content towards the achievements of the current occupants.

57 Affectionate, chatty profiles of their country homes by noble ladies were common from the 1880s onwards. See, e.g., the Duchess of Rutland on Belvoir in *English Illustrated Magazine*, 10 (1892–3), 804–10, 932–8, Lady Middleton on Wollaton in *Pall Mall Magazine*, 22 (1900), 148–64; further sketches from the *English Illustrated* were collected by Elizabeth

Balch in *Glimpses of Old English Homes* (1890), and from the *Pall Mall* by A. H. Malan in *Famous Homes of Great Britain* (1900) and *More Famous Homes* (1902). These sketches, unlike the mid-Victorian periodical literature, were rarely if ever connected to public access or visiting – they were, like the profiles discussed in the preceding note, about private houses, though with a slightly higher aesthetic content.

58 Surtees, *Coutts Lindsay.*

59 The most personal treatment is Henley, *Rosalind*, but see also Roberts, *Radical Countess*, and Surtees, *Artist and the Autocrat.*

60 The best recent account of the Souls, from which I draw my impressions, is Lambert, *Unquiet Souls*; see esp. 132–6 for their relationship to their houses.

61 Alsop, *Lady Sackville*, 114–16.

62 For which see Dakers, *Clouds*, esp. ch. 2 (for the world of the aesthetic aristocrat – the Howards' circle – c.1870) and ch. 7 (ditto – the Souls – c.1900).

63 Abdy and Gere, *Souls*, 118–19, 121, noting the contrast with Clouds; Dakers, *Clouds*, 247–9.

64 Conway, *Episodes in a Varied Life*, 103–4; see also Conway's defence of his restorationism in his article on Brinsop Court in *Country Life*, 7 Nov. 1914, 614–22. There is an interesting discussion of the Souls' influence on later restorationism in Cornforth, *Inspiration of the Past*, 20–25; the subject is taken up again below, ch. 6.

65 See below, pp. 184–91, for discussion of the Tattershall Castle affair and subsequent debates over preservation legislation. Another Soul who took a public position in favour of historic preservation was George Wyndham, who characterized country houses as virtual 'local museums'; see below, pp. 167–8.

66 Cornforth, *Search for a Style*, 94; Cooper, *Autobiography*, 64.

67 It is, indeed, the continuing prestige of this criticism that prevents scholars even a century later from taking the Victorian idea of heritage seriously: see Roy Strong's complaint, voiced with regard to Victorian history painting in *And when did you last see your father?* some fifteen years ago, and hardly noticed.

68 On links between Pre-Raphaelitism and architecture, see Girouard, *Sweetness and Light*, 13–15.

69 Girouard, *Victorian Country House*, 67.

70 Saint, *Norman Shaw*, 25–6, 32. See also Marks, *Life and Letters of Walker*, 122–5, for the magnetic attraction these little colonies exerted on other painters but also for the financial hurdles they presented.

71 Saint, *Norman Shaw*, 32–4.

72 See, for instance, the parallel designs of George Devey which sprang out of his work for the De L'Isles at Penshurst from around 1848. Allibone, *Devey*, 27–41, 77.

73 Burnand, *Happy Thoughts*, 162–92. Cf. Stacy Marks's account of the summer in *Pen and Pencil Sketches*, I, 162–9; Smith, *Art and Anecdote*, 160–63; also Hillier, 'St John's Wood Clique'.

74 E.g. Burnand's *Happy-Thought Hall* (1872), this time lampooning a winter house-party in an Elizabethan house with 'a fine collection of moths', mildew, mice, rats and ghosts.

75 Gillett, *Victorian Painter's World*, 16–17, 78.

76 Thompson, *Morris*, 173–4.

77 Adam, *Mrs Carr's Reminiscences*, 172–3.

78 On Limpsfield and the intellectual migration in general, see Marsh, *Back to the Land*, 28–31.

79 Letter to E. R. Robson, 1862, quoted by Girouard, *Sweetness and Light*, 15.

80 For some scholarly parallels, see Burrow, '"The Village Community"'. But historians' sense of the usefulness of the past – and, as Burrow demonstrates, their own

81 An early version of this narrative can be found in Stevenson, *House Architecture* (1880), e.g., I, 16–17, 21, 71–6, 163–82, and esp. 284–348, establishing the pedigree both of Old English for rural and Queen Anne for urban architecture. Stevenson is relatively undogmatic; as a professional architect, he also resists the worship of the craftsman which is to come; a generation later, the same narrative has been fossilized, e.g. in Ditchfield, *Manor Houses of England*, 28–36, which builds on Stevenson.

82 Howard, 'Painters' Preferred Places', offers a statistical analysis of the trend at the Royal Academy shows towards depiction of lowland, esp. in southern England, from the last quarter of the nineteenth century.

83 The importance of proximity to the metropolis is evident across a wide range of sources, including Escott's *Society in the English Country House* (where houses further afield are not discussed because they lack a 'stately present'), the tourist writings of Allan Fea and J. J. Hissey and the obsession with the Cotswolds of the Arts and Crafts movement proper.

84 Stevenson, *House Architecture*, 69.

85 Hissey, *Untravelled England*, 443; Fea, *Picturesque Old Houses*, 144–6.

86 *Our Own Country*, III, 179.

87 *Historic Houses*, 198.

88 Clifton-Taylor, 'Architectural Touring with the Little Guides', 246–9.

89 Ditchfield, *Vanishing England*, 176–8; also his *Manor-Houses of England*, 3–6.

90 Fea, *Picturesque Old Houses*, 188; Revd W. H. Hutton, 'Compton Winyates', *Cornhill Magazine*, n.s., 15 (1903), 135–6.

91 Fea, *Recollections*, 190–92.

92 Ibid., for Fea's own story; his early manor-house sketches are collected in *English Country Nooks and Old Storied Houses* (1886), which had

appeared originally in *The Tourist and Traveller* (writing as 'The Antiquarian Tourist' and 'Wanderer') and in his own journal, *The Antiquary*. See also his later collection, *Picturesque Old Houses* (1902).

93 See the works of Fletcher Moss, a Manchester city councillor and antiquarian, e.g. *Pilgrimages in Cheshire and Shropshire* (1901) and *Pilgrimages to Old Homes* (1903).

94 Moss, *Pilgrimages to Old Homes*, 218; 'Little Morton Hall', *Country Life*, 23 April 1904, 504.

95 Ditchfield, *Vanishing England*, 5, 7.

96 *Spectator*, 17 Aug. 1901, 220–21 (reviewing one of Moss's volumes); Fea, *Picturesque Old Houses*, 75–6.

97 Fea, *Recollections*, 115–16, 169–71, 262–3.

98 Cornforth, *Search for a Style*, 13–20, 50–2, 58; Christopher Hussey, 'The Late H. Avray Tipping, Gardener and Antiquary', *Country Life*, 25 Nov. 1933, 567–8.

99 'Castle Howard', *Country Life*, 13 Feb. 1904, 234–42.

100 See, for instance, a kind of policy statement by C. J. Cornish (who wrote some of the profiles before Tipping monopolized them), 'In English Homes', *Country Life*, 11 June 1904, 870–74. Cornish praises the 'far more catholic appreciation of architecture' characteristic of his day, pays homage to Wren and Adams (sic), but still conventionally depreciates 'formal and rather dead classicism' and dwells upon the English vernacular tradition. A similar bias is evident in Tipping's collection of profiles, *English Homes of the Early Renaissance* (1912).

101 Muthesius, *English House*, 60, 124–6, 194–6.

102 Tillyard, *Impact of Modernism*, 36–40.

103 Blomfield, *Short History of Renaissance Architecture*, 298–303; see also Girouard, *Sweetness and Light*, 224–7, stimulating on the fragmentation of the Arts and Crafts influenced styles.

104 Hissey, *English Holiday with Car and Camera*, 4–5. *Untravelled England*

(1906) was the first of Hissey's motor-tours.

105   See ch. 7.

106   Marsh, *Back to the Land*, 148. See, further, MacCarthy, *Simple Life*.

107   Muthesius, *English House*, 27–30, 195–6. It is thus doubly misleading to use Muthesius to characterize the Edwardian period as 'an age of nostalgia and romantic patriotism, of yearning for the old ways of rural life and for the old manners of building', as does Cornforth, *Search for a Style*, 14–15, 18–19. Muthesius thought the Arts and Crafts style was popular only so long as it remained modern-minded; when it retreated into nostalgia, it lost its public support.

## CHAPTER 4

1   Baldwin Brown, *Care of Ancient Monuments*, esp. 24–7, 31–2, 148–52.

2   Arguments for the ubiquity of her-itage consciousness in this period often hinge on the claim that they were evident 'across the ideological spectrum', but on examination this appears to mean each point on the spectrum had its tiny, impotent aes-thetic minority – in addition to the usually far more culturally and politi-cally significant philistine majority; see, e.g., Wiener, *English Culture*, *passim*, providing the material for Boyes, *Imagined Country*, 63, 65, 86 n. 4, or Lowenthal, *Past is a Foreign Country*, 103–5, but with a *caveat* at xxvi.

3   Evans, *Our Old Nobility*, 1907 edn, 228–9.

4   Evans, *Radical Fights*.

5   This new Radicalism was at first inspired as much by Henry George's hostility to rent as by any socialist hostility to profit. It also drew on an older critique of landed wealth as deriving from spoliation and taxa-tion, which had not however made much of an impact on Parliamentary politics before 1867. See Offer, *Prop-erty and Politics*, ch. 12, for one dis-cussion. I leave aside here the debate over whether Radicalism's goal in taxing land was to reduce total taxa-tion or to raise new revenue.

6   Levine, *Amateur and the Professional*, 119–21.

7   *Hansard*, 3rd ser., 232: 1542 [7 March 1877]. The same argument was made with reference to a country house, i.e. Byron's Newstead Abbey. See also Earl De La Warr in ibid., 251: 784 [11 March 1880].

8   Chippendale, 'Making of the First Ancient Monuments Act', gives an excellent account of the genesis and implementation of the Act; see also Thompson, *Pitt-Rivers*, ch. 6.

9   Chippendale, 'Making of the First Ancient Monuments Act', 23, refuses to make this distinction, but a close analysis of the lists reveals it. Of the 24 non-registrants, 18 hailed from the landed gentry or peerage, but only 14 of 36 registrants. Some names figure in both lists.

10   Pitt-Rivers to George Payne, 20 Dec. 1895, quoted by Bowden, *Pitt-Rivers*, 99–100.

11   The Metropolitan Commons Act 1866 provided for regulatory schemes over commons around London, but was never implemented in defiance of the manorial lord; the Commons Acts 1876 and 1899 also retained the lord's veto and, by enabling local authorities to buy up commons, actually expedited land-lord compensation. A compulsory bill, introduced by the Liberals in 1871 and again in 1872, to block all further enclosure of common land was denounced as 'spoliation' by Lord Salisbury and thrown out by the Lords.

12   Eversley, *Commons, Forests and Foot-paths*; on the Ashridge escapade, see Inglis-Jones, *Augustus Smith*, 154–67. I owe a debt here to John Davis's unwritten paper, 'The Battle of Catford Heath'.

13   Offer, *Property and Politics*, 332–48; Marsh, *Back to the Land*, 27–40.

14   Bassett, *Historical Records*, iv.

15 For some exaggerations of SPAB's importance, see Wright, *On Living in an Old Country*, 48–50; Dellheim, *Face of the Past*, 85; Tinniswood, *Country-House Visiting*, 167–8; Murray, 'Ancient Monuments Protection Act', 65–6; Lowenthal, *Past is a Foreign Country*, 104. An excellent corrective is now being provided in the work of Chris Miele, e.g. 'First Conservation Militants' and ' "A Small Knot of Cultivated People" '.

16 C. R. Peers (Chief Inspector of Ancient Monuments) to Lord Beauchamp, 23 Nov. 1912: PRO, WORK 14/1270.

17 Madsen, *Restoration and Anti-Restoration*, 92–103; Muthesius, 'Origins of the German Conservation Movement'; Denslagen, *Architectural Restoration*, esp. 142–4.

18 I do not attempt here a comprehensive survey of Radical views on taxation; for that, see Offer, *Property and Politics*, upon which I have relied selectively. My interest here is restricted to those portions of the Radical critique that fell on the landed estate, and particularly on houses and chattels. There is also an important deviation between the temper of Irish and Scottish radicalism – which retains a nationalist and 'historicist' flavour – and the English variety, for which see Dewey, 'Celtic Agrarian Legislation', though note (p. 68) that even in Scotland the 'virus of systematic selfishness' had undermined the Scottish crofters' historical feeling. Irish ancient monuments' legislation was for this reason more comprehensive.

19 'Re Knole Assessments: Particulars of Assessments of various large mansions taken from the valuation lists of the various parishes', Sackville MSS, U269/E375. The lowest value found was for the smaller Bedgebury at £403, the highest Cobham at £740. These valuations were undoubtedly low, but still above the extreme cases cited in the debate – Blenheim at virtually *nil* rateable value (its park of 2,400 acres rated at £2,580) and Beaufront Castle in Northumberland at only £84, whereas its smaller (more lettable) neighbour Stagshaw Close House at £220. *Hansard*, 3rd ser., 303: 1664–5 [23 March 1886].

20 For the status of the death duties before the estate duties of 1889 and 1894 were levied, see Buxton, *Finance and Politics*, II, 292–8.

21 For the extent of land under settlement, the latest estimate is by Offer, 'Farm tenure and land values', 10.

22 Value for succession duty was calculated by multiplying the annual rental value of the land by the numbers of years' life expectancy of the inheritor (calculated from a standard annuity table). Note again that 'rental value' of houses and parkland was generally quite low; Chatsworth was valued at £873 for purposes of succession duty in 1891. After 1889, there was another duty – Estate Duty – levied on all property in large estates, but only at 1 per cent. Thus, the valuation of Chatsworth house and park when the 7th Duke of Devonshire died in 1891 was £873 × 11 (life expectancy of the 8th Duke) = £9603 for succession duty, and £873 × $24\frac{2}{5}$ (the multiplier agreed for calculating land value from annual rental) = £21,313 for estate duty. The 8th Duke then paid £144 ($1\frac{1}{2}$ per cent succession duty) +£213 (1 per cent estate duty) = £357 total death duties on Chatsworth house and park. See 'Succession and Estate Duty on Chatsworth', annexed to Duke of Devonshire to Sir William Harcourt, 21 May 1894: Harcourt MSS, dep. 79, cf. copies in Chatsworth MSS, 8th Duke's ser. As far as I can tell, the Duke paid nothing at all on the contents of Chatsworth, which were treated as settled personalty with no effective value, although (unusually) the Devonshire estates were not under settlement. For this and the valuation of the agricultural estates,

see the 7th Duke's full death duty account in PRO, IR 59/151.

23 *Hansard*, 3rd ser., 303: 1686–7, 1696–8 [23 March 1886].

24 On Harcourt's motives and the technical details of his 1894 budget package, see Daunton, 'Politics of Harcourt's Budget'. Contemporary legal experts were in some doubt about whether a settled estate would be subject to Estate Duty, if the settlement were 'composite' – that is, broken and re-made at regular intervals, as was indeed the common practice in many landed families. As the principal legal expert put it, 'at the outset, Parliament seems to have found it impossible to avoid according a certain measure of favoured treatment to such property'. Soward, *Law and Practice of Estate Duty*, 4th edn, 56–7, 92–4. But the immediate problem for owners was that all settled property, including works of art, would be liable to Estate Duty at least *once* – at the first succession after 1894. Thus the pressure for exemption in 1896: see below, pp. 167–8.

25 'The Duke of Devonshire at Buxton', *The Times*, 14 June 1894, 7. Similar views had been expressed by Lord Arundell of Wardour in a letter to *The Times*, 15 May 1894, and were then echoed by, among others, the Conservative *Saturday Review*, 16 June 1894.

26 'The Democratic World', *Reynolds's Newspaper*, 24 June 1894, 3.

27 'Mr John Morley at Rotherham', *The Times*, 28 June 1894, 6. The same point was made by the Treasury official Sir Edward Hamilton, a friend of Devonshire's. Hamilton, *Diary*, 146.

28 *Hansard*, 4th ser., 26: 733–4 [2 July 1894].

29 'The Duke of Marlborough Again', *Reynolds's Newspaper*, 1 June 1884, 5. The occasion was the purchase of twelve pictures for the National Gallery from one of the early Blenheim sales.

30 *Hansard*, 4th ser., 26: 1349–50 [10 July 1894]; also 4th ser., 26: 729–30, 732 [2 July 1894]. This was a fairly common Liberal argument. See, also, 'Hamilton Palace Sale', *Arts and Letters* (1882), 320; A. Birrell in *Hansard*, 4th ser., 42: 995–6 [7 July 1896].

31 Leader, *Daily Chronicle*, 16 June 1894, 4.

32 The exemption, as finally formulated, covered objects of national, historical or scientific interest bequeathed to universities, local authorities or national institutions.

33 See ch. 5 on the extent of country-house access in this period.

34 *Hansard*, 4th ser., 26: 726–36, 1344–57, 1361–72, 1381–8 [2, 10 July 1894]. The only direct representative of a great house to intervene was Lord Cranborne, son of the Tory leader Lord Salisbury, who, like Devonshire, was rather proud of Hatfield's history of accessibility and rather more artistically minded than his father.

35 Alsop, *Lady Sackville*, 122–3.

36 Even Milner at the Inland Revenue was surprised by the very large amounts collected on settled personalty in the first year of operation of the new Estate Duty. He had under-estimated how well heirlooms had evaded duty under the old system: Alfred Milner to Sir Michael Hicks-Beach, 'Finance Act 1894. Experience of the first year of the new Estate Duty', 12 Aug. 1895, PRO, IR 74/2; Alfred Milner to Sir William Harcourt, 9 Feb. 1894: Harcourt MSS, dep. 70.

37 *Hansard*, 4th ser., 39: 1079–80 [16 April 1896]; 42: 988–1001, 1494–1501 [7, 14 July 1896].

38 Soward, *Law and Practice of Estate Duty*, 4th edn, 35–6.

39 Alsop, *Lady Sackville*, 144, 226, 241.

40 PRO, WORK 14/132, 135, for Office of Works' attitude, 1892–1900, and Lord Beauchamp's prefatory memorandum to Report of the Inspector of Ancient Monuments for

the Year Ending 31 Mar. 1911, *PP* (1911), x.

41  Dellheim, *Face of the Past*, 106.

42  Local authorities had been permitted to acquire buildings for museums since the Museums Act 1845, an early Radical victory. See Minihan, *Nationalization of Culture*, 90–93. The major historic buildings acquired before the First World War by local authorities, mostly for this purpose, were: Chillington Manor House (Maidstone, 1857–70, used as museum), Aston Hall (Birmingham, 1864, used as museum), Nottingham Castle (the shell of a Georgian building in the middle of the city, bought for municipal purposes, 1878), Clifton Park (Rotherham, 1893, incidental to park, used as museum), Abington (Northampton, 1894, Olden Time manor house, used as museum), Hall-in-th'-Wood (Bolton, 1900, used as museum), Heaton Hall (Manchester, 1902, incidental to park, used as museum), Towneley Hall (Burnley, 1902, incidental to park, used as museum), Marble Hill House (London County Council, 1902, incidental to park).

43  Joint Select Committee on Ancient Monuments Consolidation and Amendment Bill, *PP* (1912–13), VI, 428.

44  On Kirkstall and the argument for SPAB's provincial influence, see Dellheim, *Face of the Past*, 94–110; the Ruskinian influence detected in the *Birmingham Daily Post*'s comment, p. 107, is there, but builds on Birmingham's pre-Ruskinian heritage consciousness, already in place during the Aston Hall episode; Dellheim's second case study, on the medieval churches of York, 112–29, gives little evidence of local feeling.

45  H. Avray Tipping, 'Heaton Park, Lancs., II', *Country Life*, 5 Sept. 1925, 358–60.

46  *Heaton Park, Manchester: Official Handbook* (1928), 11; *Buildings of England, South Lancs.*, 265, 328.

47  The Bromley Palace agitation was whipped up by C. R. Ashbee, a follower of William Morris who had founded the Guild of Handicraft in 1888. It led to the establishment of the Committee for the Survey of the Memorials of Greater London, a combination of watchdog and documentary body, which published the monumental *Survey of London* in many volumes from 1900. The Bromley Palace Room joined its Olden Time predecessor at the V&A, the 'Inlaid Chamber' from Sizergh Castle.

48  Westminster had broken with the Liberals over Home Rule, but remained a Liberal Unionist. On the early years of the Trust, see Gaze, *Figures in a Landscape*, chs 1–3; Jenkins and James, *From Acorn to Oak Tree*, chs 1–2; Waterson, *National Trust*, chs 1–2, the latter offering most detail on Hill and Hunter's preparatory efforts.

49  State powers were so feeble that little conflict of interest was felt between State and Trust until after the Second World War. For early promotion of preservationist legislation on a continental model, see Executive Committee Minutes, 10 June, 1 Dec. 1897: National Trust MSS; the Trust was also active in promoting legislation after the Tattershall Castle affair, for which see below, p. 187.

50  The comparison was made by government in the 1930s, when the disparity had widened further. See below, pp. 238–9.

51  Not until the 1920s did *any* landowners see the National Trust as a means of sheltering themselves from rising taxation under the cloak of culture, and this was the view of only a small minority until the 1950s. It is a mistake to backdate postwar development to the Trust's early years, as do Offer, *Property and Politics*, 342; Wright, *On Living in an Old Country*, 50–53; Cannadine, *Decline and Fall*, 369.

52  This was still evident as late as the Second World War, when land-

53 owners complained that the Trust was substituting for private ownership: see below, pp. 322–3. As an example of early doubts, see the Duchess of Cleveland's objections recorded in Executive Committee Minutes, 17 Feb. 1897: National Trust MSS.

53 See, e.g., the debate over landed absenteeism in *The Nineteenth Century and After*, 51 (1902), 149–59, 411–20.

54 E.g. Shaw's *Major Barbara* (1905) and the first chapters of Wells's *Tono-Bungay* (1909); also Hilaire Belloc, *Emmanuel Burden* (1904). On the other side, society novels celebrating Britain's 'government of country house' were on the decline; Mrs Humphry Ward, this genre's greatest exponent, wrote her 'last significant work of fiction' in 1904. Sutherland, *Mrs Humphry Ward*, 242.

55 Wells's attitudes here were, however, highly complex; his hatred of the servant's condition, as he experienced it when visiting his mother at Uppark, warred with his admiration for the rationalism of the eighteenth-century, represented for him by Uppark's classical proportions and encyclopedic library. See West, *H. G. Wells*, 155–70, 225–7, 283–4. Gill, *Happy Rural Seat*, 101–8, treats Wells's country houses rather too monolithically as centres of civilization.

56 *The Island Pharisees* (1904), *The Country House* (1907) and *The Patricians* (1911); Masterman, *Condition of England*, 49–52; see also the discussions in Gill, *Happy Rural Seat*, 115–20, and Kelsall, *Great Good Place*, 159–60, which are too ready to assume that the critique of country-house owners 'emptied' the house of social meaning and made it accessible as 'a unifying sign of culture'.

57 Quoted by Douglas, ' "God Gave the Land to the People" ', 151–2.

58 On Harcourt's intervention, Murray, *People's Budget*, 161 (and *passim* for the full provisions of the Budget).

59 Lloyd George, *The Budget and the People*.

60 Lloyd George, *The Rural Land Problem*, 11.

61 Gilbert, 'Reform of British Land-holding and the Budget of 1914'; Emy, 'Land Campaign'.

62 Lucas, *Highways and Byways in Sussex*, 69, 96–7; Green, *Tyranny of the Countryside*, 39–40, 74–7.

63 The landmark works were the Hammonds' *Village Labourer* (1911) and Tawney's *Agrarian Problems in the Sixteenth Century* (1912); see the excellent discussion in Clarke, *Liberals and Social Democrats*, 154–63, noting the debt of the Land Inquiry Report to the work of these historians.

64 Masterman, *Condition of England*, 199–208; see also Masterman on 'The English City' and R. C. K. Ensor on 'The English Countryside' in Oldershaw, *England*, Ensor rather more optimistic about the persistence and viability of a 'peasant' countryside.

65 Cannadine, *Decline and Fall*, 452–5.

66 Phillips, *Diehards*.

67 Thompson, *English Landed Society*, 321–6, takes the 'declining confidence' view; cf. Spring, 'Land and Politics', 42, arguing that only during the war was 'the English aristocracy's sense of purpose for the first time seriously shaken'.

68 Cornforth, *Search for a Style*, 25.

69 Green, *Kenneth Grahame*, 240–48, 259–63; see also ch. 5 for Grahame's Arts and Crafts background, esp. 118–9 for an excellent assessment of the aesthetic minority's relationship to the wider world. A similar analysis could be applied to Alfred Austin's *Haunts of Ancient Peace* (1902), also widely cited as evidence of Edwardian rural nostalgia, but like *Willows* a clearly partisan tract, with its diatribes against Collectivism, Gladstone, the motor car, American

tourists and the new-style aristocratic barbarian, while Austin is keen to defend the remaining old-style paternalists; see, e.g., 1–2, 18–19, 64–6, 88–94, 138–42.

70 The SPAB had precisely eight more members in 1910 than in 1900; the Trust complained in 1910 about the 'very small income provided for the National Trust by annual subscriptions', *15th Annual Report* (1909–10), 15–16; in contrast, the National Art-Collections Fund, devoted to buying aristocratic art for urban galleries on the open market, grew very rapidly at this time, especially in 1908–9.

71 Mackail and Wyndham, *Life and Letters*, II, 583.

72 On the Fabianizing of the Arts and Crafts, see Britain, *Fabianism and Culture*. The younger Fabians known as 'Neo-Pagans' were more countrified, but their tastes ran to camping and nude mixed bathing rather than antiquarianism and 'Olde England' – which was too close to the 'beer and cricket' village life they scorned. See Delany, *Neo-Pagans*, which is not always careful to maintain this distinction.

73 NA-CF, *4th Annual Report* (1907), 11.

74 Urban authorities were still not permitted to acquire historic buildings as such, but they were allowed to take into account 'the preservation of objects of historical interest or natural beauty' in making their town planning schemes. See the 4th Schedule of the 1909 Act, 9 Edw. VII c. 44.

75 *Hansard*, 5th ser., 4: 905 [23 Nov. 1909]. After 1909, use of the chattels exemption jumped dramatically, presumably due to both the new eligibility of free estates and the enhanced attraction for settled estates under higher rates of tax. 'Report of the Committee of Trustees of the National Gallery on the Retention of Important Pictures in this Country', *PP* (1914–16), XXIX, 382.

76 Exhaustively catalogued, for instance, in Baldwin Brown, *Care of Ancient Monuments*.

77 Masterman, *Condition of England*, 82–3, 254–62; Trevelyan's testimony, 3 July 1912, to Joint Select Committee on Ancient Monuments Consolidation and Amendment Bill, *PP* (1912–13), VI, 402–4.

78 G. H. Duckworth's testimony to Joint Select Committee, *PP* (1912–13), VI, 408.

79 'Report on Historical Monuments in the County of Herts. Lines upon which it is suggested that the Report should be drafted', 7 July 1909; minutes of the Sub-Commission on English Secular Monuments, 29 June 1909; these and cuttings of press reports on the Hertfordshire publication can be found in PRO, AE 1/4.

80 Confidential memorandum, RCHM(E) to [?Harcourt], 10 March 1910: PRO, WORK 14/2270; Report of the Inspector of Ancient Monuments for the Year Ending 31 Mar. 1911, *PP* (1911), X, 267.

81 This account is pieced together from the file on Tattershall in National Trust MSS, 140, and from notices in *The Times*, mostly between 5 Sept. and 3 Oct. 1911 (also 7, 25 Nov., 22 Dec. 1911 and 6 June 1912); for details of Curzon's transactions, Tattershall Castle (National Trust) MSS, Lincolnshire Archives Office (quoted from catalogue in National Register of Archives); see also Ronaldshay, *Life of Lord Curzon*, III, 74–5.

82 Boulting, 'Law's Delays', 19–20; Kennet, *Preservation*, 22–3; Lowenthal, *Past is a Foreign Country*, 394.

83 *The Times*, 22 Sept. 1911, 6.

84 *Westminster Gazette*, 14, 16, 21 Sept. 1911. The *Manchester Guardian*, 22 Sept. 1911, was not much more sympathetic.

85 *The Standard*, Sept. 1911, *passim*; the only substantial notice about Tattershall on 22 Sept.

86 In 1899 the CPS had merged with the National Footpaths Preservation

Society (founded 1884); it was renamed the Commons and Footpaths Preservation Society and footpath work – protecting public access to private land – became one of its principal functions. See Eversley, *Commons, Forests and Footpaths*, 298–302.

87  Robert Hunter to Canon Rawnsley, 23 Sept. 1911: National Trust MSS, 140; *Manchester Guardian*, 9 Jan. 1912.

88  *Westminster Gazette*, 22 Sept. 1911.

89  Commons bills in *PP* (1911), I, 81; (1912–13), I, 57, 63; (1913), I, 121, 143; (1914), I, 129; Lords bills (no text) in *LJ* (1911–12), 517; (1912–13), 57, 71–2, 101; (1913), 55.

90  Duke of Rutland, 'The Preservation of Ancient Monuments', *The Times*, 12 Nov. 1911, 3, and testimony before Select Committee, 23 Nov. 1912, *PP* (1912–13), VI, 474–5.

91  Blomfield in testimony before Select Committee, 16 Oct. 1912, *PP* (1912–13), VI, 466–8; Gotch in *Country Life*, 9 Jan. 1909, 70, which is disputed by Tipping, 16 Jan. 1909, 105, though earlier *Country Life*, too, had decried excessive regulation of private owners, e.g. 7 Dec. 1901, 751.

92  *Hansard*, 5th ser., 11 [Lords]: 871–83 [30 April 1912]; 14 [Lords]: 446–8 [28 May 1913].

93  Baldwin Brown, *Care of Ancient Monuments*, 25–6.


CHAPTER 5

1  Stead, *Splendid Paupers*, 4, 79.

2  Ibid., 71–2.

3  '"The Splendid Paupers": The Story of Its Genesis and Its Moral', *Review of Reviews*, 10 (July–Dec. 1894), 609–10. For Radical criticisms, see *Westminster Gazette*, 3 Dec. 1894, 3; 8 Dec. 1894, 2; there was also some comment in the *Daily Chronicle*. *Reynolds's Newspaper*, 2 Dec. 1894, 2, was rather approving.

4  'The Splendid Paupers: The Effect of the Fall in Prices on Rural Life', *Review of Reviews*, 11 (Jan.–June 1895), 83–90.

5  Ibid. and 164–6, 294–5, 336. The *Westminster Gazette* felt that the survey 'bear[s] out our view of the case': 17 Jan. 1895, 3.

6  Gower, *Reminiscences*, II, 15–17.

7  Eaton, Alton, Knole, Belvoir and Newstead were certainly at or near the 10,000 level; Chatsworth, Haddon, Aston and Warwick far above it. Parks drawing huge crowds in summer (some also offering access to the house) included Woburn, Trentham, the Dukeries, Enville, Dunham Massey, Cassiobury, Alderley Edge, Hagley, Arundel, Battle Abbey, Hatfield, Lumley and Cliveden.

8  Duke of Devonshire to Joseph Paxton, 8 March 1858; Sarah to Joseph Paxton, 10 March 1858: Paxton MSS, 1335–6.

9  T. H. Rabone, Alton Towers, to Speed, 15 Sept. 1883; Henry Clark, Blenheim, to Speed, 15 Sept. 1883; J. Hatton, Burghley, to Gilson Martin, 18 Sept. 1883; F. Selwood, Eaton, to [Speed], 24 Sept. 1883: Chatsworth MSS, AS/890.

10  Ibid., George Glass, Enville, to Speed, 25 Sept. 1883.

11  Ibid., W. Ingram, Belvoir, to Speed, 21 Sept. 1883.

12  Ibid., A. M. Wing to [Gilson Martin], 14 Sept. 1883.

13  Ibid., Gilson Martin to A. M. Wing, 21 Oct. 1884; Charles Edwards, in *Historic Houses*, 112. It is possible that, while the very large numbers were kept up in the park, a limit on numbers being shown around the *house* was achieved. Some isolated visitors' books for the 1880s show only 5,000 or so names a year for house visitors, mostly small parties, and none at all at weekends. But large excursions, if they were admitted, would not have shown up in such books. In any case, the 8th Duke was again admitting huge numbers – shown around in groups

14  Carnegie, *American Four-in-Hand*, 199.

15  G. Stevens to T. Speed, 18 Sept. 1883: Chatsworth MSS, AS/890.

16  The cases can be followed in a file marked 'Sackville Estate', Sackville MSS, U269/Z33. I have simplified the narrative somewhat.

17  There is a hint of this in Lord Ronald Gower, 'Knole Park', *The Dark Blue*, 4 (1873), 20, 25.

18  *Account of the Disturbances at Knole*, 7–8.

19  I have to thank David Killingray for discussing with me in advance of publication his excellent article on the Knole Disturbances ('Knole Park Access Dispute'). Our research on this incident was concurrent and we have shared information where we had not already overlapped.

20  Fea, *Recollections*, 110–11.

21  *Sevenoaks Chronicle*, 20 June 1884, leader.

22  *Sevenoaks Chronicle*, 14 Sept. 1883, 9; 21 Sept. 1883, 6; 5 Nov. 1883, 6; 19 Oct. 1883, 6; *Account of the Disturbances*, 7.

23  E. Walford, 'Knole Park and its Owners', *Kentish Fire*, 3 Nov. 1883, 162–3.

24  *Sevenoaks Chronicle*, 5 Oct. 1883, 5; 12 Oct. 1883, 4.

25  Compiled from report in the *Sevenoaks Chronicle*, 20 June 1884, moderately sympathetic to the rioters, and *Account of the Disturbances*, which gives Sackville's version.

26  The interview first appeared in the London paper, the *Evening News*, 9 July 1884, and was reprinted in the pamphlet, *Account of the Disturbances*.

27  *Sevenoaks Chronicle*, 7 Nov. 1884. The civil action was not finally settled until the next year; for details of the settlement, see Killingray, 'Knole Park Access Dispute', 74.

28  Walford, 'Knole Park and its Owners', *Kentish Fire*, 3 Nov. 1883, 162; Evans, *Our Old Nobility*, 73–4.

29  E.g. *The World*, 14 Nov. 1883; *Vanity Fair*, 28 June 1884; *Life*, 14 Aug. 1884.

30  *Sevenoaks Chronicle*, 20 June, 8 Aug. 1884.

31  *Review of Reviews*, 11 (Jan.–June 1895), 294–5.

32  See, e.g., Evans, *London Rambler*, 12, 14–15, 51–2, 73.

33  Carr, *Stray Memories*, 53.

34  O'Connor, *Astors*, 367–8, 382–3.

35  *Review of Reviews*, 11 (Jan.–June 1895), 86, echoed by other correspondents, e.g. M. Fooks of Darlington.

36  Ibid., 88–9. Quote from R. S. Gold, Warwick, flatly contradicted by George Morley, Leamington; other evidence suggests Gold was closer to the mark.

37  Ibid., 86.

38  Muthesius, *English House*, 81.

39  Shackleton, *Four on a Tour*, 202–3.

40  Knebworth, for example; also the largely ruined Battle Abbey, where the American tenant severely restricted but did not end visiting.

41  Cooper, *Autobiography*, 30–31, 37–8.

42  Visitors' List, 1906–11: Chatsworth MSS. This is probably not a reliable guide to numbers, but it gives some indication of the practice then prevailing. For Chatsworth between the wars, see below, ch. 6.

43  House Showing Account Book, 1883–96: Eaton MSS, 960.

44  See below, pp. 218–19, for the dispute about charging at Warwick Castle.

45  Cf. Knight, *Excursion Companion*, pt xv, 20–22, with Hissey, *English Holiday*, 194–7.

46  Burghley House Visitors' Books, 1883–94, 1895–1919.

47  The house was closed 1908–10, during another contest over its title, so that on reopening in 1910 numbers bobbed up again to around 3,000. For the numbers and analysis of the visitors, Knole Visitors' Books, 1889–1910: Sackville MSS, U269/E19/4–5. For the comings and goings of the Sackvilles, which rather

romanticizes Victoria Sackville-West's devotion to the house and its public, see Alsop, *Lady Sackville*.

48   Lady Carlisle to C. Luckhurst, 11 June 1909; to Nurse Dudley, 22 July 1909: Castle Howard MSS, F9/2/8, 201.

49   *Sevenoaks Chronicle*, 5 Oct. 1883, 5.

50   S. A. Byles, 'Farnley Hall', *Magazine of Art*, 10 (1886–7), 300.

51   Visitors' Book, 18 July 1889: Chatsworth MSS.

52   In contrast, the weekday tourists are quiet and deferential, but overall the openness of Retby is portrayed as boringly old-fashioned, an early Victorian relic. Glyn, *Visits of Elizabeth*, 207, 216–20.

53   Shackleton, *Four on a Tour*, 333–4.

54   'The Public in Private Grounds', *The Times*, 19 Aug. 1913, 5, and subsequent correspondence, 21, 23, 26 Aug.; 3, 6 Sept. 1913.

55   Requests for permission to bring parties filed separately in Hatfield MSS, estate papers, from 1884; Dugdale, *Family Homespun*, 102–3.

56   Survey of excursionists' requests; also West Ward Conservative Club, Huddersfield, to Lord Salisbury, 19 May 1887, and London Welsh Sunday School Union to Lord Salisbury, 9 Aug. 1887: Hatfield MSS, N17.

57   W. Ingram to Thomas Speed, 21 Sept. 1883: Chatsworth MSS, AS/890.

58   Brown, *Tourist Rambles*, 1st ser. (1878) and 2nd ser. (1885); Tinniswood, *Country-House Visiting*, 143–4, portrays the YTS as a band of innocent trippers – but it was quite different from the many contemporary excursion clubs to which he assimilates it, and its indiscriminate interest in country houses was virtually unique.

59   Graham Wallas, 'Dunster and Its Castle', *English Illustrated Magazine*, 9 (1891–2), 694.

60   Dunster Castle Visitors' Books, 1871–86, Cleeve Abbey Visitors' Books, 1898–1910: Dunster Castle MSS.

61   Visitors' Books, 1854–1897: Long MSS.

62   New Castle Visitors' Book, 1844–1902; Old Castle Visitors' Book, 1879–1904: Wardour Castle MSS; Hardy, *Jude the Obscure*, 189–90. I have to thank Mr S. D. Hobbs of the Wiltshire County Record Office for drawing this episode to my attention.

63   Estate Accounts, 1869–1907: Wilton MSS; Thompson, *English Landed Society*, 97, attributes the decline in numbers to the wearing away of novelty, but Wilton had long been open, probably continuously since the eighteenth century – what was novel in the 1860s was the one shilling charge, which left a record in the account books.

64   Visitors' Books, 1874–1890, 1908–14: Petworth MSS, 2898, 2900.

65   Geoffrey Winterwood, 'Wilton House', *Good Words*, 35 (1894), 455; Lucas, *Highways and Byways in Sussex*, 102.

66   *Estates Gazette*, 7 July 1894, 6. Pevsner reckons that Water Eaton is neither unusually complete nor built in 1510.

67   Town Clerk, Leamington Spa, to Earl of Warwick, 8 July 1885: Warwick Castle MSS, CR1886/743; *Warwick and Warwickshire Advertiser*, 11 July 1885, 5.

68   William Fosbery to Earl of Warwick, 15 June, 19 July 1885: Warwick Castle MSS, CR1886/637.

69   William Fosbery to Earl of Warwick, 27 July 1885: Warwick Castle MSS, CR1886/637; 'Warwick Castle, Receipts and Payments connected with the Admission of the Public', 1885–90: Warwick Castle MSS, CR1886/TN1135, shows how well the year-round schedule was kept in the first years. Petworth House later followed Warwick's example in hiring commissionaires as guides.

70   Ibid., for the numbers; comment in the Birmingham press reprinted in *Warwick and Warwickshire Advertiser*, 15 Aug. 1885, 5; William Fosbery to Earl of Warwick, 13, 20, 25 Aug.

1885: Warwick Castle MSS, CR 1886/637.

71 Admission Accounts, 1885–1890, 1897–1903, 1903–1915: Warwick Castle MSS, CR1886/TN1135, 645, 847.

72 Earl of Warwick to Revd G. Bridgeman, 11 June 1885 [draft]: Warwick Castle MSS, CR1886/743.

73 Warwick, *Afterthoughts*, 96–7.

74 'Auto-telephatic' was his actual word, but he meant telepathy, not telephony: W. T. Stead, '"The Splendid Paupers": The Story of Its Genesis and Its Moral', *Review of Reviews*, 10 (July–Dec. 1894), 609–10. Lady Warwick sensibly disclaimed having had any such spiritual communication. *Life's Ebb and Flow*, 109–10. The coinage 'splendid paupers' was in fact Harcourt's, some years previously.

75 Warwick, *Life's Ebb and Flow*, 207–8, and *Afterthoughts*, 241.

76 Warwick, *Life's Ebb and Flow*, 203–6. Such pageants had begun to pop up in the 1880s, under Arts and Crafts influence and sometimes aristocratic patronage; the Lindsays were again active in this sphere. Judge, 'May Day and Merrie England', 137–9; Withington, *English Pageantry*, II, 122–5, 159, 194.

77 For the 1906 pageant, see the *Leamington Chronicle*, 6 July 1906. It formed part of a short-lived vogue for spectacular civic pageants that swept the country in 1905–11, but was thereafter diluted by commercialization and non-historical content: see Withington, *English Pageantry*, II, 194–8, 228; Parker, *Several of My Lives*, 294–8.

78 Admission Accounts, 1885–1890, 1897–1903, 1903–1915: Warwick Castle MSS, CR1886/TN1135, 645, 847.

CHAPTER 6

1 Forster, 'Mrs Miniver', 292–3.

2 Here I am much indebted to Light, *Forever England*, which I hope marks the beginning of a new assessment of English culture between the wars; see esp. 8, 47, 146. See also Samuel, 'Exciting to be English', xviii–xxv, and Potts, '"Constable Country"'.

3 Lawrence, *Lady Chatterley*, 156.

4 The top level – on fortunes over £2 million – was reduced to 40 per cent, but all of the higher rates up to £1 million were increased; agricultural land (including, normally, the country house) was, however, exempted from the increased rates.

5 Cooper, *British Agricultural Policy*.

6 Clemenson, *English Country Houses*, 111.

7 Clemenson, 'Diminishing Derbyshire Estates', 118.

8 Waller, *Dukeries Transformed*, 65–73.

9 Suburbanization has yet to be treated on a national scale. Jackson, *Semi-Detached London*, is an excellent study of the most important region.

10 The meanings of suburban style have also been generally neglected; Richards, *Castles on the Ground*, was an early appreciation that has not been bettered.

11 Also counterposed to the neo-Georgian style adopted for (lower-status) council housing and the modernist style favoured by the avant-garde.

12 This paragraph is based on a survey of *Country Illustrated* (1921–39), *The Countryside Review* (1922–7), *Town and Country* (1923–7), *Illustrated Country Review* (1923–7), *The Country House and Estate* (1923–7), *Town and Country News* (1925–36), *Town and Country Homes* (1926–33).

13 *Country Life*, 23 Aug. 1930, 223.

14 On the organization of rural leisure in Germany, see, e.g., Applegate, *Nation of Provincials*; for America, Nash, *Wilderness and the American Mind*, 3rd edn, ch. 9, on the re-assessment of wilderness as useful to modern civilization from the 1890s. Howkins, 'Discovery of Rural England', 62, argues for the uniqueness of English urban interest in the

countryside, but considers only the French alternative; note Potts's criticism, '"Constable Country"', 162, 182 n. 2, and Trentmann, 'Civilization and its Discontents', 592–3, for some useful comparisons with Germany, which still exaggerate British anti-modernism.

15  Walker, 'Outdoor Movement'; Pimlott, *Englishman's Holiday*, 211–15.

16  Pimlott, *Englishman's Holiday*, 237–8.

17  'Note on Number of Visitors Etc. at the More Popular Monuments': PRO, WORK 14/2314.

18  Charles Luckhurst to Lord Rhayader, 4 July 1938; to E. W. Habershon, 4 July 1938; to Geoffrey Russell, 2 Aug. 1938: Castle Howard MSS, F10/35.

19  *The Times*, 5 May 1932, 12; 8 Aug. 1936, 13.

20  E.g. There are 600 travel diaries in county record offices, of which 400 date from the nineteenth and only 40 from the twentieth century. Gard, *Observant Traveller*, xi.

21  Given his tremendous audience, Morton has been strangely neglected by posterity; he did not even warrant a *DNB* notice. See Pawle, 'H. V. Morton', for the only memoir that I have been able to find. Cunningham, *British Writers*, 228–9, lumps Morton together with far more aggressively nostalgic writers. Giles and Middleton, *Writing Englishness*, 74–5, is an improvement. Charles Perry of the University of the South, Tennessee, is working on a more serious treatment of Morton.

22  Morton, *In Search of England*, quotes from vii–xi, 278.

23  Mais also has been denied a *DNB* entry, but see his memoirs, *All the Days of My Life* (1937), esp. 181–6, and *Buffets and Rewards* (1952), 55–6, 96, 115, 136–41, 151. The 1932 broadcasts were published as *This Unknown Island*.

24  On the BBC's resistance to a more militant preservationist stance, see below, pp. 271–2, 275.

25  See the excellent treatment in Lowerson, 'Battles for the Countryside', 268–75.

26  Walker, 'Outdoor Movement', 148–52; Lowerson, 'Battles for the Countryside', 270–71; Sheail, *Rural Conservation*, 194–6; Trentmann, 'Civilization and its Discontents', 585–91.

27  My reading of rambling and hiking publications interprets them as to some extent reacting against the musty antiquarianism of Arts and Crafts inspired guidebooks.

28  Massingham, *Remembrance*, esp. 33–6, 43–5, 62, 76, 85.

29  Squire in *Journal of the Royal Society of Arts*, 80 (1931–2), 837; Williams-Ellis, *Architect Errant*, 176–7. See also Sheail, *Rural Conservation*, 18, for a more positive view of Squire's efforts.

30  Trevelyan, *Must England's Beauty Perish?*, 21; *Call and Claims of Natural Beauty*, 27–8; also Cannadine's shrewd overall assessment, *Trevelyan*, esp. 151–3, 178–9.

31  A proposal made by Bailey at the Executive Committee, 16 Dec. 1919; though never formally acted upon, it characterizes the Trust's work in the 1920s pretty accurately. Executive Committee Minutes, National Trust MSS.

32  Williams-Ellis, *England and the Octopus*, 107–8.

33  M. Lovett Turner, '"England Under Trust"', *Somerset Countryman*, April 1939, 21–2.

34  E.g. Harper, *Mansions of Old Romance*, 286 ('Society for the Preservation of Places of Natural Beauty and Historic Interest'); 'Note by Lord Salisbury', 10 Jan. 1936: Hatfield MSS, S(4)/157/12 ('Ancient Monuments Protection Society').

35  E.g. Ormsby-Gore, the First Commissioner of Works, in *The Times*, 16 July 1935, 13 (see also 'The Preservation of England', leader, ibid., 17).

36  *Report of the Ancient Monuments Advisory Committee, 1921*, 3–4, 14,

19–20, 27–9. A copy of this report can be found in PRO, WORK 14/2469.

37 Lord Crawford to Sir Lionel Earle, 29 May 1921: PRO, WORK 14/2312; Lord Crawford to Douglas Sladen, 30 Jan. 1922: Crawford MSS, 97/38. The Beauchamp Report had been commissioned by Crawford's predecessor as First Commissioner, Sir Alfred Mond.

38 For the Treasury position, see PRO, T 162/262, esp. H. Gatliff to E. C. Cleary, 22 Sept. 1924, E. C. Cleary to M. Fass, 4 Oct. 1924; for subsequent Office of Works arguments, see PRO, WORK 14/2312, esp. M. Connolly, 'Notes on Memorandum', 12 Feb. 1925, Sir Lionel Earle to First Commissioner, 12 Jan., 11 June 1927.

39 E.g. Schwarz, 'Language of Constitutionalism'; Howkins, 'Discovery of Rural England', 82–4; Wiener, *English Culture*, 100–2, 108–9; Rich, 'A question of life and death', 500–1; Cannadine, 'First Hundred Years', 16–18.

40 McKibbin, 'Class and Conventional Wisdom', stresses the negative, anti-socialist message, Williamson, 'Doctrinal Politics of Stanley Baldwin', the more positive, moral and Christian content.

41 Ibid., 192–5, though Williamson sees also some 'traditional squirearchical' content alongside his invocations of 'the common people'.

42 Williams-Ellis, *Architect Errant*, 180–81.

43 Clough Williams-Ellis, 'British and Beastly: A Review of Reviews', *London Mercury*, 37 (1937), 348; *Country Life*, 4 Feb. 1928, 124; see also Trevelyan, *Must England's Beauty Perish?*, 22; *Call and Claims of National Beauty*, 27–8, 31; 'Amenities and the State'; R. C. K. Ensor, 'Rural England and its Saviours', *London Mercury*, 38 (1937–8), 483, 492; Nevill, *English Country House Life*, 41.

44 Harper, *Mansions of Old Romance*, 25.

45 Lee, *Social Leaders and Public Persons*, 92–5, 103.

46 Lee gleaned some of his conclusions from *Cheshire Life*, which had become by 1936 'a gossip journal for the "smart set"', and the same process can be detected in similar publications (often connected with the Rural Community Council movement), e.g. *Derbyshire Countryside* (from 1931), *Warwickshire Journal* (from 1938), *Nottinghamshire Countryside* (from 1937).

47 See Rural Community Council magazines which retained their rural character longer than the 'suburbanized' magazines in n. 46, e.g. *Gloucestershire Countryside* (from 1931), *Somerset Countryman* (from 1932).

48 Sutherland, *Looking Back*, 86–7.

49 On the sales of Rufford and Clumber, see *The Times*, 5 Feb. 1938, 9; 17 Feb. 1938, 16; 24 Aug. 1938; and *Country Life*, 20 Aug. 1938, 189; 10 Sep. 1938, 244.

50 Cannadine, *Decline and Fall*, 132–5.

51 Ibid., 369 (but cf. the contradictory contention, 693–5); for similar claims, see Tinniswood, *Country-House Visiting*, 11; Waterson, *Country House Remembered*, 23–8; and the weaker claim made by Thompson, 'English Landed Society IV', 5.

52 John Stevenson, 'Our Changing Countryside: Vanished Glories of Great Estates', *Town and Country Planning*, 1 (1932–3), 118–19. Stevenson was General Secretary of the Incorporated Auctioneers and Landed Property Agents.

53 *Country Life*, 7 June 1919, 638; see also 4 Feb. 1928, 124.

54 Christopher Hussey, 'The Decay of English Country Life', *Quarterly Review*, 241 (1924), 332–6. See also Arthur Bryant, 'The English Squire', *Listener*, 10 (1933), 668, and a *Country Life* leader (presumably by Hussey), 'The Peril of the Countryside', 29 May 1926, 728.

55 Nevill, *English Country House Life*,

42–5; also Williams-Ellis, *England and the Octopus*, 85.

56　Vincent, *Crawford Papers*, 544.

57　See, e.g., his comments on the taste of Lord Skelmersdale, Lord Northampton and the Duke of Norfolk in ibid., 496, 582, 585.

58　Ibid., 529, 532. See also Lord Derby's comment on his town house, ibid., 543.

59　*Nottingham Journal*, 13 Sept. 1930, 9.

60　Pope-Hennessy, *Crewe*, 176.

61　On the value of the Wollaton sale, see *Country Life*, 7 June 1924, 420; on the Bramshill sale, Hussey, 'The Fate of Bramshill', ibid., 17 Aug. 1935, 168–73.

62　*Country Life*, 18 April 1925, 622; 20 June 1925, 1006; 15 Aug. 1925, 268. The local authority took over Bramall some years later.

63　Ibid., 9 April 1921, 445; Clemenson, *English Country Houses*, 136.

64　Gaze, *Figures in a Landscape*, 92–3.

65　Clemenson, *English Country Houses*, 135–6, 140–41; Harris, 'Gone to Ground', 16.

66　*The Field*, 28 March 1931, Country House and Estate Supplement, 12.

67　This was *Country Life*'s alternative to *The Field*'s more aggressive position; see, e.g., 31 Jan. 1920, 152.

68　Blunden, *Countess of Warwick*, 263.

69　*Country Life*, 2 Feb. 1935, 108.

70　See the discussion in *The Times* in early 1927: 14 Jan., 8; 15 Jan., 6 (letter from G. M. Trevelyan); 17 Jan., 19; 20 Jan., 9; 21 Jan., 15; 22 Jan., 7.

71　Hon. Patrick Balfour, 'How to Save Our Country Houses', *Country Life*, 6 Feb. 1932, 156; the editors did not dismiss his ideas out of hand, 140.

72　John Stevenson, 'Our Changing Countryside', *Town and Country Planning*, 1 (1932–3), 120.

73　*Country Life*, 11 Sept. 1937, 263.

74　Tinniswood, *Country House Visiting*, 156–8, claims that many more houses were opening, but he is only able to substantiate this by counting all castles, abbeys, gardens, etc. (including ruins and publicly owned monu-

ments). Contemporary claims to this effect – e.g. by *Country Life*, *The Field*, the National Trust, etc. – were exaggerated in order to justify tax remissions. My count is based on a systematic search of national and county guides and reveals an obvious divergence of private houses (closing) and publicly owned sites (rapidly expanding).

75　Flower, *Debrett's Stately Homes*, 21.

76　Morton, *I Saw Two Englands*, 163–4; Rhodes James, *Chips*, 204–5.

77　*High Peak News*, 14 March 1925, 3–4; 21 March 1925, 3–4; 28 March 1925, 5; 19 April 1925, 5; *Derby and Chesterfield Reporter*, 20 March 1925, 4.

78　*High Peak News*, 6 June 1925, 4.

79　*The Times*, 18 Jan. 1926, 11; 31 Dec. 1926, 5; 12 Aug. 1927, 13; 19 Aug. 1927, 13; 7 Aug. 1928, 8; 6 Aug. 1929, 13.

80　Mais, *This Unknown Island*, 80; Hobhouse, *Shell Guide to Derbyshire*, 27–8.

81　Parker, *English Summer*, 28–31, 128–9, 134–5, 138, 140–43, 151, 287–8, 293, 308, 324. See also Laughlin, *So You're Going to England*, 429, 495, 498.

82　Chatsworth Librarian's testimony to Gowers Committee, 5 Nov. 1949; PRO, T 219/180. Tinniswood, *Country House Visiting*, 182–3, claims that in the 1930s 'it was not uncommon for annual visitor figures at major properties to reach 15,000, or even 20,000, on a basis of thirty or thirty-six open days a year'. It would be interesting to know what properties he had in mind.

83　Visitors' Book, 1911–29: Sackville MSS, U269/E19/6; Visitors' Books, 1921–39: Petworth MSS, 2901–3.

84　Visitors' Books, 1925–36: Castle Howard MSS, F8/140/1–2.

85　'Note on Number of Visitors Etc. at the More Popular Monuments', Dec. 1930: PRO, WORK 14/2314.

86　*Historic Houses* (1976), 3–4; Vincent, *Crawford Papers*, 582; Brodrick, *Near to Greatness*, 211.

87 NA-CF, *27th Annual Report* (1930), 8, 11–12, begins to comment on the appeal of the 'treats', and especially the value of novelty (admission to houses normally closed to the public).

88 See reports on the scheme in *Country Life*, 18 June 1927, 986–93; 5 May 1928, 642–5; 28 Nov. 1931, 581; 16 Dec. 1933, 643; 25 May 1935, 534; 23 Nov. 1935, 528; 31 Dec. 1938, 646.

89 *The Times*, 7 Aug. 1928, 8; 6 Aug. 1929, 13.

90 Somers-Cocks, *Eastnor*, 265–9.

91 Temple Newsam had nearly 100,000 visitors in its peak year of 1928–9, though it was nearly bereft of contents; its chief attractions were a ghost and slender associations with Mary Queen of Scots. City of Leeds, Public Libraries, Art Gallery and Museum, *Annual Reports*, 1927–33; information from James Lomax.

92 Barrow, *Gossip*, 81, 87.

93 Tourist accounts, 1916–39: Warwick Castle MSS, TN852, 851, 848; Lord Warwick's testimony to the Gowers Committee, 17 Aug. 1949: PRO, T 219/183.

94 'Such as Knole', *Country Life*, 4 Feb. 1928, 124, presumed to be Hussey.

95 A memory of Lady Digby's, kindly passed on by Rachel Crawshay of the National Gardens Scheme.

96 Literary scholars have concluded – somewhat arbitrarily, in my view – that when the country house became emptied of social meaning, it was free to be refilled with spiritual meaning, as if literature abhors a vacuum. Kelsall, *Great Good Place*, 161. While this may have been true of James, Forster, Woolf *et al.*, it does not appear to apply so automatically to lesser mortals.

97 Max Baker to *The Times*, 13 June 1924, 11.

98 W. Thornton-Smith to *The Times*, 17 Feb. 1926, 10.

99 Williams-Ellis, *England and the Octopus*, 81.

100 Trevelyan to *The Times*, 15 Jan. 1927, 6.

101 H. Avray Tipping, 'Hamilton Palace, Lanarkshire, I', *Country Life*, 7 June 1919, 662; Lady Margaret Sackville, 'The Park', *Country Life*, 28 July 1917, 78 (the house is not named, but Hamilton Palace is almost certainly her subject).

102 *Country Life*, 22 July 1922, 99.

103 *The Times*, 29 March 1921, 11.

104 *Country Life*, 17 Sept. 1927, 414; *The Times*, 21 March 1929, 29.

105 Tinniswood, *Country-House Visiting*, 174–5.

106 Executive Committee Minutes, 15 Oct. 1917, 18 June 1918, 20 Jan. 1920, 15 Feb., 19 April 1921, 17 Jan. 1922: National Trust MSS.

107 Ibid., 14 Dec. 1925, 13 Dec. 1926, 11 April 1927, 9 July 1928. Even more shockingly, there was 'minimal' public response to a later appeal to save Little Moreton Hall, the half-timbered dream admired equally by devotees of the Olden Time and of the Arts and Crafts. Lees-Milne, *People and Places*, 89–90.

108 Executive Committee Minutes, 9 Nov., 14 Dec. 1925: National Trust MSS.

109 Saunders, 'Metroland', 168–9.

110 Raphael Samuel, 'English Heritage's Folly', *The Times*, 22 Aug. 1994; Carswell, *Saving of Kenwood*, 71–3, 93–4, 106–15.

111 *Sunday Times*, 23 Sept. 1928.

112 Miers, *Report on Public Museums*, 23, 25.

113 *Nottingham Journal*, 27 Feb. 1919; 4; 3 Sept. 1924, 4.

114 Kitson and Pawson, *Temple Newsam*, 31–2. See also G. E. H. Rawlins, 'Cities and Country Seats', *Town Planning Review*, 10 (1923–4), 119–22, 189–91, singling out the preservation of Temple Newsam and Aston for special praise.

115 James Lees-Milne, 'Memorandum on Temple Newsam', 15 Oct. 1937: National Trust MSS, 36/1PF. Temple Newsam's presentation was put on a new and much better foot-

ing in the following year; see below, ch. 9, n. 57.

116  Woolf, *Diaries*, III, 335 [2 Dec. 1930].

117  Williams, *Country and the City*, 249–50.

118  Light, *Forever England*, 80–82.

119  Wilde, 'Canterville Ghost'; see also Taggart, *Saturday Evening Ghost*, a 1936 theatrical adaptation of Wilde's story, much jokier and less emotional.

120  Eric [Keown], 'Sir Tristram Goes West', *Punch*, 9 May 1932; *The Ghost Goes West* (dir. René Clair, 1936) was written by an American, Robert Sherwood.

121  Morton, *In Search of England*, 269–70.

122  *Punch*, 6 July 1932, 11. The cartoon was naturally reprinted in hikers' magazines.

123  Cornforth, *Inspiration of the Past*, 20–46, discusses these and other knots of restorationists.

124  Sackville-West, *The Heir*, esp. 98–110. Note the premonitions of this story in 'A Kentish Manor House' by Vita's kinswoman Lady Margaret Sackville, *Country Life*, 1 Nov. 1910, 466–7.

125  Woolf, 'Reading', 144–5. This essay dates from 1919, before Woolf came under Sackville-West's influence; it therefore reflects Woolf's own reaction to 'England changing hands'.

126  Sackville-West, *English Country Houses*, 8–9, 37–8, 42–7; see also her cousin Edward's extraordinary denunciation of the larger eighteenth-century country houses in *Architects' Journal*, 2 Dec. 1931, 735–8.

127  Lord Lascelles's 1921 appeal to the NA-CF to take up the cause of country houses fell on deaf ears, and aroused the anger of its chairman Sir Robert Witt. NA-CF, *20th Annual Report, 1923*, 10–13; Lord Harewood to Lord Lothian, 27 Feb. 1936: Lothian MSS, GD40/18/311/608–11. For other early defences, see Helm, *Homes of the Past* (the author was literally a client of Lord Curzon's) and Spender, *Man and Mansions*.

## CHAPTER 7

1  Williams-Ellis, *Architect Errant*, 92–5; Brandon, 'A Twentieth-Century Squire'; Cannadine, *Trevelyan*, esp. ch. 4, for George, but also gives more insight into this side of Charles's character than the political biography by A. J. A. Morris; on Hilton Young, see his entry in the *DNB* (by his son Wayland).

2  There is no proper history of the CPRE, but interest in its early years is now strong: see, e.g., Sheail, *Rural Conservation*; Matless, 'Ages of English Design'; Jeans, 'Planning and the English Countryside'.

3  Patrick Abercrombie, 'Planning of Town and Country: The Contrast of Civic and Landscape Design', *Town Planning Review*, 14 (1930), 8–9.

4  Trevelyan, *Call and Claims of Natural Beauty*, 26–7.

5  Williams-Ellis, *England and the Octopus*, 12–13, 77–9.

6  G. M. Trevelyan to E. Hilton Young, 3 July 1934: cited by Cannadine, *Trevelyan*, 178.

7  N. Buxton to G. Lansbury, ? Nov. 1929: PRO, WORK 14/2270.

8  'Notes on an interview between representatives of the SPAB and the First Commissioner of Works', 26 July 1929: PRO, WORK 14/2313.

9  F. J. E. Raby, Memorandum for Sir Lionel Earle, 30 Jan. 1930: PRO, WORK 14/2313; Arthur Greenwood to Ramsay MacDonald, 9 May 1930, Sir Lionel Earle, Memorandum for Ramsay MacDonald, 11 Sept. 1930: PRO, PRO 30/69/691.

10  Vincent, *Crawford Papers*, 586.

11  Sheail, *Rural Conservation*, 53–70, 115–16.

12  Hilda Matheson to C. R. Ashbee, 6 March 1929: BBC Written Archives Centre, 910 (RCONT1)/Ashbee.

Matheson and Ashbee were brought together by their mutual friend Vita Sackville-West. The full course of the BBC's campaign, which began in Feb. 1929 and ended in August 1931, can be followed in this file.

13 Butler, *Lothian*, 144–7; Lothian to Lloyd George, 30 April 1930: Lothian MSS, GD40/17/250, f. 480. See also ibid., ff. 482–3, for Lothian's further proposals privately to Lloyd George, and publicly in *The Times*.

14 Duke of Montrose, 'The Future of the Landowner: I. Land for Death Duties', *Country Life*, 12 April 1930, 541–2, part of a discussion organized by the CPRE.

15 *Country Life*, 14 May 1932, 531; also 25 June 1932, 712–13.

16 For an excellent survey of the Act and its workings, see Sheail, *Rural Conservation*, 71–9; the details here rather undermine Sheail's upbeat conclusion about the 1932 regime, ibid., 228–38.

17 Ibid., 239–41. See also Cullingworth, *Environmental Planning*, I, 167–8.

18 Reginald Fletcher (later Lord Winster), a Liberal who had recently gone over to Labour, in *Hansard*, 5th ser., 320: 464–5 [10 Feb. 1937].

19 *The Times*, 25 Jan. 1932, 8.

20 *Country Life*, 30 Jan. 1932, 111.

21 These discussions can be followed in PRO, HLG 52/700, esp. 'Town and Country Planning Bill. Conversation with Lord Cranborne . . .', 2 Feb. 1932, 'Lord Cranborne's letter to "The Times"', n.d., 'Town and Country Planning Bill. Clause 17', 23 June 1932.

22 PRO, HLG 52/1194; *Hansard*, 5th ser., 320: 421–2 [10 Feb. 1937].

23 Ibid., 320: 467–72; Evelyn Sharp's memoranda for the Town and Country Planning Advisory Committee, 1938: PRO, HLG 52/709.

24 NA-CF, *32nd Annual Report, 1935*, 13.

25 There were six broadcasts on countryside preservation in 1929, seven in 1930, two in 1931, none that I can identify in 1932, Howard Marshall's series in 1933 (see the following note) and one pro-and-con round table discussion in 1934.

26 On the dropping of Ashbee and the CPRE, see BBC Written Archives Centre, 910 (RCONT1)/Ashbee, incl. correspondence from Lionel Fielden explaining the genesis of Marshall's series; Howard Marshall, 'Vanishing England', *Listener*, 25 Oct.–29 Nov. 1933, and cf. leader in 25 Oct., 614, correspondence in 8 Nov., 720, 22 Nov., 801–2, 6 Dec. 1933, 880; Betjeman, *Letters*, I, 113; on the toning down of preservationist rhetoric, see BBC Written Archives Centre, R51/425 ('Preservation of the Countryside'), quotes from J. M. Rose-Troup to W. E. G. Murray, 25 Nov. 1935. 'Holiday Ideas Discussed' ran on Mondays, May–June 1935.

27 Wiener, *English Culture*, 73–5; Green, *Children of the Sun*, 253–5.

28 Massingham, *English Countryside*, I, 6. Massingham's volume was thus more nostalgically preservationist than other countryside books of the 1930s; cf. Priestley, *Beauty of Britain*, a Batsford book, or the hiking-oriented *Books of the Open Air* series published by Alexander Maclehose.

29 Luckin, *Questions of Power*, 114–15, 165–7; Matless, 'Ages of English Design'.

30 National Trust, Annual Reports, 1928–36, and Reports of the Publicity Committee in Executive Committee Minutes, 10 Jan. 1930, 9 Jan. 1933: National Trust MSS. The National Trust now calculates its membership history somewhat differently, but the new figures still give as the period of most rapid growth 1933–6.

31 'The Living Past', *Landscape and Garden*, 3 (1936), 13; '"This England"', *Landscape and Garden*, 4 (1937), 205.

32 Williams-Ellis, *Britain and the Beast*,

NOTES TO PAGES 277–84

2, 66–9, 76, 84–5, 126. See also Williams-Ellis's discussion of the continuing planning vs. nationalization debate at xiv–xvii.

33 W. A. Eden, 'The English Landscape in the Life of the Community', *Town Planning Review*, 15 (1933), 279–80, 285; also Eden's review of Joad in *Town Planning Review*, 16 (1934–5), 152–3; 'Modern Architectural Research and Landscape Planning', *Landscape and Garden*, 5 (1938), 101; G. A. Jellicoe, 'Creating Our Landscape', ibid., 139.

34 Eden, 'English Landscape', 279–80. Here I confine myself to the rediscovery of the Georgian tradition in landscape design, but there was a parallel resurgence of interest in Georgian town planning, for which see below, n. 36.

35 Clough Williams-Ellis was an exception: as an architect of neo-Georgian country houses, he had a connoisseur's appreciation of the original article; see *England and the Octopus*, 80–90, and *Britain and the Beast*, 91–100, though in the latter he admits that the younger generation is better reached through natural beauty than appeals to taste or history.

36 For urban Georgianism, see Summerson, *Georgian London*, 1988 edn, 285–306; Mandler, 'Summerson'; Richards, 'Architectural Controversies'; Watkin, *Rise of Architectural History*, 120–34.

37 Even *The Times*, no organ of urbanism and modernism, urged Georgians to limit their preservation to examples of civic design. 'The Georgian Boom' [leader], 10 Feb. 1938, 15.

38 Green, *Children of the Sun*, xvii, 3–4, 201–2, for some instances of this claim, though Green is dealing with a wider movement which he calls 'dandyism', of which the Georgian revival is only a part. Calloway, *Twentieth-Century Decoration*, is more careful in characterizing the Baroque and Regency revivals of the interwar period as 'avant-garde taste', but a

thorough study of the relationship between 'avant-garde taste' and a wider market is still needed.

39 Cornforth, *Inspiration of the Past*, gives useful background, which is necessarily coloured by his emphasis on revivalism; see also Aslet, *Last Country Houses*, 263–6, 272–4, 281–2. I am here collapsing together various revivals of styles from Baroque to Regency as 'Georgian': for specifics, see Calloway, *Twentieth-Century Decoration*, esp. 141–3, 182–5, 200–6.

40 'Contemporary Architecture' [leader], *House and Garden*, Jan. 1923, 10; 'The Architecture Club Exhibition' [leader], ibid., March 1923, 94; 'The Lesson of the Adams' [leader], ibid., April 1923, 140.

41 NA-CF, *Annual Reports*, 1918–30, when membership peaked before the Slump hit hard.

42 Watkin, *Rise of Architectural History*, 115–34.

43 Curiously, the section on the classical revival in Watkin, ibid., is entitled 'Classicism and the Country House' – a bit of retrospective wishful thinking, because the section in question quite properly says nothing at all about the country house.

44 'Saving Historic Buildings; Sir R. Blomfield's Plea', *The Times*, 15 Feb. 1923, 7.

45 On Georgian preservationism between the wars, see Summerson, *Georgian London*, 1988 edn, 293–9.

46 Green, *Children of the Sun*, 229–31, 253–5; Carpenter, *Brideshead Generation*, 294–309.

47 Waugh, *Labels*, 55–6. In defence of Arthur Waugh, it was he who published John Betjeman's parallel tirade against Arts and Crafts fashions, *Ghastly Good Taste*, discussed below.

48 Betjeman, 'An Aesthete's Apologia', his 'aesthetic autobiography', published as a prologue to the 1970 edn of *Ghastly Good Taste*.

49 Betjeman, *Ghastly Good Taste*, esp. 1–10, 110–12. A similar message is implicit in *Antiquarian Prejudice* (1939), a blast against the compro-

mises of mass culture, including the pseudo-traditionalism of the interwar suburb.

50 See the surveys of Betjeman's aesthetic propaganda in Carpenter, *Brideshead Generation*, 210–18, and Hillier, *Young Betjeman*, 259–79.

51 Betjeman, *Shell Guide to Devon*, 16.

52 Steegmann, *Rule of Taste*, esp. 20, 182–4.

53 John Cornforth, 'The Husseys and the Picturesque – II', *Country Life*, 17 May 1979, 1322.

54 Dutton, *Hampshire Manor*, 5.

55 Cornforth, 'Husseys and the Picturesque'; Hussey, *Picturesque*.

56 Dutton, *Hampshire Manor*, 80–101.

57 Cornforth, *Inspiration of the Past*, 63; Calloway, *Twentieth-Century Decoration*, 62, 184–5, 200–2.

58 Hussey, *Fairy Land*, 5, 15–17, 30–42.

59 Cornforth, *Search for a Style*, 83; Christopher Hussey, 'The Decay of English Country Life', *Quarterly Review*, 241 (1924), 340–41.

60 Cornforth, *Search for a Style*, 80–85, discusses this juncture; see further on Hussey and modernism his articles in *Country Life*, 22 Oct. 1981, 1366–68, and 29 Oct. 1981, 1468–70. But Cornforth is less interested in the changing approach to preservationism.

61 *Country Life*, 2 June 1923, 758, 760, on Bramshill.

62 See also Harry Batsford and Charles Fry's *Homes and Gardens of England* (1932), in many respects a premonition of Dutton's book.

63 Dutton, *English Country House*, 1–5, 30, 53, 68–70.

64 *Country Life*, 4 Feb. 1928, 124; 8 June 1935, 584.

65 Byron, *Appreciation of Architecture*, 60–61.

66 Byron, '"That Incomparable Architect" Sir Christopher Wren', *Country Life*, 24 Sept. 1932, 339–40.

67 '"A National Style"' [leader], *Country Life*, 3 Oct. 1934, 236.

68 Hussey, 'Decay of English Country Life', 335–6.

69 Hobhouse, *Shell Guide to Derbyshire*, 23–4, 27–8.

70 *Country Life*, 9 Jan. 1926, 39; 4 Feb. 1928, 124; 18 Jan. 1930, 70; 9 April 1932, 400.

71 Oswald, *Country Houses of Kent*, xi–xii. Hussey's *Old Homes* (1928) was also aimed at stimulating country-house tourism.

72 A second edition appeared in 1935. See above, ch. 6, for more discussion of the extent of country-house visiting between the wars, and for a warning against taking contemporary propaganda as documentary material.

73 Holden and Dutton, *French Chateaux*, 10 and *passim*; cf. duc de Noailles, 'La Demeure Historique', *Country Life*, 21 March 1936, 296–7. It was also said that the châteaux of Belgium were more accessible than English country houses and there was thus 'a very general appreciation of the fact that they are part of a common national heritage': 'Chateaux of Belgium', *Observer*, 23 July 1939.

74 *Country Life*, 25 May 1929, 728; 18 Jan. 1930, 70; 25 Jan. 1930, 114; 19 April 1930, 559; 9 April 1932, 400; 5 May 1934, 449.

75 See the discussion in *Hansard*, 5th ser., 240: 1247–65 [25 June 1930] and 254: 533–4 [24 June 1931].

76 This was the case at Knebworth – see *The Times*, 25 Jan. 1932, 9, 12 April 1932, 17; it also applies loosely to Arundel and Alnwick Castles (uninhabitable and unlettable). As argued above, ch. 6, houses moved in and out of the public domain according to the vagaries of the letting market throughout the interwar years. Cobham Hall in Kent had been open earlier, because unlet, and then closed when the Earl of Darnley moved back into residence.

77 'Death Duties on Country House Property: A Way Out for Owners – Demolition?', *The Field*, 28 May 1932, 795. Also 28 March 1931, Country House and Estate Supplement, 1.

78  Butler, *Lothian*, 144–52.

79  Baker, *Architecture and Personalities*, 199.

80  Butler, *Lothian*, 152–6, 251.

81  See the reports of the speech, with different emphases, in *The Times*, 20 July 1934, 9, and *Country Life*, 28 July 1934, 80.

82  *The Times*, 26 July 1934, 13.

83  *Country Life*, 8 Sept. 1934, 238; a similar reaction from Sir John Squire in a book review in the *Sunday Times*, 29 July 1934, 10, was one of the few press comments on the Lothian scheme outside of the columns of *The Times* and *Manchester Guardian*, traditionally more alert to aesthetic issues.

84  *The Field*, 11 Aug. 1934, 332.

85  Ronald Nall-Cain, 'The Future of Country Houses', *Country Life*, 18 Aug. 1934, 163; see also letter from Jeremiah Colman of Gatton, ibid., 180.

86  *Country Life*, 15 Sept. 1934, 265, 287; 22 Sept. 1934, 290, 312. It did publish two letters in support of country-house tourism from owners with open houses: Lord De L'Isle of Penshurst and Lord Northampton of Compton Wynyates. But opposition was registered by Lord Leconfield of Petworth and the Duke of Rutland, and later by nearly all the owners canvassed by the National Trust in 1935–6; see below, pp. 303–4.

87  This predated the protests from owners against the French model. See *Country Life*, 18 Aug. 1934, 159, 164–5; 29 Sept. 1934, 325; 16 March 1935, 258; 6 April 1935, 339.

88  Both Zetland's overture and Treasury discussions over Wallington can be traced in PRO, T 152/567.

89  Ibid., 'Board of Inland Revenue, "Note"', with Chamberlain's annotation; see also, for some hints on Chamberlain's thinking, his contemporaneous speech to the Town Planning Institute in *Journal of the Town Planning Institute*, 21 (1934–5), 20–21.

90  See the report of Ormsby-Gore's speech in *The Times*, 16 July 1935, 13, and leader, 'The Preservation of England', 17; also correspondence 1 Aug. 1935, 15; 14 Aug. 1935, 9; 20 Aug. 1935, 8.

91  Neville Chamberlain to Lord Zetland, 10 Oct. 1935, enclosing 'Memorandum A. Note on Detailed Proposals of National Trust' and 'Memorandum B': PRO, HLG 126/66.

92  I think that Gaze, *Figures in a Landscape*, 122, and Waterson, *National Trust*, 108, put this backwards, crediting the more ambitious scheme to Zetland, whereas the plan for 'a Country Houses Association' he drew up in late 1935 was only a response to the Office of Works' 'Memorandum B'. In fact, he had tried to steer clear of this idea until Chamberlain insisted upon it. Zetland to Chamberlain, 11 Nov. 1935; Chamberlain to Zetland, 29 Nov. 1935: PRO, HLG 126/66.

93  Methuen's early activities in the country-house sphere can be traced in Corsham Court MSS, D50/1; quote from Dowager Lady Methuen to Lord Methuen, 5 Nov. 1934.

94  Lothian to Matheson, 29 Nov. 1935: Lothian MSS, GD40/17/311, ff. 590–91.

95  Correspondence between Methuen, Hussey and Matheson, Jan.–Feb. 1936: Corsham Court MSS, D50/1; Methuen to Lothian, 8 Jan., Matheson to Lothian, 18 Feb. 1936: Lothian MSS, GD40/17/311, ff. 593–5, 607; Matheson, 'Country Houses', 18 Jan. 1936, and 'Country Houses Scheme', 10 Feb. 1936: PRO, HLG 126/66.

96  'Note by Lord Salisbury', 10 Jan. 1936: Hatfield MSS, S(4)/157/12; Methuen's notes on the private meeting, 24 Feb. 1936: Corsham Court MSS, D50/1; reports of the public meeting, held 25 Feb., in *The Times*, 26 Feb. 1936, 9, and *Country Life*, 7 March 1936, 240.

97  Lees-Milne, 'Early Years of the Country Houses Scheme' and *People*

*and Places*, give the fullest existing accounts.

98  Lees-Milne, *Another Self*, 37–9, 53–4, 64–5, 93–5. For another angle on the Rousham incident, see Hillier, *Young Betjeman*, 248–9. Lees-Milne's genius for retrospective self-fashioning makes it difficult to evaluate claims such as the one quoted here – but his general aesthetic loyalties in the 1930s are clear enough, even if they were not shaped in just the way he makes out.

99  These also tended to be most optimistic about the income from tourism, though none had any experience.

100  Lord Salisbury to D. M. Matheson, 23 July 1936: Hatfield MSS, S(4)/159/19.

101  Edward Knox to Gen. Gerald Kitson, 31 March 1937: Corsham Court MSS, D50/2.

102  James Lees-Milne, 'Report on the Progress of the Country Houses Scheme', 10 Oct. 1936: PRO, HLG 126/67; Lees-Milne's reports on visits to houses, 1936–9, in National Trust MSS, 36/1PF, others scattered through the sequence of files numbered 36 and in individual property files.

103  Harewood to Lothian, 27, 29 Feb. 1936, 7 March 1936: Lothian MSS, GD40/17/311, ff. 608–11, 615–17, 621–9.

104  James Hunter Blair to Sir Edgar Bonham-Carter, 22 July 1938: National Trust MSS, 36.

105  *Hansard*, 5th ser., 111 [Lords]: 957–69 [28 Feb. 1939], 112 [Lords]: 529–64 [30 March 1939], 113 [Lords]: 439–46 [13 June 1939]; quotes at 112: 541–6, 550–51, 113: 439–40.

106  Lees-Milne memorandum, Longleat, 15 Sept. 1936: National Trust MSS, 36/1PF.

107  Lees-Milne, *People and Places*, 68–70.

108  See, e.g., Methuen's notes on the early meetings of the Committee, Corsham Court MSS, D50/1, where discussion of public opinion occasionally intruded ('rate-free Houses would not be popular in the Provinces'), although, importantly, public opinion was not much regarded one way or the other until wartime. Also Methuen's comments in *Landscape and Garden*, 3 (Autumn 1936), 153–4.

109  Lees-Milne to Methuen, 7 June 1937: Corsham Court MSS, D50/2; see also G. M. Trevelyan's characteristic 'Prefatory Note' to the souvenir catalogue, *British Country Life*.

110  The broadcast publicized the visit of a Demeure Historique delegation to England. See Methuen's complaints about National Trust publicity in Corsham Court MSS, D50/3, and Lees-Milne's patient replies there and (8 Aug. 1938) in D50/2.

111  There is a draft shooting script for the film, dated 7 May 1937, in Corsham Court MSS, D50/1. Vita Sackville-West reported vaguely that her secretary had seen the film – '"Time moves on" or something like that'. Sackville-West to Methuen, 19 July 1938: Corsham Court MSS, D50/3.

112  *Hansard*, 5th ser., 320: 419–81 [10 Feb. 1937], a three-and-a-half hour debate, during which country houses only rarely came up; for reactions (also slighting country houses), see, e.g., *Country Life*, 20 Feb. 1937, 189; *Listener*, 3 March 1937, 390.

113  E. J. Maude to the Minister, 24 July 1937; Evelyn Sharp to W. R. Frazer, 25 Sept. 1937; Sharp, 'Preservation of the Countryside' and 'Notes for Report on the Adequacy of the Existing Powers for the Preservation of the Countryside': PRO, HLG 52/709; see also Sheail, *Rural Conservation*, 88–93.

114  *Hansard*, 5th ser., 326: 1353–4 [14 July 1937].

115  Zetland combined a historical argument for Olden Time houses and an aesthetic argument for classical houses. This was followed by a letter from the tour operator Sir Henry Lunn calling for the nationalization of the great houses. *Sunday Times*, 29 Aug. 1937, 12; 3 Sept. 1937, 14.

116  *Landscape and Garden*, 3 (Autumn 1936), 153–4.

## CHAPTER 8

1  Waugh, *Brideshead Revisited*, 9–22, 325–31; Waugh to Tom Driberg, 11 Aug. 1945: *Letters of Evelyn Waugh*, 210.

2  The story of wartime use has now been told twice, by Seebohm, *The Country House: A Wartime History*, and Robinson, *The Country House at War*.

3  For literary reactions differing from Waugh's, see Christopher Harvie, 'A Great House Shaken', *New Statesman*, 2 Dec. 1988, 37–9, and Wright, *Journey Through Ruins*, 51–2, though both Harvie and Wright, writing in the 1980s, felt that this literature was almost immediately eclipsed after the war by the *Brideshead* vision.

4  Lees-Milne, *Prophesying Peace*, 210.

5  On building licences, see Robinson, *Latest Country Houses*, 14–16.

6  Duke of Northumberland's testimony to Gowers Committee, 29 July 1949: PRO, T 219/183.

7  For an interesting contemporary survey of death-duty liability and avoidance, see Watson, *Agricultural Death Duties*, esp. ch. 5 (on handing over to the National Trust), ch. 7 (on the limited liability of mansion houses) and ch. 8 (on the enhanced liability of estate companies).

8  E.g. Seebohm, *The Country House: A Wartime History*, 172–3.

9  Lees-Milne, *Caves of Ice*, 174; Lord Leicester to Lord Methuen, 20 Nov. 1945: Corsham Court MSS, D49/1.

10  'The National Trust and the Preservation of Historic Country Houses: A Review and a Forecast', Feb. 1943: National Trust MSS, 36/1PF. This copy is annotated in Lees-Milne's hand, and the text is well-informed, but the author was probably Malcolm Mackenzie. See Lord Methuen to Mackenzie, 3 June 1944: Corsham Court MSS, D50/6.

11  Lord Esher, 'The Country Houses Scheme', 17 Feb. 1942; Lees-Milne to Esher, 2 Aug. 1943: National Trust MSS, 36/1PF, 36.

12  On the scheme in wartime, see, in addition to Lees-Milne's diaries, his *People and Places*, 13–16 and *passim*, esp. the chapters on Knole and West Wycombe; also the minutes of the Country Houses Committee in National Trust MSS.

13  D. M. Matheson, 'The Future of the National Trust': Corsham Court MSS, D50/6; James Lees-Milne, 'Country Houses', 12 Nov. 1944; Minutes of the Country Houses Committee, 19 Dec. 1944: National Trust MSS, 36/1PF.

14  Calder, *Myth of the Blitz*, ch. 9, a subtle but still I feel, misguided analysis, partly resting on Potts, '"Constable Country"'; Wiener, *English Culture*, 74–7; Schwarz, 'Language of Constitutionalism', 17–18; Chase, 'This is no claptrap'.

15  For differing verdicts on Scott, Uthwatt and the 1947 machinery, see Sheail, *Rural Conservation*, 22–5, 205–12, Cullingworth, *Environmental Planning*, I, 15–21, 41, 251–7, Hall, *Containment of Urban England*, II, 35–70, Mandler, 'Politics and the English Landscape'.

16  This group appears to be neither Salisbury's Watching Committee, of which Young would not have been a member, nor one of R. A. Butler's consultative committees on the future of Toryism, which were not set up until 1942.

17  G. M. Young to Lord Herbert, 11 Jan. 1941; 31 Dec. 1941; 21 Dec. 1942: Wilton MSS, 2057/E2/10; Young, *Country and Town*, esp. 12–16.

18  Lord Herbert, 'Memorandum', July 1941, Lord Herbert to Lord Portal, 20 Oct. 1942: Wilton MSS, 2057/E2/10. Similar ideas were promoted by an all-party agricultural policy group led by Lord De La Warr in 1943 and by the Tory Reform Committee, chaired by the landowner

Lord Hinchingbrooke: De La Warr et al., *Post-War Agricultural Policy; Forward – by the Right!*, 9, 12; R. Tree et al., *The Husbandman Waiteth.*

19  E.g. leaders in *Country Life*, 17 Sept. 1943, 500; 18 Aug. 1944, 280; Brian Vesey-Fitzgerald, 'The Control of Land Use', *The Field*, 3 Feb. 1945, 112–3; Lord Brocket's letter to *The Field*, 4 March 1944, 251; but cf. the more hostile pieces by Mark Beaumont, 5 Feb. 1944, 136–8; 8 Aug. 1944, 32–4.

20  See correspondence in *The Times*, 6 March 1943, 5; 10 March 1943, 5; 17 March 1943, 5; 19 March 1943, 5; *Country Life*, 19 March 1943, 520, with correspondence 9 April 1943, 668–9, also leader in *Country Life*, 6 Aug. 1943, 236.

21  R. G. Proby to Duke of Norfolk, 15 April 1942: Wilton MSS, 2057/F.2/ 10. Proby became chairman of the Country Landowners' Association in the following year.

22  Zetland and Norman were here opposing a proposed government audit of country houses in 1941. The audit was an idea of Kenneth Clark's, to find wartime employment for his friends John Betjeman and John Piper. Although backed by Lord Reith, it was aborted by objections from the Trust and others, unlike a parallel proposal to record scenes of 'vanishing England' in a more Arts and Crafts mould: on the latter, see Mellor *et al.*, *Recording Britain*; and on the former, National Trust MSS, 1245, notably Lord Zetland to D. M. Matheson, 8 Sept. 1941 ('an enquiry into the civic possibilities of a man's private estate . . . is just the sort of thing to arouse his suspicion and resentment'); also similar sentiments in R. C. Norman to Matheson, 3 Sept. 1941. This is the scheme mentioned in Betjeman, *Letters*, 1, 290, which the editor was unable to identify.

23  Yet as a huge Georgian house, Wentworth Woodhouse was still aesthetically as well as socially suspect – in Vita Sackville-West's eyes, among others. Sackville-West, *English Country Houses*, 8–9, 44–5; see also *Country Life*, 6 Sept. 1946, 432.

24  L. E. Morris to D. M. Matheson, 1 Nov. 1943, and subsequent correspondence between Matheson, Morris, Julian Huxley and R. M. Barrington-Ward, Nov.–Dec. 1943: National Trust MSS, 36. See also the correspondence involving Matheson in *New Statesman*, 9 Oct. 1943, 234; 30 Oct., 286; 6 Nov., 302.

25  *Sunday Pictorial*, 4 June 1944, 4; Lees-Milne, *Prophesying Peace*, 87–8.

26  James Lees-Milne, 'We Must Stop This Ruin', *Sunday Pictorial*, 16 Sept. 1945, 6; correspondence in Sept. 1945 from A. J. Rae, Mrs L. M. Logan, Alan Ely, A. R. Drane: National Trust MSS, 36.

27  E. H. Phillips of Current Affairs Ltd, 'The National Trust', Feb. 1944: Corsham Court MSS, D50/6.

28  Lord Zetland, letter to *The Times*, 2 Feb. 1943, 5. See also James Lees-Milne, 'Future Uses for Country Houses', 28 Sept. 1943: National Trust MSS, 36/1PF.

29  National Trust, *49th Annual Report* (1944), 9–10; 'Treasures in Trust', *The Times*, 22 Sept. 1944, 5.

30  James Lees-Milne, 'Country Houses', 12 Nov. 1944: National Trust MSS, 36/1PF; Minutes of the Country Houses Committee, 19 Dec. 1944: National Trust MSS; Lees-Milne, *Prophesying Peace*, 144.

31  Methuen's annotations to 'The National Trust and the Preservation of Historic Country Houses: A Review and a Forecast', probably around June 1944. See n. 10 above. See also the Lords' debate on historic preservation, instigated by Methuen, in which there was much discussion of suitable alternative use: *Hansard*, 5th ser., 137 [L]: 1061–88 [21 Nov. 1945].

32  Mark Girouard, 'Country House Crisis?', *Architectural Review*, Oct. 1974, 243–4. See also Clemenson,

*English Country Houses and Landed Estates*, 137–9, suggesting that about 10 per cent of the national stock of country houses was demolished between 1945 and 1960.

33	Ibid., 155–6.

34	'Country Houses Considered in 1939 by National Trust as of First Importance' and 'Country Houses listed in 1939 as of first importance no longer in private ownership', 7 July 1952: PRO, HLG 103/119; James Lees-Milne to J.F.W. Rathbone, 2 Oct. 1950: National Trust MSS, 36/3; Ministry of Housing and Local Government, 'The Destruction of Historic Houses', 11 April 1953: PRO, WORK 14/2218. The 1939 list was by no means definitive, but it does reflect prevailing views of which houses were most worth saving.

35	Lees-Milne, *Caves of Ice*, 196; Lees-Milne, *Midway on the Waves*, 29.

36	Melville, *Castle in the Air*, and *Merely Melville*, 129–35, for the production and reaction.

37	Notably George Mallaby, who served briefly after the war as Matheson's successor as Secretary. See Lees-Milne, *Caves of Ice*, 5–6. Harold Nicolson, by then a member of the Country Houses Committee, could also sound defeatist notes. See, e.g., his 'Marginal Comment' column in the *Spectator*, 15 Aug. 1947, 204.

38	Samuel, *Theatres of Memory*, 288, quoting a retrospective piece of rationalization by a National Trust functionary, suggests, 'From the point of view of the National Trust . . . the landslide Labour victory of 1945 was an unquestioned good'. This turns grudging accommodation into open enthusiasm. For more or less the opposite view, see Wright, *Journey Through Ruins*, ch. 6.

39	Minihan, *Nationalization of Culture*, ch. 7, gives the best account of Labour's postwar cultural policies, but a monographic treatment is needed (and is being worked on by Richard Weight); see also for the

mood among the liberal intelligentsia, Annan, *Our Age*, esp. 215–20.

40	On listing, Saint, 'How Listing Happened'; on the NBR, Summerson's introduction to *50 Years of the NBR*; the expansion of the Ministry of Works' ambitions has to be followed in the PRO.

41	Summerson, 'The Past in the Future'. At the same time, Summerson was urging the National Trust to do more to conserve historic towns by preserving not only individual buildings but groups of buildings as well: Summerson, 'Town Buildings', 102.

42	The work of the new National Register of Archives in facilitating these transfers is discussed by Dick Sargent, 'National Register of Archives', 2–9.

43	Information from Sir John Summerson.

44	The immediate fruits of these researches included Pevsner's *Buildings of England* series, which began publication with the Cornwall volume (1951); Gunnis's *Dictionary of British Sculptors, 1660–1851* (1951); Summerson's *Architecture in Britain, 1530 to 1830* (1953); and Colvin's *Biographical Dictionary of English Architects, 1660–1840* (1954).

45	From Summerson's unpublished autobiography, copy in author's possession; the owner was not in fact a baronet.

46	Information from Lawrence Stone.

47	Lees-Milne, *Age of Adam*, v.

48	Watkin, *Rise of Architectural History*, chs 5 and 6 discusses some of these connections.

49	Banham, 'Revenge of the Picturesque'; see also Potts, ' "Constable Country" ', 178–9.

50	John Summerson, 'The Preservation of Georgian and Victorian Architecture', *The Chartered Surveyor*, 90 (1958), 606; 'The Critics', Home Service, 9 July 1950, script in BBC Written Archives Centre. Pevsner could be more sentimental about country houses: see, e.g., his frankly nostalgic Third Programme broadcast on the Dukeries, 7 Nov. 1948, reprinted as Pevsner, 'The Dukeries' – though his treatment of the same properties in the Nottinghamshire volume (1951) of the *Buildings of England* is more realistic – or his satire on government inaction (under the pseudonym Peter F. R. Donner) in *Architectural Review*, 113 (1953), 213–15.

51 By 1950, the BBC's leading 'heritage' broadcasters were Vesey-Fitzgerald (97 Home Service broadcasts, 1 Third Programme), Summerson (51 and 8) and Betjeman (35 and 13); the figures appear in the file on a proposed 'Heritage of Britain' series for the Festival year of 1951 in BBC Written Archives Centre.

52 Geoffrey Grigson, 'Country Broadcasts', *Country Life*, 8 July 1949, 102; see also 'Country Radio Programmes on Record', *Warwickshire Journal*, Autumn 1945, 81, 'Broadcasting and the Countryman', *Somerset Countryman*, Oct.–Dec. 1949, 165. The subject index at the BBC Written Archives Centre reveals a distinct upsurge in country-house programming from 1950; see below, p. 371.

53 Helen Lowenthal's testimony to the Gowers Committee, 9 June 1949: PRO, T 219/179. Lowenthal had been running adult education classes on country houses since 1947, and in 1952 she founded with Sir George Trevelyan a regular summer school on the history of the country house, based at Attingham. On the latter, see Beard, *Attingham*.

54 Pimlott, *Dalton*, esp. 455–6, 553–4.

55 See, e.g., Dalton to Sir E. Bridges, 17 Nov. 1945; Dalton's annotation to B. Trend to Dalton, 20 Feb. 1946; 'Summary for talk with Prime Minister', 12 March 1946: PRO, T 171/386; Sir B. Gilbert, 'National Estate Fund', 8 Jan. 1946; Budget Committee Report, 'National Estate Fund', n.d., with Dalton annotations: T 171/388.

56 Typescript, 'Budget Broadcast', 9 April 1946: Dalton MSS, 9/2/4–12.

See also Dalton's speech in *Hansard*, 5th ser., 421: 1839 [9 April 1946].

57 For the invitation to G. D. H. Cole to speak to the Trust's AGM and overtures to Clement Attlee through his private secretary Evan Durbin in 1943, see National Trust MSS, 1215; for failed negotiations with the Ministry of Works and also the Planning Ministry, see ibid., also Matheson's memorandum, 25 Feb. 1944: Corsham Court MSS, D50/6, and correspondence in 1945 in National Trust MSS, 36.

58 [James Lees-Milne and Lord Esher], 'Historic Country Houses: Question of Government Subsidy. Memorandum by the National Trust', n.d. [Feb. 1946]; Minutes of the Finance Committee, 15 March 1946; G. Mallaby, 'The National Trust: Memorandum for the Chancellor of the Exchequer', 22 March 1946: National Trust MSS, 1215.

59 Correspondence between Hugh and Ruth Dalton: Dalton MSS, D/N/1.

60 B. Trend to G. Mallaby, 9 May 1946; Minutes of the Finance Committee, 10 May 1946: National Trust MSS, 1215.

61 *Hansard*, 5th ser., 422: 2243 [16 May 1946].

62 R. C. Norman to G. Mallaby, 20 March 1946: National Trust MSS, 1215; Lord Crawford to Hugh Dalton, 21 May, 5 July, 30 July 1946; G. Mallaby to Lord Crawford, 3 June 1946; Lord Crawford to G. M. Trevelyan, 4 June 1946; Hugh Dalton to Lord Crawford, 11 July 1946: Crawford MSS, 101/25 (some corrected from copies in National Trust MSS, 1215).

63 Lord Crawford to Oliver Bevir, 30 July 1946: Crawford MSS, 101/25; Lees-Milne, *Caves of Ice*, 67. The Trust was much more upbeat in public; see its *51st Annual Report* (1946), 6–7.

64 James Lees-Milne, 'Country Houses and the Government', 7 June 1948; H. J. F. Smith, 'Comments on Mr

Lees-Milne's Memorandum', 9 June 1948: National Trust MSS, 36/3.

65 The endowments problem remained a tricky one, as the only endowment funds provided by the NLF came in the form of farms contiguous to the house. These houses had often to be supported from other sources: grants from the Pilgrim Trust and other charities, partial endowment by the former owner (especially if residence was to be retained), local authority grants, and, after 1953, Historic Buildings Council maintenance grants.

66 Lees-Milne, *People and Places*, 135–40; *Hansard*, 5th ser., 436: 39–40 [15 April 1947]; Lees-Milne, *Caves of Ice*, 160.

67 The acquisition of Audley End can be followed in PRO, T 218/418; quotes from Sir Eric de Normann to Sir Alan Barlow, 3 Oct. 1946, 30 Dec. 1947.

68 *Hansard*, 5th ser., 447: 1678 [23 Feb. 1948].

69 The Harewood files at the PRO are still closed, presumably out of excessive deference to royal interests, but see Lees-Milne's 'Rough notes . . . of the Meeting at the Treasury on 16 March, 1948' in National Trust MSS, 36/3, and the history of the case in PRO, T 218/10, esp. E. W. Playfair to Sir E. de Normann, 20 Oct. 1951.

70 Information from Sir Edward Playfair; Lees-Milne, *Midway on the Waves*, 18.

71 Ibid., 24–5; B. D. Fraser's brief for 'Chancellor of the Exchequer's Meeting with Lord Crawford . . . 12th May 1948': PRO, T 219/176.

72 B. D. Fraser, [Memorandum on Legislation to Extend Use of NLF for Houses], 31 May 1948; P. D. Proctor to Sir B. Gilbert and Sir E. Bridges, with annotations by Cripps, 17 June 1948; Chancellor of Exchequer, 'Preservation of Houses of Architectural or Historic Interest', 14 July 1948: PRO, T 219/176.

73 Discussion of membership of the committee in PRO, T 219/176.

74 Herbert Morrison to Sir Stafford Cripps, 21 Aug. 1948, in ibid.

75 Lees-Milne, *Midway on the Waves*, 136, 138. Blunt was appointed to the Historic Buildings Committee in October, shortly after being named to Gowers, but Lees-Milne and Esher had in fact been seeking an art expert for their committee since June; see Lees-Milne to Esher, 2 June, 12 Oct. 1948: National Trust MSS, 36.

76 Minutes of the Gowers Committee in PRO, T 219/183; memoranda of evidence in T 219/177–9.

77 See in ibid. submissions from Sir R. Hoare, Lord Northampton, M. W. Wickham-Boynton, Ronald Tree, Duke of Marlborough, Major Le G. G. W. Horton-Fawkes, Lord De L'Isle, Christopher Hussey, Lord Hinchingbrooke, Sir Algar Howard, Lord Spencer, Duke of Devonshire, Sir Harold Wernher, Duke of Northumberland, Duke of Wellington, the Land Union and Central Landowners' Association.

78 Sir E. de Normann to F. J. E. Raby, 12 Nov. 1948, with memorandum by Raby: PRO, HLG 126/16; 'Committee on Houses of National Importance. Memorandum by the Ministry of Works', 28 Feb. 1949: PRO, T 219/177.

79 There was an abortive attempt to negotiate privately a line of demarcation between Ministry and Trust: see Sir E. de Normann to F. J. Root, 23 Feb. 1949, and R. A. Barker to A. Miller, 8 March 1949: PRO, HLG 126/16.

80 Memorandum by James Lees-Milne with comments and redraft by Harold Nicolson; memorandum by Lord Esher and 'Reflections on Mr Lees-Milne' [all c. Jan. 1949]: National Trust MSS, 36/3; H. J. Smith and C. J. Gibbs, 'Country Houses and the Government', 4 Feb. 1949: Crawford MSS, 101/24;

Lees-Milne, *Midway on the Waves*, 154, 155; 'Notes of a meeting', 11 Feb. 1949: National Trust MSS, 36/3.

81  'Committee on Houses of National Importance: The National Trust. Evidence', 17 March 1949: PRO, T 219/178; Lees-Milne, *Midway on the Waves*, 169–70; Minutes of Gowers Committee, 29 April 1949: PRO, T 219/183.

82  H. M. Treasury, *Report of the Committee on Houses of Outstanding Historic or Architectural Interest*, published 23 June 1950, esp. 3–6, 28–36.

83  See the survey of press reaction in *Country Life*, 30 June 1950, 1954.

84  Lees-Milne was shortly to leave the Trust's full-time employment for life as a part-time tax exile, and to some extent this unmuzzled him. For his views at this time, see James Lees-Milne, 'Can England's Great Country Houses be Saved?', *Listener*, 10 Aug. 1950, 193–4 (a Third Programme broadcast); James Lees-Milne to J. F. W. Rathbone, 2 Oct. 1950: National Trust MSS, 36/3; James Lees-Milne to Lord Methuen, 12 April 1951: Corsham Court MSS, D49/5.

85  *The Times*, 23 June 1950, 7; for a criticism very close to ministers' thinking, see the leader, 'Historic Houses', *New Statesman*, 1 July 1950, 2.

86  Minute by Cripps, 29 April 1950: PRO, T 218/86.

87  Minute by Dalton, 29 May 1950: PRO, HLG 103/114. See also Hugh Dalton to Hugh Gaitskell, 20 Dec. 1950: Dalton MSS, 9/9/115, copy with enclosure in PRO, T 219/176.

88  Hugh Gaitskell, 'Gowers Report', 5 Jan. 1951, in response to even stronger language from his Financial Secretary Douglas Jay, 10 Dec. 1950: PRO, T 219/176.

89  See the range of options presented in E. W. Playfair to Sir Edward Bridges, 'The Gowers Report', 30 Nov.

1950, and Bridges's cover-note to Gaitskell and Jay, 6 Dec. 1950: PRO, T 219/176.

90  Gaitskell's final decision is reported in 'Gowers Report. Note of Conclusions of a Meeting', 17 Jan. 1950: PRO, T 218/87, but he is still having to tone down Playfair's rhetoric in April – see his annotations to Playfair's draft of reply to a Parliamentary Question, 24 April 1951: T 218/89. Playfair never lost his faith in Gowers's original proposal for tax reliefs.

91  Copies of minutes, Lord President's Committee, 20 April 1951, and Cabinet, 23 April 1951: PRO, WORK 14/2205.

92  'Eccles is a queer fish': Lord Crawford to R. A. Butler, 15 Sept. 1952: PRO, T 218/11, among other expressions of frustration.

93  David Eccles to Hugh Molson, 20 Nov. 1951; Eccles to Sir Harold Emmerson, 27 Feb. 1952; [Eccles], 'Historic Houses – New Legislation' [draft], 21 April 1952: PRO, WORK 14/2358; 'Note of a Meeting', 18 Aug. 1952; Eccles to Molson, 8 Sept. 1952: WORK 14/2359; *Hansard*, 5th ser., 510: 2208–9 [6 Feb. 1953].

94  'Cabinet: Historic Buildings Committee. Minutes of a Meeting', 6 March 1953: PRO, T 218/13.

95  National Trust, *57th Annual Report* (1952), 19–20; for press reaction, see *Daily Herald*, 20 Sept. 1952, 2; *Daily Telegraph*, 20 Sept. 1952, 6; *Daily Graphic*, 20 Sept. 1952, 4; *Nottingham Guardian*, 20 Sept. 1952; *Observer*, 21 Sept. 1952, 6; *News Chronicle*, 22 Sept. 1952, 2; *Evening Chronicle* [Newcastle], 25 Sept. 1952, 16. The Planning Ministry was irritated with the 'enormous Press given to the Trust's Annual Report' which gave 'a rather distorted picture' of the effectiveness of listing historic buildings. Miss I. V. Kuhlicke to R. R. Fedden, 3 Oct. 1952: PRO, HLG 103/119.

96 The *Yorkshire Evening Post, Evening Standard, News Chronicle, Daily Mail, Liverpool Daily Post, Western Mail, Birmingham Post, East Anglian Daily Times* and *Nottingham Guardian* all ran items on the Colegate debate on 6–7 Feb. 1953, and there were also leaders pressing for action in *Manchester Guardian*, 6 Feb.; *Yorkshire Post*, 7 Feb.; *Sheffield Telegraph*, 7 Feb.; *Northern Echo*, 7 Feb.; *Daily Telegraph*, 7 Feb.

97 *Hansard*, 5th ser., 510: 2202–9 [6 Feb. 1953]; see also Methuen's motion, 5th ser., 102 [Lords]: 548–78 [14 May 1953]. The Treasury's characterization of the scheme is from John Boyd-Carpenter to R. A. Butler, 4 Feb. 1953: PRO, T 218/12.

98 The Treasury had agreed to release £5 million of the National Land Fund for the Labour plan: E. W. Playfair to Sir Bernard Gilbert, 30 Oct. 1951: PRO, T 218/10; £500,000 p.a. had been the HBC budget proposed by Gaitskell: Copy of Lord President's Committee minute, 20 April 1951: WORK 14/2205.

99 *Hansard*, 5th ser., 517: 761–2 [3 July 1953].

100 From Lascelles's evidence to the Select Committee on Estimates, Subcommittee E, 9 March 1960, but deleted by him from the printed version! See Confidential Proof of Lascelles's evidence: PRO, HLG 126/556.

101 Initial membership is discussed in PRO, HLG 126/117 and HLG 103/97; quote from Sir Harold Emmerson to Sir David Eccles, 30 July 1953: HLG 126/117.

102 Hugh Molson to Sir David Eccles, 16 Sept. 1953; Lord Crawford to Hugh Molson, 21 Sept. 1953; 'Mr Rathbone's Names', 22 Sept. 1953: PRO, HLG 126/117.

103 In the following paragraphs I have drawn on John Summerson, 'The Preservation of Georgian and Victorian Architecture', *The Chartered Surveyor*, 90 (May 1958), 607–10;

Historic Buildings Council for England, 11*th Annual Report* (1963); Christopher Hussey, 'Ten Years of Preservation: The Work of the Historic Buildings Councils', *Country Life Annual* 1964, 8–11; Cornforth, *Country Houses*, 32–5, 39–40.

104 On the public-access servitude, see PRO, HLG 126/50, esp. 'Arrangements for Opening Historic Buildings to the Public', 29 Jan. 1957, and Lord Cholmondeley to C. D. E. Keeling, 27 April 1954; HLG 126/106, esp. correspondence with M. W. Harford of Little Sodbury Manor, 1957, winning relaxation of access conditions; also HLG 126/550 on houses open only by appointment.

105 For the operation of the means test, see PRO, HLG 126/10.

106 On Ragley, see Barker, *One Man's Estate*, 18–20; the relevant HBC files are still closed.

107 A prime example is Badminton, which received a grant in 1960, was opened on a minimal basis in the 1960s and 1970s, but today is not regularly open to the public.

108 See, e.g., 'Charity Begins at the Stately Home', *Evening Standard*, 13 Aug. 1952, 9; 'A Rich Man's Dilemma Ends in a Poor Man's Burden', *Daily Express*, 10 Dec. 1952; '£10,000 in Clerks for Stately Homes', *Daily Express*, 18 June 1953, 2; 'Now the Dukes Go on the Dole', *Daily Express*, 19 June 1953, 4; 'Nobles on the Dole', *Evening Standard*, 29 March 1954, 4; 'You Foot the Bill But They Shut You Out', *Sunday Express*, 4 Aug. 1957, 4; 'Why should we let them cash in on our heritage?', *Sunday Express*, 6 Sept. 1959; 'Are the stately showmen making money?', *Evening Standard*, 21 Feb. 1962, 3.

109 Eccles's annotation to Sir Eric de Normann to Sir David Eccles, 20 June 1953: PRO, WORK 14/2220; Jenkins and James, *From Acorn to Oak Tree*, 196–7.

110 See the summary of press coverage in

'Publicity', 1960: PRO, HLG 126/
22.

111   See, e.g., 'Allies in a Good Cause',
      *The Times*, 13 Nov. 1954, 7; 'The
      State and Stately Homes', *Economist*,
      8 June 1957, 865-7; John Betjeman,
      'Country House Heritage', *Daily
      Telegraph*, 7 April 1958; Christopher
      Hussey, 'What Buildings are Worth
      Preserving?', *The Times*, 13 Nov.
      1961, 14. Also the rare and subdued
      debate in *Hansard*, 5th ser., 198 [L]:
      546-57 [6 July 1956].

112   The level of the ration can be fol-
      lowed in the HBC's *Annual Reports*;
      its origins are discussed in PRO, T
      218/313 and HLG 126/546.

113   See, e.g., the dampening correspond-
      ence with the National Trust for
      Scotland in Nov. 1958 and with
      Lord Verulam of the Ancient Monu-
      ments Society in Dec. 1959:
      National Trust MSS, 36/3, 36.

114   *Daily Telegraph*, 29 May 1957, 18 July
      1957; *The Times*, 5 June 1957, 10; 18
      June 1957, 10.

115   For the arguments that follow, see
      also Mandler, 'Nationalising the
      Country House'.

116   Information from Sir John
      Summerson; see also Chuter Ede's
      worries about the HBC's neglect of
      village and townscape in *Hansard*, 5th
      ser., 634: 1356-7 [14 Feb. 1961].

117   See, e.g., A. R. Wagner and A. C.
      Acworth, ' "Economy" and the
      Gowers Report', 2 Jan. 1951: PRO,
      HLG 103/114; [A. C. Acworth],
      'Monuments and Buildings (Protec-
      tion) Bill. Memorandum Submitted
      by the Georgian Group', 12 Sept.
      1951: WORK 14/2208; 'Observa-
      tions by the Georgian Group on the
      Ministry's Memorandum', 17 June
      1953: WORK 14/2209.

CHAPTER 9

1   From the preface to the 1960 reissue,
    reprinted in subsequent editions.

2   Self and Storing, *State and the Farmer*,
    20-21, 67-71, 81-3. The 45 per cent

rebate regularized the *ad hoc* practice,
maintained since 1925, of exempting
agricultural land from increases in
death-duty rates. See Watson, *Agricultural Death Duties*, 18-20.

3   Cannadine, *Decline and Fall*, 649,
    asserts the opposite. Yet the propor-
    tion of owner-occupied acreage in
    England and Wales rose from 11 per
    cent in 1914 to 36 per cent in 1927
    but only to 38 per cent by 1950 and
    49 per cent by 1960. Furthermore,
    as farms were taken in hand, more
    estate-owners were becoming
    owner-occupiers. In Clemenson's
    large sample, there was about as
    much sale activity in 1919-23 as in
    1945-55. Clemenson, *English Coun-
    try Houses*, 111-13; also Thompson,
    *English Landed Society*, 332, 337.

4   Records of landownership are so
    poor that it is possible to come to
    varying conclusions about the scale
    of retention by the aristocracy: cf.
    the relative optimism of Thompson,
    'English Landed Society I', 12, 23, or
    Newby, *Green and Pleasant Land*, 38-
    40, and the relative pessimism
    of Habakkuk, *Marriage, Debt and the
    Estates System*, 699-702, or
    Cannadine, *Decline and Fall*, 641-2,
    649. The latter is certainly too pessi-
    mistic, suggesting that only one-third
    of the peerage still owned estates in
    1956, a statistic he appears to extract
    from Bush, *English Aristocracy*, 157-8.
    But as Bush himself points out, the
    peerage, 'profusely' extended in the
    twentieth century for political
    reasons, no longer represents the class
    of great landowners. In contrast, a
    systematic survey of surviving great
    estates in the mid-1950s shows that
    over 80 per cent were still held by
    their pre-1900 historic owners. Simi-
    lar surveys in the 1970s showed that
    over half of historic landowners still
    owned estates of some kind, and half
    of the historic great landowners still
    owned great estates. See Denman,
    *Estate Capital*, 121-2; Clemenson,
    *English Country Houses*, 118-24;
    Wells, 'Landed Gentry', xxiii-iv; also

Perrott, *Aristocrats*, 134, 149, 160, still has 43 per cent of the *peerage* owning estates in 1968, two-thirds of whom held more than 5,000 acres.

5   Self and Storing, *State and the Farmer*, 185–6; Bence-Jones, 'Trust of Land-owning', xviii; Montagu, *Gilt and the Gingerbread*, 192–6. Denman, *Estate Capital*, gloomy both about rents and investment, was based on surveys in the early 1950s before the move to taking in hand was evident.

6   Thompson, 'English Landed Society IV', 22; Self and Storing, *State and the Farmer*, 177–92; Lowe et al., *Countryside Conflicts*, 32–45.

7   See the survey of the gentry by Wells, 'Landed Gentry', xxiii–vi, and (more impressionistically) of the aristocracy by Bence-Jones and Montgomery-Massingberd, *British Aristocracy*, 229–31.

8   On the superficiality of profession-alization on great estates, see Self and Storing, *State and the Farmer*, 190–92, and from a different point of view on the 1950 and 1960s, Lord Coke: 'In those days very few estates were business-orientated or commercially-minded. That came later . . .' Levin, *Raine and Johnnie*, 185.

9   Andrew Cox, *Adversary Politics and Land*, 109–12.

10  Bence-Jones, 'Trust of Landowning', xviii.

11  Denman, *Estate Capital*, took the tra-ditional view and conveniently excluded rising land values in his cal-culation of estates' integrity in the 1950s; but noted in passing, p. 73, that even before 1939 larger estates had funded 35 per cent of their improvements from land sales, and the proportion was likely to be higher after 1945, higher still after Denman's 1957 study.

12  Self, 'Town Planning in Retreat', 213–14; Bence, 'Trust in Land-owning', xvi.

13  Lowe et al., *Countryside Conflicts*, 32–6.

14  Reitlinger, *Economics of Taste*, I, 219–20, 226–30, 235–6.

15  Harling, *Historic Houses*, 180.

16  The *douceur* for offers of land and buildings was lower – 10 per cent – reflecting the fact that owners did not have the option of exporting land and buildings.

17  Derbyshire people objected to what they saw as the national museums looting their local treasures, which were a tourist-draw. See the summary of the controversy in *Burlington Magazine*, 99 (1957), 327–8, and, for a local perspective, *Derbyshire Countryside*, Oct. 1957, 26–7.

18  Robinson, *Latest Country Houses*, 29.

19  Jones, *Britain's Heritage*, 77.

20  Robinson, *Country House At War*, 168–70; cf. Clemenson, *English Country Houses*, 138–9; also Cornforth, *Country Houses*, 4 (270 'notable' houses in England demol-ished since the war), Mark Girouard's estimate in *Architectural Review*, 156 (1974), 243 (470 houses demolished 1945–60, another 240 in 1960–74), and the exchange between Marcus Binney, J. M. Robinson and James Lees-Milne in *Country Life*, 21 Nov. 1974, 1598–9; 16 Jan. 1975, 156; 30 Jan. 1975, 275.

21  I have calculated from Robinson's gazetteer that eighty-nine new houses replaced sold or demolished old ones while eighty-two were alterations of old houses. Robinson, *Latest Country Houses*, 197–234.

22  Clemenson, *English Country Houses*, 157–8. From Clemenson's figures for sale and demolition, we can say roughly that a quarter had left before 1945, half left after and a quarter stayed.

23  Lees-Milne, *Midway on the Waves*, 227; Howard, 'Castle Howard'.

24  Flower, *Debrett's Stately Homes*, 124, 160; Robinson, *Latest Country Houses*, 178–85.

25  Cecily Blathwayt to Lord Methuen, 18 Nov. 1954: Corsham Court MSS, D49(m).

26  Denman, *Estate Capital*, 106.

27  Examples of the latter include West Wycombe, Sudbury and Ickworth.

28 Leatham, *Burghley*, 100–13, 234–6.

29 For example, the prewar inhabitants of Chatsworth, Woburn Abbey, Castle Howard and Ragley. The aesthetic 7th Duke of Wellington knew full well that he was the first of his line since the 2nd Duke to give any thought to the appearance of Stratfield Saye: see Bence-Jones, *Ancestral Houses*, 213. There are of course counter-examples, homes of prewar aesthetes – one thinks of Haddon and Althorp – but the aesthetic aristocrat was a rare bird before 1939.

30 Robinson, *Latest Country Houses*, 41–51.

31 On Phillimore and 'alteration', Robinson, *Latest Country Houses*, 124–31; on Knowsley, *Sunday Times*, 17 May 1953; on Rudding, *Daily Telegraph*, 14 Jan. 1954, 10.

32 Correspondence between Methuen, Lansdowne, H. C. M. Tapper of the Bowood Estate and Hugh Wortham of the *Daily Telegraph*, 1954–6: Corsham Court MSS, D49(l); *The Times*, 24, 28, 29 June 1955; 1 July 1955; *Sunday Times*, 26 June 1955; *Daily Telegraph*, 26 July 1955; 2 July 1956; *Country Life*, 7 July 1955, 4.

33 The sale at Christie's was held 12 Oct. 1994; for the fortunes of the Bowood estate, see *Country Life*, 15 June 1972, 1546–50, 26 July 1979, 273. The estate is now formally in the hands of the heir, Lord Shelburne.

34 E.g., in Parliament, Lord Methuen, *Hansard*, 5th ser., 170[L]: 990–5 [8 March 1951], Lord Lambton and Henry Channon, 510: 227–30 [6 Feb. 1953], Lords Winster, Montagu of Beaulieu and Brocket, 182[L]: 760–61, 774–80 [9 June 1953].

35 See the memorandum of the Central Landowners' Association, 30 April 1949, and testimony from representatives of the Land Union, Minutes of the Gowers Committee, 19 April 1949: PRO, T 219/179, 183.

36 Marquess of Bath to Sir Harold

Wernher, 12 Aug. 1952, forwarded to David Eccles: PRO, WORK 14/2216.

37 As of 1974, neither De L'Isle nor Warwick had received any grant; Salisbury only a little; Bath reluctantly took a £40,000 grant in the mid-1960s to fight death-watch beetle. Cornforth, *Country Houses*, 34; Montagu, *Gilt and the Gingerbread*, 106.

38 De L'Isle, Warwick and Salisbury's testimony to Gowers Committee, 21 April, 17 July 1949; 10 March 1950: PRO, T 219/183; Lord Salisbury to Lord Methuen, 5 May 1951: Corsham Court MSS, D49/5; Lord Salisbury to David Eccles, 16 Dec. 1952: PRO, WORK 14/2210. The same view was held at this period by W. F. Deedes, who changed his mind as a result of his membership of the Historic Buildings Council. *Hansard*, 5th ser., 634: 1380 [14 Feb. 1961].

39 See above, p. 274; Lord Salisbury to R. A. Butler, 25 Jan. 1953: PRO, T 218/12; also *Hansard*, 5th ser., 170[L]: 995–9 [8 March 1951].

40 *Hansard*, 5th ser., 182[L]: 770–71 [9 June 1953].

41 The story can be traced from Dec. 1951 to Nov. 1952 in Corsham Court MSS, D49/6, including Wernher's wounded response to the article by Victor Sims, 'The Stately Homes of England (Inc.)', *Sunday Chronicle*, 9 March 1952, 4; Wernher was the chairman, Lord Warwick vice-chairman, Lord Montagu secretary of the original committee. After the scheme's collapse, Wernher tried to carry on for a while as a soloist. See also correspondence in PRO, WORK 14/2216, and Montagu's comments in *Gilt and the Gingerbread*, 203.

42 See below, p. 398. James Lees-Milne also raised the possibility of an association of owners after his retirement from full-time work for the National Trust, but Methuen discouraged him. Lees-Milne to Methuen, 12

April 1951; Methuen to Lees-Milne, 16 April 1951: Corsham Court MSS, D49/5, D50/8.

43  Lady Exeter, 'The Future of Great Country Houses – I', *Country Life*, 9 Nov. 1945, 812–14, also letter in 31 May 1946, 1000; Minutes of the Gowers Committee, 30 March 1949: PRO, T 219/178; Leatham, *Burghley*, 14, 20–21.

44  Harling, *Historic Houses*, 21–4; Minutes of the Gowers Commmittee, 21 April 1949: PRO, T 219/183.

45  Lord St Levan to Lord Methuen, 9 Nov. 1945: Corsham Court MSS, D49/1; Montagu, *Gilt and the Gingerbread*, 48–9.

46  Minutes of the Gowers Committee, 9–10 Mar. 1950: PRO, T 219/183; Harling, *Historic Houses*, 42–3.

47  Tourist accounts, 1939–55: Warwick Castle MSS, CR 1886/TN 848, 707; Minutes of the Gowers Committee, 17 Aug. 1949: PRO, T 219/183.

48  At the time of the Gowers Committee, Warwick Castle and Penshurst, and possibly St Michael's Mount, were allowed by the Inland Revenue to set maintenance expenses against tourist income (Schedule D, Case I). The claim was allowed if a house was being shown commercially, but the definition of commercialism varied considerably between local tax inspectors. Later, houses had generally to be open one hundred days a year to qualify, and this remained a grievance through the 1970s. See, further, n. 83 below.

49  See his survey in January 1947, National Trust MSS, 36; also his *People and Places*, passim.

50  James Lees-Milne to Lord Methuen, 29 Oct. 1945; R. R. Fedden to J. F. W. Rathbone, 13 July 1955: National Trust MSS, 36.

51  Lees-Milne, *People and Places*, 177–82; Lees-Milne, *Caves of Ice*, 160. For early criticisms, see John Summerson's Third Programme broadcast, printed in *The Listener*, 8 May 1947, 700–11, and correspondence in *Country Life*, 13 May 1947, 1118–9, 4

July 1947, 36–7, 25 July 1947, 187, and, later, the Beaverbrook Press attacks cited in ch. 8, n. 108.

52  Report on the 1949 season in National Trust MSS, 36/3; examples of good publicity from Charlecote in *Warwickshire Journal*, Oct.–Dec. 1946, 156, and Mais, *Arden and Avon*, 45–50.

53  For lists, see Roger Cary, 'Country Houses Open to the Public', *Burlington Magazine*, 92 (1950), 209–13; *The Times*, 15, 18, 25 April; 13 May 1950; *Come to Britain* (1950), a joint publication of the *The Times* and the British Travel Association, 22. Cary was a BBC talks producer with a particular passion for country houses and his long list is excessively generous. Even accepting his data, a maximum of ninety-eight houses on his list qualify as country houses open to the public; *The Times'* lists ran to sixty-seven houses, *Come to Britain* eighty-two. My own estimates, here and elsewhere, are based on cross-comparisons of all the sources cited and exclude historic buildings that are not country houses or open only by appointment. For radio broadcasts, see n. 56 below; for an early league table, see *Daily Telegraph*, 9 Aug. 1950; there were also league tables in the *Daily Express*, and see leader in *The Times*, 4 June 1952, on the league-table phenomenon.

54  See Anthony Emery, '25 Years of *Historic Houses Castles and Gardens*', in *Historic Houses* (1976); circulation claim from J. H. Lewis to A. W. Cunliffe, 8 Dec. 1960: PRO, HLG 126/550. The British Travel Association list, published by *The Times* in *Come to Britain* (1950), did not appear in *Come to Britain* (1951) but transferred to the Coach Guide; the 1952 list was printed as a separate pamphlet by Index Publishers as the first in the still extant serial *Historic Houses, Castles and Gardens*. The *Country Life* series begins with Nares, *Country Houses*, and continued until

the 1960s; *Country Life* also published illustrated books based on its lists and edited by Christopher Hussey.

55 The *Daily Telegraph* began to run a regular stately-home roundup (with league table) in the autumn. For examples of media scrutinies of the business in this period, see John Summerson, 'The Open House', *New Statesman*, 18 June 1955, 847–8; 'All in a Day's Work: The Stately Homes of England', Home Service broadcast, 19 Sept. 1955; 'Half-Crown Houses', feature on *Woman's Hour*, Light Programme broadcast, 4 June 1957; Norman Shrapnel, 'Visiting Stately Homes', *Manchester Guardian*, 6, 9 Sept. 1957; 'The Stately Home Business: An Inquiry into a Postwar Industry', Home Service broadcast, 7 July 1959; 'Stately Home as Big Business', *The Times*, 15 Sept. 1959.

56 Before 1950, the rare broadcast on a country-house topic was likely to take an educational standpoint: e.g. Pevsner's talks or a *Woman's Hour* series in early 1950 on alternative uses. But in 1950 and 1951 there were about twenty broadcasts a year on country houses, increasingly leisure-oriented, in 1952 over thirty, and in 1957 over forty. My estimates from the Radio Subject Index, BBC Written Archives Centre, s.v. Famous Buildings.

57 On municipalized country houses after the war, see Cornforth, *Country Houses*, 44–6, and R. Rowe, 'Public Country House Museums', *Museums Journal*, 70 (1970–71), 125. More work needs to be done on these country-house museums to pin down the chronology of their changing presentation. A pioneer was Temple Newsam House which, under Philip Hendy, was shown as early as 1938–9 with 'its necessary complement of pictures and furniture' on loan from private owners of other houses. Leeds City . . . , *Annual Report* (1938–9), 1–2.

58 E.g., in the first category, the Duke

of Buccleuch's Boughton, Earl Bathurst's Cirencester, the Marquess of Cholmondeley's Houghton; hardly any of the Victorian houses were open. Other conspicuous non-openers were the Stopford-Sackvilles' Drayton House, the Earl of Stamford's Dunham Massey, the Duke of Wellington's Stratfield Saye and (except for a short period) the Earl of Radnor's Longford Castle. Many of these houses opened after 1974: see below, pp. 407–8.

59 Chatsworth had 85,000 and Longleat 135,000 in their first year of opening, 1949; Blenheim and Warwick Castle were at the same level by 1951.

60 Montagu, *Gilt and the Gingerbread*, 85–7; National Trust, *Annual Report, 1967–1968*. These are figures for England. For figures from the early 1970s, see below, p. 398.

61 Minutes of the Gowers Committee, 28 July 1949: PRO, T 219/183; Burnett, *Longleat*, 179–82; Marquess of Bath, 'The "Why" of Tourism at Longleat', *Historic Houses* (1980); interview with Bath in Montagu, *Gilt and the Gingerbread*, 104–17; Harling, *Historic Houses*, 65–7; see also, for early publicity, 'Now It's "Open House" at this Ancestral Mansion', *News of the World*, 24 April 1949.

62 Montagu, *Gilt and the Gingerbread*, 47–65.

63 Ibid., 30, 100–3; Duke of Bedford, 'Woburn Abbey' and *Silver-Plated Spoon* (neither very informative); for an early example of publicity, see 'Duke Talks about His 2s.6d.-a-Head Visitors', *Sunday Dispatch*, 17 June 1955.

64 Montagu, *Gilt and the Gingerbread*, 85–7, 91–9.

65 'Country Houses as Tourist Assets', *Country Life*, 20 May 1965, 1202.

66 The Wolterton case is discussed in PRO, HLG 126/4, and by Montagu, *Gilt and the Gingerbread*, 129; for Little Sodbury, see PRO, HLG 126/106.

67 'Arrangements for Opening Historic

Buildings to the Public', 9 Jan. 1957: PRO, HLG 126/50.

68  Harling, *Historic Houses*, 183–7; Marjorie Mockler, 'Opening a Smaller House', *Historic Houses* (1976), 6–7.

69  Levin, *Raine and Johnnie*, 18–20.

70  Major Le G. G. W. Horton-Fawkes to the Gowers Committee, March 1949: PRO, T 219/178. Cf. the nearly identical sentiments voiced by his predecessor at Farnley in the 1880s, above, pp. 211–12.

71  James Lees-Milne, 'Don't Kill the Goose, or Hints to Owners', *Historic Houses* (1968), 3–4.

72  Lord Herbert to C. F. G. Max-Muller, 28 July 1955: BBC Written Archives Centre, R30/'Historic Houses'.

73  Earl of Warwick's testimony (dating commercialization to 1906, when the system was reorganized, rather than 1885 when it was instituted), Minutes of the Gowers Committee, 17 Aug. 1949: PRO, T 219/183.

74  My own experience of owners is that they still view visiting as a post-1945 phenomenon, with, again, some knowledge of 'polite' visiting as described to them in *Country Life*. They tend to be unaware of Victorian tourism even if visitors' books stuffed with names are sitting on the shelves of their libraries.

75  James Lees-Milne, 'Don't Kill the Goose, or Hints to Owners', *Historic Houses* (1968), 3–4. For other admissions along these lines, see *Country Life*, 21 April 1950, 1106; Montagu, *Gilt and the Gingerbread*, 22–3.

76  'Preserving a Seat', *Daily Telegraph*, 24 June 1955; March, 'Goodwood House', 171. Later on the same page, March refers to landowners' 'moral duty' to open their historic houses, something of an afterthought.

77  Norman Wymer, 'Preserving an Ancestral Estate', *Country Life*, 26 Dec. 1952, 2094–5.

78  Harling, *Historic Houses*, 141–5.

79  Burnett, *Longleat*, 182.

80  Technically, businesses were considered under Case I of Schedule D; otherwise, Case VI of Schedule D was available, allowing only expenses directly attributable to opening (such as the cost of guides). There was also a maintenance claim for the house open to all estate owners under Schedule A, until 1963, and (for those who elected to retain it) after that date as well.

81  Tourist accounts, 1953–61: Wilton MSS, A1/202, 216.

82  E.g. 'Memorandum from the Land Union on the Preservation of Historic Houses', 26 Jan. 1953: PRO, WORK 14/2217; Cornforth, *Country Houses*, 86–91; Culme-Seymour, 'The House and the Estate', 141; Young, *Country House in the 1980s*, 81.

83  Information on this subject is limited for the earlier period of opening; in the 1970s, Cornforth, *Country Houses*, 86, estimated that as few as twenty houses could claim expenses under Case I, a guess since quoted repeatedly as fact, but Butler, *Economics of Country Houses*, 66–7, found a much wider benefit in his representative sample, and Sayer, *Disintegration*, 84–5, found sixty-two beneficiaries of Case I out of a non-representative sample of only ninety-two!

84  Hertford, 'Ragley Hall'.

85  Montagu, *Gilt and the Gingerbread*, 129–30.

86  On 'neo-romanticism', see Hewison, *In Anger, passim*, but esp. 65–6 on the country house (also the same author's *Heritage Industry*, 63–4).

87  This was more a 1960s than a 1950s phenomenon, but see the references in n. 55 above, also Norman MacKenzie, 'The Stately Homes of England', *New Statesman*, 9, 16 June 1951.

88  In the 1950s, at least, preservationists hardly felt in a majority even in intellectual circles. See, for instance, the mixed verdicts on the intellectuals rendered at 'Perils and Prospects in Town and Country', a Royal

Society of Arts conference held in October 1956, proceedings excerpted in *Journal of the Royal Society of Arts*, 105 (1956–7), 73–120.

89 On the failure of rural recreational planning, see John Heeley, 'Planning for Tourism in Britain: An Historical Perspective', *Town Planning Review*, 52 (1981), 61–79; Cherry, *Environmental Planning*, II, 109–25 (particularly damning given Cherry's usual circumspection).

90 'Open Country' file, 1955, esp. memorandum by Charles Parker, 28 Jan. [1955] and David Gretton to Robin Whitworth, n.d.: BBC Written Archives Centre, M5/92. I have only been able to scratch the surface of the BBC's outpouring of leisure-oriented programming in the 1950s, and a good deal more work remains to be done.

91 Hudson, 'Economics of the National Trust', 29–32. The correlation breaks down after 1964; see below, pp. 388–9, 411–12. Like all such correlations, it does not demonstrate that economic growth *caused* NT growth, only that the two grew *pari passu*.

92 Cornforth, *Country Houses*, 113–15, 118.

93 Montagu, *Gilt and the Gingerbread*, 150–54.

94 John Summerson, 'The Open House', *New Statesman*, 18 June 1955, 847–8.

95 'Palpable History', *Country Life*, 4 Oct. 1962, 760.

96 Lilian M. Eason, 'Chastleton: A House of Character', *Gloucestershire Countryside*, April 1949, 212–3, 230; publicity scrapbook, 1950–53: Hatfield MSS; publicity file, May 1951: Wilton MSS, H4/11.

97 'Where Shall We Go?' file, May–Aug. 1953: BBC Written Archives Centre, N8/50.

98 Kay Cicellis, 'Two Englands Apart: I. "Tea in the Grecian Hall"', *Geographical Magazine*, 29 (1956–7), 299–302.

99 John Summerson, 'The Open House', *New Statesman*, 18 June 1955, 847–8.

100 This is based on a tiny sample of Listener Research reports for 1952–3 in the BBC Written Archives Centre (LR/52/914, 53/1248, 53/1415, 53/1498); again, much more research could be done.

101 Publicity scrapbook, 1950–53: Hatfield MSS.

102 National Trust, *Annual Reports 1967–8, 1968–9*.

103 *Connoisseur*, May 1957, 209 (emphasis in original).

104 'The decorative arts and the country house musuem', *Museums Journal* 70, (1970–71), 125–7.

105 *Country Life* readers were expected to know their Gobelins. 'Country House Collections', *Country Life*, 20 June 1952, 1896.

106 Garth Christian, 'The Countryside under Invasion', *Country Life*, 21 April 1966, 930–32; Hudson, 'Economics of the National Trust', 29–33.

107 *Country Life*, 3 Oct. 1968, 803.

108 There are not as yet any truly comparative studies of postwar development and the environmentalist reaction, but a good start is made in Diefendorf, *Rebuilding Europe's Bombed Cities*. For surveys of British developments, see Cullingworth, *Environmental Planning*, IV; Hall et al., *Containment of Urban England*, II; Cox, *Adversary Politics and Land*. The roots of conservation are emphasized in Esher, *Broken Wave*, esp. 72–88, and Samuel, *Theatres of Memory*. For developments in other countries (but without explicit comparative discussion), see Kain, *Planning for Conservation*.

109 Quotes from Betjeman, 'I accuse these grey-faced men of Britain', *Daily Express*, 12 March 1962, 8, one of hundreds of articles and broadcasts on this theme in Betjeman's oeuvre. Note that the Beaverbrook press was at this point losing its hostility to preservationism.

110 James Lees-Milne, 'Who cares for

England?', *The Listener*, 19 March 1964, 457–9. At this early date, the *Listener* was not yet ready to endorse his line, querying whether it was 'axiomatic that the preservation of the countryside is the top priority', when 'industrial modernization, economic efficiency, and adequate living space' were all still necessary. Ibid., 460.

111  James Lees-Milne, 'Landed Properties and Proprietors', xxiii; 'How to Stop the Vandals', *Sunday Times*, 28 Aug. 1966, 25; 'Don't Kill the Goose, or Hints to Owners', *Historic Houses* (1968), 3–4.

112  Quoted by Jenkins and James, *From Acorn to Oak Tree*, 199.

113  'Address given by John Smith . . . 29 March 1962', copy in Crawford MSS, 101/27.

114  For Rathbone's desire to recruit young country gents, see J. F. W. Rathbone to Lord Methuen, 5 Nov. 1958: Corsham Court MSS, D50/9, and J. F. W. Rathbone to W. G. Hayter, 21 July 1964: Crawford MSS, 101/24. To judge from his annotations on the latter, Crawford found Rathbone's stipulations 'rather ridiculous'. For Rawnsley's appointment, see Gaze, *Figures in a Landscape*, 207–8; Jenkins and James, *From Acorn to Oak Tree*, 221–2; Weideger, *Gilding the Acorn*, 129–33.

115  John Smith to Lord Crawford, 12 March 1963; 22 May 1964: Crawford MSS, 101/27.

116  Smith felt Rathbone's administration was amateurish and gave the wrong impression, but he was further discomforted by Rathbone's effeminacy, a discomfort shared to a lesser degree by Crawford. See Jenkins and James, *From Acorn to Oak Tree*, 200–3, though they are still coy about Rathbone's homosexuality.

117  J. F. W. Rathbone to Lord Crawford, 28 April 1965; Lord Rosse to Lord Crawford, 8 March 1965: Crawford MSS, 101/24.

118  Rawnsley was even franker about his distaste for 'the strong homosexual element' on the Trust's staff, at least when recounting the story much later to Paula Weideger: see *Gilding the Acorn*, 142.

119  Jenkins and James, *From Acorn to Oak Tree*, 228–9.

120  For complementary accounts of the Rawnsley affair, see Gaze, *Figures in a Landscape*, ch. 16; Jenkins and James, *From Acorn to Oak Tree*, ch. 10; Weideger, *Gilding the Acorn*, ch. 4.

121  From the *Guardian*'s report of the 1966 AGM, 14 Nov. 1966, 2.

122  John Grigg, 'Trust and Public', *Guardian*, 16 Jan. 1967, 14; Lord Montagu of Beaulieu, 'Can the Trust Survive the Leisure Boom?', *Sunday Times*, 19 Jan. 1969, 12; *Country Life*, 25 June 1970, 1237.

123  Crossman, *Diaries*, II, 458. Crossman's inside sympathizer was Michael Trinick (not Trinnick as in the *Diaries*), Regional Secretary for Devon and Cornwall, who unusually combined the functions of both agent and representative.

124  Hewison, *Heritage Industry*, and Weideger, *Gilding the Acorn*, have been the most substantial critics, but I think it is fair to say that public opinion has not been widely exercised by the issue since the early 1970s.

125  William Proby, 'The Fiscal Climate for Country Houses since 1965', *Apollo*, 130 (1989), 404.

126  Cherry, *Environmental Planning*, II, 126–40, 160.

127  Montagu, *Gilt and the Gingerbread*, 203–5. The seriousness of this book has not often been recognized, obscured for one thing by its jokey title.

128  Victoria Brittain, 'How to survive in the stately home jungle', *The Times*, 1 July 1972, 14.

129  Illustrations of the new-style stately-home business of the 1960s and 1970s can be found in March, 'Goodwood House'; Harewood,

*Tongs and the Bones*, 301–6; Lytton Cobbold, 'Knebworth House'; Lytton Cobbold, *Board Meetings in the Bath*.

130 Cornforth's paraphrase in *Country Houses*, 57.

131 Melly, *Revolt into Style*, 104; on the 'New Aristocracy', see Booker, *Neophiliacs*, including both its earlier, more classless image, 22–8, and a later, 'gilded' phase, 266–8.

132 Montagu, *Gilt and the Gingerbread*, 156–9; Harling, *Historic Houses*, 105; Reyner Banham, 'Brideshead Reviolated', *New Society*, 1 July 1982, 22–3, comparing Brideshead's 'forelock-tugging mystique' to earlier television and film uses of Chiswick.

133 Sutherland, *Landowners*; Perrott, *Aristocrats*; Harling, *Historic Houses*; and, a positive celebration, Bence-Jones and Montgomery Massingberd, *British Aristocracy*. All date from 1968–9.

134 For contemporary statements of anxiety, see Montagu, *Gilt and the Gingerbread*, 129–32; James Lees-Milne, 'Don't Kill the Goose, or Hints to Owners', *Historic Houses* (1968), 3–4; Bence-Jones and Montgomery-Massingberd, *British Aristocracy*; Mary Warnock, 'Englishman's Castles', Radio 3 broadcast reprinted in *The Listener*, 11 May 1972, 614–5; as discussed below, pp. 403–5, the crisis of 1974 was very largely triggered by these anxieties, which are plentifully evident in Cornforth, *Country Houses*, and Strong et al., *Destruction*.

135 Cornforth, *Country Houses*, 100–3.

136 Hugh Wontner, 'Foreword' to *Historic Houses* (1969); Cornforth, *Country Houses*, 113–15.

137 Kennet, *Preservation*, esp. 52, 88–9; also his statement in the Lords, *Hansard*, 5th ser., 292 [L]: 334–9 [15 May 1968].

138 There is as yet no thoroughgoing discussion of the course of preservation policy in the 1960s and 1970s, but see Andreae, 'From Comprehensive Development', and, for a first-hand account, Kennet, *Preservation*. The bare bones of policy can be followed through the *Annual Reports* of the HBC for England.

139 HBC for England, *Annual Report* (1972–3).

140 Marcus Binney, 'Lost to the Nation? The Fate of Great Houses', *Country Life*, 8 Nov. 1973, 1426–8; a similar worry was expressed in John Cornforth's 1974 report, *Country Houses*, preface.

EPILOGUE

1 Andreae and Binney, *Tomorrow's Ruins?*, 1.

2 Christopher Booker, 'Mad for Conservation' and 'Something Old, Something New', *Spectator*, 12 Feb. 1977, 12–13 and 5 March 1977, 12–13, for some early if eccentric reflections on the conservation 'mania'; the earliest use I have found of 'heritage industry' is from an article with that title by David White, *New Society*, 17 Dec. 1981, 485–6, though the critical usage was popularized by Hewison, *Heritage Industry*, published in 1987.

3 On the property boom, esp. in farmland, see Michael Hanson, 'The Estate Market: Surveying the Seventies', *Country Life*, 20 Dec. 1979, 2420–1; also Massey and Catalano, *Capital and Land*, 1–3, for eye-opening statistics unaffected by the authors' Marxist analysis.

4 The left-wing Minister for the Arts gives the best existing account of this episode in Jenkins, *Culture Gap*, 140–60.

5 Cornforth, *Country Houses*, 73.

6 The ideas behind the exhibition, though not the content of the exhibition itself, can be found in Strong et al., *Destruction*.

7 For some contemporary reviews, mostly critical in some way, see Philip Howard, 'The fall of the

houses of England', *The Times*, 30 Sept. 1974, 16; Caroline Tisdall, 'Englishmen's Castles', *Guardian*, 9 Oct. 1974, 12; [Benedict Nicolson], 'The Decline and Fall of the Country House', *Burlington Magazine*, 116 (1974), 633; Evan Anthony, review of *Destruction* exhibition, *Spectator*, 19 Oct. 1974, 503; Magnus Magnusson, 'Kept in Amber?', *Spectator*, 16 Nov. 1974, 633; [Colin Amery], 'A Place in the Country', and Mark Girouard, 'Country House Crisis?', *Architectural Review*, 156 (1974), 205–6, 243–4. It should be stressed that a middlebrow paper such as the *Daily Mail* could still entirely ignore both book and exhibition.

8 Cormack, *Heritage in Danger*, 44–5, discusses the HHA agitation.

9 E.g. Earl of March, 'Country houses: Dead or alive?', *Daily Telegraph*, 3 Oct. 1974, 15.

10 For some carefully formulated arguments, see Binney, *Our Vanishing Heritage*, 9, 17; John Harris and Marcus Binney, letter to the *Guardian*, 14 Oct. 1974, 12; Jones, *Britain's Heritage*, 91–3. Binney's colleagues in the *Destruction* book were not always so careful: for provocative defences of squirearchy, see James Lees-Milne (of course), 'Country House in our Heritage', 11, 13–14; Sir Michael Culme-Seymour, 'House and the Estate', 141; Strong's introduction, esp. 10–11, is a bit more cautious. John Harris got into trouble for describing squirearchy as 'one of the happiest social structures that Western man has ever achieved': see Tisdall's review in the *Guardian*, 9 Oct. 1974, 12.

11 Andreae, 'From Comprehensive Development'.

12 The new arrangements are described in *Capital Taxation and the National Heritage*; also Binney and Martin, *The Country House*, 16–19.

13 Michael Hanson, 'Honour, Manor and Lordship: The Great Estates – I: Arundel', *Country Life*, 3 July 1980, 6–8.

14 Cornforth, 'Private Ownership and the Future', 38; Marcus Binney, 'Empty rooms', *Connoisseur*, 198 (1978), 230; Harry Teggin, 'Domus Britannicus: What future for the English country house?', *Architects' Journal*, 24 Jan. 1979, 172; *Britain's Historic Buildings*, 10; Christopher Buxton, 'Preserving – and Living in – Historic Houses', *Journal of the Royal Society of Arts*, 129 (1980–81), 246; Michael Saunders Watson, 'Historic Houses Ten Years On', *Historic Houses* (1984), 3–4; Sayer and Massingberd, *Disintegration*, 13.

15 See, e.g., 'Sales from Country Houses', *Country Life*, 19 June 1980, 1380; Young, *Country House in the 1980s*, 148.

16 On the background to the Mentmore affair, see Binney and Martin, *The Country House*, 12–13; Cormack, *Heritage in Danger*, 2nd edn, 72–5.

17 The first quote was attributed to Peter Shore, Secretary of State for the Environment, though he repudiated it: *New Statesman*, 4 Feb. 1977, 147; 11 Feb. 1977, 189; the second comes from the *Daily Mail*'s coverage of the sale, 19 May 1977, 22–3, a reminder that aesthetic appreciation of Mentmore came a distant third to hype and politics in 'Mentmore mania'.

18 Andreae and Binney, *Mentmore for the Nation*, the SAVE pamphlet, was executed within two weeks of the sale announcement in January 1977.

19 Jones, *Britain's Heritage*, gives an excellent insider's view of Parliamentary debates on the heritage after the Mentmore fiasco.

20 Young, *Country House in the 1980s*, 143; Sayer and Massingberd, *Disintegration*, vii–viii, 8–10; Hugh Massingberd, 'Time to start listing families', *Spectator*, 25 July 1992, 13–15. Wright, *On Living in an Old Country*, 146–53, has a good discussion of the tension between pro- and anti-heritage Conservatisms; Hewison, *Heritage Industry*, 99–

105, stresses their complementarity. See also Everett's criticism in *Tory View of Landscape*, 218–19.

21 On the early years of the NHMF, see Jones, *Britain's Heritage*, 204–35; for its uses on country houses, Sayer and Massingberd, *Disintegration*, 42–8, 71–2.

22 See reports of survey data in *English Heritage Monitor* (1992), 45; (1994), 48; similar findings in Myerscough, *Economic Importance*, 29–30; cf. the higher figures in Merriman, *Beyond the Glass Case*, 47–52.

23 As early as 1977, the General Household Survey found that visiting historic buildings was the second most popular outdoor leisure pursuit, after walking (ahead of dancing, swimming and visits to the seaside), though it had been behind the seaside as a summer activity in 1973. On the other hand, the historic buildings figure was considerably lower in 1987. *Country Life*, 2 June 1977, 1488; *English Heritage Monitor* (1979), 26; (1990), 41. There are now many different surveys of 'heritage consumerism' made on different bases and it is difficult to compare them; see the annual reports of the *English Heritage Monitor* and the less regular reports on *Cultural Trends* made by the Policy Studies Institute. A more dispassionate and longer-term study of the data is needed; Merriman, *Beyond the Glass Case*, is an important starting-point.

24 *Heritage Outlook*, Jan./Feb. 1981, 20.

25 Adaptations of Jane Austen, George Eliot, Henry James, D. H. Lawrence and E. M. Forster since the 1970s have tended to give more prominence to country-house settings than earlier adaptations of the same authors.

26 Lees-Milne, *Mingled Measure*, 200–201; Walker, *Arts TV*, 63; Samuel, *Theatres of Memory*, 235.

27 For analyses of country-house fashions, see Hewison, *Heritage Industry*, ch. 3, and Samuel, *Theatres of Memory*, pt 1; I also owe a debt here to discussions with Louise Ward about her MA research on country-house style.

28 For promotions of squire's style as appropriate for the modern consumer, see Seebohm and Sykes, *English Country*, and Massingberd, *Field Book*, published in 1987 and 1988 respectively.

29 The homeliness of country houses and the limits to tourism are themes in Cornforth, *Country Houses*; Earl of March, 'Historic Houses: Living Homes or Empty Shells?', *Historic Houses* (1976); Harry Teggin, 'Domus Britannicus: What future for the English country house?', *Architects' Journal*, 24 Jan. 1979, 165–200; Christopher Buxton, 'Preserving – and Living in – Historic Houses', *Journal of the Royal Society of Arts*, 129 (1980–81), 245–58; Sayer and Massingberd, *Disintegration*.

30 See, for example, J. Carter Brown's introduction to Jackson-Stops, *Treasure Houses*, and McClung, 'Country-House Arcadia'; for criticisms, see Linda Colley, 'The Cult of the Country House', *Times Literary Supplement*, 15 Nov. 1985, 1293, and, a little later, F. M. L. Thompson, 'The Long Run of the English Aristocracy', *London Review of Books*, 19 Feb. 1987, 6–7, and Patrick Wright, 'The "heritage-thinking" that spells national decline', *Listener*, 24 Sep. 1987, 12–14.

31 E.g. Jackson-Stops, 'Temples of the Arts'; Cornforth, 'The Backward Look'. An exception is Tinniswood, *Country House Visiting*, which is frank about the differences between eighteenth- and nineteenth-century taste, but still manages to knit both phases into a continuous tradition of appreciation uninterrupted by the nadir of 1880–1950: see below, n. 33.

32 The quote is from Ruskin's *Praeterita*, 1, ch. 1; for recent citations, see, e.g., Cornforth, *Country Houses*, 130; Binney and Jackson-Stops, 'The Last Hundred Years', 75; Lees-Milne, *The Country House*, ix.

33  Writers about the country house in the twentieth century can hardly ignore this, so must fall back on the argument that the English character or instinct was temporarily obscured between the 1880s and the 1940s – e.g. Tinniswood, *Country-House Visiting*, 175, where the 'popular imagination' is captivated by country houses while the 'forces of progress and social change' (unpopular? unEnglish?) are tearing them down. An alternative is to focus on small knots of connoisseurs (as in Cornforth, *Inspiration of the Past* and *Search for a Style*). Note also Jackson-Stops's tortuous explanation of how 'the innate conservatism of the British character, which might have been expected to protect such a peculiarly British phenomenon' (and indeed has been invoked for such a purpose by the same author) can also explain demolition: Jackson-Stops, 'The Fight Is Still On', 12; cf. Binney and Jackson-Stops, 'The Last Hundred Years', 75, 77.

34  This applies to Wiener, *English Culture* and Hewison, *Heritage Industry*; also in part to Wright, *On Living in an Old Country*, though the latter is concerned to break out of what he perceives as a sterile (if pervasive) 'aristocratic and high-bourgeois sense of history as decline' (70–71). A swerve in the opposite direction is made by Samuel, *Theatres of Memory*, in which 'heritage' becomes almost completely benign and democratic.

35  Samuel, *Theatres of Memory*, seems to me right to stress the transnational and ideologically complex roots of heritage-consciousness, but wrong to minimize these English specificities. See Patrick Wright's review in the *Guardian*, 4 Feb. 1995, 29.

36  Although, as Gillian Naylor has pointed out to me, the general revaluation of neglected pasts in late twentieth-century Europe has rehabilitated eighteenth-century aristocratic taste in other countries, too –

sometimes as part of a search for common European roots.

37  This conclusion incorporates and expands comments in Mandler, 'Nationalising the Country House'.

38  Sayer and Massingberd, *Disintegration*. The report was commissioned after Nicholas Ridley's dismissal of historic owners in 1988; a three-year research project was funded by Christie's, Humberts and Dixon Wilson and culminated in this 1993 publication. Its argument has been vigorously pursued by Hugh Montgomery-Massingberd in the *Daily Telegraph* and in less likely quarters by William Proby of the HHA: see, e.g., 'Weekend FT' in *Financial Times*, 29–30 July 1995, 'Property' in *Observer*, 13 Aug. 1995.

39  Cornforth, 'Private Ownership', 35–8; Bence-Jones and Montgomery-Massingberd, *British Aristocracy*, 237.

40  See, e.g., 'The SAVE Report', *Architects' Journal*, 17–24 Dec. 1975, esp. 1296; Jones, *Britain's Heritage*, 91–3; Binney, *Our Vanishing Heritage*, 17–46.

41  Charles Clover, 'Trust, but no Confidence', *Spectator*, 2 Nov. 1991, 9–10; Weideger, *Gilding the Acorn*, 105–11, 115–17.

42  See the 1980 'Montagu Report' on alternative uses, *Britain's Historic Buildings*, 10–12; Young, *Country House in the 1980s*, 109–26; Andreae and Binney, *Tomorrow's Ruins?*; Andreae et al., *Silent Mansions*; Binney and Martin, *The Country House*; Binney and Milne, *Vanishing Houses*, 68–71; Binney and Jackson-Stops, 'The Last Hundred Years', 77.

43  See the arguments advanced by Colin Amery and Mark Girouard in *Architectural Review*, 156 (1974), 205–6, 243–4, largely forgotten since the intervening mania; also Newby, *National Trust*, for some healthily evolutionary ideas about the future uses of the National Trust's properties.

44    In 1986, there were over 350 pri-
      vately owned châteaux (and just over
      100 publicly or charitably maintained
      châteaux) open to the public in
      France; this compares with approxi-
      mately 200 privately owned country
      houses (and another 150 publicly or
      charitably maintained houses) open
      in England. French figures calculated
      from de Vignaud, *Historic Houses*.

# SELECT BIBLIOGRAPHY

This bibliography lists only sources cited in the notes. It gives locations of manuscript collections, titles of serials and full titles of works referred to by short titles in the notes. It does not list individual articles from serials (except for short-titled scholarly articles) nor works given full titles in the notes (e.g. works mentioned for information but not cited).

## *Manuscript Collections*

BBC Written Archives Centre, Caversham Park, Berkshire

Burghley Visitors' Books, Burghley House, Northamptonshire

Castle Howard MSS, Castle Howard, North Yorkshire

Chatsworth MSS, Chatsworth House, Derbyshire

Corsham Court MSS, Wiltshire Record Office, Trowbridge

Crawford MSS, National Library of Scotland, Edinburgh

Dalton MSS, British Library of Political and Economic Science, London

Darnley MSS, Kent Archives Office, Strood

Dunster Castle MSS, Somerset Record Office, Taunton

Eaton MSS, Eaton Hall, Cheshire

Ernst of Westcombe MSS, Somerset Record Office, Taunton

Harcourt MSS, Bodleian Library, Oxford

Hatfield MSS, Hatfield House, Hertfordshire

Hippisley of Ston Eaton MSS, Somerset Record Office, Taunton

Long MSS, Wiltshire Record Office, Trowbridge

Lothian MSS, Scottish Record Office, Edinburgh

Lovelace–Byron Deposit, Bodleian Library, Oxford

National Trust MSS, National Trust for Places of Historic Interest or Natural Beauty, London

Paxton MSS, Chatsworth House, Derbyshire

Petworth MSS, Petworth House, Sussex

Public Record Office, Kew:
Ancient Monuments Papers [AE]
Housing and Local Government Papers [HLG]
Inland Revenue Papers [IR]
Ramsay MacDonald Papers [PRO 30]
Treasury Papers [T]
Office and Ministry of Works Papers [WORK]

Sackville MSS, Centre for Kentish Studies, Maidstone

Tattershall Castle (National Trust) MSS, Lincolnshire Archives Office [catalogue in National Register of Archives, London]

Temple Newsam Visitors' Book, Temple Newsam House, Leeds

Thomas Cook Travel Archive, London

Wardour Castle MSS, Wiltshire Record Office, Trowbridge

Warwick Castle MSS, Warwickshire Record Office, Warwick

Wilton MSS, Wiltshire Record Office, Trowbridge

## Newspapers, Magazines and other Serials

All the Year Round

Apollo

Architects' Journal

Architectural Review

Art Journal

Arts and Letters

Baedeker's Great Britain

Bentley's Miscellany

Birmingham Daily Gazette

Birmingham Daily Post

The Buildings of England, founding ed. N. Pevsner

Burlington Magazine

Cassell's Magazine

The Chartered Surveyor

Come to Britain

Connoisseur

Cook's Excursionist and Tourist Advertiser

Cornhill Magazine

The Country House and Estate

Country Illustrated

Country Life

Country Life Annual

The Countryside Review

Cultural Trends (Policy Studies Institute)

Daily Chronicle

Daily Express

Daily Graphic

Daily Herald

Daily Mail

Daily Telegraph

The Dark Blue

Derby and Chesterfield Reporter

The Derbyshire Countryside

East Anglian Daily Times

The Echo

The Economist

English Heritage Monitor (English Tourist Board)

English Illustrated Magazine

Estates Gazette

Evening Chronicle (Newcastle)

Evening Standard

The Field

Financial Times

Fraser's Magazine

The Galaxy

Geographical Magazine

The Gloucestershire Countryside

Godey's Magazine and Lady's Book

Good Words

The Graphic

Hansard's Parliamentary Debates

Heritage Outlook (Civic Trust)

High Peak News

Historic Buildings Council for England, Annual Reports

Historic Houses Castles and Gardens in Great Britain and Ireland [Historic Houses]

House and Garden

Howitt's Journal

Illustrated Country Review

Illustrated London News

Journal of the Royal Society of Arts

*Journal of the Town Planning Institute*
*Journals of the House of Lords*
*Kentish Fire*
*Landscape and Garden*
*Leamington and Warwickshire
    Chronicle*
Leeds City Art Gallery and Temple
    Newsam House, *Annual Reports*
*Leicestershire Mercury*
*The Leisure Hour*
*Life: A Weekly Journal of Society . . .*
*The Listener*
*Little Guides* (Methuen)
*Liverpool Daily Post*
*London Journal*
*London Mercury*
*London Review of Books*
*Magazine of Art*
*Manchester Guardian*
*The Metropolitan*
*The Mirror of Literature, Amusement,
    and Instruction*
*Murray's Handbooks*
*Museums Journal*
National Art-Collections Fund,
    *Annual Reports*
*National Sunday League Record*
National Trust for Places of Historic
    Interest or Natural Beauty, *Annual
    Reports*
*New Monthly Magazine*
*New Society*
*New Statesman*
*News Chronicle*
*News of the World*
*The Nineteenth Century and After*
*Northern Echo*
*Nottingham Guardian*
*Nottingham Journal*
*The Nottinghamshire Countryside*
*The Observer*
*Once a Week*

*Pall Mall Magazine*
*Parliamentary Papers*
*Penny Magazine*
*Radio Times*
*Review of Reviews*
*Quarterly Review*
*Reynolds's Miscellany*
*Reynolds's Newspaper*
*Royal Leamington Spa Courier*
*Saturday Magazine*
*Saturday Review*
*Sevenoaks Chronicle*
*Sheffield Telegraph*
*The Sketch*
*The Somerset Countryman*
*The Spectator*
*The Standard*
*Sunday Chronicle* (Manchester)
*Sunday Dispatch*
*Sunday Express*
*Sunday Pictorial*
*Sunday Times*
*The Times*
*Times Literary Supplement*
*The Tourist and Traveller*
*Town and Country*
*Town and Country Homes*
*Town and Country News*
*Town and Country Planning*
*Town Planning Review*
*Vanity Fair*
*Vogue House and Garden Book*
*Ward and Lock Guides*
*Warwick and Warwickshire Advertiser*
*The Warwickshire Journal*
*Western Mail*
*Westminster Gazette*
*The World: A Journal for Men and
    Women*
*Yorkshire Gazette*
*Yorkshire Post*

## Books and Scholarly Articles

Abdy, Jane, and Charlotte Gere, *The Souls* (London, 1984)

*An Account of the Disturbances at Knole, with Letters and Press Opinions on the Subject* (Scarborough, 1884)

Adonis, Andrew, 'Aristocracy, Agriculture and Liberalism: The Politics, Finances and Estates of the Third Lord Carrington', *Historical Journal*, 31 (1988), 871–97

Aldin, Cecil, *Old Manor Houses* (London, 1923)

[Allen, Grant] 'Cecil Power', *Philistia*, 3 vols (London, 1884)

Allibone, Jill, *Anthony Salvin: Pioneer of Gothic Revival Architecture, 1799–1881* (Columbia, Missouri, 1987)

Allibone, Jill, *George Devey: Architect, 1820–1886* (Cambridge, 1991)

Alsop, Susan Mary, *Lady Sackville: A Biography* (London, 1978)

Altick, Richard D., *The English Common Reader: A Social History of the Mass Reading Public, 1800–1900* (Chicago, 1957)

Altick, Richard D., 'From Aldine to Everyman: Cheap Reprint Series of the English Classics, 1830–1906', orig. pub. 1958, in *Writers, Readers, and Occasions* (Columbus, Ohio, 1989)

Anderson, Olive, 'The Political Uses of History in Mid Nineteenth-Century England', *Past and Present*, 36 (April 1967), 87–105

Anderson, Patricia, *The Printed Image and the Transformation of Popular Culture, 1790–1860* (Oxford, 1991)

Andreae, Sophie, 'From Comprehensive Development to Conservation Areas', in Michael Hunter (ed.), *Preserving the Past: The Rise of Heritage in Modern Britain* (Stroud, 1996)

Andreae, Sophie, and Marcus Binney, *Tomorrow's Ruins?: Country Houses at Risk* (London, 1978)

Andreae, Sophie, and Marcus Binney (eds), *Mentmore for the Nation* (London, 1977)

Andreae, Sophie, Marcus Binney and Catherine Griffiths, *Silent Mansions: More Country Houses at Risk* (London, 1981)

Andrews, Malcolm, *The Search for the Picturesque: Landscape Aesthetics and Tourism in Britain, 1760–1800* (Aldershot, 1989)

Annan, Noël, *Our Age* (London, 1990)

Applegate, Celia, *A Nation of Provincials: The German Idea of Heimat* (Berkeley, 1990)

Arnold, Matthew, *Culture and Anarchy* (1st edn, 1869; New York, 1983)

Ashbee, C. R., *American Sheaves and English Seed Corn* (London, 1902)

Aslet, Clive, *The Last Country Houses* (New Haven and London, 1982)

Aston Hall and Park Co. Ltd., *Report of the Investigation Committee, Appointed by the Shareholders at the Annual Meeting, March 28th, 1860* (Birmingham, 1860)

Austin, Alfred, *Haunts of Ancient Peace* (London, 1902)

Axon, W. E. A., *William Harrison Ainsworth: A Memoir* (London, 1902)

Bailey, Peter, *Leisure and Class in Victorian England*, 2nd edn (London, 1987)

Baker, Herbert, *Architecture and Personalities* (London, 1944)

Balch, Elizabeth, *Glimpses of Old English Homes* (London, 1890)

Banham, Reyner, 'Revenge of the Picturesque: English Architectural Polemics, 1945–1965', in John Summerson (ed.), *Concerning Architecture* (London, 1968)

Bann, Stephen, *The Clothing of Clio: A Study of the Representation of History in Nineteenth-Century Britain and France* (Cambridge, 1984)

Bann, Stephen, *The Inventions of History: Essays on the Representation of the Past* (Manchester, 1990)

[Barham, Richard Harris] 'Thomas Ingoldsby', *The Ingoldsby Legends* (1st edn, 1840–7; London, 1960)

Barker, Dennis, *One Man's Estate: The Preservation of an English Inheritance* (London, 1983)

Barrow, Andrew, *Gossip: A History of High Society from 1920 to 1970* (New York, 1978)

Bassett, Philippa, *List of the Historical Records of the Society for the Protection of Ancient Buildings* (Birmingham and Reading, 1980)

Batsford, Harry, and Charles Fry, *Homes and Gardens of England* (London, 1932)

Beard, Geoffrey, *Attingham: The First Forty Years, 1952–1991* (London, 1991)

Bedford, Duke of, *A Silver-Plated Spoon* (London, 1959)

Bedford, Duke of, 'Woburn Abbey', in Roy Strong et al. (eds), *The Destruction of the Country House, 1875–1975* (London, 1974)

Bence-Jones, Mark, *Ancestral Houses* (London, 1984)

Bence-Jones, Mark, 'The Trust of Landowning', in *Burke's Landed Gentry*, ed. Peter Townend, 18th edn, vol. 1 (London, 1965)

Bence-Jones, Mark, and Hugh Montgomery-Massingberd, *The British Aristocracy* (London, 1979)

Bennett, E. N., *Problems of Village Life* (London, [1914])

Bermingham, Ann, *Landscape and Ideology: The English Rustic Tradition, 1740–1860* (Berkeley, 1986)

Betjeman, John, *Ghastly Good Taste; Or, A Depressing Story of the Rise and Fall of English Architecture* (1st edn, 1933; London, 1986)

Betjeman, John, *Letters*, ed. Candida Lycett Green, 2 vols (London, 1994–95)

Betjeman, John (ed.), *Cornwall Illustrated in a Series of Views, of Castles, Seats of the Nobility, Mines, Picturesque Scenery, Towns, Public Buildings, Churches, Antiquities, etc.*, Shell Guide to Cornwall (London, 1934)

Betjeman, John (comp.), *Devon: A Shell Guide* (London, 1936)

Binney, Marcus, *Our Vanishing Heritage* (London, 1984)

Binney, Marcus, and Gervase Jackson-Stops, 'The Last Hundred Years', in Gervase Jackson-Stops (ed.), *The Treasure Houses of Britain: Five Hundred Years of Private Patronage and Art Collecting* (New Haven and London, 1985)

Binney, Marcus, and Kit Martin, *The Country House: To Be or Not To Be* (London, [1982])

Binney, Marcus, and Emma Milne (eds), *Vanishing Houses of England: A Pictorial Documentary of Lost Country Houses* (London, 1982)

Blomfield, Reginald, *Memoirs of an Architect* (London, 1932)

Blomfield, Reginald, *A Short History of Renaissance Architecture in England, 1500–1800* (London, 1900)

Blunden, Margaret, *The Countess of Warwick* (London, 1967)

Booker, Christopher, *The Neophiliacs* (London, 1969)

Boos, Florence S., 'Alternative Victorian Futures: "Historicism", *Past and Present* and *A Dream of John Ball*', in Florence S. Boos (ed.), *History and Community: Essays in Victorian Medievalism* (New York, 1992)

Boulting, Nikolaus, 'The Law's Delays: Conservationist Legislation in the British Isles', in Jane Fawcett (ed.), *The Future of the Past: Attitudes to Conservation, 1174–1974* (London, 1976)

Bowden, Mark, *Pitt Rivers* (Cambridge, 1991)

Boyes, Georgina, *The Imagined Village: Culture, Ideology and the English Folk Revival* (Manchester, 1993)

Brady, J. H., *A Visitor's Guide to Knole* (Sevenoaks, 1839)

Brandon, P. F., 'A Twentieth-Century Squire in His Landscape', *Southern History*, 4 (1982), 191–220

Briggs, Asa, *Saxons, Normans and Victorians* (Hastings and Bexhill, 1966)

Britain, Ian, *Fabianism and Culture: A Study in British Socialism and the Arts, c.1884–1918* (Cambridge, 1982)

*Britain's Historic Buildings: A Policy for their Future Use* (London, 1980)

'British Archaeological Association', *Journal of the British Archaeological Association*, 1 (1845), i–xv

*British Country Life throughout the Centuries* (London, 1937)

Brodrick, Alan Houghton, *Near to Greatness: A Life of the Sixth Earl Winterton* (London, 1965)

Brown, G. Baldwin, *The Care of Ancient Monuments* (Cambridge, 1905)

Brown, Ivor, and George Fearon, *Amazing Monument: A Short History of the Shakespeare Industry* (London, 1939)

Brown, J., *Tourist Rambles in Yorkshire, Lincolnshire, Durham, Northumberland, and Derbyshire* (London and York, 1878)

Brown, J., *Tourist Rambles in the Northern and Midland Counties, Second Series* (London and York, 1885)

Burgess, Thomas, *An Essay on the Study of Antiquities*, 2nd edn (Oxford, 1782)

Burke, John Bernard, *A Visitation of the Seats and Arms of the Noblemen and Gentlemen of Great Britain*, 4 vols (London, 1852–5)

Burn, W. L., *The Age of Equipoise: A Study of the Mid-Victorian Generation* (London, 1964)

Burnand, F. C., *Happy-Thought Hall* (London, 1872)

Burnand, F. C., *Happy Thoughts* (London, 1868)

Burnand, F. C., *Records and Reminiscences, Personal and General* (London, 1904)

Burnett, David, *Longleat: The Story of an English Country House* (London, 1978)

Burrow, J. W., *A Liberal Descent: Victorian Historians and the English Past* (Cambridge, 1981)

Burrow, J. W., '"The Village Community" and the Uses of History in Late Nineteenth-Century England', in Neil McKendrick (ed.), *Historical Perspectives: Studies in English Thought and Society* (London, 1974)

Bush, M. L., *The English Aristocracy: A Comparative Synthesis* (Manchester, 1984)

Butler, J. R. M., *Lord Lothian, 1882–1940* (London, 1960)

Butler, John, *The Economics of Historic Country Houses* (London, 1980)

Buxton, Sydney, *Finance and Politics: An Historical Study, 1783–1885*, 2 vols (London, 1888)

Byron, Robert, *The Appreciation of Architecture* (London, 1932)

Calabrella, Baroness de, *Evenings at Haddon Hall* (London, 1846)

Calder, Angus, *The Myth of the Blitz* (London, 1991)

Cannadine, David, 'Aristocratic Indebtedness in the Nineteenth Century: The Case Re-Opened', *Economic History Review*, 2nd ser., 30 (1977), 624–50

Cannadine, David, 'The First Hundred Years', in Howard Newby (ed.), *The National Trust: The Next Hundred Years* (London, 1995)

Cannadine, David, *The Decline and Fall of the British Aristocracy* (New Haven and London, 1990)

Cannadine, David, *G. M. Trevelyan* (London, 1992)

*Capital Taxation and the National Heritage* (London, 1977)

Cardigan, Earl of, *The Wardens of Savernake Forest* (London, 1949)

Carnegie, Andrew, *An American Four-in-Hand* (London, 1883)

Carpenter, Humphrey, *The Brideshead Generation: Evelyn Waugh and his Friends* (London, 1989)

Carr, Alice, *J. Comyns Carr: Stray Memories* (London, 1920)

Carr, Alice, *Mrs J. Comyns Carr's Reminiscences*, ed. Eve Adam (London, 1925)

Carswell, John, *The Saving of Kenwood and the Northern Heights* (Henley-on-Thames, 1992)

Cecil, Lord David, *The Cecils of Hatfield House* (London, 1973)

Chambers, Douglas, *The Planters of the English Landscape Garden* (New Haven and London, 1993)

Chancellor, Valerie E., *History for their Masters: Opinion in the English History Textbook, 1800–1914* (Bath, 1970)

Chandler, Alice, *A Dream of Order: The Medieval Ideal in Nineteenth-Century English Literature* (London, 1971)

Channon, Henry, *'Chips': The Diaries of Sir Henry Channon*, ed. Robert Rhodes James (London, 1967)

Chapman, Raymond, *The Sense of the Past in Victorian Literature* (London, 1986)

Chase, Malcolm, 'This is no claptrap: This is our heritage', in Christopher Shaw and Malcolm Chase (eds), *The Imagined Past: History and Nostalgia* (Manchester, 1989)

Cherry, Gordon E., *Environmental Planning, 1939–1969: II. National Parks and Recreation in the Countryside* (London, 1975)

Chippendale, Christopher, 'The Making of the First Ancient Monuments Act, 1882, and its Administration under General Pitt-Rivers', *Journal of the British Archaeological Association*, 136 (1983), 1–55

Clark, Kenneth, *The Gothic Revival: An Essay in the History of Taste*, 3rd edn (1st edn, 1928; London, 1962)

Clarke, Peter, *Liberals and Social Democrats* (Cambridge, 1978)

Clemenson, Heather A., 'Diminishing Derbyshire Estates', *Geographical Magazine*, 53 (1980–81), 115–18

Clemenson, Heather A., *English Country Houses and Landed Estates* (London, 1982)

Clifton-Taylor, Alec, 'Architectural Touring with the Little Guides', in John Summerson (ed.), *Concerning Architecture* (London, 1968)

Colley, Linda, *Britons: Forging the Nation, 1707–1837* (New Haven and London, 1992)

Collins, Michael, 'English Art Magazines before 1901', *The Connoisseur* (March 1976), 198–205

Conway of Allington, Lord, *Episodes in a Varied Life* (London, 1932)

Cooke, G. A., *Topographical and Statistical Description of the County of Kent* (London, 1810)

Cooke, G. A., *Topographical and Statistical Description of the County of Kent* (London, 1822)

Cooper, Andrew Fenton, *British Agricultural Policy, 1912–36: A Study in Conservative Politics* (Manchester, 1989)

Cooper, Diana, *Autobiography* (Wilton, 1979)

Cormack, Patrick, *Heritage in Danger* (London, 1976; new ed., 1978)

Cornforth, John, 'The Backward Look', in Gervase Jackson-Stops (ed.), *The Treasure Houses of Britain: Five Hundred Years of Private Patronage and Art Collecting* (New Haven and London, 1985)

Cornforth, John, *Country Houses in Britain: Can they Survive?* (London, 1974)

Cornforth, John, *The Inspiration of the Past: Country House Taste in the Twentieth Century* (Harmondsworth, 1985)

Cornforth, John, *The Search for a Style: Country Life and Architecture, 1897–1935* (London, 1988)

Cox, Andrew, *Adversary Politics and Land: The Conflict over Land and Property Policy in Post-War Britain* (Cambridge, 1984)

Crawford, 27th Earl of, *The Crawford Papers: The Journals of David Lindsay, 27th Earl of Crawford . . . during the years 1892 to 1940*, ed. John Vincent (Manchester, 1984)

Crook, J. Mordaunt, 'John Britton and the Genesis of the Gothic Revival', in John Summerson (ed.), *Concerning Architecture* (London, 1968)

Crook, J. Mordaunt, *The Dilemma of Style: Architectural Ideas from the Picturesque to the Post-Modern* (London, 1989)

Crossman, Richard, *The Diaries of a Cabinet Minister*, 3 vols (London, 1975–7)

Cruse, Amy, *After the Victorians* (London, 1938)

Cullingworth, J. B., *Environmental Planning, 1939–1969: I. Reconstruction and Land Use Planning 1939–1947* (London, 1975)

Cullingworth, J. B., *Environmental Planning, 1939–1969: IV. Land Values, Compensation and Betterment* (London, 1980)

Culme-Seymour, Sir Michael, 'The House and the Estate', in Roy Strong et al. (eds), *The Destruction of the Country House, 1875–1975* (London, 1974)

Cunningham, Hugh, *Leisure in the Industrial Revolution* (London, 1980)

Cunningham, Valentine, *British Writers of the Thirties* (Oxford, 1988)

Curzon of Kedleston, Marquess, and H. Avray Tipping, *Tattershall Castle, Lincolnshire* (London, 1929)

Dakers, Caroline, *Clouds: The Biography of a Country House* (New Haven and London, 1993)

Daniels, Stephen, *Fields of Vision: Landscape Imagery and National Identity in England and the United States* (Cambridge, 1993)

Martin Daunton, 'The Politics of Harcourt's Budget, 1894', in N.B. Harte and R. Quinault (eds), *Land and Society in Britain, 1700–1914* (Manchester, 1996)

Delany, Paul, *The Neo-Pagans: Friendship and Love in the Rupert Brooke Circle* (London, 1987)

De La Warr, Lord, et al. *A Post-War Agricultural Policy for Great Britain* (London, 1943)

Delgado, Alan, *The Annual Outing and Other Excursions* (London, 1977)

Dellheim, Charles, *The Face of the Past: The Preservation of the Medieval Inheritance in Victorian England* (Cambridge, 1982)

Denman, D. R., *Estate Capital: The Contribution of Landownership to Agricultural Finance* (London, 1957)

Denslagen, Wim, *Architectural Restoration in Western Europe: Controversy and Continuity* (Amsterdam, 1994)

Devonshire, Deborah, Duchess of, *The House: A Portrait of Chatsworth* (London, 1982)

Dewey, C. J., 'Celtic Agrarian Legislation and the Celtic Revival: Historicist Implications of Gladstone's Irish and Scottish Land Acts, 1870–1886', *Past and Present*, 64 (Aug. 1974), 30–70

Diefendorf, Jeffry M. (ed.), *Rebuilding Europe's Bombed Cities* (London, 1990)

Ditchfield, P. H., *Vanishing England* (London, 1910)

Ditchfield, P. H., *The Manor Houses of England* (London, 1910)

Dodd, Philip, 'Englishness and the National Culture', in Robert Colls and Philip Dodd (eds), *Englishness: Politics and Culture, 1880–1920* (London, 1986)

Dorson, Richard M., *The British Folklorists: A History* (London, 1968)

Douglas, Roy, '"God Gave the Land to the People"', in A. J. A. Morris (ed.),

*Edwardian Radicalism, 1900–1914: Some Aspects of British Radicalism* (London, 1974)

Draper, Marie P. G., and W. A. Eden, *Marble Hill House and its Owners* (London, 1970)

Dugdale, Blanche E. C., *Family Homespun* (London, 1940)

Dutton, Ralph, *The English Country House* (London, 1935)

Dutton, Ralph, *A Hampshire Manor: Hinton Ampner* (London, 1968)

Dutton, Ralph, and Angus Holden, *English Country Houses open to the Public* (London, 1934)

Dutton, Ralph, and Angus Holden, *English Country Houses open to the Public*, 2nd edn, rev. and enlarged (London, 1935)

Easby, Rebecca Jeffrey, 'The Myth of Merrie England in Victorian Painting', in Florence S. Boos (ed.), *History and Community: Essays in Victorian Medievalism* (New York, 1992)

Eastlake, Charles L., *A History of the Gothic Revival* (London, 1872)

Eastlake, Elizabeth, Lady, *Journals and Correspondence of Lady Eastlake*, ed. Charles Eastlake Smith, 2 vols (London, 1895)

Ellis, S. M., *William Harrison Ainsworth and His Friends*, 2 vols (London, 1911)

Emy, H. V., 'The Land Campaign: Lloyd George as a Social Reformer, 1900–14', in A. J. P. Taylor (ed.), *Lloyd George: Twelve Essays* (London, 1971)

Engen, Rodney K., *Dictionary of Victorian Engravers, Print Publishers and Their Works* (Cambridge, 1979)

Ensor, R. C. K., 'The English Countryside', in Lucian Oldershaw (ed.), *England: A Nation* (London and Edinburgh, 1904)

Escott, T. H. S., *England: Its People, Polity, and Pursuits*, 2 vols (London, [1879])

Escott, T. H. S., *Society in the Country House* (London, 1907)

Esher, Lionel, *A Broken Wave: The Rebuilding of England 1940–1980* (London, 1981)

Evans, Howard, *The London Rambler and Footpath Guide* (London, 1884)

Evans, Howard, *Our Old Nobility* (London, 1907)

Evans, Howard, *Radical Fights of Forty Years* (London, 1913)

Evans, Joan, *A History of the Society of Antiquaries* (Oxford, 1956)

Evans, Joan, 'The Royal Archaeological Institute: A Retrospect', *Archaeological Journal*, 106 (1949), 1–11

Everett, Nigel, *The Tory View of Landscape* (New Haven and London, 1994)

Eversley, Lord, *Commons, Forests and Footpaths* (London, 1910)

Fabricant, Carole, 'The Literature of Domestic Tourism and the Public Consumption of Private Property', in Felicity Nussbaum and Laura Brown (eds), *The New Eighteenth Century: Theory, Politics, English Literature* (New York, 1987)

Fairclough, Oliver, *The Grand Old Mansion: The Holtes and Their Successors at Aston Hall, 1618–1864* (Birmingham, 1984)

Fea, Allan, *Picturesque Old Houses* (London, 1902)

Fea, Allan, *Recollections of Sixty Years* (London, 1927)

*Fifty Years of the National Buildings Record* (London, 1991)

Fleishman, Avrom, *The English Historical Novel: Walter Scott to Virginia Woolf* (Baltimore, 1971)

Flower, Sibylla Jane, *Debrett's The Stately Homes of Britain* (Exeter, 1982)

Forster, E. M., 'Mrs. Miniver', in *Two Cheers for Democracy* (Harmondsworth, 1976)

Fox, Celina, *Graphic Journalism in England during the 1830s and 1840s* (New York and London, 1988)

Franklin, Jill, *The Gentleman's Country House and its Plan, 1835–1914* (London, 1981)

Franklin, Jill, 'The Liberty of the Park', in Raphael Samuel (ed.), *Patriotism: The Making and Unmaking of British National Identity. Vol. III: National Fictions* (London, 1989)

'G. U.', *A Visit to Haddon Hall in 1838; Or, a Description of a Baronial Mansion of the Olden Time* (Derby, 1838)

Gard, Robin (ed.), *The Observant Traveller: Diaries of Travel . . . in the County Record Offices of England and Wales* (London, 1989)

Gaze, John, *Figures in a Landscape: A History of the National Trust* (London, 1988)

Geddie, John, *The Royal Palaces, Historic Castles and Stately Homes of Great Britain* (Edinburgh, 1913)

Gerard, Jessica, *Country House Life: Family and Servants, 1815–1914* (Oxford, 1994)

Gilbert, Bentley B., 'David Lloyd George: The Reform of British Landholding and the Budget of 1914', *Historical Journal*, 21 (1978), 117–41

Giles, Judy, and Tim Middleton (eds), *Writing Englishness, 1900–1950* (London, 1995)

Gill, Richard, *Happy Rural Seat: The English Country House and the Literary Imagination* (New Haven, 1972)

Gillett, Paula, *The Victorian Painter's World* (Gloucester, 1990)

Girouard, Mark, 'Attitudes to Elizabethan Architecture, 1600–1900', in John Summerson (ed.), *Concerning Architecture* (London, 1968)

Girouard, Mark, 'Living With the Past: Victorian Alterations to Country Houses', in Jane Fawcett (ed.), *The Future of the Past: Attitudes to Conservation, 1174–1974* (London, 1976)

Girouard, Mark, *The Return to Camelot: Chivalry and the English Gentleman* (New Haven and London, 1981)

Girouard, Mark, *Sweetness and Light: The 'Queen Anne' Movement, 1860–1900* (Oxford, 1977)

Girouard, Mark, *The Victorian Country House*, 2nd edn (New Haven and London, 1981)

Glyn, Elinor, *The Visits of Elizabeth* (London, 1900)

Goodall, Frederick, *Reminiscences* (London, 1902)

Goss, W. H., *The Life and Death of Llewellynn Jewitt* (London, 1889)

Gower, Lord Ronald, *My Reminiscences*, 2 vols (London, 1883)

Gower, Lord Ronald, *Old Diaries, 1881–1901* (London, 1902)

Green, F. E., *The Tyranny of the Countryside* (London, 1913)

Green, Martin, *Children of the Sun: A Narrative of Decadence in England after 1918* (New York, 1976)

Green, Peter, *Kenneth Grahame* (London, 1959)

*Guide to Hatfield House*, 5th edn (Hertford, 1894)

*Guide to Holkham* (Norwich, 1861)

Habakkuk, John, *Marriage, Debt, and the Estates System: English Landownership, 1650–1950* (Oxford, 1994)

Hale, J. R., *England and the Italian Renaissance: The Growth of Interest in its History and Art*, repr. edn (1st edn, 1954; London, 1963)

*The Half-Holiday Hand-Book; A Guide to the Principal Places of Interest, Churches, Ruins, Parks, Villages, etc.* (Manchester, [1846])

Hall, Peter, et al., *The Containment of Urban England*, 2 vols (London, 1973)

Hall, S. C., *The Baronial Halls, Picturesque Edifices, and Ancient Churches of England*, 3 vols (London, 1845–6)

Hamilton, Edward, *The Destruction of Lord Rosebery: From the Diary of Sir Edward Hamilton, 1894–1895*, ed. David Brooks (London, 1986)

*Handbook to Aston Hall, Museum and Park* (Birmingham, 1871)

*Handy Guide to Tamworth Castle* (Tamworth, [1899])

Hardy, Thomas, *Jude the Obscure* (1st edn, 1896; Harmondsworth, 1978)

Harewood, Lord, *The Tongs and the Bones: The Memoirs of Lord Harewood* (London, 1981)

Harley, Basil, and Jessie, *A Gardener at Chatsworth: Three Years in the Life of Robert Aughtie, 1848–1850* (n.p., 1992)

Harling, Robert, *Historic Houses: Conversations in Stately Homes* (London, 1969)

Harper, Charles G., *Mansions of Old Romance* (London, 1930)

Harris, John, 'English Country House Guides, 1740–1840', in John Summerson (ed.), *Concerning Architecture* (London, 1968)

Harris, John, 'Gone to Ground', in Roy Strong et al. (eds), *The Destruction of the Country House, 1875–1975* (London, 1974)

Harris, Jose, *Private Lives, Public Spirit: A Social History of Britain 1870–1914* (Oxford, 1993)

*Heaton Park, Manchester: Official Handbook* (Cheltenham, [1928])

Helm, W. H., *Homes of the Past* (London, 1921)

Hemans, Felicia [Browne], *The Works of Mrs Hemans*, 7 vols (Edinburgh, 1839)

Hemingway, Andrew, *Landscape Imagery and Urban Culture in Early Nineteenth-Century Britain* (Cambridge, 1992)

Henley, Dorothy, *Rosalind Howard, Countess of Carlisle* (London, 1958)

Hertford, Marquess of, 'Ragley Hall', in Roy Strong et al. (eds), *The Destruction of the Country House, 1875–1975* (London, 1974)

Hewison, Robert, *The Heritage Industry: Britain in a Climate of Decline* (London, 1987)

Hewison, Robert, *In Anger: British Culture in the Cold War, 1945–60* (New York, 1981)

Hillier, Bevis, 'The St. John's Wood Clique', *Apollo*, 80 (1964), 490–5

Hillier, Bevis, *Young Betjeman* (London, 1988)

Hilton, Boyd, *The Age of Atonement: The Influence of Evangelicalism on Social and Economic Thought, 1784–1865* (Oxford, 1988)

Hissey, James John, *An English Holiday with Car and Camera* (London, 1908)

Hissey, James John, *Untravelled England* (London, 1906)

*Historic Houses of the United Kingdom: Descriptive, Historical, Pictorial* (London, 1891)

*An Historical and Descriptive Guide to Warwick Castle*, 15th edn (Warwick, 1877)

Hobhouse, Christopher, *Shell Guide to Derbyshire: A Series of Views of Castles, Seats of the Nobility, Mines, Picturesque Scenery, Towns, Public Buildings, Churches, Antiquities, etc.* (London, 1935)

Holden, Angus, and Ralph Dutton, *French Chateaux open to the Public* (London, 1936)

Holme, Charles (ed.), *Old English Mansions* (London, 1915)

Horn, Pamela, *Joseph Arch (1826–1919): The Farm Workers' Leader* (Kineton, 1971)

Howard, George, 'Castle Howard', in Roy Strong et al. (eds), *The Destruction of the Country House, 1875–1975* (London, 1975)

Howard, Peter, 'Painters' Preferred Places', *Journal of Historical Geography*, 11 (1985), 138–54

Howard of Penrith, Lord, 'Lessons from Other Countries', in Clough Williams-Ellis (ed.), *Britain and the Beast* (London, 1937)

Howitt, William, *The Rural Life of England*, 2 vols (London, 1838)

Howitt, William, *Visits to Remarkable Places: Old Halls, Battle Fields, and Scenes Illustrative of Striking Passages in English History and Poetry* (London, 1840)

Howitt, William, *Visits to Remarkable Places: Old Halls, Battle Fields, and Scenes Illustrative of Striking Passages in History and Poetry, Second Series* (London, 1842)

Howkins, Alun, 'The Discovery of Rural England', in Robert Colls and Philip Dodd (eds), *Englishness: Politics and Culture 1880–1920* (London, 1986)

Howkins, Alun, 'J. M. W. Turner at Petworth: Agricultural Improvement and the Politics of Landscape', in John Barrell (ed.), *Painting and the Politics of Culture* (Oxford, 1992)

Hudson, John, 'The Economics of the National Trust: A Demand Curve for a History Club', *Scottish Journal of Political Economy*, 36 (1989), 19–35

Hunt, John Dixon, 'Picturesque Mirrors and the Ruins of the Past', in *Gardens and the Picturesque: Studies in the History of Landscape Architecture* (Cambridge, Mass., 1992)

Hunter, Michael, 'The Preconditions of Preservation: A Historical Perspective', in David Lowenthal and Marcus Binney (eds), *Our Past Before Us: Why Do We Save It?* (London, 1981)

Hussey, Christopher, *The Fairy Land of England* (London, 1924)

Hussey, Christopher, *The Picturesque: Studies in a Point of View* (London, 1927)

Hussey, Christopher (ed.), *The Old Homes of Britain: The Southern Counties (Kent, Sussex, Hampshire, Surrey and Middlesex)* (London, 1928)

Hutton, Ronald, *The Stations of the Sun: A History of the Ritual Year in Britain* (Oxford, 1996)

Inglis-Jones, Elisabeth, *Augustus Smith of Scilly* (London, 1969)

Jacks, Leonard, *The Great Houses of Nottinghamshire and the County Families* (Nottingham, 1881)

Jackson, Alan A., *Semi-Detached London: Suburban Development, Life and Transport, 1900–39*, 2nd edn (Didcot, 1991)

Jackson-Stops, Gervase, 'The Fight is Still On', in Marcus Binney and Emma Milne (eds), *Vanishing Houses of England: A Pictorial Documentary of Lost Country Houses* (London, 1982)

Jackson-Stops, Gervase, 'Temples of the Arts', in Gervase Jackson-Stops (ed.), *The Treasure Houses of Britain: Five Hundred Years of Private Patronage and Art Collecting* (New Haven and London, 1985)

Jackson-Stops, Gervase (ed.), *The Treasure Houses of Britain: Five Hundred Years of Private Patronage and Art Collecting* (New Haven and London, 1985)

James, Henry, *English Hours* (1st edn, 1905; London, 1960)

James, Louis, *Fiction for the Working Man, 1830–1850* (Oxford, 1963)

Janowitz, Anne, *England's Ruins: Poetic Purpose and the National Landscape* (Oxford, 1990)

Jeans, D. N., 'Planning and the Myth of the English Countryside, in the Interwar Period', *Rural History*, 1 (1990), 249–64

Jenkins, Hugh, *The Culture Gap: An Experience of Government and the Arts* (London, 1979)

Jenkins, Jennifer, and Patrick James, *From Acorn to Oak Tree: The Growth of the National Trust, 1895–1994* (London, 1994)

Jewitt, Llewellyn [*sic*], *The Illustrated Guide to Haddon Hall* (Manchester, [1904])

Jewitt, Llewellywn [*sic*], *Guide to Alton Towers and the Surrounding District* (Edinburgh, 1869)

Jewitt, Llewellynn, and S. C. Hall, *The Stately Homes of England* (London, 1874)

Jewitt, Llewellynn, and S. C. Hall, *The Stately Homes of England, 2nd Series* (London, 1877)

Joad, C. E. M., 'The People's Claim', in Clough Williams-Ellis (ed.), *Britain and the Beast* (London, 1937)

Jones, Arthur, *Britain's Heritage: The Creation of the National Heritage Memorial Fund* (London, 1985)

Jones, T. E., *A Descriptive Account of the Literary Works of John Britton* (London, 1849)

Joyce, Patrick, *Democratic Subjects: The Self and the Social in Nineteenth-Century England* (Cambridge, 1994)

Joyce, Patrick, *Visions of the People: Industrial England and the the Question of Class, 1840–1914* (Cambridge, 1991)

Judge, Roy, 'May Day and Merrie England', *Folklore*, 102 (1991), 131–48

Kain, Roger (ed.), *Planning for Conservation* (London, 1981)

Kelsall, Malcolm, *The Great Good Place: The Country House and English Literature* (Hemel Hempstead, 1993)

Kennet, Wayland, *Preservation* (London, 1972)

Ketton-Cremer, R. W., *Norfolk Assembly* (London, 1957)

Keynes, J. M., 'Art and the State', in Clough Williams-Ellis (ed.), *Britain and the Beast* (London, 1937)

Killingray, David, 'Rights, "Riot" and Ritual: The Knole Park Access Dispute, Sevenoaks, Kent, 1883–5', *Rural History*, 5 (1994), 63–79

Kitson, Sydney D., and Edmund D. Pawson, *Temple Newsam*, 2nd edn (Leeds, 1928)

Klancher, Jon P., *The Making of English Reading Audiences, 1790–1832* (Madison, Wisconsin, 1987)

[Knight, Charles], *Knight's Excursion Companion: Excursions from London, 1851* (London, 1851)

Knight, Charles (ed.), *Old England: A Pictorial Museum of Regal, Ecclesiastical, Municipal, Baronial, and Popular Antiquities*, 2 vols (London, [1860])

Lambert, Angela, *Unquiet Souls: The Indian Summer of the British Aristocracy, 1880–1918* (London, 1984)

Laughlin, Clara E., *So You're Going to England! And if I were going with you there are things I'd invite you to do* (Boston, 1926)

Lawrence, D. H., *Lady Chatterley's Lover* (1st edn, 1928; Harmondsworth, 1994)

Leatham, Victoria, *Burghley: The Life of a Great House* (London, 1992)

Lee, Amice, *Laurels and Rosemary: The Life of William and Mary Howitt* (London, 1955)

Lee, J. M., *Social Leaders and Public Persons: A Study of County Government in Cheshire since 1888* (Oxford, 1963)

Lees-Milne, James, *The Age of Adam* (London, 1947)

Lees-Milne, James, *Ancestral Voices* (London, 1975)

Lees-Milne, James, *Another Self* (London, 1970)

Lees-Milne, James, *Caves of Ice* (London, 1983)

Lees-Milne, James, 'The Country House in Our Heritage', in Roy Strong et al. (eds), *The Destruction of the Country House, 1875–1975* (London, 1974)

Lees-Milne, James, 'The Early Years of the Country Houses Scheme', in G. Jackson-Stops (ed.), *The National Trust Year Book, 1976–7* (London, 1977)

Lees-Milne, James, 'Landed Properties and Proprietors', in *Burke's Landed Gentry*, ed. Peter Townend, 18th edn, vol. 1 (London, 1965)

Lees-Milne, James, *Midway on the Waves* (London, 1985)

Lees-Milne, James, *A Mingled Measure: Diaries, 1953–1972* (London, 1994)

Lees-Milne, James, *People and Places: Country House Donors and the National Trust* (London, 1992)

Lees-Milne, James, *Prophesying Peace* (London, 1977)

Lees-Milne, James (comp.), *The Country House* (Oxford, 1982)

Leslie, Charles Robert, *Autobiographical Recollections*, 2 vols (London, 1860)

Levin, Angela, *Raine and Johnnie: The Spencers and the Scandal of Althorp* (London, 1993)

Levine, Philippa, *The Amateur and the Professional: Antiquarians, Historians and Archaeologists in Victorian England, 1838–1866* (Cambridge, 1986)

Lewin, Thomas, *A Practical Treatise on the Law of Trusts*, 8th edn, ed. F. A. Lewin (London, 1885)

Lieven, Dominic, *The Aristocracy in Europe, 1815–1914* (New York, 1992)

Light, Alison, *Forever England: Femininity, Literature and Conservatism Between the Wars* (London, 1991)

Lloyd George, David, *The Budget and The People; A Speech . . . Authorized Verbatim Report* (London, 1909)

Lloyd George, David, *The Rural Land Problem: What It Is; A Speech . . . Authorized Edition* (London, 1913)

Lloyd George, David, *The Rural Land Problem: The Remedy; A Speech . . . Authorized Edition* (London, 1913)

Loudon, John Claudius, *In Search of English Gardens: The Travels of John Claudius Loudon and his Wife Jane* (London, 1990)

Lowe, Philip et al., *Countryside Conflicts: The Politics of Farming, Forestry and Conservation* (Aldershot, 1986)

Lowenthal, David, *The Past is a Foreign Country* (Cambridge, 1985)

Lowerson, John, 'Battles for the Countryside', in Frank Gloversmith (ed.), *Class, Culture and Social Change: A New View of the 1930s* (Brighton, 1980)

Lucas, E. V., *Highways and Byways in Sussex* (London, 1904)

Luckin, Bill, *Questions of Power: Electricity and Environment in Inter-War Britain* (Manchester, 1990)

Lytton Cobbold, Chryssie, *Board Meetings in the Bath: The Knebworth House Story* (London, 1986)

Lytton Cobbold, David, 'Knebworth House', in Roy Strong et al. (eds), *The Destruction of the Country House, 1875–1975* (London, 1975)

Maas, Jeremy. 'S. C. Hall and the *Art Journal*', *The Connoisseur* (March 1976), 206–9

MacCarthy, Fiona, *The Simple Life: C.R. Ashbee in the Cotswolds* (London, 1981)

McClung, William A., 'The Country-House Arcadia', in Gervase Jackson-Stops et al. (eds), *The Fashioning and Functioning of the British Country House* (Hanover, N. H., and London, 1989)

Mackail, J. W., and Guy Wyndham, *Life and Letters of George Wyndham*, 2 vols (London, [1925])

McKibbin, Ross, 'Class and Conventional Wisdom: The Conservative Party and the "Public" in Inter-war Britain', in *The Ideologies of Class: Social Relations in Britain, 1880–1950* (Oxford, 1990)

Madsen, Stephan Tschudi, *Restoration and Anti-Restoration* (Oslo, 1976)

Mais, S. P. B., *All the Days of My Life* (London, 1937)

Mais, S. P. B., *Arden and Avon* (London, 1951)

Mais, S. P. B., *Buffets and Rewards: An Autobiographical Record (1937–1951)* (London, 1952)

Mais, S. P. B., *This Unknown Island* (London, 1932)

Mandler, Peter, '"In the Olden Time": Romantic History and English National Identity, 1820–1850', in Laurence Brockliss and David Eastwood (eds), *A Union of Multiple Identities* (Manchester, 1997)

Mandler, Peter, 'John Summerson (1904–1992): The Architectural Critic and the Quest for the Modern', in Susan Pedersen and Peter Mandler (eds), *After the Victorians: Private Conscience and Public Duty in Modern Britain* (London, 1994)

Mandler, Peter, 'Nationalising the Country House', in Michael Hunter (ed.), *Preserving the Past: The Rise of Heritage in Modern Britain* (Stroud, 1996)

Mandler, Peter, 'Politics and the English Landscape since the First World War', *Huntington Library Quarterly*, 55 (1992), 459–76

March, Earl of, 'Goodwood House', in Roy Strong et al. (eds), *The Destruction of the Country House, 1875–1975* (London, 1974)

Marks, Henry Stacy, *Pen and Pencil Sketches*, 2 vols (London, 1894)

Marks, John George, *Life and Letters of Frederick Walker, A.R.A.* (London, 1896)

Marsh, Jan, *Back to the Land: The Pastoral Impulse in England, from 1880 to 1914* (London, 1982)

Massey, Doreen, and Alejandrina Catalano, *Capital and Land: Landownership by Capital in Great Britain* (London, 1978)

Massingham, H. J., *Remembrance: An Autobiography* (London, 1941)

Massingham, H. J. (ed.), *The English Countryside* (London, 1939)

Masterman, C. F. G., *The Condition of England* (London, 1909)

Masterman, C. F. G., 'The English City', in Lucian Oldershaw (ed.), *England: A Nation* (London and Edinburgh, 1904)

Matless, David, 'Ages of English Design: Preservation, Modernism and Tales of their History, 1926–1939', *Journal of Design History*, 3 (1990), 203–12

Meisel, Martin, *Realizations: Narrative, Pictorial, and Theatrical Arts in Nineteenth-Century England* (Princeton, 1983)

Mellor, David, Gill Saunders and Patrick Wright, *Recording Britain: A Pictorial Domesday of Pre-War Britain* (Newton Abbot, 1990)

Melly, George, *Revolt into Style* (London, 1970)

Melville, Alan [W. M. Caverhill], *Castle in the Air: A Comedy* (London, 1951)

Melville, Alan, *Merely Melville: An Autobiography* (London, 1970)

Merriman, Nick, *Beyond the Glass Case: The Past, the Heritage and the Public in Britain* (Leicester, 1991)

Miele, Chris, '"A Small Knot of Cultivated People": William Morris and the Ideologies of Protection', *Art Journal*, 54 (1995), 73–79

Miele, Chris, 'The first conservation militants: William Morris and the Society for the Protection of Ancient Buildings', in Michael Hunter (ed.), *Preserving the Past: The Rise of Heritage in Modern Britain* (Stroud, 1996)

Miers, Henry, *A Report on the Public Museums of the British Isles* (Edinburgh, 1928)

Miller, William, *Jottings of Kent* (London, 1864)

Minihan, Janet, *The Nationalization of Culture* (London, 1977)

Mitford, Nancy (ed.), *The Ladies of Alderley* (London, 1938)

Moir, Esther, *The Discovery of Britain: The English Tourists, 1540–1840* (London, 1964)

Montagu of Beaulieu, Lord, *The Gilt and the Gingerbread, or How to Live in a Stately Home and Make Money* (London, 1967)

Montague, C. E., *The Right Place* (London, 1924)

Montgomery-Massingberd, Hugh, *The Field Book of Country Houses and Their Owners: Family Seats of the British Isles* (Exeter, 1988)

Morton, H. V., *I Saw Two Englands* (London, 1942)

Morton, H. V., *In Search of England*, 23rd edn revised (London, 1936)

Morris, A. J. A., *C. P. Trevelyan, 1870–1958: Portrait of a Radical* (New York, 1977)

Moss, Fletcher, *Pilgrimages to Old Homes, Mostly on the Welsh Border* (Didsbury, 1903)

Munby, A. N. L., 'The Library', in Roy Strong et al. (eds), *The Destruction of the Country House, 1875–1975* (London, 1974)

Murray, Bruce K., *The People's Budget 1909/10: Lloyd George and Liberal Politics* (Oxford, 1980)

Murray, Tim, 'The History, Philosophy and Sociology of Archaeology: The Case of the Ancient Monuments Protection Act (1882)', in Valerie Pinsky and Alison Wylie (eds), *Critical Traditions in Contemporary Archaeology* (Cambridge, 1989)

Muthesius, Hermann, *The English House*, abridged and ed. Dennis Sharp (1st edn, 1904–5; Oxford, 1987)

Muthesius, Stefan, 'The origins of the German conservation movement', in Roger Kain (ed.), *Planning for Conservation* (London, 1981)

Myerscough, John, *The Economic Importance of the Arts in Britain* (London, 1988)

Nares, Gordon, *Country Houses Open to the Public* (London, 1951)

Nash, Joseph, *Architecture of the Middle Ages* (London, 1838)

Nash, Joseph, *Descriptions of the Plates of the Mansions of England in the Olden Time* (London, 1849)

Nash, Joseph, *The Mansions of England in the Olden Time*, 4 vols (London, 1839–49)

Nash, Joseph, *The Mansions of England in the Olden Time*, 4 vols, ed. J. Corbet Anderson (London, 1869–72)

Nash, Joseph, *The Mansions of England in the Olden Time*, ed. Charles Holme (London, 1906)

Nash, Joseph, *The Mansions of England in the Olden Time*, intro. by Reginald Blomfield (London, 1912)

Nash, Joseph, *A Series of Views Illustrative of Pugin's Examples of Gothic Architecture* (London, 1830)

Nash, Roderick, *Wilderness and the American Mind*, 3rd edn (New Haven and London, 1982)

Nevill, Lady Dorothy, *The Reminiscences of Lady Dorothy Nevill*, ed. Ralph Nevill (London, 1906)

Nevill, Lady Dorothy, *Under Five Reigns*, ed. Ralph Nevill (London, 1912)

Nevill, Ralph, *English Country House Life* (London, 1925)

Nevinson, Henry Woodd, *Rough Islanders, Or the Natives of England* (London, 1930)

Newby, Howard, *Green and Pleasant Land? Social Change in Rural England* (London, 1985)

Newby, Howard (ed.), *The National Trust: The Next Hundred Years* (London, 1995)

Newman, Gerald, *The Rise of English Nationalism: A Cultural History, 1740–1830* (New York, 1987)

*Notes on the History of Chillington Manor* (Maidstone, 1919)

O'Connor, Harvey, *The Astors* (New York, 1941)

O'Neill, D. J., *How Aston Hall and Park Were Saved* (Birmingham, 1910)

Offer, Avner, 'Farm tenure and land values in England, c. 1750–1950', *Economic History Review*, 44 (1991), 1–20

Offer, Avner, *Property and Politics, 1870–1914* (Cambridge, 1981)

*Official Guide to Aston Hall and Park* (Birmingham, 1858)

Oldfield, Susan H., *Some Records of the Later Life of Harriet, Countess Granville* (London, 1901)

Olmsted, Frederick Law, *Walks and Talks of an American Farmer in England* (New York, 1852)

Oswald, Arthur, *Country Houses of Dorset* (London, 1935)

Oswald, Arthur, *Country Houses of Kent* (London, 1933)

*Our Own Country: Descriptive, Historical, Pictorial*, 6 vols (London, 1878–83)

Ousby, Ian, *The Englishman's England: Taste, Travel and the Rise of Tourism* (Cambridge, 1990)

Palmer, W. T., *Tramping Derbyshire* (London, 1934)

Parker, Louis N., *Several of My Lives* (London, 1928)

Parker, Cornelia Stratton, *English Summer* (New York, 1931)

Pawle, Gerald, 'H. V. Morton – Fleet Street and After', *Blackwood's Magazine*, 326 (1979), 120–28

Perrott, Roy, *The Aristocrats* (London, 1968)

Pevsner, Nikolaus, 'The Dukeries', in John Morris (ed.), *From the Third Programme* (London, 1956)

Phillips, Gregory D., *The Diehards: Aristocratic Society and Politics in Edwardian England* (Cambridge, Mass., 1979)

*Pictorial and Descriptive Guide to Sherwood Forest and 'The Dukeries' (The Land of Robin Hood)* (London, 1893)

*The Pictorial Guide to Gravesend and its Rural Vicinity: A Holiday Handbook* (London, 1845)

Piggott, Stuart, 'The Origins of the English County Archaeological Societies', in

*Ruins in a Landscape* (Edinburgh, 1976)

Pimlott, Ben, *Hugh Dalton*

Pimlott, J. A. R., *The Englishman's Holiday: A Social History* (London, 1947)

Pinney, R. G., *Britain – Destination of Tourists?* (London, 1944)

Pope-Hennessy, James, *Lord Crewe, 1858–1945: The Likeness of a Liberal* (London, 1955)

Portland, 6th Duke of, *Men Women and Things* (London, 1937)

Potts, Alex, '"Constable Country" Between the Wars', in Raphael Samuel (ed.), *Patriotism: The Making and Unmaking of British National Identity. III: National Fictions* (London, 1989)

Priestley, J. B. (ed.), *The Beauty of Britain* (London, 1935)

Pugh, R. B., '*The Victoria History*: Its Origins and Progress', in *Victoria History of the Counties of England: General Introduction*, ed. R. B. Pugh (London, 1970)

Pugin, A. Welby, *The True Principles of Pointed or Christian Architecture* (1st edn, 1841; London, 1853)

Punter, John, 'A History of Aesthetic Control: Part 1, 1909–1953', *Town Planning Review*, 57 (1986), 351–81

Radnor, Helen, Countess-Dowager of, *From a Great-Grandmother's Armchair* (London, [1928])

Rae, W. Fraser, *The Business of Travel: A Fifty Years' Record of Progress* (London, 1891)

Raleigh, John Henry, 'What Scott Meant to the Victorians', *Victorian Studies*, 7 (1963–4), 7–34

Rance, Nicholas, *The Historical Novel and Popular Politics in Nineteenth-Century England* (London, 1975)

Rayner, S., *The History and Antiquities of Haddon Hall* (Derby, 1836)

Redgrave, F. M., *Richard Redgrave: A Memoir* (London, 1891)

Reitlinger, Gerald, *The Economics of Taste. I: The Rise and Fall of Picture Prices, 1760–1960* (London, 1961)

Reitlinger, Gerald, *The Economics of Taste. II: The Rise and Fall of Objets D'Art Prices since 1750* (London, 1963)

[Rhodes, Ebenezer], *Modern Chatsworth; or, the Palace of the Peak* (Sheffield, 1837)

Rich, Paul, 'A question of life and death to England: Patriotism and the British Intellectuals, c.1886–1945', *New Community*, 15 (1989), 491–508

Richards, J. M., 'Architectural Criticism in the 1930s', in John Summerson (ed.), *Concerning Architecture* (London, 1968)

Richards, J. M., *The Castles on the Ground: The Anatomy of Suburbia*, 2nd edn (1st edn, 1946; London, 1973)

Richards, J. M., *Memoirs of an Unjust Fella* (London, 1980)

Roberts, Charles, *The Radical Countess: The History of the Life of Rosalind Countess of Carlisle* (Carlisle, 1962)

Robinson, John Martin, *The Country House At War* (London, 1989)

Robinson, John Martin, *The Latest Country Houses* (London, 1984)

Ronaldshay, Earl of, *The Life of Lord Curzon*, 3 vols (London, 1928)

Ruddick, William, 'Sir Walter Scott's Northumberland', in J. H. Alexander and David Hewitt (eds), *Scott and His Influence* (Aberdeen, 1983)

Russell, Bertrand, and Patricia Russell (eds), *The Amberley Papers*, 2 vols (London, 1937)

Rutland, Janetta, Duchess of, *The Collected Writings of Janetta Duchess of Rutland*, 2 vols (Edinburgh and London, 1901)

Sackville-West, Vita, *English Country Houses* (London, 1941)

Sackville-West, Vita, *The Heir* (1st edn, 1922; London, 1987)

Saint, Andrew, 'How Listing Happened', in Michael Hunter (ed.), *Preserving the Past: The Rise of Heritage in Modern Britain* (Stroud, 1996)

Saint, Andrew, *Richard Norman Shaw* (New Haven and London, 1976)

Samuel, Raphael, 'Introduction: Exciting to be English', in Raphael Samuel (ed.), *Patriotism: The Making and Unmaking of British National Identity. I: History and Politics* (London, 1989)

Samuel, Raphael, *Theatres of Memory: I. Past and Present in Contemporary Culture* (London, 1994)

Sanders, Andrew, *The Victorian Historical Novel, 1840–1880* (London, 1978)

Sargent, Dick, 'The National Register of Archives', *Historical Research*, Special Supplement 13 (1995), 1–35

*The Saturday Half-Holiday Guide to London and the Environs* (London, 1868)

*The Saturday Half-Holiday Guide*, 10th edn (London, 1879)

Saunders, Matthew, 'Metroland: Half-Timbering and Other Souvenirs in the Outer London Suburbs', in David Lowenthal and Marcus Binney (eds), *Our Past Before Us: Why Do We Save It?* (London, 1981)

Sayer, Michael, and Hugh Massingberd, *The Disintegration of a Heritage: Country Houses and their Collections, 1979–1992* (Norwich, 1993)

Schwarz, Bill, 'The Language of Constitutionalism: Baldwinite Conservatism', in *Formations of Nation and People* (London, 1984)

Scott, George Gilbert, *Remarks on Secular and Domestic Architecture, Present and Future* (London, 1857)

Scott, Walter, *Poetical Works*, ed. J. Logie Robertson (London, 1904)

Seebohm, Caroline, *The Country House: A Wartime History, 1939–45* (London, 1989)

Seebohm, Caroline, and Christopher Simon Sykes, *English Country* (London, 1987)

Self, Peter, 'Town Planning in Retreat', *Political Quarterly*, 27 (1956), 209–15

Self, Peter, and Herbert J. Storing, *The State and the Farmer* (London, 1962)

Shackleton, Robert, and Elizabeth, *Four on a Tour in England* (New York, 1914)

Shaw, George Bernard, 'Heartbreak House and Horseback Hall', intro. to *Heartbreak House* (1st edn, 1919; Harmondsworth, 1964)

Sheail, John, *Rural Conservation in Inter-War Britain* (Oxford, 1981)

Simmons, James C., 'Of Kettledrums and Trumpets: The Early Victorian Followers of Scott', *Studies in Scottish Literature*, 6 (1968–9), 47–59

Smith, Anthony D. (ed.), *Nationalist Movements* (London, 1976)

Smith, M. H. Stephen, *Art and Anecdote: Recollections of William Frederick Yeames, R. A., His Life and His Friends* (London, [1927])

Smith, R. J., *The Gothic Bequest: Medieval Institutions in British Thought, 1688–1863* (Cambridge, 1987)

Somers-Cocks, Henry L., *Eastnor and its Malvern Hills* (Hereford, 1923)

Soward, Alfred W., *The Law and Practice of the Estate Duty (Finance Acts, 1894 to 1900)*, 4th edn (London, 1900)

Spender, Harold, *Man and Mansions* (London, 1924)

Spring, David, 'Aristocracy, Social Structure, and Religion in the Early Victorian Period', *Victorian Studies*, 6 (1962–3), 263–80

Spring, David, 'Land and Politics in Edwardian England', *Agricultural History*, 58 (1984), 17–42

Spring, David, 'Ralph Sneyd: Tory Country Gentleman', *Bulletin of the John Rylands Library*, 38 (1955–6), 535–55

Spring, Eileen, 'Landowners, Lawyers, and Land Law Reform in Nineteenth-Century England', *American Journal of Legal History* (1977), 40–59

Sproule, Anna, and Michael Pollard, *The Country House Guide: Family Homes in the Historic Houses Association* (London, 1988)

[Stead, W.T.], *The Splendid Paupers: A Tale of the Coming Plutocracy* (London, 1894)

Steegman, John, *The Artist and the Country House* (London, 1949)

Steegman, John, *Victorian Taste: A Study of the Arts and Architecture from 1830 to 1870*, repr. edn (1st edn, as *Consort of Taste*, 1950; London, 1970)

Steegmann, John [*sic*], *The Rule of Taste from George I to George IV* (London, 1936)

Stevenson, J. J., *House Architecture*, 2 vols (London, 1880)

Stone, Lawrence, 'The Public and the Private in the Stately Homes of England, 1500–1990', *Social Research*, 58 (1991), 227–51

Stone, Lawrence, and Jeanne C. Fawtier Stone, *An Open Elite? England, 1540–1880* (Oxford, 1984)

Stowe, Harriet Beecher, *Sunny Memories of Foreign Lands* (London, 1854)

*The Stranger's Guide or Description of Alton Towers, Staffs.* (London, 1850)

Street, A. G., 'The Countryman's View', in Clough Williams-Ellis (ed.), *Britain and the Beast* (London, 1937)

Strong, Roy, *And when did you last see your father?: The Victorian Painter and British History* (London, 1978)

Strong, Roy, Marcus Binney and John Harris (eds), *The Destruction of the Country House, 1875–1975* (London, 1974)

*Summer Excursions in the County of Kent along the banks of the Rivers Thames and Medway* (London, 1847)

Summerson, John, *Georgian London*, new edn (London, 1988)

Summerson, John, *John Nash: Architect to King George IV*, 2nd edn (London, 1949)

Summerson, John, 'The Past in the Future', in *Heavenly Mansions and other Essays on Architecture* (1st pub. 1949; New York, 1963)

Summerson, John, 'Town Buildings', in James Lees-Milne (ed.), *The National Trust: A Record of Fifty Years' Achievement* (London, 1945)

Surtees, Virginia, *The Artist and the Autocrat: George and Rosalind Howard, Earl and Countess of Carlisle* (Wilton, 1988)

Surtees, Virginia, *Coutts Lindsay, 1824–1913* (Norwich, 1993)

Sutherland, Douglas, *The Landowners* (London, 1968)

Sutherland, Duke of, *Looking Back* (London, 1958)

Sutherland, John, *Mrs Humphry Ward: Eminent Victorian, Pre-eminent Edwardian* (Oxford, 1991)

Taggart, Tom, *The Saturday Evening Ghost: A Comedy in Three Acts* (New York, 1936)

Tallents, Stephen, *The Projection of England* (London, 1932)

Thompson, E. P., *William Morris: Romantic to Revolutionary*, 2nd edn (London, 1976)

Thompson, F. M. L., *English Landed Society in the Nineteenth Century* (London, 1963)

Thompson, F. M. L., 'English Landed Society in the Twentieth Century. I. Property: Collapse and Survival', *Transactions of the Royal Historical Society*, 5th ser., 40 (1990), 1–24

Thompson, F. M. L., 'English Landed Society in the Twentieth Century. IV. Prestige Without Power?', *Transactions of the Royal Historical Society*, 6th ser., 3 (1993), 1–22

Thompson, M. W., *General Pitt-Rivers: Evolution and Archaeology in the Nineteenth Century* (Bradford-on-Avon, 1977)

Tillyard, Stella, *The Impact of Modernism, 1900–1920: Early Modernism and the Arts and Crafts Movement in Edwardian England* (London, 1988)

Tinniswood, Adrian, *A History of Country House Visiting: Five Centuries of Tourism and Taste* (Oxford and London, 1989)

Trainor, Richard, 'Peers on an Industrial Frontier: The Earls of Dartmouth and of Dudley in the Black Country, c. 1810 to 1914', in David Cannadine (ed.), *Patricians, Power and Politics in Nineteenth-Century Towns* (Leicester, 1982)

Tree, R., J. S. Wedderburn and C. York, *The Husbandman Waiteth: A Statement on Agricultural Policy on Behalf of the Tory Reform Committee* (London, 1944)

Trentmann, Frank, 'Civilization and Its Discontents: English Neo-Romanticism and the Transformation of Anti-Modernism in Twentieth-Century Western Culture', *Journal of Contemporary History*, 29 (1994), 583–625

Trevelyan, G. M., 'Amenities and the State', in Clough Williams-Ellis (ed.), *Britain and the Beast* (London, 1937)

Trevelyan, G. M., *The Call and Claims of Natural Beauty* (London, 1931)

Trevelyan, G. M., *Must England's Beauty Perish? A Plea on Behalf of the National Trust . . .* (London, 1929)

Turner, T. Hudson, and John Henry Parker, *Some Account of Domestic Architecture in England*, 3 vols (Oxford, 1851–9)

de Vignaud, Bertrand (ed.), *The Historic Houses, Castles and Gardens of France: The Official Guide to Sites Open to the Public* (Twickenham, 1986)

Vincent, David, *Literacy and Popular Culture: England 1750–1914* (Cambridge, 1989)

Wainwright, Clive, *The Romantic Interior: The British Collector at Home, 1750–1850* (New Haven and London, 1989)

Walker, Helen, 'The Popularisation of the Outdoor Movement, 1900–1940', *British Journal of Sports History*, 2 (1985), 140–53

Walker, John A., *Arts TV: A History of Arts Television in Britain* (London, 1993)

Walker, Mack, *German Home Towns: Community, State, and General Estate, 1648–1871* (Ithaca, NY, 1971)

Waller, Robert J., *The Dukeries Transformed* (Oxford, 1983)

Walton, John K., *The English Seaside Resort: A Social History, 1750–1914* (Leicester, 1983)

Warwick, Frances, Countess of, *Afterthoughts* (London, 1931)

Warwick, Frances, Countess of, *Life's Ebb and Flow* (London, 1929)

Warwick, Frances, Countess of, *Warwick Castle and its Earls*, 2 vols (London, 1903)

Waterfield, Giles, 'The Town House as Gallery of Art', *London Journal*, 20 (1995), 47–66

Waterson, Merlin (ed.), *The Country House Remembered: Recollections of Life Between the Wars* (London, 1985)

Waterson, Merlin, *The National Trust: The First Hundred Years* (London, 1994)

Watkin, David, *The Rise of Architectural History* (London, 1980)

Watson, W. Walker, *Agricultural Death Duties: A Handbook for Landowners* (London, [1951])

Watts, Alaric Alfred, *Alaric Watts: A Narrative of His Life*, 2 vols (London, 1884)

Waugh, Evelyn, *Brideshead Revisited* (1st pub. 1945; Harmondsworth, 1962)

Waugh, Evelyn, *Labels: A Mediterranean Journal*, new edn (1st ed., 1930; London, 1974)

Waugh, Evelyn, *The Letters of Evelyn Waugh*, ed. Mark Amory (London, 1980)

Weideger, Paula, *Gilding the Acorn: Behind the façade of the National Trust* (London, 1994)

Wells, W. A. A., 'The Landed Gentry: A Personal Synopsis', in *Burke's Landed Gentry*, 18th edn, III (London, 1972)

West, Anthony, *Gloucestershire: A Shell Guide* (London, 1939)

West, Anthony, *H. G. Wells: Aspects of a Life* (New York, 1984)

Wetherall, David, 'From Canterbury to Winchester: The Foundation of the Institute', in Blaise Vyner (ed.), *Building on the Past: Papers Celebrating 150 Years of the Royal Archaeological Institute* (London, 1994)

Wiener, Martin J., *English Culture and the Decline of the Industrial Spirit, 1850–1980* (Cambridge, 1981)

Williams, Raymond, *Culture and Society, 1780–1950* (London, 1958)

Williams, Raymond, *The Country and the City* (London, 1973)

Williams-Ellis, Clough, *Architect Errant* (London, 1971)

Williams-Ellis, Clough, *England and the Octopus* (London, 1928)

Williams-Ellis, Clough, 'Houses and Parks – National and Private', in Clough Williams-Ellis (ed.), *Britain and the Beast* (London, 1937)

Williamson, Tom, and Liz Bellamy, *Property and Landscape: A Social History of Land Ownership and the English Countryside* (London, 1987)

Withington, Robert, *English Pageantry: An Historical Outline*, 2 vols (Cambridge, Mass., 1918–20)

Woodcock, Gwen, *Historic Haunts of England* (London, 1938)

Woodring, Carl Ray, *Victorian Samplers: William and Mary Howitt* (Lawrence, Kansas, 1952)

Woolf, Virginia, *The Diary of Virginia Woolf*, ed. Anne Olivier Bell, 5 vols (London, 1977–84)

Woolf, Virginia, 'The Memoirs of Lady Dorothy Nevill', in *The Essays of Virginia Woolf, I: 1904–1912*, ed. Andrew McNeillie (London, 1986)

Woolf, Virginia, 'Reading', in *The Captain's Death Bed and Other Essays* (London, 1950)

Wright, Patrick, *A Journey Through Ruins: The Last Days of London* (London, 1991)

Wright, Patrick, *On Living in an Old Country* (London, 1985)

[Wright, Thomas] 'The Journeyman Engineer', 'Bill Banks's Day Out', in Andrew Halliday (ed.), *The Savage-Club Papers for 1868* (London, 1868)

Young, G. M. (ed.), *Country and Town: A Summary of the Scott and Uthwatt Reports* (Harmondsworth, 1943)

Young, G. M., *Stanley Baldwin* (London, 1952)

Young, John, *The Country House in the 1980s* (London, 1981)

## ACKNOWLEDGEMENTS

A truly interdisciplinary work, as I hope this is, inevitably incurs far-flung debts. I must first thank my most constant historian-friends. It was Stella Tillyard who, over tea at the Swimming-Pool Library, helped me to make out the earliest glimmerings of this book. John Brewer has since read nearly all of its manifestations in draft. Between them they have provided years of gossip, childcare, football, more tea, sympathy and, always, stimulation. Mark Mazower offered the same generous measure of companionship and controversy on two continents. Susan Pedersen explored with me tracts of twentieth-century cultural and intellectual history that had been unfamiliar to us both and now seem like home.

Then I must acknowledge the time and care others have taken to guide me through their own fields. Michael Hunter took an early interest and provided many vital leads into the literature of 'heritage'. Charles Saumarez Smith did the same for architectural history. Giles Waterfield exposed me to the Attingham Summer School and endured long conversations about country-house museums when coaches stalled in traffic. Louise Ward talked to me about her research on country-house styles in interior decoration, Becky Conekin about tourism after the Second World War, and Jennifer Hall about aristocratic culture in the nineteenth century. W. G. Lister laid bare his meticulous research into nineteenth-century guidebooks. David Feldman and Miles Taylor read carefully and commented practically on draft chapters covering the Victorian period. Peter Stansky read even more extensively and supplied his characteristic flow of criticisms on matters great and small. Daniel Johnson kindly steered my way books on architecture historic and modern. For discussing with me their personal contributions to the history I have written about, I am very grateful to the late Sir John Summerson, the late Sir James (J. M.) Richards, James Lees-Milne, Sir Edward Playfair, Lawrence Stone, Sir Howard Colvin and Rachel Crawshay.

I have had a number of opportunities to try out my ideas on

audiences of various kinds and I thank them all for their comments. Particularly helpful were the students and staff on the MA course in the History of Design run jointly by the Royal College of Art and the Victoria and Albert Museum, the people I met at the Huntington Library symposium, 'An English Arcadia', in the autumn of 1991 when I was just beginning my research, and those at the Attingham Summer School in 1995 when I was nearing the end.

Permission to use the manuscript materials listed in the bibliography is gratefully acknowledged. Librarians and archivists of course provide more than access: they know their sources better than casual researchers and many have given me invaluable advice. I would like to single out Janette Harley of the National Trust, Eeyan Hartley of Castle Howard, Peter Day of the Devonshire Collections at Chatsworth, Stephen Hobbs of the Wiltshire Record Office, Kenneth Dunn of the National Library of Scotland, James Lomax of Temple Newsam House, Jill Lomer of the Thomas Cook Travel Archive, and Robin Harcourt Williams of Hatfield House.

None of this would have been possible without time for research and writing. I have to thank the US National Endowment for the Humanities for a fellowship in 1992–3, and since then more leave and support both moral and material from my heads of department at London Guildhall University, successively Renée Gerson and Iwan Morgan.

Yale University Press authors are, notoriously, satisfied authors, and I am no exception. Much of the credit for this is owing to Gillian Malpass, an editor (and, in this case, designer) who cares about her books and works for them at an almost frightening pitch. Among her many contributions was the procuring of two highly constructive criticisms from anonymous referees. She also procured the services of Celia Jones, both as copy-editor and as picture researcher, in the one capacity pruning, in the other adorning my prose, with imagination and good humour. And behind these faces with whom the author works directly are others, both in London and in New Haven, who also deserve my thanks.

Finally, there are two families I could not have done without. My continuing debt to the family in which I grew up is of course hardly expressible in words, though I might mention specifically the early education in historic architecture that I gained from my mother, very much in the parish church, small manor house and cottage taste described in the middle chapters of this book. I have incurred more recent debts to my wife's family, the Ehrlichs, without whose subtle influences I doubt whether I would have taken up cultural history. I want to thank especially Felicity, for a stream of suggestions and press cuttings; Cyril, for many ideas about how to practise cultural history (including when to count and when not to); and Doreen, for sources from art history that I would otherwise have missed. For the most important Ehrlich I reserve my dedication.

# PHOTOGRAPH CREDITS

By permission of the British Library: 1 (578.d.5), 3 (Add. MS 15548, f.49), 10 (1208.I.2), 19 (1347.I.26), 20–21 (PP.600.bb), 23 (747.f.7), 24 (PP.600.bb), 26 (557.h.5), 27 (126), 32 (1421), 40 (7806.ccl), 47 (LD46), 49 (PP.5939.aa), 52 (269), 61 (9013.G), 63 (197), 70 (WP.9256), 85 (251); National Trust Photographic Library (photo: Courtauld Institute of Art): 2; Mansell Collection: 4, 6, 30; from Joseph Nash, *The Mansions of England in the Olden Time*, ed. C. Holme (London, Paris and New York, 1906): 5, 9, 13–18, 39 (top); © Crown copyright: UK Government Art Collection: 8; from *Old English Mansions*, ed. Charles Holme (London, Paris and New York, 1915): 22; British Architectural Library, RIBA, London: 25; from the Castle Howard Collection: 28, 29, 56; Devonshire Collection, Chatsworth. Reproduced by permission of the Chatsworth Settlement Trustees: 34; Birmingham Central Library: 35, 36, 37; Victoria and Albert Museum: 39 (bottom); B.T. Batsford Ltd (photo.: RCHME): 41; The Country Life Picture Library: 44, 53, 66; from Max Beerbohm, *Things Old and New* (London, 1923): 46; National Trust Photographic Library: 48, 74; from George Du Maurier, *English Society Sketched* (London, 1877): 51, 54; Hulton Getty Collection: 55, 57, 59, 69, 75, 88, 93, 97, 98; RCHME © Crown Copyright: 60, 82; courtesy of CTE (Carlton) Ltd and the Sam Goldwyn Company (photo: BFI Stills): 64; from Council for the Preservation of Rural England, *The Thames Valley from Cricklade to Staines: A Survey* (London, 1929): 67; Council for the Protection of Rural England: 68; Wiltshire Record Office, Trowbridge: 71; Malvernian Society: 72; Express Newspapers plc: 78, 89; Johansen Publishing: 79; By kind permission of the Duke of Westminster OBE TD DL: 81; A.F. Kersting: 83, 84; Lord Montagu of Beaulieu: 87; *The Geographical Magazine* (1956–7, pp. 300–01): 90, 91, 92; reproduced by kind permission of Schweppes Ltd: 94; from Marcus Binney, *Our Vanishing Heritage* (London 1984): 95; from Goodwood House, courtesy of the Trustees: 96

# INDEX

Pages with illustrations are *italicized*